MW00777010

Al-Fuṣūl

CHAPTERS *from* THE LIFE *of the* MESSENGER ﷺ

Authored by Al-Imām, Al-Ḥāfidh,

ABUL-FIDĀʾ ISMĀʿĪL IBN ʿUMAR IBN KATHĪR AL-QURASHĪ

Born 701 H — Died 774 H (رَحِمَهُ ٱللَّهُ)

Translated by Ash-Shaikh, Al-Mutarjim

ABŪ TALHAH DĀWŪD IBN RONALD BURBANK

Born 1963 CE / 1383 H
Died 2011 CE / 1432 H (رَحِمَهُ ٱللَّهُ)

Al-Fuṣūl

CHAPTERS *from* THE LIFE *of the* MESSENGER 

الفُصُولُ فِي سِيرَةِ الرَّسُولِ صَلَّى ٱللَّهُ عَلَيْهِ وَسَلَّمَ

SECOND EDITION — NOVEMBER 2022 CE • RABĪʿ ATH-THĀNĪ 1444 AH

Published by Salafi Publications
Twitter — @SalafiPubs
Website — SalafiPublications.Com

Distributed by the Salafi Bookstore and Islamic Centre
472 Coventry road, Small Heath, Birmingham, UK, B10 0UG
Email Address — info@salafibookstore.com
Phone Number — (+44) 121 773 0033
Website — SalafiBookstore.com
Twitter — @SalafiBookstore

Design, typeset, maps, & diagrams done in-house at Salafi Publications
Printed and bound by Mega Print in Turkey

May Allāh reward the family who donated in order to defray the cost of this book's publishing. May Allāh bless their living and have mercy upon the ones who have passed away.

ISBN: 978-1-902727-70-7

Transliteration Table

Consonants

ء ʾ ★	د d	ض dh	ك k
ب b	ذ dh	ط t	ل l
ت t	ر r	ظ dh	م m
ث th	ز z	ع ʿ	ن n
ج j	س s	غ gh	هـ h
ح h	ش sh	ف f	و w
خ kh	ص s	ق q	ي y

★ — The *hamzah* may be denoted as a "right half-ring" (ʾ) — for example, in the words: Muʾmin, and Qurʾān.

It may also be denoted by way of an open vowel at the start of a word — for example, in the words: Anas, and Islām.

Vowels

SHORT	ـَ a	ـِ i	ـُ u
LONG	ـَا ā	ـِي ī	ـُو ū
DIPHTHONGS	ـَو aw	ـَي ay / ai	

Table of Contents

Publisher's Note 11

Regarding Footnotes and Endnotes 13

Eulogy of Shaikh Abū Talhah Dawūd Burbank and his Wife; Umm Talhah 15

Preface Regarding the Importance of Sīrah 25

Introduction of the Verifiers: Samīr Az-Zuhayrī & Dr. Bāsim Al-Jawābirah 31

The Biography of Ibn Kathīr (رَحِمَهُ ٱللَّهُ) 56

Volume One — The Life of the Prophet Muhammad (صَلَّى ٱللَّهُ عَلَيْهِ وَسَلَّمَ) & his Military Expeditions ... 65

A Mention of His (صَلَّى ٱللَّهُ عَلَيْهِ وَسَلَّمَ) Lineage 66

Chapter: The Birth of Allāh's Messenger (صَلَّى ٱللَّهُ عَلَيْهِ وَسَلَّمَ), his Suckling, and his Early Years 74

Chapter: His Being Raised as a Prophet 77

Chapter: The Aggression of the Mushrikūn Against the Weak Ones from Amongst the Muslims 81

The Hijrah (Migration) To Abyssinia 82

Chapter: The Boycotting Of Banū Hāshim And Banul-Muttalib By The Quraysh 84

Chapter: The Departure Of Allāh's Messenger (صَلَّى ٱللَّهُ عَلَيْهِ وَسَلَّمَ) To At-Tā'if 85

Chapter: The Night-Journey & the Ascent Through the Heavens (Al-Isrā' Wal-Mi'rāj) & the Prophet's Presenting Himself to the Tribes 87

Chapter: An Account Concerning Suwayd Ibn As-Sāmit 89

Chapter: The First Pledge (Bai'ah) Of Al-'Aqabah 90

Chapter: The Hijrah (Migration) of Allāh's Messenger صَلَّى ٱللَّهُ عَلَيْهِ وَسَلَّمَ 94

Chapter: The Prophet's (صَلَّى ٱللَّهُ عَلَيْهِ وَسَلَّمَ) Entry into Al-Madīnah 97

Chapter: The Prophet's (صَلَّى ٱللَّهُ عَلَيْهِ وَسَلَّمَ) Settling In Al-Madīnah 98

Chapter: The Brotherhood Established Between The Muhājirīn And The Ansār 99

Chapter: The Obligation of Jihād 101

Chapter: The First of The Military Expeditions And The Raiding Parties 102

Chapter: The Military Expedition Of Buwāt 103

Chapter: The Raiding Party of 'Abdullāh Ibn Jah-sh (رَضِيَ ٱللَّهُ عَنْهُ) 105

Chapter: The Changing Of The Qiblah (Direction Of Prayer), and the Obligation Of Fasting 107

Chapter: The Major Battle of Badr 108

Chapter: The Number of People Present At Badr 119

Chapter: The Expedition Of Banū Sulaym 121
Chapter: The Expedition Of As-Sawīq 121
Chapter: The Expedition Of Dhī Amarr 122
Chapter: The Expedition Of Buhrān 122
Chapter: The Expedition Of Banū Qaynuqā' 122
Chapter: The Killing Of Ka'b Ibn Al-Ashraf, The Jew 123
Chapter: Comprising the Battle of Uhud, in Abridged Form 125
Chapter: The Expedition Of Hamrā' Al-Asad 134
Chapter: The Expedition Of Ar-Rajī' 136
Chapter: The Expedition of Bi'r Ma'ūnah 138
Chapter: The Expedition Of Banun-Nadīr 141
Chapter: The Military Expedition of Dhātur-Riqā' — and it is the Expedition to Najd 144
Chapter: Badr of the Appointment (Badrul-Maw'id) 148
Chapter: The Expedition of Dūmatul-Jandal 149
Chapter: Comprising an Abridgement of the Battle of the Trench (Al-Khandaq) 150
Chapter: Containing a Mention of the Expedition of Banū Quraydhah 158
Chapter: The Killing of Abū Rāfi' Sallām Ibn Abil-Huqayq 165
Chapter: The Expedition of Banū Lahyān 166
Chapter: The Expedition of Dhī Qarad 167
Chapter: The Expedition of Banul-Mustaliq or Al-Muraysī' 169
Chapter: The Expedition Of Al-Hudaybiyah 175
Chapter: The Expedition Of Khaybar 180
Chapter: The Conquest Of Fadak 183
Chapter: The Conquest Of Wādī Al-Qurā 184
Chapter: 'Umratul-Qadā' (The 'Umrah Performed In Accordance With the Terms of the Agreement) 184
Chapter: The Expedition Sent To Mu'tah 185
Chapter: The Conquest Of Makkah 189
Chapter: The Expedition of Khālid to Banū Jadhīmah 199
Chapter: The Expedition of Khālid Against Al-'Uzzā 199
Chapter: The Expedition of Hunayn 200

Chapter: The Expedition Of At-Ṭā'if 206
Chapter: The Expedition of Tabūk, and it is the Expedition of Hardship (Ghazwatul-'Usrah) 210
Chapter: The Arrival of the Deputation of Thaqīf 216
Chapter: The Hajj of Abū Bakr As-Siddīq 217
Chapter: The Farewell Hajj (Hajjatul-Wadā') 219
Chapter: His Passing Away — (صَلَّى ٱللَّٰهُ عَلَيْهِ وَسَلَّمَ) 224

VOLUME TWO — His Circumstances, Characteristics, & the Matters Particular to him 233
Chapter: His (صَلَّى ٱللَّٰهُ عَلَيْهِ وَسَلَّمَ) Performing Hajj & 'Umrah 233
Chapter: The Number of his Military Expeditions and the Armies Which He Sent Out 234
Chapter: The Signs of his Prophethood 235
Chapter: His Foretelling of Future Events 244
Chapter: The Earlier Scriptures Sent Down from the Heavens Foretelling of Allāh's Messenger (صَلَّى ٱللَّٰهُ عَلَيْهِ وَسَلَّمَ) 246
Chapter: His (صَلَّى ٱللَّٰهُ عَلَيْهِ وَسَلَّمَ) Children 251
Chapter: Regarding his Wives (رَضِيَ ٱللَّٰهُ عَنْهُنَّ) 253
Chapter: The Slaves He Owned 264
Chapter: His (صَلَّى ٱللَّٰهُ عَلَيْهِ وَسَلَّمَ) Servants 265
Chapter: The Scribes of the Revelation 265
Chapter: The Mu'adhdhins 266
Chapter: A Mention of the Emissaries he Sent to the Kings of the Distant Lands 266
Chapter: His (صَلَّى ٱللَّٰهُ عَلَيْهِ وَسَلَّمَ) She-Camels and Horses 268
Chapter: His Weaponry 271
Chapter: Regarding His Outward Appearance 272
Chapter: And as for his Pure Manners 275
Chapter: A Mention of the Places Which he (صَلَّى ٱللَّٰهُ عَلَيْهِ وَسَلَّمَ) Visited and These are the Prophetic Journeys. 278
Chapter: Summary of his Hijrah and Other Expeditions 283
Chapter: The Ways in Which he (صَلَّى ٱللَّٰهُ عَلَيْهِ وَسَلَّمَ) Heard the Revelation 283
Chapter: Those Who Heard From him (صَلَّى ٱللَّٰهُ عَلَيْهِ وَسَلَّمَ) 289
Chapter: The Number of the Muslims When he (صَلَّى ٱللَّٰهُ عَلَيْهِ وَسَلَّمَ) Passed Away 290

Chapter: The Matters Particular to Allāh's Messenger (صَلَّى ٱللَّهُ عَلَيْهِ وَسَلَّمَ) 292

The First Category — Those Matters Which Were Specific to him to the Exclusion of the Other Prophets 295

Chapter: The State of the Prophets in their Sleep and in their Graves 310

The Second Category — That Which was Particular to him, to the Exclusion of his Nation, though the other Prophets may share with him in some of it 312

The Book Of Īmān (True Faith): 312

Chapter: The Book of Purification 321

The Book of the Prayer 329

The Book of Zakāt 339

The Book of Fasting 340

The Book of Hajj 341

The Book of Foods 343

And Regarding Gifts: 348

And Regarding the Laws of Inheritance 349

The Book of Marriage 350

And Regarding Jihād 366

And Regarding Rulings (Al-Ahkām): 369

Chapter: An Indication of the Types of Intercession (Ash-Shafā'ah) Which Our Prophet Muhammad (صَلَّى ٱللَّهُ عَلَيْهِ وَسَلَّمَ) Will Be Granted 377

Appendix One — The Islamic Months 389

Appendix Two — Timeline of Key Events in the Life of the Messenger (صَلَّى ٱللَّهُ عَلَيْهِ وَسَلَّمَ) 390

Appendix Three — The Lineage of the Prophet (صَلَّى ٱللَّهُ عَلَيْهِ وَسَلَّمَ) 414

Appendix Four — The Ten Companions Promised Paradise 416

Appendix Five — The Wives of Allāh's Messenger (صَلَّى ٱللَّهُ عَلَيْهِ وَسَلَّمَ) — May Allāh be pleased with them all 419

Appendix Six — The Children of Allāh's Messenger (صَلَّى ٱللَّهُ عَلَيْهِ وَسَلَّمَ) 422

Appendix Seven — Maps & Diagrams 426

Endnotes 430

Translator's References 589

Publisher's Note

In the Name of Allāh, the Possessor of Vast Mercy, the One who bestows mercy upon whom He wills.

Before you is the translation of the book *Al-Fusūl Fī Sīratir-Rasūl* (*Chapters from the Life of the Messenger*) by the great Imām, Al-Hāfidh Ibn Kathīr (رَحِمَهُ ٱللَّهُ). It was translated over a number of years by the erudite translator of English descent; the Shaikh, Abū Talhah Dāwūd Burbank, who passed away with his wife whilst performing Hajj with the brothers from Salafi Publications in 2011 CE — may Allāh have mercy upon them both. The process of preparing this book for publication took a number of years, however we are honoured to finally be able to present this translation to the respected readers, and we hope that Allāh causes it to be a means for good, and that He rewards both the original author and the translator for their enormous efforts.

The translator has added extensive notes where appropriate to clarify authenticity of narrations, provide useful definitions, or points of benefit derived from the Sunnah and the works of the scholars. These have been placed in the footnotes, and the longer ones at the back of the book in a section entitled *Endnotes*. Breadcrumbs have been placed in the pages of the main translation section, which point the reader to the corresponding endnote and its page number.

It is important to note that this book was translated many years ago, and the station of some of the people referenced in the footnotes and endnotes may have changed since that time. Certain individuals whom the translator used as references were at the time deemed people who were strong in creed and upon the correct path, however they have since strayed from the correct path — may Allāh guide us and guide them. In any case, it is advised that the Muslim maintain upmost vigilance as it relates to whom he or she takes their knowledge from. As is reported from the great Imām, Muhammad Ibn Sīrīn (رَحِمَهُ ٱللَّهُ): *"Indeed this knowledge is religion — so be aware of whom you take your religion from."*

With that we leave the respected reader to embark upon the study and reflection over this tremendous work.

Regarding Footnotes and Endnotes

The translator has added extensive notes where appropriate to clarify authenticity of narrations, provide useful definitions, or points of benefit derived from the Sunnah and the works of the scholars.

These have been placed in the footnotes, and the longer ones at the back of the book in a section entitled *Endnotes*. Breadcrumbs have been placed in the pages of the main translation section, which point the reader to the corresponding endnote and its page number.

This translation has been produced using the following three printed Arabic editions, from which footnotes have been extracted and abridged. The source for a footnote or endnote is indicated by the letters that precede it.

1. (MK)(MM) The edition of Dār Ibn Kathīr and Maktabah Dārit-Turāth, 4th edition 1405 H; with the notes and checking of Muhammad Al-'Eid Al-Khatrāwī and Muhiyyuddīn Mostū (412 pages).
2. (BJ)(SZ) The edition of Maktabatul-Ma'ārif Lin-Nashr Wat-Tawzī', 1st edition, 1420 H; with the notes and checking of Dr. Bāsim Ibn Faysal Al-Jawābirah and Samīr ibn Amīn Az-Zuhayrī (367 pages).
3. (SH) The edition of Gharās Lin-nashr Wat-Tawzī', 1st edition, 1424 H; with the notes and checking of Salīm ibn 'Eid al-Hilālī (648 pages).
4. (DB) Footnotes included by the translator (Abū Talhah Dāwūd Burbank رَحِمَهُ ٱللَّهُ) from other sources are referenced.

Eulogy of Shaikh Abū Talhah Dāwūd Burbank and his Wife; Umm Talhah

An article written by Abū Khadeejah ʿAbdul-Wahid on the day of their passing.

Abū Talhah Dāwūd Burbank and his wife passed away earlier today, Tuesday 1st November 2011 (5th Dhul-Hijjah 1432H) — may Allāh shower them both with His abundant Mercy.

(Their Janāzah will be prayed at the Haram Masjid in Makkah, after Fajr on Wednesday 6th Dhul-Hijjah, Inshā-Allāh)

The eyes shed tears, there is sadness and grief in the heart, but we only say things pleasing to our Lord. Indeed we are saddened by the passing away of our brother Abū Talhah (رَحِمَهُ ٱللَّهُ), and his wife (رَحِمَهَا ٱللَّهُ).

> إِنَّا لِلَّهِ وَإِنَّا إِلَيهِ رَاجِعُون
>
> "Indeed to Allāh we belong and to Him we shall return."

Allāh (the Most Perfect and the Most High) said,

> وَبَشِّرِ الصَّابِرِينَ ۝ الَّذِينَ إِذَا أَصَابَتْهُم مُّصِيبَةٌ قَالُوا إِنَّا لِلَّهِ وَإِنَّا إِلَيْهِ رَاجِعُونَ ۝
> أُولَـٰئِكَ عَلَيْهِمْ صَلَوَاتٌ مِّن رَّبِّهِمْ وَرَحْمَةٌ ۖ وَأُولَـٰئِكَ هُمُ الْمُهْتَدُونَ ۝
>
> "And give glad tidings to the patient — those who, when afflicted with a calamity, say 'Indeed to Allāh we belong and to Him we shall return.' It is those who will be rewarded with blessings and mercy from their Lord. And it is those who are the guided ones." — **Sūrah Al-Baqarah 2:155-157**

Allāh's Messenger (ﷺ) said: "To Allāh belongs what He took, and to Him belongs what He gave. Everything is recorded with him for an appointed term."[1]

Both Abū Talhah and Umm Talhah were in a state of Ihrām, calling out the talbiyah — a proclamation wherein one audibly calls out the affirmation of Allāh's Tawhīd; his sole right to being worshipped. The Messenger of Allāh (ﷺ) stated on an occasion when a Companion died in a state of Ihrām:

> "Wash him with water and sidr (lotus), and shroud him in two garments. Do not embalm or perfume him, and do not cover his head or face. He will be resurrected on the Day of Judgment making the Talbiyah." — **Al-Bukhārī and Muslim**

They passed away in this month of Dhul-Hijjah on their way to Hajj in these most virtuous days of the world — days in which righteous deeds are most beloved to Allāh, the Most Merciful, the Most Majestic; as has been stated by the Prophet (ﷺ).

As they were traveling to Makkah, the bus they were on caught fire, and thereafter both of them were killed. Allāh's Messenger (ﷺ) stated:

> وَصَاحِبُ الْحَرِيقِ شَـهِيدٌ
>
> "Death from burning is a Shahādah (martyrdom)..."[2]

I have known Abū Talhah and his family (Umm Talhah) for twenty years. He has been my teacher, my friend, my confidant, an adviser, a support for myself and my family throughout this time. In the depths of battles practically throughout the whole of the nineties, he stood firm against the people of misguidance and bidʿah, translating material in clarification of the truth, and propagating the truth, without any compromising or fearing the blame of the blamers.

---

1 — *Ahkāmul-Janā'iz* of Imām Al-Albānī.

2 — *Sunan Abī Dāwūd: 3111.* Declared *'sahīh'* by Imām Al-Albānī.

He stood firm against the Sūfīs, the Ashʿarīs, the Khawārij and the Shīʿah. He translated the works of the scholars both past and present, making clear the path of Ahlus-Sunnah wal-Jamāʿah. He defended the honour of the scholars such as Shaikh Ibn Bāz, Shaikh Al-Albānī, Shaikh Muqbil bin Hādī and Shaikh Rabīʿ Al-Madkhalī when the partisans and the innovators in the West tried to dishonour and discredit them. He became a symbol and a sign of Salafiyyah in the West — and we do not praise anyone beyond Allāh, the Most High.

He was a prolific translator, having translated scores of books of the Scholars. From them was *At-Tawassul* of Shaikh Al-Albānī (رَحِمَهُ ٱللَّهُ), and thereby clarified the belief of Ahlus-Sunnah in opposition to the grave worshippers and Sūfīs. He translated *The Reality of Sūfism* of Shaikh Muhammad bin Rabīʿ Al-Madkhalī (حفظه الله), he translated *The Explanation of the Three Principles* of Shaikh Ibn Uthaimīn (رَحِمَهُ ٱللَّهُ), he translated *The Methodology of the Prophets in Calling to Allāh* of Shaikh Rabīʿ Al-Madkhalī (حفظه الله), he translated the seminal work; *The Explanation of the Creed* of Imām Al-Barbahārī (رَحِمَهُ ٱللَّهُ), and much more besides.

In the nineties, when the daʿwah was still in its infancy, many people left the Salafī Manhaj, preferring the paths of innovation — Dāwūd (رَحِمَهُ ٱللَّهُ) saw them come and saw them go, but he would not join them in their opposition. Rather, he would advise those who were once upon this path of Sunnah, and would show great concern for them so that they would not choose a path of misguidance. He would make duʿā for them, and then leave their affair to Allāh, and stop his association with them, only for the sake of Allāh.

He would not compromise with them, nor praise those who opposed this blessed Manhaj. He was the first person to translate the rudūd (refutations) of Shaikh Muqbil, Shaikh Al-Albānī and Shaikh Rabīʿ against Jamʿiyyah Ihyāʾ At-Turāth Al-Islāmī[1] — and their bidʿah was stemmed and almost cut off in the UK by way of these translations (by

---

1 — A Kuwaiti organisation who propogated their misguided Ikhwānī ideology internationally, using their vast funds, and their media and publishing apparatus.

the permission of Allāh). Allāh had blessed him with skills of translation that I have not seen equaled in the West, and Allāh knows best.

The Scholars loved and praised him and spoke highly of him, and were saddened at his passing away as has been narrated from many of the scholars — not least Shaikh Rabīʿ Ibn Hādī Al-Madkhalī, and Shaikh ʿUbaid Ibn ʿAbdillāh Al-Jābirī. In fact, Shaikh ʿUbaid Al-Jābirī invited his sons to give them words of comfort and advice in the days following the passing of their parents.

From those scholars who held our companion in high regard was Shaikh Muqbil Ibn Hādī Al-Wādiʿī (رَحِمَهُ ٱللَّهُ), who heard of the excellence of Dāwūd and wrote a tazkiyah (commendation) for him nearly fifteen years ago!

Shaikh ʿAbdus-Salām Burjiss Āl ʿAbdil-Karīm (رَحِمَهُ ٱللَّهُ) used to sit with us and advice us with the importance of knowledge and adhering to the Salafi Manhaj — and he loved the company of Abū Talhah, as did other scholars who mae visits to Birmingham. Shaikh ʿAbdus-Salām (رَحِمَهُ ٱللَّهُ), who was a former judge and scholar of Riyadh, would visit us from time to time in Birmingham, oftentimes bringing gifts, and knowing the shyness of Dāwūd, he would ask me to pass the gift to him on his behalf.

I recall back in 1999, when I was in Kuwait, sitting in a gathering of mashāyikh and they had heard that one of the children of Abū Talhah had become ill — so they spoke well of him and made duʿāʾ for his child. Then they asked me to convey their salutations to him.

He started teaching regularly in the mid 90s upon the advice of some of the mashāyikh, after they saw that the people of partisanship had left us and scattered, and we were few in number who remained upon the Sunnah and Salafiyyah. So they encouraged him to step up and teach the people what he possessed of knowledge, and call the people to Salafiyyah. So we set up classes, and only a handful sat in those durūs of ours in the early days — as this was in the era of the split from JIMAS, and was after Ihyāʾ At-Turāth (with the help of Suhaib Hasan and Green Lane Mosque) had poisoned many of the people with their hizbiyyah.

But Abū Talhah persisted and continued, not flinching from the immense task ahead of him. The Mashāyikh requested from me to remain close to Abū Talhah, to support him, encourage him and strengthen him in his determination.

Slowly but surely the numbers grew, the da'wah spread, the opposers were silenced, as the truth became clearer and clearer, and the da'wah of the scholars took root — and all praise is due to Allāh. Abū Talhah would teach from the well-known books, such as *Kitābut-Tawhīd* of Shaikh-ul-Islām Muhammad bin 'Abdul-Wahhāb, *Al-'Aqīdatul-Wāsitiyyah* of Ibn Taymiyyah, *Riyādhus-Sālihīn* of An-Nawawī, *As-Sahīhah* of Shaikh al-Albānī and many others. With these efforts and the efforts of others, and by the Grace of Allāh, Birmingham became a destination for Salafis in the UK, an island of Salafiyyah in this land.

People traveled and moved with their families to Birmingham. The scholars heard of the efforts being made and when asked about the da'wah in Europe, they would praise the efforts of the brothers in Birmingham at 'Salafi Publications', and encourage co-operation with them (as was advised by Shaikh Muqbil) and even living amongst them, if one could not migrate to a Muslim land (as was advised by Shaikh 'Ubaid and others). We worked collectively and tirelessly in disseminating the Salafi da'wah: Abū Talhah, Abū Hakeem, Abū 'Iyād (and others), and there is no doubt regarding the prominent and exceptional role Abū Talhah (رَحِمَهُ ٱللَّٰهُ) played in conveying this da'wah over the last 20 years.

Abū Talhah (رَحِمَهُ ٱللَّٰهُ) continued and never stopped calling the people to the 'aqīdah, the manhaj, the fiqh, the akhlāq (manners) and the ādāb (etiquette) of the Salaf — not for one moment have I known him to be upon anything other than that. He was firm upon the Sunnah, not compromising — if he knew something to be the haqq, he would hold to it with his molar teeth. Though he lived far from it, he would still walk miles to reach the Masjid As-Salafi, hoping for the reward from Allāh and a removal of sin for every step that he took — may Allāh have mercy on him. I would ask him, "Dāwūd, why do you not learn to drive?"

He would respond, "No thank you, I'm fine walking," and we would laugh.

He would not carry a mobile phone, and had no interest in having one, as he knew it would occupy him away from *"more important matters"*. He would rarely travel out of Birmingham for daʿwah, and on several occasions he would seek our advice before traveling. He was a loving and caring husband and father, with a beautiful sense of humor. He was full of information, and we would talk for hours sometimes about the Dīn and worldly matters of interest, but never was he lewd or foul.

He was conscious of time and being on time and not wasting time. In the trips to visit the Mashāyikh of Saudi Arabia, I would share the hotel room with him, we would talk for hours about the affairs of daʿwah — and then sometimes he would disappear, and we would not see him for hours. Then he'd reappear clutching bags of books that he had picked up at some obscure bookshop in Makkah or Madinah, before proceeding to sit down, and flick through them for hours. He'd return to the UK, quite often with overweight luggage! We'd have fun discussing the various scenarios to expect at the airport when our bags are weighed. He would say, "Well if Abū Hakeem can get away with it, so will I — Inshā-Allāh!".

In 2001, as the month of Dhul-Hijjah approached, Abū Talhah called me and said, "I've got some news. I'm going to Hajj, Inshā-Allāh."

I replied, "Māshā'Allāh Dāwūd! Excellent news!"

He said, "Would you like to come along?"

I responded, "Love to Dāwūd, but can't really afford it right now. Maybe next year."

So he said, "I will arrange the tickets — just say yes."

I said, "I don't want to put anyone through difficulty."

He said, "So you're coming, Inshā-Allāh."

So I gave in! This spirit of generosity and giving remained til the end — (رَحِمَهُ ٱللَّهُ).

It was the most enjoyable and memorable Hajj I have performed. We stayed in some strange apartments (!), and never left each other's sides throughout the nearly four weeks, and we used often to recall that Hajj trip of ours, and reminisce and smile. That Hajj we performed alongside several other brothers, including Abū Amān, Abū Hammād, Jamāl-ud-Dīn, Abū ʿAbdil-Karīm, Maqsūd, ʿAbdul-Hamīd and others. After that Hajj, there was never a time that Abū Talhah went to Makkah and Madinah, except that Abū Hakeem, Abū ʿIyād, and myself accompanied him.

He was from the founders of Al-Maktabah As-Salafiyyah (Salafi Publications) and a pillar of its early success, as his translations and research were an invaluable part of the daʿwah. It is amazing looking back at where we began in the early 90s, and how much we have gone through (and all praise is due to Allāh), that Salafiyyah has tens of thousands of adherents now in the UK — and to think that Allāh had decreed Abū Talhah (رَحِمَهُ ٱللَّهُ) to be a leading figure in that call. My brothers and sisters, make no mistake: he (رَحِمَهُ ٱللَّهُ) remained steadfast till the last. And we praise no one beyond Allāh.

I invited him to my home only a few weeks ago — him, his family and his children — and they spent the day with us till just before Maghrib. We spoke about the early days of the daʿwah when we were isolated, yet Allāh gave us resolve, and we spoke of the durūs in those days; classes that were based around the manhaj of tasfiyah (purification from falsehood) and tarbiyah (nurturing upon the truth). We spoke of how the people abandoned us and prevented us, and how the Mashāyikh stuck by us and would advise us, and then we would return back 're-charged' and enthused with energy — walhamdulillāh! May Allāh bless and preserve our mashāyikh.

We spoke of the sittings with the scholars, when Abū Talhah, Abū Hakeem, Abū ʿIyād, Hasan As-Somālī and myself would go regularly to Saudi Arabia and sit with the scholars; the Hajj and ʿUmrahs that we made together; the happy times and the tough battles — all memories that we cherished dearly. And how we have grown into middle-age upon this daʿwah, and how many scholars have passed away; and how old the living ones have become.

We spoke about Shaikh Rabīʿ (حَفِظَهُ اللَّه) a lot, and Abū Talhah expressed how much love he had for the Shaikh, and how angered he is at those who speak ill of him, and of Shaikh ʿUbaid and others. We spoke about natural health and issues related to natural medicine, as he was a proponent of natural foods and healthy living. He loved our brother Abū ʿIyād and would praise him often for his efforts in the daʿwah and his translations, and in bringing to the forefront the importance of Prophetic medicine and healthy living by eating healthily. We spoke, in this visit of his to my home, about where to get hold of organic and raw food, and we exchanged websites of organic suppliers. His sons sat, listened and participated in our discussions with polite and useful comments, showing the excellent tarbiyah (nurturing) of the parents upon their children. We spoke for hours, in the pleasure of each other's company.

Umm Talhah (رَحِمَهَا ٱللَّهُ) was a caring and careful mother; a joyful character who loved her children and cared immensely for the Sunnah and its implementation in the home. A day before she left for Hajj, she rang our home and spoke to my wife about how she was so overjoyed that Allāh, the Most Perfect and Most High, had given her another opportunity to perform Hajj — this endeavour for Allāh's sake. May Allāh unite these two loving parents with their children once more in the highest and most noble company, in the highest level of Jannah.

By Allāh, my brothers and sisters, I do not know of anyone in the West more meticulous in acting upon the Sunnah than Abū Talhah — he would know fine details of how the Messenger (صَلَّى ٱللَّهُ عَلَيْهِ وَسَلَّمَ) walked, talked, ate and behaved and he would follow him in that precisely. He was from the shyest of the people, from the most humble and with the least concern for the world and its glitter. I do not say this out of flattery for anyone, nor to raise a person above his level, but rather from my truthful knowledge of him. And this is something that was witnessed by the scholars, who would mention this to us about Abū Talhah (رَحِمَهُ ٱللَّهُ) in his absence, and they would praise his humility. Both myself and Abū Hakeem have heard this from our mashāyikh.

There is no doubt that we are saddened at the loss of our brother and his wife, especially those of us in the arena of daʿwah! My brothers such as Abū Hakeem, Abū ʿIyād, Hasan As-Somālī, Kashiff Khan, the brothers of Al-Maktabah As-Salafiyyah (may Allāh preserve them all), as well as those who attend the durūs and frequent the Masjid, have all expressed their sadness at the departure of this beloved brother and his wife. Myself and Abū Hakeem have received calls and messages from all across the UK, and the USA, Canada, KSA, Kuwait, the Caribbean, and Sri Lanka (to name a few) mentioning their sadness at the loss of our brother and sister — yet we utter only those words which please our Lord, the Mighty and Majestic.

O Allāh! Forgive Abū Talhah and forgive Umm Talhah, elevate their position amongst the guided ones, and raise good successors for them from their offspring. Forgive us and them, O Lord of the worlds, expand and illuminate their graves, for them both. Allāhumma Amīn!

Abū Khadeejah 'Abdul-Wāhid Alam

First written on the 1st November 2011.
Edited since then, and edited for the purpose of this book.
Birmingham, United Kingdom.

Post Script — Written by Abū Khadeejah 'Abdul-Wahid

Fact — Abū Talhah translated Shaikh Muqbil's refutations on 'Abdur-Rahmān 'Abdul-Khāliq and Jam'iyyah Ihyā' At-Turāth in 1996; articles which was distributed under the moniker: *'The Blazing Meteor'* series.

Fact — Abū Talhah translated Shaikh Muqbils' refutation on 'Abdullāh As-Sabt of Jam'iyyah Ihyā' At-Turāth in 1997.

Fact — Abū Talhah translated Shaikh Muqbil's refutations on Suhaib Hasan and Al-Hidāyah in 1997.

Fact — Abū Talhah translated Shaikh Rabī''s first critique of Suhaib Hasan and Jam'iyyah Ihyā' At-Turāth in 1997 after Hajj.

Fact — Abū Talhah translated sections from Shaikh Rabī''s book; *Jamā'ah Wāhidah Lā Jamā'āt*, in refutation of the head of Jam'iyyah Ihyā' At-Turāth; 'Abdur-Rahmān 'Abdul-Khāliq in 1998.

Fact — Abū Talhah translated portions of Shaikh 'Abdus-Salām Burjis's *Mu'āmalāt Al-Hukkām*, in refutation of the Qutubīs and those who called for revolt and revolution in the mid to late 1990's.

Fact — Abū Talhah prevented any amalgamation with Muhammad Surūr, after he had read the magazine entitled *As-Sunnah,* of this takfīrī in the early nineties — and found it to be in contradiction to the Sunnah!

Fact — Abū Talhah translated portions of the book *Al-Qutubiyyah* in refutation of the Qutubīs such as Safar Al-Hawālī and Salmān Al-'Awdah who were attacking the major scholars.

Fact — Abū Talhah translated the fatwa of Shaikh Ibn Bāz (رَحِمَهُ ٱللَّهُ) calling upon the authorities to prevent Safar and Salmān from delivering lectures, classes and their tapes from being distributed.

Fact — Abū Talhah translated many of Shaikh Rabī''s refutations against Sayyid Qutub and Al-Mawdūdī. His translation of *Manhaj Al-Anbiyā'* is a case in point.

Fact — Abū Talhah translated Shaikh Al-Albānī's refutations on Jam'iyyah Ihyā' At-Turāth and 'Abdur-Rahmān 'Abdul-Khāliq.

— And much more besides. Documented in his own handwriting (رَحِمَهُ ٱللَّهُ).

Preface Regarding the Importance of Sīrah

Excerpt from a Lecture of Shaikh Fawzān in Which he Details Some of the Important Benefits of Studying the Sīrah

In the name of Allāh, the Extremely Merciful, the Bestower of Mercy.

All praise is truly and deservedly for Allāh, and all extolment is for Him — He the Majestic and Most High; for He is the One Who bestows all favours, and He is the One Who shows beneficence, and He is the One Who bestows all blessings: and from the greatest of His blessings upon us is that He sent Muhammad (صَلَّى ٱللَّٰهُ عَلَيْهِ وَسَلَّمَ) to us as a guide, a bearer of glad tidings, and a warner:

> وَمَا أَرْسَلْنَاكَ إِلَّا رَحْمَةً لِّلْعَالَمِينَ
>
> MEANING: "And We sent you not except as a mercy to the creation." — SURAH AL-ANBIYĀ' (21): 107

> لَّقَدْ كَانَ لَكُمْ فِي رَسُولِ اللَّهِ أُسْوَةٌ حَسَنَةٌ لِّمَن كَانَ يَرْجُو اللَّهَ وَالْيَوْمَ الْآخِرَ وَذَكَرَ اللَّهَ كَثِيرًا
>
> MEANING: "There is certainly in Allāh's Messenger a fine example for you to follow, for those who hope for Allāh's reward and His Mercy in the Hereafter, and who remember Allāh frequently." — SŪRAH AL-AHZĀB (33): 21

And I testify that none has the right to be worshipped except Allāh, alone with no partner; and I testify that Muhammad is the Slave of Allāh, and

His Messenger, and His chosen one, and one especially beloved to Him. Through him Allāh (the Majestic and Most High) removed Shirk and its army. Through him Allāh (the Majestic and Most High) established Tawhīd and its people; and through him, He gave the people the ability to see, after they had been blind; and the people became guided, after having been astray.

So what a tremendous favour He (عَزَّوَجَلَّ) bestowed upon us in sending Muhammad (صَلَّى ٱللَّهُ عَلَيْهِ وَسَلَّمَ) as a Messenger to us, and how tremendously indebted to Muhammad (صَلَّى ٱللَّهُ عَلَيْهِ وَسَلَّمَ) is his nation.

So if they were to surrender themselves, their children, their families, and their wealth as a ransom for him they would not fulfil his (صَلَّى ٱللَّهُ عَلَيْهِ وَسَلَّمَ) right. Is he not the one who found us upon the brink of falling into the Fire, and he rescued us from it? May Allāh extol our Prophet Muhammad as abundantly as befits the direction that he gave, the knowledge that he taught, and the clear explanation that he brought.

We testify that he conveyed the Message, fulfilled his trust, truly and sincerely advised the nation, and he strove and fought truly for Allāh's sake. He left us upon pure, white guidance: its night is just like its day; no one deviates from it, after he (صَلَّى ٱللَّهُ عَلَيْهِ وَسَلَّمَ) left us upon it, except that he is destroyed.

And may Allāh extol those who follow them upon good until the Day of Recompensing, and may He make us from them, through the Mercy of the Most Merciful of those who are merciful.

To proceed:

Then I ask Allāh (the Majestic and Most High) that He should make me and you from those to whom He gives a humble and submissive heart, and supplications that are heard. O Allāh! Make us from those whose hearts are humble and submissive to You, and whose hearts soften at Your remembrance. O Allāh! And facilitate for us that we are guided aright in our affair: for we cannot make any movement, and we do not possess any ability, except with Your aid. We seek Your refuge from intending to exalt ourselves upon the earth or intending corruption. And we ask You that You save us from error, and from having foolish opinions, and from being far from what is correct. Indeed, You are the One Who guides to correctness.

> وَمَن يَهْدِ اللَّهُ فَهُوَ الْمُهْتَدِ
>
> MEANING: "And whomever Allāh guides then he is the one who is truly guided." — **Sūrah Al-Isrā' (17): 97**

Then at the start of this lecture I thank the honourable brothers in the Office of Da'wah and Guidance in the area of Al-Kharaj for inviting me for this lecture, and for the importance which they gave to it; and this is not surprising, since they are eager upon good, and they are represented by the virtuous brother Shaikh 'Abdur-Rahmān As-Saghīr, and likewise the virtuous brother, the Shaikh who is the imām of the mosque, and likewise the rest of the honourable brothers.

So I ask Allāh (عَزَّوَجَلَّ) for an increase in His bounty for them; and that He accepts from them whatever efforts they have made, and their movements to propagate the truth and the guidance.

Then the topic of this lecture is '**Principles for Understanding the Sīrah of the Chosen Messenger** (صَلَّى ٱللَّهُ عَلَيْهِ وَسَلَّمَ)' — and this lecture is not a sermon of admonition, rather it is a lecture to lay down principles for the topic of the Sīrah of the Prophet (صَلَّى ٱللَّهُ عَلَيْهِ وَسَلَّمَ). So perhaps, therefore, everyone will derive benefit from it, but particular benefit will be derived by those who have some relation to, or connection to knowledge, the Sunnah, the Sīrah, and to Da'wah and guidance; and there is no doubt that the Sīrah of the chosen Messenger (صَلَّى ٱللَّهُ عَلَيْهِ وَسَلَّمَ) is something to which the scholars have given importance in the earlier and later times, and that is because through the way and behaviour of the chosen Messenger (صَلَّى ٱللَّهُ عَلَيْهِ وَسَلَّمَ) matters are made clear, and He (the Majestic and Most High) said:

> لَّقَدْ كَانَ لَكُمْ فِي رَسُولِ اللَّهِ أُسْوَةٌ حَسَنَةٌ
>
> MEANING: "There is certainly in Allāh's Messenger a fine example for you to follow." — **Sūrah Al-Ahzāb (33): 21**

Therefore giving importance to the Sīrah is something essential, since through the Sīrah, and through giving importance to it, awareness is gained of all his conditions (عَلَيْهِ ٱلصَّلَاةُ وَٱلسَّلَامُ) from his birth to his passing away (عَلَيْهِ ٱلصَّلَاةُ وَٱلسَّلَامُ). Likewise through the Sīrah, the Muslim will come to know what the Prophet (صَلَّى ٱللَّهُ عَلَيْهِ وَسَلَّمَ) and his Companions did for the propagation of the Religion, and what they endured for it, and the sacrifices they made, such that they left the nation after them upon a plain and clear affair. So Islām did not spread with ease, rather he (عَلَيْهِ ٱلصَّلَاةُ وَٱلسَّلَامُ) exerted effort for it, and was aided by his Lord (عَزَّ وَجَلَّ); and his honourable Companions exerted themselves for it, and this will become apparent to you in the Sīrah.

Another reason why importance should be given to the Sīrah is that awareness of the Sīrah of the chosen Messenger (عَلَيْهِ ٱلصَّلَاةُ وَٱلسَّلَامُ) and awareness of the lives of the Companions along with him (صَلَّى ٱللَّهُ عَلَيْهِ وَسَلَّمَ), will stimulate in the hearts of the people of Īmān (true Faith) strength of Īmān, and strength of certainty; and that no matter how serious their problems become, and no matter how strong Satan and his army become, then they have a fine example to follow in Allāh's Messenger (صَلَّى ٱللَّهُ عَلَيْهِ وَسَلَّمَ), and they have a fine example in the honourable Companions. Indeed some of the Companions complained to the Prophet (صَلَّى ٱللَّهُ عَلَيْهِ وَسَلَّمَ) of the severe harm, which they were experiencing from the Quraysh. So he (صَلَّى ٱللَّهُ عَلَيْهِ وَسَلَّمَ) said:

> "In the times before you a man would be brought forth and he would be sawn into two halves, between his flesh and bones, and that would not cause him to turn back from his Religion. So by the One in Whose hand is my soul! Allāh will certainly complete this affair until a rider may travel from Makkah to Sanʿā" — or he said: "from Egypt to Makkah — not fearing anyone except Allāh, the Majestic and Most High."

So this makes it clear that there being a large number of people is not a condition for the truth; and that no matter what befalls the Believer from the plots of Satan, or from numerous desires, or from multiple temptations, then this only incites him to cling more tenaciously to the Religion of Allāh (عَزَّ وَجَلَّ), for the Companions (رَضِيَ ٱللَّهُ عَنْهُمْ) did not abandon their Religion. They did not abandon singling out Allāh with all worship (Tawhīd), and they did not abandon freeing themselves from Shirk (directing any form of worship to other than Allāh). They did not abandon what befell them — may Allāh's Pleasure be upon them. So what about the state of the people of this age — those who perhaps abandon something from the Religion for the slightest temptations.

So examining and reading the Sīrah instils in the Believer strength of certainty, and strengthens his readiness to remain firm upon the Religion. Likewise it instils in the heart of the believer strong esteem for and pride in the Religion of Islām; and that he has honour because of establishing the Tawhīd of Allāh (the Majestic and Most High), and that he has honour because of what his heart contains from awareness and knowledge of Allāh, and his believing truly in Muhammad (صَلَّى ٱللَّهُ عَلَيْهِ وَسَلَّمَ) and in that which He (عَزَّ وَجَلَّ) sent down to His Messenger:

> وَلِلَّهِ الْعِزَّةُ وَلِرَسُولِهِ وَلِلْمُؤْمِنِينَ
>
> MEANING: "And might and honour are for Allāh, and for His Messenger, and the Believers." — **Sūrah Al-Munafiqūn (63): 8**

So these are some of the many benefits, which every Believer will derive from looking into the Sīrah of the chosen Messenger (صَلَّى ٱللَّهُ عَلَيْهِ وَسَلَّمَ).

Therefore, the principle is that reading the Sīrah is not a case of just reading stories and narratives, but rather it is a case of reading to take admonition and to derive lessons. So points of benefit are to be taken from the Sīrah, and from it is to be taken whatever will benefit the Believer, and that which will instil in him good qualities, guidance, and adherence to the truth:

> فَاسْتَمْسِكْ بِالَّذِي أُوحِيَ إِلَيْكَ ۖ إِنَّكَ عَلَىٰ صِرَاطٍ مُّسْتَقِيمٍ ۝ وَإِنَّهُ لَذِكْرٌ لَّكَ وَلِقَوْمِكَ ۖ وَسَوْفَ تُسْأَلُونَ
>
> MEANING: "So cling, O Muhammad (صَلَّى ٱللَّهُ عَلَيْهِ وَسَلَّمَ), to that which your Lord revealed to you. Indeed, you are upon a straight path; and this Qur'ān is an honour for you and your people and you will all soon be asked about your action upon it." — **Sūrah Az-Zukhruf (43): 43-44**

So the people of knowledge have given attention to the various aspects of the Sīrah, because of its great importance.

Then what is meant by *'the Sīrah'* is whatever is reported from the Prophet (صَلَّىٱللَّهُعَلَيْهِوَسَلَّمَ), and from his Companions, and from the Tābi'īn and those who came after them, in description of the life of the Prophet (صَلَّىٱللَّهُعَلَيْهِوَسَلَّمَ), and his behaviour, and his condition, from his (صَلَّىٱللَّهُعَلَيْهِوَسَلَّمَ) birth until Allāh (the Majestic and Most High) took his soul.

So the Sīrah is, therefore, a narrative of what the Prophet (صَلَّىٱللَّهُعَلَيْهِوَسَلَّمَ) was upon from when he was born, until Allāh (عَزَّوَجَلَّ) took his soul. It contains an explanation of what occurred at his birth and of the appearance of miracles when he was born and of the portents of his (صَلَّىٱللَّهُعَلَيْهِوَسَلَّمَ) suckling, and a mention of his condition, and of his mother and his paternal uncle, and the like of that. It contains a mention of his (صَلَّىٱللَّهُعَلَيْهِوَسَلَّمَ) life and his behaviour whilst young, until Allāh (عَزَّوَجَلَّ) raised him as a Prophet; and a description of his manners and characteristics before he was raised as a Prophet.

Likewise the Sīrah is a narrative of his (صَلَّىٱللَّهُعَلَيْهِوَسَلَّمَ) condition, from the time when Allāh (عَزَّوَجَلَّ) raised him as a Prophet; so he conveyed the call of Allāh, and he had patience upon that and what he experienced from harm; and how he conveyed the message, and the means which he used to convey the message, until he migrated to Al-Madīnah; and from his migration to Al-Madīnah, and his establishment of the first Islamic state, until Allāh (عَزَّوَجَلَّ) took his soul.

INTRODUCTION OF THE VERIFIERS:

Samīr Az-Zuhayrī & Dr. Bāsim Al-Jawābirah

All praise is for Allāh. We praise Him, we seek His aid, and we ask for His forgiveness. We seek Allāh's refuge from the evils of our selves and from the evil consequences of our deeds. Whomever Allāh guides then none can misguide him, and whomever He misguides then none can guide him. I testify that none has the right to be worshipped except Allāh, alone, having no partner; and I testify that Muhammad is His Slave and His Messenger.

> يَا أَيُّهَا الَّذِينَ آمَنُوا اتَّقُوا اللَّهَ حَقَّ تُقَاتِهِ وَلَا تَمُوتُنَّ إِلَّا وَأَنتُم مُّسْلِمُونَ
>
> THE MEANING OF THIS VERSE: "O you who believe in Allāh and His Messenger! Fear and be dutiful to Allāh, by obeying Him and avoiding disobedience to Him, as He deserves to be feared (Obey Him and do not disobey Him; give thanks to Him and do not show ingratitude; remember Him and do not forget Him); and do not die except as Muslims: obediently submitting to Him, and worshipping Him alone."[1] — **Sūrah Āl-'Imrān (3): 102**

---

1 — DB The meaning and explanation given for verses of the Qur'ān is abridged from *Jāmi' Al-Bayān* — the tafsīr (exegesis) of Imām Muhammad ibn Jarīr At-Tabarī (d. 310H) (رَحِمَهُ ٱللَّهُ), and from the other reliable tafsīrs — such as the tafsīr of Imām Al-Baghawī (d. 516H) and the tafsīr of the author — Al-Hāfidh Ibn Kathīr (d. 774H) (رَحِمَهُ ٱللَّهُ).

يَا أَيُّهَا النَّاسُ اتَّقُوا رَبَّكُمُ الَّذِي خَلَقَكُم مِّن نَّفْسٍ وَاحِدَةٍ وَخَلَقَ مِنْهَا زَوْجَهَا وَبَثَّ مِنْهُمَا رِجَالًا كَثِيرًا وَنِسَاءً ۚ وَاتَّقُوا اللَّهَ الَّذِي تَسَاءَلُونَ بِهِ وَالْأَرْحَامَ ۚ إِنَّ اللَّهَ كَانَ عَلَيْكُمْ رَقِيبًا

MEANING: "O Mankind! Fear and be dutiful to your Lord, Who alone created you from a single person (Ādam), and from him He created his mate, and from these two He produced many men and women; and fear and be dutiful to Allāh through Whom you ask each other for your rights, and beware of cutting ties of kinship. Allāh is always a Watcher over you." — **Sūrah An-Nisā' (4): 1**

يَا أَيُّهَا الَّذِينَ آمَنُوا اتَّقُوا اللَّهَ وَقُولُوا قَوْلًا سَدِيدًا ۝ يُصْلِحْ لَكُمْ أَعْمَالَكُمْ وَيَغْفِرْ لَكُمْ ذُنُوبَكُمْ ۗ وَمَن يُطِعِ اللَّهَ وَرَسُولَهُ فَقَدْ فَازَ فَوْزًا عَظِيمًا

MEANING: "O you who believe in Allāh and His Messenger! Fear and be dutiful to Allāh and speak with truth and justice, and He will rectify your deeds for you and forgive your sins; and whoever obeys Allāh and His Messenger has attained tremendous success." — **Sūrah Al-Ahzāb (33): 70-71**

To proceed: Then the truest speech is the Book of Allāh (عَزَّوَجَلَّ), and the best way is the way of Muhammad (صَلَّىٱللَّهُعَلَيْهِوَسَلَّمَ); and the worst of affairs are those things which are new introductions (into the Religion) and every new introduction is an innovation, and every innovation is misguidance, and all misguidance will be in the Fire.

Then Allāh (the Mighty and Majestic) has commanded us to take the noblest one of mankind as an example, and to follow him (صَلَّىٱللَّهُعَلَيْهِوَسَلَّمَ), so He (the One free of all imperfections and the Most High) said:

لَّقَدْ كَانَ لَكُمْ فِي رَسُولِ اللَّهِ أُسْوَةٌ حَسَنَةٌ لِّمَن كَانَ يَرْجُو اللَّهَ وَالْيَوْمَ الْآخِرَ وَذَكَرَ اللَّهَ كَثِيرًا

MEANING: "There is certainly in Allāh's Messenger a fine example for you to follow, for those who hope for Allāh's reward and His Mercy

> in the Hereafter, and who remember Allāh frequently." — **Sūrah Al-Ahzāb (33): 21**

So this āyah, which restricts the fine example to the Prophet (صَلَّىٱللَّهُعَلَيْهِوَسَلَّمَ), gives nobility to the Believers, and makes it clear that this example applies and is restricted to them alone. So this is a Favour from the Lord of the whole of creation upon the Believers.

Then from the completion of taking him (صَلَّىٱللَّهُعَلَيْهِوَسَلَّمَ) as an example is to know and study his Sīrah, and that is because of its tremendous benefit for the life of the Muslim, as will follow.

So here are some brief glimpses of important introductory points that the student of knowledge of the Sīrah needs.

Firstly: The Sīrah and the Sunnah

[ONE] The 'Sunnah' in the language means: *'A path and a way of acting, whether it be praiseworthy or blameworthy.'*

With this meaning comes the Saying of He (عَزَّوَجَلَّ):

> سُنَّةَ اللَّهِ فِي الَّذِينَ خَلَوْا مِن قَبْلُ ۖ وَلَن تَجِدَ لِسُنَّةِ اللَّهِ تَبْدِيلًا
>
> MEANING: "That was Allāh's Way (Sunnah) with those who passed away before; and you will not find any change in Allāh's Way." — **Sūrah Al-Ahzāb (33): 62**

Another example of this is his (صَلَّىٱللَّهُعَلَيْهِوَسَلَّمَ) saying: "Whoever establishes a fine precedent (sunnah) in Islām, then for him shall be its reward and the reward of those who act upon it after him, without anything being reduced from their rewards; and whoever establishes an evil precedent in Islām, then upon him shall be its sin and the sin of those who act upon it after him, without anything being reduced from their sin." — Reported by Muslim (no. 1017) as a hadīth of Jarīr.

[TWO] The 'Sunnah' in the technical sense means: *'Everything that is established from the Prophet Muhammad (صَلَّىٱللَّهُعَلَيْهِوَسَلَّمَ) from sayings, actions, and tacit approvals.'*

[THREE] The 'Sīrah' in the language means: *'A path and a way of acting, whether it be praiseworthy or blameworthy'*, or it is: *'the condition which a person, or other than him, is upon'*; so it should be noticed that 'Sunnah' and 'Sīrah' in the linguistic sense have the same meaning.

[FOUR] The 'Sīrah' in the technical sense means: *'Knowledge of all the conditions of the Prophet (صَلَّىٰٱللَّهُعَلَيْهِوَسَلَّمَ), in detail, from the time of his birth until his death, and whatever is connected to that.'*

So by means of this comprehensive knowledge of the Sīrah of the Prophet (صَلَّىٰٱللَّهُعَلَيْهِوَسَلَّمَ): knowledge of the condition of his people before Islām, and of his lineage, his birth, his being sent as a Prophet, his military expeditions, his call, his manners, and so on, the Muslim becomes able to correctly follow his Prophet (صَلَّىٰٱللَّهُعَلَيْهِوَسَلَّمَ). This will also inspire confidence in the heart of the Muslim that what he is following him upon is not open to error, and is not open to any doubt, since the one who is being followed is the Prophet (صَلَّىٰٱللَّهُعَلَيْهِوَسَلَّمَ), who is rendered free from error.

Secondly: The Connection Between the Prophetic Sīrah & the Sunnah

[ONE] The Prophetic Sīrah stands apart from the Sunnah in its covering all the stages of the life of the Prophet (صَلَّىٰٱللَّهُعَلَيْهِوَسَلَّمَ), from the day of his birth — indeed from before that, and what accompanied his birth, and affirmation of his lineage: his forefathers, and their status amongst the Arabs, and the nobility of (his lineage); and a mention of his (صَلَّىٰٱللَّهُعَلَيْهِوَسَلَّمَ) description; and his servants and the slaves he owned; and the description of his apartments, and the roads which he walked upon, and the wells which he drank from; and his shoes, his riding-beasts, and so on.

[TWO] The Sunnah stands apart from the Sīrah with regard to the ahādīth of rulings (*ahkām*), creed and beliefs (*Al-'Aqā'id*), manners (*Al-Ādāb*), and encouragements and deterrents (*At-Targhīb wat-Tarhīb*), and so on.

[THREE] The Sunnah stands apart in the fact that everything in it is a proof, however this proof will vary in accordance with the levels of the five rulings , since it is Revelation from the Lord of the whole of creation (just as occurs in His Saying — He the Most High said: MEANING *"It is but Revelation revealed,"*) contrary to the Sīrah, which contains some things that the Muslim is not required to follow, and which he is not duty-bound to take as an example.

[FOUR] However these two: the Sunnah and the Sīrah come together in some affairs, such as: explanation of his (ﷺ) fine manners, the description of his clothing, the manner in which he ate, how he drank, how he slept, and so on.

Thirdly: The Connection Between the Sīrah and History (At-Tārīkh)

The Prophetic Sīrah has a strong connection to Islamic history since it represents a part of this history, so it has the connection of a part of the whole.

So the books of history are the works which give importance to relating the historical events of the nations and states, and the history of mankind from the time of the creation of Ādam, generally, until the time of the author. As for the Prophetic Sīrah then it relates to the time when the Prophet (ﷺ) lived, and to whatever pertains to him (ﷺ).

Fourthly: The Fruits of Studying the Sīrah

[ONE] Through study of the Sīrah it becomes possible to follow his (ﷺ) example more completely. He (the Most High) said:

> لَّقَدْ كَانَ لَكُمْ فِي رَسُولِ اللَّهِ أُسْوَةٌ حَسَنَةٌ لِّمَن كَانَ يَرْجُو اللَّهَ وَالْيَوْمَ الْآخِرَ
> وَذَكَرَ اللَّهَ كَثِيرًا
>
> MEANING: "There is certainly in Allāh's Messenger a fine example for you to follow, for those who hope for Allāh's reward and His Mercy in the Hereafter, and who remember Allāh frequently." — **SŪRAH AL-AHZĀB (33): 21**

[TWO] Actualization of the servant's love of his Lord — the Mighty and Majestic, which cannot be completed except through following the Messenger of Allāh (ﷺ); and this will not come about except through knowledge and awareness of his characteristics, meaning through study of the Sīrah. Allāh (the Mighty and Majestic) said:

> قُلْ إِن كُنتُمْ تُحِبُّونَ اللَّهَ فَاتَّبِعُونِي يُحْبِبْكُمُ اللَّهُ
>
> MEANING: "Say to them O Muhammad: If you truly love Allāh then follow me, then Allāh will love you." — **Sūrah Āl-Imrān (3): 31**

[THREE] Knowledge and awareness of many of the rulings of the Legislation, which came through Āyahs of the Qur'ān and Prophetic ahādīth, and the manner in which they are to be implemented — as they were implemented by the Prophet (صَلَّى ٱللَّهُ عَلَيْهِ وَسَلَّمَ).

[FOUR] Studying the Prophetic Sīrah aids a person upon awareness of the abrogating and the abrogated texts (*An-Nāsikh wal-Mansūkh*), whether in the Noble Qur'ān or in the Prophetic Sunnah.

[FIVE] Deriving benefit from the admonitions and the lessons which are to be found throughout the Sīrah, and which are equally applicable to the individual Muslim and to the Islamic society as a whole.

[SIX] Knowledge and awareness of the signs of his (صَلَّى ٱللَّهُ عَلَيْهِ وَسَلَّمَ) Prophethood, and of the miracles by which Allāh (the Mighty and Majestic) aided him. This increases Īmān and strengthens it.

[SEVEN] Study of the Prophetic Sīrah is an aid to acquiring awareness of the underlying reasons behind the Legislation and its wisdom; and studying it likewise produces awareness of the reasons for the sending down of Āyahs, and of the incidents behind some of the ahādīth.

[EIGHT] Through study of the Prophetic Sīrah the Muslim will come across the severity of the hostility shown by the Disbelievers and the People of the Book towards Islām and the Muslims: this will become apparent through awareness of their plots and their goals. The Muslim will also come across the Jihād of the Prophet (صَلَّى ٱللَّهُ عَلَيْهِ وَسَلَّمَ) and the Jihād of his Companions to break the strength of the Disbelievers, and to remove every obstacle that prevents the call of Islām from reaching the whole of mankind.

Fifthly: The Sources of the Sīrah, and the Most Important Works Written About it

1 — The Noble Qur'ān

The Noble Qur'ān contains many Āyahs which deal with the Sīrah of the Prophet (ﷺ), relating to before he was sent as a Prophet and afterwards. The Qur'ān also deals with the religious, political, and social life of the Arabs before Islām; and there is a great deal in the Qur'ān concerning the Prophetic military expeditions: their initial stages, their results, and their effects. It also completely illuminates the stance of the Hypocrites and Hypocrisy in Al-Madīnah.

Furthermore, the text of the Qur'ān is something definite with regard to its establishment, and it has a degree of sanctity not reached by other texts. So therefore there is no doubt that it is the most important, the greatest, and the most authentic source from the sources of the Sīrah.

Then there are a number of works that have been written concerning Sīrah in the light of the Qur'ān, from them;

- *As-Sīrat An-Nabawiyyah fī Daw'il Qur'ān was-Sunnah* of Muhammad Abū Shuhbah
- *Sīratur-Rasūl* (ﷺ) *Suwar Muqtabasah minal-Qur'ānil-Karīm* of Muhammad 'Izzat Darūzah
- *As-Sīratun-Nabawiyyatul-'Atirah fil-āyātil-Qur'āniyyah Al-Musattarah* of Shaikh Muhammad Ibrāhīm Shaqrah.

2 — The Books of the Noble Prophetic Ahādīth

These works gather the sayings of the Prophet (ﷺ), his actions, and his tacit approvals; and many of them contain a mention of his Sīrah and his military expeditions.

Some of these works devote a whole book, or a number of chapters to aspects of his (ﷺ) Sīrah, such as: the book of Jihād, the book of Military Expeditions, the book of the Virtues of the Prophet (ﷺ) and the Virtues of his Companions, and other chapters and books within these works of hadīth.

These books also contain many narrations that relate particularly to the Sīrah, and they are to be found throughout these books, in accordance with the choice and arrangement of the author.

From these books of hadīth are: the *Sahīh* of Al-Bukhārī, the *Sahīh* of Muslim, the *Sunan* of An-Nasā'ī, the *Sunan* of Abū Dāwūd, the *Sunan* of At-Tirmidhī, the *Sunan* of Ibn Mājah, the *Musnad* of Ahmad, the *Musnad* of Abū Ya'lā, the *Sahīh* of Ibn Khuzaymah, the *Sahīh* of Ibn Hibbān, the *Mustadrak 'alas-Sahīhayn* of Al-Hākim, *Al-Ahādīthul-Mukhtārah* of Al-Maqdisī, *Al-Musannaf* of 'Abdur-Razzāq, *Al-Musannaf* of Ibn Abī Shaybah, the three *Mu'jams* (*Al-Kabīr*, *Al-Awsat*, and *As-Saghīr*) of At-Tabarānī, and other works.

3 — The Books of 'Shamā'il' (Prophetic Characteristics)

They are the books which comprise the ahādīth and reports relating to the attributes and manners of the Prophet (صَلَّىٰ ٱللَّٰهُ عَلَيْهِ وَسَلَّمَ), and his conditions, and his way and behaviour, from the time of his birth until his (صَلَّىٰ ٱللَّٰهُ عَلَيْهِ وَسَلَّمَ) death. They do not deal with his (صَلَّىٰ ٱللَّٰهُ عَلَيْهِ وَسَلَّمَ) military expeditions, nor with his life as a whole — as is the case with the books of military expeditions and Sīrah.

Then from the most famous of these books are:

- *Ash-Shamā'ilul-Muhammadiyyah* of At-Tirmidhī, the compiler of the *Sunan* (d. 279 H). It has been published, and it has been abridged by Shaikh Muhammad Nāsiruddīn Al-Albānī who removed the unauthentic ahādīth from it.
- *Al-Anwār fī Shamā'ilin-Nabiyyil-Mukhtār* of Al-Baghawī, the compiler of *Sharhus-Sunnah* (d. 516 H).
- *Ash-Shifā' bit-ta'rīf fī huqūqil-Mustafā* of Al-Qādī 'Iyād (d. 544 H).
- *Ash-Shamā'il* of Ibn Kathīr (d. 774 H), included within his book *Al-Bidāyah wan-Nihāyah.*

4 — The Books of the Signs of Prophethood (Dalā'ilun-Nubuwwah)

These are also books devoted by their authors to a specific aspect relating to the Prophet (صَلَّى ٱللَّهُ عَلَيْهِ وَسَلَّمَ), and it is the aspect of his miracles, and the signs proving his Prophethood.

Concerning this, very many books have been written, but the most comprehensive books compiled concerning that, even though they include Sīrah along with the signs of Prophethood, are:

- *Dalā'ilun-Nubuwwah* of Abū Nu'aym (d. 430 H);
- *Dalā'ilun-Nubuwwah* of Imām Al-Bayhaqī (d. 458 H), and it is one of the most extensive and comprehensive of them;
- *Dalā'ilun-Nubuwwah* of Abul-Qāsim Ismā'īl ibn Muhammad Al-Asbahānī (d. 535 H).

5 — The Books of Military Expeditions (Al-Maghazī) and Events of the Sīrah, and the Most Famous Works on this, from the Earlier and Later Times

The material contained in these books is generally found scattered throughout the books of hadīth. However, the scholars and imāms of hadīth gave special attention to the Sīrah of the Messenger (صَلَّى ٱللَّهُ عَلَيْهِ وَسَلَّمَ), and this began very early on and continued until they devoted specific works to it.

Some of the Companions gave a great deal of attention and importance to the topic of Sīrah. Amongst them were Ibn 'Abbās, Ibn 'Umar, Al-Barā', and others (رَضِيَ ٱللَّهُ عَنْهُمْ).

As for the Tābi'īn, then they took this importance given to the Prophetic Sīrah from the Companions (رَضِيَ ٱللَّهُ عَنْهُمْ) and wrote works concerning it, and then they were followed upon that by those who succeeded them and those who came afterwards.

So at the forefront of them are:

[ONE] 'Urwah ibn Az-Zubayr, who was one of the imāms, the reliable narrators of hadīth, and the seven famous jurists, (d. 94 H). Dr. Muhammad Mustafā Al-A'zamī has gathered the reports of 'Urwah on the Sīrah, as narrated by Abul-Aswad, and has published it as a book entitled *Maghāzī Rasūlillāh* (ﷺ) *li-'Urwah ibn Az-Zubayr biriwāyati Abil-Aswad yatīm 'Urwah*;

[TWO] Muhammad ibn Muslim ibn Shihāb Az-Zuhrī (d. 124 H). He was from the major imāms of hadīth, and the first one to gather the '*musnads*' (collections of hadīth from each individual Companion). Dr. Suhayl Zakkār has gathered the narrations of Az-Zuhrī from the source works, and has published them in a book entitled *Al-Maghāzī An-Nabawiyyah*.

Imām At-Tahāwī said in *Sharh Ma'āniyyil-āthār* (3/112): "The narrations of Maghāzī revolve around 'Ikrimah — the mawlā of Ibn 'Abbās — and Az-Zuhrī."

[THREE] Mūsā ibn 'Uqbah. He was reliable as a narrator, a jurist, an imām concerning the military expeditions, (d. 141 H). He was one of the students of Az-Zuhrī and wrote a book of the military expeditions. A part of it has reached us and has been published by the orientalist Edward Sachau in the year 1904 C.E. with the title *Al-Muntaqā min Maghāzī Mūsā ibn 'Uqbah* from a manuscript which he found in Berlin.

Also Dr. Akram Al-'Umarī gathered many of his narrations and published them as a research paper in the journal of the college of Islamic Studies in Baghdad, No. 1 (1387 H).

[FOUR] Muhammad ibn Is-hāq ibn Yasār Al-Muttalibī (d. 150 H). He grew up in Al-Madīnah An-Nabawiyyah, and he gathered a great deal from the scholars, and he gave extra attention to Sīrah and the history of the people. He used to ask the young and the old, the men and the women, until he gathered a tremendous amount of knowledge of that. He studied under Abān ibn 'Uthmān ibn 'Affān, and Nāfi' — the mawlā of Ibn 'Umar — and Az-Zuhrī, and he saw Anas and Ibn Al-Musayyib.

He travelled a great deal, and therefore he gathered abundant knowledge and was alone in reporting some things, to the exclusion of others. For this reason, some of the people of knowledge spoke about him, whereas others declared him to be reliable. What is most correct is that he is '*hasan*' in his narrations of hadīth when he clearly states that he heard the narration directly.

He wrote concerning the Sīrah and he became famous for that, and he authored a book that is well known as *The Sīrah of Ibn Is-hāq*, whose title was actually *Al-Mubtada' wal-Bahth fil-Maghāzī* — a part of which has been published. So this book acquired fame and became known everywhere throughout the levels of Islamic society, and everyone who wrote about the Sīrah afterwards took benefit from it. The reason for the fame of the Sīrah of Ibn Is-hāq relates to a number of factors:

His extensive knowledge and his status in the field of knowledge, and because he took from the major scholars of hadīth, such as Az-Zuhrī and Abān ibn 'Uthmān, and in particular those who gave special attention to the Prophetic Sīrah.

He used to combine the different narrations that reached him about a particular event, and report them as a single continuous narrative — without distinguishing the narration of each separate narrator.

So in this way he made Sīrah a complete and comprehensive narrative. So therefore, it quickly entered the heart of the listener and was easier to understand, to take on, and to memorize.

He brought narrations and events in accordance with the order in which they occurred, and he took this from his teacher Az-Zuhrī who wrote his Sīrah in accordance with years and chapters; and this was done for the first time in his time.

The abridgement of Ibn Hishām added elegance and polish to it, and opened the way for the scholars to benefit from it. So they began to explain it, study it, and add notes to it, and it began to be narrated again.

So Ibn Hishām (رَحِمَهُ ٱللَّهُ) carried out a great work in arranging and abridging it. He removed that which was unauthentic, in particular the falsely concocted poems, and he added things for which there was a need. So this work produced such a profound effect that the people forgot the Sīrah of Ibn Is-hāq and instead called it the Sīrah of Ibn Hishām.

[FIVE] Muhammad ibn ʿUmar Al-Wāqidī (d. 207 H). Most of the verifiers of hadīth criticized him severely with regard to narrating hadīth, whilst some of them declared him to be reliable. Therefore, Al-Hāfidh [Ibn Hajr] said in *At-Taqrīb*: "Abandoned despite his extensive knowledge."

Ibn Sayyidin-Nās quoted nearly all of the sayings about him, those criticizing him and those declaring him reliable, and he defended him, and gave strength to his position.

He wrote *Kitābul-Maghāzī* that has been published in three volumes, with the verification of the orientalist Dr. Marsden Jones.

As for the most important qualities that gave a special status to Al-Wāqidī, from amongst the compilers of the Sīrah and the military expeditions, then they are:

- He mentions the names of those he reported his narrations from;
- the precise arrangements that he gives to events and their various details;
- he specifies the date of the battle;
- he mentions geographic details about the battle or the military detachment that he is speaking about;
- he mentions further details relating to the battle. So he mentions the names of those whom the Prophet (ﷺ) left in charge of Al-Madīnah; and he mentions the lines of poetry said by the Muslims during the fighting; and the Āyahs of the Qurʾān that came down on the occasion, and he explains those Āyahs.

Perhaps these reasons also lead to him being criticized since he had been preceded in these matters.

THE MOST IMPORTANT PRESENT DAY WORKS OF SĪRAH:

The present-day works on Sīrah fall into two categories:

[ONE] Works that abridge and refine the Sīrah, such as:

- *Taqrībus-Sīratin-Nabawiyyah* of Ibn Hishām;

- *Mukhtasar Sīratir-Rasūl* of Imām Muhammad ibn ʿAbdul-Wahhāb, and he wrote an extremely fine introduction to it;
- *Tahdhīb Sīrah Ibn Hishām* of ʿAbdus-Salām Hārūn.

[TWO] Works that are restricted to what is authentically established from the Prophetic Sīrah:

- *As-Sīratun-Nabawiyyatus-Sahīhah* of Dr. Akram Diyāʾ Al-ʿUmarī;
- *Sahīhus-Sīratin-Nabawiyyah* of Muhammad ibn Rizq At-Tarahūnī;
- *Sahīhus-Sīratin-Nabawiyyah* of Ibrāhīm Al-ʿAliyy;
- *As-Sīratun-Nabawiyyah fī dawʾil-masādiril-Asliyyah* of Dr. Muhammad Rizqullāh Ahmad, and this is the most extensive and the best of them. He has clearly expended great effort, for which he is to be thanked, in producing it; and we have benefitted from the introduction of the book, and from the points of benefit, the points of wisdom, and the lessons that he mentioned throughout the book. So may Allāh reward him with good, and place it upon the scale of his (good) deeds.

[THREE] General works on the Sīrah by present-day writers which gather whatever is reported concerning a particular topic from the topics of Sīrah, which the author researches.

These are mostly written as university research papers, such as: *The Battle of Badr: Research and Verification*, *The Battle of Tabūk*, and so on.

[FOUR] Other present-day works, which concentrate upon an explanation of extraction of the lessons and precepts from the Sīrah, without focussing upon distinguishing what is authentic from them.

So from these are:

- *As-Sīratun-Nabawiyyah: Durūs wa ʿibar* of Mustafā As-Sibaʾī;
- *Hādhal-Habīb yā Muhibb* of Shaikh Abū Bakr Al-Jazāʾirī;
- *Fiqhus-Sīrah* of Al-Būtī, and Shaikh Muhammad Nāsiruddīn Al-Albānī has discussed it critically in a book entitled *Difāʿun ʿanil-hadīthin-Nabawī was-Sīrah war-Radd ʿalā jahālātid-Duktūril-Būtī fī*

Kitābihi Fiqhis-Sīrah (A Defence of the Prophetic Hadīth and the Sīrah, and a Refutation of the Ignorant Statements of Dr. Al-Būtī in his book 'Fiqhus-Sīrah');

- *Fiqhus-Sīrah* of Muhammad Al-Ghazālī, and its ahādīth have been researched by Shaikh Muhammad Nāsiruddīn Al-Albānī;
- *Ar-Rahīqul Makhtūm* of Safiyyur-Rahmān Al-Mubārakfūrī.

[FIVE] Works which strive to gather the Sīrah of the Messenger (صَلَّى ٱللَّٰهُ عَلَيْهِ وَسَلَّمَ) from the Qur'ān and the Sunnah whilst attempting to verify the narrations, such as: *As-Sīrah An-Nabawiyyah fī daw'il-kitāb was-Sunnah* of Dr. Muhammad Abū Shuhbah.

[SIX] Books of the affairs particular (*Khasā'is*) to the Prophet (صَلَّى ٱللَّٰهُ عَلَيْهِ وَسَلَّمَ) and his virtues — These books with what they contain from characteristics, affairs that are particular, and signs of Prophethood, can be benefitted from with regard to one of the aspects of the Prophetic Sīrah.

So from these works are:

- *Nihāyatus-Sūl fī Khasā'isir-Rasūl* (صَلَّى ٱللَّٰهُ عَلَيْهِ وَسَلَّمَ) of Ibn Dihyah Al-Kalbī (d. 633 H),
- *Ghāyatus-Sūl fī Khasā'isir-Rasūl* (صَلَّى ٱللَّٰهُ عَلَيْهِ وَسَلَّمَ) of Ibn Al-Mulaqqin (d. 723 H),
- *Bidāyatus-Sūl fī tafdīlir-Rasūl* (صَلَّى ٱللَّٰهُ عَلَيْهِ وَسَلَّمَ) of Al-'Izz Ibn 'Abdis-Salām (d. 660 H).

[SEVEN] Books of History (*At-Tārīkh*) — These are works that generally begin by speaking about the beginning of the creation, and end with the age of the author. Some of these works bring reports with connected chains of narration and others are without connected chains.

So from the works with connected chains are:

- *Tārīkhul-Umam wal-Mulūk* ("*Tārīkhut-Tabarī*"), (d. 310 H),
- *Tārīkh Khalīfah ibn Khayyāt Al-'Asfarī* (d. 240 H).

And from the works which do not bring connected chains of narration:

- *Al-Kāmil* of Ibn Al-Athīr (d. 630 H),
- *Al-Bidāyah wan-Nihāyah* of Ibn Kathīr (d. 774 H),
- *Tārīkhul-Islām* of Adh-Dhahabī (d. 748 H).

[EIGHT] Books concerning the Companions — These books mention the names and biographies of the Companions, such as:

- *Al-Āhād wal-Mathānī* of Ibn Abī ʿĀsim (d. 287 H),
- *Maʿrifatus-Sahābah* of Abū Nuʿaym (d. 430 H),
- *Al-Istīʿāb fī maʿrifatil-As-hāb* of Ibn ʿAbdil-Barr (d. 463 H),
- *Usdul-Ghābah fī maʿrifatis-Sahābah* of Ibn Al-Athīr (d. 630 H),
- *Al-Isābah fī tamyīzis-Sahābah* of Ibn Hajr Al-ʿAsqalānī (d. 852 H).

[NINE] The Books of Tabaqāt (Levels of Narrators) — These comprise a mention of the Shaikhs, and their conditions, and their narrations, level by level and era by era, until the time of the author. The most important of these works are:

- *At-Tabaqātul-Kubrā* of Muhammad ibn Saʿd (d. 230 H),
- *Kitābut-Tabaqāt* of Khalīfah ibn Khayyāt Al-ʿAsfarī (d. 240 H).

[TEN] The Books of History of the Haramayn — These are books which are written by their authors concerning the history of Makkah Al-Mukarramah and Al-Madīnah An-Nabawiyyah, and the relics contained in them, and the events, and occurrences that happened in them, before and after Islām. There are many of these, and from those that have been printed are:

- *Tārīkh Makkah* of Abul-Walīd Muhammad ibn ʿAbdillāh Al-Azraqī (d. 250 H),
- *Tārīkh Makkah* of Abū ʿAbdillāh Al-Fākihī (d. 280 H),
- *Tārīkhul-Madīnah* of ʿUmar ibn Shabbah (d. 262 H),

Other Books

46 And finally, there are other books that it is possible to benefit from with regard to the Prophetic Sīrah; however, their benefit is limited, because either they are not specific to this affair, or because they only contain a small amount of Sīrah — indeed it may be a very slight amount, and it will usually have been taken from previous sources.

So these books are:

[ONE] The books of history of other cities, such as *Tārīkh Dimashq* of Ibn ʿAsākir (d. 571 H), and *Tārīkh Baghdād* of Al-Khatīb Al-Baghdādī (d. 463 H).

[TWO] The books of refined manners, whether poetry or prose. The most important of these are: *Kitābul-Aghānī* of Abul-Faraj Al-Asbahānī (d. 356 H), *Kitābul-ʿIqdul-Farīd* of Ahmad ibn Muhammad ibn ʿAbd Rabbihi Al-Qurtubī (d. 327 H); and reliance cannot be placed upon these books since they include many unauthentic and even fabricated ahādīth.

[THREE] The books of geography, and they are the dictionaries of places. These are useful for awareness of tribes and clans and their dispersion, and awareness of the names of places and their distances within the Arabian Peninsula.

[FOUR] The books of lineages: books which bring about awareness of the lineages, and of the places of the tribes, and they contain a small amount of material relating to the Sīrah, such as *Al-Ansāb* of As-Samʿānī (d. 562 AH).

Then from the Important Reference Works for Sīrah Throughout the Ages are:

- The writings of Shaikhul-Islām Ibn Taimiyyah, and in particular what he wrote in *Al-Jawābus-Sahīh liman baddala Dīnal-Masīh* and in *As-Sārimul Maslūl fī Shātimir-Rasūl*. So in that regard reference can be made to the book *Maʾāthir Shaikhil-Islām Ibn Taimiyyah wa*

As-hābihi fī Kitābatis-Sīratin-Nabawiyyah of Dr. ʿAbdur-Rahmān ibn ʿAbdil-Jabbār Al-Firyawāʾī.

- *As-Sīratun-Nabawiyyah wa Akhbāril-Khulafā* of Ibn Hibbān (d. 354 AH).
- *Jawāmiʿus-Sīrah* of Ibn Hazm (d. 456 H).
- *Talqīh Fuhūmil-Athar fī ʿUyūnit-Tārīkh was-Siyar* of Ibnul-Jawzī (d. 597 H).
- *Ar-Rawdul-Unuf fī tafsīris-Sīratin-Nabawiyyah Libni Hishām* of As-Suhaylī (d. 581 H)
- *ʿUyūnul-Athar fī funūnil-Maghāzī wash-Shamāʾil was-Siyar* of Ibn Sayyidin-Nās (d. 734 H)
- *Subulul-Hudā war-Rashād fī Sīrati Khayril-ʿIbād* of As-Sālihī (d. 942 H).
- *Sharhul-Mawāhibil-Ladunniyyah* of Al-Qustalānī (d. 1122 H).

Sixthly: The Particular Characteristics and Distinguising Qualities of the Prophetic Sīrah

[ONE] The authenticity of this Sīrah in its broad outlines and its fine details, and that is because a large part of it occurs in the Book of Allāh, the Mighty and Majestic — which is not approached by falsehood from before or behind — and [whatever is within this Sīrah] which does not occur in the Book of Allāh (the Mighty and Majestic) has received great attention from the people of knowledge regarding its authenticity and its understanding.

[TWO] This Sīrah covers all the stages of his (صَلَّى ٱللَّهُ عَلَيْهِ وَسَلَّمَ) life and whatever relates to it. So along with its total clarity it does not leave any minor or major incident, from his birth to his (صَلَّى ٱللَّهُ عَلَيْهِ وَسَلَّمَ) death; and this is not the case with anyone else from the creation besides him (صَلَّى ٱللَّهُ عَلَيْهِ وَسَلَّمَ).

[THREE] This Sīrah has had specific and independent works written on it that draw it closer and make it easier for the one who desires to learn it.

Seventhly: The State of the World Prior to the Sending of the Prophet (صَلَّى ٱللَّهُ عَلَيْهِ وَسَلَّمَ)

The world before his being sent as a Prophet was in a tragic state. The two religions that were widespread at that time (Judaism and Christianity) had been severely perverted, and in addition to this idolatry had become widespread in many areas.

Likewise, corruption of manners had spread over the whole world and was manifest in everything from the religious and worldly life. Also, oppression had spread far and wide, and the class/caste system, and falsely seizing people's property, and wantonness, and philosophies built upon idolatry.

Then the Peninsula — the Arabian Peninsula — was not any better, since the idol-worshippers were its leaders. Each tribe had an idol which it worshipped, so *Wudd* was worshipped by Banū Kalb ibn Murrah at Dūmatul-Jandal; *Suwā'* was worshipped by Banū Hudhayl at Ruhāt; *Yaghūth* was worshipped by Banū An'am from Tay'; and *Ya'ūq* by Banū Khaywān, the Hamdāniyūn; and *Nasr* by the tribe of Dhul-Kilā' — the Himyarites.

These were also the idols worshipped by the people of Nūh, just as Allāh (عَزَّوَجَلَّ) said:

> وَقَالُوا لَا تَذَرُنَّ آلِهَتَكُمْ وَلَا تَذَرُنَّ وَدًّا وَلَا سُوَاعًا وَلَا يَغُوثَ وَيَعُوقَ وَنَسْرًا ۝ وَقَدْ أَضَلُّوا كَثِيرًا
>
> MEANING: "And the people of Nūh said: *'Do not leave off worshipping your objects of worship. Do not abandon Wadd, not Suwā', not Yaghūth, and Ya'ūq, and Nasr';* and they lead many astray." — **Sūrah Nūh (53): 19-20**

So they came to be worshipped by the Arabs afterwards, as Al-Bukhārī narrated (no. 4929) from Ibn 'Abbās (رَضِيَ ٱللَّهُ عَنْهُمَا).

It was 'Amr ibn Luhayy Al-Khuzā'ī who first changed the Religion of Ibrāhīm (صَلَّى ٱللَّهُ عَلَيْهِ وَسَلَّمَ), and led the people to worship the idols.

Also from the famous idols of the Arabs in the times of Ignorance was *Hubal*, which was worshipped by the Quraysh; and the Quraysh also had *Isāf* and *Nā'ilah*.

The Arabs also had buildings which they venerated just like the veneration of the Ka'bah. So the Quraysh and Banū Kinānah had *Al-'Uzzā*, and Thaqīf had *Al-Lāt* in At-Tā'if, and the Aws and the Khazraj had *Manāt*. So these are the idols mentioned in His saying (the Mighty and Majestic):

> أَفَرَأَيْتُمُ اللَّاتَ وَالْعُزَّىٰ ۝ وَمَنَاةَ الثَّالِثَةَ الْأُخْرَىٰ
>
> MEANING: "Have you seen *Al-Lāt* and *Al-'Uzzā*, and *Manāt* — the third, the other one?!" — **Sūrah An-Najm (53): 19-20**

And there are many other idols, and whoever wishes to know more then let him refer to *Kitābul-Asnām* of Al-Kalbī.

However, some remnants of the Religion of Ibrāhīm remained with the Arabs, such as: veneration of the House and performing Tawāf around it, the Hajj and 'Umrah, sacrificing the sacrificial animals, and other than this. However, they introduced distortions into these acts, such as their performing the Tawāf naked and their turning their Prayer at the house into whistling and clapping, and other than this.

The Arabs were also not free of corrupt and evil social practices such as the drinking of intoxicants, gambling, burying daughters alive, marrying two sisters at the same time, marrying wives inherited from their fathers, and other practices well-known from them. These things are mentioned in the Book of Allāh (عَزَّوَجَلَّ), and in the Sunnah of the Prophet (صَلَّىٰ ٱللَّٰهُ عَلَيْهِ وَسَلَّمَ), and in the poetry of their poets.

Along with this, though, it is not to be denied that they were people of bravery, courage, and chivalrous manners. Their state of ignorance was not the same as the state of ignorance of others, which was founded upon complicated philosophies. Indeed, despite it, they used to love virtues, and they would give precedence to people who adhered to virtue, and they acknowledged the status of those who possessed fine manners. Before Prophethood, they used to call the Prophet (صَلَّىٰ ٱللَّٰهُ عَلَيْهِ وَسَلَّمَ) *'the truthful and trustworthy one'*. They would also refuse to accept injustice, and to submit to other nations. They likewise possessed sounder intellects, clemency, deliberateness, bravery, and courage.

They were also people of a single unifying language that contained magic and eloquence, and they did not used to deny the existence of Allāh — the Perfect and Most High.

So it is perhaps these characteristics that enabled them to bear the message of Islām, and not the other nations; and Allāh — the One free of all imperfections and the Most High — is more Exalted and knows best.

The Distinctive Characteristics of the Book 'Al-Fusūl'

[ONE] The book is divided into two parts:

- The First Part: The Sīrah of the Messenger (صَلَّى ٱللَّهُ عَلَيْهِ وَسَلَّمَ) and his military expeditions.
- The Second Part: The Signs of his Prophethood, his characteristics, and the things particular to him.

[TWO] This book is not an abridgement of, or an extraction from *Al-Bidāyah wan-Nihāyah,* but rather it is an independent book that stands on its own merit. The author compiled it from the works of the fine scholars who preceded him.

[THREE] Despite its small size, it is replete with information; it is comprehensive and beneficial.

[FOUR] It is simple in its style.

[FIVE] It narrates events and occurrences in sequence.

[SIX] Ibn Kathīr took benefit from the previous works, but he avoided reports with weak chains of narration. He sometimes mentions them, however, and then draws attention to them, or he criticizes them.

Validation Of The Ascription Of The Book To The Author [1]

Ibn Kathīr (رَحِمَهُ ٱللَّهُ) made an indication towards this book in his tafsīr of Sūratul-Ahzāb, saying: "And all of this is affirmed in detail - with its evidences, ahādīth, and full explanation, in the book of Sīrah which we have written in a brief and simple form, and all praise is for Allāh and all favour is from Him."

And Ibn Kathīr mentioned it in his history (6/271).

Also, Hājī Khalīfah mentioned it in *Kashfuz-Zunūn* (2/192), and he called it: *Al-Fusūl fī Sīratir-Rasūl* (صَلَّى ٱللَّهُ عَلَيْهِ وَسَلَّمَ)*;* and Ibnul-ʿImād said in *Ash-Shadharāt* (6/231): "And he has a small Sīrah."

A Description Of The Manuscripts:

In this edition, we have relied upon two handwritten manuscripts:

[THE FIRST]: Which is described herein as *'the primary source'* (*Al-Asl*). This is a manuscript in the Sulaymāniyyah Library[2] in Turkey. It consists of 114 pages,[3] and its script is Persian in style, and it is very carefully written. Its transcriber has added the vowel points to it, and has very carefully transcribed it, and checked it against the source manuscript which he transcribed it from, which in our view was the original manuscript copy of the author (رَحِمَهُ ٱللَّهُ); and this becomes clear from the many transcriptions brought by the transcriber which he introduces with his saying: "An annotation from the manuscript of the author, in his own handwriting."

He also confirmed the places reached in the reading of the text, which shows that the manuscript was read to Ibn Kathīr in *Dārul-Hadīth-il-*

---

1 — [DB] This is taken from the edition of *Al-Fusūl,* with the checking of Mustafā ʿAbdul-Hayy, produced by M. Dārul-Watan Lin-nashr (1st Edition 1424H).

2 — [DB] Manuscript no. 3339. (Salīm Al-Hilālī numbers it as '2339'. However, what is apparent from the manuscript, and what occurs in the Sulaymāniyyah Library index of manuscripts is '3339', as it is numbered in the edition checked by Muhammad Al-Khatrāwī and Muhiyyuddīn Mostū and the edition checked by Mustafā ʿAbdul-Hayy).

3 — [DB] Each page having 17 lines of writing.

Ashrafiyyah in Damascus, and these are pointed out in the annotations to the manuscript from which it was transcribed.

The transcriber has also mentioned some annotations that he ascribes to the books of Sīrah and biographies.

As for the words or sentences which were missed during transcription, then he rectified this when reading out the text for correction. He then appended these to the footnotes, following them with the word *'correction'*, in the manner that is well known in transcribing manuscripts.

This manuscript has the headings, and likewise the beginnings of sections written in red. Also, the transcriber does not adhere to a single form of sending *salāt* upon the Messenger. So sometimes he writes it as 'صَلَّى ٱللَّهُ عَلَيْهِ وَسَلَّمَ', and sometimes he writes it as 'عَلَيْهِ ٱلسَّلَامُ'; however, we have written it always in the first form, as this is what is found throughout the second manuscript.

A fault with this manuscript, however, is that some of its pages have become lost, even though they have been replaced in a different script.

The manuscript is dated as having been written in the year 784H.

[THE SECOND]: Which is indicated by (م).[1] It is a manuscript of the 'Ārif Hikmat Library in Al-Madīnah An-Nabawiyyah. It consists of 56 pages, each page having 25 lines of writing; and they are 20.5 cm x 14 cm [i.e. 8" x 5 ½"] in size. Its script is Persian in style, and its headings are written in red. It is a more recent manuscript, having been written in the year 1101 H.[2]

---

1 — DB References to slight variations between the manuscripts have been omitted in this translation.

2 — DB In his introduction Salīm Al-Hilālī mentions another manuscript that he relied upon, in addition to these two, saying: "The manuscript of the Sulaymāniyyah Library (no. 59) which consists of 62 pages, each page having 21 lines (of text). It was written in clear Persian-style script in the year 813 H, and it was given as a *waqf* (religious endowment) to the Haramayn by the Sultan Mahmūd Khān. This manuscript was the source manuscript for the... ['Ārif Hikmat] manuscript and I have indicated it by (ح)."

Our Work In Producing The Book

1) We have given particular care and attention to verifying the text of the book, and to checking it against the two handwritten manuscripts that have already been described.

2) Since the author (رَحِمَهُ ٱللَّهُ) restricted himself, in the chapter headings of the book, to using the word *'Fasl'* (division/section/chapter) his book is rightfully entitled *Al-Fusūl fī Sīratir-Rasūl* (*Chapters from the Life of the Messenger*); we saw fit, however, for clarification and to make it easier to index, to add a title to each chapter. We indicate there being additions, and add them only if we are unable to highlight some [initial] speech of the author which indicates the contents of the chapter.

3) We quote the references for the verses.

4) We mention the sources of the ahādīth. If the hadīth occurs in the two *Sahīhs*, or in one of them, then we suffice with that. If it occurs outside the two *Sahīhs* then we bring more extensive referencing for the hadīth, in accordance with need, and we mention a ruling upon the hadīth or the narration.

5) In the footnotes we mention some points of wisdom and lessons for most of the events of the Sīrah and the military expeditions.[1]

6) We have added further notes to identify, for example, some important person or place, or to explain a difficult word, and so on.

7) We have written this short introduction in which we have included some points that we felt the student of Sīrah needed.

8) We have written an abridged biography of Al-Hāfidh Ibn Kathīr (رَحِمَهُ ٱللَّهُ).

And finally we ask Allāh, the Mighty and Majestic that He brings benefit through this book, and that He rewards its author (رَحِمَهُ ٱللَّهُ) with the best reward; and that He makes our deeds purely and sincerely for His Noble Face; just as we ask Him — He the One free of all imperfections and the Most High — that He grants us that we follow in a fine manner

---

1 — [DB] These have not been included in the translation.

the noblest one of the creation: Muhammad (ﷺ); and that He resurrects and gathers us beneath his (ﷺ) banner.

Indeed, He [Allāh] is the finest Patron-Lord and Master, and the finest Helper.

THE TWO VERIFIERS:
Bāsim Al-Jawābirah,
Samīr Az-Zuhayrī

Title page of the ʿĀrif Hikmat Library manuscript.

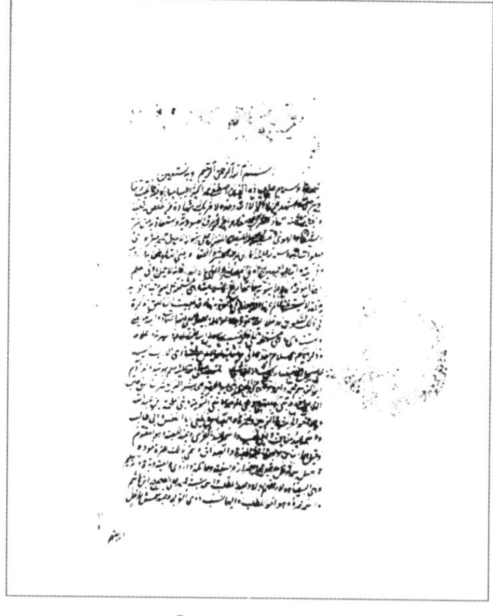

Second page of the ʿĀrif Hikmat Library manuscript, containing the author's introduction.

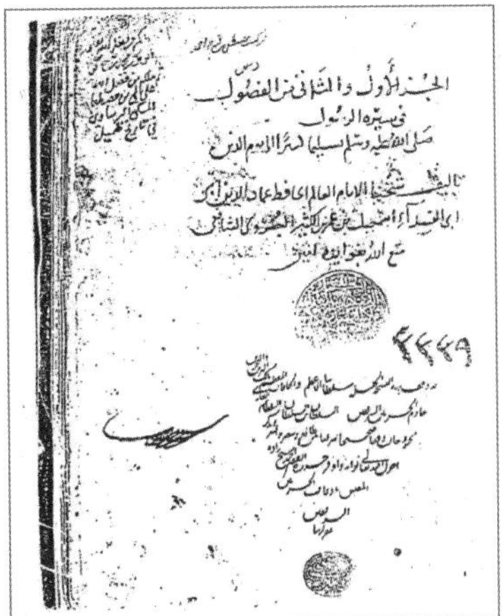

Title page of the Sulaymaaniyyah manuscript (no. 3339).

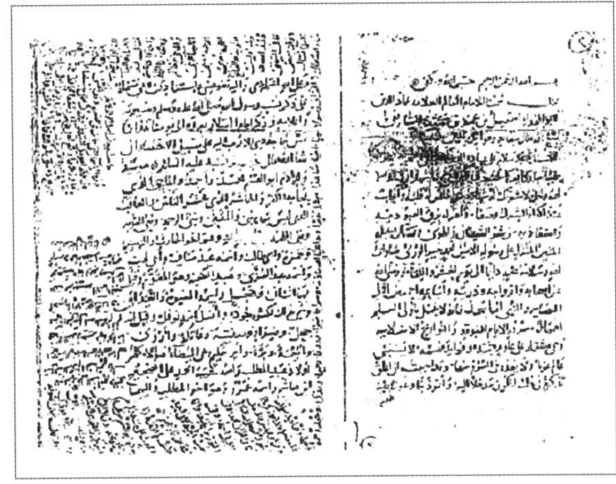

First two pages of the Sulaymaaniyyah manuscript (no. 3339).

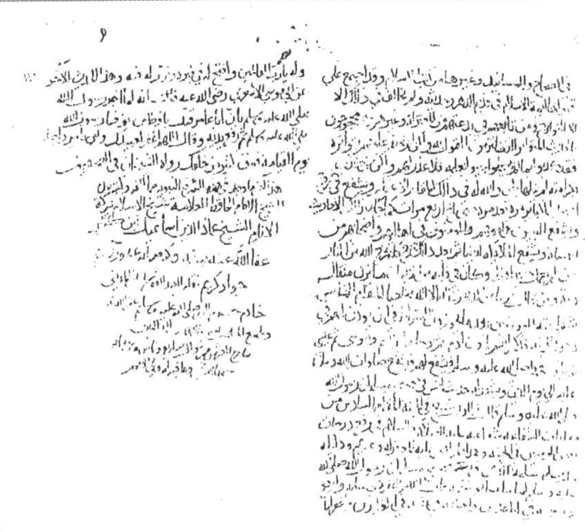

Last two pages of the Sulaymaaniyyah manuscript (no. 3339).

Second page of the Sulaymaaniyyah manuscript (no. 59), containing the author's introduction.

Final page of the Sulaymaaniyyah manuscript (no. 59).

The Biography of Ibn Kathīr (رَحِمَهُ ٱللَّهُ)

Written by Samīr Az-Zuhayrī and Dr. Bāsim Al-Jawābirah

He is: the Imām, the Hāfidh, the Shaikh of the Muhaddithīn, the Historian, the Explainer of the Qur'ān, 'Imāduddīn Abul-Fidā' Ismā'īl ibn 'Umar ibn Kathīr ibn Daw' ibn Kathīr ibn Zar', Al-Qurashī; Al-Busrawī, then Ad-Dimashqī, the jurist, Ash-Shāfi'ī.[1] He was born in Mijdal, a village to the east of Busrā — which is a town in the province of Damascus, in the year 701 H, where his father was a Khatīb.

After the death of his father he moved, along with his brother Kamāluddīn 'Abdul-Wahhāb, to Damascus, in the year 707 H.

He memorized the whole of the Qur'ān at the age of ten, and he read the different recitations, and he excelled in tafsīr.

He married Zaynab the daughter of Al-Hāfidh Abul-Hajjāj Al-Mizzī, and he closely accompanied him and learned from him. He gave great attention to the science of hadīth, and qualified under him in it. He also accompanied Shaikhul-Islām Taqiyyuddīn Ibn Taimiyyah and was a special student of his and defended him, and he followed him upon many of his opinions. He used to deliver verdicts in accordance with his

---

1 — Refer for his biography to: [I] *Tadhkiratul-Huffāz* (4/1508); [II] *Al-Mu'jamul-Mukhtass* (no. 86); [III] *Dhayl Tabaqātil-Huffāz* of Al-Husaynī (p. 57); [IV] *Dhayl Tabaqātil Huffāz* of As-Suyūtī (p. 361); [V] *Tabaqātush-Shāfi'iyyah* of Al-Qādī Shuhbah (no. 638); [VI] *Ad-Durarul-Kāminah* of Al-Hāfidh Ibn Hajr (1/399); [VII] *Inbā'ul-Ghumr* of Al-Hāfidh Ibn Hajr (1/45); [VIII] *Shadharātudh-Dhahab* of Ibnul-'Imād (6/231); [IX] *An-Nujūmuz-Zāhirah* of Ibnu Taghrībardī (11/123-124); [X] *Al-Badrut-Tāli'* of Ash-Shawkānī (1/153); [XI] *Hadiyyatul-'Ārifīn* (1/215); [XII] *Ar-Raddul-Wāfir* (no. 48); [XIII] *Al-A'lām* of Az-Ziriqlī (1/317); [XIV] *Mu'jamul-Mu'allifīn* (2/283).

view concerning the question of the three simultaneous divorces, that they count as a single divorce, and he was put to trial on account of this and suffered harm.

He gave attention to memorising the texts; and to awareness of the chains of narration, the hidden defects in narrations, the narrators, and to history, to the extent that he excelled in all of that whilst he was still a youth. He delivered verdicts, taught and debated. He excelled in Fiqh, Tafsīr, and Arabic Grammar. He closely studied the narrators and the hidden defects in narrations.

He became the shaikh of the Sālihiyyah School after the death of Adh-Dhahabī, and the shaikh of Dārul-Hadīth Al-Ashrafiyyah for a short while after the death of As-Subkī. Then this was taken from him after it was seized by Kamāluddīn Al-Maʿarrī.

His Scholarly Status

Ibn Kathīr had prominent status as is clear from the institutions of knowledge he headed, and the mosques in which he taught, and the works of Tafsīr, History, and Hadīth that he authored.

As for the schools that he took charge of, then they were: The Ashrafiyyah School of Hadīth, the School of As-Sālihiyyah, the school of An-Najībiyyah, the school of At-Tankaziyyah, and the school of An-Nūriyyah Al-Kubrā.

These were schools sought after by the students of knowledge from the east and the west, and their Shaikhs and teachers had high status. None were allowed to teach in them except those who were firmly grounded in knowledge and whose position amongst the scholars was established. Therefore, the scholars respected him and the hearts of the students of knowledge were attentive to him.

As for the mosques in which he delivered his lessons, then the most famous of them were 'Al-Jāmiʿ Al-Amawī'; the mosque of Ibn Hishām, the Jāmiʿ mosque of Tankaz, the Jāmiʿ mosque of Al-Fūqānī — and he used to deliver the Khutbah in it also.

This being in addition to his writings, which have filled the earth with knowledge, and from which people have benefitted in his lifetime and after his death.

The Scholars Praise Of Him

Adh-Dhahabī said: "The jurist, the muftī, the muhaddith. He gave special attention to the narrators, to the texts, and to acquiring knowledge of Fiqh. He elucidated, wrote works, debated, authored, explained (the Qur'ān), and attained precedence."

He also said: "The imām, the jurist, the muhaddith, the singular and outstanding scholar. He was a jurist knowledgeable in various fields, a precise muhaddith, a critical and verifying explainer (of the Qur'ān). He produced beneficial works. He was well aware of Fiqh, and had good understanding of Arabic and the Fundamentals (of Fiqh). He memorized a good portion of the texts, of Tafsīr, and the narrators. He heard (narrations) from me, and had good memorisation."[1]

Ibn Hajjī said: "I never came to him except that I benefitted from him, and I was his constant companion for six years."

Ibn Habīb said, as quoted from him by Imām Ibn Hajr:[2] "He was an imām, frequent upon *tasbīh*[3] and *tahlīl*,[4] and he was at the head of the scholars of explanation (of the Qur'ān). He heard, gathered, and authored. People strove to listen to his sayings. He spoke in a manner that delighted, he narrated, and he brought benefit. The pages of his verdicts were sent to the lands, and he became famous for precision and verification. He attained leadership in knowledge in History, Hadīth, and Tafsīr."

---

1 — *Al-Mu'jamul-Mukhtass* (no. 86)

2 — *Inbā'ul-Ghumr* (1/39)

3 — (DB) Saying *'Subhānallāh'*: (I declare Allāh free of all imperfections).

4 — Saying *'Lā ilāha illā Allāh'* (None has the right to be worshipped except Allāh).

Abul-Mahāsin Ad-Dimashqī said: "He delivered verdicts and taught. He debated and excelled in Fiqh, Tafsīr, and Grammar. He carefully studied the narrators and the hidden defects of narrations."[1]

Al-Hāfidh Ibn Hajr said: "He could bring a great deal to mind, and he joked in a fine manner. His works spread throughout the lands within his lifetime, and the people derived benefit through him after his death."[2]

Al-ʿAynī said, as quoted from him by Ibn Taghrībardī: "He was the example amongst the scholars and the great memorizers, and the reference point for the people of meanings and wordings. He heard, gathered, compiled, taught, narrated, and wrote works. He had an abundance of knowledge and awareness of Hadīth, Tafsīr, and History. He became famous for precision and verification. He attained the limit in knowledge of History, Hadīth, and Tafsīr; and he wrote many beneficial works."[3]

His ʿAqīdah (Creed And Belief)

He (رَحِمَهُ ٱللَّهُ) was upon the ʿAqīdah of the Salafus-Sālih (the Pious Predecessors). This is proven by his tremendous Tafsīr, which is the most excellent tafsīr that has made the ʿAqīdah of the Salaf manifest. An example of that is his saying, in his explanation of His Saying, He the Most High:

> ثُمَّ اسْتَوَىٰ عَلَى الْعَرْشِ
>
> MEANING: "Then He ascended over the Throne"

"Regarding this we follow the position of the Salafus-Sālih: Mālik, Al-Awzāʿī, Ath-Thawrī, Al-Layth ibn Saʿd, Ash-Shāfiʿī, Ahmad, Is-hāq ibn Rāhawaih, and others from the imāms of the Muslims, in the earlier and the later times: (and it is to let them pass) without saying how (*takyīf*), without declaring resemblance to the creation (*tashbīh*), and without

1 — *Dhayl Tadhkiratil-Huffāz* (no. 58)

2 — *Inbāʾul-Ghumr* (1/39); *Ad-Durarul-Kāminah* (1/400)

3 — *An-Nujūmuz-Zāhirah* (11/123)

negating the attributes (*ta'ṭīl*). Furthermore, what is immediately apparent to the minds of those who hold that the Creator resembles the creation is something negated for Allāh, the Most High, since nothing from the creation resembles Allāh:

> لَيْسَ كَمِثْلِهِ شَيْءٌ ۖ وَهُوَ السَّمِيعُ الْبَصِيرُ
>
> MEANING: 'There is nothing like unto Him, and He is the All-Hearing, the All-Seeing.'"

His Most Important Teachers

Ibn Kathīr studied under many famous major Shaikhs, and the most important of them are:

- Shaikhul-Islām Taqiyyuddīn Ahmad Ibn 'Abdil-Halīm Ibn 'Abdis-Salām Ibn Taimiyyah, who died in 728H. Al-'Irāqī said within his biography of Ibn Kathīr: "He was an especially close student of Shaikh Taqiyyuddīn Ibn Taimiyyah, and he defended him, and he followed him upon many of his views."
- The Imām, Al-Hāfidh, the Muhaddith of Shām, Jamāluddīn, Abul-Hajjāj Yūsuf Ibn Az-Zakī 'Abdir-Rahmān Al-Mizzī, who died in 742 H. Ibn Kathīr closely accompanied him, and married his daughter.
- The Imām, Al-Hāfidh, the Muhaddith, the Historian of Islām, Shamsuddīn, Abū 'Abdillāh Muhammad ibn Ahmad ibn 'Uthmān Adh-Dhahabī, At-Turkumānī in his origin, Ad-Dimashqī. The author of beneficial works such as *Siyar A'lāmin-Nubalā'*, *Tārīkhul-Islām,* and *Mīzānul-I'tidāl.* He died in 748 H.
- Abul-'Abbās Ahmad ibn Abī Tālib ibn Ni'mah ibn Hasan ibn 'Alī An-Najjār, who was well-known as 'Ibnush-Shahnah'. He lived for a hundred years, and died in 730 H.

His Most Important Students

- Shihāb-ud-Dīn Abul-ʿAbbās, Ahmad Ibn Hijjiyy Ibn Mūsā Ibn Ahmad As-Saʿdī Al-Hasbānī Ad-Dimashqī — the Hāfidh and the historian of Islām. He had numerous authorships; from them is his explanation of *Al-Muharrar* of Ibn ʿAbdil-Hādī. He died in 816 H.
- Shihāb-ud-Dīn, Muhammad Ibn Ahmad Ibn Muhammad Ibn Ahmad Al-Harīrī Ad-Dimashqī — well-known as As-Silāwī.He was the Overseer of the judiciary of Baʿlabak (Heliopolis, Lebanon), then of the judiciary of Al-Madīnah, then he had various positions in [different] judiciaries. He died in 765 H.
- Abul-Mahāsin Al-Husainī, Muhammad Ibn ʿAlī Ibn Al-Hasan Ibn Hamzah Ibn Hamd Ad-Dimashqī. He died in 765 H.

His Authorships (and the most famous of them)

Ibn Kathīr filled the Islamic library with beneficial works. Some of them have been printed, and others remain in manuscript form. The most important of his printed works are:

- *Tafsīrul-Qurʾānil-ʿAdhīm,*
- *Al-Bidāyah wan-Nihāyah,*
- *Ikhtisār ʿUlūmil-Hadīth,*
- *Fadāʾilul-Qurʾān,*
- *Tuhfatut-Tālib bimukhtasar Ibnil-Hājib,*
- *Ahādīthut-Tawhīd war-Radd ʿalā Ahlish-Shirk,*
- *Al-Fusūl fī Sīratir-Rasūl* (صَلَّىٱللَّهُعَلَيْهِوَسَلَّمَ),
- *Sīrah ʿUmar ibn ʿAbdil-ʿAzīz;*

— and he has many works that remain in manuscript form.

His Death

Ibn Kathīr (رَحِمَهُٱللَّهُ) died on the day of Thursday, the 26th of Shaʿbān, in the year 774 H, in Damascus, and he was buried therein.

VOLUME ONE

The Life of the Prophet Muhammad (صَلَّى ٱللَّهُ عَلَيْهِ وَسَلَّمَ) & his Military Expeditions

VOLUME ONE

The Life of the Prophet Muhammad (صَلَّى ٱللَّهُ عَلَيْهِ وَسَلَّمَ) & his Military Expeditions

In the name of Allāh, the Extremely Merciful, the Bestower of Mercy. Allāh is sufficient for me, and He suffices.

Our Shaikh, the Imām, the great scholar, the 'Allāmah, 'Imāduddīn Abul-Fidā' Ismā'īl ibn 'Umar ibn Kathīr Ash-Shāfi'ī (may Allāh grant that he remains and continues to bring benefit — āmīn) said:

All praise is for Allāh, and may He send peace and security upon those servants of His whom He chose. All praise is for Allāh, very great praise, pure praise and blessed praise, such as our Lord loves and is pleased with.

And I bear witness that none has the right to be worshipped except Allāh, alone, with no partner attributed to Him. The testification of one who makes his heart pure and sincere for Him, and who has the pollution of Shirk cleared away from him and is made pure; one who affirms that he is a slave to and a worshipper of Him; and one who seeks His refuge from the evil of Satan, and from desires; and who clings to the strong Rope which He sent down upon His trustworthy Messenger Muhammad — the best of Mankind — may Allāh extol and send peace and security upon him, continually, until the Day of the Gathering and the Meeting.

And may Allāh be pleased with his Companions, and his wives, and his descendants, and all of his followers: the people of insight and intelligence.

To proceed, then it is not befitting that those possessing knowledge neglect knowledge and awareness of the days of Prophethood and the

Islamic histories which comprise many branches of knowledge and many points of benefit, such that the scholars will not be without need of them, and there will not be any excuse for being negligent of them.

Therefore I desired that I should write a small book as a reminder in that regard, so that it should serve as an introduction to those matters and as a model and aid for that; and my dependence is upon Allāh, and to Him I surrender my affair and I rely upon Him.

So they include a mention of the lineage of the Messenger of Allāh (صَلَّىٱللَّهُعَلَيْهِوَسَلَّمَ) and his life history, and the signs of his Prophethood, and a mention of the days of Islām after him — until this day of ours — which is greatly needed by the people of intelligence, writing it in abridged form, if Allāh (the Most High) wishes.

A Mention of His (صَلَّىٱللَّهُعَلَيْهِوَسَلَّمَ) Lineage

Then he was the best and noblest of the sons of Ādam.[1]

Abul-Qāsim, Muhammad, and Ahmad,[2] and *Al-Māhī* (the one through whom disbelief was wiped away), and *Al-Hāshir* (the one *after*[3] whom the people will be resurrected) and *Al-ʿĀqib* (the one after whom there is no Prophet) and *Al-Muqaffī* (the one who follows on from the previous Prophets), and *Nabiyyur-Rahmah* (the Prophet of Mercy), and *Nabiyyut-*

---

1 — [SH] As occurs in the hadīth reported by Imām Muslim (no. 2278/3) from Abū Hurairah (رَضِيَٱللَّهُعَنْهُ) from the Prophet (صَلَّىٱللَّهُعَلَيْهِوَسَلَّمَ): "I will be the noble chief of the descendants of Ādam on the Day of Resurrection; and I am the first one for whom the grave will open; and I will be the first intercessor, and the first one whose intercession will be accepted."

2 — Muhammad and Ahmad are two names derived from *'Al-Hamd'* (praise) — see Endnote 1 on page 430.

3 — [SH] An important addition which occurs in the clear authentic ahādīth, and through it the wording and the meaning are rendered sound; meaning: the people will be gathered after him and after the time of his Prophethood; or it is an indication towards the hadīth of the Major Intercession: that the people will be gathered, but judgement will not be passed upon them until he (صَلَّىٱللَّهُعَلَيْهِوَسَلَّمَ) intercedes for them. So Allāh will accept his Intercession — to the exclusion of the rest of the people.

Tawbah (the Prophet of Repentance), and *Nabiyyul-Malhamah* (the Prophet of Great War),[1] the son of:

'Abdullāh — who was the brother of Al-Hārith, Az-Zubayr, Hamzah, and Abū Tālib — whose name was 'Abd-Manāf; and Abū Lahab — whose name was 'Abdul-'Uzzā; and 'Abdul-Ka'bah — who was Al-Muqawwam, or it is said they are two different people; and Hajl — whose name was Al-Mughīrah; and Al-Ghaydāq — who was given that name because of his great generosity, and his original name was Nawfal, and it is said that he was actually Hajl; and Dirār; and Safiyyah; and 'Ātikah; and Arwā; and Umaymah; and Barrah; and Umm Hakīm — who was Al-Baydā'; all of them being children of:

'Abdul-Muttalib — and his name was Shaybatul-Hamd[2] upon the correct saying; [and he was] the son of:

Hāshim — whose name was 'Amr, and he was the brother of Al-Muttalib, and it is to these two that the 'closest kindred' (Dhul-Qurbā) have their ascription, and of 'Abd-Shams, and Nawfal, the four of them being the sons of:

'Abd Manāf — the brother of 'Abdul-'Uzzā, and 'Abdud-Dār, and 'Abd, the sons of:

Qusayy — and his name was Zayd, and he was the brother of Zuhrah, and they were the two sons of:

Kilāb — the brother of Taym and Yaqazah — Abū Makhzūm, the three of them being the sons of:

Murrah — the brother of 'Adiyy and Husays, and they were the sons of:

Ka'b — the brother of 'Āmir, and Sāmah, and Khuzaymah, and Sa'd, and Al-Hārith, and 'Awf; the seven of them being the sons of:

---

1 — This name is established from a hadīth of Hudhayfah Ibn Al-Yamān (رَضِيَ اللَّهُ عَنْهُ). See **Endnote 2 on page 430** for this narration and other points of benefit related to these names and monikers.

2 — [SH] (meaning: *'Praiseworthy whiteness of the hair'*) because he had a lock of white hair.

Lu'ayy — the brother of Taym Al-Adram; the two sons of:

Ghālib — the brother of Al-Hārith, and Muhārib; the sons of:

Fihr — the brother of Al-Hārith, the two sons of:

Mālik — the brother of As-Salt and Makhlad, the sons of:

An-Nadr — the brother of Mālik, and Malkān, and ʿAbd Manāt, and others; the sons of:

Kinānah — the brother of Asad, Asadah, and Al-Hūn; the sons of:

Khuzaymah — the brother of Hudhayl, the son of:

Mudrikah — and his name was ʿAmr; and he was the brother of Tābikhah — whose name was ʿĀmir, and Qimmaʿah; the three of them being the sons of:

Ilyās — the brother of An-Nās, who was ʿAylān, the father of all of Qays, both of them being sons of:

Mudar — the brother of Rabīʿah; and they were the two clear descendants of Ismāʿīl; and the brother of Anmār, and Iyād, who both settled in Yemen; the four sons of:

Nizār — the brother of Qudāʿah, in the saying of the majority of the scholars of lineages, the two of them being the sons of:

Maʿadd — the son of:

ʿAdnān.

So all of the tribes of the Arabs are ascribed to and descended from those we have mentioned from the descendants of ʿAdnān. This was clarified fully by Al-Hāfidh Abū ʿUmar An-Namarī (رَحِمَهُ ٱللَّهُ) in his book *Al-Inbā' bi Maʿrifati Qabā'il-ir-Ruwāt.*

And Quraysh, upon the saying of the majority of the scholars of lineages, are those descended from Fihr ibn Mālik ibn An-Nadr ibn Kinānah; and they composed the line of poetry in that regard:

> *Qusayy, upon my life, was called the gatherer,*
>
> *through him Allāh gathered all the tribes descended from Fihr.*

However, it is otherwise said: rather the one from whom the whole of Quraysh are descended is An-Nadr ibn Kinānah, and this was held by the majority of the jurists and the verifiers.

They use as evidence in that regard the hadīth which Abū ʿUmar ibn ʿAbdul-Barr[1] (رَحِمَهُ ٱللَّهُ) mentioned from Al-Ashʿath ibn Qays (رَضِيَ ٱللَّهُ عَنْهُ) who said: "I came to Allāh's Messenger (صَلَّى ٱللَّهُ عَلَيْهِ وَسَلَّمَ) in the deputation of Kindah, and I said: *'Are you not from us, O Messenger of Allāh?'*[2]

He said:

> 'No, we are the sons of An-Nadr ibn Kinānah, we will not take ascription from our mothers and we will not leave off ascribing ourselves to our forefathers.'"[3]

And is reported by Ibn Mājah in his *Sunan* with a *'hasan'* (good) chain of narration, and it contains the wording: "So Al-Ashʿath used to say: *'I will not have any man brought to me who denies that a man descended from An-Nadr ibn Kinānah is from Quraysh except that I will lash him with the prescribed punishment.'*"[4]

---

1 — He is the great scholar of Al-Andalus (Adalusia: Southern Spain) and its imām. Read more about him in Endnote 3 on page 431.

2 — [SH] Because the mother of ʿAbd Mannaf-Hubayy bint Hulayl Ibn Habashiyyah was from Khuzāʿah, and it is a Yemeni tribe; and likewise Kindah is Yemeni. So Al-Ashʿath ibn Qays thought that this resulted in the Messenger (صَلَّى ٱللَّهُ عَلَيْهِ وَسَلَّمَ) sharing their lineage. So Allāh's Messenger (صَلَّى ٱللَّهُ عَلَيْهِ وَسَلَّمَ) clarified to him that the correct and legislated lineage is through the fathers, and not through the mothers; and Allāh knows best.

3 — [SH] It is *'sahīh'*: Reported by ʿAbdullāh Ibn Al-Mubārak in his *Musnad* (96/161), At-Tayālisī in his *Musnad* (2/377-378/1145) and by way of him by Al-Bayhaqī in *Dalāʾilun-Nubuwwah* (1/173), and As-Samʿānī in *Al-Ansāb* (1/49), and Ibn Abī Shaybah in his *Musnad* (2/362/872) and from him by Ibn Mājah (2/181/2612), and Ahmad (5/211 & 212) and by way of Hammād ibn Salamah: from ʿAqīl Ibn Talhah: from Muslim ibn Haysam: from Al-Ashʿath with it.

4 — [DB] Declared *'hasan'* by Shaikh Al-Albānī in his checking of *Sunan Ibn Mājah* and in *Al-Irwāʾ* (no.2368) and *As-Sahīhah* (no.2375).

And it is otherwise said that the whole of Quraysh are united at Ilyās ibn Mudar ibn Nizār; or it is otherwise said: rather they are united at his father Mudar.

These are two sayings found amongst the students of Ash-Shāfi'ī and they are both mentioned by Abul-Qāsim 'Abdul-Karīm Ar-Rāfi'ī in his *Sharh* as being two such sayings; however they are both something strange.

Then as for the tribes of Yemen such as Himyar, Hadramawt, Saba' and so on, then they are descended from Qahtān; they are not descended from 'Adnān.

As for Qudā'ah, then there are three sayings about them. So it is said that they are from the descendants of 'Adnān, and it is also said that they are from the descendants of Qahtān, or it is said: they have a third route of descent being neither from these, nor from those; and this is something strange. It was mentioned by Abū 'Umar and others.

Chapter: His (صَلَّىٰ ٱللَّهُ عَلَيْهِ وَسَلَّمَ) Lineage Beyond Adnān

So as for this lineage that we have quoted, going back to 'Adnān; then there is no doubt about it nor any dispute. It is established by many indisputable (*mutawātir*) lines of transmission and by consensus (*ijmā'*).

Rather, the affair open to question is what comes beyond that. However there is no disagreement between the scholars of lineage and others besides them from the people of knowledge from the People of the Book about the fact that 'Adnān was from the descendants of Ismā'īl — the Prophet of Allāh, who was the one who was due to be sacrificed — in the correct saying from the two sayings of the Companions and the Imāms; and Ismā'īl was the son of Ibrāhīm — the specially beloved one (Khalīl) of the Most Merciful (عَلَيْهِ ٱلصَّلَاةُ وَٱلسَّلَامُ).[1]

1 — Read the speech of Ibn Al-Qayyim and Ibn Taymiyyah regarding the difference of opinion that has occurred over whether it was Is-hāq (عَلَيْهِ ٱلسَّلَامُ) or Ismā'īl (عَلَيْهِ ٱلسَّلَامُ) who was designated for sacrifice — **Endnote 4 on page 432**.

There is also disagreement about how many forefathers there are between the two of them,[1] and in that regard, there are a number of sayings.

So the largest number mentioned is that there were forty forefathers, and the smallest number mentioned is that they were seven forefathers; or it was otherwise said: nine; and it was said: fifteen; and then they disagree about their names.

And some of the Salaf and the Imāms disliked that the lineage be mentioned beyond ʿAdnān. So it is related from Mālik ibn Anas Al-Asbahī, the Imām (رَحِمَهُ ٱللَّهُ), that he disliked that.

Imām Abū ʿUmar Ibn ʿAbdil-Barr said in his book *Al-Inbāh*: "And what is held by the scholars of this affair regarding the lineage of ʿAdnān is that they say:

> "ʿAdnān was the son of Udad, the son of Muqawwim, the son of Nāhūr, the son of Tayrah, the son of Yaʿrub, the son of Yashjub, the son of Nābit, the son of Ismāʿīl, the son of Ibrāhīm — the specially beloved one (Khalīl) of the Most Merciful, the son of Tārih, who was Āzar, the son of Nāhūr, the son of Shārūkh, the son of Rāʿū, the son of Fālikh, the son of ʿAybar, the son of Shālah, the son of Arfakhshadh, the son of Sām, the son of Nūh, the son of Lāmak, the son of Mattūshalakh, the son of Akhnūkh (who was Idrīs, the Prophet (عَلَيْهِ ٱلسَّلَامُ) as they claim, and Allāh knows best, and he was the first of the descendants of Ādam to be given Prophethood after Ādam and Shīth, and the first one who wrote with the pen) the son of Yard, the son of Mahlayl, the son of Qaynan, the son of Yānish, the son of Shīth, the son of Ādam (صَلَّىٰ ٱللَّهُ عَلَيْهِ وَسَلَّمَ).'

This is how Muhammad ibn Is-hāq ibn Yasār Al-Madanī, the author of *As-Sīratun-Nabawiyyah* mentioned it, and as did others from the scholars of lineage.

Then Abul-ʿAbbās ʿAbdullāh Ibn Muhammad An-Nāshī, the Muʿtazilī, composed that within a poem in which he praised Allāh's Messenger

---

1 — DB i.e Between ʿAdnān and Ismāʿīl (عَلَيْهِ ٱلسَّلَامُ).

(صَلَّى ٱللَّهُ عَلَيْهِ وَسَلَّمَ) and Imām Abū 'Umar[1] quoted it, and likewise our Shaikh[2] in his abridgement and it is an eloquent poem that begins:

> *I praise Allāh's Messenger, seeking by praise of him*
>
> *to acquire for myself a plentiful share of good from One Who rewards generously;*[3]
>
> *I have praised a person who stands out alone in praise,*
>
> *Having surpassed those far and near by his attributes.*

So all the tribes of the Arabs join together with him at 'Adnān, so therefore Allāh (the Most High) said:

> لَّا أَسْأَلُكُمْ عَلَيْهِ أَجْرًا إِلَّا الْمَوَدَّةَ فِي الْقُرْبَىٰ
>
> MEANING: "Say I do not ask for any reward for calling you to the truth, but rather I remind you to observe the ties of kinship between us." — **Sūrah Ash-Shūrā (42): 23**

Ibn 'Abbās (رَضِيَ ٱللَّهُ عَنْهُمَا) said: "There was no branch of Quraysh except that Allāh's Messenger (صَلَّى ٱللَّهُ عَلَيْهِ وَسَلَّمَ) had a tie of close kinship to them."[4]

Then he was Allāh's chosen one from amongst them, just as Muslim reports in his *Sahīh* from Wāthilah ibn Al-Asqa' (رَضِيَ ٱللَّهُ عَنْهُ) who said: Allāh's Messenger (صَلَّى ٱللَّهُ عَلَيْهِ وَسَلَّمَ) said: "Allāh chose Kinānah from the descendants of Ismā'īl, then from Kinānah he chose Quraysh. Then from Quraysh He chose Banū Hāshim. Then He chose me from Banū Hāshim."[5]

Likewise the Banū Isrā'īl: their Prophets and others besides them join with him at Ibrāhīm, the specially beloved (عَلَيْهِ ٱلصَّلَاةُ وَٱلسَّلَامُ), within whose offspring Allāh placed Prophethood and the Book.

---

1 — i.e. Imām Abū 'Umar Yūsuf ibn 'Abdul-Barr An-Namarī, died 463 H (رَحِمَهُ ٱللَّهُ).

2 — i.e. Al-Imām, Al-Hāfidh Abul-Hajjāj Yūsuf Al-Mizzī, died 742 H (رَحِمَهُ ٱللَّهُ).

3 — i.e Allāh.

4 — Reported by Al-Bukhārī (no. 4818)

5 — Reported by Muslim (no. 2276)

Likewise Allāh, the Perfect and Most High, commanded the Banū Isrā'īl upon the tongue of Mūsā (عَلَيْهِ السَّلَامُ), and it is in the Tawrāt — as is mentioned by more than one of the scholars who have gathered the reports from the earlier Prophets foretelling of his (صَلَّى اللَّهُ عَلَيْهِ وَسَلَّمَ) coming — that Allāh (the Most High) said to them that which has the meaning: "I will raise for you, from the children of your brother, a Prophet: you should all listen to him, and I will make him very great."[1]

Then no one has been born from the descendants of Ismā'īl who was greater than Muhammad (صَلَّى اللَّهُ عَلَيْهِ وَسَلَّمَ). Indeed, no one has been born from the descendants of Ādam, nor will anyone be born until the establishment of the Hour, who is greater than him (صَلَّى اللَّهُ عَلَيْهِ وَسَلَّمَ). So it is authentic from him that he said: "I am the best of the descendants of Ādam, and I am not boasting: Ādam and those after him from the Prophets will be beneath my banner."[2]

And it is authentic from him that he said: "(I will stand) in a station where the whole of the creation, even Ibrāhīm, will be eager for me."[3]

This is the praiseworthy station (*Al-Maqāmul-Mahmūd*)[4] which Allāh — the Most High — promised him, and it is the Greater Intercession (*Ash-Shafā'atul-'Udhmā*) wherein he will intercede for the whole of the creation that Allāh should relieve them from the standing in the place of the Gathering by beginning judgement upon them, as is mentioned in detail in the authentic ahādīth from him (صَلَّى اللَّهُ عَلَيْهِ وَسَلَّمَ).[5]

And his (صَلَّى اللَّهُ عَلَيْهِ وَسَلَّمَ) mother was Āminah, the daughter of Wahb, the son of 'Abd Manāf, the son of Zuhrah, the son of Kilāb, the son of Murrah.

---

1 — SH [*Deuteronomy* — CHAPTER 18]

2 — Reported by At-Tirmidhī (no. 3148) as a hadīth of Abū Sa'īd Al-Khudrī (رَضِيَ اللَّهُ عَنْهُ), and by others, and declared *'sahīh'* because of supporting narrations by Shaikh Al-Albānī: *Sahīh Sunanit-Tirmidhī, As-Sahīhah* (no.1571).

3 — DB Reported by Muslim (no. 820), as a hadīth of Ubayy ibn Ka'b (رَضِيَ اللَّهُ عَنْهُ) with its like.

4 — DB Refer to āyah 79 of Sūrah Al-Isrā' (17).

5 — SH Al-Bukhārī (no.4476 and 4712), and Muslim (no. 193 and 194) as a hadīth of Anas ibn Mālik and Abū Hurairah (رَضِيَ اللَّهُ عَنْهُمَا).

CHAPTER:

The Birth of Allāh's Messenger (صَلَّى ٱللَّهُ عَلَيْهِ وَسَلَّمَ), his Suckling, and his Early Years

Allāh's Messenger was born on Monday the second of Rabīʿul-Awwal; or it is said: on the eighth; or it is said: on the tenth; or it is said: on the twelfth day. As for Az-Zubayr ibn Bakkār, then he said: *"He was born in Ramadān,"* and this is strange. As-Suhaylī quoted it in his *Rawd.*[1]

And that was in *'the Year of the Elephant'*, occurring fifty days afterwards; or it is otherwise said: fifty-eight days afterwards; or it is said: ten years afterwards; or it is said: thirty years after the (incident of the) elephant; or it is said: forty years afterwards.

However, what is correct is that he was born in the Year of the Elephant. Ibrāhīm Ibnul-Mundhir Al-Hizāmī — the Shaikh of Al-Bukhārī, Khalīfah ibn Khayyāt, and others quote consensus upon this.

His father died whilst he was still in the womb, or it is otherwise said: [he died] a few months after his birth, or it is said: a year later, or it is said two years — however what is well known is the first saying.[2]

They sought to find someone from (the tribe of) Banū Saʿd to breast-feed him, and so he was breast-fed by Halīmah As-Saʿdiyyah, as we report with an authentic chain of narration; and he resided with her for

---

1 — BJ SZ See *Ar-Rawdul-Unuf*: (1/282)

2 — The first saying is clearly proven by many evidences, which can be seen in ENDNOTE 5 ON PAGE 433.

about four years, and his heart was split open there — so she returned him to his mother.[1]

His mother went with him to al-Madīnah to visit his maternal uncles, and she died at Al-Abwā', whilst returning to Makkah. At this time he was six years, three months and ten days old, or it is said: rather [he was] four years (old).

And Muslim reported in his *Sahīh*: that Allāh's Messenger (صَلَّى ٱللَّهُ عَلَيْهِ وَسَلَّمَ) when he passed by Al-Abwā' whilst going towards Makkah in the Year of the Conquest, sought permission from his Lord to visit the grave of his mother, so He granted him permission. So he wept and caused those around him to weep, and he had with him a thousand whose heads were covered; meaning that they were wearing helmets.[2]

So when his mother died he was looked after by Umm Ayman,[3] and she was a slave woman belonging to him, whom he inherited from his father; and he was taken into guardianship by his grandfather 'Abdul-Muttalib. Then when Allāh's Messenger (صَلَّى ٱللَّهُ عَلَيْهِ وَسَلَّمَ) reached eight years old, his grandfather died, having entrusted his paternal uncle Abū Tālib with him, since he was the full-brother of 'Abdullāh.[4]

So he became his guardian, and he took full care of him, and supported him fully when Allāh raised him as a Prophet. This was despite the fact that he continued upon Shirk until he died. So for that reason Allāh reduced his punishment, as is authentic in the hadīth in that regard.[5]

---

1 — See **Endnote 6 on page 433** for the hadīth wherein the Messenger (صَلَّى ٱللَّهُ عَلَيْهِ وَسَلَّمَ) describes the splitting of the heart.

2 — See **Endnote 7 on page 435** for the story of the Prophet's (صَلَّى ٱللَّهُ عَلَيْهِ وَسَلَّمَ) visit to his mother's grave, and the advice he gave to the Companions (رَضِيَ ٱللَّهُ عَنْهُمْ).

3 — Who was Umm Ayman? See **Endnote 8 on page 436**.

4 — DB i.e. the father of Allāh's Messenger (صَلَّى ٱللَّهُ عَلَيْهِ وَسَلَّمَ).

5 — BJ SZ Al-Bukhārī (no. 3883) and Muslim (no. 209) report from Al-'Abbās Ibn 'Abdul-Muttalib that he said: "O Messenger of Allāh! Have you benefitted Abū Tālib at all, since he used to defend you and become angry for you (and in a narration: and aid you)?" He said: "Yes, he is in a shallow part of the Fire; and if it were not for me, he would have been in the lowest depth of the Fire."

And his uncle went out with him to Shām for the purpose of trade when he was twelve years old; and that was from his complete concern for him, since there was no one to look after him if he had left him in Makkah. So both he and those who went along with him to Shām saw such signs regarding him (صَلَّى ٱللَّٰهُ عَلَيْهِ وَسَلَّمَ) that it led his uncle to take care of him even more carefully and to have even greater concern for him. So At-Tirmidhī reported in his *Jāmiʿ* with a chain of narration whose narrators are reliable, that a cloud gave him shade, and trees leaned over to shade him, and Bahīrah the monk gave glad tidings regarding him, and commanded his uncle to go back with him for fear that the Jews should see him and strike him with some harm. So the hadīth has a preserved basis, however it contains other additions.[1]

Then he went out to Shām for a second time to trade on behalf of Khadījah bint Khuwaylid, going along with her slave Maysarah, on the basis of the profits being shared. So Maysarah saw things from him that amazed him, so when he returned he informed his mistress about what he had seen. So she desired that he should marry her, hoping for the good that Allāh had gathered for her and which was more than any person could imagine. So Allāh's Messenger (صَلَّى ٱللَّٰهُ عَلَيْهِ وَسَلَّمَ) married her, being at the time twenty-five years old.

Furthermore, Allāh (the One free of all imperfections) had safeguarded his chastity, preserved him from a young age, and kept him pure from the pollution of the Days of Ignorance and from every fault; and bestowed upon him every beautiful characteristic, to the extent that he was known amongst his people as *'The Trustworthy One'* (*Al-Amīn*) because of what they witnessed from his purity, truthfulness in speech, and trustworthiness. This was the case to such an extent that when the Quraysh rebuilt the Kaʿbah, when he was thirty-five years old, and they reached the place of the Black Stone they argued about who should put the stone in its place. So each tribe said: "We should place it!"

---

1 — Shaikh Al-Albānī said concerning the hadīth in *Sahīh Sunanit-Tirmidhī* (no.3620): "Authentic (*'sahīh'*) except that the mention of Bilāl in it is incorrect, as has been mentioned."

Then they agreed that whoever was first to enter upon them should be the one to place it. So it was Allāh's Messenger (صَلَّى ٱللَّهُ عَلَيْهِ وَسَلَّمَ). So they said: *"The Trustworthy One has come,"* and they were satisfied with him. So he ordered them to bring a cloth and he placed the Black Stone in the centre of it. Then he ordered that each tribe should raise a side of the cloth. Then he (صَلَّى ٱللَّهُ عَلَيْهِ وَسَلَّمَ) took the Stone and put it in its place.[1]

Chapter: His Being Raised as a Prophet

When Allāh (the Most High) willed that He should have mercy upon the servants and bestow honour upon him, by sending him as a Messenger to the whole of the creation, He caused solitude to become beloved to him. So he began devoting himself to worship in the cave Hirā', as used to be done by those who worshipped in that time — just as Abū Tālib said in his famous poem that rhymes on the letter *'Lām'*:

> *And by Thawr, and the One who set Thabīr firmly in its place;*
>
> *and by those going up to ascend Hirā' and those descending.*

So the truth came to him suddenly whilst he was in the cave of Hirā', in Ramadān, at the age of forty. So the Angel came to him and said to him; "Recite!"

So he said: "I am not able to recite."

So he pressed him tightly, to the limit he could bear, then he released him and said: "Recite!"

He replied: *"I am not able to recite,"* and this happened three times. Then he said:

---

1 — [BJ][SZ] It is *'sahīh'* with its witnesses, reported by Ahmad (3/425), and Al-Hākim (1/458) with a strong chain of narration from Mujāhid from his master, and it was declared *'sahīh'* by Al-Hākim. It also has a witness as a hadīth of 'Alī (رَضِيَ ٱللَّهُ عَنْهُ), reported by At-Tayālisī (no. 113), Al-Hākim (1/458-4590, and Al-Bayhaqī in *Ad-Dalā'il* (2/56); and it has a *'mursal'* witness from Ibn Shihāb in *Ad-Dalā'il* also.

ٱقْرَأْ بِٱسْمِ رَبِّكَ ٱلَّذِي خَلَقَ ۝ خَلَقَ ٱلْإِنسَـٰنَ مِنْ عَلَقٍ ۝ ٱقْرَأْ وَرَبُّكَ ٱلْأَكْرَمُ ۝
ٱلَّذِي عَلَّمَ بِٱلْقَلَمِ ۝ عَلَّمَ ٱلْإِنسَـٰنَ مَا لَمْ يَعْلَمْ

MEANING: "Recite in the Name of your Lord Who created everything. He created mankind from a clot. Recite and your Lord is the Most Honourable and Generous. He Who has taught by means of the pen. He has taught mankind that which he knew not." — **Sūrah Al-'Alaq (96): 1-5**

So Allāh's Messenger (ﷺ) returned with it, and the skin of his collarbone was trembling, and he informed Khadījah of it and said: "I feared for my intellect."

So she reassured him and said: "Receive good news. No, by Allāh! Allāh would never disgrace you; for you maintain ties of kinship, and you are truthful in speech, and you look after orphans and you aid those suffering from calamities."

So she recounted a number of other fine characteristics of his, having faith in him, and to aid him upon the truth. So she was the first one to believe in him — may Allāh be pleased with her and honour her.

Then Allāh's Messenger (ﷺ) remained for as long as Allāh wished, not seeing anything further, and the Revelation ceased coming to him. So he felt great grief at that and went out a number of times to throw himself from the tops of the mountains.[1] This was because of his yearning for what he had seen the first time, i.e. the sweetness of what he had witnessed from Allāh's Revelation to him.

So it has been said that the period of the cessation of Revelation was close to two years, or more. Then the Angel appeared to him, sitting upon a seat between the heavens and the earth, and he reassured him and informed him that he was truly the Messenger of Allāh. So when Allāh's Messenger (ﷺ) saw him he feared him, and went back to Khadījah and said: *"Cover me up! Envelop me with blankets!"*

---

1 — This is not correct and is inauthentic. See **Endnote 9 on page 436** for the speech of the scholars regarding this claim.

So Allāh sent down upon him:

> يَا أَيُّهَا الْمُدَّثِّرُ ۝ قُمْ فَأَنذِرْ ۝ وَرَبَّكَ فَكَبِّرْ ۝ وَثِيَابَكَ فَطَهِّرْ
>
> MEANING: "O you covered in garments! Arise and warn! And exalt your Lord (by worshipping Him alone). And purify your garments."
> — SŪRAH AL-MUDATTHIR (74): 1-4[1]

So the initial state was the state of Prophethood and inspired Revelation.

Then, in this āyah, Allāh commanded him to warn his people and to call them to Allāh. So he (ﷺ) set about his duty and stood, establishing obedience to Allāh in the most complete manner. So he called the old and the young, the free and the slaves, the men and the women, the black and the red, to Allāh. So servants of Allāh from every tribe responded to him. So the one who achieved the honour of preceding them in that was Abū Bakr — ʿAbdullāh ibn ʿUthmān At-Taymī (رَضِيَ ٱللَّهُ عَنْهُ). He aided him upon the Religion of Allāh, and called along with him to Allāh — upon clear knowledge and insight. So ʿUthmān Ibn ʿAffān, Talhah, and Saʿd ibn Abī Waqqās responded to Abū Bakr.

As for ʿAlī, then he accepted Islām whilst young — at the age of eight years, or it is said: he was older than that. It is said that he accepted Islām before Abū Bakr, or it is otherwise said: (no that is not the case). So whatever the case, then his Islām was not like the Islām of As-Siddīq, since he was under the care of Allāh's Messenger (ﷺ): he took him from his uncle in order to assist him during a year of drought.

Likewise, Khadījah and Zayd ibn Hārithah accepted Islām. Also the priest Waraqah ibn Nawfal accepted Islām, and believed in what he found from Allāh's Revelations, and he wished that he had been a youth; and this was when the Revelation first descended.[2]

Furthermore, At-Tirmidhī narrated that Allāh's Messenger (ﷺ) saw him in a dream in a fine condition, and there occurs in a hadīth

---

1 — BJ SZ Refer to: *Sahīhul-Bukhārī* (no. 3, 4 and 6982) and *Sahīh Muslim* (nos. 160 and 161).

2 — SH Reported by Al-Bukhārī (no. 3) and Muslim (no. 252/160).

that Allāh's Messenger (صَلَّى ٱللَّهُ عَلَيْهِ وَسَلَّمَ) said: "I saw the priest wearing white clothes."[1]

And there occurs in the two *Sahīhs* that he [i.e. Waraqah] said: *"This is the Spirit which came to Mūsā Ibn 'Imrān,"* when Khadījah took him (صَلَّى ٱللَّهُ عَلَيْهِ وَسَلَّمَ) to him, and Allāh's Messenger (صَلَّى ٱللَّهُ عَلَيْهِ وَسَلَّمَ) narrated to him what he had seen with regard to Jibrīl (عَلَيْهِ ٱلسَّلَامُ).

So those who were such that Allāh opened their hearts to Islām entered into Islām; doing so upon light, insight and seeing (the truth) openly.

So the foolish ones from the people of Makkah subjected them to harm and torture, and Allāh defended His Messenger (صَلَّى ٱللَّهُ عَلَيْهِ وَسَلَّمَ) and protected him by means of his paternal uncle Abū Tālib. This was because he was a noble who was obeyed by them, and was one of the prominent persons amongst them. So they did not dare to upset him by assaulting Muhammad (صَلَّى ٱللَّهُ عَلَيْهِ وَسَلَّمَ) for they knew the love that he had for him. Furthermore, it was from the Wisdom of Allāh that he should remain upon their religion, because of the benefit that lay in that.

So this was the case, and Allāh's Messenger (صَلَّى ٱللَّهُ عَلَيْهِ وَسَلَّمَ) called to Allāh night and day, secretly and openly. Nothing could hinder him or turn him back from that, and he was not repelled in Allāh's cause by the rebuke of anyone.

---

1 — BJ SZ It is *'da'īf'* (unauthentic): reported by Ahmad (6/65) and At-Tirmidhī (no. 2288) as a hadīth of 'Ā'ishah (رَضِيَ ٱللَّهُ عَنْهَا) and it was declared weak by At-Tirmidhī by his saying: *"It is a 'gharīb' hadīth: 'Uthmān Ibn 'Abdir-Rahmān is not held to be strong by the people of hadīth."* I say: It is also declared to be weak because of its being *'mursal'*, and it was declared to be *'da'īf'* by Shaikh Al-Albānī in *Da'īf Sunanit-Tirmidhī*.

DB Al-Hākim reported in *Al-Mustadrak* (2/609) from 'Ā'ishah (رَضِيَ ٱللَّهُ عَنْهَا) that the Prophet (صَلَّى ٱللَّهُ عَلَيْهِ وَسَلَّمَ) said: *"Do not abuse Waraqah, for I saw one or two gardens [i.e. in Paradise] for him."* Declared authentic by Shaikh Al-Albānī in *As-Sahīhah* (no. 405).

CHAPTER:

The Aggression of the Mushrikūn Against the Weak Ones from Amongst the Muslims

However, the harm of the Mushrikūn became severe upon those who believed; and they put a group of them through great trials to the extent that they would beat them, throw them down upon the heat of the ground, and place a great rock upon their chests when it was extremely hot. Then when one of them was set free he would not be able to sit because of the severe pain. So they would say to one of them (i.e. those being tortured): *'Al-Lāt is the one deserving of your worship, not the One Whom you worship'*, so he would reply under compulsion: *'Yes!'*

To the extent that a dung beetle would pass by and they would say: *'This is the one deserving of your worship besides Allāh'*, and he would reply: *'Yes!'*

Also the foul enemy of Allāh — Abū Jahl 'Amr ibn Hishām — passed by Sumayyah, the mother of 'Ammār, whilst she was being tortured along with her husband and son, and he stabbed her in her private parts with a spear and killed her — may Allāh be pleased with her, and her son, and her husband.

So whenever Abū Bakr would pass by one of the slaves who was being tortured he would buy him from his owners and then set him free. So from them was Bilāl and his mother Hamāmah, and 'Āmir ibn Fuhayrah, Umm 'Abs, Zinnīrah, An-Nahdiyyah and her daughter, and a slave-girl belonging to Banū 'Adiyy whom 'Umar used to torture for her acceptance of Islām, [and that was] before he himself accepted Islām.

So it reached the extent that his father Abū Quhāfah said: "O my son! I see you setting free slaves who are weak, so if only you freed people of strength so that they would defend you!"

So Abū Bakr said: *"I want what I want"*. So it is said that there was sent down concerning him:

> وَسَيُجَنَّبُهَا الْأَتْقَى ۝ الَّذِي يُؤْتِي مَالَهُ يَتَزَكَّىٰ
>
> MEANING: "And the one dutiful to Allāh will be protected from the Fire. He who spends his wealth to seek to purify himself." (to the end of the Sūrah) — **Sūrah Al-Layl (92): 17-18** [1]

The Hijrah (Migration) To Abyssinia

So when the trial became severe Allāh (the Perfect and Most High) granted them permission to migrate to Abyssinia[2] which is to the west of Makkah, between the two lands lies the deserts of the Sudan and the ocean, which extends from Yemen to Al-Qulzum (the Gulf of ʿAqabah).

So the first one who left, fleeing with his Religion to Abyssinia was ʿUthmān Ibn ʿAffān (رَضِيَ ٱللَّهُ عَنْهُ), and with him was his wife Ruqayyah, the daughter of Allāh's Messenger (صَلَّى ٱللَّهُ عَلَيْهِ وَسَلَّمَ), and other people followed him; or it is otherwise said: rather the first one who migrated to the land of Abyssinia was Abū Hātib ibn ʿAmr ibn ʿAbd Shams ibn ʿAbd Wudd ibn Nasr ibn Mālik. Then afterwards Jaʿfar ibn Abī Tālib and groups of people (may Allāh be pleased with them and cause them to be pleased) went over, and they numbered eighty and odd men.

Muhammad ibn Is-hāq mentioned Abū Mūsā Al-Ashʿarī ʿAbdullāh ibn Qays amongst those who migrated to Abyssinia! So I do not know what led him to that?! So this is an affair that is clear and would not

---

1 — Dr. Akram Diyāʾ Al-ʿUmarī said concerning this narration in *As-Sīratun-Nabawiyyah* (1/156): *"Al-Hākim: Al-Mustadrak (2/525-526) with a 'hasan' chain of narration;"* and it was likewise declared *'hasan'* by the author of *Al-Istīʿāb fī Bayānil-Asbāb* in that book (3/517).

2 — DB Present day Northern Ethiopia.

remain hidden even from someone having less standing than him in this field. Therefore, Al-Wāqidī and others from the scholars of the military campaigns criticised that from him, and said: Abū Mūsā migrated from Yemen to Abyssinia, joining Ja'far, as is clearly stated in the *Sahīh* as a narration of his (رَضِيَ ٱللَّهُ عَنْهُ).[1]

So the Muhājirūn (those who migrated) withdrew to the kingdom of As-hamah[2] the Negus, so he gave them shelter and treated them honourably — so they were safe with him.

So when the Quraysh came to know of this they sent after them 'Abdullāh ibn Abī Rabī'ah and 'Amr ibn 'Ās, bearing presents and valuable gifts from their land for the Negus, so that he would send them [i.e. those who had migrated] back to them.

However, he refused to do that, so they tried to get the heads of his army to convince him on their behalf; but he still refused their request.[3] So they slandered them to him and said: "They say something very serious concerning 'Īsā; they say that he was a slave!"

So he brought the Muslims to his gathering and their head was Ja'far ibn Abī Tālib (رَضِيَ ٱللَّهُ عَنْهُ), and said: "What is it that those people say is your saying about 'Īsā?!"

So Ja'far recited Sūrah *'Kāf-Hā-Yā-'Ayn-Sād'*.[4]

So when he finished the Negus took a small splinter of wood from the ground and said: "This is no more than what is stated in the Tawrāt [Torah], not even by the amount of this splinter. Then he said: "Go freely, for you are safe in my land; whoever abuses you will be fined!"

He also said to 'Amr and 'Abdullāh: *"By Allāh, if you were to give me a mountain of gold I would not surrender them to you two,"* then he

---

1 — See: *Sahīhul-Bukhārī* (no. 3136) and *Sahīh Muslim* (no. 2502).

2 — SH Its meaning in Arabic is 'a gift', and *'An-Najjāshī'* (the Negus) was the title given to the kings of Abyssinia.

3 — For the story of An-Najjāshī's rise to power, see **Endnote 10 on page 437**.

4 — Also known as Sūrah Maryam, the nineteenth chapter of the Qur'ān.

commanded that their gifts be returned to them, and they went back in disgrace: frustrated and in a wretched state.[1]

Chapter: The Boycotting Of Banū Hāshim And Banul-Muttalib By The Quraysh

Then Hamzah — the paternal uncle of Allāh's Messenger and a large number of people accepted Islām, and Islām became widespread. So when the Quraysh saw this it upset them. So they gathered and made a joint agreement against the offspring of Hāshim and 'Abdul-Muttalib (the two sons of 'Abd Manāf), that they would not trade with them, or inter-marry with them, or speak to them, or sit with them until they surrendered Allāh's Messenger (صَلَّى ٱللَّهُ عَلَيْهِ وَسَلَّمَ) to them. They wrote this upon a parchment and suspended it from the ceiling of the Ka'bah. It is said that it was written by Mansūr ibn 'Ikrimah ibn 'Āmir ibn Hāshim ibn 'Abd Manāf or it is otherwise said: rather by An-Nadr ibn Al-Hārith. So Allāh's Messenger (صَلَّى ٱللَّهُ عَلَيْهِ وَسَلَّمَ) made supplication against him and his hand became paralysed.

So (the clans of) Banū Hāshim and Banul-Muttalib, their Believers and their Disbelievers, except for Abū Lahab — may Allāh curse him — withdrew to the mountain pass of Abū Tālib, being besieged and in a condition of great hardship for a period of about three years. So it was there that Abū Tālib wrote his famous poem:

> *'May Allāh reward 'Abd Shams and Nawfal for us...'*

Then some people of Quraysh worked for the abolition of the document, and the one who took charge of that was Hishām ibn 'Amr [ibn Rabī'ah] ibn Hārith ibn Hubayyib ibn Nasr[2] ibn Mālik ibn Hisl ibn 'Āmir ibn Lu'ayy. He went for that purpose to Mut'im ibn 'Adiyy and a group of Quraysh, and they responded to that.

---

1 — [BJ][SZ] This was reported by Ibn Is-hāq (1/357) and from him by Ahmad (1/201) with a longer wording, and its chain of narration is *'hasan'*.

[DB] Declared *'hasan'* by Shaikh Al-Albānī in *Sahīhus-Sīratin-Nabawiyyah*. (p. 180)

2 — [SH] That is what occurs in the Sulaymāniyyah Library manuscript (no. 3339), whereas the other two manuscripts have *"Judhaymah."*

And Allāh's Messenger (صَلَّى ٱللَّهُ عَلَيْهِ وَسَلَّمَ) informed his people that Allāh had sent some termites upon that parchment which had eaten everything of it except where there was a mention of Allāh (the Mighty and Majestic), and that was found to be so.

Then Banū Hāshim and Banul-Muttalib returned to Makkah, and a state of peace was attained, against the will of Abū Jahl 'Amr ibn Hishām.

Also, a report reached those who were in Abyssinia that the Quraysh had accepted Islām, so a group of them came back to Makkah. However, they found that the trials and hardships were just the same as before. So they remained in Makkah until they migrated to Al-Madīnah, except for As-Sakrān ibn 'Amr — the husband of Sawdah bint Zam'ah, for he had died in Makkah after returning from Abyssinia, before the migration to Al-Madīnah; and except for Salamah ibn Hishām and 'Ayyāsh ibn Abī Rabī'ah, for they were withheld in Makkah — being from the poor and weak; and except for 'Abdullāh ibn Makhramah ibn 'Abdul-'Uzzā, for he was imprisoned. Then on the day of Badr he fled from the Mushrikūn and joined the Muslims.

Chapter: The Departure Of Allāh's Messenger (صَلَّى ٱللَّهُ عَلَيْهِ وَسَلَّمَ) To At-Tā'if

At the time the agreement was abolished, Khadījah (رَضِيَ ٱللَّهُ عَنْهَا) died, and Abū Tālib died, with three days between the two events. So then the harm inflicted upon Allāh's Messenger (صَلَّى ٱللَّهُ عَلَيْهِ وَسَلَّمَ) by the foolish ones from his people became severe, and they made assaults upon him.[1]

So then Allāh's Messenger (صَلَّى ٱللَّهُ عَلَيْهِ وَسَلَّمَ) departed for At-Tā'if so that they should shelter him and aid him against his people and defend him from them. So he called them to Allāh (the Mighty and Majestic) but they did not accept anything from that which he requested from them. rather

---

1 — SH This is indicated by what Al-Hākim reported (2/622), and Al-Bayhaqī in *Dalā'ilun-Nubuwwah* (2/349-350), and Ibn 'Asākir in *Tārīkh Dimashq* (70/250), and others, as a hadīth of 'Ā'ishah (رَضِيَ ٱللَّهُ عَنْهَا) from the Prophet (صَلَّى ٱللَّهُ عَلَيْهِ وَسَلَّمَ) that he said: *"The Quraysh did not have the courage to make attacks upon me until Abū Tālib died."* I say: Its chain of narration is good.

they harmed him so greatly that the harm of his own people was not any greater than the harm that they assaulted him with.[1]

So he left them and re-entered Makkah under an agreement of protection from Al-Mutʿim ibn ʿAdiyy ibn Nawfal ibn ʿAbd Manāf, and he called (the people) to Allāh. So At-Tufayl ibn ʿAmr Ad-Dawsī accepted Islām, and Allāh's Messenger (صَلَّى ٱللَّهُ عَلَيْهِ وَسَلَّمَ) made supplication for him that Allāh should grant him a sign. So Allāh placed light upon his face, so he said: *"O Messenger of Allāh! I fear that they will say that this is a disfigurement."* So he made supplication for him, and the light moved to his whip. So he was the one known as *'The Possessor of Light'*.[2]

So At-Tufayl called his people to Islām and some of them accepted Islām, and he remained in his land until Allāh granted the Conquest of Khaybar to His Messenger. Then he came along with them; and they were around eighty families.[3]

---

1 — The Messenger (صَلَّى ٱللَّهُ عَلَيْهِ وَسَلَّمَ) considered this day to be from the most severe periods of his life as he elaborated to ʿĀ'ishah (رَضِيَ ٱللَّهُ عَنْهَا). See **Endnote 11 on page 439**.

2 — BJ SZ Refer to his biography in *Al-Isābah* (3/286), and the story of the light is mentioned by Ibn Is-hāq (1/421) without a chain of narration, and Ibn Hajr mentions weak chains of narration for it.

3 — SH Reported by Al-Bukhārī (no. 2937, 4392, 6397), Muslim (no. 2524) (...) from Abū Hurairah (رَضِيَ ٱللَّهُ عَنْهُ) who said: "When At-Tufayl and his companions came to Allāh's Messenger (صَلَّى ٱللَّهُ عَلَيْهِ وَسَلَّمَ) he said: *'Daws have been obstinate and refused, so make supplication to Allāh against them.'* So Allāh's Messenger (صَلَّى ٱللَّهُ عَلَيْهِ وَسَلَّمَ) faced the Qiblah and raised his hands. So the people said: *'They are destroyed!'* But he said: *'O Allāh! Guide the Daws and bring them along.'*"

CHAPTER:

The Night-Journey & the Ascent Through the Heavens (Al-Isrā' Wal-Mi'rāj) & the Prophet's Presenting Himself to the Tribes

And Allāh's Messenger (صَلَّى ٱللَّهُ عَلَيْهِ وَسَلَّمَ) was taken on the Night Journey (Al-Isrā'), bodily — in the correct saying from the two sayings of the Companions and the scholars[1] from the Sacred Mosque (Al-Masjidul-Harām) to Jerusalem, riding Al-Burāq[2] whilst being accompanied by Jibrīl (عَلَيْهِ ٱلسَّلَامُ). So he dismounted there and led the Prophets in Prayer in Jerusalem.

Then he was taken up that night from there to the lowest heaven, and then to the next one, then to the third, then the fourth, then the fifth, then the next, then the seventh; and he saw the Prophets in their stations in the heavens. Then he was taken up to the Farthest Lote-Tree (*'Sidratul-Muntahā'*) and he saw Jibrīl there in the form upon which Allāh created him; and Allāh made the Prayers obligatory upon him that night.[3] And the scholars disagree about whether he saw his Lord (the Mighty and Majestic) or not, about which they have two sayings.

---

1 — Read Endnote 12 on page 440 for the speech of Al-Hāfidh Ibn Hajr and Al-Qādhī 'Iyād regarding the position of the Salaf on this matter.

2 — Al-Bukhārī narrated (no. 3887) as a hadīth of Mālik ibn Sa'sa'ah (رَضِيَ ٱللَّهُ عَنْهُ) that the Prophet (صَلَّى ٱللَّهُ عَلَيْهِ وَسَلَّمَ) described Al-Burāq saying: "A white animal smaller than a mule and larger than a donkey. Its stride was as wide as the distance it could see..."

3 — [BJ] [SZ] Refer to *Sahīhul-Bukhārī* (no. 3887) and *Sahīh Muslim* (no.164).

So it is authentic from Ibn ʿAbbās that he said: *"He saw his Lord"*[1] and there occurs in one narration from him: *"He saw him with his heart."*[2]

And there occurs in the two *Sahīhs* from ʿĀ'ishah (رَضِيَ ٱللَّهُ عَنْهَا) that she criticised that saying from those who say it.[3]

And both she and Ibn Masʿūd said: *"He saw Jibrīl."*[4] And Muslim reported in his *Sahīh* as a hadīth of Qatādah; from ʿAbdullāh ibn Shaqīq: from Abū Dharr who said: "I asked Allāh's Messenger (صَلَّى ٱللَّهُ عَلَيْهِ وَسَلَّمَ): *'Did you see your Lord?'*

He replied: *'Light! How could I see Him?!'*" — and in one narration: "I saw light."[5]

So this hadīth is sufficient with regard to this matter.[6]

Then when Allāh's Messenger (صَلَّى ٱللَّهُ عَلَيْهِ وَسَلَّمَ) entered the morning amongst his people, he informed them of the greater signs which Allāh had showed him.[7] So their calling him a liar, their harm, and their boldness in attacking him only increased in severity.

And Allāh's Messenger (صَلَّى ٱللَّهُ عَلَيْهِ وَسَلَّمَ) presented himself to the tribes on the days of the rites of the pilgrimage, and he would say:

---

1 — [BJ][SZ] It is reported by Ibn Khuzaymah (p. 130), At-Tirmidhī (no. 3279), An-Nasā'ī in [*Al-Kubrā*] (no. 11537), Ibn Abī ʿĀsim in *As-Sunnah* (no. 441) and others, and it is authentic from Ibn ʿAbbās, as the author said.

2 — [BJ][SZ] Reported by Muslim (no. 176).

3 — [SH] Reported by Al-Bukhārī (nos. 4855 & 7380) and Muslim (no.177).

4 — [SH] Reported by Al-Bukhārī (nos. 4856 & 4857) and Muslim (nos. 174 & 175).

5 — [BJ][SZ] Reported by Muslim (no.178).

6 — There was no real disagreement between the Companions with regards to the matter of the Messenger (صَلَّى ٱللَّهُ عَلَيْهِ وَسَلَّمَ) seeing His Lord — see **Endnote 13 on page 441**.

7 — When the Messenger of Allāh (صَلَّى ٱللَّهُ عَلَيْهِ وَسَلَّمَ) returned from the Night Journey, he was questioned regarding it by the enemy of Allāh; Abū Jahl — see **Endnote 14 on page 441** for the narration.

> "Is there any man who will take me to his people and defend me so that I can convey the Message of my Lord, since Quraysh have prevented me from conveying the Message of my Lord."

So his uncle Abū Lahab — may Allāh curse him — would follow behind him saying to the people: "Do not listen to him for he is a great liar!"

So the tribes of the Arabs were on their guard against him because of what they heard about him from Quraysh: that he was a liar, that he was a sorcerer, that he was a soothsayer, that he was a poet; lies that they themselves invented and threw against him.

So those who had no ability to distinguish gave ear to them. However, those possessing intellect bore witness when they heard and understood his speech, that what he said was the truth, and that those people were inventing lies against him, and so they accepted Islām.

So from that which Allāh did for his allies from the Aws and the Khazraj is that they used to hear from their confederates from the Jews of Al-Madīnah that a Prophet was going to be raised in this time. They also used to threaten them that he was going to come and wage war against them, and they said: *'We will kill you fighting along with him, with the killing that happened to 'Ād and Iram.'* And the Ansār used to love the House, just as the Arabs loved it, but as for the Jews then they did not.

So when the Ansār saw Allāh's Messenger (صَلَّى ٱللَّهُ عَلَيْهِ وَسَلَّمَ) calling the people to Allāh — the Most High, and they saw the clear signs of truthfulness upon him they said: "This, by Allāh is the one the Jews threatened you with. So don't let them precede you in believing in him."

Chapter: An Account Concerning Suwayd Ibn As-Sāmit

Suwayd ibn As-Sāmit was a brother of the (Clan of) Banū 'Amr ibn 'Awf from the Aws, and he came to Makkah. So Allāh's Messenger (صَلَّى ٱللَّهُ عَلَيْهِ وَسَلَّمَ) called him to Islām, but he neither distanced himself nor responded. Then he returned to Al-Madīnah and was killed in one of their wars; and this Suwayd was a maternal cousin of ʿAbdul-Muttalib.[1]

The Islām Of Iyās Ibn Muʿādh And The Story Of Abul-Haysar

Then Abul-Haysar Anas ibn Rāfiʿ came to Makkah along with some youths from his people, from Banū ʿAbdul-Ash-hal seeking to make an alliance, so Allāh's Messenger (صَلَّىٰٱللَّهُعَلَيْهِوَسَلَّمَ) called them to Islām. So from them Iyās ibn Muʿādh, who was a young youth, said: "O people! This is, by Allāh, better than what we came for."

So Abul-Haysar struck him, and rebuked him. So he fell silent. Then they did not obtain the alliance, so they returned to their land: to Al-Madīnah. So it is said that Iyās died as a Muslim.

Chapter: The First Pledge (Baiʿah) Of Al-ʿAqabah

Then during the Pilgrimage, at Al-ʿAqabah,[2] Allāh's Messenger (صَلَّىٰٱللَّهُعَلَيْهِوَسَلَّمَ) met six men from the Ansār; all of them were from the Khazraj, and they were: Abū Umāmah Asʿad ibn Zurārah ibn ʿUdas, ʿAwf ibn Al-Hārith ibn Rifāʿah — and he was Ibn ʿAfrāʾ, and Rāfiʿ ibn Mālik ibn Al-ʿAjlān, Qutbah ibn ʿĀmir ibn Hadīdah, ʿUqbah ibn ʿĀmir ibn Nābī, and Jābir ibn ʿAbdillāh ibn Riʾāb.

So Allāh's Messenger (صَلَّىٰٱللَّهُعَلَيْهِوَسَلَّمَ) called them to Islām so they accepted Islām, hastening to good. Then they returned to Al-Madīnah and called to Islām, so Islām became widespread there to the extent that no household remained except that Islām entered it.

---

1 — [SH] It is not established that Suwayd ibn As-Sāmit accepted Islām; and refer to: *As-Sīratun-Nabawiyyah* (2/39), and *Al-Isābah* (2/134).

2 — [DB] Yāqūt Al-Hamawī said in *Muʿjamul-Buldān* (4/134) "As for the ʿAqabah (mountain pass) in Makkah where the pledge was given to the Prophet (صَلَّىٰٱللَّهُعَلَيْهِوَسَلَّمَ), then it is a mountain pass between Minā and Makkah. It is about two miles from Makkah, and there is a mosque there; and from there the Jamratul-ʿAqabah is pelted with small pebbles."

Then the following year twelve men of them came: the first six, except for Jābir ibn ʿAbdillāh ibn Riʾāb, and along with them was Muʿādh ibn Al-Hārith ibn Rifāʿah — the brother of the aforementioned ʿAwf; and Dhakwān ibn ʿAbd Qays ibn Khaldah, and this Dhakwān remained in Makkah until he performed the migration to Al-Madīnah, so it is said that he is a 'Muhājir' from the Ansār; and ʿUbādah ibn As-Sāmit ibn Qays; and Abū ʿAbdir-Rahmān Yazīd ibn Thaʿlabah. So they are ten from the (tribes of the) Khazraj.

And two were from the (tribes of the) Aws, and they were: Abul-Haytham Mālik ibn At-Tayyihān, and ʿUwaym ibn Sāʿidah.

So they gave the pledge of allegiance to Allāh's Messenger (صَلَّىٱللَّهُعَلَيْهِوَسَلَّمَ) with the *'Pledge of the Women'*, and they had not yet been commanded with fighting.[1]

So when they went back to Al-Madīnah, Allāh's Messenger (صَلَّىٱللَّهُعَلَيْهِوَسَلَّمَ) sent along with them ʿAmr ibn Umm Maktūm and Musʿab ibn ʿUmayr to teach the Qurʾān to those amongst them who had accepted Islām, and to call to Allāh — the Mighty and Majestic. So the two of them resided with Abū Umāmah Asʿad ibn Zurārah; and Musʿab ibn Umayr used to lead them in the Prayer, and one day he led them in the Jumuʿah Prayer when they were forty in number.[2]

So many people accepted Islām at the hands of these two. From them was Usayd ibn Al-Hudayr and Saʿd ibn Muʿādh; and on that day, because of the Islām of these two, the whole of Banū ʿAbdil-Ash-hal accepted Islām — the men and the women — except for *'Al-Usayram'* who was ʿAmr ibn Thābit ibn Waqsh, for his Islām was delayed until the Day of Uhud. He accepted Islām on that day and fought and was killed before he had prostrated a single prostration for Allāh. So the Prophet (صَلَّىٱللَّهُعَلَيْهِوَسَلَّمَ) was

---

1 — The wording of the Pledge is reported in the *Sahīhayn* and can be read in ENDNOTE 15 ON PAGE 443.

2 — DB Reported by Abū Dāwūd (no. 1069) and Ibn Mājah (1082), and declared *'hasan'* by Shaikh Al-Albānī.

informed of him and said: "He performed little action but was rewarded greatly."[1]

The Second Pledge Of Al-ʿAqabah

So Islām increased greatly in Al-Madīnah and became apparent, then Musʿab ibn ʿUmayr returned to Makkah. Then that year a large number of people from the Ansār, from the Muslims and the Mushrikūn, gathered for the Pilgrimage, and the leader of the people was Al-Barāʾ Ibn Maʿrūr (رَضِيَ ٱللَّهُ عَنْهُ).

So when it was the night of Al-ʿAqabah, during the first third of it, seventy three man and two women came secretly to Allāh's Messenger (صَلَّى ٱللَّهُ عَلَيْهِ وَسَلَّمَ). So they gave the pledge to Allāh's Messenger (صَلَّى ٱللَّهُ عَلَيْهِ وَسَلَّمَ), keeping it a secret from their people and from the Disbelievers of the Quraysh, that they would defend him just as they defended their own wives, children, and women folk.[2]

So the first one who gave him the pledge on that night was Al-Barāʾ ibn Maʿrūr, and he had the distinction of emphasizing the pledge and being quick to give it.

And Al-ʿAbbās — the paternal uncle of Allāh's Messenger (صَلَّى ٱللَّهُ عَلَيْهِ وَسَلَّمَ) — was present to confirm and emphasize the pledge, even though he was still at that time upon the religion of his people!

And Allāh's Messenger (صَلَّى ٱللَّهُ عَلَيْهِ وَسَلَّمَ) chose from them on that night twelve chiefs, and they were: Asʿad ibn Zurārah ibn ʿUdas, Saʿd ibn Ar-Rabīʿ ibn ʿAmr, ʿAbdullāh ibn Rawāhah ibn Umruʾul-Qays, Rāfiʿ ibn Mālik ibnil-ʿAjlān, Al-Barāʾ ibn Maʿrūr ibn Sakhr ibn Khansāʾ, ʿAbdullāh ibn ʿAmr ibn Harām — who was the father of Jābir and had accepted Islām that night (رَضِيَ ٱللَّهُ عَنْهُ), Saʿd ibn ʿUbādah ibn Dulaym, Al-Mundhir ibn ʿAmr ibn Khunays, and ʿUbādah ibn As-Sāmit; so these were nine from

---

1 — It is not clear that Allāh's Messenger (صَلَّى ٱللَّهُ عَلَيْهِ وَسَلَّمَ) was referring to ʿAmr Ibn Thābit with this speech, and more detail can be found in Endnote 16 on page 443.

2 — Read Endnote 17 on page 444 for the amazing and heart-moving narration of the events of that day.

the (tribes of) the Khazraj. And from the Aws three, and they were: Usayd ibn Al-Hudayr ibn Simāk, Sa'd ibn Khaythamah ibn Al-Hārith, and Rifā'ah ibn 'Abdil-Mundhir ibn Zubayr; or it is said: rather Abul-Haytham ibn At-Tayyihān in place of him; then the people followed them.

And the two women were: Umm 'Umārah Nasībah bint Ka'b ibn 'Amr, whose son — Habīb ibn Zayd ibn 'Āsim ibn Ka'b — was killed by Musaylamah, and Asmā' bint 'Amr ibn 'Adiyy ibn Nābī. So when the pledge was completed they asked permission of Allāh's Messenger (صَلَّى ٱللَّهُ عَلَيْهِ وَسَلَّمَ) to attack those present at the (pass of) Al-'Aqabah, but he did not permit them to do that.[1]

Rather, permission was given after it, to the Muslims from the people of Makkah, for them to migrate to Al-Madīnah; so the people hastened to do that. So the first one from the people of Makkah who departed for Al-Madīnah was Abū Salamah ibn 'Abdil-Asad, along with his wife Umm Salamah. However, she was caught, and kept back from him, and prevented from joining him for one year, and her son was taken away from her. Then after a year, she departed and went with her son to Al-Madīnah, and she was escorted by 'Uthmān ibn Abī Talhah. It is, however, otherwise said that Abū Salamah migrated before the Last (pledge of) Al-'Aqabah, so Allāh knows best. Then the people departed in successive groups, following each other.

---

1 — (SH) Reported by Ibn Is-hāq in *As-Sīrah* and from him by Ahmad (3/460-462) and Ibn Hibbān. And declared *'hasan'* by Shaikh Al-Albānī in *Sahīh Mawāridiz-Zam'ān* (no. 1900).

CHAPTER:

The Hijrah (Migration) of Allāh's Messenger صَلَّى ٱللَّٰهُ عَلَيْهِ وَسَلَّمَ

So no Muslims remained in Makkah except for Allāh's Messenger (صَلَّى ٱللَّٰهُ عَلَيْهِ وَسَلَّمَ), Abū Bakr and ʿAlī (رَضِيَ ٱللَّٰهُ عَنْهُمَا); and these two remained because of his order for them to do so; and except for those who were held against their will by the Mushrikūn.

Abū Bakr (رَضِيَ ٱللَّٰهُ عَنْهُ) had made ready the requirements for the journey for himself and for Allāh's Messenger (صَلَّى ٱللَّٰهُ عَلَيْهِ وَسَلَّمَ), awaiting the permission of Allāh (the Mighty and Majestic) for His Messenger (صَلَّى ٱللَّٰهُ عَلَيْهِ وَسَلَّمَ) to depart. So one night the Mushrikūn intended to attack Allāh's Messenger (صَلَّى ٱللَّٰهُ عَلَيْهِ وَسَلَّمَ), and they positioned some people to wait outside his door so that when he came out they would kill him. However when he came out towards them none of them saw him. It is also mentioned in a hadīth that he sprinkled dust on the head of each of them,[1] and then he escaped to the house of Abū Bakr (رَضِيَ ٱللَّٰهُ عَنْهُ).

Then the two of them escaped through a window in[2] the house of Abū Bakr during the night, and they had hired ʿAbdullāh ibn Urayqat who was an experienced and proficient guide who knew the way to the land of Al-Madīnah well. So they entrusted him with that even though he remained upon the religion of his people, and they handed over their riding camels to him and arranged to meet him at the cave of Thawr after three days.

---

1 — Dr. Akram Diyāʾ Al-ʿUmarī said in *As-Sīratun-Nabawiyyah As-Sahīhah* (1/207): "*Sīrah ibn Hishām* (1/483) with a chain of narration that is authentic to Muhammad ibn Kaʿb Al-Qurazī, however it is mursal (i.e. since he was a Tābiʿī)."

2 — DB *As-Sīratun-Nabawiyyah* (2/205) has: *"At the back of his house."*

So when they reached the cave Allāh caused all news about them to remain hidden from the Quraysh, so they did not know where they had gone. Also, ʿĀmir ibn Fuhayrah began grazing some sheep belonging to Abū Bakr wherever they had passed to cover their tracks, and Asmā, the daughter of Abū Bakr carried food for them to the cave. Also, ʿAbdullāh ibn Abī Bakr listened out for whatever was being said in Makkah and then went and informed them, so they would be on their guard based upon that.

Then the Mushrikūn came looking for them towards Thawr and the places in that area, until they came to the mouth of the cave and their feet were level with Allāh's Messenger (ﷺ) and his companion, but Allāh caused them to be blind to the mouth of the cave.

And it is said — and Allāh knows best — that a spider had covered the entrance of the cave and that two pigeons had made nests over the entrance.[1]

So that is the explanation of His Saying, He (the Most High):

> إِلَّا تَنصُرُوهُ فَقَدْ نَصَرَهُ اللَّهُ إِذْ أَخْرَجَهُ الَّذِينَ كَفَرُوا ثَانِيَ اثْنَيْنِ إِذْ هُمَا فِي الْغَارِ إِذْ يَقُولُ لِصَاحِبِهِ لَا تَحْزَنْ إِنَّ اللَّهَ مَعَنَا ۖ فَأَنزَلَ اللَّهُ سَكِينَتَهُ عَلَيْهِ وَأَيَّدَهُ بِجُنُودٍ لَّمْ تَرَوْهَا وَجَعَلَ كَلِمَةَ الَّذِينَ كَفَرُوا السُّفْلَىٰ ۗ وَكَلِمَةُ اللَّهِ هِيَ الْعُلْيَا ۗ وَاللَّهُ عَزِيزٌ حَكِيمٌ
>
> MEANING: "If you do not aid him (Muhammad (ﷺ) then Allāh certainly aided him when the Disbelievers drove him out: the second of two when they were in the cave, when he (ﷺ) said to his companion (Abū Bakr رضي الله عنه): *"Do not grieve, Allāh is with us"*. So Allāh sent down His tranquillity upon him, and strengthened

1 — BJ SZ And it is *'gharīb jiddan'* (very singular/weak) as Ibn Kathīr said in *Al-Bidāyah* (3/180)"

SH The story of the two pigeons and the story of the spider is *'munkar'* (weak and contrary to what is correct); and refer necessarily to *Al-Bidāyah wan-Nihāyah* (3/181), and *Ad-Daʿīfah* (of Shaikh Al-Albānī) (nos. 1128 and 1129).

> him with armies of Angels which you did not see; and He made the saying of those who disbelieved the lowest; whereas the Word of Allāh is uppermost; and Allāh is the Mighty, the Wise." — **Sūrah At-Tawbah (9): 40**

And that was because Abū Bakr (رَضِيَ ٱللَّهُ عَنْهُ), because of his great concern, wept when the Mushrikūn passed close by, and said: "O Messenger of Allāh! If one of them were to look towards the place of his feet he would see us!"

So the Prophet (صَلَّى ٱللَّهُ عَلَيْهِ وَسَلَّمَ) said to him: "O Abū Bakr! What do you think about two for whom the third is Allāh?!"

Then after three days Ibn Urayqat came to them with the two riding-camels, so they mounted them and Abū Bakr had ʿĀmir ride along with him upon a single camel, and Ad-Dīlī[1] proceeded in front of them upon his own riding camel.

Quraysh offered a reward of a hundred camels for anyone who could capture either Muhammad (صَلَّى ٱللَّهُ عَلَيْهِ وَسَلَّمَ) or Abū Bakr (رَضِيَ ٱللَّهُ عَنْهُ). So when they passed by the area of (the tribe of) Mudlij, Surāqah ibn Mālik ibn Juʿshum, the chief of the Mudlij saw them. So he mounted his fastest horse and chased after them. Then he came close to them, and heard the recitation of the Prophet (صَلَّى ٱللَّهُ عَلَيْهِ وَسَلَّمَ) — and Abū Bakr (رَضِيَ ٱللَّهُ عَنْهُ) turned around frequently, being fearful for Allāh's Messenger (صَلَّى ٱللَّهُ عَلَيْهِ وَسَلَّمَ), whereas he (صَلَّى ٱللَّهُ عَلَيْهِ وَسَلَّمَ) did not turn around. So Abū Bakr said: "O Messenger of Allāh! Here is Surāqah ibn Mālik; he has caught up with us."

So Allāh's Messenger (صَلَّى ٱللَّهُ عَلَيْهِ وَسَلَّمَ) made supplication against him, so the front legs of his horse sank into the ground. So he said: "I know that what has happened to me is because of your supplication, so make supplication to Allāh for me, and it will be upon me to repel the people from the two of you."

So Allāh's Messenger (صَلَّى ٱللَّهُ عَلَيْهِ وَسَلَّمَ) made supplication for him and he was set free. He also asked Allāh's Messenger (صَلَّى ٱللَّهُ عَلَيْهِ وَسَلَّمَ) to write a document for him, which Abū Bakr then inscribed for him upon an animal hide.

---

1 — [DB] i.e. Ibn Urayqat.

Then he went back to the people and said: *"I have checked this area for you already."* Then on the year of the Farewell Hajj he came as a Muslim, and he handed over to Allāh's Messenger (ﷺ) the document that he had written for him. So Allāh's Messenger (ﷺ) paid him what he had promised him, and he was deserving of that.[1]

Also whilst on this journey Allāh's Messenger (ﷺ) passed by the tent of Umm Maʿbad, and he took a siesta at her place. So she saw signs of his Prophethood in what occurred with her sheep: they started to give milk plentifully at a time of drought — astonishing![2]

Chapter: The Prophet's (ﷺ) Entry into Al-Madīnah

News of his departure from Makkah and his coming towards them reached the Ansār, so every day they used to go out to the lava plain to await him. So when it was Monday the twelfth of Rabīʿ Al-Awwal, at the head of thirteen years of his Prophethood, Allāh's Messenger (ﷺ) came to them whilst the heat of the forenoon was at its peak. The Ansār had gone out that day, but after remaining for a long time, they returned to their homes.

So the first one who saw him was a man of the Jews, who was upon the roof of his fortified house. So he called out at the top of his voice: "O Banū Qaylah![3] Here is the one you are waiting for!"

So the Ansār went out with their weapons, and met him and greeted him as their Prophet.

So Allāh's Messenger (ﷺ) alighted and stayed in Qubā' with Kulthūm ibn Al-Hidm, or it is said; with Saʿd ibn Khaythamah.

---

1 — [SH] Refer to *Sahīhul-Bukhārī* (no. 3615) and *Sahīh Muslim* (no. 2009).

2 — [BJ][SZ] Ibn Kathīr said in *Al-Bidāyah* (3/209) concerning the story of Umm Maʿbad: *"Her story is famous and narrated through chains of narrations which strengthen each other,"* and refer to her story in the following references: *Mustadrakul-Hākim* (3/9), *Ad-Dalā'il* of Abū Nuʿaym (no. 238).

3 — [SH] The Aws and the Khazraj, ascribing them to a grandmother of theirs called Qaylah.

So the Muslims came to give salutations to Allāh's Messenger (ﷺ) and most of them had never seen him. So some of them, or most of them, thought that Abū Bakr was him, because he had a great deal of grey hair. Then when the heat became severe Abū Bakr stood holding a garment to shade Allāh's Messenger (ﷺ) so the people realised then which one was the Messenger of Allāh (عَلَيْهِ الصَّلَاةُ وَالسَّلَامُ).[1]

Chapter: The Prophet's (ﷺ) Settling In Al-Madīnah

So Allāh's Messenger (ﷺ) remained in Qubā' for some days, and it is said: for fourteen days; and it is then that he found his mosque: the mosque of Qubā'. Then he rode onwards in accordance with Allāh's (the Most High) command to him, and the Jumu'ah became due upon him whilst he was amongst Banū Sālim ibn 'Awf. So he prayed it in the [place of the] mosque which lies in the wadi of Rānūnā.[2]

So the people of that locality encouraged him to alight and settle with them, but he said: *"Let her proceed, for she is under orders."* So his camel continued on its way with him. He did not pass by any abode from the abodes of the Ansār except that they encouraged him to stay with them, but he would say: *"Let her proceed, for she is under orders."*[3]

---

1 — (SH) Refer to *Sahīhul-Bukhārī* (no. 3906).

2 — (SH) A wadi which begins northwest of Qubā' and meets up with the wadi of Buthān close to Al-Madīnah. The Jumu'ah mosque is present there today.

3 — (BJ)(SZ) *Da'īf* (unauthentic): Reported by Sa'īd ibn Mansūr (no. 2978), and reported by way of him by At-Tabarānī (no.3568) and Al-Bayhaqī in *Ad-Dalā'il* (2/509) from 'Attāf ibn Khālid who said: Siddīq ibn Mūsā narrated to me: from 'Abdillāh ibn Az-Zubayr, with it. I say: Adh-Dhahabī said concerning Siddīq ibn Mūsā: *'He is not a proof';* and it has a witness from a hadīth of Anas ibn Mālik, which is reported by Al-Bayhaqī in *Ad-Dalā'il* (2/508), except that its chain of narration contains Ibrāhīm ibn Surmah who was declared to be a liar by Ibn Ma'īn; and a third from Ibn 'Umar in *Al-Kāmil* of Ibn 'Adiyy (2/591), but its chain contains two weak narrators. Then there occurs in *Sahīhul-Bukhārī* (no. 3906): *"Then he (ﷺ) rode his riding-camel, and the people walked along with him, until it knelt down in (the place of) the mosque of the Messenger (ﷺ) in Al-Madīnah,"* — and refer to *Fat-hul-Bārī* (7/245-246).

So when it came to the place where the mosque is today it knelt down. However, he (صَلَّى ٱللَّهُ عَلَيْهِ وَسَلَّمَ) did not dismount until it had got up again, moved on a little, turned and had come back to the first place and knelt down. Then he (صَلَّى ٱللَّهُ عَلَيْهِ وَسَلَّمَ) dismounted. This was in the dwelling-place of Banun-Najjār, so Abū Ayyūb (رَضِيَ ٱللَّهُ عَنْهُ) carried the baggage of Allāh's Messenger (صَلَّى ٱللَّهُ عَلَيْهِ وَسَلَّمَ) into his house.

Allāh's Messenger (صَلَّى ٱللَّهُ عَلَيْهِ وَسَلَّمَ) bought the place of the mosque, and it had been a drying-ground for dates, and he built the mosque; and the apartments for the family of Allāh's Messenger (صَلَّى ٱللَّهُ عَلَيْهِ وَسَلَّمَ) were built to the side of it.

As for ʿAlī (رَضِيَ ٱللَّهُ عَنْهُ), then he stayed in Makkah until he had restored, on behalf of Allāh's Messenger (صَلَّى ٱللَّهُ عَلَيْهِ وَسَلَّمَ), all the goods that had been deposited with him for safekeeping, and other than that. Then he came and joined Allāh's Messenger (صَلَّى ٱللَّهُ عَلَيْهِ وَسَلَّمَ).[1]

Chapter: The Brotherhood Established Between The Muhājirīn And The Ansār

Allāh's Messenger (صَلَّى ٱللَّهُ عَلَيْهِ وَسَلَّمَ) made a treaty with the Jews present in Al-Madīnah, and he wrote that down upon a document;[2] and their scholar ʿAbdullāh ibn Salām (رَضِيَ ٱللَّهُ عَنْهُ) accepted Islām,[3] whereas most of them disbelieved, and they were three tribes: Banū Qaynuqāʿ, Banun-Nadīr, and Banū Quraydhah.

---

1 — [SH] Ibn Is-hāq mentioned that this was a saying that reached him, as occurs in *Al-Bidāyah wan-Nihāyah.*

2 — [SH] Shaikh Al-Albānī (رَحِمَهُ ٱللَّهُ) said in *Difāʿ ʿAnil-hadīthin-Nabawī was-Sīrah* (pp. 25-26): "This is something whose authenticity is not known, since Ibn Hishām related it in his *Sīrah*, saying: *'Ibn Is-hāq said...'*, and he mentioned it like that without a chain of narration, so it is *'muʿdal'* (has two or more consecutive missing links in its chain). Also, Ibn Kathīr quotes it (3/224-225) from Ibn Is-hāq, and does not add anything further as a reference for it, contrary to his usual practice. So this indicates that it is not something well-known to the people of knowledge and awareness of the Sīrah and the chains of narration."

3 — For the hadīth of ʿAbdullāh Ibn Salām accepting Islām, see ENDNOTE 18 ON PAGE **445**.

And Allāh's Messenger (صَلَّى ٱللَّهُ عَلَيْهِ وَسَلَّمَ) established brotherhood between the Muhājirīn and the Ansār.[1] So in the beginning of Islām they used to inherit from each other upon the basis of this brotherhood in a way that took precedence over the ties of kinship.[2]

And Allāh (the Perfect and the Most High) made the Zakāt obligatory at that time, as a mercy upon the poor and needy Muhājirīn.

Ibn Hazm mentioned this as having occurred at this time. However, one of the memorizers from the scholars of hadīth said that he was unaware of when the Zakāt was made obligatory.

---

1 — [SH] Reported by Al-Bukhārī (nos. 1968 and 2293) and Muslim (no. 2528).

2 — [SH] Reported by Al-Bukhārī (nos. 2292 and 2294) and Muslim (no. 2529).

CHAPTER:

The Obligation Of Jihād

Then when Allāh's Messenger (ﷺ) became settled amongst the Ansār in Al-Madīnah, and they took on the responsibility of defending him from everyone, all of the Arabs strove against them and opposed them from every aspect.

So Allāh (the Perfect) had already given permission to the Muslims for Jihād in Sūratul-Hajj, which was sent down in Makkah, in His saying (He the Most High):

> أُذِنَ لِلَّذِينَ يُقَاتَلُونَ بِأَنَّهُمْ ظُلِمُوا ۚ وَإِنَّ اللَّهَ عَلَىٰ نَصْرِهِمْ لَقَدِيرٌ
>
> MEANING: "Permission to fight is given to those Believers who are fought against, because they have been wronged, and Allāh is fully able to give them victory." — **Sūrah Al-Hajj (22): 39**

So when they came to Al-Madīnah, and they came to have strength and support, then Allāh obligated Jihād upon them, as He (the Most High) said in Sūratul-Baqarah:

> كُتِبَ عَلَيْكُمُ الْقِتَالُ وَهُوَ كُرْهٌ لَّكُمْ ۖ وَعَسَىٰ أَن تَكْرَهُوا شَيْئًا وَهُوَ خَيْرٌ لَّكُمْ ۖ وَعَسَىٰ
> أَن تُحِبُّوا شَيْئًا وَهُوَ شَرٌّ لَّكُمْ ۗ وَاللَّهُ يَعْلَمُ وَأَنتُمْ لَا تَعْلَمُونَ
>
> MEANING: "Jihād is obligated upon you, though it is disagreeable to you, but it may be that you dislike something that is good for you; and it may be that you love something that is bad for you. Allāh knows and you do not know." — **Sūrah Al-Baqarah (2): 216**

Chapter: The First Of The Military Expeditions And The Raiding Parties

102 So the first military expedition which Allāh's Messenger (صَلَّى ٱللَّهُ عَلَيْهِ وَسَلَّمَ) took part in was:

The Military Expedition (Ghazwah) Of Al-Abwā'[1]

And it occurred in (the month of) Safar in the second year of the Hijrah (Migration). He himself went out,[2] and when he reached Waddān he made a peace agreement with Banū Damrah ibn 'Abd Manāt ibn Kinānah, with their chief Makhshiyy[3] ibn 'Amr. Then he returned to Al-Madīnah, having not encountered any fighting. He had left in charge of it Sa'd ibn 'Ubādah (رَضِيَ ٱللَّهُ عَنْهُ).

The Raiding Party Of Hamzah (رَضِيَ ٱللَّهُ عَنْهُ)

Then he sent his paternal uncle Hamzah (رَضِيَ ٱللَّهُ عَنْهُ) with a raiding party of thirty riders from the Muhājirīn, there being no Ansārī amongst them, towards the seashore, and he encountered Abū Jahl ibn Hishām — who had with him over three hundred riders.

So Makhshiyy ibn 'Amr Al-Juhanī[4] intervened between them, since he had a peace treaty with both groups.

---

1 — It is also called *'The Expedition of Waddān'*. See more in **Endnote 19 on page 448**.

2 — [DB] Imām Ibnul-Qayyim said in *Zādul-Ma'ād* ((3/164): "His banner was carried by Hamzah ibn 'Abdil-Muttalib and it was white. He left Sa'd ibn 'Ubādah in charge of Al-Madīnah, and he went out with the Muhājirūn exclusively, in order to attack a caravan of the Quraysh, but he did not encounter any fighting."

3 — [MK][MM] The three manuscripts have *'Majdī ibn 'Umar'*, so the correction is from *As-Sīratun-Nabawiyyah* of Ibn Hishām (2/241) and *As-Sīratun-Nabawwiyyah* of Ibn Kathīr (2/356).

4 — [MK][MM] The three manuscripts have 'Majdī ibn 'Amr', as has preceded, and the correction is from *As-Sīratun-Nabawiyyah* of Ibn Hishām (2/245) and *As-Sīratun-Nabawiyyah* of Ibn Kathīr (2/359).

The Raiding Party Of ʿUbaydah Ibn Al-Hārith (رَضِيَ ٱللَّهُ عَنْهُ)

And he sent ʿUbaydah ibn Al-Hārith ibn Al-Muttalib, in Rabīʿul-Ākhir, with sixty or eighty riders, who were also from the Muhājirīn, towards some water in the Hijāz below Thaniyyatul-Marah. So they encountered a very large body of the Quraysh headed by ʿIkrimah ibn Abī Jahl, or it is said: rather by Mikraz ibn Hafs. However no fighting occurred between them, except that Saʿd ibn Abī Waqqās shot an arrow at the Mushrikīn that day, so it was the first arrow to be fired in Allāh's cause.[1]

Furthermore, on that day, Al-Miqdād ibn ʿAmr Al-Kindī and ʿUtbah ibn Ghazwān (رَضِيَ ٱللَّهُ عَنْهُمَا) escaped from the Disbelievers and joined the Muslims.

So these two raids were the first time a flag was tied by Allāh's Messenger (صَلَّى ٱللَّهُ عَلَيْهِ وَسَلَّمَ), however there is disagreement about which of them came first.[2]

It is otherwise stated that these two occurred in the first year of the Hijrah, and that is the saying of Ibn Jarīr At-Tabarī, and Allāh — the Most High — knows best.

Chapter: The Military Expedition Of Buwāt

Then Allāh's Messenger (صَلَّى ٱللَّهُ عَلَيْهِ وَسَلَّمَ) went out on the military expedition of Buwāt.[3] So he went out himself and left in charge of Al-Madīnah As-Sāʾib ibn ʿUthmān ibn Mazʿūn. So he proceeded until he came to Buwāt, in the direction of Radwā, then he returned and had not encountered any fighting.

---

1 — [BJ][SZ] See *Sahīhul-Bukhārī* (nos. 4326 and 4327).

2 — [BJ][SZ] Amongst those who stated that the raid of Hamzah (رَضِيَ ٱللَّهُ عَنْهُ) came first are: Mūsā ibn ʿUqbah, Abū Maʿshar and Al-Wāqidī; whereas Ibn Is-hāq, At-Tabarī, and Ibn Hibbān placed the raiding party of ʿUbaydah before the raid of Hamzah.

3 — [BJ][SZ] It is a mountain from the mountains of (the tribe of) Juhaynah, towards the mountain of Radwā, which is a huge mountain at Yanbuʿ.

[DB] He (صَلَّى ٱللَّهُ عَلَيْهِ وَسَلَّمَ) went out on this expedition to attack a caravan of the Quraysh. [*Zādul-Maʿād*: (3/165)]

The Military Expedition Of Al-ʿUshayrah

104 Then after it came the military expedition of Al-ʿUshayrah (العشيرة) or it is said that it is with a *ʻsīnʼ* without dots [i.e. ʿUsayrah (عسيرة)], or it is said: Al-ʿUshayrāʾ (العشيراء).

He (صَلَّى اللَّهُ عَلَيْهِ وَسَلَّمَ) went out himself during Jumādal-Ūlā until he reached it, and it is a place in the valley of Yanbuʿ. So he remained there for the rest of the month and for some nights from Jumādal-Ākhirah; and he made a treaty with Banū Mudlaj, then he returned and did not encounter any fighting. He had left in charge of Al-Madīnah Abū Salamah ibn ʿAbdil-Asad. And there occurs in *Sahīh Muslim* as a hadīth of Abū Is-hāq As-Sabīʿī who said:

> "I said to Zayd ibn Arqam: *'How many military expeditions did Allāh's Messenger (صَلَّى اللَّهُ عَلَيْهِ وَسَلَّمَ) go on?'* So he said: *'Nineteen military expeditions, the first of them being Al-Usayr or Al-ʿUshayr.'*"

The Military Expedition Of The First Badr

Then about ten days afterwards, he went out to the first Badr, and that was because Kurz ibn Jābir Al-Fihrī made a raid upon the pasturing animals of Al-Madīnah. So he went out in search of him and reached a valley called Safawān in the direction of Badr. However, Kurz evaded him so he returned, and he had left in charge of Al-Madīnah Zayd ibn Hārithah (رَضِيَ اللَّهُ عَنْهُ).

The Raiding Party Of Saʿd Ibn Abī Waqqās

And he sent out Saʿd ibn Abī Waqqās (رَضِيَ اللَّهُ عَنْهُ) in pursuit of Kurz ibn Jābir, as it is said, and Allāh knows best; or it is otherwise said: Rather, he sent him out for a different purpose.[1]

---

1 — [BJ][SZ] Ibn Is-hāq said: "He sent him in a group of eight men of the Muhājirīn. So he proceeded until he reached Al-Kharrār in the land of the Hijāz." See *Sīrah Ibn Hishām* (2/212).

Chapter: The Raiding Party Of ʿAbdullāh Ibn Jah-sh (رَضِيَٱللَّهُعَنْهُ)[1]

Then Allāh's Messenger (صَلَّىٱللَّهُعَلَيْهِوَسَلَّمَ) sent ʿAbdullāh ibn Jah-sh ibn Riʾāb Al-Asadī and eight of the Muhājirīn, and he wrote a letter for him and commanded him not to read it until he had travelled for two days; then he was to read it and not compel any of his companions. So he did that, and when he opened the letter he found in it:

> When you look at this letter of mine then proceed until you reach Nakhlah — between Makkah and At-Tāʾif, and lie in wait there for the Quraysh, and find out their news for us.

So he said: *"Hearing and obeying"*, and he informed his companions of that, and told them that he was not going to compel them, (and said):

> "Whoever wishes for martyrdom then let him continue, and whoever dislikes death then let him go back; and as for myself then I am going to go forward."

So they all proceeded.

Then on the way Saʿd ibn Abī Waqqās and ʿUtbah ibn Ghazwān lost a camel of theirs which they were riding by turns, so they stayed behind looking for it. ʿAbdullāh ibn Jah-sh, though, continued until he reached Nakhlah. So a caravan of Quraysh which carried raisins, leather, and merchandise passed by, and in it were ʿAmr ibn Al-Hadramī, and ʿUthmān and Nawfal — the two sons of ʿAbdullāh ibn Al-Mughīrah, and Al-Hakam ibn Kaysān — the slave belonging to Banul-Mughīrah. So the Muslims held consultations and said: "We are in the last day of Rajab, the sacred month, so if we fight them then we will have violated the sacred month; but if we leave them tonight, then they will enter the Sacred Precincts (Al-Haram)."

So they agreed that they should attack them, so one of them fired an arrow at ʿAmr Al-Hadramī and killed him; and they took ʿUthmān and Al-Hakam as prisoners, but Nawfal escaped.

---

1 — (SH) In the Sulaymāniyyah Library manuscript (no. 3339), the chapter on the change of the Qiblah is placed before this chapter.

Then they returned with the caravan and the two captives, and they had separated the *'khumus'* [the share of one fifth to be handed over to the Messenger (صَلَّى ٱللَّهُ عَلَيْهِ وَسَلَّمَ)]. So this was the first war-booty taken in Islām, and the first *'khumus'* in Islām, and the first enemy killed in Islām, and the first captives to be taken in Islām. However, the Messenger of Allāh (صَلَّى ٱللَّهُ عَلَيْهِ وَسَلَّمَ) criticised them for what they had done; but they (رَضِيَ ٱللَّهُ عَنْهُمْ) had been acting upon the basis of personal deduction (*ijtihād*) in what they did.

The Quraysh severely blamed and criticised that action, and said: *'Muhammad has violated the sacred month'*. So Allāh (the Mighty and Majestic) sent down concerning that:

> يَسْـَٔلُونَكَ عَنِ ٱلشَّهْرِ ٱلْحَرَامِ قِتَالٍ فِيهِ ۖ قُلْ قِتَالٌ فِيهِ كَبِيرٌ ۖ وَصَدٌّ عَن سَبِيلِ ٱللَّهِ
> وَكُفْرٌۢ بِهِۦ وَٱلْمَسْجِدِ ٱلْحَرَامِ وَإِخْرَاجُ أَهْلِهِۦ مِنْهُ أَكْبَرُ عِندَ ٱللَّهِ
>
> MEANING: "They ask you about fighting in the sacred month. Say: Fighting in it is something serious. However, preventing people from Allāh's path, and disbelieving in Him, and preventing access to the Sacred Mosque, and expelling its people, are all worse with Allāh than fighting in the sacred month." — **Sūrah Al-Baqarah (2): 217**

He (the One free of all imperfections) says: even though what occurred was something wrong, since fighting in the sacred month is a grave matter with Allāh, then what you are doing, O people of Shirk: preventing people from Allāh's path, and disbelieving in Him, and preventing access to the Sacred Mosque, and expelling Muhammad and his companions — who are the true people of the Sacred Mosque — is worse with Allāh than fighting in the sacred month.

Then Allāh's Messenger (صَلَّى ٱللَّهُ عَلَيْهِ وَسَلَّمَ) accepted the share of the fifth from the booty, and he accepted payment of ransom for those two captives.[1]

---

1 — For a discussion on the authenticity of this, see **Endnote 20 on page 449**.

Chapter: The Changing Of The Qiblah (Direction Of Prayer), And The Obligation Of Fasting

In Shaʿbān of this year the Qiblah was changed from Jerusalem to the Kaʿbah, and that was sixteen, or it is said seventeen months after his arrival in Al-Madīnah; these two (sayings) occur in the two *'Sahīhs'*.[1]

So the first person who prayed towards it was Abū Saʿīd ibn Al-Muʿallā and a companion of his, as reported by An-Nasāʾī. That was because they had heard Allāh's Messenger (صَلَّى ٱللَّهُ عَلَيْهِ وَسَلَّمَ) addressing the people and reciting to them that the Qiblah had been changed. (He said:)

> "So I said to my companions: *'Come let us pray two rakʿahs and be the first ones to pray towards it.'*"

So we moved out of sight and prayed towards it. Then Allāh's Messenger (صَلَّى ٱللَّهُ عَلَيْهِ وَسَلَّمَ) descended and led the people in the Dhuhr Prayer that day.[2] And the fast of Ramadān was made obligatory, and the Zakātul-Fitr was made obligatory, to be given a day before it.[3]

---

1 — [BJ][SZ] Al-Bukhārī (no.4492), Muslim — and the context in his (no.525) — reported from Al-Barāʾ ibn ʿĀzib (رَضِيَ ٱللَّهُ عَنْهُ) that he said: "We prayed along with Allāh's Messenger (صَلَّى ٱللَّهُ عَلَيْهِ وَسَلَّمَ) towards Jerusalem for sixteen or seventeen months. Then we were directed to turn towards the Kaʿbah."

2 — [BJ][SZ] *'Daʿīf'* (unauthentic). It is reported by An-Nasāʾī in *At-Tafsīr* (no.24), At-Tabarānī in *Al-Kabīr* (22/770), and Al-Bazzār (no. 419 — *Al-Kashf*) by way of Marwān ibn ʿUthmān — who was weak: that ʿUbayd ibn Hunayn informed him: from Abū Saʿīd ibn Al-Muʿallā, with it.

3 — [DB] i.e. before ʿEidul-Fitr.

[SH] The author (رَحِمَهُ ٱللَّهُ) is indicating the hadīth of Ibn ʿUmar (رَضِيَ ٱللَّهُ عَنْهُ) occurring in *Sahīhul-Bukhārī* (3/375/1511) and *Sahīh Muslim* (2/677/984) with the wording: *"The Prophet (صَلَّى ٱللَّهُ عَلَيْهِ وَسَلَّمَ) obligated the charity of Al-Fitr..."*, and there occurs at its end: *"...and they used to give it before the (day of) Fitr by a day or two days"*, and this is the wording of Al-Bukhārī.

CHAPTER:

The Major Battle of Badr

Wherein we will mention a summary of the second battle of Badr, and it is the great battle, through which Allāh separated between the truth and falsehood, and gave strength to Islām, and repelled Disbelief and its people.

So it occurred when it reached Allāh's Messenger (صَلَّى ٱللَّهُ عَلَيْهِ وَسَلَّمَ), in Ramadān of this second year, that a caravan of Quraysh was returning from Shām accompanied by Abū Sufyān Sakhr ibn Harb, with thirty or forty men of Quraysh. So it was a tremendous caravan carrying a large amount of wealth belonging to Quraysh. So he (صَلَّى ٱللَّهُ عَلَيْهِ وَسَلَّمَ) encouraged the people to go out to it, and he commanded that whoever had a riding beast ready should go out. However he did not make a great deal of preparation for it: he went out with only three hundred and ten and odd men, on the eighth of Ramadān. He left in charge of Al-Madīnah and the prayer Ibn Umm Maktūm. Then when he reached Ar-Rawhā' he sent Abū Lubābah ibn 'Abdil-Mundhir back and appointed him to take charge of Al-Madīnah.[1]

He did not have any horses with him besides the horse of Az-Zubayr and the horse of Al-Miqdād ibn Al-Aswad Al-Kindī, and he had seventy camels. Two or three men or more would take turns to ride a single camel. So Allāh's Messenger (صَلَّى ٱللَّهُ عَلَيْهِ وَسَلَّمَ), 'Alī, and Marthad ibn Abī

---

1 — [BJ][SZ] Ar-Rawhā' is thirty-six miles from Al-Madīnah, as occurs in a hadīth reported by Muslim (no.388); and Abū Lubābah [Rifā'ah] ibn 'Abdil-Mundhir was a famous companion, and was one of the chiefs (at the pledge of 'Aqabah). He lived until the Khilāfah of 'Alī (رَضِيَٱللَّهُعَنْهُ).

Marthad Al-Ghanawī took turns to ride upon a single camel;[1] and Zayd ibn Hārithah, Anasah,[2] and Abū Kabshah — the freed slaves of Allāh's Messenger (صَلَّى ٱللَّهُ عَلَيْهِ وَسَلَّمَ) — took turns to ride a male camel; and Abū Bakr, 'Umar, and 'Abdur-Rahmān ibn 'Awf were upon another camel (and so on).

He (صَلَّى ٱللَّهُ عَلَيْهِ وَسَلَّمَ) gave the battle-flag to Mus'ab ibn 'Umayr, and one banner to 'Alī ibn Abī Tālib, and the other banner to a man from the Ansār; whereas the banner of the Ansār that day was in the hand of Sa'd ibn Mu'ādh; and he placed Qays ibn Abī Sa'sa'ah in charge of the infantry.

So he (صَلَّى ٱللَّهُ عَلَيْهِ وَسَلَّمَ) proceeded, until when he approached As-Safrā'[3] he sent Basbas[4] ibn 'Amr Al-Juhanī, who was a confederate of Banū Sā'idah, and 'Adiyy ibn Abiz-Zaghbā' Al-Juhanī, who was a confederate of Banun-Najjār, to Badr to seek out any information about the caravan.

As for Abū Sufyān, then the news that Allāh's Messenger (صَلَّى ٱللَّهُ عَلَيْهِ وَسَلَّمَ) had come out and was heading towards him had reached him. So he hired Damdam ibn 'Amr Al-Ghifārī to go to Makkah to call Quraysh to come and defend the caravan from Muhammad and his companions. So the call for help reached the people of Makkah and they came out quickly. So all of them came out; from their notable people no one remained behind except Abū Lahab, who sent a man who was indebted to him in his place. They also gathered others from the tribes of the Arabs around

---

1 — [BJ][SZ] This is what Ibn Is-hāq said, as occurs in *As-Sīrah* (2/225); whereas there occurs in *As-Sunanul-Kubrā* of An-Nasā'ī (no. 8807), *Musnad Ahmad* (1/411), and *Musnad Abī Ya'lā* (no. 5359), and others with a *'hasan'* chain of narration: "Abū Lubābah" instead of "Marthad ibn Abī Marthad".

2 — [BJ][SZ] In some books, such as *Zādul-Ma'ād* it is miswritten as *'and his son';* and he is Anasah, the freed slave (*mawlā*) of the Prophet (صَلَّى ٱللَّهُ عَلَيْهِ وَسَلَّمَ). He used to request permission for those wishing to enter. They are agreed that he was present at Badr, and they disagree about when he died.

3 — [BJ][SZ] It is a valley, or a village, which has many date palms, crops, and abundant good, and there are springs there. It is above Yanbu', in the direction of Al-Madīnah, and it is a place of the tribe of Juhaynah.

4 — There is disagreement regarding his name; see ENDNOTE 21 ON PAGE 449.

them, and no clan of the tribe of Quraysh remained behind except for Banū ʿAdiyy, from which not a single person went out along with them.

So they departed from their homes just as Allāh (the Mighty and Majestic) said:

> رِئَاءَ النَّاسِ وَيَصُدُّونَ عَن سَبِيلِ اللَّهِ
>
> MEANING: "Boastfully, to be seen by the people, and to hinder people from Allāh's path." — **Sūrah Al-Anfāl (8):47**

So they came out in a state of adornment and great rage and proceeded towards Allāh's Messenger (صَلَّى ٱللَّهُ عَلَيْهِ وَسَلَّمَ) and his companions who wished to seize their caravan, and had just a short while ago seized ʿAmr ibn Al-Hadramī and the caravan that was with him. So Allāh brought them together (in battle), even though they did not go out with that in mind, for the wise purpose He desired, just as He (the Most High) said:

> وَلَوْ تَوَاعَدتُّمْ لَاخْتَلَفْتُمْ فِي الْمِيعَادِ ۙ وَلَٰكِن لِّيَقْضِيَ اللَّهُ أَمْرًا كَانَ مَفْعُولًا
>
> MEANING: "Even if you had made a mutual appointment to meet you would have failed to meet, but you met so that Allāh should accomplish a matter already ordained." — **Sūrah Al-Anfāl (8):42**

Then when news of the coming out of the Quraysh reached Allāh's Messenger (صَلَّى ٱللَّهُ عَلَيْهِ وَسَلَّمَ) he consulted his Companions. So many of the Muhājirīn spoke, and they spoke well. Then he consulted them (again), and he wished to see what the Ansār would say. So Saʿd ibn Muʿādh (رَضِيَ ٱللَّهُ عَنْهُ) quickly spoke up and said:

> "O Messenger of Allāh! It is as if you are intending us. Then, by Allāh, O Messenger of Allāh, if you sought that we should cross this ocean then we would plunge into it along with you. So proceed forward with us, O Messenger of Allāh, upon Allāh's blessing."

So he (صَلَّى ٱللَّهُ عَلَيْهِ وَسَلَّمَ) was pleased at that and said:

> "Proceed and receive glad tidings, since Allāh has promised me one of the two groups."[1]

Then Allāh's Messenger (صَلَّى ٱللَّهُ عَلَيْهِ وَسَلَّمَ) rode until he camped close to Badr, and he (صَلَّى ٱللَّهُ عَلَيْهِ وَسَلَّمَ) rode out along with a man of his Companions seeking news, then he turned back. In the evening he sent ʿAlī, Saʿd, and Az-Zubayr to the well of Badr to seek news, and they returned with two slaves belonging to Quraysh, returning whilst Allāh's Messenger (صَلَّى ٱللَّهُ عَلَيْهِ وَسَلَّمَ) was standing in prayer. So his Companions asked the two of them: "To whom do you belong?"

So they replied: "We are water-carriers of Quraysh."

So the Companions of Allāh's Messenger (صَلَّى ٱللَّهُ عَلَيْهِ وَسَلَّمَ) disliked that, and wanted them to belong to the caravan of Abū Sufyān so that it would be near to them and they could capture it, since this would be less trouble than having to fight against the re-enforcements. So they began beating the two of them, and when they had been soundly beaten, they both said: "We belong to Abū Sufyān."

So then, they left them alone and then asked them again, so they replied: "*We belong to Quraysh.*" When Allāh's Messenger (صَلَّى ٱللَّهُ عَلَيْهِ وَسَلَّمَ) finished his Prayer, he said: "By the One in Whose Hand is my soul! You beat them when they were telling the truth, and you left them when they lied!"

Then he said to the two of them: "Inform me where Quraysh are."

So they said: "Behind this sand-hill." He said; "How many are the people?"

They replied: "We do not know that." He said: "How many (camels) do they slaughter each day?"

They said *"One day it was ten, and the next [day it was] nine."* So he (صَلَّى ٱللَّهُ عَلَيْهِ وَسَلَّمَ) said: "The people are between nine hundred and a thousand."[2]

---

1 — For details regarding the authenticity of this narration and other details, see **Endnote 22 on page 450**.

2 — See **Endnote 23 on page 451** for an in-depth look at the authenticity of this narration.

As for Basbas ibn ʿAmr and ʿAdiyy ibn Abiz-Zaghbāʾ, then they came to the well of Badr and they heard a girl say to her companion: "Will you not pay me what you owe me?"

So the other girl said: *"The caravan will arrive tomorrow or the day after tomorrow, and then I will pay you back,"* and Majdī ibn ʿAmr attested to her speaking the truth.

So the two of them returned with what they had heard, and they were followed by Abū Sufyān who said to Majdī ibn ʿAmr: *"Have you perceived anyone from the Companions of Muhammad?"* He said: "No, except that two riders halted by that hill."

So Abū Sufyān went off to where they had been and picked up a piece of the dung left by their camels and crumbled it between his fingers. So he found date-stones in it and said: "This, by Allāh, is the camel fodder of Yathrib."[1]

So he changed the direction of the caravan towards the coast and escaped, and he sent a message to Quraysh that he and the caravan were safe, and commanded them to go back.

So that reached the Quraysh, but Abū Jahl refused that and said: "By Allāh, we shall not return until we have arrived at the well of Badr and have remained there for three days; and until we have drank wine and had singing girls play for us, so that the Arabs will always have awe of us."

However, Al-Akhnas ibn Sharīq went back along with all of his people, Banū Zuhrah, and said: "You only came out to defend your caravan, and it has escaped."

So no one from the clan of Zuhrah was present at Badr except for the two paternal uncles of Muslim ibn Shihāb ibn ʿAbdillāh — the father of Az-Zuhrī[2] for they were present that day and were killed as Disbelievers.

---

1 — (DB) i.e. Al-Madīnah.

2 — Az-Zuhrī being Muhammad ibn Muslim ibn ʿUbaydillāh ibn ʿAbdillāh ibn Shihāb, Al-Qurashī, Az-Zuhrī. The famous scholar and memoriser of hadīth from the Tābiʿīn, who passed away in 124H.

So he (صَلَّى ٱللَّٰهُ عَلَيْهِ وَسَلَّمَ) beat the Quraysh to the well of Badr, and he stopped at the closest well. So Al-Hubāb ibn ʿAmr said: "O Messenger of Allāh! This stopping place where you have halted, did Allāh command you with it or is it just a stopping place which you have taken as a stratagem of war and as a plan?"

So he (صَلَّى ٱللَّٰهُ عَلَيْهِ وَسَلَّمَ) said: "Rather, a stopping place that I have taken as a stratagem of war and as a plan."

So he said: "This is not the place to stop, so proceed forward with us until we come to the well closest to the enemy and let us camp by it; and let us block up and bury the wells behind us. Then let us build a reservoir around this one and let it fill with water so that we can drink and they will not be able to drink." So Allāh's Messenger approved of that idea of his.[1]

Then Allāh prevented the Quraysh from reaching the water by sending a great downpour of rain. So it came as a punishment upon the Disbelievers and a blessing upon the Muslims, since it caused the earth to become firm and compacted for them.[2]

A shelter was built for Allāh's Messenger (صَلَّى ٱللَّٰهُ عَلَيْهِ وَسَلَّمَ) to occupy, and he (صَلَّى ٱللَّٰهُ عَلَيْهِ وَسَلَّمَ) walked around the battlefield and showed them the places where the chiefs of the enemy were going to fall, one by one, saying: "This is the place where so and so will be killed tomorrow — if Allāh wills, and this is the place where so and so will be killed, and this is where so and so will be killed."[3]

ʿAbdullāh ibn Masʿūd said: "So by the One who sent him with the truth, not a single one of them missed the place which Allāh's Messenger (صَلَّى ٱللَّٰهُ عَلَيْهِ وَسَلَّمَ) had indicated for him."

---

1 — This was declared as weak by Imām Al-Albānī, and you can see more detail in Endnote 24 on page 453.

2 — See the commentary of Al-Hāfidh Ibn Kathīr regarding this event: Endnote 25 on page 453.

3 — [BJ][SZ] Muslim reported its like (no.1778), as a hadīth of Anas ibn Mālik (رَضِيَ ٱللَّٰهُ عَنْهُ) and (no. 2873), as a hadīth of ʿUmar ibn Al-Khattāb (رَضِيَ ٱللَّٰهُ عَنْهُ).

Allāh's Messenger (صَلَّى ٱللَّهُ عَلَيْهِ وَسَلَّمَ) spent that night praying towards the trunk of a tree there, and it was the night prior to Friday the seventeenth of Ramadān. Then when he entered the morning and Quraysh came with their forces he (صَلَّى ٱللَّهُ عَلَيْهِ وَسَلَّمَ) said: "O Allāh! This is Quraysh: they have come forward in their pride and arrogance showing open hostility to You and showing open hostility to your Messenger."[1]

It was the desire of Hakīm ibn Hizām[2] and 'Utbah ibn Rabī'ah that Quraysh should return without there being any fighting. However, Abū Jahl refused that, and he and 'Utbah spoke ill of each other in that regard.

Also, Abū Jahl ordered the brother of 'Amr ibn Al-Hadramī to seek vengeance for the blood of his brother 'Amr, so he uncovered his backside and screamed out: ***"Alas for 'Amr! Alas for 'Amr!"*** Thus, he provoked the fury of the people and war became unavoidable.

So Allāh's Messenger (صَلَّى ٱللَّهُ عَلَيْهِ وَسَلَّمَ) straightened the rows and then returned to the shelter with Abū Bakr alone. Sa'd ibn Mu'ādh and some of the Ansār stood at the door of the shelter to defend Allāh's Messenger (صَلَّى ٱللَّهُ عَلَيْهِ وَسَلَّمَ).

'Utbah and Shaybah — the two sons of Rabī'ah — and Al-Walīd came out, all three of them seeking single handed combat. So three of the Muslims from the Ansār went forth to them, and they were 'Awf and Mu'awwidh — the two sons of 'Afrā', and 'Abdullāh ibn Rawāhah. So they said to them: "Who are you?"

So they said: "From the Ansār."

So they replied: "Noble opponents, however we desire sons of our uncle."

So 'Alī, 'Ubaydah ibn Al-Hārith and Hamzah went forth to fight them. So 'Alī killed Al-Walīd, and Hamzah killed 'Utbah or it is said: Shaybah;

---

1 — [BJ][SZ] Ibn Is-hāq brings it without a chain *As-Sīrah* (2/233) and Adh-Dhahabī indicated its weakness in *Al-Maghāzī* by saying: *'as they claim.'*

2 — [SH] He was the son of the brother of Khadījah bint Khuwaylid — the Mother of the Believers (رَضِيَ ٱللَّهُ عَنْهَا) — and he was a close friend of Allāh's Messenger (صَلَّى ٱللَّهُ عَلَيْهِ وَسَلَّمَ) before he became a Prophet and afterwards. He accepted Islām (رَضِيَ ٱللَّهُ عَنْهُ) on the Day of the Conquest (of Makkah) and he passed away in Al-Madīnah in the year 54H.

whereas ʿUbaydah and his adversary traded two blows, and each of them wounded the other. So Hamzah and ʿAlī turned upon him and finished him off, and they carried ʿUbaydah away. His leg had been severed, and his wound bled until he died at As-Safrā' — (رَحِمَهُ ٱللَّهُ *wa* رَضِيَ ٱللَّهُ عَنْهُ).[1—2]

There occurs in the *Sahīh* that ʿAlī (رَضِيَ ٱللَّهُ عَنْهُ) used to interpret His saying (He the Most High):

> هَٰذَانِ خَصْمَانِ ٱخْتَصَمُوا فِي رَبِّهِمْ
>
> MEANING: "These two adversaries disputed regarding their Lord." — **SŪRAH AL-HAJJ (22):19**

— to mean their single-handed combat on the day of Badr.[3]

So there is no doubt that this Āyah occurs in Sūratul-Hajj, which was sent down in Makkah, and Badr occurred after that. However, their single-handed combat is something that is one of the first and foremost affairs entering within the meaning of the Āyah.

Then the flames of war were fanned and the fighting became severe, and aid descended. Allāh's Messenger (صَلَّى ٱللَّهُ عَلَيْهِ وَسَلَّمَ) exerted in making supplication, and he earnestly beseeched to the extent that his *ridā'* (shoulder-wrapper) was falling from his shoulders. So Abū Bakr put it back, saying: *"O Messenger of Allāh! Your entreaties to your Lord are sufficient, for He will certainly fulfil His promise to you,"* and Allāh's Messenger (صَلَّى ٱللَّهُ عَلَيْهِ وَسَلَّمَ) was saying:

---

1 — SH A valley towards Al-Madīnah. It contains many date palms and crops, and lies on the route of the pilgrims. It is one riding stage from Badr. (*Muʿjamul-Buldān*: 3/412)

2 — There is a difference of opinion regarding the authenticity of this event; see **ENDNOTE 26 ON PAGE 454**.

3 — SH Reported by Al-Bukhārī in his *Sahīh* (no.3965) as a hadīth of ʿAlī (رَضِيَ ٱللَّهُ عَنْهُ); and also by Al-Bukhārī (no. 3966) and Muslim (no.3033) as a hadīth of Abū Dharr (رَضِيَ ٱللَّهُ عَنْهُ).

> "O Allāh if this group are destroyed, You will not be worshipped upon the earth."[1]

So that is His saying — He the Most High:

> إِذْ تَسْتَغِيثُونَ رَبَّكُمْ فَاسْتَجَابَ لَكُمْ أَنِّي مُمِدُّكُم بِأَلْفٍ مِّنَ الْمَلَائِكَةِ مُرْدِفِينَ
>
> MEANING: "Remember when you beseeched your Lord for aid, and He answered you saying: *'I will reinforce you with a thousand angels following each other in succession.'*" — **Sūrah Al-Anfāl (8):9**

Then Allāh's Messenger (ﷺ) was seized by slumber briefly, then he raised his head saying: "Receive glad tiding O Abū Bakr! This is Jibrīl (coming) with dust upon his front teeth."[2]

Also Satan appeared to the Quraysh in the guise of Surāqah ibn Mālik ibn Juʿshum — the chief of Mudlij (tribe). So he promised them protection and enticed them to continue upon their way.

This was because they feared that Banū Mudlij would attack their families and property from behind them. So this is His Saying — He the Most High:

> وَإِذْ زَيَّنَ لَهُمُ الشَّيْطَانُ أَعْمَالَهُمْ وَقَالَ لَا غَالِبَ لَكُمُ الْيَوْمَ مِنَ النَّاسِ وَإِنِّي جَارٌ لَّكُمْ فَلَمَّا تَرَاءَتِ الْفِئَتَانِ نَكَصَ عَلَىٰ عَقِبَيْهِ وَقَالَ إِنِّي بَرِيءٌ مِّنكُمْ إِنِّي أَرَىٰ مَا لَا تَرَوْنَ
>
> MEANING: "And remember when Satan made their deeds seem fair to them and said: *'No one from the people can overcome you today, and I am a protector for you.'* However, when the two armies came in sight of each other he turned on his heels and fled, and said: *'I have nothing*

---

1 — BJ SZ Reported by Muslim (no. 1763) as a hadīth of ʿUmar ibn Al-Khattāb (رَضِيَ اللَّهُ عَنْهُ) and its like is reported by Al-Bukhārī (no. 2915) as a hadīth of Ibn ʿAbbās (رَضِيَ اللَّهُ عَنْهُ).

2 — BJ SZ Reported by Al-Amawī in *Al-Maghāzī* with a *'hasan'* chain of narration, as Shaikh Al-Albānī mentioned in his notes upon *Fiqhus-Sīrah* (p.243).

> *to do with you. I see that which you do not see.'"* — **Sūrah Al-Anfāl (8):48**

That was because he saw the Angels when they descended to fight, and he saw that which he was incapable of countering, so he fled.[1] So the Angels fought as Allāh had commanded them to, so men from the Muslims would be pursuing an enemy fighter when he would suddenly fall dead in front of them. So Allāh gifted the Muslims with the shoulder blades of the Mushrikīn, and the first of them to flee was Khālid ibn Al-A'lam who was caught and taken prisoner. So the Muslims pursued them, killing and taking captives, and they killed seventy of them and took seventy captives, and they captured their booty.

So from those who were killed from the Mushrikīn, from those whom Allāh's Messenger (صَلَّى ٱللَّٰهُ عَلَيْهِ وَسَلَّمَ) had pointed out where they would fall [the previous day] were: Abū Jahl, who was Abul-Hakam 'Amr ibn Hishām — may Allāh's curse be upon him; he was killed by Mu'ādh ibn 'Amr ibn Al-Jamūh and Mu'awwidh ibn 'Afrā'; and Abdullāh ibn Mas'ūd finished him off, and decapitated him and brought his head to Allāh's Messenger (صَلَّى ٱللَّٰهُ عَلَيْهِ وَسَلَّمَ), and that pleased him;[2] and 'Utbah and Shaybah the two sons of Rabī'ah, and Al-Walīd ibn 'Utbah, and Umayyah ibn Khalaf, so Allāh's Messenger (صَلَّى ٱللَّٰهُ عَلَيْهِ وَسَلَّمَ) ordered that they be dragged and thrown into the ditch. Then he stood over them at night, and he reproached them, and rebuked them and said:

> "What an evil kinsfolk you were towards your Prophet: you called me a liar whereas the people believed me; you deserted me whereas the

---

1 — [SH] Reported by Ibn Abī Hātim in his *Tafsīr* (51715/9157), At-Tabarī in *Jāmi'ul-Bayān* (9/14), and Al-Bayhaqī in *Dalā'ilun-Nubuwwah* (3/78-79) with chains of narration from 'Abdullāh ibn Sālih who said: Mu'āwiyah ibn Sālih narrated to us: from 'Alī ibn Abī Talhah: from Ibn 'Abbās, with it.

I say: This is a *'hasan'* chain of narration because of the slight speech concerning Mu'āwiyah ibn Sālih and 'Alī ibn Abī Talhah and it has been declared to have a weakness which does not actually harm it.

2 — Refer to *Sahīhul-Bukhārī* (nos. 3141 and 3963) and *Sahīh Muslim* (no.1752 and 1800).

> people aided me; and you expelled me from my home whereas the people gave me shelter."[1]

Then Allāh's Messenger (صَلَّىٱللَّهُعَلَيْهِوَسَلَّمَ) camped on the battlefield for three days.[2]

Then he departed with the booty and the captives, having placed in charge of that ʿAbdullāh ibn Kaʿb ibn ʿAmr An-Najjārī; and concerning the battle of Badr, Allāh sent down Sūratul-Anfāl. Then when Allāh's Messenger (صَلَّىٱللَّهُعَلَيْهِوَسَلَّمَ) reached As-Safrāʾ he shared out the booty, as he was commanded to by Allāh — the Most High. He also commanded that An-Nadr ibn Al-Hārith should be beheaded whilst captive, because of the great corruption he was guilty of and the harm that he had caused to Allāh's Messenger (صَلَّىٱللَّهُعَلَيْهِوَسَلَّمَ). So his sister (or it is said his daughter) Qutaylah lamented him in a famous poem mentioned by Ibn Hishām. So they claim that when it reached Allāh's Messenger (صَلَّىٱللَّهُعَلَيْهِوَسَلَّمَ) he said: "If I had heard it before I would not have killed him."[3]

Then he halted at ʿIrquz-Zubyah,[4] he commanded that ʿUqbah ibn Abī Muʿayt should also be beheaded whilst captive.[5]

Then Allāh's Messenger (صَلَّىٱللَّهُعَلَيْهِوَسَلَّمَ) consulted his Companions regarding the captives: what should he do with them?

So ʿUmar ibn Al-Khattāb (رَضِيَٱللَّهُعَنْهُ) advised that they should be killed, whereas Abū Bakr As-Siddīq (رَضِيَٱللَّهُعَنْهُ) advised that ransom money

---

1 — For more detail regarding the authenticity of this narration, see **Endnote 27 on page 454**.

2 — Reported by Al-Bukhārī (no.3976) and Muslim (no. 2875).

3 — [BJ][SZ] The hadīth is not authentic since it was quoted by Ibn Hishām without a chain of narration.

4 — [SH] A place close to Ar-Rawhāʾ, three miles away from it, in the direction of Al-Madīnah.

5 — [BJ][SZ] Concerning An-Nadr and ʿUqbah, Ibn Kathīr said in *Al-Bidāyah* (3/306): "These two men were from the worst of Allāh's servants; and from those most severe in Disbelief, obstinate rejection, transgression, envy, and mockery of Islām and its people — may Allāh's curse be upon them."

should be accepted for them. So Allāh's Messenger (ﷺ) inclined towards what Abū Bakr said, and Allāh permitted that for them.

Allāh (the Perfect) rebuked that mildly however, in His Saying:

> مَا كَانَ لِنَبِيٍّ أَن يَكُونَ لَهُ أَسْرَىٰ حَتَّىٰ يُثْخِنَ فِي الْأَرْضِ ۚ تُرِيدُونَ عَرَضَ الدُّنْيَا وَاللَّهُ يُرِيدُ الْآخِرَةَ ۗ وَاللَّهُ عَزِيزٌ حَكِيمٌ
>
> MEANING: "It is not for a Prophet to take captives from the Mushrikīn until he has greatly slaughtered and overcome his enemies in the land. You (Believers) desire the goods of this world, whereas Allāh desires the Hereafter for you, and Allāh is All-Mighty, All-Wise." — **Sūrah Al-Anfāl (8):67**

Also, Muslim narrated a long hadīth in his *Sahīh* from Ibn ʿAbbās, which contains an explanation of this. So Allāh's Messenger (ﷺ) set the ransom as four hundred (*dirhams*) for each of them.[1]

So Allāh's Messenger (ﷺ) returned to Al-Madīnah aided, victorious, and having been given assistance; and Allāh had raised high His Word; and He had given him authority and mighty aid. So therefore, a great number of the people of Al-Madīnah accepted Islām, and therefore ʿAbdullāh ibn Ubayy ibn Salūl and his party of Hypocrites entered into Islām, as an outward pretence.

Chapter: The Number Of People Present At Badr

[The total number of people present at Badr was:]

From the Muslims: three hundred and ten and odd (~310): from the Muhājirīn eighty-six men (86), and from the Aws sixty-one men (61), and from the Khazraj one hundred and seventy men (170).

The reason why the number of the men of Aws was less than the number of the Khazraj, even though they were fiercer than them and more

---

1 — [DB] Refer to *Sahīh Muslim* (no.1763). As for the mention of the figure of four hundred (*dirhams*), then it is reported by Abū Dāwūd (no. 2691). Shaikh Al-Albānī (رحمه الله) said concerning this report: "'It is *sahīh*' apart from the four hundred (*dirhams*)."

patient in fighting, was that their homes lay in the outlying areas of Al-Madīnah. So when the call to go out was given, it was easier for the Khazraj because of the closeness of their homes.

Then the scholars of military campaigns and expeditions differ greatly with regard to those who were present at Badr, and with regard to their number, and with regard to the names of some of them.

So they have been mentioned by Az-Zuhrī, Mūsā ibn 'Uqbah, Muhammad ibn Yasār, Muhammad ibn 'Umar Al-Wāqidī, Sa'īd ibn Al-Amawī — in his *Maghāzī*, and by Al-Bukhārī and a number of the early scholars.

Also Ibn Hazm mentions them in detail, as I have mentioned them, in *Kitābus-Sīrah* and he claimed that eight of them were not personally present at Badr — but rather that Allāh's Messenger (ﷺ) gave them a share of the booty, and he mentioned amongst them: 'Uthmān, Talhah and Sa'īd ibn Zayd.

One of those who gave attention to that in the finest manner, from the later scholars, was the Shaikh, the Imām, Al-Hāfidh Diyā'ud-Dīn Abū 'Abdillāh Muhammad ibn 'Abdil-Wāhid Al-Maqdisī (رَحِمَهُ ٱللَّهُ). So he devoted a small volume to them, and he included it in his *Ahkām* also.[1]

As for the Mushrikūn, then their number was, as he (عَلَيْهِ ٱلسَّلَامُ) said, between nine hundred and a thousand (~900 — 1000). Furthermore, fourteen (14) men of the Muslims were killed that day: six (6) from the Muhājirīn, six (6) from the Khazraj, and two (2) from the Aws.[2]

The first one to be killed on that day was Mihja', the mawlā of 'Umar ibn Al-Khattāb or it is said: it was a man from the Ansār whose name was Hārithah ibn Surāqah.

---

1 — [BJ][SZ] This volume and *Al-Ahkām* are still in the realm of manuscripts.

2 — In *Jawāmi'us-Sīrah*, Ibn Hazm makes mention of some of the names of those martyred at Badr. See **Endnote 28 on page 455** for the list.

From the Mushrikūn seventy (70) were killed, or it is said: fewer than that, and a like number were taken captive also.[1]

And Allāh's Messenger (ﷺ) completed the affair of Badr and the captives in (the month of) Shawwāl.

Chapter: The Expedition Of Banū Sulaym

Then seven days after its completion he (ﷺ) went out in person to attack Banū Sulaym. So he stayed there for three nights and then he returned, not having encountered any fighting. He had left in charge of Al-Madīnah Sibāʿ ibn ʿUrfutah, or it is said: Ibn Umm Maktūm.[2]

Chapter: The Expedition Of As-Sawīq

And when Abū Sufyān returned to Makkah, and Allāh caused His punishment to befall his companions at Badr, Abū Sufyān vowed that he would not pour any water upon his head until he had made an attack upon Allāh's Messenger (ﷺ).[3]

So he went out with two hundred riders and halted at the edge of Al-ʿUrayd,[4] and he spent a single night amongst Banun-Nadīr, staying with Sallām ibn Mishkam who gave him drink and provided him with information about the people. Then he rejoined his companions in the morning, and he ordered the cutting down of some date palms, and he

---

1 — [MK][MM] There occurs in *Sahīhul-Bukhārī* (no.3986) from Al-Barāʾ ibn ʿĀzib (رَضِيَ ٱللَّهُ عَنْهُ) that he said: "The Prophet (ﷺ) and his Companions struck the Mushrikūn on the day of Badr with a loss of one hundred and forty (140): seventy captives (70) and seventy killed (70)."

2 — Ibn Kathīr said in *As-Sīratun-Nabawiyyah* (2/511): "And this is the saying of the majority."

3 — [DB] Meaning that he would not have sexual relations and thus make it necessary upon himself to take a bath, until he had taken revenge. [*Sīrah Ibn Hishām* (3/47) and *As-Sīratun-Nabawiyyah* (p. 211) of Ibn Hibbān].

4 — [SH] A valley on the north-eastern edge of Al-Madīnah, and there is now a mosque there bearing the name.

killed a man of the Ansār and a person who was an ally of his, and then he went back.

Allāh's Messenger (صَلَّى ٱللَّٰهُ عَلَيْهِ وَسَلَّمَ) had received warning of him and therefore went out with the Muslims to seek him. So he reached Qarqaratul-Kudr (The Plain of the Sand Grouse).[1]

However Abū Sufyān and the Mushrikūn escaped him, but (to do so) they had to discard a great amount of their provisions, such as parched and ground barley (As-Sawīq), so it was therefore called the expedition of *'As-Sawīq'*. It occurred in the month of Dhul-Hijjah of the second year of the Hijrah. Then he (صَلَّى ٱللَّٰهُ عَلَيْهِ وَسَلَّمَ) returned to Al-Madīnah, having left Abū Lubābah in charge of it.

Chapter: The Expedition Of Dhī Amarr

Then he (صَلَّى ٱللَّٰهُ عَلَيْهِ وَسَلَّمَ) remained in residence for the rest of Dhul-Hijjah, and then he took a military expedition to Najd intending to attack (the tribe of) Ghatafān, and he left 'Uthmān ibn 'Affān in charge of Al-Madīnah. He stayed in Najd for the whole of Safar of the second year, and then he returned having not encountered any fighting.

Chapter: The Expedition Of Buhrān

Then he (صَلَّى ٱللَّٰهُ عَلَيْهِ وَسَلَّمَ) went out in Rabī'ul-Ākhir to attack Quraysh, and he left Ibn Umm Maktūm in charge of Al-Madīnah. So he reached Buhrān, a mine in Al-Hijāz, and then he came back not having encountered any fighting.

Chapter: The Expedition Of Banū Qaynuqā'

Banū Qaynuqā', one of the groups of the Jews in Al-Madīnah, broke their covenant. They were traders and goldsmiths, and they were around seven hundred fighters in number. So Allāh's Messenger (صَلَّى ٱللَّٰهُ عَلَيْهِ وَسَلَّمَ) went out to lay siege to them, and he left Bashīr ibn 'Abdil-Mundhir

---

1 — [BJ] [SZ] A place in the direction of Al-Ma'dan, eight riding stages from Al-Madīnah; and it is said: It is a watering place belonging to Banū Sulaym.

in charge of Al-Madīnah. So he (صَلَّى ٱللَّهُ عَلَيْهِ وَسَلَّمَ) besieged them for fifteen nights, and then they agreed to surrender and accept his (صَلَّى ٱللَّهُ عَلَيْهِ وَسَلَّمَ) judgement.

So ʿAbdullāh ibn Ubayy ibn Salūl interceded on their behalf, since they had been confederates of the Khazraj, and he was the leader of the Khazraj, so Allāh's Messenger (صَلَّى ٱللَّهُ عَلَيْهِ وَسَلَّمَ) allowed him to intercede for them; and they lived at the edge of Al-Madīnah.[1]

Chapter: The Killing Of Kaʿb Ibn Al-Ashraf, The Jew

As for Kaʿb ibn Al-Ashraf the Jew, then he was a man of (the tribe of) Tayyiʾ, and his mother was from Banun-Nadīr. So he used to abuse Allāh's Messenger (صَلَّى ٱللَّهُ عَلَيْهِ وَسَلَّمَ) and the Believers, and he composed love-poems mentioning the believing women. After the battle of Badr, he went to Makkah, and provoked the people against Allāh's Messenger and the Believers. So Allāh's Messenger (صَلَّى ٱللَّهُ عَلَيْهِ وَسَلَّمَ) encouraged the Muslims to kill him, and said: *"Who will deal with Kaʿb ibn Ashraf, since he has annoyed Allāh and His Messenger?"* [2]

So some men of the Ansār, and then from the Aws, went forth to deal with him; and they were Muhammad ibn Maslamah, and ʿAbbād ibn Bishr ibn Waqsh, and Abū Nāʾilah — whose name was Silkān ibn Salāmah ibn Waqsh — and these two were brothers to Kaʿb ibn Al-Ashraf through breastfeeding, and Al-Hārith ibn Aws ibn Muʿādh, and Abū ʿAbs ibn

---

1 — DB Imām Ibnul-Qayyim said in *Zādul-Maʿād* (3/126-127): "So they surrendered upon the basis of accepting the judgement of Allāh's Messenger (صَلَّى ٱللَّهُ عَلَيْهِ وَسَلَّمَ) concerning their necks, their property, their wives, and their children. So he ordered that their hands should be tied behind their backs. Then ʿAbdullāh ibn Ubayy spoke concerning them with Allāh's Messenger (صَلَّى ٱللَّهُ عَلَيْهِ وَسَلَّمَ) and he urged and implored him, so he gifted them to him; and he commanded that they should leave Al-Madīnah and not live as his neighbours in it. So they departed and went to Adhriʿāt in the land of Shām, and they had hardly settled there before most of them died. They were goldsmiths and traders, and were about seven-hundred fighting men in number, and their home was at the edge of Al-Madīnah."

2 — SH Reported by Al-Bukhārī in his *Sahīh* (no. 4037) and Muslim in his *Sahīh* (no. 1801) as a hadīth of Jābir ibn ʿAbdillāh (رَضِيَ ٱللَّهُ عَنْهُمَا).

Jabr. So he (صَلَّى ٱللَّٰهُ عَلَيْهِ وَسَلَّمَ) gave them permission to say whatever speech they wished in order to trick him, and that there would be no blame upon them.

So they went to him and got him to come down from his fortress during the night, and they spoke to him with words that gave him the false impression that they were speaking against Allāh's Messenger (صَلَّى ٱللَّٰهُ عَلَيْهِ وَسَلَّمَ), so he felt secure with them. So when they had him in their grasp, they killed him — may Allāh curse him.

Then they came back at the end of the night, and it was a moonlit night, and they came to Allāh's Messenger whilst he was standing in Prayer. So when he finished he supplicated for them.

Al-Hārith ibn Aws had been wounded by some of the swords of his companions, so he (عَلَيْهِ ٱلصَّلَاةُ وَٱلسَّلَامُ) spat lightly upon his wound, and he was cured immediately.

Then in the morning, the Jews began speaking about his killing, so he (صَلَّى ٱللَّٰهُ عَلَيْهِ وَسَلَّمَ) gave permission for the killing of the Jews.

CHAPTER:

Comprising the Battle of Uhud, in Abridged Form

It was a battle during which Allāh tested His servants — the Believers — and through it, He distinguished the Believers from the Hypocrites.

It came about after the Quraysh had experienced the killing of their chiefs at Badr, and they had been struck by a disaster which they had no expectation of; and then Abū Sufyān ibn Harb became their head, because of the absence of elders. So he came, as we have mentioned, to the outskirts of Al-Madīnah for the expedition of As-Sawīq. However, he did not achieve what he desired, and so he began to gather the Quraysh, and to provoke them against Allāh's Messenger (ﷺ) and the Muslims. So he gathered three thousand of the Quraysh, their confederate tribes, and the Ahābīsh.[1] They all came along, and they brought their womenfolk so that they would not flee. Then he set off with them towards Al-Madīnah, and camped close to Mount Uhud at

---

1 — (SH) There occurs in *Lisānul-'Arab* (6/278): "Hubshī is a mountain below Makkah. It is said that the *'Ahābīsh of Quraysh'* were named after it. This is because the Banul-Mustaliq and the Banul-Hūn ibn Khuzaymah gathered by it, and made an oath of alliance with the Quraysh. They swore a pledge in Allāh's name: *'We shall be a single hand together against others; for as long as the night is dark and the day is bright, and for as long as Hubshī remains in its place.'* So they were called the Hubshī adherents of Quraysh, being named after the mountain."

a place called ʿAynayn,[1] and that was in (the month of) Shawwāl of the third year.

So Allāh's Messenger (ﷺ) consulted his companions about whether he should go out to confront them, or remain within Al-Madīnah. So a group of the noblest ones from the Companions, from those who missed going out on the day of Badr, advised going out to meet them; and they kept on urging him to do that. ʿAbdullāh ibn Ubayy ibn Salūl, however, advised remaining within Al-Madīnah, and a group of the Companions shared that view of his. However, the others were persistent in urging Allāh's Messenger (ﷺ), so he got up, entered his house, put on his armour, and then came out to them. By now, the resolve of some of those people had wavered, so they said: *"O Messenger of Allāh! If you wish to remain in Al-Madīnah then do so."* So he said: "It is not right for a Prophet, when he has put on his armour, that he should take it off until he has fought."[2]

And a man from Banun-Najjār was brought to Allāh's Messenger (ﷺ) and he prayed over him, and that was the day of Jumuʿah;[3]

---

1 — MK MM It is a small hill just to the south of Uhud, being separated from it by the wādī of Qanāt. It was called Jabal ʿAynayn (The Hill of Two Springs) because of the two springs that existed next to it. It is known today as Jabalur-Rumāt (The Hill of the Archers) because of the fact that Allāh's Messenger (ﷺ) placed the group of archers upon it.

2 — DB Shaikh Al-Albānī said in his checking of *Fiqhus-Sīrah* (p. 169): "Ibn Hishām reported it (2/126-128): from Abū Is-hāq: from Az-Zuhrī and others, in *mursal* form. It is also reported in fully connected form by Ahmad (3/351) by way of Abuz-Zubayr: from Jābir with its like, and its chain of narration is to the standard of Muslim except for the fact that Abuz-Zubayr is a *'mudallis'* and reports it with *"anʿanah'*. However, it has a supporting witness as a hadīth of Ibn ʿAbbās which is reported by Al-Bayhaqī — as occurs in Al-Bidāyah (4/11) — with a *'hasan'* chain of narration. So the hadīth is *'sahīh'*, and it is also reported by Ahmad (1/271) and Al-Hākim (2/128-129, 296, 297) and he declared it authentic, and Adh-Dhahabī agreed."

3 — DB Ibn Kathīr said in *As-Sīratun-Nabawiyyah* (3/27): "So the people persisted with Allāh's Messenger (ﷺ) until he entered and put his armour on, and that was on the day of Jumuʿah, after he had completed the Prayer; and a man from Banun-Najjār called Mālik ibn ʿAmr had died that day, so he prayed over him."

and he left Ibn Umm Maktūm in charge of Al-Madīnah. He went out to Uhud with a thousand men, and along the way, ʿAbdullāh ibn Ubayy deserted, with around three hundred men, and returned to Al-Madīnah. So ʿAbdullāh ibn ʿAmr ibn Harām, the father of Jābir (رَضِيَ ٱللَّهُ عَنْهُمَا) went after them, rebuking them and urging them to return. However they said: *"If we knew that you were really going to fight then we would not be going back,"* so when they refused to obey him, he left them and abused them.

Allāh's Messenger (صَلَّى ٱللَّهُ عَلَيْهِ وَسَلَّمَ) went on with those who remained with him until he halted at the ravine of Uhud, at the bank of the wādī leading to the mountain, and he placed his back to Uhud, and he forbade the people from fighting until he commanded them.

Then in the morning, he (صَلَّى ٱللَّهُ عَلَيْهِ وَسَلَّمَ) prepared and arranged his companions for the fighting. Amongst them, there were fifty horsemen.[1] In charge of the archers, who were fifty in number, he placed ʿAbdullāh ibn Jubayr Al-Awsī; and he commanded him and his companions that they should not move from their places, and that they should guard the backs of the Muslims against any attack from their direction.[2]

He (صَلَّى ٱللَّهُ عَلَيْهِ وَسَلَّمَ) wore two coats of chain mail on that day, one on top of the other.[3] He gave the battle-flag to Musʿab, the brother of Banū ʿAbdid-Dār; and in charge of one wing he placed Az-Zubayr ibn Al-

---

1 — DB Al-Hāfidh Ibn Hajr said *Fathul-Bārī* (7/350): "His saying (the archers): in the narration of Zuhayr: *'And they were fifty men'*, this is what is dependable; and it occurs in Az-Zād that the fifty refers to the number of horsemen on that day, and this is a clear mistake; and Mūsā ibn ʿUqbah stated clearly that they had no horses at Uhud." [Refer to: *Dalāʾilun-Nubuwwah* of Al-Bayhaqī (3/209).]

2 — BJ SZ Refer to *Sahīhul-Bukhārī* (no.3039), and it contains his (صَلَّى ٱللَّهُ عَلَيْهِ وَسَلَّمَ) saying to the archers: "Even if you see us being snatched away by birds then do not leave your places until I send a message to you; and if you see that we have defeated the enemy and trodden them underfoot, then still do not leave your place until I send a message to you."

3 — For more detail regarding these two chain-mail coats, see **Endnote 29 on page 456**.

ʿAwwām, and in charge of the other wing Al-Mundhir ibn ʿAmr: *'The One Who Hastens to Death'* (*Al-Muʿniq Liyamūt*).[1]

He had the youths presented to him that day, and he gave permission (to fight) to some of them and sent others back. From those he permitted were: Samurah ibn Jundab and Rāfiʿ ibn Khadīj, and they were both fifteen years old; and from those he sent back on that day were: Usāmah ibn Zayd ibn Hārithah, Usayd ibn Zuhayr, Al-Barāʾ ibn ʿĀzib, Zayd ibn Arqam, Zayd ibn Thābit, ʿAbdullāh ibn ʿUmar, ʿArābah ibn Aws, and ʿAmr ibn Hazm; and then he permitted them on the day of the Trench (Al-Khandaq).

The Quraysh also made preparations, and they were three thousand in number — as we have mentioned, amongst them two hundred horsemen. So they placed Khālid ibn Al-Walīd in charge of their right wing and ʿIkrimah ibn Abī Jahl in charge of their left wing.

The first one of the Mushrikūn to come forward that day was Abū ʿĀmir Ar-Rāhib ('The Monk'), whose name was ʿAbd ʿAmr ibn Sayfī, who had been the head of the Aws in the times of Ignorance, and had been a person who devoted himself to worship in seclusion. However when Islām came he disgraced himself and did not enter into it. Rather, he showed open hostility towards the Prophet (ﷺ), so he (ﷺ) made supplication against him. So he left Al-Madīnah and went to the Quraysh, provoking them against Allāh's Messenger (ﷺ) and encouraging them to fight against him, in addition to the hatred that they already had for Allāh's Messenger and his Companions. He also promised the Mushrikūn that he would persuade his people of the Aws to come over to their side on the day of the battle, and that they would come back to him. So when he arrived, with the slaves of the people of Makkah and those who had pledged at the mountain of Hubshī to fight along with them, he presented himself to his people. So they said to him: *"May Allāh not bring bliss to your eye, O wicked one!"* So he said: *"My*

---

1 — SH This was his title and he was a famous Companion, being from the Ansār, from the Khazraj. He was present at the Pledge of Al-ʿAqabah where he was one of the chiefs. He was present at Badr and Uhud, and was martyred on the day of *Biʾr Maʿūnah*.

people have been afflicted with evil after my leaving them." Then he fought fiercely against the Muslims.

The call of recognition of the Muslims that day was: ***"Put to death! Put to death!"***[1]

On that day Abū Dujānah Simāk ibn Kharashah and Hamzah, the paternal uncle of Allāh's Messenger (ﷺ): the Lion of Allāh and the Lion of His Messenger — may Allāh be pleased with him and cause him to be pleased — showed great courage in fighting; and likewise ʿAlī ibn Abī Tālib; and a group of the Ansār, from them: An-Nadr ibn Anas and Saʿd ibn Ar-Rabīʿ — may Allāh be pleased with them all.

So the initial outcome of the day was in favour of the Muslims, and against the Disbelievers, who were defeated and sent fleeing backwards until they reached their women.

So when the companions of ʿAbdullāh ibn Jubayr saw this, they said: "O people, the spoils! The spoils!"

So ʿAbdullāh ibn Jubayr reminded them of the earlier command of Allāh's Messenger (ﷺ) to them concerning that. However, they thought that the Mushrikūn would not return, and that they would be unable to make a stand after that, so therefore they went in search of booty.[2]

---

1 — [BJ][SZ] This is what is mentioned by the scholars of sīrah such as Ibn Hishām (3/76) and others, but it is something that I do not find reported in connected form as being restricted to the Day of Uhud. Rather it was reported by Abū Dāwūd (nos. 2596 and 2638), An-Nasāʾī in *Al-Kubrā* (no. 8862), Ibn Mājah (no. 2840), and others: from Salamah ibn Al-Akwaʿ that this was their battle-call during their night-time attack upon the (tribe of) Hawāzin under the authority of Abū Bakr (رضي الله عنه), and it is *'sahīh'*.

So perhaps this recognition call was used by the Muslims in all of their battles, or most of them, since Ibn Abī Shaybah reported (12/503) and Ad-Dārimī (2/219) with a *'sahīh'* chain of narration from Salamah also that: *"Our call of recognition along with Khālid ibn Al-Walīd was* ***'Amit' (Put to death)!"***

2 — See **Endnote 30 on page 456** for more regarding the bravery and courage of ʿAbdullāh Ibn Jubayr.

Then the cavalry of the Mushrikūn made a charge and found the gap empty of archers. They therefore passed by and were able to make an attack, and they all came through. So what Allāh willed to happen occurred, and those whom Allāh honoured with martyrdom from the Believers were martyred; so a group of the finest Companions were killed, but the majority of them were put to flight.[1]

So the Mushrikūn were free to attack Allāh's Messenger (صَلَّى ٱللَّهُ عَلَيْهِ وَسَلَّمَ) and his (noble) face was injured, his right lower lateral incisor tooth was broken by a stone, and his helmet was crushed into his pure head.[2]

The Mushrikūn pelted him with stones until he fell upon his side, and he fell into one of the pits which Abū 'Āmir, the wicked one, had dug as a plot against the Muslims. So 'Alī took hold of his arm and Talhah ibn 'Ubaydillāh clasped him in his arms.

Those who took it upon themselves to cause harm to Allāh's Messenger (صَلَّى ٱللَّهُ عَلَيْهِ وَسَلَّمَ) were 'Amr ibn Qami'ah and 'Utbah ibn Abī Waqqās; or it is said that it was 'Abdullāh ibn Shihāb Az-Zuhrī, the father of the paternal uncle of Muhammad ibn Muslim ibn Shihāb Az-Zuhrī, who wounded him (صَلَّى ٱللَّهُ عَلَيْهِ وَسَلَّمَ); and Mus'ab was killed in front of him, so he (صَلَّى ٱللَّهُ عَلَيْهِ وَسَلَّمَ) handed the flag to 'Alī ibn Abī Tālib.

Also, two rings of the chain-mail of the helmet were crushed into his (صَلَّى ٱللَّهُ عَلَيْهِ وَسَلَّمَ) face; so Abū 'Ubaydah pulled them out by biting upon them, which caused his two front teeth to fall out, and the break in his teeth made him more handsome; and Mālik ibn Sinān — the father of Abū Sa'īd Al-Khudrī — sucked out the blood from his (صَلَّى ٱللَّهُ عَلَيْهِ وَسَلَّمَ) wound.

The Mushrikūn reached Allāh's Messenger (صَلَّى ٱللَّهُ عَلَيْهِ وَسَلَّمَ), so a group of about ten of the Muslims stood in front of him, defending him, and they were killed.[3]

---

1 — DB Al-Bukhārī reported (no. 3039), within a hadīth of Al-Barā' ibn 'Āzib (رَضِيَ ٱللَّهُ عَنْهُ) *"So none remained with Allāh's Messenger except for twelve men; and they killed seventy of us."*

2 — BJ SZ That is reported by Al-Bukhārī (no.2911) and Muslim (no. 1790) as a hadīth of Sahl ibn Sa'd (رَضِيَ ٱللَّهُ عَنْهُ).

3 — SH Muslim (no. 1789) reports its like as a hadīth of Anas ibn Mālik (رَضِيَ ٱللَّهُ عَنْهُ).

Then Talhah fought against them fiercely until he beat them away from him (صَلَّى ٱللَّٰهُ عَلَيْهِ وَسَلَّمَ); and Abū Dujānah Simāk ibn Kharashah used his back as a shield for him (صَلَّى ٱللَّٰهُ عَلَيْهِ وَسَلَّمَ), so arrows were striking his back and he did not move — رَضِيَ ٱللَّٰهُ عَنْهُ.

On that day Sa'd ibn Abī Waqqās (رَضِيَ ٱللَّٰهُ عَنْهُ) fired well-aimed arrows that struck and inflicted losses, so Allāh's Messenger (صَلَّى ٱللَّٰهُ عَلَيْهِ وَسَلَّمَ) said: "Shoot! May my father and my mother be a ransom for you!"[1]

Also on that day the eye of Qatādah ibn An-Nu'mān Az-Zafarī[2] was struck out, so he went with it to Allāh's Messenger (صَلَّى ٱللَّٰهُ عَلَيْهِ وَسَلَّمَ) and he restored it with his (عَلَيْهِ ٱلصَّلَاةُ وَٱلسَّلَامُ) noble hand, and it became the soundest and best of his two eyes.[3]

Furthermore, Satan — may Allāh curse him — called out at the top of his voice: ***'Muhammad has been killed.'*** So this produced an effect upon the hearts of many of the Muslims, and most of them fled; and Allāh's command occurred.

Anas ibn An-Nadr passed by some of the Muslims who had laid down their arms, so he said: "What are you waiting for?"

So they said: "Allāh's Messenger (صَلَّى ٱللَّٰهُ عَلَيْهِ وَسَلَّمَ) has been killed."

So he said: "What will you do with life after him? Stand and die upon that which he died upon!"

Then he went forward to fight the enemy and he met Sa'd ibn Mu'ādh and said: *"O Sa'd! By Allāh! I can smell the fragrance of Paradise coming from the direction of Uhud!"* So he fought until he was killed (رَضِيَ ٱللَّٰهُ عَنْهُ), and he was found with seventy wounds.[4]

---

1 — [BJ][SZ] Reported by Al-Bukhārī (no. 4055) and Muslim (no. 2412).

2 — [SH] A Companion who fought at Badr. He was one of the famous archers and was present at all of the battles. He died in Al-Madīnah in 23H.

3 — [DB] Ibn Is-hāq narrated that 'Āsim ibn 'Umar ibn Qatādah said: "The eye of Qatādah ibn An-Nu'mān was struck out that day such that it hung upon his cheek." — *Sīrah Ibn Hishām* (3/87).

4 — [BJ][SZ] Refer to *Sahīhul-Bukhārī* (no. 2805) and *Sahīh Muslim* (no.1903).

'Abdur-Rahmān ibn 'Awf also suffered around twenty wounds on that day: some of them were to his leg, such that he limped from that until he died (رَضِيَ ٱللَّهُ عَنْهُ).

Allāh's Messenger (صَلَّى ٱللَّهُ عَلَيْهِ وَسَلَّمَ) then came towards the Muslims, and the first person to recognise him from beneath his helmet was Ka'b ibn Mālik (رَضِيَ ٱللَّهُ عَنْهُ) who called out at the top of his voice: "O Muslims! Receive good news! This is Allāh's Messenger (صَلَّى ٱللَّهُ عَلَيْهِ وَسَلَّمَ)!"

So Allāh's Messenger (صَلَّى ٱللَّهُ عَلَيْهِ وَسَلَّمَ) indicated to him to be silent. So the Muslims gathered around him and accompanied him to the ravine where he had camped, amongst them was Abū Bakr, 'Umar, 'Alī, Al-Hārith ibn As-Simmah[1] and others.

Then, as he ascended the mountain, Ubayy ibn Khalaf reached him, riding upon a fast horse called Al-'Awd. The foul one had claimed that whilst upon it he would kill Allāh's Messenger (صَلَّى ٱللَّهُ عَلَيْهِ وَسَلَّمَ). So when he drew close, Allāh's Messenger (صَلَّى ٱللَّهُ عَلَيْهِ وَسَلَّمَ) took the spear from the hand of Al-Hārith ibn As-Simmah and struck him with it. It struck the place of his collarbone, and the enemy of Allāh went back defeated. So the Mushrikūn said to him: "By Allāh! You are alright."

So he said: "By Allāh! If my wound had struck all of the people of (the market place of) Dhul-Majāz then they would all die! For indeed he told me previously that he was going to kill me."

So he continued with it until he died at Sarif, whilst returning to Makkah — may Allāh curse him.[2]

---

1 — [MK][MM][SH] He is Al-Hārith ibn As-Simmah ibn 'Amr ibn 'Atīk Al-Ansārī Al-Khazrajī. He went out with Allāh's Messenger (صَلَّى ٱللَّهُ عَلَيْهِ وَسَلَّمَ) on the day of Badr; however, he was injured at Ar-Rawhā. So Allāh's Messenger (صَلَّى ٱللَّهُ عَلَيْهِ وَسَلَّمَ) sent him back; and he gave him a share of the booty. He was present with him at Uhud and stood firm that day. He was martyred at Bi'r Ma'ūnah (رَضِيَ ٱللَّهُ عَنْهُ).

2 — [SH] Reported by Ibn Is-hāq in *As-Sīrah* (3/771-772: Ibn Hishām) from Ibn Shihāb Az-Zuhrī with it. I say: Its chain of narration is weak as it is *'mursal'*. [...] In summary these *'mursal'* reports do not establish proof, and Allāh knows best.

ʿAlī (رَضِيَ ٱللَّهُ عَنْهُ) brought some water to Allāh's Messenger (صَلَّى ٱللَّهُ عَلَيْهِ وَسَلَّمَ) to wash away the blood from him, but he found that it had an odour so he refused it.[1]

He (صَلَّى ٱللَّهُ عَلَيْهِ وَسَلَّمَ) wanted to climb upon a rock there, but he was unable to because of his condition and because of the two coats of chain mail he was wearing that day. So Talhah sat under him to enable him to climb upon it.[2]

The time of the Prayer became due, so he led them in the Prayer whilst sitting. Then the Mushrikūn went off to their camels, took the road to Makkah, and departed towards it. All of this occurred on Saturday.

On that day around seventy Muslims were martyred,[3] from them Hamzah the paternal uncle of Allāh's Messenger (صَلَّى ٱللَّهُ عَلَيْهِ وَسَلَّمَ). He was killed by Wah-shī, the slave belonging to Banū Nawfal; and for that, he was set free. Then later on, he accepted Islām, and was one of those who killed Musaylamah Al-Kadhdhāb — upon whom be Allāh's curse.[4]

And (also from those martyred were:) ʿAbdullāh ibn Jah-sh, the confederate of Banū Umayyah; and Musʿab ibn ʿUmayr; and ʿUthmān ibn ʿUthmān who was Shammās ibn ʿUthmān al Makhzūmī — he was called *'Shammās'* (shining like the sun) because of the handsomeness of his face. So these four were from the Muhājirīn, and the rest were from the Ansār — may Allāh be pleased with all of them. So he buried them

---

1 — For the narration which lends more detail to this event, see **Endnote 31 on page 457**.

2 — BJ SZ Reported by At-Tirmidhī (no. 1692 and 3738) and Ahmad (1/165) with a *'hasan'* chain of narration and it contains his (صَلَّى ٱللَّهُ عَلَيْهِ وَسَلَّمَ) statement: *"Talhah has made it binding for himself"* —meaning: Talhah has done such deeds as have made Paradise certain for him.

3 — SH Reported by Al-Bukhārī (no. 3986) as a hadīth of Al-Barā' ibn ʿĀzib (رَضِيَ ٱللَّهُ عَنْهُمَا); and (no. 4078) as a hadīth of Anas ibn Mālik (رَضِيَ ٱللَّهُ عَنْهُ).

4 — Refer to *Sahīhul-Bukhārī* (no. 4072)

with their blood and wounds upon them, and did not pray over them that day.[1]

On that day, a group of the prominent Companions fled, from them 'Uthmān ibn 'Affān (رَضِيَ ٱللَّهُ عَنْهُ), and Allāh (the One Free of all imperfections) stated that He has pardoned them, so He (the Mighty and Majestic) said:

> إِنَّ الَّذِينَ تَوَلَّوْا مِنكُمْ يَوْمَ الْتَقَى الْجَمْعَانِ إِنَّمَا اسْتَزَلَّهُمُ الشَّيْطَانُ بِبَعْضِ مَا كَسَبُوا ۖ وَلَقَدْ عَفَا اللَّهُ عَنْهُمْ ۗ إِنَّ اللَّهَ غَفُورٌ حَلِيمٌ
>
> MEANING: "Those of you who turned back on the day when the two armies met at Uhud were prompted to flee by Satan, because of some sins they had earned, and indeed Allāh has pardoned them. Allāh is the One Who forgives extensively, the Most Forbearing."[2] — **SŪRAH ĀLI 'IMRĀN (3): 155**

And He (the One Free of all imperfections) has mentioned this battle in Sūrah Āli 'Imrān, where He says:

> وَإِذْ غَدَوْتَ مِنْ أَهْلِكَ تُبَوِّئُ الْمُؤْمِنِينَ مَقَاعِدَ لِلْقِتَالِ ۗ وَاللَّهُ سَمِيعٌ عَلِيمٌ
>
> MEANING: "And when you left your household to station the Believers at their positions for fighting, and Allāh is All-Hearing, All-Knowing."[3] — **SŪRAH ĀLI 'IMRĀN (3): 121**

Chapter: The Expedition Of Hamrā' Al-Asad

Then, when Allāh's Messenger (صَلَّى ٱللَّهُ عَلَيْهِ وَسَلَّمَ) entered the morning of Sunday, he summoned the Muslims to go out in pursuit of the enemy, to

---

1 — (SH) Reported by Al-Bukhārī in his *Sahīh* (no. 1343) from Jābir ibn 'Abdillāh (رَضِيَ ٱللَّهُ عَنْهُمَا) and there is disagreement about this matter between the people of knowledge. Refer to the speech of Al-Hāfidh Ibn Hajr concerning the hadīth in *Fat-hul-Bārī*.

2 — 'Abdullāh Ibn 'Umar was asked regarding those who fled on the Day of Uhud. See **ENDNOTE 32 ON PAGE 457**.

3 — Imām Ibn Al-Qayyim mentions some points of benefit extracted from the events of the Battle of Uhud. Read them at **ENDNOTE 33 ON PAGE 458**.

put Fear into them. So this was the expedition of Hamrā' Al-Asad. He ordered that no one should go out with him except those who had been present at Uhud.[1] So no one did go out along with him except those who had been at Uhud, apart from Jābir ibn 'Abdillāh, whose father had left him in charge of his daughters, and his father was killed on the day of Uhud. So he asked permission of Allāh's Messenger (صَلَّى ٱللَّهُ عَلَيْهِ وَسَلَّمَ) to go out to Hamrā' Al-Asad, and he granted him permission.

So the Muslims went forth just as he (صَلَّى ٱللَّهُ عَلَيْهِ وَسَلَّمَ) had commanded them, still suffering from their wounds, until he reached Hamrā' Al-Asad, which is eight miles from Al-Madīnah. So that is His Saying — He the Most High:

> ٱلَّذِينَ ٱسْتَجَابُوا لِلَّهِ وَٱلرَّسُولِ مِن بَعْدِ مَا أَصَابَهُمُ ٱلْقَرْحُ ۚ لِلَّذِينَ أَحْسَنُوا مِنْهُمْ وَٱتَّقَوْا أَجْرٌ عَظِيمٌ
>
> MEANING: "Those who responded to Allāh and the Messenger after being wounded: for those of them who are doers of good, and who fear and are dutiful to Allāh, there is a tremendous reward."[2] — **Sūrah Āli 'Imrān (3): 172**

Ma'bad ibn Abī Ma'bad Al-Khuzā'ī passed by Allāh's Messenger (صَلَّى ٱللَّهُ عَلَيْهِ وَسَلَّمَ) and his Companions, so he allowed him to pass, and to reach Abū Sufyān and the Mushrikūn at Ar-Rawhā'. He informed them that

---

1 — DB Al-Hāfidh Ibn Hajr said in *Fathul-Bārī* (7/374): "He went forth to put fear into the enemy; and to cause them to think that what had befallen them [i.e. the Muslims] had not weakened them to such an extent that they were not able to pursue the enemy..."

2 — Refer to *Sahīhul-Bukhārī* (no. 4077).

Allāh's Messenger (ﷺ) and his Companions had come out in pursuit of them.[1]

So this broke the spirit of the Quraysh, when prior to this they had wanted to return to Al-Madīnah; but this caused them to abandon that and they carried on returning to Makkah.

He (ﷺ) also captured Mu'āwiyah ibn Al-Mughīrah ibn Abil-'Ās, and he commanded that he should be beheaded whilst captive; and he was the father of 'Ā'ishah who was the mother of 'Abdul-Mālik ibn Marwān; and he did not execute anyone else on this occasion.

Chapter: The Expedition Of Ar-Rajī'

Then, after Uhud, he (ﷺ) sent out the expedition of Ar-Rajī', and this was in the (month of) Safar in the fourth year. It came about because he (ﷺ) had sent some men to (the tribes of) 'Adal and Al-Qārah,[2] due to them requesting that from Allāh's Messenger (ﷺ) when they came to see him, and they mentioned that there were some Muslims amongst them. So he sent six men, upon the saying of Ibn Is-hāq, whereas Al-Bukhārī said in his *Sahīh* that they were ten; and Abul-Qāsim As-Suhaylī said: *"This is what is correct."*

---

1 — DB Imām Ibnul-Qayyim said in *Zādul-Ma'ād* (3/242): "Ma'bad ibn Abī Ma'bad Al-Khuzā'ī came to Allāh's Messenger (ﷺ) and accepted Islām. So he ordered him to catch up with Abū Sufyān and to dishearten him. So he met him at Ar-Rawhā', and he did not know that he had accepted Islām. So he said: *'What is behind you, O Ma'bad?'* So he said: *'Muhammad and his Companions. They are burning with fury against you, and have brought out such a force as they have never brought out before; and their companions, who left them behind, have regretted what they did.'*"

2 — SH Ibn Hishām said in *As-Sīrah* (3/852): "'Adal and Al-Qārah are from (the tribe of) Al-Hūn ibn Khuzaymah ibn Mudrikah."

He appointed as their leader Marthad ibn Abī Marthad Al-Ghanawī (رضي الله عنه)[1] and amongst them was Khubayb ibn ʿAdiyy. So they went off with them. However, when they reached Ar-Rajīʿ, which is a watering place belonging to (the tribe of) Hudhayl in a district of the Hijāz[2] at Al-Had'ah, they betrayed them and called (the tribe of) Hudhayl to attack them. So they came and surrounded them, and they killed most of them; and some amazing signs were seen in their affair — may Allāh be pleased with them all. From them, Khubayb ibn ʿAdiyy, and another man (and he was Zayd ibn Ad-Dathinnah) were taken captive.

So they took the two of them and sold them as slaves in Makkah, and this was done on account of the Disbelievers of Quraysh, who these two had killed on the day of Uhud.

So as for Khubayb (رضي الله عنه), then he remained imprisoned with them, and then they gathered together to kill him. So they took him to At-Tanʿīm[3] in order to crucify him. So he requested that they should allow him to pray two rakʿahs, and they permitted him. So he prayed the two (rakʿahs), then he said: "By Allāh! Were it not that you would say that I did it out of fear, I would have prolonged it."

---

1 — [SH] Ibn Is-hāq reported in *As-Sīrah* (3/852-853): "ʿĀsim ibn ʿUmar ibn Qatādah narrated it to me, in *'mursal'* form."

So this is what the author (رحمه الله) held to be correct in *Al-Bidāyah wan-Nihāyah* (5/501-502), even though it is *'mursal'*, and it is unauthentic (*daʿīf*).

Furthermore it is established in *Sahīhul-Bukhārī* (nos. 3045, 3989, 4086) that Allāh's Messenger (صلى الله عليه وسلم) appointed ʿĀsim ibn Thābit Al-Ansārī (رضي الله عنه) as their leader; and this was declared correct by As-Suhaylī in *Ar-Rawdul-Unuf* (6/184); and this is what is correct and well known, contrary to what the author (رحمه الله) said; and refer to *Al-Fat-h* (7/380).

2 — [SH] There occurs in *Sahīhul-Bukhārī* (no. 4086) that it is between ʿUsfān and Makkah.

3 — [BJ][SZ] There occurs in *Sahīhul-Bukhārī* (no. 4086): *"So when they took him out of the sacred precincts to kill him"* — and At-Tanʿīm is the closest point lying outside the scared precincts. These days it is a well-known place and has the Mosque of ʿĀ'ishah, which is the place from which ʿĀ'ishah (رضي الله عنها) performed ʿUmrah during her Hajj with the Prophet (صلى الله عليه وسلم), in accordance with his command.

Then he said:

> "I do not care, when I am killed as a Muslim, in what manner my death for Allāh's sake occurs.
>
> Since that is for the sake of the One worshipped truly, and if He wishes He may bless my torn limbs."

Also, Abū Sufyān said to him: "Would it please you that Muhammad were with us being beheaded, and you instead were with your family?"

So he said:

> "By Allāh! It would not even please me that instead of this, I were amongst my family, whilst Muhammad were at his place suffering even the prick of a thorn!"[1]

Then they appointed someone to guard his body. So ʿAmr ibn Umayyah came and managed to carry his body away by night, by means of a ruse, and he buried him.[2]

And as for Zayd ibn Ad-Dathinnah (رَضِيَ اللَّهُ عَنْهُ), then he was bought by Safwān ibn Umayyah, who then killed him in revenge for his father.[3]

Chapter: The Expedition of Biʾr Maʿūnah

Also in this (month of) Safar the expedition of Biʾr Maʿūnah was sent out. The reason for it was that Abū Barāʾ ʿĀmir ibn Mālik — who they called *'The One Who Plays with Spears'* — came to Allāh's Messenger (صَلَّى اللَّهُ عَلَيْهِ وَسَلَّمَ) in Al-Madīnah. So he (صَلَّى اللَّهُ عَلَيْهِ وَسَلَّمَ) called him to Islām; but he did not accept Islām, nor did he refuse outright. So he said: "O Messenger of Allāh! If you were to send your Companions to the people

---

1 — [SH] Reported by Al-Bayhaqī in *Dalāʾilun-Nubuwwah* (3/326) with a chain of narration that is weak due to its being *'mursal'*.

2 — [BJ][SZ] That is reported in *Al-Musnad* (4/139), *Ad-Dalāʾil* of Al-Bayhaqī (3/332), and At-Tabarānī in *Al-Kabīr* (no. 4193). However, it is a narration of Ibrāhīm ibn Ismāʿīl ibn Mujammiʿ Al-Ansārī who is weak. It is also reported by Al-Wāqidī in *Al-Maghāzī* as part of a long narration.

3 — Concerning this expedition, refer to *Sahīhul-Bukhārī* (3045 & 4086).

of Najd to call them to your Religion, then I have hope that they would respond to them."

So he said: "I fear for them from the people of Najd."

So Abū Barā' said: "I will give them my guarantee of protection."[1]

So he (صَلَّىٰ ٱللَّٰهُ عَلَيْهِ وَسَلَّمَ) sent, upon the saying of Ibn Is-hāq, forty men from his Companions; and there occurs in the two *Sahīhs*: seventy men;[2] and that is what is correct, and he appointed as their leader Al-Mundhir ibn 'Amr, one of Banū Sā'idah who had the title *'Al-Mu'niq Liyamūt'* (*The One Who Hastens to Die*) — (may Allāh be pleased with them all) — and they were from the most excellent and virtuous Muslims and the reciters of the Qur'ān.

So they set out, and they stopped off at Bi'r Ma'ūnah (and it lies between the land of Banū 'Āmir and the rocky lava-plain of Banū Sulaym), and they sent forth from it Harām ibn Milhān, the brother of Umm Sulaym, with a letter from Allāh's Messenger (صَلَّىٰ ٱللَّٰهُ عَلَيْهِ وَسَلَّمَ) to the enemy of Allāh; 'Āmir ibn At-Tufayl. So he did not even look at it, but commanded that he be killed. So a man stabbed him with a spear and killed him. So as the blood spurted out he said: "I have succeeded, by the Lord of the Ka'bah!"[3]

The enemy of Allāh, 'Āmir, also called the (tribe of) Banū 'Āmir to fight against those who remained. However, they did not respond to him because of Abū Barā''s grant of protection. So he called the Banū Sulaym, and the clans of 'Usayyah, Ri'l, and Dhakwān responded to him, and they surrounded the Companions of Allāh's Messenger (صَلَّىٰ ٱللَّٰهُ عَلَيْهِ وَسَلَّمَ). So they fought until they were all killed (رَضِيَ ٱللَّٰهُ عَنْهُمْ) except for Ka'b ibn Zayd, from Banun-Najjār, who was later found and carried away injured

---

1 — (DB) Shaikh Al-Albānī said in his notes upon *Fiqhus-Sīrah* (p. 298): "Ibn Hishām reported it (2/114) from Ibn Is-hāq with a *'mursal'* chain which is *'sahīh'*. It is likewise reported by At-Tabarānī from Ibn Is-hāq, as occurs in *Al-Majma'* (6/128-129); and At-Tabarānī reported it also as a hadīth of Ka'b ibn Mālik (رَضِيَ ٱللَّٰهُ عَنْهُ) with its like. Al-Haythamī said: 'Its narrators are those of the *Sahīh*.'"

2 — (BJ)(SZ) Refer to *Sahīhul-Bukhārī* (no. 4088) and *Sahīh Muslim* (no. 677).

3 — (SH) Reported by Al-Bukhārī (no. 4091) and Muslim in abridged form (no. 677).

from amongst the dead. So he lived until he was killed on the day of the Trench (*Al-Khandaq*).

ʿAmr ibn Umayyah Ad-Damrī and Al-Mundhir ibn Muhammad ibn ʿUqbah were pasturing the camels of the Muslims, and they saw birds circling over the place of the incident. So Al-Mundhir ibn Muhammad went there and fought against the Mushrikūn until he was killed along with his Companions, and ʿAmr ibn Umayyah was taken captive. When he informed them that he was from (the tribe of) Mudar, ʿĀmir (Ibn At-Tufayl) lopped off his forelock and set him free from slavery — as he claimed — to fulfil a pledge he had made to his mother to free a slave.

ʿAmr ibn Umayyah then returned, and when he reached Al-Qarqarah, at the beginning of Al-Qanāt,[1] he stopped off beneath some shade. Two men from Banū Kilāb, or it is said: from Banū Sulaym, came and halted along with him there. Then whilst they slept, ʿAmr killed them both, thinking that he was achieving revenge for his companions. However, he later found out that they had received an agreement of peace and security from Allāh's Messenger (صَلَّى ٱللَّٰهُ عَلَيْهِ وَسَلَّمَ) which he was not aware of. Then when he arrived he informed Allāh's Messenger (صَلَّى ٱللَّٰهُ عَلَيْهِ وَسَلَّمَ) of what he had done, so he said: "You have killed two men for whom I shall pay blood money."[2]

So this was the reason for the expedition of Banun-Nadīr, as occurs in the *Sahīh*.[3]

Az-Zuhrī claimed that the expedition of Banun-Nadīr occurred six months after Badr, but this is not the case. Rather that which occurred six months after Badr was the expedition of Banū Qaynuqāʿ. As for Banun-Nadīr, then it occurred after Uhud; just as Quraydhah occurred after the Trench, and Khaybar occurred after Al-Hudaybiyah, and the

---

1 — [MK][MM] A wādī (dry riverbed) to the north of Al-Madīnah, running from east to west. It is to the south of Uhud.

2 — [SH] Reported by Ibn Is-hāq in *As-Sīrah* (3/867-869) (...) and it is *'mursal'* with a *'sahīh'* isnād.

3 — As mentioned by Al-Bukhārī in a chapter heading: *The Book of Military Expeditions (Al-Maghāzī): Chapter 14*

expedition against the Byzantines in the year of Tabūk came after the Conquest of Makkah.

Furthermore he (عَلَيْهِ ٱلسَّلَامُ) at the point of death, ordered the expulsion of the Jews and the Christians from the Arabian Peninsula.[1]

Chapter: The Expedition Of Banun-Nadīr

Allāh's Messenger (صَلَّىٰ ٱللَّهُ عَلَيْهِ وَسَلَّمَ) went out himself to Banun-Nadīr, to seek their assistance in paying the blood money for those two who were killed, because of the sworn-alliance between the two men and them. So they said: *'Yes.'*

So he (صَلَّىٰ ٱللَّهُ عَلَيْهِ وَسَلَّمَ), Abū Bakr, 'Umar, 'Alī, and a group of his Companions (رَضِيَ ٱللَّهُ عَنْهُمْ) sat beneath a wall of theirs. So they [i.e. the Jews of Banun-Nadīr] gathered secretly and said: *"Which man will throw this mill-stone down upon Muhammad and kill him?"*

So 'Amr ibn Jihāsh — may Allāh curse him — volunteered to do that. However, Allāh informed His Messenger of what they intended to do to him, so he (صَلَّىٰ ٱللَّهُ عَلَيْهِ وَسَلَّمَ) got up immediately from amongst his Companions, and did not stop until he entered Al-Madīnah. Then a man came, stating that he had seen him (صَلَّىٰ ٱللَّهُ عَلَيْهِ وَسَلَّمَ) entering within the walls of Al-Madīnah, so Abū Bakr and those with him got up and followed him.

So he (صَلَّىٰ ٱللَّهُ عَلَيْهِ وَسَلَّمَ) informed them of what Allāh had told him concerning the affair of the Jews, and he urged the people to fight against them. So he went out, and he left Ibn Umm Maktūm in charge of Al-Madīnah, and this was in (the month of) Rabī'ul-Awwal. He then besieged them for six nights from it.

---

1 — What is intended here is that the Non-Muslims are prevented from residing in Hijāz in particular and not the entire Arabian Peninsula. See Endnote 34 on page 461.

It was at this time that drinking intoxicants became forbidden;[1] this was mentioned by Ibn Hazm; however, I have not seen this being stated by anyone else besides him.

Meanwhile, ʿAbdullāh ibn Ubayy ibn Salūl and his companions from the Hypocrites sent a secret message to Banun-Nadīr, saying: *'We are with you: we will fight along with you, and if you are expelled, we will go out along with you.'* They were therefore deceived by them into having false hopes, and they retreated to their fortresses.

So he (ﷺ) commanded that their date palms be cut down and burnt.[2]

So then, they requested of Allāh's Messenger (ﷺ) that he should banish them, but spare their lives; and that they be allowed to carry away whatever their camels could carry, except for armour. So he accepted that from them.

So their elders, such as Huyayy ibn Akhtab and Sallām ibn Abil-Huqayq, departed with their families and wealth and went to Khaybar, which they took control of; and a group of them went to Shām (Palestine/Syria).

None of them accepted Islām except for two men, who were: Abū Saʿd ibn Wahb and Yāmīn ibn ʿUmayr ibn Kaʿb, who offered a reward for anyone who killed his paternal cousin ʿAmr ibn Jihāsh, because of his intending to make an attempt on the life of Allāh's Messenger (ﷺ). So these two retained their property.

---

1 — [SH] Ibn Is-hāq reported it in *As-Sīrah* (3/872-873: Ibn Hishām), saying: *"Yazīd ibn Rūmān narrated it to me"*, and its chain of narration is weak, as it has a break of two or more successive narrators.

2 — [BJ][SZ] As reported by Al-Bukhārī (no.4031) and Muslim (no.1746), as a hadīth of Ibn ʿUmar (رَضِيَ اللَّهُ عَنْهُمَا) who said: "Allāh's Messenger (ﷺ) burnt and cut down the date palms of Banun-Nadīr, at Al-Buwayrah, so there was sent down:

> مَا قَطَعْتُم مِّن لِّينَةٍ أَوْ تَرَكْتُمُوهَا قَائِمَةً عَلَىٰ أُصُولِهَا فَبِإِذْنِ اللَّهِ
>
> MEANING: 'Whatever you cut down of their date palms, or left standing upon their trunks, then it was by Allāh's command.'" — **SŪRAH AL-HASHR (59): 5**

Allāh's Messenger (صَلَّى ٱللَّهُ عَلَيْهِ وَسَلَّمَ) divided the property of the rest between the first Emigrants (Muhājirīn) exclusively, except that he gave something to Abū Dujānah and to Sahl ibn Hunayf — who were both from the Ansār — because of their being poor and needy.[1]

Furthermore, the property of Banun-Nadīr was *Fai'* (booty obtained without fighting) since the Muslims did not have to ride upon horses or camels to acquire it.[2]

Then concerning this expedition Allāh (the One free of all imperfections) sent down Sūratul-Hashr, and ʿAbdullāh ibn ʿAbbās (رَضِيَ ٱللَّهُ عَنْهُمَا) used to call it Sūrah Banin-Nadīr.[3]

Also, Allāh's Messenger (صَلَّى ٱللَّهُ عَلَيْهِ وَسَلَّمَ) supplicated, whilst standing in the Prayer, for one month against those who had killed the reciters: those killed at Bi'r Maʿūnah.

---

1 — [BJ][SZ] Reported by Abū Dāwūd (no. 3004) within a long hadīth concerning the events of Banun-Nadīr and its chain of narration is *'sahīh'*. However, it does not state the name of the two Companions.

2 — [SH] Meaning without fighting, combat or hardship. Rather, they walked to it on foot, and did not ride horses or camels, just as He (the Most High) said:

> وَمَا أَفَاءَ اللَّهُ عَلَىٰ رَسُولِهِ مِنْهُمْ فَمَا أَوْجَفْتُمْ عَلَيْهِ مِنْ خَيْلٍ وَلَا رِكَابٍ
>
> MEANING: "And whatever Allāh gave as booty to His Messenger from them, then you made no expedition for it upon horses or camels." — **Sūrah Al-Hashr (59): 6**

3 — [BJ][SZ] As occurs in *Sahīhul-Bukhārī* (no. 4029) and *Sahīh Muslim* (no. 3031).

Chapter: The Military Expedition of Dhātur-Riqā' – and it is the Expedition to Najd[1]

So he went out in Jumādal-Ūlā of the fourth year to attack (the tribes of) Muhārib and Banū Tha'labah ibn Sa'd ibn Ghatafān, and he left Abū Dharr Al-Ghifārī in charge of Al-Madīnah.[2]

So he proceeded until he reached Nakhl[3] and he met a force of Ghatafān, and they faced each other. However, no fighting took place between them, but he prayed the Fear Prayer that day — as mentioned by Ibn Is-hāq and others from the people of Sīrah.[4]

So this is problematic since there occurs in the narration of Ash-Shāfi'ī, Ahmad, and An-Nasā'ī from Abū Sa'īd; that Allāh's Messenger (صَلَّى ٱللَّهُ عَلَيْهِ وَسَلَّمَ) was prevented by the Mushrikūn on the day of the Trench from praying the Dhuhr, 'Asr, Maghrib, and 'Ishā' Prayers, so he prayed them all together, and that was before the Fear Prayer came down.[1]

They said: The Fear Prayer came down at 'Usfān, as was narrated by Abū 'Ayyāsh Az-Zuraqī who said: "We were with the Prophet (صَلَّى ٱللَّهُ عَلَيْهِ وَسَلَّمَ) at 'Usfān, and he prayed the Dhuhr Prayer there; and on that day Khālid ibn Al-Walīd was in charge of the Mushrikūn. So they said: 'We have found a time when they are inattentive.'

Then they said: 'They have another Prayer after this which is more beloved to them than their wealth and their children.'

---

1 — There is a disagreement about when this expedition occured, which is dicussed in *Al-Fat-h* — see ENDNOTE 35 ON PAGE 462.

2 — What is more correct is that it was left to 'Uthmān Ibn 'Affān, and Abū Dharr (رَضِيَ ٱللَّهُ عَنْهُ) narrates the reason why he was not deputised to that role in a beautiful narration which you can read in ENDNOTE 36 ON PAGE 462.

3 — [BJ][SZ] A place in Najd from the lands of Ghatafān.

4 — [SH] Reported by Ibn Is-hāq in *As-Sīrah* (3/885-886: Ibn Hishām) without a chain of narration.

1 — [BJ][SZ] *'Sahīh'*: Reported by Ash-Shāfi'ī in *Al-Umm* (1/75), and in *Al-Musnad* (1/196-197); and by Ahmad in *Al-Musnad* (3/25); and Nasā'ī (2/17) with a *'sahīh'* chain of narration.

[DB] Shaikh Al-Albānī said in *Sahīh Sunanin-Nasā'ī:* "*sahīh.*"

So it came down — meaning the Fear Prayer — between Dhuhr and 'Asr.

So he led us in the 'Asr Prayer, and we separated into two groups..."— and he mentioned the hadīth (in its entirety). It was reported by Imām Ahmad, Abū Dāwūd, and An-Nasā'ī.[1]

And from Abū Hurairah (رَضِيَ ٱللَّهُ عَنْهُ) who said: "Allāh's Messenger (صَلَّى ٱللَّهُ عَلَيْهِ وَسَلَّمَ) had camped at a place between Dajanān and 'Usfān,[2] and he had encircled the Mushrikūn. So the Mushrikūn said: *'They have a Prayer which is more beloved to them than their sons and their virgins, so unite and attack them all at once.'* So Jibrīl (عَلَيْهِ ٱلسَّلَامُ) came and ordered him to divide his Companions into two halves" — and he mentioned the complete hadīth. It was reported by An-Nasā'ī, and by At-Tirmidhī who said: "It is '*hasan sahīh*.'"[3]

It is also known, without any disagreement, that the expedition of 'Usfān occurred after the Trench, so this necessitates that Dhātur-Riqā' happened after it; indeed after Khaybar.[4]

This is supported by the fact that Abū Mūsā Al-Ash'arī and Abū Hurairah (رَضِيَ ٱللَّهُ عَنْهُمَا) were present on it.

As for Abū Mūsā Al-Ash'arī, then there occurs in the *Sahīhayn* from him that he was present on the expedition of Dhātur-Riqā', and that they wrapped pieces of cloth around their injured feet, and that it was named on account of this.[5]

---

1 — [BJ] [SZ] *'Sahīh'*: Reported by Ahmad (4/59-60), and Abū Dāwūd (no. 1236), and An-Nasā'ī (3/177-178) with a *'sahīh'* chain of narration.

[DB] Declared *'sahīh'* by Shaikh Al-Albānī in his *Sahīh Sunan Abī Dāwūd*.

2 — [BJ] [SZ] (Dajanān) is a mountain or a hill twenty-five miles from Makkah [*Mu'jamul-Buldān*]; and 'Usfān is a village between Makkah and Al-Madīnah.

3 — Reported by An-Nasā'ī (3/174), and At-Tirmidhī (no.3035). Declared *'sahīh'* by Shaikh Al-Albānī in *Sahīh Sunanit-Tirmidhī*.

4 — There is some disagreement about this point, but what is more correct is that it did indeed occur after Khaybar. See **Endnote 37 on page 462**.

5 — [BJ] [SZ] Reported by Al-Bukhārī (no.4128) and Muslim (no. 1816).

And as for Abū Hurairah, then Marwān ibn Al-Hakam said that he asked Abū Hurairah: "Did you pray the Fear prayer along with Allāh's Messenger (صَلَّىٱللَّهُعَلَيْهِوَسَلَّمَ)?"

So he said: "Yes."

He said: "When was that?"

He said: *"In the year of the expedition to Najd…"*—and he mentioned one form of the Fear Prayer. This was reported by Ahmad, Abū Dāwūd, and An-Nasā'ī.[1]

Also, some historians say that the Expedition of Dhātur-Riqā' occurred more than once, so one expedition took place before the Trench, and another took place after it.

I say: However, it would not be correct that he prayed the Fear Prayer during the first if the hadīth is authentic, which states that it became obligatory at 'Usfān.

They also mention, among the incidents that occurred on this expedition, the story of Jābir's camel and how he sold it to Allāh's Messenger.[2]

However, this is a subject for examination since it is reported that this occurred during the expedition of Tabūk,[3] except that what is mentioned here is more appropriate, since his father was killed at Uhud and had left behind (Jābir's) sisters, so he needed to marry someone quickly who could take care of them for him.[4]

And from them is a hadīth of Jābir also, with regard to the man whose wife they took as a captive, and who swore that he would spill the blood of the

---

1 — [BJ] [SZ] *'Sahīh'*: Reported by Ahmad (2/320), Abū Dāwūd (no. 1240), and An-Nasā'ī (3/173) with a *'sahīh'* chain of narration.

[DB] Declared *'sahīh'* by Shaikh Al-Albānī in *Sahīh Sunanin-Nasā'ī.*

2 — For the details of this narration, see Endnote 38 on page 463.

3 — For the details of the apparent weakness in this narration, see Endnote 39 on page 463.

4 — Al-Hāfidh Ibn Hajr holds this view of events and you can see his speech at Endnote 40 on page 463.

Companions of Muhammad (ﷺ). So he came during the night, and Allāh's Messenger (ﷺ) had assigned two men as lookouts for the Muslims, to guard against the Disbelievers; and they were ʿAbbād ibn Bishr and ʿAmmār ibn Yāsir (رضي الله عنهما). So the man fired an arrow at ʿAbbād, whilst he was standing in Prayer, so he pulled it out and did not break his Prayer. This happened three times, and he did not leave his Prayer until he said the Salutation. Then he alerted his companion who said: "Subhānallāh! (I declare Allāh free of all imperfections!) Why did you not alert me?"

He said: "I was reciting a certain Sūrah and I disliked to break it."[1]

Also from them is the narration concerning Ghawrath ibn Al-Hārith, who intended to kill Allāh's Messenger (ﷺ) whilst he was taking a mid-day nap beneath a tree. So he brandished his sword and wanted to strike him, but Allāh prevented him and his hand was held back. Then Allāh's Messenger (ﷺ) awoke from his sleep and called his Companions, who gathered around him. So he informed them about him, and of Ghawrath's attempting to kill him. In spite of all this, he (ﷺ) set him free, and pardoned him.[2]

So this occurred during the expedition of Dhātur-Riqāʿ, except that it was the one which happened after the Trench, as is shown by what they report in the two *Sahīhs*, from Jābir ibn ʿAbdillāh (رضي الله عنه) who said: "We were travelling along with Allāh's Messenger (ﷺ) until we came to Dhātur-Riqāʿ."

He said: "When we came to a shady tree we would leave it for Allāh's Messenger (ﷺ)."

---

1 — Declared *'hasan'* by Imām Al-Albānī — see **Endnote 41 on page 464** for more details.

2 — Reported by ʿAbd Ibn Humayd in his *Musnad* (3/48-49/ no. 1094: *Muntakhab*) Ahmad (3/364-365 & 390), At-Tahāwī in *Sharh Maʿāniyyil-Āthār* (1/315), Abū Yaʿlā in his *Musnad* (3/312-313/1778), Ibn Hibbān in his *Sahīh* (7/138-139/no. 2883; *Al-Ihsān*) (...) by way of Abū ʿAwānah: Abū Bishr narrated to us; from Sulaymān ibn Qays: from Jābir with it. This chain of narration is *'sahīh'*, its narrators are reliable, and it has been criticised with that which is not a justification for criticism.

He said: "So a man from the Mushrikūn came whilst the sword of Allāh's Messenger (صَلَّىٱللَّهُعَلَيْهِوَسَلَّمَ) was suspended upon a tree. So he took the sword and brandished it, and said to Allāh's Messenger (صَلَّىٱللَّهُعَلَيْهِوَسَلَّمَ): *'Do you Fear me?!'*

He said: *'No.'*

He said: *'Then who will protect you from me?'*

He said: *'Allāh.'*"

He [Jābir] said: "So the Companions of Allāh's Messenger (صَلَّىٱللَّهُعَلَيْهِوَسَلَّمَ) threatened him, and he put the sword back in its sheath, and hung it up."

He said: "So the call to Prayer was given, and he led one group in two rakʿahs, then they retreated; and he led the other group in two rakʿahs."

So it was four rakʿahs for Allāh's Messenger, and two rakʿahs for the people; and the wording is that of Muslim.[1]

Chapter: Badr of the Appointment (Badrul-Mawʿid)

When departing on the day of Uhud, Abū Sufyān called out: "You have an appointment with us at Badr next year."

So Allāh's Messenger (صَلَّىٱللَّهُعَلَيْهِوَسَلَّمَ) commanded one of his Companions to respond to him with: "Yes."

So when it was Shaʿbān of this year, Allāh's Messenger (صَلَّىٱللَّهُعَلَيْهِوَسَلَّمَ) went out, and arrived at Badr for the appointment. He left in charge of Al-Madīnah ʿAbdullāh ibn ʿAbdillāh ibn Ubayy. He remained there for eight nights, then he returned, and did not encounter any fighting. This was because Abū Sufyān had come out with Quraysh, but whilst upon the way they decided to go back, on account of a drought that they were suffering from that year. So they went back. So this expedition is called the 'The Third Badr', and 'Badr of the Appointment'.

---

1 — Reported by Al-Bukhārī (no. 4136) and Muslim (no. 843).

Chapter: The Expedition of Dūmatul-Jandal

He (صَلَّىٱللَّهُعَلَيْهِوَسَلَّمَ) went out to Dūmatul-Jandal[1] in Rabīʿul-Awwal of the 149
fifth year. Then after travelling some distance he came back, and did not encounter any fighting. He had left Sibāʿ ibn ʿUrfutah in charge of Al-Madīnah.

---

1 — Ibnul-Qayyim said in *Zādul-Maʿād* (3/255): "Allāh's Messenger (صَلَّىٱللَّهُعَلَيْهِوَسَلَّمَ) went out to it in Rabīʿul-Awwal of the fifth year. This was because it reached him that an army, which wanted to approach Al-Madīnah, had gathered there. It is at a distance of fifteen nights from Al-Madīnah, and of five nights from Damascus."

CHAPTER:

Comprising an Abridgement of the Battle of the Trench (Al-Khandaq)[1]

During which Allāh tried and tested His believing servants, and shook them; and He planted true Faith (*Īmān*) firmly in the hearts of His beloved, obedient servants; and He made manifest that which the people of Hypocrisy sought to conceal, and He exposed them and rebuked them. Then He sent down His Aid, and gave His Servant victory, and He alone defeated the allied enemies (*Al-Ahzāb*). He gave honour to His army and threw back the Disbelievers, and He protected the Believers from the evil of their plots; and that was through His Favour and Beneficence.

He also forbade and prevented them, with both His Legislative and His Universal Decree[2] from coming out to make an attack upon the believers after it.[3] Rather, He caused them to be defeated, and He caused His Party to be those who overcome, and all praise is for Allāh the Lord of the whole of creation.

---

1 — [SH] Al-Bukhārī said: "Chapter: The Battle of the Trench (Al-Khandaq) and it is Al-Ahzāb (The Allied Enemies)."

Al-Hāfidh Ibn Hajr said in *Fat-hul-Bārī*: "Meaning that it has two names, and it is just as he said (...). And concerning this event Allāh (the Most High) sent down the first part of Sūratul-Ahzāb."

2 — For a brief explanation of these two types of Allāh's Decree, see **Endnote 42 on page 464**.

3 — [BJ] [SZ] Al-Bukhārī reported (no. 4110), as a hadīth of Sulaymān ibn Surad (رَضِيَ اللَّهُ عَنْهُ) who said: "I heard the Prophet (صَلَّى اللَّهُ عَلَيْهِ وَسَلَّمَ) say, when the allied enemies were driven away from him: *'From now onwards we will go out to attack them, and they will not come to attack us. We shall proceed against them.'*"

It occurred in the fifth year, in Shawwāl of that year, upon what is most correct from the two sayings of the scholars of military campaigns and expeditions.[1]

The evidence for this is that there is no disagreement concerning the fact that Uhud occurred in Shawwāl of the third year; and what the scholars of military expeditions have mentioned has already preceded, concerning Abū Sufyān arranging to meet them in the following year at Badr, and that he (ﷺ) went out to meet them. However, they failed to turn up because of the drought that year in their land. So they delayed coming until this year.

Abū Muhammad ibn Hazm Al-Andalusī said in his *Maghāzī*: *"This is the saying of the scholars of military expeditions,"* — then he said: *"But what is correct, about which there is no doubt, is that it occurred in the fourth year."*

This was also the saying of Mūsā ibn 'Uqbah. Then Ibn Hazm used as evidence the hadīth of Ibn 'Umar: "I was presented before the Prophet (ﷺ) on the day of Uhud, when I was fourteen years old, and he did not permit me (to fight); and I was presented before him on the day of the Trench, when I was fifteen years old, and he permitted me,"[2] — and (Ibn Hazm commenting upon this) said: "So it is correct that between the two there was but a single year."

I say: This hadīth is reported in the two *Sahīhs,* however it does not prove that which he claimed, since the condition he (ﷺ) applied for permission to fight was attainment at the age of fifteen. So he did not permit those who had not reached it, but permitted those who had reached it. So since Ibn 'Umar was not amongst those who had reached that age on the day of Uhud he did not permit him. But when he had attained that age on the day of the Trench he permitted him. However, this does not negate his having exceeded it by a year, or two years, or three, or more than that. So it is as if he had said: *'I was presented to him*

---

1 — [SH] The author (رَحِمَهُ ٱللَّهُ) said in *Al-Bidāyah wan-Nihāyah* (6/9): "This was stated by Ibn Is-hāq, 'Urwah ibn Az-Zubayr, Qatādah, Al-Bayhaqī, and others from the earlier and later scholars."

2 — [BJ][SZ] Reported by Al-Bukhārī (no. 2664), and Muslim (no. 1868).

on the day of the Trench and I was an adult', — or: *'one of those suitable for war.'*

It has also been said: "On the day of Uhud, he was at the beginning of his fourteenth year, and on the day of the Trench, he was at the end of his fifteenth year."

However, this is open to question, and the first answer is seen to be stronger if one carefully considers and is fair, and Allāh knows best.

The reason for the battle of the Trench was that a group of Jews of Banun-Nadīr, whom he (صَلَّى ٱللَّهُ عَلَيْهِ وَسَلَّمَ) had banished from Al-Madīnah and sent to Khaybar, as we have already mentioned, and they were their nobles — such as Sallām ibn Abil-Huqayq, Sallām ibn Mishkam, Kinānah ibn Ar-Rabīʿ, and others — went out to the Quraysh in Makkah and incited them to wage war upon Allāh's Messenger (صَلَّى ٱللَّهُ عَلَيْهِ وَسَلَّمَ). They promised that they would aid them, so they responded to them. Then they went off to (the tribe of) Ghatafān and called them, and they responded also. So the Quraysh came out, and their leader was Abū Sufyān ibn Harb; and the leader of Ghatafān was ʿUyainah ibn Hisn. Altogether, they numbered about ten thousand men.

So when Allāh's Messenger (صَلَّى ٱللَّهُ عَلَيْهِ وَسَلَّمَ) heard of their coming he ordered the Muslims to dig a (defensive) trench (Khandaq) to prevent the Mushrikūn from entering Al-Madīnah. This was based upon the advice of Salmān Al-Fārisī (رَضِيَ ٱللَّهُ عَنْهُ). So the Muslims worked on it, hastening to complete it before the Disbelievers could attack. During its digging a number of distinct signs were seen,[1] an explanation of which would be lengthy, and clear proofs of Prophethood that are *'mutawātir'* (reported by large numbers of narrators at every stage of transmission.) When it had been completed, the Mushrikūn arrived and positioned themselves around Al-Madīnah, just as Allāh (the Most High) said:

إِذْ جَاءُوكُم مِّن فَوْقِكُمْ وَمِنْ أَسْفَلَ مِنكُمْ

---

1 — DB Amongst the miracles which occurred during the digging of the Trench, is what is mentioned in the narrations reported by Al-Bukhārī (nos. 4101 & 4102).

MEANING: "When they came upon you from above you and from below you." — **Sūrah Al-Ahzāb (33):10**

Allāh's Messenger (صَلَّى ٱللَّٰهُ عَلَيْهِ وَسَلَّمَ) went out and took up a defensive position behind the Trench, along with — in the correct saying — three thousand of the inhabitants of Al-Madīnah.

Ibn Is-hāq claimed that he only had seven hundred along with him, but this is a mistake that refers to Uhud, and Allāh knows best.[1]

So they placed their backs to (Mount) Sal',[2] and he commanded that the women and the children be placed in the forts of Al-Madīnah, and he placed in charge of it Ibn Umm Maktūm (رَضِيَ ٱللَّٰهُ عَنْهُ).

Meanwhile, Huyayy ibn Akhtab An-Nadrī went to Banū Quraydhah. So he met Ka'b ibn Asad, their chief, and kept persuading him until he broke the covenant which existed between him and Allāh's Messenger (صَلَّى ٱللَّٰهُ عَلَيْهِ وَسَلَّمَ); and Ka'b joined forces with the Mushrikūn to fight against Allāh's Messenger (صَلَّى ٱللَّٰهُ عَلَيْهِ وَسَلَّمَ). So they became overjoyed at that.

Allāh's Messenger (صَلَّى ٱللَّٰهُ عَلَيْهِ وَسَلَّمَ) sent the two Sa'ds: Ibn Mu'ādh, and Ibn 'Ubādah, and Khawāt ibn Jubayr, and 'Abdullāh ibn Rawāhah to find out for him whether Banū Quraydhah had indeed broken the covenant or not. So when they approached them they found them showing open hostility and treachery. So each side reviled the other, and the Jews — may Allāh's curse be upon them — spoke ill of Allāh's Messenger (صَلَّى ٱللَّٰهُ عَلَيْهِ وَسَلَّمَ). So Sa'd ibn Mu'ādh reviled them, and they departed and left them. He (صَلَّى ٱللَّٰهُ عَلَيْهِ وَسَلَّمَ) had already ordered them that if it was the case that they had broken their agreement, then they were not to mention that openly, and so adversely affect the morale of the Muslims and cause listlessness, but rather they should indicate it by indirect speech. So when they came to him he said: "What lies behind you?"

---

1 — [BJ][SZ][SH] This is what Al-Hāfidh ibn Kathīr said, and Ibnul-Qayyim states the same in *Zādul-Ma'ād*. However, that which occurs in Ibn Is-hāq's *Sīrah* (3/243) is his statement that they numbered three thousand.

2 — [SH] There occurs in *Mu'jamul-Buldān* (3/236): "Sal' is a mountain by the market place of Al-Madīnah."

So they said: *"Adal and Al-Qārah!"*—by which they meant their treachery towards the Companions at Ar-Rajīʿ. So the Muslims took this as a serious affair, and the matter became severe, and the danger became great. So they were just as Allāh (the Most High) said:

> هُنَالِكَ ابْتُلِيَ الْمُؤْمِنُونَ وَزُلْزِلُوا زِلْزَالًا شَدِيدًا
>
> MEANING: "Then the Believers were tried and were shaken with a mighty shaking." — **Sūrah Al-Ahzāb (33):11**

Hypocrisy then appeared and increased, and some of Banū Hārithah sought permission of Allāh's Messenger (ﷺ) to return to Al-Madīnah, on account of their houses. They said that they were exposed, since no barrier existed between them and the enemy. Also, Banū Salimah almost gave up hope, but then Allāh made both groups firm.

The Mushrikūn besieged Allāh's Messenger (ﷺ) for a month, but there was no fighting between them because of the barrier of the Trench, by means of which Allāh kept them apart; except that some riders from Quraysh, from them ʿAmr ibn ʿAbd Wudd Al-ʿĀmirī and a group along with him, came towards the Trench. So when they stood over it they said: *'This is a stratagem unknown to the Arabs.'* Then they searched for a narrow part of the trench, and they leapt down and crossed it. So their horses led them to the salty ground between the Trench and Salʿ, and they called for a single-handed combat. So ʿAlī ibn Abī Tālib went forward to fight ʿAmr ibn ʿAbd Wudd, and he fought him and Allāh killed him at his hands. On that day, he was an old man of over a hundred years old, and in the days of Ignorance, no one could challenge him in bravery.

As for the others, then they fled back to their people from the direction in which they had come. So this was the beginning of the humiliation that Allāh gave to them.

At that battle the call of recognition of the Muslims was; ***'Hā-Mīm. They will not be aided!'***[1]

When the situation became prolonged for the Muslims, Allāh's Messenger (صَلَّى ٱللَّٰهُ عَلَيْهِ وَسَلَّمَ) desired to make peace with 'Uyainah ibn Hisn and Al-Hārith ibn 'Awf, the two leaders of Ghatafān, upon the basis that they should receive one third of the fruits of Al-Madīnah, in return for their departing along with their people. So negotiations to persuade them were taking place but the affair had not been concluded. So he (صَلَّى ٱللَّٰهُ عَلَيْهِ وَسَلَّمَ) consulted the two Sa'ds concerning that, and they both said:

> "O Messenger of Allāh! If Allāh has commanded you with this then we will hear and obey; but if it is something which you are arranging for our benefit, then we and those people used to be upon committing Shirk with Allāh, and upon the worship of the idols. Yet they had no hope of eating any of its fruits unless they were being entertained as guests or they bought them. So now that Allāh has given us nobility with Islām, and guided us to it, and given us honour by means of you and it, shall we now hand over our wealth to them? By Allāh, we shall give them nothing except the sword!"

So he (صَلَّى ٱللَّٰهُ عَلَيْهِ وَسَلَّمَ) said: *"It is something I was arranging for your benefit"*— and he held their view (رَضِيَ ٱللَّٰهُ عَنْهُمَا) to be sound, and he did not do anything from that.[2]

Then Allāh — the One free of all imperfections, and all praise is for Him — brought about an affair with which He caused them to have mutual distrust and by which He broke apart their unity.

---

1 — BJ SZ *Sahīh*: Reported by An-Nasā'ī in *Al-Kubrā* (no. 8861 & 10453), and its chain of narration contains Sharīk ibn 'Abdillāh. However it is reported by Abū Dāwūd (no. 2597), An-Nasā'ī (6/361), and At-Tirmidhī (no. 1682) with a *'sahīh'* chain of narration.

2 — SH Reported by Ibn Is-hāq in *As-Sīrah* (3/903-904: Ibn Hishām) who said: "'Āsim ibn 'Umar ibn Qatādah and one whom I do not suspect narrated to me: From Az-Zuhrī with it. Its chain of narration is weak (*da'īf*) as it is *'mursal'*."

So Nuʿaym ibn Masʿūd ibn ʿĀmir Al-Ghatafānī (رَضِيَ اللَّهُ عَنْهُ) came to the Prophet (صَلَّى اللَّهُ عَلَيْهِ وَسَلَّمَ) and said: "O Messenger of Allāh! I have accepted Islām so order me with whatever you wish."

So he (صَلَّى اللَّهُ عَلَيْهِ وَسَلَّمَ) said:

> "You are only one man, so cause them to distrust each other and leave us if you are able to, for war is trickery."[1]

So he went immediately to Banū Quraydhah, and he had been a companion of theirs in the days of Ignorance, and entered upon them, and they were not aware of his Islām. So he said: "O Banū Quraydhah! You have waged war upon Muhammad, but as soon as the Quraysh gain an opportunity, they are going to return to their land. They will leave you to Muhammad, and he will then take revenge upon you."

They said: "Then what are we to do, O Nuʿaym?"

He said: "Do not associate with them in fighting unless they give you (some of their men) as hostages."

They said: "You have given excellent advice!"

Then he went off to the Quraysh, and said to Abū Sufyān and to them: "Are you aware of my affection for you and my sincerity towards you?"

So they said: "Yes."

He said: "The Jews have started to regret what they have done regarding their breaking their agreement with Muhammad and his companions, and they have sent a message to him that they are going to take hostages from amongst you, and then hand them over to him. Then they are going to aid him against you!"

Then he went to his own people (the tribe of) Ghatafān and said the like of that to them.

So on the night prior to Saturday in Shawwāl, they [i.e. Quraysh] sent a message to the Jews, saying: "We are not in a land suitable for us to

---

1 — For more elaboration regarding the statement *'War is trickery,'* see **Endnote 43 on page 466**.

remain in it, so come out with us in the morning and let us put an end to this man."

So the Jews sent a reply to them: "Today is the day of Saturday and furthermore we will not join you in fighting until you send some hostages to us."

So when the messengers came to them with that message the Quraysh said: "By Allāh! Nuʿaym ibn Masʿūd spoke the truth to us!"

So they sent the message to the Jews: *"By Allāh! We will not send a single person to you. So come out along with us!"* So Banū Quraydhah said: *"By Allāh! Nuʿaym has spoken the truth"*—and they refused to fight along with them.

Furthermore, Allāh (the Mighty and Majestic) sent against the Quraysh and those with them an army (of Angels) and a strong wind, which shook them. Nothing of theirs remained upright. So their tents, their tent-ropes, their cooking pots and everything else could not withstand (the wind). When they saw that, they departed that same night.

Also, he (صَلَّى ٱللَّهُ عَلَيْهِ وَسَلَّمَ) sent Hudhayfah ibn Al-Yamān to find out their news for him, so he found them just as we have described.

He also saw Abū Sufyān warming his back against a fire, and if Hudhayfah had wished, he could have killed him. Then he came back to Allāh's Messenger (صَلَّى ٱللَّهُ عَلَيْهِ وَسَلَّمَ) during the night and informed him that they were departing.[1]

So when he entered the morning Allāh's Messenger (صَلَّى ٱللَّهُ عَلَيْهِ وَسَلَّمَ) went into Al-Madīnah and the people laid down their arms. So Jibrīl (عَلَيْهِ ٱلسَّلَامُ) came to Allāh's Messenger (صَلَّى ٱللَّهُ عَلَيْهِ وَسَلَّمَ) whilst he was taking a bath in the apartment of Umm Salamah and said: *"Have you laid down your arms?*

1 — Hudhaifah (رَضِيَ ٱللَّهُ عَنْهُ) tells the story of the cold and bitter night that he was sent out for reconnaisance — read his words at **Endnote 44 on page 467**.

As for us, then we have not laid down our arms yet. Go out to those people" — meaning Banū Quraydhah.[1]

Chapter: Containing a Mention of the Expedition of Banū Quraydhah

So he (صَلَّى ٱللَّٰهُ عَلَيْهِ وَسَلَّمَ) immediately went out towards them, and he commanded that no one should pray the ʿAsr Prayer, and its time had already begun, except at Banū Quraydhah.

So the Muslims went off in successive groups; and some of them prayed the ʿAsr Prayer on the way, saying: *"Allāh's Messenger (صَلَّى ٱللَّٰهُ عَلَيْهِ وَسَلَّمَ) did not intend from us that we should leave the Prayer, rather he wanted us to proceed quickly."* Others, however, did not pray until they reached Banū Quraydhah and the sun had set.

So he (صَلَّى ٱللَّٰهُ عَلَيْهِ وَسَلَّمَ) did not rebuke either of the two groups.[2]

Ibn Hazm said:[3] "And these were the ones who attained what is correct; whereas the others made a mistake, but are still rewarded; and Allāh knows that if we had been there then we would not have prayed the ʿAsr Prayer except at Banū Quraydhah, even if that had been some days later."

I say: As for Ibn Hazm then he is excused since he was one of the eminent ones of the Dhāhirīs, and so he was unable to diverge from this text.

However, holding one of these actions to be more correct than the other is a matter requiring examination, since he (صَلَّى ٱللَّٰهُ عَلَيْهِ وَسَلَّمَ) did not rebuke

---

1 — [SH] Reported with this wording by Imām Ahmad (6/131 & 280), and ʿAbd ibn Humayd in his *Musnad* (3/225/no. 1486: *Muntakhab*) through two chains of narration from Hammād ibn Salamah: from Hishām ibn ʿUrwah: from his father: from ʿĀʾishah, with it.

This chain of narration is authentic to the standard of Muslim. It is also reported by Al-Bukhārī in his *Sahīh* (no. 4117 & 4122) and Muslim in his *Sahīh* (no.1769) through different chains of narration from Hishām, with its like.

2 — [BJ][SZ] Reported by Al-Bukhārī (no. 4119) and Muslim (no. 1770) as a hadīth of Ibn ʿUmar (رَضِيَ ٱللَّٰهُ عَنْهُمَا).

3 — [SH] In *Jawāmiʿus-Sīratin-Nabawiyyah* (p.152).

either of the two groups. So those who declare every *'mujtahid'*[1] to be correct, then upon their saying, both attained what is correct and there is no declaring one to be more correct than the other. Whereas the one who says that correctness will be attained by one side only — and this is the truth about which there can be no doubt or disputing, because it has many proofs in the Book and the Sunnah — then upon his saying, it must certainly be the case that one of the two groups will receive two rewards for attaining the correctness, whereas for the other group there will be one reward.

So we say (and successful attainment of correctness is granted by Allāh) those who prayed the 'Asr Prayer in its due time gained the success of coming first since they complied with his (صَلَّى ٱللَّهُ عَلَيْهِ وَسَلَّمَ) command to hasten to the Jihād, and they performed the Prayer in its due time — especially since it was the 'Asr Prayer, which Allāh (the Perfect) has emphasized careful observance of in His Book, in His saying:

> حَافِظُوا عَلَى الصَّلَوَاتِ وَالصَّلَاةِ الْوُسْطَىٰ
>
> MEANING: "Be constant upon observance of the Prayers, and upon the Middle Prayer." — **SŪRAH AL-BAQARAH (2):238**

And it (the Middle Prayer) is the 'Asr Prayer, upon the correct and certain saying — if Allāh wills — from amongst the ten and odd sayings, whose careful observance is mentioned in the Sunnah.

So if it is said: At that time it was permissible to delay the Prayer for Jihād, just as he (صَلَّى ٱللَّهُ عَلَيْهِ وَسَلَّمَ) delayed the 'Asr and the Maghrib Prayer on the day of the Trench, because of preoccupation with the Jihād; and the Dhuhr Prayer also, as occurs in a hadīth reported by An-Nasā'ī through two chains of narration.[2]

---

1 — i.e. the scholar who strives to extract the legislated ruling from the texts of the Legislation: *Kitābul-'Ilm* of Shaikh Muhammad ibn Sālih Al-'Uthaymīn (p. 176-177).

2 — [SH] Reported by An-Nasā'ī in *Al-Mujtabā* (2/17) and in *Al-Kubrā* (no. 1625), and by Abū Dāwūd At-Tayālisī in his *Musnad* (no. 2345) [...] by way of Ibn Abū Dhi'b: from Sa'īd Al-Maqburī: from 'Abdur-Rahmān ibn Abī Sa'īd Al-Khudrī; from his father [...]: This chain of narration is *'sahīh'*, its narrators are reliable.

Then the response is: Even if we were to accept this, and that he did not leave it due to forgetfulness that day, then still it grieved him, since when 'Umar ibn Al-Khattāb (رَضِيَٱللَّهُعَنْهُ) said to him: "O Messenger of Allāh! I have not been able to perform the 'Asr Prayer until the sun is almost setting!"

Then he said: "By Allāh! I have not prayed it either."[1]

So this gives the impression that he (صَلَّىٱللَّهُعَلَيْهِوَسَلَّمَ) had forgotten about it because of what he was preoccupied with, as occurs in the two *Sahīhs* from 'Alī (رَضِيَٱللَّهُعَنْهُ) who said: Allāh's Messenger (صَلَّىٱللَّهُعَلَيْهِوَسَلَّمَ) said on the day of the Allied Enemies (*Al-Ahzāb*):

> "They have preoccupied us from the Middle Prayer: The 'Asr prayer. May Allāh fill their bellies and their graves with fire!"[2]

So, in summary, those who prayed the 'Asr Prayer upon the way brought the evidences together and understood the meaning, so they receive the reward twice over; whereas the others were observing his specific command, so they have one reward — may Allāh be pleased with all of them and cause them to be pleased.

Allāh's Messenger (صَلَّىٱللَّهُعَلَيْهِوَسَلَّمَ) gave the battle-flag that day to 'Alī ibn Abī Tālib (رَضِيَٱللَّهُعَنْهُ),[3] and he left Ibn Umm Maktūm in charge of Al-Madīnah.[4]

He set up camp at the forts of Banū Quraydhah, and he besieged them for twenty-five nights.

Their chief, Ka'b ibn Asad, presented three choices to them: either they should submit and enter along with Muhammad into his Religion;

---

1 — [BJ][SZ] Reported by Al-Bukhārī (no.596) and Muslim (no. 631) as a hadīth of Jābir ibn 'Abdillāh (رَضِيَٱللَّهُعَنْهُمَا).

2 — [BJ][SZ] Reported by Al-Bukhārī (no. 6396) and Muslim (no. 627) .

3 — [SH] Ibn Is-hāq mentioned it in *As-Sīrah* (3/913: Ibn Hishām), and the author quoted it from him, also, in *Al-Bidāyah wan-Nihāyah* (6/76) — without a chain of narration.

4 — [SH] Ibn Is-hāq reported it in *As-Sīrah* (3/913), saying: *"Az-Zuhrī narrated to me..."* and he mentioned the story, which contained this part.

or they should kill their offspring, and go out on horseback and fight until they were all killed or escaped, and then acquire new children and wives; or otherwise that they should make a sudden attack upon Allāh's Messenger (ﷺ) and his Companions, on Saturday, when the Muslims would feel secure from their evil. However, they refused to accept any of these from him.

Huyayy ibn Akhtab had also entered the fortress along with them when the Quraysh departed. He had previously promised them this in order to persuade them to break their covenant. So now they began abusing Allāh's Messenger (ﷺ), and they caused his Companions to hear that. Allāh's Messenger (ﷺ) wanted to address them, but ʿAlī (رضي الله عنه) said to him: *"Do not approach them, O Messenger of Allāh,"* — for fear that he would hear something from them. So he said: "If they were to see me, they would not say anything."

So when they saw him none of them were able to say anything.[1]

Then he (ﷺ) sent Abū Lubābah ibn ʿAbdil-Mundhir Al-Awsī to them, since they were confederates of the Aws. So when they saw him they stood in front of him, weeping: their men and their women, and they said: "O Abū Lubābah! What do you see that we should do? Shall we submit to the judgement of Muhammad?"

So he said: *"Yes"*, and he indicated with his hand towards his throat, meaning that it would result in their slaughter. He immediately regretted this action and got up in haste. He did not return to Allāh's Messenger (ﷺ), but instead came to the mosque in Al-Madīnah and tied himself to one of the pillars of the mosque; and he swore an oath that no one would set him free except Allāh's Messenger (ﷺ) with his own hand, and that he would never again enter the territory of Banū Quraydhah.

---

1 — [SH] Mūsā ibn ʿUqbah reported it in his *Maghāzī*, as occurs in *Al-Bidāyah wan-Nihāyah* (5/76-78), and Al-Bayhaqī reported it from him in *Dalāʾilun-Nubuwwah* (4/11-14) from Az-Zuhrī with it. I say: This is *'mursal'* with a *'sahīh'* chain of narration.

It is also reported by Al-Bayhaqī (4/14) with a *'hasan'* chain of narration from ʿUrwah ibn Az-Zubayr with it in *'mursal'* form. Ibn Is-hāq also mentions it in his *Sīrah* (3/914-915) without a chain of narration.

So when this reached Allāh's Messenger (ﷺ) he said: *"Leave him until Allāh accepts his repentance."* So this affair continued until Allāh accepted his repentance (رَضِيَ اللَّهُ عَنْهُ).[1]

Then Banū Quraydhah surrendered and submitted to the judgement of Allāh's Messenger (ﷺ).

On that same night Tha'labah and Usayd, the two sons of Sa'yah, and Asad ibn 'Ubayd accepted Islām — and they were a group from (the clan of) Banū Hadl, from the tribe of the paternal uncles of Quraydhah and An-Nadīr. Also that night, 'Amr ibn Su'dā Al-Quradhī departed and went off, and it is not known where he went to, and he had refused to join them in breaking their covenant.

So when they surrendered and accepted his (ﷺ) judgement, the Aws said: "O Messenger of Allāh! You treated Banū Qaynuqā' as you know, and they were the confederates of our brothers the Khazraj. Whereas these are our confederates."

So he said: "Will you not be satisfied that a man from amongst you should pass judgement regarding them?"

---

1 — SH Reported by Ibn Is-hāq in *As-Sīrah* (3/914-915: Ibn Hishām) and from him by Al-Bayhaqī in *Ad-Dalā'il* (4/15). He said: "My father, Is-hāq ibn Yasār narrated to me: from Ma'bad ibn Ka'b ibn Mālik Al-Ansārī, with a longer wording."

I say: This is *'mursal'* with a *'sahīh'* chain of narration. The second part: the story of Abū Lubābah has witnesses, from them: (a report) from 'Ā'ishah (رَضِيَ اللَّهُ عَنْهَا) reported by Ibn Abī Shaybah in *Al-Musannaf* (no. 18643), Ahmad in his *Musnad* (6/141-142), ibn Sa'd in *At-Tabāqātul-Kubrā* (3/421-432), and Ibn Hibbān in his *Sahīh* (no. 7028: *Ihsān*) by way of Muhammad ibn 'Amr: from his father: from his grandfather: from 'Ā'ishah with it.

I say: This is a *'hasan'* chain when used as a witness and a supporting narration; 'Amr ibn 'Alqamah is *'maqbūl'* (acceptable is supported) as occurs in *At-Taqrīb*. It has a further witness from a *'mursal'* narration of Qatādah reported by Sa'īd ibn Mansūr in his *Sunan* (no. 987). [...]

And a third witness from a *'mursal'* narration of Mūsā ibn 'Uqbah, reported by Al-Bayhaqī in *Ad-Dalā'il* (4/12-14)[...] So in summary the hadīth is *'sahīh'* due to its supporting narrations, and Allāh knows best. (See: *As-Sahīhah* (no. 67) of Shaikh Al-Albānī).

So they said: "Yes indeed!"

He said: "Then that is for Saʿd ibn Muʿādh."

At that time, he had been wounded in the medial vein of his forearm, and Allāh's Messenger (صَلَّى ٱللَّهُ عَلَيْهِ وَسَلَّمَ) had set up a tent for him in the mosque so that he would be close by, so that he would be able to visit him whilst he was ill. So he (صَلَّى ٱللَّهُ عَلَيْهِ وَسَلَّمَ) sent for him and he was brought, and they had seated him upon a donkey. His brothers from the Aws were around him, encircling him, and were saying: "O Abū ʿAmr! Treat our allies well!"

So when they persisted with him he said: *"It is time for Saʿd that he should not be distracted for Allāh's sake by the blame of anyone!"* So some of the men from his people went off to Banū ʿAbdil-Ash-hal announcing to them that it was the end of Banū Quraydhah. So when he came close to Allāh's Messenger, he (صَلَّى ٱللَّهُ عَلَيْهِ وَسَلَّمَ) said: "Stand up to your chief."[1]

So the Muslims stood up to him and said: "O Saʿd! Allāh's Messenger (صَلَّى ٱللَّهُ عَلَيْهِ وَسَلَّمَ) has appointed you to pass judgement upon Banū Quraydhah."

So he said: "Do you agree to bind yourselves by Allāh's covenant that you will accept the judgement which I give?"

They said: "Yes."

He said: "And it will be binding upon the one who is over here?"

And he indicated in the direction of Allāh's Messenger (صَلَّى ٱللَّهُ عَلَيْهِ وَسَلَّمَ) out of respect for him. So Allāh's Messenger (صَلَّى ٱللَّهُ عَلَيْهِ وَسَلَّمَ) said: "Yes."

---

1 — [DB] Shaikh Al-Albānī said concerning the *isnād* of Imām Ahmad's report of the hadīth in his *Musnad* (6/141-142) with the wording: *"Stand up to your chief and help him to get down"* — "I say: And this is a *'hasan'* chain of narration" — and he said concerning this wording: "It has become well-known to use this hadīth as evidence that it is legislated to stand up for a person who enters. However, if you carefully consider the context of the incident then it will become clear to you that this is a baseless argument from many angles. The strongest of them is his (صَلَّى ٱللَّهُ عَلَيْهِ وَسَلَّمَ) saying: *'And help him to get down,'* for it is a decisive text proving that the command to stand up to Saʿd was in order that they should help him down on account of his ailment. This is why Al-Hāfidh [Ibn Hajr] said: *'This addition destroys seeking to use the story of Saʿd as a proof for the standing about which there is disagreement.'"* (*As-Sahīhah*: 1/1/146, no. 67)

So Sa'd said: "I pass judgement upon them that their fighters should be killed, and their wives and children should be taken captive."

So Allāh's Messenger (صَلَّى ٱللَّهُ عَلَيْهِ وَسَلَّمَ) said:

> "You have passed judgement upon them with the Judgement of Allāh, from above seven heavens."

So Allāh's Messenger (صَلَّى ٱللَّهُ عَلَيْهِ وَسَلَّمَ) commanded that those who had grown pubic hair from amongst them should be killed, and those who had not grown pubic hair should be left.[1]

So their heads were struck off in the trenches that had been dug where the market place of Al-Madīnah is today — it is said: between seven and eight hundred.

None of their women were killed except one woman. She was Banānah the wife of Al-Hakam Al-Quraydhī, and she had thrown a millstone down upon the head of Suwayd ibn As-Sāmit[2] and killed him — may Allāh curse her.[3]

He distributed the wealth of Banū Quraydhah amongst the Muslims: one who went to fight on foot received a single share, and one who fought on horseback received three shares; and amongst the Muslims there were thirty-six mounted soldiers.[4]

When they had finished with them Allāh answered the supplication of the righteous servant Sa'd ibn Mu'ādh, for when he was injured he said:

---

1 — [DB] Reported by Abū Dāwūd (no. 1404) as a hadīth of 'Atiyyah Al-Quraydhī (رَضِيَ ٱللَّهُ عَنْهُ), and declared *'sahīh'* by Shaikh Al-Albānī.

2 — [BJ] [SZ] That is what occurs in the two manuscripts, whereas in *As-Sīrah* there occurs that he was *'Khallād ibn Suwayd'*, and that is what is correct.

3 — [BJ] [SZ] The hadīth concerning her killing was reported by Ibn Is-hāq in *As-Sīrah* (3/266), and from him by Abū Dāwūd (no. 2671) and Ahmad in *Al-Musnad* (6/277), as a hadīth of 'Ā'ishah (رَضِيَ ٱللَّهُ عَنْهَا), and its chain of narration is *'hasan'*. It was declared *'hasan'* by Shaikh Al-Albānī.

4 — [SH] "Ibn Is-hāq mentioned it in *As-Sīrah* (3/923: Ibn Hishām), and the author related it from him, and was silent concerning it, in *Al-Bidāyah wan-Nihāyah* (6/96) — without a chain of narration."

"O Allāh if You have left behind any fighting with Quraysh, then cause me to remain for it; but if You have raised fighting between us and them, then cause my wound to flow copiously, but do not cause me to die until You grant me satisfaction regarding Banū Quraydhah."

So he (صَلَّى ٱللَّهُ عَلَيْهِ وَسَلَّمَ) had cauterized his wound, but then it burst open and he died from it (رَضِيَ ٱللَّهُ عَنْهُ).[1]

So Allāh's Messenger (صَلَّى ٱللَّهُ عَلَيْهِ وَسَلَّمَ) and the Muslims accompanied his funeral, and he is the one for whom the Throne of the Most Merciful shook[2] from joy at the arrival of his soul (may Allāh be pleased with them and cause them to be pleased).

On the Day of the Trench and the Day of Quraydhah about ten men were martyred — may Allāh be pleased with them all — *Āmīn*.[3]

Chapter: The Killing of Abū Rāfiʿ Sallām Ibn Abil-Huqayq[4]

Allāh (and all praise is for Him) killed Kaʿb ibn Al-Ashraf, the enemy of Allāh, at the hands of some men of the Aws — as we have already mentioned — after the battle of Badr. And Abū Rāfiʿ Sallām ibn Abil-Huqayq was one of those who had incited the Allied Enemies against Allāh's Messenger (صَلَّى ٱللَّهُ عَلَيْهِ وَسَلَّمَ), and he had not been killed along with Banū Quraydhah, as his companion Huyayy ibn Akhtab had been killed. So the Khazraj desired to kill him, seeking to obtain a reward equal to that of the Aws. For Allāh (the One free of all imperfections) caused these two groups to strive to outdo each other in front of Allāh's

---

1 — [BJ][SZ][SH] Reported in *Sahīhul-Bukhārī* (no.4122) and *Sahīh Muslim* (no. 1769) as a hadīth of ʿĀʾishah (رَضِيَ ٱللَّهُ عَنْهَا).

2 — [BJ][SZ] Reported by Al-Bukhārī (no.3803) and Muslim (no.2466) as a hadīth of Jābir ibn ʿAbdillāh (رَضِيَ ٱللَّهُ عَنْهُمَا).

3 — For a list of those martyred, see **Endnote 45 on page 468**.

4 — [DB] The author (رَحِمَهُ ٱللَّهُ) entitled this chapter in his *As-Sīratun-Nabawiyyah* (3/256): "The killing of Abū Rāfiʿ Sallām ibn Abil-Huqayq the Jew — may Allāh curse him — in a fortress of his in Khaybar, and he was a famous trader in the land of the Hijāz."

Messenger (ﷺ). So they requested the permission of Allāh's Messenger (ﷺ) to kill him, so he granted them permission.

So he assigned some men to attack him; all of them were from Banū Salimah. They were: ʿAbdullāh ibn ʿAtīk and he was their leader — by his (ﷺ) command, ʿAbdullāh ibn Unays, Abū Qatādah Al-Hārith ibn Ribʿī, Masʿūd ibn Sinān, and Khuzāʿī ibn Aswad — a confederate of theirs.

So they went out until they came to him at Khaybar and he was in a fortified villa of his. So they attacked him at night and killed him, and they returned to Allāh's Messenger (ﷺ), each one of them claiming that he had killed him. So he said: "Show me your swords."

So when they had showed him, he said concerning the sword of ʿAbdullāh ibn Unays: "This one has killed him. I see the traces of food upon it."

ʿAbdullāh ibn Unays had forced his sword down upon him until he heard his backbone snap, and the enemy of Allāh was saying: ***"Enough! Enough!"*** Meaning: You have done enough to me.[1]

Chapter: The Expedition of Banū Lahyān

Then he (ﷺ) went out six months after Quraydhah, and that was in Jumādal-Ūlā of the sixth year — in the correct saying — to attack Banū Lahyān, to take revenge for the companions of Ar-Rajīʿ who have been mentioned previously. So he proceeded until he descended upon their territory in a valley called Ghurān, which is between Amaj[2] and ʿUsfān. So he found that they had taken up defensive positions on the tops of mountains, so he left them and rode on with two hundred riders

---

1 — For a detailed report of this military operation as conveyed by ʿAbdullāh ibn Unays, see **Endnote 46 on page 468**.

2 — [SH] A large town comprising many farms and date-palm groves. It is upon a large wādī, and is populated by (the tribe of) Khuzāʿah.

until he descended upon ʿUsfān. He also sent two riders to descend upon Kurāʿ An-Namīm.[1] Then he (ﷺ) returned to Al-Madīnah.[2]

Chapter: The Expedition of Dhī Qarad

Then a few nights after he had arrived back in Al-Madīnah, ʿUyainah ibn Hisn, with some men of Banū ʿAbdullāh ibn Ghatafān made an attack upon the milch-camels[3] of the Prophet (ﷺ) which were found at Ghābah.[4]

So he led them away and killed the man who was guarding them, and he was a man of (the tribe of) Ghifār, and captured his wife. So the first person who was alerted to them was Salamah ibn ʿAmr ibn Al-Akwaʿ Al-Aslamī (رَضِيَ ٱللَّهُ عَنْهُ). So he chased after them on foot and they were not able to out outstrip him, and he began firing arrows at them and saying:

> "(Take it and) I am Ibnul-Akwaʿ, and today is the day for destruction of the vile folk!"

Meaning: the base people; and he was able to recover most of what they had taken.

When the cries (for aid) were heard in Al-Madīnah, Allāh's Messenger (ﷺ) went out with a group of riders and met Salamah ibn Al-Akwaʿ, and they took the milch-camels back. So the Prophet (ﷺ) reached a watering place called 'Dhū Qarad.'[5]

---

1 — SH A place between Rābigh and Al-Juhfah

2 — SH Ibn Is-hāq reported it in *As-Sīrah* (3/956-957: Ibn Hishām) saying: "From ʿĀsim ibn ʿUmar ibn Qatādah, and ʿAbdur-Rahmān ibn Abī Bakr: from ʿAbdullāh ibn Kaʿb ibn Mālik, with it, within some lengthy speech." I say: Its chain of narration is weak.

3 — SH She-camels which give milk, on account of their having recently given birth or being pregnant.

4 — SH A place of dense shrubs and thickets of tamarisk, to the north-west of Uhud.

5 — DB Yāqūt Al-Hamawī said in *Muʿjamul-Buldān:* "Dhū Qarad is a watering place two nights away from Al-Madīnah in the direction of Khaybar (...) And Al-Qādī [ʿIyād] said: *'Dhū Qarad is about a day's journey from Al-Madīnah.'*"

He slaughtered one of the milch-camels that they had retaken, and he camped there for a day and a night. Then he returned to Al-Madīnah.[1]

During this expedition Al-Akhram, who was Muhriz ibn Nadalah (رَضِيَ ٱللَّهُ عَنْهُ), was killed.[2] He was killed by ʿAbdur-Rahmān ibn ʿUyainah, who then jumped upon his horse. Then Abū Qatādah attacked ʿAbdur-Rahmān and killed him; and he regained the horse, which belonged to Mahmūd ibn Maslamah.

Also, the woman who had been captured returned upon a camel belonging to Allāh's Messenger (صَلَّى ٱللَّهُ عَلَيْهِ وَسَلَّمَ), and she had made a vow that if Allāh saved her upon it she would sacrifice it. So Allāh's Messenger (صَلَّى ٱللَّهُ عَلَيْهِ وَسَلَّمَ) said: *"What a bad reward she would give it. There is no oath for the son of Ādam regarding that which he does not own, nor regarding something sinful"* — and he took his camel back.[3]

And Muslim reported in his *Sahīh* from Salamah ibn Al-Akwaʿ that he said concerning this incident: *"So we returned to Al-Madīnah, and then we did not remain except for three nights until we went out to (attack) Khaybar,"*[4] and perhaps this is what is correct, and Allāh (the Most High) knows best.

---

1 — SH Ibn Is-hāq reported it in *As-Sīrah* (3/958-962: Ibn Hishām), with this wording, with weak chains of narration. The hadīth concerning the milch-camels is reported by Al-Bukhārī (no. 4194) and Muslim (no. 1806) as a hadīth of Yazīd ibn Abī ʿUbayd: from Salamah (رَضِيَ ٱللَّهُ عَنْهُ) with a more complete and longer wording.

2 — MK MM Muhriz ibn Nadalah ibn ʿAbdillāh Al-Asadī, the confederate of Banū ʿAbd Shams. He was present at Badr, Uhud, and Al-Khandaq, and was martyred at Dhī Qarad in 6H at the age of 37: Refer to *Usdul-Ghābah* (4/307).

3 — SH Reported by Muslim (no. 1641), within a long hadīth, as a narration of ʿImrān ibn Husayn (رَضِيَ ٱللَّهُ عَنْهُ).

4 — BJ SZ Reported by Muslim (no. 1807) as a hadīth of Salamah ibn Al-Akwaʿ and it mentions the events of this expedition and others, and Al-Bukhārī gave as a chapter heading for this expedition: *"Chapter: The Expedition of Dhātul-Qarad, and it is the Expedition where they Attacked the Milch-Camels of the Prophet (صَلَّى ٱللَّهُ عَلَيْهِ وَسَلَّمَ), which Occurred Three Days Before Khaybar."*

Chapter: The Expedition of Banul-Mustaliq or Al-Muraysīʿ

Then he (صَلَّى ٱللَّهُ عَلَيْهِ وَسَلَّمَ) went to attack the (clan of) Banul-Mustaliq from the (tribe of) Khuzāʿah in Shaʿbān of the sixth year,[1] or it is said: it happened in Shaʿbān of the fifth year; and the first is more correct, and it was the saying of Ibn Is-hāq and others.

He left in charge of Al-Madīnah Abū Dharr, or it is said: Numaylah ibn ʿAbdillāh Al-Laythī.

So he attacked them, and they were caught unawares at an oasis of theirs called ʿAl-Muraysīʿ', which is in the direction of Qudayd towards the coast. So he killed those of them whom he killed, and he took the women and children as captives.[2]

The call of recognition for the Muslims that day was ***"Amit! Amit!"*** — ***"Put to death! Put to death!"***[3]

So amongst the captives was Juwayriyah, the daughter of Al-Hārith ibn Abī Dirār — the King[4] of the (clan of) Banul-Mustaliq. She fell to the share of Thābit ibn Qays ibn Shammās, who agreed to free her upon receipt of a stipulated payment. So Allāh's Messenger (صَلَّى ٱللَّهُ عَلَيْهِ وَسَلَّمَ) paid on her behalf, and married her. She therefore became *'Ummul-*

---

1 — For more information regarding this event, and some commentary regarding the referencing, see ENDNOTE 47 ON PAGE 470.

2 — [SH] As occurs in *Sahīhul-Bukhārī* (no.2541) and *Sahīh Muslim* (no.1730), as a hadīth of ʿAbdullāh ibn ʿUmar (رَضِيَ ٱللَّهُ عَنْهُمَا)

[DB] The wording in the two *Sahīhs* is: "He killed their fighting men and took their women and children captive."

3 — [SH] This was stated by Ibn Hishām in *As-Sīrah* (3/970) without a chain of narration, and it has already preceded with us that this was the call of recognition for the Muslims in some battles, and was perhaps so in most of them, and Allāh knows best.

4 — [MK][MM] There occurs in *Zādul-Maʿād* (2/125) and *Jawāmiʿus-Sīrah* (p. 204): *"The chief of the (tribe of) Banul-Mustaliq"* — and this wording is more precise since kingship was unknown to Khuzāʿah.

Mu'minīn' (Mother of the Believers). Because of this, the Muslims set free a hundred families of the Banul-Mustaliq who had accepted Islām.[1]

Then, whilst he (ﷺ) was returning, the foul one — ʿAbdullāh ibn Ubayy ibn Salūl — said: *"When we return to Al-Madīnah the more honourable one will expel the meaner one from it"* — referring (in derogatory terms) to Allāh's Messenger (ﷺ). So Zayd ibn Arqam reported it to Allāh's Messenger (ﷺ), and then ʿAbdullāh ibn Ubayy came, seeking to excuse himself and swearing that he hadn't said it. So Allāh's Messenger (ﷺ) remained silent regarding him until Allāh (the Mighty and Majestic) sent down affirmation of the truthfulness of Zayd ibn Arqam in Sūratul-Munāfiqīn.[2] And from the incidents that occurred during this expedition was:

The Incident of the Slanderous Lie (*'Al-Ifk'*)

Which was invented by ʿAbdullāh ibn Ubayy, this filthy one, and his companions. So, the Mother of the Believers ʿĀ'ishah bint Abī Bakr As-Siddīq (رَضِيَ ٱللَّهُ عَنْهَا) had gone out on this journey along with Allāh's Messenger (ﷺ), and she was carried in a covered camel-litter (howdah). So they had stopped off at some place and then they wanted to move on at the start of the day. She had, however, gone off to a place suitable for relieving herself; and then when she returned she found that she had lost a necklace belonging to her sister Asmā', which she had lent to her. She therefore went off to search for it, in the place where she had been. Meanwhile, the group of people who travelled with her returned, and together lifted the empty camel-litter and secured it upon the camel. They did not find its lightness strange since they were helping each other, and because at that time ʿĀ'ishah (رَضِيَ ٱللَّهُ عَنْهَا) was not heavy; rather she was a very young woman, aged fourteen.

So when she returned, having found the necklace, she did not see anyone at the camping place. So she sat down at the place of camping

1 — Imām Al-Albānī declared this to be a *'hasan'* chain of narration. For more detail, see Endnote 48 on page 471.

2 — This shows the permissibility of reporting forbidden speech to the one who has been spoken about in certain circumstances. See Endnote 49 on page 471.

and said (to herself) that they would soon miss her and therefore come back for her; and Allāh causes His command to occur, and He is Wise in whatever He wishes to occur.

She was then overcome by drowsiness and was not awoken except by Safwān ibn Al-Mu'attal As-Sulamī, then Adh-Dhakwānī,[1] calling out *'Innā lillāhi wa innā ilaihi rāji'ūn'* (*'Indeed we belong to Allāh, and to Him we shall return'*). He had halted for rest towards the rear of the people, and he used to sleep heavily — as is reported about him in a narration of Abū Dāwūd.[2]

So when he saw Ummul-Mu'minīn he said: "Indeed we belong to Allāh, and to Him we shall return! The wife of Allāh's Messenger (صَلَّى ٱللَّهُ عَلَيْهِ وَسَلَّمَ)?!"

Then he made his camel kneel down, drawing it close to her, and she rode upon it. He did not speak a single word to her, and all she heard from him was his saying: "Indeed we belong to Allāh, and to him we shall return."

Then he led her along until they arrived and found that the army had camped at the time of the beginning of noon. So when the people saw that, the Hypocrites spoke with that which Allāh will punish them for; and 'Abdullāh ibn Ubayy — the filthy one — along with the disgrace he had already been guilty of on this expedition, spoke about it, made it open news, propagated it, and made it apparent.

So the affair occurred as is mentioned at length in the two *Sahīhs*[3] as a hadīth of Az-Zuhrī: from Sa'īd ibn Al-Musayyib, 'Urwah ibn Az-Zubayr, 'Alqamah ibn Waqqās Al-Laythī, and 'Ubaydullāh ibn 'Abdullāh ibn 'Utbah, all of them from 'Ā'ishah (رَضِيَ ٱللَّهُ عَنْهَا), As-Siddīqah (the eminently true and truthful woman), the daughter of As-Siddīq (the eminently true and truthful man), the woman declared innocent from above the

---

1 — SH He is Safwān As-Sulamī, Adh-Dhakwānī; he was present at Al-Khandaq and the expeditions after in the days of Allāh's Messenger (صَلَّى ٱللَّهُ عَلَيْهِ وَسَلَّمَ) and he was present at the conquest of Damascus. He was martyred in Armenia in 19H.

2 — DB Reported by Abū Dāwūd (no. 2459) and declared *'sahīh'* by Shaikh Al-Albānī.

3 — The long story of the Ifk is detailed in **Endnote 50 on page 471**.

seven heavens of what the people of the slanderous lie accused her of during this expedition in His Saying (He the Most High):

> إِنَّ ٱلَّذِينَ جَآءُو بِٱلْإِفْكِ عُصْبَةٌ مِّنكُمْ ۚ لَا تَحْسَبُوهُ شَرًّا لَّكُم ۖ بَلْ هُوَ خَيْرٌ لَّكُمْ
>
> MEANING: "Those who brought forth the slanderous lie are a group from amongst you. Do not consider it something bad for you; rather it is something good for you." — **SŪRATUN-NŪR (24):11**

So when Allāh (the Most High) sent that down, and this was more than a month after they had returned from this expedition, then those who had spoken with the slanderous lie were lashed, and amongst those who were lashed was Mistah ibn Uthāthah and Hamnah bint Jah-sh.

Prior to that Allāh's Messenger (صَلَّى ٱللَّٰهُ عَلَيْهِ وَسَلَّمَ) had ascended the minbar and given an address to the Muslims, and had sought assistance against ʿAbdullāh ibn Ubayy and his companions, saying:

> "Who will assist me against a man who harms me with regard to my family. By Allāh, I have not known anything but good about my family; and they have mentioned a man whom I have known nothing but good about, and he does not enter upon my family except along with me."

So Saʿd ibn Muʿādh — the brother of Banū ʿAbdil-Ash-hal — stood up and said: "O Messenger of Allāh! I will assist you against him. So if he is from the Aws then we will strike his neck, and if he is from our brothers from the Khazraj then you can command us and we will do what you command."

So Saʿd ibn ʿUbādah stood up and said: "By Allāh's eternity you have lied! You will not kill him, and you will not be able to kill him; and if he were from your group then you would not wish that he be killed!"

So Usayd ibn Al-Hudayr said: "By Allāh! We will certainly kill him; since you are a hypocrite arguing in defence of the Hypocrites!"

So both groups became so angry that they almost started fighting each other. Then Allāh's Messenger (صَلَّى ٱللَّٰهُ عَلَيْهِ وَسَلَّمَ) kept trying to calm them down until they became calm — until the end of the hadīth.

This is what occurs in the two *Sahīhs*: that the one who spoke to Saʿd ibn ʿUbādah was Saʿd ibn Muʿādh. So this is a problem, which many of the scholars of military expeditions have found problematic, since none of them differ concerning the fact that he died after Banū Quraydhah, which occurred after Al-Khandaq, and that was in the fifth year — in the correct saying.

Then there is no doubt that the incident of the false slander occurred during this expedition of Banul-Mustaliq, which is the expedition of Al-Muraysīʿ. Az-Zuhrī said: *"During the expedition of Al-Muraysīʿ."* So the people have differed concerning how to respond to this. So Mūsā ibn ʿUqbah said, in what Al-Bukhārī quoted from him, that the expedition of Al-Muraysīʿ occurred in the fourth year; and this is contrary to (the saying of) the majority.[1]

Then there is something in the hadīth which negates what he said, since she said: *"And that was after the (Legislation of the) Hijāb came down"*, and there is no disagreement about the fact that it came down on the morning after he (صَلَّى ٱللَّهُ عَلَيْهِ وَسَلَّمَ) consummated his marriage to Zaynab bint Jah-sh; and he (صَلَّى ٱللَّهُ عَلَيْهِ وَسَلَّمَ) asked Zaynab bint Jah-sh about ʿĀʾishah in that regard.

So she said: "I will guard my hearing and my sight."

ʿĀʾishah said: "And she was the one who was my rival from amongst the wives of the Prophet (صَلَّى ٱللَّهُ عَلَيْهِ وَسَلَّمَ)."

---

1 — SH Al-Hāfidh (Ibn Hajr) said in *Al-Fat-h* (7/430): "This is what Al-Bukhārī mentioned, and it is as if it was a slip of the pen, and that he intended to write 'the fifth year' but instead wrote 'the fourth year'; since what occurs in the *Maghāzī* of Mūsā ibn ʿUqbah through a number of chains of narration, which Al-Hākim Abū Saʿīd An-Naysābūrī and Al-Bayhaqī in *Ad-Dalāʾil* and others report, is *'the fifth year'*."

The historians mentioned that he married her[1] in Dhul-Qaʿdah of the fifth year. So this nullifies what he said, and the problem is not resolved.[2]

As for Imām Muhammad ibn Is-hāq ibn Yasār, then he said that the expedition of Banul-Mustaliq occurred in the sixth year, and he mentioned the incident of the slanderous lie within it, except that he said: *"From Az-Zuhrī: from ʿUbaydullāh ibn ʿAbdillāh ibn ʿUtbah: from ʿĀʾishah"* — and he mentioned the hadīth.

He said: *"So Usayd ibn Al-Hudayr stood up and said: 'I will assist you against him,'"* and he did not mention Saʿd ibn Muʿādh.

Abū Muhammad ibn Hazm said, *"This is what is correct, about which there is no doubt; whereas that, in our view, was a mistake,"* and he spoke at length concerning that, whilst acknowledging that the mention of Saʿd is reported through authentic chains of narration.

I say: And it is just as he said, if Allāh wills.

So there are a number of ahādīth that contain mistakes of this type, which do not alter a legislated ruling, and the people have pointed most of them out; and some have tried to provide answers for them with implausible responses; and Allāh (the One free of all imperfections and the Most High) knows best.

---

1 — DB i.e. Zaynab bint Jahsh (رَضِيَ اللَّهُ عَنْهَا).

2 — DB Al-Hāfidh Ibn Hajr in *Fat-hul-Bārī* (7/430) resolved the difficulty in the dates given for this expedition, the presence of Saʿd ibn Muʿādh, the marriage of Zaynab and the subsequent obligation of the Hijāb, by saying: "The incident of the Slanderous Lie occurred in the fifth year, since the hadīth states clearly that the incident occurred after the coming down of the Hijāb; and the Hijāb came about in Dhul-Qaʿdah of the fourth year — upon the saying of a group. So Al-Muraysīʿ occurred after that, so it is correct that it occurred in the fifth year. As for the saying of Al-Wāqidī that the Hijāb came about in Dhul-Qaʿdah of the fifth year, then this is rejected. Khalīfah, Abū ʿUbaydah, and others state with certainty that it was in the third year. So we have three sayings concerning the Hijāb; the most well-known of them is (that it was in) the fourth year and Allāh knows best."

CHAPTER:

The Expedition Of Al-Hudaybiyah

In Dhul-Qa'dah of the sixth year Allāh's Messenger (صَلَّى ٱللَّهُ عَلَيْهِ وَسَلَّمَ) went out to perform 'Umrah along with one thousand and more men. It is said: with one thousand and five hundred (1500), or it is said: *'and four hundred'* (1400), or it is said: *'and three hundred'* (1300); and there are other sayings.[1]

As for the one who claimed that he went out along with seven hundred, then he made a mistake.[2]

So when the Mushrikūn came to know of this, they gathered their scattered associated tribes and went out from Makkah to block and prevent him from performing 'Umrah that year. They sent Khālid ibn Al-Walīd forward in charge of some of their cavalry to Kurā' Al-Ghamīm.[3]

---

1 — SH All of these sayings are confirmed in the two *Sahīhs* in a number of narrations. Refer to *Sahīhul-Bukhārī* (nos. 4150-4155, & 4157, & 4158), and *Sahīh Muslim* (nos. 1856 & 1857).

DB Al-Hāfidh Ibn Hajr in *Fat-hul-Bārī* (7/440), and likewise An-Nawawī, harmonised the narrations by saying that their number was between 1400 and 1500.

2 — SH It was the saying of Ibn Is-hāq, and no one agreed with him upon it.

3 — DB Yāqūtul-Hamawī said in *Mu'jamul-Buldān*: "A place at the edge of the Hijāz between Makkah and Al-Madīnah, and it is a valley eight miles before 'Usfān."

However, he (صَلَّىٰ ٱللَّٰهُ عَلَيْهِ وَسَلَّمَ) took a different route, to avoid him, and he (صَلَّىٰ ٱللَّٰهُ عَلَيْهِ وَسَلَّمَ) arrived at Al-Hudaybiyah.[1]

Then he and the Mushrikūn sent messages back and forth until Suhayl ibn ʿAmr came. So he made an agreement with him that he would go back and depart from them that year, and that he would perform ʿUmrah the following year. So he (صَلَّىٰ ٱللَّٰهُ عَلَيْهِ وَسَلَّمَ) accepted that which he requested, because of the blessing and benefit which Allāh — the Mighty and Majestic — placed in that.

However a group of the Companions disliked that, from them ʿUmar ibn Al-Khattāb (رَضِيَ ٱللَّٰهُ عَنْهُ). So he went to argue against it with Abū Bakr As-Siddīq, and then with him (صَلَّىٰ ٱللَّٰهُ عَلَيْهِ وَسَلَّمَ). So his (صَلَّىٰ ٱللَّٰهُ عَلَيْهِ وَسَلَّمَ) response was just the same as that of As-Siddīq (رَضِيَ ٱللَّٰهُ عَنْهُ): that he (صَلَّىٰ ٱللَّٰهُ عَلَيْهِ وَسَلَّمَ) was the Slave of Allāh and His Messenger, and that he would not disobey Him, and that He would certainly aid him. And Al-Bukhārī reported the hadīth fully in his *Sahīh*.[2]

So Suhayl ibn ʿAmr attained from him the agreement that he would depart and leave them that year, and would perform the ʿUmrah the following year, with the condition that he could not enter Makkah unless their swords were packed away in their sheaths, and that he could remain no longer than three days, and that a state of peace should be established between him and the people for a period of ten years.[3]

---

1 — [DB] Al-Hudaybiyah is the name of a well, twenty-two kilometres (c. 14 miles) north-west of Makkah: *As-Sīratun-Nabawiyyatus-Sahīhah* (2/434) of Dr. Akram Diyāʾ Al-ʿUmarī. It is referred to as 'Al-Hudaybi**y**ah' and also 'Al-Hudaybi**yy**ah', both being correct. [*Fat-hul-Bārī* (7/439), *Tahdhībul-Asmā wal-Lughāt* (3/77)]

2 — [BJ][SZ] Reported by Al-Bukhārī (nos. 2731 & 2732)

3 — [SH] This length, which Ibn Is-hāq mentioned as being the time limit of the peace-treaty, is what is dependable. This is what Ibn Saʿd stated, and Al-Hākim reported it as a hadīth of ʿAlī himself.

However, there occurs in the *Maghāzī* of Ibn ʿĀʾidh, as a hadīth of Ibn ʿAbbās and others, that it was for two years, and the same occurs with Mūsā ibn ʿUqbah. So the two (sayings) are harmonised by the fact that what Ibn Is-hāq said was the time period agreed in the peace-treaty; whereas that which Ibn ʿĀʾidh and others mentioned was the actual period which the peace lasted, until it was broken at the hands of the Quraysh.

So this truce was one of the greatest of victories for the Muslims, just as ʿAbdullāh ibn Masʿūd (رَضِيَ ٱللَّهُ عَنْهُ) said.[1]

So, upon that basis, whoever wished could enter into an alliance with Allāh's Messenger (صَلَّى ٱللَّهُ عَلَيْهِ وَسَلَّمَ), and whoever wished could enter into an alliance with the Quraysh. So (the tribe of) Khuzāʿah were amongst those who entered into an alliance with him (صَلَّى ٱللَّهُ عَلَيْهِ وَسَلَّمَ), and (the tribe of) Banū Bakr entered into an alliance with the Quraysh.

Also [from the conditions was] that none of them should come to him, even if he be a Muslim, except that he should return him to them; and that if anyone from the Muslims went over to them, then they were not to send him back.

So Allāh (the One free of all imperfections) affirmed all of that, apart from the exception He made regarding the Believing women who migrated: He forbade that they be sent back to the Disbelievers, and He prohibited them for the Disbelievers that day.[2]

So this is a rare example of what is mentioned in the Principles (of Fiqh) concerning restriction and particularization (*takhsīs*) of something in the Sunnah by the Qurʾān. Then there are some of them who counted it as being abrogation (*naskh*), as was the position of Abū Hanīfah and some of the people of Usūl (Principles of Fiqh).

However, it is not what is held by the majority of the later people; and disagreement in that regard is something slight, since it only amounts to a discussion concerning wording.

Prior to the treaty, he (صَلَّى ٱللَّهُ عَلَيْهِ وَسَلَّمَ) had sent ʿUthmān ibn ʿAffān (رَضِيَ ٱللَّهُ عَنْهُ) to the people of Makkah to inform them that he had not come to fight anyone, but rather to perform ʿUmrah.

So because of the nobility of ʿUthmān (رَضِيَ ٱللَّهُ عَنْهُ) the Mushrikūn offered to allow him to perform Tawāf around the House, however he refused that,

---

1 — For more information regarding other events that were considered mighty victories for Islām, see ENDNOTE 51 ON PAGE 480.

2 — [SH] The author (رَحِمَهُ ٱللَّهُ) is referring to the verse [10] in Sūrah Al-Mumtahanah.

and said: "I will not perform Tawāf around it before Allāh's Messenger (صَلَّى ٱللَّٰهُ عَلَيْهِ وَسَلَّمَ)."

Then 'Uthmān (رَضِيَ ٱللَّٰهُ عَنْهُ) had not returned before news reached him (صَلَّى ٱللَّٰهُ عَلَيْهِ وَسَلَّمَ) that 'Uthmān had been killed. So Allāh's Messenger (صَلَّى ٱللَّٰهُ عَلَيْهِ وَسَلَّمَ) was angered by that, and he called his Companions to give a pledge to fight. So they gave him that pledge beneath a tree at that place, and it was an Egyptian Mimosa tree (*samurah*); and the number of those who gave him the pledge there was the total of all those whom we have already mentioned as having gone out with him to Al-Hudaybiyah, apart from Al-Judd ibn Qays who hid himself behind a camel of his, as a result of Hypocrisy and cowardice;[1] and apart from Abū Sarīhah Hudhayfah ibn Usayd, since he was present at Al-Hudaybiyah, but it is said that he did not give the pledge, or it is otherwise said: rather he did give the pledge.

The first one who gave the pledge on that day was Abū Sinān Wahb ibn Mihsan, the brother of 'Ukkāshah ibn Mihsan, or it is otherwise said: his son Sinān ibn Abī Sinān.

Also Salamah ibn Al-Akwa' (رَضِيَ ٱللَّٰهُ عَنْهُ) gave the pledge three times that day, as Allāh's Messenger (صَلَّى ٱللَّٰهُ عَلَيْهِ وَسَلَّمَ) commanded him to do, as is reported by Muslim from him.[2]

And he (صَلَّى ٱللَّٰهُ عَلَيْهِ وَسَلَّمَ) placed his hand[3] upon his own noble hand, then he said, "And this is on behalf of 'Uthmān."[4]

So that was greater for him than his actually witnessing that pledge in person. Allāh (the Mighty and Majestic) sent down in that regard:

> لَّقَدْ رَضِيَ اللَّهُ عَنِ الْمُؤْمِنِينَ إِذْ يُبَايِعُونَكَ تَحْتَ الشَّجَرَةِ

---

1 — [SH] Reported by Muslim in his *Sahīh* (no. 1856/69) as a hadīth of Jābir ibn 'Abdillāh (رَضِيَ ٱللَّٰهُ عَنْهُمَا).

2 — [SH] In his *Sahīh* (no. 1807) (SH).

3 — [BJ][SZ][SH] In one manuscript version [it reads]: *'one of his hands'*.

4 — [SH] Reported by Al-Bukhārī in his *Sahīh* (no. 3698) as a hadīth of Ibn 'Umar (رَضِيَ ٱللَّٰهُ عَنْهُمَا).

> MEANING: "Indeed Allāh was pleased with the Believers when they gave the pledge to you beneath the tree," — SŪRAH AL-FAT-H (48):18

— and he (صَلَّى ٱللَّهُ عَلَيْهِ وَسَلَّمَ) said: "None shall enter the Fire from those who gave the pledge beneath the tree."[1]

So this was the *'Bay'atur-Ridwān'* (The Pledge of Those who Earned Allāh's Pleasure).

And when the Prophet (صَلَّى ٱللَّهُ عَلَيْهِ وَسَلَّمَ) finished concluding the agreement with the Mushrikīn, as we have already mentioned, he prepared to remove himself from the state of ihrām which he had entered for his 'Umrah, and he commanded the people to do so. So they found it very difficult to make themselves do it, and they withheld, hoping that it would be abrogated. So the Prophet (صَلَّى ٱللَّهُ عَلَيْهِ وَسَلَّمَ) became angry at that. So he entered upon Umm Salamah and told her so. Therefore, she said: "Then you go out, O Messenger of Allāh! And slaughter your sacrifice, and shave your head, and then the people will follow you, O Messenger of Allāh!"

So he went out and did that, and the people were quick to follow his example.[2] So they all shaved their heads except for 'Uthmān ibn 'Affān and Abū Qatādah Al-Hārith ibn Rib'ī — for they cut their hair short. This was mentioned by As-Suhaylī in *Ar-Rawdul-Unuf.*[3]

So some of them were almost killing each other because of their anguish,[4] because they thought that the Mushrikūn had dictated whatever conditions they wanted to them, and that he (صَلَّى ٱللَّهُ عَلَيْهِ وَسَلَّمَ) had merely acceded to them. So this was because of their excess of bravery (رَضِيَ ٱللَّهُ عَنْهُمْ),

---

1 — [SH] Reported by Al-Bukhārī in his *Sahīh* (no. 3698) as a hadīth of Ibn 'Umar (رَضِيَ ٱللَّهُ عَنْهُمَا).

2 — [BJ][SZ] Refer to *Sahīhul-Bukhārī* (nos. 2731 & 2732).

3 — Refer to *Ar-Rawdul-Unuf* (4/55).

4 — [DB] The narration of Al-Bukhārī (no. 2731) has the wording: "So he (صَلَّى ٱللَّهُ عَلَيْهِ وَسَلَّمَ) went out, and he did not speak to anyone from them until he had done that. He slaughtered his sacrifice, and called for his barber who shaved his head. So when they saw that, they got up and sacrificed, and they shaved each others heads and were almost killing each other because of their anguish."

and their eagerness for the victory of Islām; however Allāh (the Mighty and Majestic) knows better than them the true realities of all affairs and whatever is truly beneficial.[1]

So therefore when he (صَلَّى ٱللَّهُ عَلَيْهِ وَسَلَّمَ) departed and made his way back to Al-Madīnah, Allāh (the Mighty and Majestic) sent down to him the whole of Sūratul-Fat-h with regard to that. And ʿAbdullāh ibn Masʿūd said: "You people consider the Victory to be the conquest of Makkah, but we used to consider it to be the victory of Al-Hudaybiyah."[2]

And he (رَضِيَ ٱللَّهُ عَنْهُ) spoke truthfully, since Allāh (the One free of all imperfections) made this the means for the conquest of Makkah; as we will mention later on, if Allāh (the Most High) wishes.

And He substituted this with Khaybar, as a reward brought forward and granted quickly. So the duration of their stay at Al-Hudaybiyah was for about twenty nights.

Chapter: The Expedition Of Khaybar[3]

When he (صَلَّى ٱللَّهُ عَلَيْهِ وَسَلَّمَ) returned to Al-Madīnah, he remained in residence there until Muharram of the seventh year, then at the end of it (i.e. Muharram), he went out to Khaybar.

It is however related from Mālik ibn Anas (رَحِمَهُ ٱللَّهُ) that the conquest of Khaybar occurred in the sixth year; but the majority hold that it occurred in the seventh year.

As for Ibn Hazm, then it occurs from him that it occurred in the sixth year — without doubt. So this was based upon his usage, which was

1 — For the commentary of Imām Al-Albānī as it relates to the servant having complete trust in the wisdom of Allāh's legislation, see ENDNOTE 52 ON PAGE 481.

2 — [BJ] [SZ] It occurs in *Sahīhul-Bukhārī* (no. 4150) as a statement of Al-Barāʾ (رَضِيَ ٱللَّهُ عَنْهُ).

3 — [DB] Al-Hāfidh Ibn Hajr said in *Fat-hul-Bārī* (7/464): "It is a large town with fortresses and farms, eight riding stages from Al-Madīnah in the direction of Shām (Palestine/Syria)."

Yāqūtul-Hamawī said in *Muʿjamul-Buldān*: "The name applies to a district, and this district includes seven fortresses, and farms, and many date-orchards."

that he held that the start of the Hijrah years was the month of Rabī'-ul-Awwal, during which Allāh's Messenger (صَلَّى ٱللَّهُ عَلَيْهِ وَسَلَّمَ) arrived at Al-Madīnah having performed the Hijrah. However, he was not followed upon that view, since the majority hold that dating starts from Muharram of that year.

So the first one to use that as the starting point for dates was Ya'lā ibn Umayyah in Yemen, as Imām Ahmad ibn Hanbal reported from him with a chain of narration that is *'sahīh'* up to him;[1] or it is said: 'Umar ibn Al-Khattāb (رَضِيَ ٱللَّهُ عَنْهُ), and that was in the sixteenth year as is explained in detail elsewhere.

So he (صَلَّى ٱللَّهُ عَلَيْهِ وَسَلَّمَ) travelled towards it, and he left in charge of Al-Madīnah Numaylah ibn 'Abdillāh Al-Laythī.[2]

So when he reached it he besieged it, fort by fort. So Allāh — the Mighty and Majestic — granted him victory over it,[3] and He granted it to him as war-booty such that he (صَلَّى ٱللَّهُ عَلَيْهِ وَسَلَّمَ) set aside one fifth. Then he distributed half of that amongst the Muslims, and they were only those who had been present at Al-Hudaybiyah. He kept the other half to be used at his discretion, and for the important affairs of the Muslims, for which he was responsible.

He employed the Jews who were living there, after they had requested that from him; so that instead of their being exiled, in accordance with the terms of surrender which he had accepted from them, they were to work the land, and half of the fruit or grain which it produced was to be for Allāh's Messenger (صَلَّى ٱللَّهُ عَلَيْهِ وَسَلَّمَ).[4]

---

1 — SH Al-Hāfidh (Ibn Hajr) said in *Al-Fat-h* (7/268): "Ahmad ibn Hanbal reported it with a chain of narration which is *'sahīh'* except that it is disconnected between 'Amr ibn Dīnār and Ya'lā."

2 — There is a difference of opinion over whether it was Numaylah Ibn 'Abdillāh Al-Laythī who was deputised, or if it was Sibā' ibn 'Urfutah. See ENDNOTE 53 ON PAGE 485 for more details.

3 — For more of the events that took place on that day, see ENDNOTE 54 ON PAGE 485.

4 — DB Al-Bukhārī reported (no. 4248) from 'Abdullāh: "The Prophet (صَلَّى ٱللَّهُ عَلَيْهِ وَسَلَّمَ) gave (the land of) Khaybar to the Jews (of Khaybar) on condition that they would work on it, and cultivate it, and they would have half of its yield."

And he (ﷺ) took for himself from its spoils Safiyyah bint Huyyay ibn Akhtab. So she accepted Islām, and he set her free and married her; and he consummated his marriage to her on the way back to Al-Madīnah, after she became lawful.[1]

A woman from the Jews of Khaybar, and she was Zaynab bint Al-Hārith — the wife of Sallām ibn Mishkam, gave him a gift of a poisoned cooked sheep. So when he took a bite of its shoulder, the shoulder informed him that it was poisoned. So he stopped eating, and called for the Jewish woman, and asked her: "Did you put poison into this sheep?"

So she said: "Yes."

So he said: "What made you do it?"

So she said: "I wanted to establish if you were a Prophet, in which case it would not harm you; or if you were other than that, then we would be relieved of you." So he pardoned her.[2]

It is said that Bishr ibn Al-Barā' ibn Ma'rūr was one of those who ate from it, and he died, so he killed her in retaliation for him. This was reported by Abū Dāwūd in *'mursal'* form from Abū Salamah ibn 'Abdir-Rahmān ibn 'Awf.[3]

And on the expedition of Khaybar, after they had finished fighting, Ja'far ibn Abī Tālib and his companions — those who had migrated to and remained in Abyssinia — came to the Prophet (ﷺ), and they

---

1 — SH Reported by Al-Bukhārī in his *Sahīh* (no. 371) and Muslim in his *Sahīh* (2/1043-1044 & 1045-1046) as a hadīth of Anas (رَضِيَٱللَّهُعَنْهُ).

DB Al-Hāfidh Ibn Hajr said in *Fat-hul-Bārī* (4/424): "What is meant by his saying 'she became lawful' is she became clear of her menstrual period."

2 — SH Reported by Al-Bukhārī (no. 3169) as a hadīth of Abū Hurairah, and it does not mention whether he punished her or pardoned her; and by Muslim (no. 2190) as a hadīth of Anas, and it contains the wording: "They said: *'Shall we not kill her?'* He said: *'No.'*"

3 — It is said that the Messenger (عَلَيْهِٱلسَّلَامُ) pardoned her as he did not seek retribution for the crime against himself, but when Bishr died from the poison, she was then executed. See **Endnote 55 on page 486** for more speech regarding this matter.

were accompanied by Abū Mūsā Al-Ash'arī and a group numbering more than seventy of the Ash'arī tribe.[1]

Also Abū Hurairah and others came to him (may Allāh be pleased with all of them). So he (صَلَّى ٱللَّهُ عَلَيْهِ وَسَلَّمَ) gave them a share of the spoils, just as Allāh (the Mighty and Majestic) willed.

And he (صَلَّى ٱللَّهُ عَلَيْهِ وَسَلَّمَ) said to Ja'far: *"I do not know which of the two gives me greater joy: the conquest of Khaybar, or the arrival of Ja'far,"* and when he came to him he got up and kissed him between his eyes.[2]

And about twenty men from the Muslims were martyred at Khaybar (may Allāh be pleased with all of them).[3]

Chapter: The Conquest Of Fadak

When news reached the people of Fadak[4] of what Allāh's Messenger (صَلَّى ٱللَّهُ عَلَيْهِ وَسَلَّمَ) had done with the people of Khaybar they sent a message to him requesting a peace agreement, so he responded to them. So the Muslims did not have to attack them with any camels or horses to take it. So he (صَلَّى ٱللَّهُ عَلَيْهِ وَسَلَّمَ) dealt with (its wealth) as Allāh (the Mighty and Majestic) willed that he should, and he did not distribute it.[5]

---

1 — [SH] Reported by Al-Bukhārī (no. 3136) with a different number quoted.

2 — [SH] Reported by At-Tabarānī in *Al-Mu'jamul-Kabīr* (22/82/244) and declared *'sahīh'* by our Shaikh Al-Albānī (رَحِمَهُ ٱللَّهُ) in *As-Silsilatus-Sahīhah* (6/335) because of its chains of narration and witnesses.

3 — For a list of the names of the Muslims who died at Khaybar, see Endnote 56 on page 487.

4 — [SH] Fadak is a village in the Hijāz, two or three days from Al-Madīnah: *Mu'jamul-Buldān*.

5 — [SH] Its like was mentioned by Ibn Is-hāq in *As-Sīrah* (3/1023): Ibn Hishām, without a chain of narration.

[DB] Ibn Is-hāq's report contains the wording: "So they sent a message to Allāh's Messenger (صَلَّى ٱللَّهُ عَلَيْهِ وَسَلَّمَ) asking for a peace agreement from him in exchange for half (the produce) of Fadak."

Chapter: The Conquest Of Wādī Al-Qurā

184 He returned to Al-Madīnah by way of Wādī Al-Qurā[1] and conquered it, and it is said that he fought for it, and Allāh knows best.

There occurs in the two *Sahīhs* that a slave-boy belonging to Allāh's Messenger (صَلَّى ٱللَّهُ عَلَيْهِ وَسَلَّمَ) called Midʿam, was removing the saddle of Allāh's Messenger (صَلَّى ٱللَّهُ عَلَيْهِ وَسَلَّمَ) when he was struck by an arrow fired from an unknown quarter, and was killed by it. So the people said: "Congratulations to him for the martyrdom! O Messenger of Allāh!"

So he said: "Not at all! By the One in Whose Hand is my soul! The cloak that he misappropriated from the spoils, which had been taken before the spoils were divided, is fire blazing upon him."[2]

Chapter: ʿUmratul-Qadāʾ (The ʿUmrah Performed In Accordance With the Terms of the Agreement)

When he (صَلَّى ٱللَّهُ عَلَيْهِ وَسَلَّمَ) returned to Al-Madīnah, he remained in residence there until the month of Dhul-Qaʿdah.[3] Then he went out to perform the ʿUmrah of the agreement, upon which basis he had made the agreement with Quraysh. Then there are some who declare it to have been a *qadāʾ* (compensation) to make up for the ʿUmrah of Al-Hudaybiyah which they had been prevented from; whereas others call it *"Umratul-Qisās'* (*The ʿUmrah of Retribution'*); and all (of these) are correct.

So he proceeded until he reached Makkah; and he performed ʿUmrah, performed Tawāf around the House, and left the state of ihram upon completion of his ʿUmrah. After leaving the state of ihram he married

---

1 — [SH] It is a wadi with many villages and is well known for its fertility, springs and wells. It was inhabited by Arabs and Jews.

2 — [SH] Reported by Al-Bukhārī in his *Sahīh* (no. 4234) and Muslim in his *Sahīh* (no. 115) as a hadīth of Abū Hurairah (رَضِيَ ٱللَّهُ عَنْهُ); and the narration of Muslim does not name the slave-boy. Al-Hāfidh (Ibn Hajr) said in *Al-Fat-h* (7/489-490): "The hadīth shows the seriousness of misappropriating wealth."

3 — During this time, he (صَلَّى ٱللَّهُ عَلَيْهِ وَسَلَّمَ) also sent out a number of military units, and Ibn Al-Qayyim briefly elaborates upon these missions in *Zād Al-Maʿād* — see Endnote 57 on page 489.

Maymūnah bint Al-Hārith, the Mother of the Believers; and the three day period was completed, so the Mushrikūn sent a message to him via ʿAlī (رَضِيَ اللَّهُ عَنْهُ) saying: "Get out from our land!"[1]

So he said: "How would it harm them if I were to consummate my marriage to Maymūnah with them?!"

However, they refused to allow him that; and they themselves had departed from Makkah when he (صَلَّى اللَّهُ عَلَيْهِ وَسَلَّمَ) arrived, out of their animosity towards him and their hatred of him.

So he (عَلَيْهِ الصَّلَاةُ وَالسَّلَامُ) departed, and he consummated his marriage with Maymūnah at Sarif;[2] and he returned to Al-Madīnah, having been aided and granted success.[3]

Chapter: The Expedition Sent To Mu'tah

In the month of Jumādal-Ākhirah of the eighth year, he (صَلَّى اللَّهُ عَلَيْهِ وَسَلَّمَ) sent out the army commanders to Mu'tah — and it is a town in the land of Shām — to take revenge for the killing of the Muslims at that place.[4]

So he placed Zayd ibn Hārithah, his (صَلَّى اللَّهُ عَلَيْهِ وَسَلَّمَ) freed slave, in command of the people, and he said: "If Zayd is struck down, then Jaʿfar ibn Abī

---

1 — [SH] Refer to what Al-Bukhārī reported in his *Sahīh* (no. 2699), and Muslim in his *Sahīh* (no. 1783) as a hadīth of Al-Barā' ibn ʿĀzib (رَضِيَ اللَّهُ عَنْهُمَا) regarding this incident.

2 — This sequence of events is what is most correct due to supporting reports, although there is a disputing view from Ibn ʿAbbās (رَضِيَ اللَّهُ عَنْهُمَا). For more detail see ENDNOTE 58 ON PAGE 490.

3 — There was a time limit imposed upon the Muslims of three days, after which they would have to leave Makkah — and the Messenger (صَلَّى اللَّهُ عَلَيْهِ وَسَلَّمَ) agreed to this stipulation. See ENDNOTE 59 ON PAGE 490 for the hadīth in *Sahīh Al-Bukhārī* regarding this event.

4 — Imām Ibn Al-Qayyim elaborates further on this mentioned reason for the expedition, although its authenticity is disputed. Read more at ENDNOTE 60 ON PAGE 491.

Tālib (is to take command); and if Ja'far is struck down, then 'Abdullāh ibn Rawāhah (is to take command)."[1]

So they departed with an army of around three thousand; and he (ﷺ) went out to bid them farewell, going part of the way with them. Then they proceeded until they reached Ma'ān, where news reached them that Hiraql (Heraclius) the king of the Byzantines had come out to attack them with an army of a hundred thousand; and that along with him was Mālik ibn Zāfilah with another hundred thousand of the Arab Christians, from the tribes of Lakhm and Judhām, and the tribes of Qudā'ah: Bahrā', Baliyy, and Balqayn.

So the Muslims consulted and discussed what to do there, and said: "We should write a letter to Allāh's Messenger (ﷺ) so that he can order us with some command of his, or send us reinforcements."

So 'Abdullāh ibn Rawāhah (رضي الله عنه) said:

> "O people! By Allāh, that which you came out seeking is in front of you (meaning martyrdom) and you do not fight against the people based upon your numbers or strength. Rather we do not fight them except with this Religion, with which Allāh has honoured us. So it can only be one of two fine outcomes: either victory or martyrdom!"

So the people agreed with him and proceeded.

Then when they came to the district of Al-Balqā' they encountered the massed armies of the Byzantines. So the Muslims camped at the side of the village of Mu'tah, and the Byzantines were at a village called Mashārif. Then they met and fought a tremendous battle.

The Muslim commander Zayd ibn Hārithah (رضي الله عنه) was killed with the battle flag in his hand, and so it was taken up by Ja'far. He dismounted

---

1 — [SH] Reported by Ibn Is-hāq in *As-Sīrah* (4/1042: Ibn Hishām), and from him by Al-Bayhaqī in *Dalā'ilun-Nubuwwah* (4/358-359): *"Muhammad ibn Ja'far ibn Az-Zubayr narrated to me: from 'Urwah ibn Az-Zubayr with it."* I say: This is a *'mursal'* narration with a *'sahīh'* chain of narration, and it has a witness as a hadīth of 'Abdullāh ibn 'Umar (رضي الله عنهما) with it, reported by Al-Bukhārī (no. 4261) — (...).

from a sorrel coloured horse of his and hamstrung it.[1] Then he fought until his right hand was severed. So he took the flag in his other hand, and that too was severed; then he clasped the flag, and then he was killed (رَضِيَ ٱللَّهُ عَنْهُ) at the age of thirty-three years, according to the correct saying.[2]

So ʿAbdullāh ibn Rawāhah Al-Ansārī (رَضِيَ ٱللَّهُ عَنْهُ) took the flag, and he hesitated slightly, then he went on with determination, and he fought until he was killed.

Then it is said that Thābit ibn Aqram took the flag, and that the Muslims wanted to appoint him as their commander, but he refused.[3]

So Khālid ibn Al-Walīd (رَضِيَ ٱللَّهُ عَنْهُ) took the flag,[4] and he performed a strategic retreat with the Muslims and acted with caution and skill, so that the Muslims were rescued from the enemy. So Allāh granted victory at his hands.[5]

So all of this was just as Allāh's Messenger (صَلَّى ٱللَّهُ عَلَيْهِ وَسَلَّمَ) informed his Companions in Al-Madīnah, that same day, as he was standing upon a minbar. So he announced the deaths of the commanders to them, one after the other, and his eyes were shedding tears; and the hadīth occurs in the *Sahīh*.[6]

---

1 — This was declared *'hasan'* by Imām Al-Albānī in *Sahīh Sunan Abī Dāwūd* — see **Endnote 61 on page 492** for more detail.

2 — Upon further research, it seems that this is not authentic. There is another hadīth reported by Al-Bukhārī regarding the bravery and death of Jaʿfar. Read more at **Endnote 62 on page 492**.

3 — [SH] Reported by Ibn Is-hāq in *As-Sīrah* (4/1048-1049: Ibn Hishām) with a *'hasan'* chain of narration.

4 — [BJ][SZ] And on that day, nine swords broke in his hand (رَضِيَ ٱللَّهُ عَنْهُ). Refer to *Sahīhul-Bukhārī* (no.4265).

[DB] Ibn Hazm mentioned in *Jawāmiʿus-Sīrah* (p.174): "And ʿAmr ibn Al-ʿĀs, Khālid ibn Al-Walīd, and ʿUthmān ibn Talhah ibn Abī Talhah, and they were the heads of Quraysh, had accepted Islām before that and after Al-Hudaybiyah, and after Khaybar."

5 — For more detail regarding Khālid Ibn Al-Walīd taking command, see **Endnote 63 on page 492**.

6 — [BJ][SZ] Reported by Al-Bukhārī (no. 4262) as a hadīth of Anas (رَضِيَ ٱللَّهُ عَنْهُ).

So night fell and the Disbelievers ceased fighting.

188 Then despite the great number of the enemy and the small number of the Muslims in comparison to them, only a few Muslims were killed, in accordance with what is mentioned by the historians. So they only mention, when they name them, about ten.[1]

So the Muslims returned, and Allāh protected them from the evil of the Disbelievers; and all praise and thanks for favours are for Him. Then this battle was a preparation for the battles against the Byzantines that came after it, and struck terror in the enemies of Allāh and His Messenger.

---

1 — For a list of the Muslims who were martyred at Mu'tah, see **Endnote 64 on page 493**.

CHAPTER:

The Conquest Of Makkah

We will mention in it a summary of the expedition of the conquest of Makkah, with which Allāh (the Mighty and Majestic) honoured His Messenger, and with which He brought pleasure to his eyes; and which He made a manifest sign of the raising high of His Word, the completion of His Religion, and His concern for aiding him.

That occurred because (the tribe of) Khuzāʿah, as we have already mentioned, entered into an alliance with Allāh's Messenger (صَلَّىٰٱللَّهُعَلَيْهِوَسَلَّمَ) and Banū Bakr entered into an alliance with the Quraysh; and the period of the agreement was laid down as ten years, and the people were rendered safe from each other. So one year of the agreement had passed, and about nine months of the second year, and that was not completed before Nawfal ibn Muʿāwiyah Ad-Dīlī and those who obeyed him from (the tribe of) Banū Bakr ibn ʿAbd Manāt proceeded towards, and attacked (the tribe of) Khuzāʿah at night, at a watering place of theirs called 'Al-Watīr.'

So they fought there, because of a grudge which Banū Bakr bore against Khuzāʿah from the days of Ignorance.

Furthermore, the Quraysh aided Banū Bakr against Khuzāʿah, by supplying them with weapons, and some of them secretly supported them in person. So Khuzāʿah fled to the Sacred Precincts (Al-Haram), but Banū Bakr pursued them into it. So the people of Nawfal reminded Nawfal of the Sacred Precincts and said: "Beware of your God!"

So he said that he had no God that day, (and said): "By Allāh, O Banū Bakr! You steal within the Sacred Precincts, will you not then avenge yourselves in it?"[1]

I say: this Nawfal accepted Islām after that,[2] and Allāh pardoned him; and a hadīth of his is reported in the two *Sahīhs* (رَضِيَ اللَّهُ عَنْهُ).[3]

They killed a man of Khuzā'ah called Munabbih, and Khuzā'ah sought refuge in the houses of Makkah, and they entered the house of Budayl ibn Warqā', and the house of a freed-slave of theirs called Rāfi'. So the covenant of the Quraysh was broken by that.

So 'Amr ibn Sālim Al-Khuzā'ī and Budayl ibn Warqā' Al-Khuzā'ī [and some people from Khuzā'ah][4] departed and went to Allāh's Messenger (صَلَّى اللَّهُ عَلَيْهِ وَسَلَّمَ). They informed him of what Quraysh had done, and requested that he aid them against them. So he (صَلَّى اللَّهُ عَلَيْهِ وَسَلَّمَ) responded to them and gave them the good news that he would assist them.[5] He also forewarned them that Abū Sufyān would come to him to renew the treaty, but that he would send him back without him having achieved his purpose; and that is what occurred.

This was because the Quraysh came to regret what they had done, and therefore sent Abū Sufyān to reinforce the agreement which existed between them and Muhammad (صَلَّى اللَّهُ عَلَيْهِ وَسَلَّمَ), and to extend its time period. So he went off, and when he came to 'Usfān he met Budayl ibn Warqā,

---

1 — For more detail see **Endnote 65 on page 494.**

2 — [MK][MM] He is Nawfal ibn Mu'āwiyah Ad-Dīlī. He accepted Islām and was present with the Prophet (صَلَّى اللَّهُ عَلَيْهِ وَسَلَّمَ) at the Conquest of Makkah, which was his first expedition. He settled in Al-Madīnah, and died there in the days of Yazīd ibn Mu'āwiyah. Refer to *Usdul-Ghābah* (5/47).

3 — [SH] Indicating by that the hadīth reported by Al-Bukhārī (no. 3602) and Muslim (4/2212/11) from him, that he said: "I heard Allāh's Messenger (صَلَّى اللَّهُ عَلَيْهِ وَسَلَّمَ) say: 'Amongst the Prayer(s) there is a Prayer, which if a person misses it then it is as if he has lost his family and wealth.'"

4 — [MK][MM][SH] An addition not present in the original, but necessitated by the context and found in the works of Sīrah such as *Jawāmi'us-Sīrah* of Ibn Hazm.

5 — For more detail see **Endnote 66 on page 495.**

who was returning from Al-Madīnah. Budayl, however, concealed what had been said by Allāh's Messenger (صَلَّى ٱللَّٰهُ عَلَيْهِ وَسَلَّمَ). Abū Sufyān proceeded until he came to Al-Madīnah, and he entered upon his daughter Umm Habībah, the wife of Allāh's Messenger (صَلَّى ٱللَّٰهُ عَلَيْهِ وَسَلَّمَ) — (رَضِيَ ٱللَّٰهُ عَنْهَا).

He tried to sit upon the mattress of Allāh's Messenger (صَلَّى ٱللَّٰهُ عَلَيْهِ وَسَلَّمَ), but she prevented him and said: *"You are an unclean mushrik man!"* So he said: "O my daughter, by Allāh! You have been struck by evil after having left me." [1]

Then Allāh's Messenger (صَلَّى ٱللَّٰهُ عَلَيْهِ وَسَلَّمَ) came, and he explained to him his purpose in coming. Allāh's Messenger (صَلَّى ٱللَّٰهُ عَلَيْهِ وَسَلَّمَ), however, did not reply with a single word to him. Then he went to Abū Bakr (رَضِيَ ٱللَّٰهُ عَنْهُ) and requested that he should speak to Allāh's Messenger (صَلَّى ٱللَّٰهُ عَلَيْهِ وَسَلَّمَ), but he refused. Then he went to ʿUmar (رَضِيَ ٱللَّٰهُ عَنْهُ) who responded to him with sternness, and said: "Am I to do that?! By Allāh, if I could find nothing other than an ant I would fight you with it."

So he went to ʿAlī (رَضِيَ ٱللَّٰهُ عَنْهُ) and he would not do so; and he requested from Fātimah, the daughter of Allāh's Messenger (صَلَّى ٱللَّٰهُ عَلَيْهِ وَسَلَّمَ) — (رَضِيَ ٱللَّٰهُ عَنْهَا) — that she should order her son Al-Hasan to intercede to safeguard the people, so she said: *"My son is not old enough for that, and no one can intercede and grant protection over and above Allāh's Messenger (صَلَّى ٱللَّٰهُ عَلَيْهِ وَسَلَّمَ)."* Then ʿAlī (رَضِيَ ٱللَّٰهُ عَنْهُ) indicated to him that he should himself stand and give his own guarantee of safety between the people. So he did that, and then he returned to Makkah, and informed them of what had occurred between him and them. So they said: "By Allāh! All he has done, meaning ʿAlī, is that he has made a fool of you." [2]

Then Allāh's Messenger (صَلَّى ٱللَّٰهُ عَلَيْهِ وَسَلَّمَ) made preparations for an attack against Makkah, and he asked Allāh (the Mighty and Majestic) to blind the Quraysh to any news. So His Lord (the Exalted and Most High)

---

1 — DB Shaikh Al-Albānī said in his notes upon *Fiqhus-Sīrah* (p. 405): "Daʿīf (weak): Reported by Ibn Is-hāq without a chain of narration, as occurs in *Sīrah Ibn Hishām* (2/265), and with Ibn Jarīr [At-Tabarī] (5/325-326)."

2 — *ibid.*

answered him. So it occurred that Hātib ibn Abī Balta'ah[1] wrote a letter to the people of Makkah to inform them of the intention of Allāh's Messenger (صَلَّى ٱللَّهُ عَلَيْهِ وَسَلَّمَ) to attack them, and he sent it with a woman. He did that seeking to safeguard some personal benefit that he had, and Allāh's Messenger (صَلَّى ٱللَّهُ عَلَيْهِ وَسَلَّمَ) accepted that explanation from him and believed him, since he was one of those who had fought at Badr.

So Allāh's Messenger (صَلَّى ٱللَّهُ عَلَيْهِ وَسَلَّمَ) sent out 'Alī, Az-Zubayr, and Al-Miqdād (رَضِيَ ٱللَّهُ عَنْهُمْ) and they caught that woman at Rawdah Khākh,[2] and they took this letter from her. So this was something which Allāh (the Mighty and Majestic) informed His Prophet (صَلَّى ٱللَّهُ عَلَيْهِ وَسَلَّمَ) of, and it is a sign of the trueness of his Prophethood.[3]

He (صَلَّى ٱللَّهُ عَلَيْهِ وَسَلَّمَ) went out on the tenth of Ramadān with an army of ten thousand soldiers from the Muhājirīn, the Ansār, and the tribes of the Arabs; and Muzaynah numbered over a thousand, and likewise Banū Sulaym, in the most well-known saying — may Allāh be pleased with them all. He (صَلَّى ٱللَّهُ عَلَيْهِ وَسَلَّمَ) left Abū Ruhm, Kulthūm ibn Husayn[4] in charge of Al-Madīnah.[5] He was met by his paternal uncle, Al-'Abbās,

---

1 — [MK][MM] He is Hātib ibn Abī Balta'ah, Al-Lakhmī, and the name of his father was 'Amr. He was a confederate of Banū Asad ibn 'Abdil-'Uzzā. He was present at Badr and the battles after it along with Allāh's Messenger (صَلَّى ٱللَّهُ عَلَيْهِ وَسَلَّمَ), and he was one of the fiercest of the archers amongst the Companions, and he had extensive trade in Makkah. The Prophet (صَلَّى ٱللَّهُ عَلَيْهِ وَسَلَّمَ) sent him with his letter to Al-Muqawqis, the ruler of Alexandria. He died in Al-Madīnah in 30 H. Refer to *Usdul-Ghābah* (1/360-362).

2 — [MK][MM] A place one riding stage away from Al-Madīnah in the direction of Makkah (MM/MK)

3 — [SH] Reported by Al-Bukhārī in his *Sahīh* (no. 4274) and Muslim in his *Sahīh* (no. 2494) as a hadīth of 'Alī ibn Abī Tālib (رَضِيَ ٱللَّهُ عَنْهُ).

4 — [MK][MM] He is Abū Ruhm, Kulthūm ibn Husayn Al-Ghifārī, well known by his name and by his kunyah. He accepted Islām after the arrival of Allāh's Messenger (صَلَّى ٱللَّهُ عَلَيْهِ وَسَلَّمَ) at Al-Madīnah. He was present at Uhud and was struck in the throat by an arrow, and so came to be known as *'the one struck in the throat.'* The Prophet (صَلَّى ٱللَّهُ عَلَيْهِ وَسَلَّمَ) left him in charge of Al-Madīnah twice; once during the 'Umrah of the Agreement, and once during the expedition of the Conquest of Makkah. Refer to *Usudul-Ghābah* (5/197).

5 — For more detail see **Endnote 67 on page 495**.

at Dhul-Hulayfah, or it is otherwise said: at Al-Juhfah, and he accepted Islām, and returned with him (صَلَّى ٱللَّٰهُ عَلَيْهِ وَسَلَّمَ); and he sent his family and belongings on to Al-Madīnah.

Then when he (صَلَّى ٱللَّٰهُ عَلَيْهِ وَسَلَّمَ) reached Nīqul-'Iqāb[1] his paternal cousin Abū Sufyān ibn Al-Hārith ibn 'Abdil-Muttalib came to him, along with 'Abdullāh ibn Abī Umayyah — the brother of Umm Salamah — and they had both accepted Islām, but he sent them away. However, Umm Salamah interceded for them, and mentioned to him such things about them as caused him to take pity upon them. So he accepted them, and they perfected their Islām (رَضِيَ ٱللَّٰهُ عَنْهُمَا) after they had previously been the staunchest of enemies towards him (صَلَّى ٱللَّٰهُ عَلَيْهِ وَسَلَّمَ).[2]

He (صَلَّى ٱللَّٰهُ عَلَيْهِ وَسَلَّمَ) fasted until he reached a watering place called Al-Kudayd, between 'Usfān and Amajj, on the road to Makkah. Here he broke his fast after 'Asr, upon his riding camel, so that the people should see him; and he gave permission for the people to break their fast; and then he made it binding upon them to do that.[3]

Then he (صَلَّى ٱللَّٰهُ عَلَيْهِ وَسَلَّمَ) continued until he stopped at Marraz-Zahrān where he spent the night.[4]

As for Quraysh, then Allāh blinded them to any news, however they feared and suspected that. So that night Ibn Harb,[5] Budayl ibn Warqā',

---

1 — SH A place between Makkah and Al-Madīnah close to Al-Juhfah. (*Mu'jamul-Buldān*).

2 — For more detail regarding this story, see **Endnote 68 on page 496.**

3 — SH Reported by Al-Bukhārī (nos. 4275-4279) and Muslim (no. 1113) as a hadīth of Ibn 'Abbās (رَضِيَ ٱللَّٰهُ عَنْهُمَا). An-Nawawī said in *Sharh Sahīh Muslim* (7/230): "Al-Kudayd (...) is a spring about seven riding stages from Al-Madīnah and nearly two riding stages from Makkah; and it is closer to Al-Madīnah than 'Usfān."

Al-Qādī 'Iyād said: "And 'Usfān is a large town, thirty six miles from Makkah." And Amajj is a town from the provincial towns of Al-Madīnah.

4 — DB "Marraz-Zahrān is a place one riding stage from Makkah, and it is mentioned in hadīth. 'Arrām said: 'Marr is the town and Az-Zahrān is the wadi. At Marr there are many springs, date-palms and sycamore-figs.'" — *Mu'jamul-Buldān*

5 — DB i.e. Abū Sufyān, Sakhr ibn Umayyah.

and Hakīm ibn Hizām went out to search for news. So when they saw the campfires they were doubtful regarding them. Budayl said: *"They are the fires of Khuzā'ah."* So Abū Sufyān said: *"Khuzā'ah are fewer in number than that."* Al-'Abbās was riding the mule of Allāh's Messenger (صَلَّى ٱللَّهُ عَلَيْهِ وَسَلَّمَ) that night, and he went out from the army hoping to meet someone or other. So when he heard their voices he recognised them, and said: "Abū Hanzalah!"

So Abū Sufyān recognised him and said: "Abdul-Fadl?"

He said: "Yes."

He said: "What lies behind you?"

He said: "Woe to you! This is Allāh's Messenger (صَلَّى ٱللَّهُ عَلَيْهِ وَسَلَّمَ) with (all) the people. What a woeful morning it will be for Quraysh!"

He said: "Then what can we do about it?"

He said: "By Allāh! If he catches you, he will certainly kill you. So ride behind me and accept Islām."

So he rode behind him and set off with him. He passed through the army and whenever they came to a people, they would say: *"This is the paternal uncle of Allāh's Messenger (صَلَّى ٱللَّهُ عَلَيْهِ وَسَلَّمَ) upon the mule of Allāh's Messenger (صَلَّى ٱللَّهُ عَلَيْهِ وَسَلَّمَ),"* until they passed by the camping place of 'Umar ibn Al-Khattāb (رَضِيَ ٱللَّهُ عَنْهُ). So when he saw him he said: "The enemy of Allāh? All praise is for Allāh Who has delivered you to me without any treaty or safeguard."

Al-'Abbās made the mule run, and 'Umar (رَضِيَ ٱللَّهُ عَنْهُ) ran on foot after it, but was too slow. So Al-'Abbās preceded him, and entered him into the presence of Allāh's Messenger (صَلَّى ٱللَّهُ عَلَيْهِ وَسَلَّمَ), and 'Umar followed him, and sought permission of Allāh's Messenger (صَلَّى ٱللَّهُ عَلَيْهِ وَسَلَّمَ) to strike his neck. So Al-'Abbās immediately gave him a guarantee of safety. So he and 'Umar ibn Al-Khattāb (رَضِيَ ٱللَّهُ عَنْهُمَا) exchanged disagreeable words.

So he (صَلَّى ٱللَّهُ عَلَيْهِ وَسَلَّمَ) ordered him to bring Abū Sufyān to himself in the morning. So then, in the morning, he took him to Allāh's Messenger (صَلَّى ٱللَّهُ عَلَيْهِ وَسَلَّمَ) and he asked him to accept Islām. He was hesitant for a while but then Al-'Abbās spoke sternly and he accepted Islām. Al-'Abbās said:

"O Messenger of Allāh! Abū Sufyān loves to be honoured," and therefore he (صَلَّىٰ ٱللَّٰهُ عَلَيْهِ وَسَلَّمَ) said: "Whoever enters the house of Abū Sufyān will be safe, and whoever closes his door will be safe, and whoever enters the Sacred Mosque will be safe."[1]

Ibn Hazm said: This is a textual statement that it was conquered peacefully, and not by force.

I say: This is one of the sayings of the scholars, and it is the newer saying from the position of Ash-Shāfi'ī; and a further evidence which is used to prove that is that its property was not divided into fifths, and it was not distributed.

Whereas those who hold that it was conquered by force use as evidence the fact that on that day they killed about twenty men of the Quraysh, at Al-Khandamah;[2] and they use this wording as evidence also: *"Then he will be safe."* However, the matter would be too protracted to mention in detail here; and the two Shaikhs have debated this matter, by which I mean Tājud-Dīn Al-Fazārī and Abū Zakariyyā An-Nawawī, and also the matter of the distribution of the booty.

What is important is that when he entered the morning of that day he proceeded towards Makkah, and he (صَلَّىٰ ٱللَّٰهُ عَلَيْهِ وَسَلَّمَ) had ordered Al-'Abbās to cause Abū Sufyān to stand upon a promontory of the mountain, so that he could see the armies of Islām as they passed by him.[3]

He (صَلَّىٰ ٱللَّٰهُ عَلَيْهِ وَسَلَّمَ) placed Abū 'Ubaydah ibn Al-Jarrāh (رَضِيَ ٱللَّٰهُ عَنْهُ) in charge of the vanguard, Khālid ibn Al-Walīd (رَضِيَ ٱللَّٰهُ عَنْهُ) in charge of the right wing, Az-Zubayr ibn Al-'Awwām (رَضِيَ ٱللَّٰهُ عَنْهُ) in charge of the left wing, and Allāh's Messenger (صَلَّىٰ ٱللَّٰهُ عَلَيْهِ وَسَلَّمَ) was at the centre. He had given the battle-flag to Sa'd ibn 'Ubādah (رَضِيَ ٱللَّٰهُ عَنْهُ), but then it reached him that he had said to Abū Sufyān when he passed by him: "O Abū Sufyān! Today is

---

1 — [BJ][SZ] Reported by Abū Dāwūd (no. 3022), with its full wording, as a hadīth of Ibn 'Abbās, and our Shaikh [Al-Albānī] (رَحِمَهُ ٱللَّٰهُ) declared it *'hasan'* in *Sahīh Sunan Abī Dāwūd*; and the words ascribed to the Prophet (صَلَّىٰ ٱللَّٰهُ عَلَيْهِ وَسَلَّمَ) have a similar witness reported by Muslim (no. 1780), as a hadīth of Abū Hurairah (رَضِيَ ٱللَّٰهُ عَنْهُ).

2 — [MK][MM] The name of a mountain in Makkah.

3 — See **Endnote 69 on page 497** for detail regarding authenticity.

the day of slaughter. Today the sanctity will be broken" — meaning: the sanctity of the Ka'bah.

So when Abū Sufyān complained of that to Allāh's Messenger (صَلَّىٰ ٱللَّهُ عَلَيْهِ وَسَلَّمَ) he said: "Rather this is a day when the Ka'bah shall be honoured."[1]

Therefore he commanded that the flag be taken from Sa'd and given to 'Alī, or it is said: to Az-Zubayr, and that is what is correct. He (صَلَّىٰ ٱللَّهُ عَلَيْهِ وَسَلَّمَ) ordered Az-Zubayr to enter from Kadā', in upper Makkah, and that he should plant his flag at Al-Hajūn; and he ordered Khālid to enter from Kudayy, in the lower part of Makkah, and he ordered them to fight whoever fought against them.[2]

It happened that 'Ikrimah ibn Abī Jahl, Safwān ibn Umayyah, and Suhayl ibn 'Amr gathered an opposing force at Al-Khandamah. So Khālid passed by them and fought them, and three of the Muslims were killed; and they were: Kurz ibn Jābir, who was from the Banū Muhārib ibn Fihr, and Hubaysh ibn Khālid ibn Rabī'ah ibn Asram Al-Khuzā'ī, and Salamah ibn Al-Mīlā' Al-Juhanī (رَضِيَ ٱللَّهُ عَنْهُمْ); and from the Mushrikūn thirteen men were killed, and the remainder fled.

Allāh's Messenger (صَلَّىٰ ٱللَّهُ عَلَيْهِ وَسَلَّمَ) entered Makkah riding upon his she-camel, wearing a helmet upon his head,[3] and his head was almost touching the front part of the saddle in humility to his Lord — the Mighty and Majestic.[4]

He (صَلَّىٰ ٱللَّهُ عَلَيْهِ وَسَلَّمَ) had granted a guarantee of safety to the people except for 'Abdul-'Uzzā ibn Khatal, 'Abdullāh ibn Sa'd ibn Abī Sarh, 'Ikrimah ibn Abī Jahl, Miqyas ibn Subābah, Al-Huwayrith ibn Nuqaydh, two singing girls who belonged to Ibn Khatal, and they were: Fartanā and her companion; and Sārah, the slave-girl belonging to Banū 'Abdil-Muttalib.

---

1 — DB Shaikh Al-Albānī (رَحِمَهُ ٱللَّهُ) said in *Takhrīj Fiqhis-Sīrah* (p. 413): "*Da'īf* (weak): Reported by Al-Bukhārī [no. 4280] and others as a *'mursal'* hadīth of 'Urwah."

2 — SH Reported by Al-Bukhārī (no. 4280).

3 — BJ SZ Reported by Al-Bukhārī (no. 4286) and Muslim (no. 1357) as a hadīth of Anas ibn Mālik (رَضِيَ ٱللَّهُ عَنْهُ).

4 — For details regarding the authenticity of this, see **Endnote 70 on page 497**.

He (صَلَّى ٱللَّهُ عَلَيْهِ وَسَلَّمَ) announced that their blood could lawfully be shed, and he ordered that they should be killed wherever they be found, even if they were hanging on to the cover of the Ka'bah. So Ibn Khatal was killed and he was holding on to its cover,[1] and Miqyas ibn Subābah, and Al-Huwayrith ibn Nuqaydh, and one of the two singing girls; and the rest were rendered safe. He (صَلَّى ٱللَّهُ عَلَيْهِ وَسَلَّمَ) camped in Makkah, and took a bath in the house of Umm Hāni';[2] and he prayed eight rak'ahs,[3] giving the Salutation after every two rak'ahs. So it is said that it was the Duhā Prayer,[4] and it is otherwise said: it was the Conquest Prayer.[5] As-Suhaylī said: *"And it was prayed by Sa'd ibn Abī Waqqās in the palace of Kisrā, except that he prayed eight rak'ahs with a single salutation"*,[6] and it is not as he said; rather he gave Salutation between each two rak'ahs, as Abū Dāwūd reported it.[7]

And he (صَلَّى ٱللَّهُ عَلَيْهِ وَسَلَّمَ) went out to the House, and performed the Tawāf of Arrival (*'Tawāful-Qudūm'*) around it, and did not perform the Sa'ī, and

---

1 — [BJ][SZ] Refer to *Sahīhul-Bukhārī* (no.1846) and *Sahīh Muslim* (no.1357) as a hadīth of Anas ibn Mālik (رَضِيَ ٱللَّهُ عَنْهُ).

2 — [SH] She was the daughter of Abū Tālib, and the paternal cousin of Allāh's Messenger (صَلَّى ٱللَّهُ عَلَيْهِ وَسَلَّمَ). She accepted Islām in the year of the Conquest. She was married to Hubayrah ibn 'Āmir Al-Makhzūmī, who fled to Najrān on the Day of the Conquest and died there as a Mushrik.

3 — [SH] Reported by Al-Bukhārī (no. 1176) and Muslim (no. 336/71).

4 — [SH] This is what is established as the saying of Umm Hāni' (رَضِيَ ٱللَّهُ عَنْهَا) in the two *Sahīhs*.

5 — [SH] This saying was held by Ibn Qayyim Al-Jawziyyah (رَحِمَهُ ٱللَّهُ) in *Zādul-Ma'ād* (3/410).

6 — [SH] In *Ar-Rawdul-Unuf* (7/108). [DB] As-Suhaylī said: "It was the Conquest Prayer. It is known by this name by the people of knowledge, and the generals used to pray it when they conquered a land." At-Tabarī said: "Sa'd ibn Abī Waqqās prayed (it) when he conquered Al-Madā'in and entered the palace of Kisrā; so he prayed the Conquest Prayer in it; and it is eight rak'ahs, without any separation between them, and it is not prayed with an imām."

7 — For details regarding the authenticity of this, see ENDNOTE 71 ON PAGE 498.

he was not performing ʿUmrah;[1] and he called for the keys and entered the House,[2] and he ordered that the images be cast out and erased from it[3] and on that day Bilāl gave the Adhān from on top of the Kaʿbah.[4] Then he (صَلَّى ٱللَّهُ عَلَيْهِ وَسَلَّمَ) restored the keys to ʿUthmān ibn Talhah ibn Abī Talhah, and confirmed their role of custodianship of the Kaʿbah (*As-Sidānah*).[5] And the conquest occurred with ten days of Ramadān remaining.[6] And he (صَلَّى ٱللَّهُ عَلَيْهِ وَسَلَّمَ) continued desisting from fasting for the remainder of the month, praying two rakʿahs,[7] and he commanded the inhabitants of Makkah to complete [the Prayers], as is reported by An-Nasāʾī with a *'hasan'* chain of narration from ʿImrān ibn Husayn (رَضِيَ ٱللَّهُ عَنْهُ).[8]

The next day, after the Day of the Conquest, he (صَلَّى ٱللَّهُ عَلَيْهِ وَسَلَّمَ) gave a Khutbah, and he made clear the sanctity of Makkah and that it had not been rendered permissible for anyone before him, nor would it be rendered permissible for anyone after him; and that it had only been rendered permissible for him for a single hour of the day, and that apart from that hour it was, and remains, in its state of sanctity.[9]

And he (صَلَّى ٱللَّهُ عَلَيْهِ وَسَلَّمَ) sent expeditions to those areas of the Arabs lying around Makkah, calling them to Islām.

---

1 — [SH] Reported by Muslim in his *Sahīh* (no.1780), as a hadīth of Abū Hurairah (رَضِيَ ٱللَّهُ عَنْهُ).

2 — [SH] Reported by Al-Bukhārī (no. 4289) in disconnected form, and in connected form (no. 2988), and Muslim (no. 1331) as a hadīth of Ibn ʿUmar (رَضِيَ ٱللَّهُ عَنْهُمَا).

3 — [SH] Reported by Al-Bukhārī (no. 3352) as a hadīth of Ibn ʿAbbās (رَضِيَ ٱللَّهُ عَنْهُمَا).

4 — For details regarding the authenticity of this, see **Endnote 72 on page 498**.

5 — For details regarding the authenticity of this, see **Endnote 73 on page 499**.

6 — [SH] Al-Hāfidh Ibn Hajr said in *Fat-hul-Bārī* (4/181): "What is agreed upon by the scholars of the military expeditions is that he went out on the tenth of Ramadān, and he entered Makkah on the nineteenth."

7 — [SH] The author (رَحِمَهُ ٱللَّهُ) said in *Al-Bidāyah wan-Nihāyah* (6/609): "And there is no disagreement about the fact that he (عَلَيْهِ ٱلصَّلَاةُ وَٱلسَّلَامُ) remained for the rest of the month of Ramadān shortening the Prayers and not fasting."

8 — For details regarding the authenticity of this, see **Endnote 74 on page 500**.

9 — [SH] Reported by Al-Bukhārī (no. 4295) and Muslim (no. 1354), as a hadīth of Abū Shuraih Al-ʿAdawī (رَضِيَ ٱللَّهُ عَنْهُ).

Chapter: The Expedition of Khālid to Banū Jadhīmah

So amongst these expeditions was the sending of Khālid to Banū Jadhīmah, those whom Khālid killed, who said — when he called them to Islām: *"We have left our religion (saba'nā),"* and they were unable to respond properly and say: *"We have accepted Islām (aslamnā)."*

So Allāh's Messenger (صَلَّى ٱللَّهُ عَلَيْهِ وَسَلَّمَ) paid the blood money for them, and declared himself free of what Khālid had done with them.[1]

Chapter: The Expedition of Khālid Against Al-'Uzzā

Also amongst these expeditions was the sending of Khālid against Al-'Uzzā; and it was a shrine venerated by the Quraysh, and by Kinānah, and by all of Mudar. So he, an imām (leader) and a brave man (رَضِيَ ٱللَّهُ عَنْهُ) demolished it.[2]

And 'Ikrimah ibn Abī Jahl had fled to Yemen; so his wife caught up with him, and she was a Muslim, and she was Umm Hakīm bint Al-Hārith ibn Hishām. So she persuaded him to return under a guarantee of safety

---

1 — [SH] Reported by Al-Bukhārī in his *Sahīh* (no. 4339), as a hadīth of Ibn 'Umar (رَضِيَ ٱللَّهُ عَنْهُمَا). Al-Hāfidh Ibn Hajr said in *Fat-hul-Bārī* (13/182): "Al-Khattābī said: *'The wisdom behind his (صَلَّى ٱللَّهُ عَلَيْهِ وَسَلَّمَ) freeing himself from the action of Khālid, along with the fact that he did not punish him for it — since he acted upon personal deduction (ijtihād) — is so that it should be known that he had not given him permission for that; for fear that someone might believe that it had occurred with his permission; and in order to deter anyone else from doing the like of what Khālid had done.'*"

Al-Hāfidh said: "And what is apparent is that freeing oneself from an action does not necessitate that the one who did it is sinful, or that a penalty becomes binding upon him; since one who made a mistake is not taken to be sinful, even though his action is not praiseworthy."

2 — [SH] Reported by An-Nasā'ī in *As-Sunanul-Kubrā* (no.11483), and Abū Ya'lā in his *Musnad* (no. 902), and from him by Al-Bayhaqī in *Dalā'ilun-Nubuwwah* (5/77), and Abū Nu'aym in *Dalā'ilun-Nubuwwah* (p. 469): by way of Ibn Fudayl: from Al-Walīd ibn Jumai': from Abut-Tufayl, with it. I say: This is a *'hasan'* chain of narration.

from Allāh's Messenger (ﷺ). So he accepted Islām, and he made his Islām good.[1]

Likewise, Safwān ibn Umayyah had also fled to Yemen; so 'Umayr ibn Wahb, who used to be his companion in the days of ignorance, followed him with a guarantee of safety from Allāh's Messenger (ﷺ) and persuaded him to return. Furthermore, he (ﷺ) gave him a period of respite of four months; and it was not completed before he had accepted Islām, and he made his Islām good (رضي الله عنه).[2]

Chapter: The Expedition of Hunayn[3]

When news of the Conquest of Makkah reached (the tribe of) Hawāzin, Mālik ibn 'Awf An-Nasrī gathered them together. So he was joined by the (tribe of) Thaqīf, and his people: Banū Nasr ibn Mu'āwiyah, and Banū Jusham, Banū Sa'd ibn Bakr, and a few of Banū Hilāl ibn 'Āmir; and they brought along with them their cattle and their wives, in order that they should not flee.[4]

So Durayd ibn As-Simmah (the Shaikh of Banū Jusham, who because of his age they carried along with them in a howdah, seeking the value of his opinions) when he found this to be the case he criticised Mālik ibn 'Awf An-Nasrī for that and reviled him, and said: *"If (the battle) goes in your favour, then that will not benefit you; and if it goes against you, then*

---

1 — SH It is reported by Ibn Is-hāq in *As-Sīrah* (4/1083: Ibn Hishām) who said: *"Az-Zuhrī narrated it to me."* I say: It is a *'mursal'* report with a *'sahīh'* isnād.

2 — SH Reported by Ibn Is-hāq in *As-Sīrah* (4/1083: Ibn Hishām) who said: *"Muhammad ibn Ja'far narrated to me; from 'Urwah ibn Az-Zubayr"* (with it). I say: This is a *'mursal'* report with a *'sahīh'* isnād.

3 — SH Al-Hāfidh Ibn Hajr said in *Al-Fat-h* (8/27): "Hunayn (...) is a wadi at the side of the (market place of) Dhul-Majāz. It is close to At-Tā'if; between it and Makkah is a distance of more than ten miles, and it is in the same direction as 'Arafāt."

The expedition is also named *'The Expedition of Awtās'* since it began at Hunayn and ended at Awtās. It is likewise called *'The Expedition of Hawāzin'* since they are the (tribe) who came to fight against Allāh's Messenger (ﷺ).

4 — For details regarding the authenticity of this, see Endnote 75 on page 500.

nothing will stop a defeated army from fleeing." He also encouraged them not to fight except in their own territory, but they refused to obey him in that, and they followed the opinion of Mālik ibn ʿAwf instead. So Durayd said: "This is a day I shall not witness (as a fighter), but nor will it escape me altogether."

He (صَلَّى ٱللَّٰهُ عَلَيْهِ وَسَلَّمَ) sent out ʿAbdullāh ibn Abī Hadradil-Aslamī[1] to seek out news of the people for him, and what they were intending; and Allāh's Messenger (صَلَّى ٱللَّٰهُ عَلَيْهِ وَسَلَّمَ) prepared to meet them.[2] He also loaned from Safwān ibn Umayyah some coats of chain mail[3] — it is said: a hundred, or it is said: four hundred,[4] — and he loaned from him an amount of equipment. He proceeded towards them with the ten thousand men who were present with him at the Conquest, and with two thousand of those who were pardoned on the Day of the Conquest of Makkah,[5] and Safwān ibn Umayyah was present with him at Hunayn, whilst he was still a Mushrik.

---

1 — SH He was ʿAbdullāh ibn Abī Hadrad ibn ʿUmayr ibn Hawāz ibn Aslam. He was present at Al-Hudaybiyah, and Khaybar, and the later battles along with Allāh's Messenger (صَلَّى ٱللَّٰهُ عَلَيْهِ وَسَلَّمَ). He died in 71 H.

2 — For details regarding the authenticity of this, see **Endnote 76 on page 501**.

3 — For details regarding the reporting of this, see **Endnote 77 on page 501**.

4 — SH I say: Rather what is correct is that he loaned thirty coats of chain mail from him, as occurs in the preceding hadīth of Yaʿlā ibn Umayyah. As for those who say *'a hundred'*, then this is based upon what Ibn Is-hāq mentioned in *As-Sīrah* (4/1103). The author said in *Al-Bidāyah wan-Nihāyah* (7/9): *"This is how Ibn Is-hāq mentioned it, without a chain of narration."* I say: Yūnus ibn Bukayr narrated it from him with a full chain of narration, as preceded a short while ago, however its chain of narration is weak because of the weakness of Ahmad ibn ʿAbdil-Jabbār; and I have not seen anyone who said *'four hundred.'*

5 — SH (Refer to what) Al-Bukhārī reported (no. 4337) and Muslim (no. 1059/ 135), as a hadīth of Anas ibn Mālik (رَضِيَ ٱللَّٰهُ عَنْهُ).

It occurred in Shawwāl of this year, and he left in charge of Makkah ʿAttāb ibn Asīd ibn Abil-ʿĪs ibn Umayyah ibn ʿAbd Shams,[1] who was about twenty years old.

During that journey of his (صَلَّى ٱللَّهُ عَلَيْهِ وَسَلَّمَ), he passed by a tree venerated by the Mushrikūn, called *'Dhātu Anwāt,'*[2] so some of the ignorant bedouins said: "Make for us a *Dhātu Anwāt* just as they have a *Dhātu Anwāt*."

So he [صَلَّى ٱللَّهُ عَلَيْهِ وَسَلَّمَ] said: "You have said, by the One in Whose Hand is my soul, the like of what the people of Mūsā said: *'Make for us an object of worship just as they have objects of worship.'* You will certainly follow the ways of those who came before you."[3]

Then he (صَلَّى ٱللَّهُ عَلَيْهِ وَسَلَّمَ) proceeded until he drew level with Hunayn, and it is a steep-sided valley (wādī) from the valleys of Tihāmah, and Hawāzin lay in wait to ambush them there. It was during the time of the darkness before dawn and they attacked the Muslims, doing so in unison. So the Muslims fled without even turning to each other.[4] So this is as stated by He — the Most High:

---

1 — [MK][MM] He was ʿAttāb ibn Abil-ʿĪs ibn Umayyah ibn ʿAbd Shams. He accepted Islām on the day of the Conquest of Makkah, and he was a brave and intelligent man, and was one of the nobles from the Arabs in the early part of Islām. He remained as governor of Makkah from the time when the Messenger (صَلَّى ٱللَّهُ عَلَيْهِ وَسَلَّمَ) placed him in that position until he died, towards the end of the days of ʿUmar.

2 — [MK][MM] *'Anwāt'* is the plural of *'Nawt'*, which is that which is hung/suspended upon something. The tree was called this because the disbelievers of Quraysh and other Arabs used to come to it every year and hang their weapons upon it, and perform sacrifices by it, and remain there for a day.

3 — For details regarding the authenticity of this, see **Endnote 78 on page 502**.

4 — [SH] Reported by Ibn Is-hāq in *As-Sīrah* (4/1104-1105: Ibn Hishām), and from him Ahmad in his *Musnad* (3/376-377), Abū Yaʿlā in his *Musnad* (no. 1862) and (...) saying; ʿĀsim ibn ʿUmar ibn Qatādah narrated to me: from ʿAbdur-Rahmān ibn Jābir ibn ʿAbdillāh: from his father (Jābir) with it.

I say: This is a *'sahīh'* chain of narration, as our Shaikh Al-Albānī (رَحِمَهُ ٱللَّهُ) said in *Takhrīj Fiqhis-Sīrah* (pg. 422).

لَقَدْ نَصَرَكُمُ اللَّهُ فِي مَوَاطِنَ كَثِيرَةٍ ۙ وَيَوْمَ حُنَيْنٍ ۙ إِذْ أَعْجَبَتْكُمْ كَثْرَتُكُمْ فَلَمْ تُغْنِ
عَنكُمْ شَيْئًا وَضَاقَتْ عَلَيْكُمُ الْأَرْضُ بِمَا رَحُبَتْ ثُمَّ وَلَّيْتُم مُّدْبِرِينَ

MEANING: "And (He aided you) on the day of Hunayn, when you were amazed at your great number, but it did not avail you at all; and the earth, despite its vastness, became restricted for you; and then you turned and fled." — **Sūrah At-Tawbah (9):25**

That was because some of them had said: "We shall not be overcome today on account of lack of numbers."[1]

But Allāh's Messenger (ﷺ) stood firm and did not flee, and with him from the Companions were: Abū Bakr, and ʿUmar; and his paternal uncle Al-ʿAbbās, and his two sons: Al-Fadl, and Qutham; and Abū Sufyān ibn Al-Hārith ibn ʿAbdil-Muttalib, and his son Jaʿfar, and others.[2]

On that day he (ﷺ) was riding a mule which had been given to him as a gift by Farwah ibn Nufāthah Al-Judhāmī, and he was spurring it on with his feet to keep it turned towards the enemy; and Al-ʿAbbās was holding on to its bridle to stop it from going forward; and he (ﷺ) was calling out his name, saying: ***"I am the Prophet, it is no lie. I am the (grand-) son of ʿAbdul-Muttalib!"***[3]

Then he ordered Al-ʿAbbās, who had a strong voice, to call out: ***"O Ansār! O companions of the tree! O companions of the Egyptian thorn-Tree!"***[4]

---

1 — For details regarding the authenticity of this, see **Endnote 79 on page 502**.

2 — [SH] This is a part of the previous hadīth of Jābir.

3 — [SH] Reported by Al-Bukhārī (no. 2864) and Muslim (no. 1776) as a hadīth of Al-Barāʾ ibn ʿĀzib (رَضِيَ ٱللَّهُ عَنْهُ); and Muslim reported it in his *Sahīh* (no. 1775), as a hadīth of Al-ʿAbbās himself, with the wording: "Al-ʿAbbās said: I was holding on to the bridle of the mule of Allāh's Messenger (ﷺ) to hold it back, so that it would not move too quickly; and Abū Sufyān was holding on to the stirrups of Allāh's Messenger (ﷺ)."

4 — [DB] An-Nawawī said in his explanation of *Sahīh Muslim*: "i.e. the tree beneath which they had given 'Bayʿatur-Ridwān' (...) on the Day of Al-Hudaybiyah."

So when the Muslims heard him, whilst they were fleeing, they turned and responded to him: ***"At your service! At your service!"***

Then if a man became unable to turn his camel around, because of the large number of those fleeing, he would dismount from his camel. He would take his coat of mail, put it on, take his sword and his shield and return on foot to Allāh's Messenger (صَلَّى ٱللَّهُ عَلَيْهِ وَسَلَّمَ).

Eventually, when a group of about a hundred of them had gathered around him they faced the Hawāzin, and they fought fiercely with them, and the battle raged.

When they returned Allāh cast terror into the hearts of Hawāzin, and they could not hold themselves;[1] and he (صَلَّى ٱللَّهُ عَلَيْهِ وَسَلَّمَ) threw a handful of gravel at them, and there was not a single one of them except that he was struck by a part of it.[2] And this has been given as the explanation of His Saying — He the Most High:

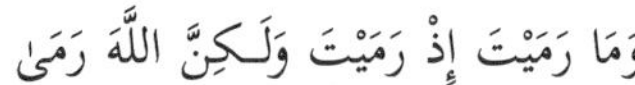

1 — [SH] Reported by Ibn Is-hāq in his *Sīrah* (4/1106-1107: Ibn Hishām): Az-Zuhrī narrated to me: from Kathīr ibn Al-ʿAbbās: from his father Al-ʿAbbās ibn ʿAbdil-Muttalib. I say: This chain of narration is *'sahīh'*, and it is reported by Muslim (no. 1775).

2 — [SH] Reported by Muslim in his *Sahīh* (no.1777) from Salamah ibn Al-Akwaʿ (رَضِيَ ٱللَّهُ عَنْهُ) who said: "We went out to fight at Hunayn along with Allāh's Messenger (صَلَّى ٱللَّهُ عَلَيْهِ وَسَلَّمَ) (...) So when they surrounded Allāh's Messenger (صَلَّى ٱللَّهُ عَلَيْهِ وَسَلَّمَ), he took a handful of earth from the ground. Then he faced them, and said: 'May the faces be disfigured.' So there was not a person amongst them whom Allāh had created except that his eyes were filled with the dust from that handful. So they turned and fled."

And it has another witness from the hadīth of Al-ʿAbbās ibn ʿAbdil-Muttalib (رَضِيَ ٱللَّهُ عَنْهُ) reported by Muslim (no. 1775/76) containing the wording: "Then Allāh's Messenger (صَلَّى ٱللَّهُ عَلَيْهِ وَسَلَّمَ) took some gravel and threw it at the faces of the disbelievers. Then he said: 'They have been defeated, by the Lord of Muhammad'" — and in one narration (no. 1775/77); "They have been defeated by the Lord of the Kaʿbah! They have been defeated, by the Lord of the Kaʿbah."

MEANING: "And you threw not, when you threw, but it was Allāh Who threw." — **SŪRAH AL-ANFĀL (8): 17**

However, that is something doubtful in my view, since the Āyah came down with regard to the story of Badr, as has preceded.

So Hawāzin fled away from the Muslims, who chased them — killing them and taking captives. So the last of the Companions had not returned to Allāh's Messenger (صَلَّى اللَّهُ عَلَيْهِ وَسَلَّمَ) before he had the captives in front of him, and he had captured their property, and their women and dependents.

Some groups of Hawāzin withdrew to Awtās, so Allāh's Messenger sent against them Abū 'Āmir Al-Ash'arī whose name was 'Ubayd, and with him his brother Abū Mūsā Al-Ash'arī who carried the battle-flag of the Muslims, along with a group of the Muslims. So they killed a large number of them, and the leader of the Muslims, Abū 'Āmir was killed. A man fired an arrow at him and it struck him in his knee, and brought about his death. So Abū Mūsā Al-Ash'arī killed the one who had killed him.[1]

Or it is otherwise said that his killer accepted Islām after that; and that he was one of ten brothers, and that Abū 'Āmir had killed the other nine before him, so Allāh knows best.[2]

When Abū Mūsā informed Allāh's Messenger (صَلَّى اللَّهُ عَلَيْهِ وَسَلَّمَ), he (صَلَّى اللَّهُ عَلَيْهِ وَسَلَّمَ) asked for forgiveness for Abū 'Āmir.[3] So Abū 'Āmir was one of four men who were martyred on the day of Hunayn. The second was: Ayman ibn Umm Ayman. The third was: Yazīd ibn Zam'ah ibn Al-Aswad; and the fourth was: Surāqah ibn Al-Hārith ibn 'Adiyy, who was from Banul-'Ajlān, from the Ansār (رَضِيَ اللَّهُ عَنْهُمْ).

---

1 — [SH] Reported by Al-Bukhārī in his *Sahīh* (no. 4323) and Muslim (no. 2498), as a hadīth of Abū Mūsā Al-Ash'arī (رَضِيَ اللَّهُ عَنْهُ).

2 — [SH] This was declared weak by Al-Hāfidh Ibn Hajr in *Fat-hul-Bārī* (8/43), and he said: *"It is contrary to what occurs in the Sahīh."* This is also indicated by the saying of the author (رَحِمَهُ اللَّهُ) here: *'It is said...'*

3 — [SH] It is a part of the hadīth of Abū Mūsā.

As for the Mushrikūn, then many of them were killed (about forty [in number]).[1]

It was during this battle that he (صَلَّى ٱللَّٰهُ عَلَيْهِ وَسَلَّمَ) said: *"Whoever kills someone may take his spoils,"*[2] — within the story of Abū Qatādah (رَضِيَ ٱللَّٰهُ عَنْهُ).

Chapter: The Expedition Of At-Tā'if[3]

As for the king of the Hawāzin, who was Malik ibn 'Awf An-Nasrī, then when his army was defeated he entered the fortress of At-Tā'if along with (the tribe of) Thaqīf. Meanwhile, he (صَلَّى ٱللَّٰهُ عَلَيْهِ وَسَلَّمَ) returned from Hunayn, but he did not enter Makkah; rather he went to At-Tā'if and besieged them.

So it is said that this continued for twenty and odd nights; or it is said: for ten and odd nights. Ibn Hazm said; "This is what is correct, without a doubt."

I say: I do not know how he declared that to be what is correct. So it is as if he took it from his (صَلَّى ٱللَّٰهُ عَلَيْهِ وَسَلَّمَ) saying to Hawāzin, when they came to him as Muslims later on: "I waited twenty nights for you."[4]

And there occurs in the *Sahīh*[5] from Anas ibn Mālik (رَضِيَ ٱللَّٰهُ عَنْهُ) who said: *"So we besieged them for forty days,"*[6] — meaning Thaqīf. So they resisted

---

1 — SH An addition occurring in the 'Ārif Hikmat Library manuscript.

2 — SH Reported by Al-Bukhārī (no. 4321) and Muslim (no. 1751), as a hadīth of Abū Qatādah (رَضِيَ ٱللَّٰهُ عَنْهُ).

3 — SH Al-Hāfidh ibn Hajr said in *Fat-hul-Bārī* (8/43): "At-Tā'if is a large, well known city. It has many grape-vines and date-palms, and it is two or three riding stages from Makkah, being to the east of it."

4 — SH Reported by Al-Bukhārī in his *Sahīh* (no. 2307 & 2308) with the wording: "*'I waited for you'*, and Allāh's Messenger (صَلَّى ٱللَّٰهُ عَلَيْهِ وَسَلَّمَ) waited for them for ten and odd nights..."

5 — SH There occurs in the Sulaymāniyyah Library manuscript (no.3339): *"The two Sahīhs."*

6 — BJ SZ It occurs in *Sahīh Muslim* (no. 1059) only and with the wording: "So we besieged them for forty nights."

and defended themselves, and they killed a group of the Muslims with arrows and other weapons.

He (ﷺ) destroyed a large amount of their visible property, and he cut down their grapevines, but he did not affect them greatly.

So he departed and left them, and went to Al-Ji'rānah.[1] So the deputation of Hawāzin came to him there as Muslims, and that was before the distribution of the booty. So he (ﷺ) gave them a choice between (taking back) their women and children, or their wealth. So they chose their women and children. So he (ﷺ) said: *"As for what is my share and the share of Banul-Muttalib, then it is for you."* So the Muhājirūn and the Ansār said: "Whatever is ours, then it is for Allāh's Messenger (ﷺ)."

However, Al-Aqra' ibn Hābis and 'Uyainah ibn Hisn and their people refused that, until he (ﷺ) caused them to become satisfied with that, and gave them something as a replacement for it. Al-'Abbās ibn Mirdās As-Sulamī wanted to do the same as they did, however Banū Sulaym did not agree with him. Rather, they were satisfied that whatever was theirs should be given to Allāh's Messenger (ﷺ).[2]

So the women and children were returned to Hawāzin,[3] and they were six thousand in number. Amongst them was Ash-Shaymā' bint Al-Hārith ibn 'Abdil-'Uzzā, who was from Banū Sa'd ibn Bakr ibn Hawāzin, and she was a sister to Allāh's Messenger (ﷺ) through breast-feeding. So he honoured her and gave her something, and she chose to return to

---

1 — [MK][MM] Al-Ji'rānah is a watering place between At-Tā'if and Makkah, and it is closer to Makkah. It is here that Allāh's Messenger (ﷺ) distributed the booty of Hunayn; and from here, he entered the state of ihrām for 'Umrah on that journey.

2 — [SH] Reported by Ibn Is-hāq in *As-Sīrah* (4/1147 & 1148: Ibn Hishām), and from him by Al-Bayhaqī in *Dalā'ilun-Nubuwwah* (5/194-195): "'Amr ibn Shu'ayb narrated to me: from his father: from his grandfather, 'Abdullāh ibn 'Amr, with it." I say: This is a *'hasan'* chain of narration. And it is reported by Al-Bukhārī (nos. 4318 and 4319), as a hadīth of Al-Miswar ibn Makhramah and Marwān ibn Al-Hakam.

3 — [SH] Reported by Ibn Is-hāq in *As-Sīrah* (4/1148-1149): Nāfi' narrated to me: from Ibn 'Umar with it. This is a *'hasan'* chain of narration. It is also witnessed to by the previous hadīth of 'Abdullāh ibn 'Amr.

her land; and Hawāzin sought from Allāh's Messenger (ﷺ) that he should treat them kindly, because of their having breast-fed him.

Then he (ﷺ) shared out the rest of the wealth amongst the Muslims, and he gave extra to a group from the nobles of Quraysh and others to consolidate their hearts upon Islām. So he would give a man a hundred camels, and another man fifty, and so on.

There also occurs in *Sahīh Muslim*: from Az-Zuhrī: that Allāh's Messenger (ﷺ) gave three-hundred camels to Safwān ibn Umayyah that day.[1] Some of the Ansār felt aggrieved, and this news reached him, so he addressed them on their own; and he reminded them of Allāh's having favoured them with their having Īmān in Him, and how Allāh had given them wealth and sufficiency after their poverty, and how He had united their hearts after their having been total enemies. So they were satisfied and felt pleased (may Allāh be pleased with them and cause them to be pleased).[2]

And Dhul-Khuwaysarah At-Tamīmī, whose name was Hurqūs, as is said, accused the Prophet (ﷺ) of being unjust in that distribution. So he (ﷺ) overlooked that from him, and was mild with him,

---

1 — [SH] Muslim (no. 2313). Muslim also reported (no. 1060), as a hadīth of Rāfi' ibn Khadīj: *"That he (ﷺ) gave a hundred camels to Safwān,"* and that is what is correct.

2 — [BJ][SZ] This occurs in a number of ahādīth, from them the hadīth of 'Abdullāh ibn Zayd (رضي الله عنه) reported by Al-Bukhārī (no. 4330) and Muslim (no.1061); and from them the hadīth of Anas ibn Mālik (رضي الله عنه) reported by Al-Bukhārī (no. 4331) and Muslim (no. 1059).

after one of the chiefs had said to him: *"Shall I not strike his neck?"* So he said: ***"No."***[1]

Then he said: "There shall emerge from the progeny of this one, a people who will recite the Qur'ān, and it will not pass beyond their throats. So wherever you find them then kill them; for there is reward in killing them, for those who kill them."[2]

He placed Mālik ibn 'Awf An-Nasrī in charge of those who accepted Islām from his people, and he had accepted Islām and made his Islām good. He also praised Allāh's Messenger (صَلَّى ٱللَّٰهُ عَلَيْهِ وَسَلَّمَ) in a poem, and Ibn Is-hāq mentioned it.

Then he (صَلَّى ٱللَّٰهُ عَلَيْهِ وَسَلَّمَ) went to perform 'Umrah from Al-Ji'rānah,[3] and he entered Makkah. Then when he had completed his 'Umrah he travelled back to Al-Madīnah. In that year, the Hajj was established for the people by 'Attāb ibn Asīd (رَضِيَ ٱللَّٰهُ عَنْهُ). So he was the first governor from the Muslims to lead the people in the Hajj.[4]

---

1 — [SH] This is established from 'Umar ibn Al-Khattāb, 'Alī ibn Abī Tālib, and Abū Sa'īd Al-Khudrī in the two *Sahīhs*, and the ahādīth concerning the Khawārij are *'mutawātir.'*

Al-Hāfidh said in *Al-Fat-h* (6/618): "His saying in this narration: *'Umar said: "Grant me, permission to strike his neck"'* does not negate his saying in that narration: *'So Khālid said...'* since it is possible that both of them made that request."

[BJ][SZ] Concerning the incident of Dhul-Khuwaysarah refer to *Sahīh Al-Bukhārī* (no. 3610) and *Sahīh Muslim* (no. 1064) — the hadīth of Abū Sa'īd Al-Khudrī (رَضِيَ ٱللَّٰهُ عَنْهُ).

2 — [BJ][SZ] Reported by Al-Bukhārī (no. 3611) and Muslim (no.1064) as a hadīth of 'Alī (رَضِيَ ٱللَّٰهُ عَنْهُ).

3 — [SH] Reported by Al-Bukhārī (no. 1778) and Muslim (no. 1253) as a hadīth of Anas ibn Mālik (رَضِيَ ٱللَّٰهُ عَنْهُ).

4 — [SH] Ibn Is-hāq mentioned it in *As-Sīrah* (4/1158: Ibn Hishām) without a chain of narration.

CHAPTER:

The Expedition of Tabūk, and it is The Expedition of Hardship (Ghazwatul-'Usrah)

When Allāh (the Mighty and Majestic) sent down to His Messenger:

> قَاتِلُوا الَّذِينَ لَا يُؤْمِنُونَ بِاللَّهِ وَلَا بِالْيَوْمِ الْآخِرِ وَلَا يُحَرِّمُونَ مَا حَرَّمَ اللَّهُ وَرَسُولُهُ وَلَا يَدِينُونَ دِينَ الْحَقِّ مِنَ الَّذِينَ أُوتُوا الْكِتَابَ حَتَّىٰ يُعْطُوا الْجِزْيَةَ عَن يَدٍ وَهُمْ صَاغِرُونَ
>
> MEANING: "Fight against those who do not truly believe in Allāh, nor in the Last Day; nor forbid that which Allāh and His Messenger have forbidden, and who do not follow the Religion of truth; from the people of the Scripture, until they hand over the jizyah submissively and in a state of being humbled." — **Sūrah At-Tawbah (9): 29**

Allāh's Messenger (ﷺ) encouraged the people of Al-Madīnah and the bedouins who lived around them to go off to fight Jihād, and he informed them of an expedition against the Byzantines. This occurred in Rajab of the ninth year, and he had not used to go on any expedition except that he would seek to disguise his purpose from the enemy, and make it appear that he intended to attack someone else. This expedition, however, was an exception, since he clearly stated his purpose to them, so that they could prepare and equip themselves to face the strength and great number of their enemy.

It came about at the time of year when the fruits had just ripened, and it had been a year of drought. So the Muslims prepared themselves for it.[1]

ʿUthmān ibn ʿAffān (رَضِيَٱللَّهُعَنْهُ) donated a large amount of wealth in charity upon this army, which was the *'army of hardship.'* So it is said that he spent a thousand dīnars.[2]

Some said that he provided a thousand riding-camels, and a hundred horses,[3] and fully equipped them to the extent that they did not miss out on a single tethering rope or bridle (رَضِيَٱللَّهُعَنْهُ).[4] So he (صَلَّىٱللَّهُعَلَيْهِوَسَلَّمَ) went out with an army of about thirty thousand, and he left in charge of Al-Madīnah Muhammad ibn Maslamah; or it is said: Sibāʿ ibn ʿUrfutah; or it is said: ʿAlī ibn Abī Tālib (رَضِيَٱللَّهُعَنْهُ). What is correct is that ʿAlī was appointed by him to remain to take charge of the women and the children. So when the Hypocrites abused him, and said: *"He has left him in charge of the women and children,"* he caught up with Allāh's Messenger (صَلَّىٱللَّهُعَلَيْهِوَسَلَّمَ) and complained to him of that, so he said:

> "Will you not be pleased that you should have with me the position that Hārūn had with Mūsā? Except that, there is no Prophet after me."[5]

ʿAbdullāh ibn Ubayy, the head of the Hypocrites, went out along with him, but after going part of the way he went back.[6]

---

1 — [SH] These lines are established in the hadīth of Kaʿb ibn Mālik (رَضِيَٱللَّهُعَنْهُ) reported by Al-Bukhārī (no. 4418) and Muslim (no. 2769).

2 — For details regarding the authenticity of this, see **Endnote 80 on page 502**.

3 — [SH] Reported by Asad ibn Mūsā in *Fadā'ilus-Sahābah*, as occurs in *Al-Fat-h* (5/408), as a *'mursal'* narration of Qatādah, and Al-Hāfidh was silent concerning it; and it contains the wording *'seventy horses'* instead of *'a hundred'*.

4 — To read more regarding the virtue of ʿUthmān (رَضِيَٱللَّهُعَنْهُ), see **Endnote 81 on page 503**.

5 — [SH] Reported by Al-Bukhārī (no. 4416) and Muslim (no. 2404), as a hadīth of Saʿd ibn Abī Waqqās (رَضِيَٱللَّهُعَنْهُ).

6 — [SH] Mentioned by Ibn Is-hāq in *As-Sīrah* (4/175: Ibn Hishām) without a chain of narration.

The women and children remained behind and did not go along with Allāh's Messenger (صَلَّى ٱللَّهُ عَلَيْهِ وَسَلَّمَ); and also those men whom Allāh excused, because they could not obtain any riding beast, nor did they have sufficient funds. Amongst them were *'Those Who Wept'* (*Al-Bakkā'ūn*), and they were seven in number: Sālim ibn 'Umayr, 'Ulbah ibn Zayd, Abū Laylā 'Abdur-Rahmān ibn Ka'b, 'Amr ibn Al-Humām, 'Abdullāh ibn Al-Mughaffal Al-Muzanī, Haramiyy ibn 'Abdillāh, and 'Irbād ibn Sāriyah Al-Fazārī (رَضِيَ ٱللَّهُ عَنْهُمْ).[1]

And the Hypocrites remained behind, as a result of Disbelief and obstinate rejection, and they numbered about eighty men. And some who disobeyed the command remained behind, such as Murārah ibn Ar-Rabī', Ka'b ibn Mālik, and Hilāl ibn Umayyah. Then Allāh accepted their repentance, fifty nights after his (صَلَّى ٱللَّهُ عَلَيْهِ وَسَلَّمَ) return.[2]

So he (صَلَّى ٱللَّهُ عَلَيْهِ وَسَلَّمَ) travelled, and on the way he passed Al-Hijr,[3] so he ordered that they should not enter their dwelling places except weeping,[4] and that they should not drink except from the well of the She-Camel;[5] and that whatever dough they had made using (water from) other than it,

---

1 — For details regarding the authenticity of this, see **Endnote 82 on page 504**.

2 — For the immense story of Ka'b ibn Mālik, told in his own words, see **Endnote 83 on page 505**.

3 — [MK] [MM] Al-Hijr is the land of Thamūd, and it is known today by the name *'Madā'in Sālih.'*

4 — [SH] Reported by Al-Bukhārī (no.4419) and Muslim (no. 2980), as a hadīth of 'Abdullāh ibn 'Umar (رَضِيَ ٱللَّهُ عَنْهُمَا) .

[DB] Al-Bukhārī's wording is: "When the Prophet (صَلَّى ٱللَّهُ عَلَيْهِ وَسَلَّمَ) passed by Al-Hijr he said: *'Do not enter the dwelling-places of those who wronged themselves, for fear that what befell them should befall you, unless you are weeping.'* Then he covered his head, and rode quickly, until he had crossed the valley."

5 — [DB] i.e. the She-Camel of Prophet Sālih (عَلَيْهِ ٱلسَّلَامُ).

then they were to feed it to the camels,[1] and he crossed it whilst covering his head.

So he (صَلَّى ٱللَّهُ عَلَيْهِ وَسَلَّمَ) reached Tabūk, where there was a spring that oozed out a trickle of water, so it was caused to flow plentifully as a blessing granted to him.[2]

This was along with the rest of the blessings that came as a result of his supplications upon this expedition, such as food being greatly increased in quantity. So food for the entire army was gathered one night, and it covered the space upon which a goat could sit. So he made supplication to Allāh (the Mighty and Majestic), and then they all ate from it, and they filled every container that could be found in that army.[1]

Likewise when they became very thirsty he supplicated to Allāh (the Most High) and a cloud came, and it rained. So they drank until they were fully satisfied and they carried water (in their water-skins). Then they found that the cloud did not exceed the army.[2] Along with many other signs that they were in great need of at that time.

However when he arrived there he did not encounter any enemy, and he saw that their entering into the land of Shām that year would be a great hardship for them.

---

1 — [SH] Reported by Al-Bukhārī (no.3379) and Muslim (no.2981), as a hadīth of Ibn ʿUmar (رَضِيَ ٱللَّهُ عَنْهُمَا). An-Nawawī said in *Sharh Sahīh Muslim* (18/111-112): "It shows an encouragement upon being mindful when passing the homes of the wrongdoers and places where punishment came down; and like it is the hastening across Wādī Muhassir (the boundary area between Minā and Muzdalifah), since the Army of the Elephant were destroyed there. So a person who passes the like of these places should be mindful, fearful, and weeping, and deriving a lesson from them and their destruction; and he should seek Allāh's refuge from that."

2 — [SH] Reported by Muslim in his *Sahīh* (no. 706), as a hadīth of Anas (رَضِيَ ٱللَّهُ عَنْهُ).

1 — [SH] Reported by Muslim in his *Sahīh* (no. 27), as a hadīth of Abū Hurairah, with longer wording, and it clearly states that it happened on the expedition of Tabūk. It is also reported by Al-Bukhārī (no. 2982), as a hadīth of Salamah ibn Al-Akwaʿ, in abridged form, and it does not specify the expedition.

2 — Imām Al-Albānī declares this to be weak — see **Endnote 84 on page 513**.

So he decided to return; and he made a peace agreement with Yuhannah ibn Ru'bah, the governor of Aylah.[1]

He also sent Khālid to Ukaydir of Dūmah,[2] and he was brought. So he made a peace treaty with him also, and sent him back.[3]

Then he (صَلَّى ٱللَّهُ عَلَيْهِ وَسَلَّمَ) returned, and after his return, he ordered the demolition of *Masjidud-Dirār* (the mosque built to cause harm).[4] It had been built so that opened out onto the house of Khidhām ibn Khālid, and it was demolished in accordance with the command of Allāh's Messenger (صَلَّى ٱللَّهُ عَلَيْهِ وَسَلَّمَ) by Mālik ibn Ad-Dukhshum — the brother of Banū Sālim, one of the men of Badr — and another man along with him, about whom they disagree.[5] It is the mosque, which Allāh forbade His Messenger from ever standing in.[6]

His return from this expedition was in Ramadān of the ninth year, and concerning it, Allāh sent down the major part of Sūratut-Tawbah; and

---

1 — DB Yāqūtul-Hamawī said in *Mu'jamul-Buldān*: "Aylah [Elat] (...) is a town on the coast of the sea of Qulzum (the Gulf of Aqabah), next to Shām. It is said that it is the end of the Hijāz and the beginning of Shām."

2 — SH It is Dūmatul-Jandal, and it is a town in Al-Jawf, an area to the north of Taymā', and it is overlooked by the fortress of Ukaydir Al-Kindī.

MK MM Allāh's Messenger (صَلَّى ٱللَّهُ عَلَيْهِ وَسَلَّمَ) came here previously on an expedition, in Rabī'ul Awwal of the fifth year, and returned without meeting an enemy.

3 — For details regarding the authenticity of this, see **Endnote 85 on page 513**.

4 — It was built by the Hypocrites to cause separation between the Muslims, and as a base for their enemies, and to harm the Mosque founded upon dutifulness to Allāh: Qubā' Mosque. Read more: **Endnote 86 on page 514**

5 — MK MM Ibn Hazm, in *Jawāmi'us-Sīrah* (p. 200), named him as Ma'an ibn 'Adiyy, or his brother 'Āsim ibn 'Adiyy — from Banul-'Ajlān.

SH Ibn Is-hāq mentioned it in *As-Sīrah* (4/1180-1184: Ibn Hishām), without a chain of narration.

6 — As occurs in His saying — He the Most High:

> لَا تَقُمْ فِيهِ أَبَدًا
>
> Meaning: "Never stand in it." — **Sūrah At-Tawbah (9):108**

Allāh (the Mighty and Majestic) rebuked those who stayed behind and did not join him (ﷺ). So He (the Mighty and Majestic) said:

> مَا كَانَ لِأَهْلِ الْمَدِينَةِ وَمَنْ حَوْلَهُم مِّنَ الْأَعْرَابِ أَن يَتَخَلَّفُوا عَن رَّسُولِ اللَّهِ وَلَا
> يَرْغَبُوا بِأَنفُسِهِمْ عَن نَّفْسِهِ ——
>
> MEANING: "It was not right for the people of Al-Madīnah and the Bedouins of the neighbourhood to remain behind and not join Allāh's Messenger, and to prefer their own lives to his life——" the Āyah, and that which follows it. — **Sūrah At-Tawbah (9): 120-121**

Then He said:

> وَمَا كَانَ الْمُؤْمِنُونَ لِيَنفِرُوا كَافَّةً ۚ فَلَوْلَا نَفَرَ مِن كُلِّ فِرْقَةٍ مِّنْهُمْ طَائِفَةٌ لِّيَتَفَقَّهُوا فِي
> الدِّينِ وَلِيُنذِرُوا قَوْمَهُمْ إِذَا رَجَعُوا إِلَيْهِمْ لَعَلَّهُمْ يَحْذَرُونَ
>
> MEANING: "It is not proper for the Believers to all go off to fight. Rather there should be a group who acquire knowledge of the Religion; and so that they may warn their people when they return to them, so that they may beware of evil." — **Sūrah At-Tawbah (9):122**

So through this, that which the people disagree about in this regard will become clearly apparent to you; which is that it is the group who went out who are the ones who acquired knowledge of the Religion, through their accompanying Allāh's Messenger (ﷺ) on this expedition; and that they warned their people when they returned, so that they could beware of evil, with that which had newly been sent down from the Religion, and Allāh — the One free of all imperfections and the Most High — knows best.

Chapter: The Arrival of the Deputation of Thaqīf

216 The deputation of Thaqīf came to Allāh's Messenger (صَلَّى ٱللَّهُ عَلَيْهِ وَسَلَّمَ) in Ramadān of this year,[1] and they accepted Islām.

The reason behind it was that ʿUrwah ibn Masʿūd, their leader, had come to Allāh's Messenger (صَلَّى ٱللَّهُ عَلَيْهِ وَسَلَّمَ) whilst he was returning from Hunayn and Tā'if, and before he reached Al-Madīnah. So he accepted Islām and made his Islām good. He then asked permission of Allāh's Messenger (صَلَّى ٱللَّهُ عَلَيْهِ وَسَلَّمَ) to return to his people, to call them to Allāh (the Mighty and Majestic).

So he gave him permission, even though he feared for him. Then when he returned to them and called them to Islām, they fired arrows at him and killed him.

Then they regretted this, and saw that they were not capable of fighting against Allāh's Messenger (صَلَّى ٱللَّهُ عَلَيْهِ وَسَلَّمَ). So they sent their deputation to him, and they came to him in Ramadān, as we have already mentioned, and they were six in number.

The first person who saw them was Al-Mughīrah ibn Shuʿbah Ath-Thaqafī. He was pasturing camels, so he left that and went with them towards Allāh's Messenger (صَلَّى ٱللَّهُ عَلَيْهِ وَسَلَّمَ), and upon the way he taught them how to give the salutation to him.

Abū Bakr As-Siddīq (رَضِيَ ٱللَّهُ عَنْهُ) preceded Al-Mughīrah, and gave the good news of their coming to Allāh's Messenger (صَلَّى ٱللَّهُ عَلَيْهِ وَسَلَّمَ).

He (صَلَّى ٱللَّهُ عَلَيْهِ وَسَلَّمَ) settled them in the mosque, and pitched a tent for them in it, and Khālid ibn Saʿīd ibn Al-ʿĀs acted as a messenger between them and him; and food would come to them from the Prophet (صَلَّى ٱللَّهُ عَلَيْهِ وَسَلَّمَ), and they would not eat until Khālid had eaten before them.

---

1 — [SH] The author (رَحِمَهُ ٱللَّهُ) said in *Al-Bidāyah wan-Nihāyah* (7/205): "This is what Mūsā ibn ʿUqbah mentioned regarding the story of ʿUrwah. However, he claimed that it occurred after the Hajj led by Abū Bakr As-Siddīq, and he was followed upon that by Abū Bakr Al-Bayhaqī, and that is very strange. What is correct is that it occurred before the Hajj of Abū Bakr, as Ibn Is-hāq mentioned, and Allāh knows best."

So they accepted Islām, but they tried to make a condition that he should leave their major idol, i.e. Al-Lāt, with them, and that it should not be destroyed; however he (ﷺ) would not agree to that. They also asked him that he should relieve them of some of the Prayers, and he would not agree to that. Then they asked him that they should not have to destroy their idol with their own hands, so he agreed to that, and he sent Abū Sufyān Sakhr ibn Harb, and Al-Mughīrah ibn Shu'bah along with them to demolish it. So the two of them demolished it.

This greatly distressed the women of Thaqīf, and they believed that some evil would befall the two of them from it.

So Al-Mughīrah ibn Shu'bah played a trick upon them when they demolished it, and he fell down as if he had been knocked unconscious. He did this in accordance with a plan he had made with Abū Sufyān, in order that they should wrongly think that (the idol) had done it. Then he stood up and put them to shame, and rebuked them (رضي الله عنه). So they accepted Islām and made their Islām good.

Furthermore, he (ﷺ) appointed as their imām (leader in Prayer) one of the six who came to him, and he was 'Uthmān ibn Abil-'Ās,[1] and he was the youngest of them in age; because of what he witnessed with regard to his eagerness upon recitation of the Qur'ān and his learning the obligatory duties. He also ordered him to appoint a mu'adhdhin (one who gives the call to prayer) who would not take any wages for his adhān, and to lead them in Prayer taking into consideration the weakest of them.[2]

Chapter: The Hajj of Abū Bakr As-Siddīq

This year he (ﷺ) sent Abū Bakr As-Siddīq (رضي الله عنه) to lead the Hajj; and he sent 'Alī (رضي الله عنه) after him with Sūrah Barā'ah: *"That after this year no Mushrik is allowed to perform Hajj, and no naked person is*

---

1 — [BJ] [SZ] As occurs in *Sahīh Muslim* (no. 468).

2 — For details regarding the authenticity of this, see Endnote 87 on page 515.

allowed to perform tawāf around the house,"[1] — and he annulled their agreements, except for agreements with a set time-limit, which were to continue for their duration.

The Successive Deputations that Came to the Messenger (ﷺ)

Also this year and the following year deputations came in succession to Allāh's Messenger (ﷺ), submitting with Islām, entering into the Religion of Allāh in crowds, just as He (the Most High) said:

> إِذَا جَاءَ نَصْرُ اللَّهِ وَالْفَتْحُ ۝ وَرَأَيْتَ النَّاسَ يَدْخُلُونَ فِي دِينِ اللَّهِ أَفْوَاجًا ۝ فَسَبِّحْ بِحَمْدِ رَبِّكَ وَاسْتَغْفِرْهُ ۚ إِنَّهُ كَانَ تَوَّابًا
>
> MEANING: "When the Help of Allāh comes and the conquest (of Makkah), and you see the people entering Allāh's Religion in crowds; then glorify and praise your Lord, and ask for His forgiveness. Indeed, He is the One Who accepts repentance repeatedly."

And he (ﷺ) sent Mu'ādh ibn Jabal to Yemen and with him Abū Mūsā Al-Ash'arī (رضي الله عنهما).[2]

And he sent messengers to the kings of the regions calling them to Islām. So the call became widespread, the Word was elevated, the Truth came, and falsehood was vanquished — indeed; falsehood will certainly perish.

---

1 — [SH] Reported by Al-Bukhārī in his *Sahīh* (nos. 1622, 4655 and 4656) and Muslim in his *Sahīh* (no. 1347), with its like, as a hadīth of Abū Hurairah (رضي الله عنه).

2 — [SH] Reported by Al-Bukhārī in his *Sahīh* (nos. 4341 and 4342) and Muslim in his *Sahīh* (no. 1733).

CHAPTER:

The Farewell Hajj (Hajjatul-Wadā')

In which we shall mention an abridgement of the Farewell Hajj, and how it was performed — with the aid of Allāh, His favour, and His granting attainment of correctness and guidance. So we say, and attainment of correctness is granted by Allāh:

....

Allāh's Messenger (صَلَّىٱللَّهُعَلَيْهِوَسَلَّمَ) prayed the Dhuhr Prayer on Thursday,[1] with six days of Dhul-Qa'dah remaining, in the tenth year in Al-Madīnah. Then he departed, along with the Muslims of Al-Madīnah who were with him, and with those who had gathered from the bedouins.

He then prayed the 'Asr Prayer at Dhul-Hulayfah[2] as two rak'ahs, and he spent the night there.[3]

Then someone[4] came to him from his Lord (the Mighty and Majestic) at that place, which is Wādī Al-'Aqīq, giving him the command from his

---

1 — For details regarding the authenticity of this, see ENDNOTE 88 ON PAGE 515.

2 — [MM][MK][SH] A place seven miles away from Al-Madīnah, and it is a part of Wādī Al-'Aqīq. It is the *'mīqāt'* (the point at which the state of *ihrām* is entered) for the people of Al-Madīnah and those who pass by on their way to perform Hajj or 'Umrah.

3 — [DB] Reported by Al-Bukhārī in his *Sahīh* (no. 1546) and Muslim in his *Sahīh* (no. 690), as a hadīth of Anas ibn Mālik (رَضِيَٱللَّهُعَنْهُ).

4 — [DB] Al-Hāfidh ibn Hajr said in *Fat-hul-Bārī* (3/392): "He was Jibrīl."

Lord (the Mighty and Majestic) that he should say in this Hajj of his: *"A Hajj within an 'Umrah."*[1]

The meaning of that is that Allāh commanded him to join the Hajj along with the 'Umrah. So he (ﷺ) entered the morning and informed the people of that.

And he had relations that day with all of his wives, and they were nine in number, or it is said: eleven; and he took a single bath.[2]

Then he took a bath and prayed two rak'ahs at the place of Prayer, and he announced that he was performing a Hajj and an 'Umrah together [i.e. *Hajj Qirān*]. This is what is reported in wording and in meaning from him (ﷺ), by sixteen Companions, from them his servant Anas ibn Mālik (رَضِيَ ٱللَّهُ عَنْهُ); and it was reported from him by sixteen of the Tābi'īn; and it is a clear and direct statement which cannot be explained away, except with something far-fetched.

As for other ahādīth which are reported, which may give the impression that he was performing an 'Umrah and then a Hajj separately (*Tamattu'*), or that he was performing Hajj on its own (*Ifrād*), then they can be explained at a place other than this.

Performing *Qirān*[3] of Hajj is what is most excellent in the view of Abū Hanīfah, and is one narration from Imām Ahmad ibn Hanbal, and is the saying of Imām Abū 'Abdillāh Ash-Shāfi'ī; and it was supported by a group of the verifiers from his companions. It is what brings about harmonization of all of the hādīths, and amongst the scholars are some who declare that it is obligatory, and Allāh knows best.[4]

---

1 — BJ SZ Reported by Al-Bukhārī (no. 1534) as a hadīth of Ibn 'Abbās (رَضِيَ ٱللَّهُ عَنْهُمَا) with the wording: "An 'Umrah within a Hajj."

2 — SH Reported by Al-Bukhārī in his *Sahīh* (270) and Muslim in his *Sahīh* (no. 1192), as a hadīth of 'Ā'ishah (رَضِيَ ٱللَّهُ عَنْهَا).

3 — DB 'Umrah and Hajj together with a single *ihrām*.

4 — For the speech of Shaikh Muhammad Nāsiruddīn Al-Albānī (رَحِمَهُ ٱللَّهُ) regarding the types of Hajj, see **Endnote 89 on page 516**.

He (ﷺ) led his sacrificial camel along from Dhul-Hulayfah, and he commanded those who had a sacrificial animal to declare that they were performing the same as what he (ﷺ) declared that he was performing.

He (ﷺ) proceeded with the people in front of him and behind him, and to his right and to his left, and they were so numerous that they could not be counted: all of them had come to carefully follow him (ﷺ).

When he (ﷺ) arrived at Makkah he performed the *'Tawāful-Qudūm'* (Tawāf of Arrival), and then performed Saʿī between As-Safā and Al-Marwah; and he commanded those who had not brought a sacrificial animal along with them to change their Hajj into an ʿUmrah, and to completely leave the state of *ihrām*. Then that they should enter the state of *ihrām* again for the Hajj at the time of their departure for Minā, and he said: "If I had known before what I know now, then I would not have brought the sacrificial animal along, and I would have made it an ʿUmrah."[1]

So this proves to you that he was certainly not performing *Tamattuʿ*, contrary to those who claim that, from the companions of Imām Ahmad and others.

Also, ʿAlī (رضي الله عنه) arrived from Yemen, and he (ﷺ) said to him: *"What did you declare as your intent?"* He said: *"With the intent to perform the same as the Prophet (ﷺ)."* So the Prophet (ﷺ) said: *"I have brought along the sacrificial animal, and I am combining ʿUmrah and*

---

1 — [SH] Reported by Al-Bukhārī in his *Sahīh* (no. 1568), and Muslim in his *Sahīh* (no. 1218), as a hadīth of Jābir ibn ʿAbdillāh (رضي الله عنه); and Al-Bukhārī divided it, and mentioned its parts in different places in his *Sahīh*, whereas Imām Muslim reported it with its full wording in one place in his *Sahīh* in a fine manner — may Allāh have mercy upon them both.

Hajj (Qirān)." This wording is reported by Abū Dāwūd and others from the imāms, with an authentic (sahīh) chain of narration.[1]

So this clearly shows *Qirān* ('Umrah and Hajj combined);[2] and 'Alī (رَضِيَ اللَّهُ عَنْهُ) brought a sacrificial animal from Yemen, and he (صَلَّى اللَّهُ عَلَيْهِ وَسَلَّمَ) made him a sharer in his sacrificial animals also, and they numbered one hundred camels.

Then he (صَلَّى اللَّهُ عَلَيْهِ وَسَلَّمَ) went out to Minā, and he spent the night there, and that was the night of Friday, the ninth of Dhul-Hijjah.

Then, in the morning, he proceeded to 'Arafah, and he gave a tremendous Khutbah at Namirah which was witnessed by about forty thousand of his Companions (may Allāh be pleased with them all) and he combined the Dhuhr and the 'Asr Prayers, and then stood in 'Arafah.

Then he spent the night in Muzdalifah, and he combined the Maghrib and the 'Ishā' Prayers that night. Then at dawn, he prayed the Fajr Prayer at the beginning of its time.

Then before the sun rose, he proceeded to Minā and pelted Jamratul-'Aqabah, and he performed the sacrifice and had his head shaved.

Then he proceeded (to the Ka'bah) and he performed the obligatory tawāf around the House, and that was the *'Tawāfuz-Ziyārah'* (Tawāf of Visitation). Then there is disagreement about where he prayed the

---

1 — [SH] Reported by Abū Dāwūd in his *Sunan* (no. 1797), An-Nasā'ī in *Al-Mujtabā* (5/148-149 and 157) and *Al-Kubrā* (no. 3691 and 3711), and Al-Bayhaqī in *Al-Kubrā* (5/15) by way of Yahyā ibn Ma'īn: from Al-Hajjāj: from Yūnus: from Abū Is-hāq As-Sabī'ī; from Al-Barā', with it.

I say this chain of narration is weak, Abū Is-hāq was a mudallis whose memory deteriorated; and he narrates it without stating that he heard it directly, and Yūnus heard from him after his memory deteriorated. However, the hadīth has a witness as a hadīth of 'Alī ibn Abī Tālib (رَضِيَ اللَّهُ عَنْهُ) himself, reported by Ibn Hibbān in his *Sahīh* (no.3777: 'Ihsān') with a *'hasan'* chain of narration; and the hadīth was declared *'sahīh'* by our Shaikh Al-Albānī (رَحِمَهُ اللَّهُ).

2 — He performed *Hajj Qirān* due to the fact that he'd brought a sacrificial animal with him on the journey to Makkah. For more detail see **Endnote 90 on page 521**.

Dhuhr Prayer that day, and this has been problematic for many of the great preservers of hadīth.[1]

Then he freed himself from everything which had been prohibited for him (صَلَّى ٱللَّهُ عَلَيْهِ وَسَلَّمَ) whilst in the state of *ihrām*. Then on the second day of Sacrifice he also gave a tremendous Khutbah,[2] and he gave them final advice, and he cautioned and warned them, and he called them to bear witness that he had indeed conveyed the Message to them.[3] So we bear witness that he did indeed convey the Message, fulfil what he was entrusted with, and sincerely advised the Ummah (may Allāh extol him and grant him perfect peace and security which persists until the day of Resurrection.)

Then he (صَلَّى ٱللَّهُ عَلَيْهِ وَسَلَّمَ) set out and departed for Al-Madīnah, and Allāh had completed His Religion.[4]

---

1 — [BJ][SZ][SH] That is because there occurs in the hadīth of Jābir, which is reported by Muslim (no. 1218), that the Prophet (صَلَّى ٱللَّهُ عَلَيْهِ وَسَلَّمَ) prayed the Dhuhr Prayer in Makkah, whereas Ibn ʿUmar stated that the Prophet (صَلَّى ٱللَّهُ عَلَيْهِ وَسَلَّمَ) prayed the Dhuhr Prayer in Minā — reported by Muslim (no. 1308). Refer to An-Nawawī's *Sharh* of Muslim (8/193), *Zādul-Maʿād* (2/280-283), and *Naylul-Awtār* (5/151).

[DB] Shaikh Al-Albānī (رَحِمَهُ ٱللَّهُ) said in his book on the rites of Hajj and ʿUmrah; *Manāsikul-Hajj wal-ʿUmrah* (p. 39): "And he prayed the Dhuhr Prayer in Makkah; and Ibn ʿUmar said: *'In Minā.'*"

"I say: Allāh knows best which of the two Allāh's Messenger (صَلَّى ٱللَّهُ عَلَيْهِ وَسَلَّمَ) did, and it is possible that he led them in Prayer twice: once in Makkah, and once in Minā, as happened in some of his (صَلَّى ٱللَّهُ عَلَيْهِ وَسَلَّمَ) battles."

2 — [BJ][SZ] Meaning: In addition to the well-known Khutbah which he (صَلَّى ٱللَّهُ عَلَيْهِ وَسَلَّمَ) gave on the Day of Sacrifice, which is reported in the two *Sahīhs* and elsewhere.

3 — For a more detailed discussion on the authenticity of this, see **ENDNOTE 91 ON PAGE 522**.

4 — And that was with the sending down of the saying of the One Who Alone is truly worshipped, the Exalted and Most High:

> الْيَوْمَ أَكْمَلْتُ لَكُمْ دِينَكُمْ وَأَتْمَمْتُ عَلَيْكُمْ نِعْمَتِي وَرَضِيتُ لَكُمُ الْإِسْلَامَ دِينًا
>
> MEANING: "This day I have perfected your Religion for you, and have completed My Favour upon you, and am pleased with Islām as your Religion." — **5: 3**

CHAPTER:

His Passing Away — (صَلَّى ٱللَّهُ عَلَيْهِ وَسَلَّمَ)

Then he (صَلَّى ٱللَّهُ عَلَيْهِ وَسَلَّمَ) remained in residence for the rest of Dhul-Hijjah, Muharram, and Safar. Then he (صَلَّى ٱللَّهُ عَلَيْهِ وَسَلَّمَ) began to suffer a painful illness whilst he was in the house of Maymūnah, on the day of Thursday. It was a severe pain which affected his noble head, and he suffered frequent severe headaches (صَلَّى ٱللَّهُ عَلَيْهِ وَسَلَّمَ). Yet despite this he still continued giving all of his wives their turns, until this became too difficult for him. Then he sought their permission to be nursed in the house of ʿĀ'ishah (رَضِيَ ٱللَّهُ عَنْهَا), and they granted him permission for that.[1]

So he continued to suffer the pain for twelve days, or it is said for fourteen days.

And As-Siddīq (رَضِيَ ٱللَّهُ عَنْهُ) was leading the people in Prayer, as he had been commanded to by him (صَلَّى ٱللَّهُ عَلَيْهِ وَسَلَّمَ);[2] and he exempted him from accompanying the army of Usāmah, which he (صَلَّى ٱللَّهُ عَلَيْهِ وَسَلَّمَ) had prepared to go off to Shām to fight against the Byzantines. So when he became ill they waited to see what would happen with him (صَلَّى ٱللَّهُ عَلَيْهِ وَسَلَّمَ), and he (صَلَّى ٱللَّهُ عَلَيْهِ وَسَلَّمَ) prayed behind As-Siddīq, whilst sitting.

---

1 — [SH] Reported by Al-Bukhārī in his *Sahīh* (nos. 198 and 2588), and Muslim in his *Sahīh* (418/91, 92), as a hadīth of the Mother of the Believers ʿĀ'ishah (رَضِيَ ٱللَّهُ عَنْهَا).

2 — [MK][MM][SH] Reported by Al-Bukhārī (no. 687) and Muslim (no.418/90), as a hadīth of ʿĀ'ishah (رَضِيَ ٱللَّهُ عَنْهَا).

His (صَلَّى ٱللَّهُ عَلَيْهِ وَسَلَّمَ) soul was taken in death during the forenoon of the day of Monday,[1] in the month of Rabīʿul-Awwal. What is famous is that it was the twelfth day, or it is said: its first day, or it is said: the second; and there are other sayings.

As-Suhaylī said something which he claimed that he had not been preceded in, which was that it is not possible, if his standing (in ʿArafah) occurred on the day of Jumuʿah (Friday) on the ninth of Dhul-Hijjah, that his death could then have been on the day of Monday, the twelfth of Rabīʿul-Awwal which came after it; whether the intervening months are counted as having been complete or incomplete,[2] or some as being complete and others in incomplete.

However, a correct response has been given for him, which is at the limit of correctness, and all praise is for Allāh. I have written it out separately, along with other responses, and it is that this occurred in accordance with the fact that the crescent moon of Dhul-Hijjah was sighted upon different days in Makkah and Al-Madīnah. So the people of Makkah saw it one day before them. So in this way the famous saying is found to be in full conformity, and all praise is for Allāh and all favours are bestowed by Him.[3]

On the day when he (صَلَّى ٱللَّهُ عَلَيْهِ وَسَلَّمَ) died, his age was sixty-three years, upon the correct saying.[4]

---

1 — [BJ][SZ][SH] Reported by Al-Bukhārī (no. 680) and Muslim (no. 419), as a hadīth of Anas ibn Mālik (رَضِيَ ٱللَّهُ عَنْهُ).

2 — [DB] i.e. of thirty days, or of twenty-nine days.

3 — [SH] However, Ibn Hajr refutes this in *Al-Fat-h* (8/129-130) and he mentions the different sayings of the scholars regarding this, so refer to that.

4 — [BJ][SZ] Reported by Al-Bukhārī (no.3536) and Muslim (no. 2349), as a hadīth of ʿĀʾishah (رَضِيَ ٱللَّهُ عَنْهَا); and by Al-Bukhārī (no. 3902) and Muslim (no. 2351) also, as a hadīth of Ibn ʿAbbās (رَضِيَ ٱللَّهُ عَنْهُمَا).

They said: And Abū Bakr, ʿUmar, ʿAlī, and ʿĀʾishah (رَضِيَ ٱللَّهُ عَنْهُمْ) also died at that age. Abū Zakariyyā An-Nawawī mentioned this in his *Tahdhīb*[1] and declared it correct, however part of that is doubtful.

And it is said: He was sixty,[2] and it is said: sixty-five;[3] and these three sayings occur in *Sahīh Al-Bukhārī* from Ibn ʿAbbās (رَضِيَ ٱللَّهُ عَنْهُمَا).[4]

So the calamity of his (صَلَّى ٱللَّهُ عَلَيْهِ وَسَلَّمَ) death was severe, and the matter was extremely serious, and the affair was terrible, and the Muslims were struck with a calamity upon the death of their Prophet.

ʿUmar ibn Al-Khattāb (رَضِيَ ٱللَّهُ عَنْهُ) refused to accept it, and said: "He has not died! Rather he will return, just as Mūsā returned to his people" — and the people were in a state of commotion.

Then As-Siddīq (رَضِيَ ٱللَّهُ عَنْهُ), the one aided and supported, initially and at the end, inwardly and outwardly, came and stood at the time of greatest need and spoke out with the truth, and addressed the people, and recited to them:

---

1 — (SH) Entitled *Tahdhībul-Asmāʾ wal-Lughāt* (1/23), and that is established in a report of Muslim (no. 2348), as a hadīth of Anas, who said: "Allāh's Messenger (صَلَّى ٱللَّهُ عَلَيْهِ وَسَلَّمَ) died at the age of sixty-three; and Abū Bakr at the age of sixty-three; and ʿUmar at the age of sixty-three."

2 — (SH) Reported by Al-Bukhārī (no. 4464, 4465), from ʿĀʾishah and Ibn ʿAbbās (رَضِيَ ٱللَّهُ عَنْهُمْ): "That the Prophet (صَلَّى ٱللَّهُ عَلَيْهِ وَسَلَّمَ) remained in Makkah for ten years, with the Qurʾān descending upon him; and for ten years in Al-Madīnah."

3 — (SH) Reported by Muslim (no. 2353), as a hadīth of Ibn ʿAbbās, containing the wording: "At the age of forty he was raised as a Prophet, then he spent fifteen years in Makkah, in security and in fear, and ten years after his migration in Al-Madīnah."

An-Nawawī said in *Tahdhībul-Asmāʾ wal-Lughāt* (1/23) "He (عَلَيْهِ ٱلسَّلَامُ) died at the age of sixty-three; or it is said: sixty-five; or it is said: sixty. However, the first is more correct and well known and the three sayings occur in the *Sahīh*. The scholars said: The harmonization between the narrations is that those who report 'sixty' are not counting the odd years; and those who report 'sixty-five' are including the years of his birth and death; and those who report 'sixty-three' do not count those two; and what is correct is sixty-three."

4 — (SH) The first and last sayings occur in *Sahīh Muslim*, and the second saying in *Sahīh Al-Bukhārī*.

وَمَا مُحَمَّدٌ إِلَّا رَسُولٌ قَدْ خَلَتْ مِن قَبْلِهِ الرُّسُلُ ۚ أَفَإِن مَّاتَ أَوْ قُتِلَ انقَلَبْتُمْ عَلَىٰ
أَعْقَابِكُمْ ۚ وَمَن يَنقَلِبْ عَلَىٰ عَقِبَيْهِ فَلَن يَضُرَّ اللَّهَ شَيْئًا ۗ وَسَيَجْزِي اللَّهُ الشَّاكِرِينَ

MEANING: "And Muhammad (ﷺ) is but a Messenger, (many) Messengers have passed away before him. If he dies or is killed, will you then turn back upon your heels as Disbelievers? And whoever turns back upon his heels will not harm Allāh in the least; and Allāh will reward those who are thankful and remain firm." — **SŪRAH ĀLI-IMRĀN (3): 144**

So it was as if the people had not heard it prior to that, and there remained no one except that he recited it.[1]

Then the Muslims went with him to the enclosure of Banū Sā'idah, where they had gathered and agreed to appoint Sa'd ibn 'Ubādah as their leader. So he[2] turned them back from that and prevented them, and he indicated to them that they should rather choose 'Umar ibn Al-Khattāb or Abū 'Ubaydah ibn Al-Jarrāh. So both of them refused that, and the Muslims, and Allāh also refused that; and the Muslims (رضي الله عنهم) gave the pledge of allegiance to him at that place. Then he came, and the people gave him the general pledge of allegiance upon the minbar.[3]

Then they began to prepare Allāh's Messenger (ﷺ) for burial, and they washed him with his shirt upon him.[4] The one who took charge of that was his uncle Al-'Abbās and his son Qutham, and 'Alī ibn Abī Tālib; and Usāmah ibn Zayd and Shuqrān - his two freed slaves - poured the water; and Aws ibn Khawlī Al-Ansārī, Al-Badrī helped in that (may Allāh be pleased with them all).[5]

---

1 — [SH] Al-Bukhārī reported the incident (no. 4454) as a hadīth of Ibn 'Abbās (رضي الله عنهما), without a mention of Mūsā.

2 — [DB] i.e. Abū Bakr As-Siddīq (رضي الله عنه).

3 — [SH] Reported by Al-Bukhārī in his *Sahīh* (nos. 3667 and 3668), as a hadīth of 'Ā'ishah (رضي الله عنها).

4 — This was declared *'sahīh'* by Imām Al-Albānī — and for more discussion see **ENDNOTE 92 ON PAGE 523**.

5 — For a discussion of the authenticity of this, see **ENDNOTE 93 ON PAGE 524**.

They shrouded him in three *Sahūlī*[1] cotton sheets, without any shirt or turban.[2] They prayed over him individually and separately,[3] and as occurs in a hadīth reported by Al-Bazzār — and Allāh knows best about its authenticity[4] — he (ﷺ) commanded them with that.

Ash-Shāfiʿī said: "They prayed over him separately, some followed by others, because of his tremendous status, and because none of them would have wished to have someone else leading them in Prayer over him."

Al-Hākim, Abū Ahmad said: "The first of them to pray over him was Al-ʿAbbās — his paternal uncle — then Banū Hāshim, then the Muhājirūn, then the Ansār, and then the rest of the people.

Then when the men had finished, the children entered, then the women.

He (ﷺ) was buried on the day of Tuesday, or it is said: on Wednesday, during the last hours of the night, in the place where he passed away in the apartment of ʿĀʾishah. This occurs in a hadīth

---

1 — [SH] An ascription to Sahūl, which is a place in Yemen famous for making garments.

2 — [SH] Reported by Al-Bukhārī in his *Sahīh* (no. 1264) and Muslim in his *Sahīh* (no. 941), as a hadīth of ʿĀʾishah (رَضِيَ اللَّهُ عَنْهَا).

3 — This was declared *'sahīh'* by Imām Al-Albānī — and for more discussion see Endnote 94 on page 524.

4 — This narration is not accepted — see Endnote 95 on page 525 for more detail as to why.

reported by At-Tirmidhī from Abū Bakr (رَضِيَ ٱللَّهُ عَنْهُ);[1] and this is something *mutawātir* to such an extent that it is something known by necessity in the Religion; and it is today within the mosque of Al-Madīnah.

---

1 — [BJ][SZ] Reported by At-Tirmidhī (no. 1018), and in *Ash-Shamā'il* (no.390), from 'Ā'ishah who said: "When Allāh's Messenger (صَلَّى ٱللَّهُ عَلَيْهِ وَسَلَّمَ) died they disagreed with regard to his burial. So Abū Bakr said: 'I heard Allāh's Messenger (صَلَّى ٱللَّهُ عَلَيْهِ وَسَلَّمَ) say something which I have not forgotten. He said:

"Allāh has not caused a Prophet to die except in the place where he loved that he should be buried."'

So they buried him in the place of his bed." It is a hadīth that is *'sahīh'* because of its witness.

[SH] Its chain is weak since 'Abdur-Rahmān ibn Abī Bakr is weak. Shaikh Al-Albānī (رَحِمَهُ ٱللَّهُ) said in *Mukhtasarush-Shamā'il* (p. 195): "However the hadīth is *'sahīh'* because of the witnesses which it has, as is explained in *Ahkāmul-Janā'iz* (pp.137-138)."

VOLUME TWO

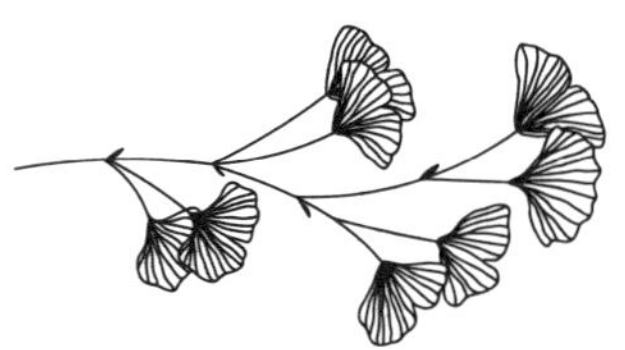

His Circumstances, Characteristics, & the Matters Particular to him

VOLUME TWO:

His Circumstances, Characteristics, & the Matters Particular to him

Chapter: His (صَلَّىٱللَّهُعَلَيْهِوَسَلَّمَ) Performing Hajj & ʿUmrah

He (صَلَّىٱللَّهُعَلَيْهِوَسَلَّمَ) did not perform Hajj after having migrated except for this Hajj of his, and it was the obligatory Hajj of Islām (Hajjatul-Islām), and the Farewell Hajj (Hajjatul-Wadāʿ).

The Hajj was made obligatory in the sixth year, upon the saying of some of the scholars; or in the ninth year, upon the saying of others from amongst them.[1]

It is also said that it was in the tenth, and this is something strange; and even stranger than it is what Imāmul-Haramayn quoted in *An-Nihāyah* as one saying from some of the companions[2] that the obligation of the Hajj came before the Hijrah.

As for his ʿUmrahs, then they were four: Al-Hudaybiyah, from which he was prevented; and the ʿUmrah of the Agreement (ʿUmratul-Qadāʾ)

---

1 — [BJ][SZ] The majority of the scholars use as evidence that the obligation of Hajj came about in the sixth year. He (the Most High) said: *"And complete the Hajj and the ʿUmrah for Allāh,"* since it came down in the sixth year, the year of Al-Hudaybiyah.

Imām Ibnul-Qayyim preferred the view, in *Zādul-Maʿād* (2/101), that the obligation of the Hajj was delayed until the ninth or the tenth year.

Refer to *Al-Majmūʿ* of An-Nawawī (7/82), *Fat-hul-Bārī* (3/442: after hadīth no. 1513), and *Naylul-Awtār* (4/313).

2 — [DB] i.e. the companions of the Shāfiʿī madh-hab.

after it; then the ʿUmrah of Al-Jiʿrānah; and then his ʿUmrah which was along with his Hajj.

He (صَلَّى ٱللَّهُ عَلَيْهِ وَسَلَّمَ) performed Hajj once before the Hijrah; or it is said: more than that, and that is more apparent, since he (صَلَّى ٱللَّهُ عَلَيْهِ وَسَلَّمَ) used to go out on the nights of the pilgrimage, calling the people to Allāh (the Most High) may Allāh extol him, and grant him extensive peace and security, continually, until the Day of Recompense.

Chapter: The Number of his Military Expeditions and the Armies Which He Sent Out

As for his military expeditions, then Muslim reported[1] as a hadīth of ʿAbdullāh ibn Buraydah ibn Al-Husayb Al-Aslamī, from his father, who said: "Allāh's Messenger (صَلَّى ٱللَّهُ عَلَيْهِ وَسَلَّمَ) went upon nineteen military expeditions. He fought in eight of them."[2]

And from Zayd ibn Arqam who said: "Allāh's Messenger (صَلَّى ٱللَّهُ عَلَيْهِ وَسَلَّمَ) went upon nineteen military expeditions. I was with him upon seventeen."[3] As for Muhammad ibn Is-hāq, then he said: "The military expeditions (*ghazawāt*) which he went upon himself were twenty seven,[4] and the armies (*buʿūth*) and army-detachments (*sarāyā*) which he sent were thirty-eight."

And Ibn Hishām added some army detachments sent, in addition to what Ibn Is-hāq mentioned, and Allāh knows best.

---

1 — SH In his *Sahīh* (no. 1814).

2 — There is a difference of opinion regarding the number of military expeditions the Messenger of Allāh (صَلَّى ٱللَّهُ عَلَيْهِ وَسَلَّمَ) fought in. See **Endnote 96 on page 525** for the speech of Imām An-Nawawī in this regard.

3 — BJ SZ Reported by Al-Bukhārī in his *Sahīh* (nos. 3949 & 4404) and Muslim (no. 1254).

4 — See the speech of Al-Hāfidh Ibn Hajr regarding the number of expeditions — **Endnote 97 on page 526**.

Chapter: The Signs of his Prophethood

With regard to the signs of his (صَلَّى ٱللَّهُ عَلَيْهِ وَسَلَّمَ) Prophethood generally, since 235
mentioning it in detail would require many volumes; and the imāms have gathered more than a thousand miracles from that.

So from the clearest and the greatest of them is the Mighty Qurʾān,[1] which is such that:

> لَّا يَأْتِيهِ الْبَاطِلُ مِن بَيْنِ يَدَيْهِ وَلَا مِنْ خَلْفِهِ ۖ تَنزِيلٌ مِّنْ حَكِيمٍ حَمِيدٍ
>
> MEANING: "Falsehood cannot come to it from before it or behind it. It is Revelation sent down by One Who is All Wise, Deserving of all praise]," — **Sūrah Fussilat (41): 42**

and its miraculous nature (*iʿjāz*) is with respect to its wording and its meaning.

As for its wording, then it is at the highest limit of eloquence of speech; and the more a person increases in knowledge and awareness of this matter, then the more his honour and respect for the Qurʾān will be in this regard. So he challenged the orators and fine-speakers in his time, along with their severe enmity towards him and their eagerness to try to show him to be a liar, to bring its like; or ten Sūrahs with its like,[2] or a

---

1 — [BJ][SZ] Al-Bukhārī reported (nos. 4981 and 7274), and Muslim (no. 152) as a hadīth of Abū Hurairah (رَضِيَ ٱللَّهُ عَنْهُ) that Allāh's Messenger (صَلَّى ٱللَّهُ عَلَيْهِ وَسَلَّمَ) said: "There was no Prophet from the Prophets except that he was given signs such that mankind would believe on account of them; but what I was given is Revelation sent to me by Allāh, and I hope that I shall be the one from them having the most followers on the Day of Resurrection."

2 — [BJ][SZ][SH] Allāh (the Most High) said:

> أَمْ يَقُولُونَ افْتَرَاهُ ۖ قُلْ فَأْتُوا بِعَشْرِ سُوَرٍ مِّثْلِهِ مُفْتَرَيَاتٍ وَادْعُوا مَنِ اسْتَطَعْتُم مِّن دُونِ اللَّهِ إِن كُنتُمْ صَادِقِينَ
>
> MEANING: "Or do they say: *'He has forged it.'* Say: Then produce ten forged Sūrahs like it, and call whomever you can besides Allāh to help you, if you are truthful." — **Sūrah Hūd (11):13**

single Sūrah,[1] and they were unable to do so; and He informed them that they would never be able to do that. Indeed, He challenged the whole of the jinn and mankind to produce its like, and they were unable to do so; and He informed them of that.

So Allāh (the Most High) said:

> قُل لَّئِنِ اجْتَمَعَتِ الْإِنسُ وَالْجِنُّ عَلَىٰ أَن يَأْتُوا بِمِثْلِ هَٰذَا الْقُرْآنِ لَا يَأْتُونَ بِمِثْلِهِ وَلَوْ كَانَ بَعْضُهُمْ لِبَعْضٍ ظَهِيرًا
>
> MEANING: "Say: 'If mankind and the jinn were to gather together to produce the like of this Qur'ān they could not produce its like, even if they helped one another,'" — **Sūrah Al-Isrā' (17):88**

— along with the other aspects which confirm its miraculous nature.

As for its meaning, then it reaches the limit of self-consistency and wisdom, and of mercifulness and benefit, and in its praiseworthy outcome and agreement, and in attaining the highest goals and nullifying evils, and in other matters. This will be apparent to one who has understanding and a sound intellect, which is free of unfounded doubts and desires — we seek Allāh's refuge from them, and we ask Him for guidance.

And from [the signs of Prophethood] is that he grew up amongst people who knew his lineage and high standing, and wherever he entered or departed from. He grew up as an orphan amongst them, being trustworthy and truthful, righteous and good, and upon rectitude: all of them acknowledged that for him, and no one would deny it except one who deliberately opposes the truth, argues for the sake of arguing, and is arrogant.

---

1 — (BJ)(SZ)(SH) He (the Perfect and Most High) said:

> وَإِن كُنتُمْ فِي رَيْبٍ مِّمَّا نَزَّلْنَا عَلَىٰ عَبْدِنَا فَأْتُوا بِسُورَةٍ مِّن مِّثْلِهِ وَادْعُوا شُهَدَاءَكُم مِّن دُونِ اللَّهِ إِن كُنتُمْ صَادِقِينَ
>
> MEANING: "And if you are in doubt about what We have sent down to our Slave then produce a Sūrah like it and call your witnesses besides Allāh, if you are truthful." — **Sūrah Al-Baqarah (2):23**

He was illiterate and could not write. He did not learn it, or associate with its people; and their town did not possess knowledge of the earlier peoples, nor anyone who knew anything from that. Yet he came to them at the age of forty and informed them of events of the past, with details and clarity. Then the scholars of the earlier books, who had full knowledge of them, those who were guided by truthfulness, testified in his favour.

Indeed most of the books, which had been sent down before him, had been distorted and changed. So that which Allāh sent down to him came, clarifying that, guarding it, and indicating the truth from it.

Along with this, he was at the limit of truthfulness and trustworthiness, and was upon fine behaviour to such an extent that the people of understanding had not seen the like of him (صَلَّى ٱللَّهُ عَلَيْهِ وَسَلَّمَ). He was, furthermore, upon the worship of Allāh, and was upon humility towards Him and humble submission. He called the people to Him and had patience, and patiently bore the harm of those who opposed him. He abstained from the worldly life, and he was upon fine and noble manners: generosity, bravery, sense of shame, goodness and dutifulness, and maintaining ties of kinship (صَلَّى ٱللَّهُ عَلَيْهِ وَسَلَّمَ); along with the rest of the manners, which have not been gathered together in any human being besides him, neither before him nor after him.

So the intellect comprehends that it would be impossible for such a person to lie against the slightest person with the smallest lie. Then how could it be possible for such a person to lie against Allāh, the Lord of the whole creation, Who informed of the painful punishment which lies with Him, and of what awaits whoever lies and invents falsehood against Him! This would not emanate except from the worst of the servants of Allāh, and those who are the most insolent and foul.

The like of this would not be hidden from children in primary schools; so how could it have remained hidden from people of wisdom and intellect: those who expended their souls and their wealth, and who left behind their children, their homelands, and their tribes for love of him and in obedience to him — may Allāh be pleased with them, and may He extol him (ﷺ) and grant him peace and security, for as long as the night and day alternate.

Also from [the signs of Prophethood] is what he (ﷺ) informed of in this tremendous Qur'ān, and in the ahādīth which are authentic from him, with regard to future Unseen events which later occurred just as he had foretold, just as one arrow-feather resembles the next; and it would be too prolonged to mention all of that here.

Also from them are the astonishing miraculous events which Allāh (the Most High) caused to occur at his hands. So from that is what Allāh (the Mighty and Majestic) informed of in His Mighty Book with regard to the splitting of the moon. This occurred because the Mushrikūn asked him for a sign, and it was during the night, so he pointed towards the moon and it separated into two parts.

Then they asked the other tribes around them (whether they had also seen it), to exclude the possibility that he had merely done magic upon them, and they informed them that they had seen the same; and this is something which the people of knowledge of narrations mention is '*mutawātir*' (reported by a very large number of people at every stage of transmission).

It was reported by a number of the Companions — may Allāh be pleased with them all.[1]

And from [the signs of Prophethood] is what appeared as a result of the blessing given to his supplications, at so many places that a mention of them would be prolonged, and numerous volumes would hardly be able to include them all.

Al-Hāfidh Abū Bakr Al-Bayhaqī (رَحِمَهُ ٱللَّهُ) compiled a fine book in that regard,[2] following the way of those who preceded him in that, just as he was followed in that by many of those who came after him (رَحِمَهُ ٱللَّهُ).

---

1 — See the takhrīj of this hadīth in ENDNOTE 98 ON PAGE 526.

2 — SH Entitled *Dalā'ilun-Nubuwwah wa ma'rifatu ahwāli Sāhibish-Sharī'ah*, which has been printed in seven volumes by Dārul-Kutubil-'Ilmiyyah in Beirut, and it needs a methodical and trustworthy checking and a strong scholarly referencing and verification — may Allāh facilitate that.

So from that is that he (صَلَّى ٱللَّٰهُ عَلَيْهِ وَسَلَّمَ) supplicated to Allāh (the Most High) concerning the young lamb which Ibn Mas'ūd had in the flock he was tending, and he mentioned Allāh's name and milked it, and it flowed with milk for him. So he drank and gave Abū Bakr a drink.[1] He also did the same with the ewe of Umm Ma'bad.[2]

And he supplicated for At-Tufayl ibn 'Amr, so a sign appeared for him, and it was a light, which shone upon the end of his whip, and it could be seen from afar.[3] And the same thing happened for Usayd ibn Al-Hudayr and 'Abbād ibn Bishr, both of whom were from the Ansār, and they had departed from his presence on a dark night.[4]

And he supplicated to Allāh against the seven who mocked him whilst he was praying, and they were killed at Badr.[5]

And he supplicated against Ibn Abī Lahab, and Allāh set upon him a wild animal in Shām, in accordance with his (صَلَّى ٱللَّٰهُ عَلَيْهِ وَسَلَّمَ) supplication.[6]

And he supplicated against Surāqah, and the front legs of his horse sank into the ground. Then he supplicated to Allāh and they were released.[7]

And he threw a handful of small pebbles at the Disbelievers of Quraysh on the day of Badr, and every one of them was struck by something from

---

1 — For details regarding the authenticity of this report, see Endnote 99 on page 527.

2 — For details regarding the authenticity of this report, see Endnote 100 on page 527.

3 — For details regarding the authenticity of this report, see Endnote 101 on page 528.

4 — [SH] Reported by Al-Bukhārī in his *Sahīh* (nos. 465, 3639, and 3805), as a hadīth of Anas (رَضِيَ ٱللَّٰهُ عَنْهُ).

5 — For details regarding the authenticity of this report, see Endnote 102 on page 528.

6 — For details regarding the authenticity of this report, see Endnote 103 on page 528.

7 — [SH] Reported by Al-Bukhārī (no. 3615) and Muslim (no. 2009) as a hadīth of Abū Bakr (رَضِيَ ٱللَّٰهُ عَنْهُ); and Al-Bukhārī reported it (no. 3906) as a hadīth of Surāqah ibn Ju'sham himself (رَضِيَ ٱللَّٰهُ عَنْهُ).

it, and Allāh routed them,[1] and he did exactly the same on the day of Hunayn.[2]

And on the day of Badr, he gave a stump of wood to ʿUkkāshah Ibn Mihsan, and it became a sharp sword in his hand.[3]

And he informed his paternal uncle Al-ʿAbbās, whilst he was being held captive, of the wealth which he and Ummul-Fadl had buried beneath the threshold of his door, and he confirmed that for him.[4]

And he informed ʿUmayr ibn Wahb that he had actually come intending to kill him, using the excuse that he had come to pay a ransom to free captives caught at Badr. So he admitted that to him, and accepted Islām at that moment (رَضِيَ اللَّهُ عَنْهُ).[5]

And on the day of Uhud, he restored the eye of Qatādah ibn An-Nuʿmān Az-Zafrī after it hung out upon his cheek, or it is said: after it fell into his hand; and it became the best one of his two eyes, and it could not be distinguished from the other one.[6]

---

1 — For details regarding the authenticity of this report, see Endnote 104 on page 529.

2 — [BJ][SZ] Reported by Muslim (no. 1775), as a hadīth of Al-ʿAbbās; and Muslim reported it also (no. 1777), as a hadīth of Salamah ibn Al-Akwaʿ.

3 — [BJ][SZ] It is *'daʿīf'*: Reported by Ibn Saʿd in *At-Tabaqāt* (1/188) in *'mursal'* form, with a weak chain of narration; and Ibn Is-hāq reported it in *As-Sīrah* (2/202) without a chain of narration, and it was from him by Al-Bayhaqī in *Ad-Dalāʾil* (3/98); and Al-Wāqidī reported it in *Al-Maghāzī* (1/93), and by way of him Al-Bayhaqī reported it in *Ad-Dalāʾil* (3/98), and Al-Wāqidī is abandoned (*matrūk*).

4 — Reported by Imām Ahmad in his *Musnad* — see detail in Endnote 105 on page 530.

5 — For details regarding the authenticity of this report, see Endnote 106 on page 530.

6 — This hadīth is considered to be of grade: *'hasan'* — see detail in Endnote 107 on page 531.

And on the day of the Trench, he fed a huge number of people, who numbered close to a thousand, from a small goat and one Sā'[1] of barley, in the house of Jābir.[2]

Also on that day, he fed with a very small number of dates, which the daughter of Bashīr brought.[3]

Likewise, he fed about eighty people from some food, which [was such a small amount that it] could almost be concealed in his noble hand.[4]

He did likewise on the morning after his marriage to Zaynab bint Jahsh.[5]

As for the day of Tabūk, then an astonishing affair occurred. He fed the whole army and they filled every available container, from an amount of food, which only covered the space that a small goat could sit upon.[6]

And he gave Abū Hurairah (رَضِيَ اللَّهُ عَنْهُ) a leather bag which he ate from throughout his life, and he frequently took provision from it in Allāh's cause, and it remained with him until the time when 'Uthmān was killed.[7]

---

1 — [DB] Ibnul-Athīr said in *An-Nihāyah fī Gharībil-Hadīth*: "The *Sā'* is repeatedly mentioned in hadīth, and it is a measure amounting to four *'mudds'* (four times what the two hands can hold)."

2 — [SH] Reported by Al-Bukhārī in his *Sahīh* (no. 4101) and Muslim in his *Sahīh* (no. 2039), as a hadīth of Jābir ibn 'Abdillāh (رَضِيَ اللَّهُ عَنْهُمَا).

3 — For details regarding the authenticity of this report, see Endnote 108 on page 532.

4 — [BJ][SZ] Reported by Al-Bukhārī (no. 3578) and Muslim (no. 2040), as a hadīth of Anas (رَضِيَ اللَّهُ عَنْهُ).

5 — [SH] Reported by Al-Bukhārī in his *Sahīh*: (no. 5163), in disconnected form, and (no. 5166) in connected form; and Muslim in his *Sahīh* (no. 1428), as a hadīth of Anas (رَضِيَ اللَّهُ عَنْهُ).

6 — [BJ][SZ][SH] Reported by Al-Bukhārī (no. 2484) and Muslim (no.1729) from Salamah ibn Al-Akwa' (رَضِيَ اللَّهُ عَنْهُ); and Muslim did not mention Tabūk.

7 — Read Endnote 109 on page 533 for details regarding this miracle.

And there were many events of this type, and singling them out with a mention would be very prolonged. So we shall, if Allāh (the Most High) wills, and we trust in Him, devote a separate specific work to that.[1]

And when they suffered a drought he supplicated to Allāh (the Most High) and he did not descend from the minbar before the rain dripped upon his (صَلَّى ٱللَّهُ عَلَيْهِ وَسَلَّمَ) beard, from the roof of the mosque. Prior to this no cloud had been seen in the sky, nor any trace of a cloud, not even to the extent of the palm (of a hand). Then, when he requested that they should be relieved from its falling directly upon them, the cloud opened and spread all around Al-Madīnah until it became like a crown encircling Al-Madīnah.[2]

And he supplicated to Allāh against the Quraysh, and they were struck with a drought so severe that it cannot be put into words, to the extent that they requested mercy from him. So he felt compassion for them, and it was removed from them.[3]

And a container of water was brought for him to make wudhū' (ablution) from. So some people came to him there, hoping to make wudhū' along with him. So he placed his hand in that water container, and it was not large enough to accommodate his whole hand. Then he supplicated to Allāh, and water flowed out from between his (صَلَّى ٱللَّهُ عَلَيْهِ وَسَلَّمَ) fingers.[4]

---

1 — SH The author (رَحِمَهُ ٱللَّهُ) devoted a specific book in his work *Al-Bidāyah wan-Nihāyah* to the signs of Prophethood, and he mentioned very many (may Allāh reward him with good); and his Shaikh, Shaikhul-Islām Ibn Taimiyyah (رَحِمَهُ ٱللَّهُ) said in *Al-Furqān*: "The like of this is plentiful, and I have gathered about a thousand miracles."

2 — BJ SZ Reported in Al-Bukhārī in his *Sahīh* (nos. 1013 and 1014) and Muslim (no. 897), as a hadīth of Anas ibn Mālik (رَضِيَ ٱللَّهُ عَنْهُ).

3 — See **Endnote 110 on page 534** for more details regarding this story.

4 — BJ SZ Reported by Al-Bukhārī (nos. 169, 195, 200, and 3572) and Muslim (no. 2279), as a hadīth of Anas ibn Mālik (رَضِيَ ٱللَّهُ عَنْهُ).

He did likewise on the day of Al-Hudaybiyah, and the army numbered one thousand and four hundred. Jābir said: "And even if we had been one hundred thousand it would have sufficed us."[1]

He did the same upon one of his journeys with a drop of water in a waterskin. The narrator said: "When he ordered me to pour it out into the container I feared that the dryness of the leather waterskin would absorb it. So he placed his hand in it, and supplicated to Allāh (the Most High). So the water flowed out from between his fingers for his Companions, until they performed wudhū' and drank."[2]

Likewise, he sent an arrow to the spring of Al-Hudaybiyah, and it was placed in it, and it flowed tremendously with water until it sufficed them.[3]

He did likewise on *'The Day of the Two Waterskins'*. He gave water to drink to his Companions, and they performed wudhū'; and he ordered one of them to take a bath required because of a wet dream; and nothing was reduced from those two waterskins, which belonged to a woman. So she went to her people and said: *"Today I have either seen the greatest sorcerer upon earth, or he is certainly a Prophet!"* Then she accepted Islām and her people accepted Islām (رَضِيَ اللَّهُ عَنْهُمْ).[4]

And there is a great deal of this type, and mentioning it all in detail would become prolonged; and in what we have mentioned there is sufficiency, if Allāh (the Most High) wills.

---

1 — [BJ] [SZ] Reported by Al-Bukhārī (nos. 3576 & 4152) and Muslim (no. 1856/72 &73), as a hadīth of Jābir, with the wording: *"We were fifteen hundred."* As for his saying: *"We were one thousand and four hundred"*, then it is as a hadīth of Al-Barā' — reported by Al-Bukhārī (no. 3577).

2 — [BJ] [SZ] Reported by Muslim (no. 3013), as a hadīth of Jābir (رَضِيَ اللَّهُ عَنْهُ).

3 — [BJ] [SZ] Reported by Al-Bukhārī (nos. 2731 and 2732), as a hadīth of Al-Miswar ibn Makhramah and Marwān — from one of the Companions of the Messenger (صَلَّى اللَّهُ عَلَيْهِ وَسَلَّمَ).

4 — [SH] Reported by Al-Bukhārī (nos. 344, 348 & 3571) and Muslim (no. 682), as a hadīth of 'Imrān ibn Al-Husayn (رَضِيَ اللَّهُ عَنْهُمَا).

Chapter: His Foretelling of Future Events

244 He also informed of future unseen events, which later happened just as he foretold that they would occur. So Allāh (the Mighty and Majestic) informed in His Book that His Religion would be made manifest and victorious, and His Word would be raised high, and that He would place in authority upon the earth those from his nation who truly believed and who performed righteous deeds,[1] and that is what happened.

And he informed that the Byzantines would defeat the Persians within three to nine years, and that is what occurred.[2]

And he (صَلَّى ٱللَّهُ عَلَيْهِ وَسَلَّمَ) informed his people, those who were with him in the mountain pass, that Allāh had caused termites to attack and devour the document, except for the mention of Allāh within it,[3] and that was found to be the case.

---

1 — (SH) In His Saying:

> وَعَدَ اللَّهُ الَّذِينَ آمَنُوا مِنكُمْ وَعَمِلُوا الصَّالِحَاتِ لَيَسْتَخْلِفَنَّهُمْ فِي الْأَرْضِ كَمَا اسْتَخْلَفَ الَّذِينَ مِن قَبْلِهِمْ وَلَيُمَكِّنَنَّ لَهُمْ دِينَهُمُ الَّذِي ارْتَضَىٰ لَهُمْ وَلَيُبَدِّلَنَّهُم مِّن بَعْدِ خَوْفِهِمْ أَمْنًا ۚ يَعْبُدُونَنِي لَا يُشْرِكُونَ بِي شَيْئًا
>
> MEANING: "Allāh has promised those who truly believe from amongst you and who perform righteous deeds that He will certainly grant them succession to authority upon the earth, just as He granted it to those before them; and that He will certainly establish for them their Religion, which He has chosen for them; and that He will certainly change their condition of fear to one of security. They worship Me alone, and do not associate anything with me." — SŪRAH AN-NŪR (24):55

2 — For details regarding the authenticity of this narration, see ENDNOTE III ON PAGE 534.

3 — (SH) Everything reported about the affair of the boycotting is *'mursal'*, and therefore there is no authentic report established concerning the specific details of the Boycott. However, the event, in its basis, is something established, as Al-Hāfidh Ibn Hajr (رَحِمَهُ ٱللَّهُ) said in *Fat-hul-Bārī* (7/193).

And on the day of Badr, the day before the actual battle, he informed of the places where the enemy fighters would be killed, one by one; and it happened just as he had stated, exactly.[1]

And he informed that the treasures of Kisrā (Khosrau) and Qaysar (Caesar),[2] would be spent in Allāh's cause,[3] and that is what happened.

And he gave the good news to his nation that their rulership would extend over the breadth of the earth,[4] and that is what happened.[5]

And he informed that the Hour would not be established until his nation has fought against a people with small eyes and flat noses. Their faces would be as if they are leather shields, and this is the appearance of the Tarters and this is what happened.[6]

And he informed that Allāh would bring about peace between two large parties of Muslims by means of Al-Hasan ibn ʿAlī (رَضِيَ اللَّهُ عَنْهُمَا),[7] and that occurred.

[And he informed of the fighting against the Khawārij, and he described to them *'Dhuth-Thudayyah'* (the man with a stump of a hand) and he was found, just as described, exactly.][8]

---

1 — BJ SZ Reported by Muslim (no. 1779) as a hadīth of Anas (رَضِيَ اللَّهُ عَنْهُ).

2 — DB Al-Hāfidh Ibn Hajr said in *Fat-hul-Bārī* (6/625): "*'Kisrā'* — with a *kasrah* on the *kāf*, and it is permissible to have a *fat-hah*, and it is a title used for everyone who became the ruler of the Persian Empire; and *'Qaysar'* (Caesar) is a title used for everyone who became the ruler of the Byzantine Empire."

3 — Reported by Al-Bukhārī and Muslim — see more detail in **Endnote 112 on page 534**.

4 — SH Reported by Muslim in his *Sahīh* (no. 2889), as a hadīth of Thawbān (رَضِيَ اللَّهُ عَنْهُ).

5 — Whether this rulership has truly extended over the Earth in its entirety is debateable, and is discussed in **Endnote 113 on page 535**.

6 — BJ SZ Reported by Al-Bukhārī (no. 2928) and Muslim (no. 2912), as a hadīth of Abu Hurairah; and by Al-Bukhārī (no. 2927), as a hadīth of ʿAmr ibn Taghlib.

7 — BJ SZ Reported by Al-Bukhārī (no. 3746 and 7109), as a hadīth of Abū Bakrah (رَضِيَ اللَّهُ عَنْهُ).

8 — See various comments regarding this in **Endnote 114 on page 535**.

And he informed that ʿAmmār would be killed by the rebellious group;[1] and he was killed on the day of Siffīn, being on the side of ʿAlī (رَضِيَ اللَّهُ عَنْهُمَا).

And he informed that a fire would emerge from the Hijāz, which would light up the necks of camels at Busrā.[2] So this fire appeared in the year six hundred and fifty something, and it was very widely reported.[3]

And I was informed from one who actually witnessed the shining of the necks of the camels in Busrā.

So may Allāh extol His Messenger (whenever He is remembered by those who remember Him).[4]

And he informed of individual events that would take place before the coming of the Hour, and a mention of them would be prolonged, and there is sufficiency in what we have mentioned, if Allāh (the Most High) wills, and reliance is upon Him.

Chapter: The Earlier Scriptures Sent Down from the Heavens Foretelling of Allāh's Messenger (صَلَّى اللَّهُ عَلَيْهِ وَسَلَّمَ)

And the previous Scriptures contain the news of him being sent, just as Allāh (the Most High) informed that this is written in the Tawrāt and the Injīl; and likewise He informed about His Prophet ʿĪsā (عَلَيْهِ السَّلَامُ) that he said:

وَمُبَشِّرًا بِرَسُولٍ يَأْتِي مِن بَعْدِي اسْمُهُ أَحْمَدُ

---

1 — SH Reported by Al-Bukhārī (no. 447) and Muslim (no. 2915), as a hadīth of Abū Saʿīd Al-Khudrī (رَضِيَ اللَّهُ عَنْهُ); and by Muslim (no. 2916), as a hadīth of Umm Salamah (رَضِيَ اللَّهُ عَنْهَا).

2 — SH Reported by Al-Bukhārī (no. 7118) and Muslim (no. 2902), as a hadīth of Abū Hurairah (رَضِيَ اللَّهُ عَنْهُ).

I say: Busrā is a well-known town in Shām, being 100 km (approx. 60 miles) to the east of Damascus.

3 — Imām An-Nawawi (رَحِمَهُ اللَّهُ) mentions this event — see Endnote 115 on page 536.

4 — SH An addition from the Sulaymāniyyah Library manuscript (no. 59), and the ʿĀrif Hikmat Library manuscript.

> MEANING: "And I give you the good news of a Messenger of Allāh who will come after me, whose name is Ahmad." — **SŪRAH AS-SAFF (61): 6**

And Al-Bukhārī reported[1] from 'Abdullāh ibn 'Amr that he found his (ﷺ) description in the Tawrāt, and he mentioned it.

And there occurs in the Tawrāt today, whose authenticity the Jews affirm, in the first book of the Scriptures, that Allāh (the Most High) manifested Himself to Ibrāhīm, and said that which has the meaning of:

> "(Arise) and proceed through the length and breadth of the earth, out of honour and respect for your son."[2]

So it is well known that no one has had authority over the east and west of the earth except for Muhammad (ﷺ), as occurs in the *Sahīh* from him that he said:

> "Allāh gathered up the earth for me so that I saw its east and its west, and the rulership of my nation shall reach whatever was shown to me from it."[3]

And there occurs in it:[4] *"Allāh (the Most High) said to Ibrāhīm (Abraham): You shall have descendants through Is-hāq (Isaac). As for Ismā'īl (Ishmael), I shall bless him, grant him increases, and make him great; and I shall make his descendants like the stars of the sky..."* — continuing until He said: *"And I shall make him great by means of Mādhmādh"* — meaning: Muhammad.

And it is said: *"By means of Ahmad;"* and it is said: *"I shall make him tremendous, tremendous;"* and it is said: *"Great, great."*

And there occurs in it: "Allāh promised Ibrāhīm that his son Ismā'īl would have the upper-hand over every nation; and every nation shall be

---

1 — See the speech of 'Abdullāh Ibn 'Amr Ibn Al-'Ās (رضي الله عنه) regarding the mention of Muhammad (ﷺ) in the Torah — ENDNOTE 116 ON PAGE 536.

2 — [BJ][SZ] [*Genesis* — CHAPTER 13: VERSES 15-18]

3 — [SH] Reported by Muslim (no. 2889).

4 — [SH] In Genesis of the Torah: [*Genesis* — CHAPTER 17: VERSE 20].

under his hand; and that he would dwell in all of the habitations of his brothers."[1]

Then the people of the Scripture, and others, know that Ismāʿīl never entered Shām,[2] nor did he overwhelm his brothers.

Rather this occurred for his descendant Muhammad (صَلَّى ٱللَّٰهُ عَلَيْهِ وَسَلَّمَ); and no one from the Arabs had sovereignty over Shām and Egypt before the nation of Muhammad (صَلَّى ٱللَّٰهُ عَلَيْهِ وَسَلَّمَ), for they were both conquered in the Khilāfah of As-Siddīq, and Al-Fārūq (رَضِيَ ٱللَّٰهُ عَنْهُمَا).

Also in the fourth book of the Tawrāt, which they have in their hands today, there occurs that which means:

> "I will raise for them, from their kin, from their brother, a Prophet who is like you, O Mūsā. I shall place My Words in his mouth."[3]

And it is known to them, and to everyone, that Allāh (the Mighty and Majestic) did not raise (any Prophet) from the offspring of Ismāʿīl except for Muhammad (صَلَّى ٱللَّٰهُ عَلَيْهِ وَسَلَّمَ).

Indeed there has not even been amongst the Children of Isrāʾīl a Prophet who was like Mūsā, except for ʿĪsā (عَلَيْهِ ٱلسَّلَامُ), and they do not affirm his Prophethood. And he was not from their brothers, rather he is ascribed to their lineage through his mother — may Allāh extol him and grant him peace and security.

So this is something certainly confirmed for Muhammad (صَلَّى ٱللَّٰهُ عَلَيْهِ وَسَلَّمَ).

Also from that is what the Tawrāt is concluded with, at the end of the fifth book, with the meaning of:

> "Allāh came from Sinai, and shone brightly from Sāʿīr, and arose from the mountains of Fārān."[4]

---

1 — [*Genesis* — Chapter 16: verse 12].

2 — DB Shām: the area of present-day Occupied Palestine, Jordan, Syria, and Lebanon.

3 — BJ SZ [*Deuteronomy* — Chapter 18: verse 17-22].

4 — BJ SZ [*Deuteronomy* — Chapter 33: verse 2].

The meaning of this is that Allāh brought His revealed Laws and His Light from Mount Sinai, upon which He spoke to Mūsā; and He shone forth from Sā'īr, which is the mountain where 'Īsā (عَلَيْهِ ٱلسَّلَامُ) was born and where he was sent as a Messenger.[1]

And He arose from the Mountains of Fārān (Paran), which is Makkah, as proven by the fact that Allāh commanded Ibrāhīm (صَلَّى ٱللَّهُ عَلَيْهِ وَسَلَّمَ) to take Ismā'īl to the mountains of Fārān.[2]

Some of the scholars use as proof for the correctness of this the fact that Allāh (the Perfect) swore an oath by these three places, and they are mentioned in succession, progressing from the lesser to the greater, in His Saying — He the Most High:

> وَالتِّينِ وَالزَّيْتُونِ ۝ وَطُورِ سِينِينَ ۝ وَهَٰذَا الْبَلَدِ الْأَمِينِ ۝
>
> MEANING: "By the fig and the olive, and by Mount Sinai, and by this secure city."

So in the Tawrāt (Torah) they are mentioned in the order in which the events occurred: the first and then the next, and in accordance with the level of light appearing from them. Whereas in the Qur'ān, when He swore by them, He mentioned the place of 'Īsā, then (that of) Mūsā, then (that of) Muhammad (may Allāh extol and grant peace and security to

---

1 — DB Yāqūt Al-Hamawī states in *Mu'jamul-Buldān* that Sā'īr is in the area of Nazareth, between Lake Tiberius (the Sea of Galilee) and Acre.

2 — BJ SZ [*Genesis* — CHAPTER 21: VERSES 20-21]

them all); because it is the custom of the Arabs, when swearing an oath, to proceed from the lesser to the greater.[1]

And likewise the Zabūr of Dāwūd (عَلَيْهِ السَّلَامُ) and the books of revelation found today in the hands of the People of the Book: they contain the glad tidings of him (صَلَّى اللَّهُ عَلَيْهِ وَسَلَّمَ), as has been informed of by those of them who accepted Islām in the earlier and more recent times.

And there occurs in the Injīl a mention of the Paraclete, who is described with the characteristics of Muhammad (صَلَّى اللَّهُ عَلَيْهِ وَسَلَّمَ) exactly.

As for the speech of Isaiah and Jeremiah, then it is very clear to everyone who reads it,[2] and all praise is for Allāh, and all bounties are from Him, and His is the decisive proof.

---

1 — [SH] The author (رَحِمَهُ اللَّهُ) said in *Tafsīrul-Qur'ānil-'Adhīm* (8/570): "Some of the imāms said: These are three places: In each one of them Allāh raised a Prophet as a Messenger from those firmest in resolve (*Ulul-'Azm*): those possessing major revealed laws.

So the first place is that of the fig and the olive, and it Jerusalem, where Allāh raised 'Īsā ibn Maryam (عَلَيْهِ السَّلَامُ); and the second is Mount Sinai, which is the Mount Sinai where Allāh spoke to Mūsā ibn 'Imrān; and the third is Makkah, which is the secure city, which is such that whoever enters it is secure; and it was where he (صَلَّى اللَّهُ عَلَيْهِ وَسَلَّمَ) was raised."

2 — [BJ] [SZ] See the speech of Isaiah in *Al-Jawābus-Sahīh* of Shaikhul-Islām Ibn Taimiyyah (رَحِمَهُ اللَّهُ) (3/326-3278).

CHAPTER:

His (صَلَّى ٱللَّٰهُ عَلَيْهِ وَسَلَّمَ) Children

A mention of his paternal uncles and paternal aunts has preceded at the mention of his (صَلَّى ٱللَّٰهُ عَلَيْهِ وَسَلَّمَ) lineage.

As for his children, then both the males and the females were born to Khadījah bint Khuwaylid (رَضِيَ ٱللَّٰهُ عَنْهَا), except for Ibrāhīm who was born to Māriyah Al-Qibtiyyah; and they are:

Al-Qāsim, after whom he took his *kunyah* — since he was the eldest of his children; then Zaynab; then Ruqayyah; then Umm Kulthūm; then Fātimah.

Then after Prophethood: ʿAbdullāh, and he is called *'The Good One, The Pure One'* (*At-Tayyib At-Tāhir*) because he was born in Islām; and it is said: At-Tāhir was other than At-Tayyib, and this was declared correct by some of the scholars.

Then Ibrāhīm was born to Māriyah. He was born for him (صَلَّى ٱللَّٰهُ عَلَيْهِ وَسَلَّمَ) in Al-Madīnah, in the eighth year; and he died aged one year and ten months,[1] and therefore he (صَلَّى ٱللَّٰهُ عَلَيْهِ وَسَلَّمَ) said: "There is a wet-nurse for him in Paradise."[2]

---

1 — [MM][MK] There occurs in *Jawāmiʿus-Sīrah* (p. 39) of Ibn Hazm: "As for Ibrāhīm, then he was born in Al-Madīnah, and he lived for two months less than two years. He died three months before the death of his father (صَلَّى ٱللَّٰهُ عَلَيْهِ وَسَلَّمَ), on the day when the sun eclipsed.

2 — [BJ][SZ] Reported by Al-Bukhārī (no. 1382) as a hadīth of Al-Barāʾ (رَحِمَهُ ٱللَّٰهُ); and by Muslim (no. 2316), as a hadīth of Anas (رَحِمَهُ ٱللَّٰهُ).

All of them died before him (ﷺ), except for Fātimah (رَضِيَ اللَّهُ عَنْهَا), for she died a short time after him. It is said: six months [after him], upon what is well known.[1] And it is said: eight months;[2] and it is said: seventy days; and it is said: seventy-five days; and it is said: three months; and it is said: a hundred days; and other than that has been said.

ʿAlī led the Prayer over her, or it is said: Abū Bakr, but that is a strange saying.

There also occurs a hadīth that she took a bath a short time before her death, and that she left instructions that she should not be bathed after her death, but this is very strange;[3] for it has been reported that ʿAlī, Al-

---

1 — [BJ][SZ] Reported by Al-Bukhārī (no. 3093) and Muslim (no. 1759), from ʿĀʾishah, as part of a long narration which states that Fātimah (رَضِيَ اللَّهُ عَنْهَا) lived on for six months after Allāh's Messenger (ﷺ).

[DB] An-Nawawī said: "All of them died before him except for Fātimah, for she lived after him for six months, upon the most correct and most famous saying." [*Tahdhībul-Asmāʾ wal-Lughāt* (1/53)]

2 — [BJ][SZ] Khalīfah ibn Khayyāt said in his *Tārīkh* (p. 96): "She died eight months after Allāh's Messenger (ﷺ); or it is said: six months after; or it is said: seventy days after."

3 — [SH] Reported by Ahmad in *Al-Musnad* (6/461-462), and in *Fadāʾilus-Sahābah* (2/725/1243); and Ibn Saʿd in *At-Tabaqātul-Kubrā* (10/28), and by way of Ibrāhīm ibn Saʿd: from Muhammad ibn Is-hāq: fromʿUbaydullāh ibn ʿAlī ibn Abī Rāfiʿ: from his father: from his mother, Salmā — and she was the nurse of Fātimah, with it.

I say: This is a weak (*daʿīf*) chain of narration; it contains a number of weaknesses:

- Firstly: Ibn Is-hāq is a *'mudallis'*, and he has narrated it with *ʿanʿanah*;
- Secondly: ʿUbaydullāh ibn ʿAlī is weak in hadīth — as occurs in *At-Taqrīb*;
- Thirdly: Its text is weak and contrary to what is correct, as will follow.

Ibn ʿAbdul-Hādī said in *Tanqīhut-Tahqīq* (2/126): "This hadīth is very *'munkar'*, it was criticized by Imām Ahmad and others."

The author said in *Al-Bidāyah wan-Nihāyah* (6/333): "As for what is related concerning her having taken a bath before her death and leaving instructions that she should not be washed after that, then it is weak (*daʿīf*): no dependence is placed upon it, and Allāh knows best."

'Abbās, Asmā' bint 'Umays — the wife of As-Siddīq, and Salmā Umm Rāfi' — who was her mid-wife, washed her; and this is what is correct.[1]

Chapter: Regarding his Wives (رَضِيَ ٱللَّهُ عَنْهُنَّ)

The first one he (صَلَّى ٱللَّهُ عَلَيْهِ وَسَلَّمَ) married was Khadījah bint Khuwaylid (رَضِيَ ٱللَّهُ عَنْهَا). So she was a true counsellor to him when he was sent as a Prophet; and she was the first to believe in him — upon the correct saying, or it is said: Abū Bakr, and this is strange.[2]

He did not marry anyone else besides her during her lifetime,[3] because of her greatness and the tremendous status which she had with him.

And there is disagreement about who had the greater excellence: she or 'Ā'ishah (رَضِيَ ٱللَّهُ عَنْهَا). So a group of the scholars preferred the view that Khadījah had the greater excellence,[4] and she died before the Hijrah (Migration).[5]

Then he married Sawdah bint Zam'ah Al-Qurashiyyah, Al-'Āmiriyyah in Makkah, after the death of Khadījah, and he consummated the marriage with her there.

---

1 — This narration was declared *'hasan'* by Imām Al-Albānī. See **Endnote 117 on page 536** for more detail.

2 — [BJ][SZ] Shaikhul-Islām Ibn Taimiyyah (rah) said in *Majmū'ul-Fatāwā* (4/462): "The first of the free, adult Muslim men to accept Islām was Abū Bakr; and of the free children 'Alī; and of the slaves Zayd ibn Al-Hārithah; and of the women Khadījah — the Mother of the Believers; and this is by agreement of the people of knowledge."

3 — Muslim reported in his *Sahīh* (no 2436), as a hadīth of 'Ā'ishah who said: "The Prophet (صَلَّى ٱللَّهُ عَلَيْهِ وَسَلَّمَ) did not marry anyone else along with Khadījah until she died."

4 — [BJ][SZ][SH] Al-Bukhārī (no. 3815) and Muslim (no. 2430) reported from 'Alī ibn Abī Tālib (رَضِيَ ٱللَّهُ عَنْهُ) who said: "I heard Allāh's Messenger (صَلَّى ٱللَّهُ عَلَيْهِ وَسَلَّمَ) say: *'The best of its women is Maryam bint 'Imrān, and the best of its women is Khadījah bint Khuwaylid.'*" Abū Kurayb said: "Wakī' pointed to heaven and to the earth."

5 — [SH] Al-Bukhārī (no. 3896) reported, and the wording is his, and Muslim (no. 1422), as a hadīth of 'Urwah ibn Az-Zubayr who said: *"Khadījah died three years before the departure of the Prophet (صَلَّى ٱللَّهُ عَلَيْهِ وَسَلَّمَ)."* This was also stated by the author in *Al-Bidāyah wan-Nihāyah* (5/300), and by Ibn Qayyim Al-Jawziyyah in *Zādul-Ma'ād* (1/105).

Then, when she grew old, he (صَلَّى ٱللَّهُ عَلَيْهِ وَسَلَّمَ) wished to divorce her, however she made an agreement with him that he would retain her upon the basis that she would grant her appointed day to ʿĀʾishah. Concerning this, there is His Saying — He the Most High:

> وَإِنِ امْرَأَةٌ خَافَتْ مِن بَعْلِهَا نُشُوزًا أَوْ إِعْرَاضًا
>
> MEANING: "And if a woman fears from her husband aversion or desertion."[1]

— the verse, came down.[2]

And she passed away at the end of the days of the Chief of the Believers ʿUmar ibn Al-Khattāb (رَضِيَ ٱللَّهُ عَنْهُ).[3]

It is alternatively said that he married ʿĀʾishah before Sawdah, however he did not consummate his marriage to her except in Shawwāl of the second year, after the Hijrah;[4] and he did not marry any virgin besides her;[5] (and the Revelation did not come to him whilst he was under the blanket of anyone besides her from his wives).[6] And he did not love

---

1 — The whole verse is:

> وَإِنِ امْرَأَةٌ خَافَتْ مِن بَعْلِهَا نُشُوزًا أَوْ إِعْرَاضًا فَلَا جُنَاحَ عَلَيْهِمَا أَن يُصْلِحَا بَيْنَهُمَا صُلْحًا ۚ
> وَالصُّلْحُ خَيْرٌ ۗ وَأُحْضِرَتِ الْأَنفُسُ الشُّحَّ ۚ وَإِن تُحْسِنُوا وَتَتَّقُوا فَإِنَّ اللَّهَ كَانَ بِمَا تَعْمَلُونَ خَبِيرًا
>
> MEANING: "And if a woman fears from her husband aversion or desertion, there is no sin upon them if they make terms of settlement between themselves — and settlement is best. And present in the souls is stinginess. But if you do good and fear Allah — then indeed Allah is ever Acquainted with what you do." — **SŪRAH AN-NISĀʾ (4): 128**

2 — See **ENDNOTE 118 ON PAGE 537** for more details regarding the authenticity of this report.

3 — This deathdate is not unanimously agreed upon — read **ENDNOTE 119 ON PAGE 537**.

4 — [SH] Reported by Muslim in his *Sahīh* (no. 1423) from a hadīth of ʿĀʾishah (رَضِيَ ٱللَّهُ عَنْهَا).

5 — [SH] Reported by Al-Bukhārī (no. 4753) from a hadīth of Ibn Abī Mulaykah, containing the wording: He (meaning Ibn ʿAbbās) said: "And he did not marry any virgin besides you."

6 — [SH] Reported by Al-Bukhārī (no. 3775) and Muslim (no. 2442).

any woman as he loved her.[1] And she had praiseworthy qualities and virtues which have been mentioned in the Qur'ān and the Sunnah, and no woman in this Ummah is known who reached her level of knowledge. She passed away in the year 57 AH, or it is said: 58 AH.

Then he married Hafsah, the daughter of ʿUmar ibn Al-Khattāb (رَضِيَ اللَّهُ عَنْهُ) in the third year after the Hijrah. He (صَلَّى اللَّهُ عَلَيْهِ وَسَلَّمَ) divorced her, and then he returned to her.[2] She died in the year 41 AH, or it is said: 50 AH, or it is said: 45 AH.[3]

Then he married Umm Salamah, and her name was Hind Al-Qurashiyyah (the daughter of Abū Umayyah, whose name was Hudhayfah; and it is said: he was Suhayl ibn Al-Mughīrah ibn ʿAbdillāh ibn ʿUmar ibn Makhzūm). That was after the death of her husband Abū Salamah: ʿAbdullāh ibn ʿAbdil-Asad ibn Hilāl ibn ʿAbdillāh (ibn ʿUmar) ibn Makhzūm, after his return from Badr.[4]

So when she finished her waiting period (*ʿiddah*), he (صَلَّى اللَّهُ عَلَيْهِ وَسَلَّمَ) gave her a proposal of marriage. So this would necessitate that this occurred at the beginning of the third year; and her son ʿUmar was the one who acted as the guardian in her marriage to him (صَلَّى اللَّهُ عَلَيْهِ وَسَلَّمَ), as was reported by An-

---

1 — [BJ][SZ] Reported by Al-Bukhārī (nos. 2662 & 4358) and Muslim (no. 2384), from ʿAmr ibn Al-ʿĀs who said: "I said: *'O Messenger of Allāh! Who is the most beloved of the people to you?'* He said: *'Āʾishah.'* I said: *'From the men?'* He said: *'Her father.'*"

2 — [BJ][SZ] It is *'sahīh'*: reported by Abū Dāwūd (no. 2283), An-Nasāʾī (no. 3562), Ibn Mājah (no. 2016), Ibn Hibbān (no. 4275), and Ad-Dārimī (no. 2269), as a hadīth of ʿUmar.

3 — [DB] The author (رَحِمَهُ اللَّهُ) said in *Al-Bidāyah wan-Nihāyah* (8/31-32), whilst mentioning the events of the year 45 H: "And the majority agree that she died in Shaʿbān of this year, at the age of 60; or it is said that she died in the time of ʿUthmān, but the first saying is more correct."

4 — Regarding the death of Abū Salamah (رَضِيَ اللَّهُ عَنْهُ); read **Endnote 120 on page 538**.

Nasā'ī, by way of Hammād ibn Salamah: from Thābit Al-Bunānī: from Ibn 'Umar ibn Abī Salamah: from his father: from Umm Salamah. [1]

I have compiled a treatise on this matter, and I have clarified that the 'Umar who is spoken of in this hadīth is actually 'Umar ibn Al-Khattāb (رَضِيَ ٱللَّهُ عَنْهُ), since he was the one who conveyed the marriage proposal of Allāh's Messenger (صَلَّى ٱللَّهُ عَلَيْهِ وَسَلَّمَ) to her. Also, Al-Wāqidī and others mentioned that her guardian (*walī*) was her son Salamah, and that is what is correct, if Allāh (the Most High) wills.

It was also mentioned that he married her without any guardian (*walī*), and Allāh knows best.

Al-Wāqidī said: She died in the year 69 AH,[2] whereas others said: During the Caliphate of Yazīd ibn Mu'āwiyah, in the year 62 AH.

Then he married Zaynab bint Jahsh in the 5th year, in Dhul-Qa'dah; or it is said: in the 3rd year, and this is weak.[3]

---

1 — [SH] Reported by Ahmad in his *Musnad* (6/317-318), An-Nasā'ī in *Al-Mujtabā* (6/81-82), and Ibn Hibbān in his *Sahīh* (no. 2949: *'Al-Ihsān'*), by way of Yazīd ibn Hārūn: from Hammād ibn Salamah with it, as part of a long story.

I say: This chain of narration is weak (*da'īf*): This Ibn 'Umar is acceptable only when supported, as occurs in *At-Taqrīb*; and it was declared *'da'īf'* by our Shaikh, the Imām Al-Albānī (رَحِمَهُ ٱللَّهُ).

2 — [SH] This is what occurs in the manuscripts, however there occurs in *At-Tabaqātul-Kubrā* (8/96): "59" and that is what is correct.

3 — [DB] Al-Hāfidh Ibn Hajr said in *Fat-hul-Bārī* (8/463): "There is no disagreement concerning the fact that the verse of Hijāb came down when he (صَلَّى ٱللَّهُ عَلَيْهِ وَسَلَّمَ) consummated his marriage to her [i.e. Zaynab bint Jahsh]," and he said (8/462): "The Hijāb came about in Dhul-Qa'dah of the third year, upon the saying of Abū 'Ubaydah and a group; and with others it was in that (month) of the fourth year — this was declared to be what is correct by Ad-Dimyātī; or it is said: rather it occurred in the fifth year," and he said (7/430): "So we have three sayings concerning the Hijāb. The most well-known of them is (that it was in) the fourth year, and Allāh knows best."

This was also the conclusion reached by Dr. Akram Diyā' Al-'Umarī in *As-Sīratun-Nabawiyyatis-Sahīhah* (2/402-403).

On the morning after her wedding the (obligation of the) Hijāb came down, as they reported in the two *Sahīhs*[1] from Anas; and he screened him away on that day, and Anas was ten years of age when Allāh's Messenger (صَلَّى ٱللَّهُ عَلَيْهِ وَسَلَّمَ) first came to Al-Madīnah. So this shows that he had attained the age of fifteen, and Allāh knows best.

Her Guardian (*Walī*) was Allāh (the Perfect and Most High), who said:

> فَلَمَّا قَضَىٰ زَيْدٌ مِّنْهَا وَطَرًا زَوَّجْنَاكَهَا
>
> MEANING: "So when Zayd had accomplished his desire from her, We gave her to you in marriage." — **Sūrah Al-Ahzāb (33): 37**

And Al-Bukhārī reported in his *Sahīh* with a chain of narration containing only three intermediary narrators, that she used to boast over the other wives of Allāh's Messenger (صَلَّى ٱللَّهُ عَلَيْهِ وَسَلَّمَ) saying: "Your families married you off, whereas Allāh married me off from above the heavens"[2] — and she was the first of the wives of Allāh's Messenger (صَلَّى ٱللَّهُ عَلَيْهِ وَسَلَّمَ) to die.[3]

Al-Wāqidī said: She died in the year 20 AH,[4] and 'Umar ibn Al-Khattāb (رَضِيَ ٱللَّهُ عَنْهُ) led the Funeral Prayer over her.

Then he married Juwayriyah bint Al-Hārith ibn Abī Dirār Al-Mustalaqiyyah, and that occurred when he led a military expedition against her people in the sixth year, at the watering place called Al-Muraysī. She fell to the share of Thābit ibn Qays ibn Shammas, and he arranged for her to buy her freedom. So she came to Allāh's Messenger

---

1 — [SH] Al-Bukhārī (no. 4791) and Muslim (no. 1428).

2 — [SH] Reported by Al-Bukhārī in his *Sahīh* (no. 7420 & 7421), as a hadīth of Anas (رَضِيَ ٱللَّهُ عَنْهُ).

3 — [BJ][SZ] Muslim reported (no. 2452), as a hadīth of 'Ā'ishah (رَضِيَ ٱللَّهُ عَنْهَا) that she said: "Allāh's Messenger (صَلَّى ٱللَّهُ عَلَيْهِ وَسَلَّمَ) said: *'The quickest of you to join me will be the one with the qura.'*" She said: "So we measured our hands to see who had the longest hand; but the one with the longest hand turned out to be Zaynab, since she used to work with her hand and spend in charity."

4 — [SH] As occurs in *At-Tabaqātul-Kubrā* (8/115).

(صَلَّى ٱللَّٰهُ عَلَيْهِ وَسَلَّمَ) seeking his help regarding the payment to set herself free. So he bought her, set her free, and married her.[1]

It is said that she died in the year 50 AH, whereas Al-Wāqidī said: In the year 56 AH.[2]

Then he married Safiyyah bint Huyayy ibn Akhtab, from the Banū Isrā'īl, a descendent of Harūn, of Banun-Nadīr, then of Khaybar (رَضِيَ ٱللَّٰهُ عَنْهَا), and that was after he chose her from the spoils of Khaybar, and this was at the beginning of the seventh year. So he set her free, and made that her dower.

So when she became lawful, whilst upon the way, he consummated his marriage to her, and he screened her with the Hijāb. So they knew that she had become one of the 'Mothers of the Believers.'[3]

Al-Wāqidī said: She died in the year 50 AH;[4] whereas others said: In the year 36 AH, and Allāh knows best.[5]

---

1 — [SH] Reported by Ibn Is-hāq in *As-Sīrah* (3/970-971: Ibn Hishām); and by way of him by Abū Dāwūd (no. 3931), Ahmad (6/277): Muhammad ibn Ja'far ibn Az-Zubayr narrated to me: from 'Urwah: from 'Ā'ishah, with it. I say: This is a *'hasan'* chain of narration; Ibn Is-hāq clearly states that he heard it directly, as you can see. Our Shaikh [Al-Albānī] (رَحِمَهُ ٱللَّٰهُ) said in *Sahīh Mawārididh-Dham'ān* (no. 1020): "It is *'hasan'*."

2 — [SH] As occurs in *At-Tabaqātul-Kubrā* (8/120).

3 — [SH] Reported by Al-Bukhārī (no. 5169) and Muslim (no. 1365/84), as a hadīth of Anas (رَضِيَ ٱللَّٰهُ عَنْهُ).

4 — [SH] As occurs in *At-Tabaqātul-Kubrā* (8/128).

5 — [DB] The author (رَحِمَهُ ٱللَّٰهُ) said in *Al-Bidāyah wan-Nihāyah* (8/47): "Al-Wāqidī said: *'She died in the year fifty'*, and others said: *'In the year thirty-six'*, and the first (saying) is more correct."

Al-Hāfidh Ibn Hajr said in *Fat-hul-Bārī* (4/278: hadīth no. 2035) : "The clear statement of 'Alī ibn Al-Husayn that she [i.e. Safiyyah] narrated to him is a refutation of those who say that she died in the year thirty-six, or before that; since 'Alī was not born until after that, in the year forty or thereabouts. What is correct is that she died in the year fifty, or it is said: after that."

And in this year (or it is said: in the one before it: the sixth year) he married Umm Habībah; and her name was Ramlah bint Abī Sufyān: Sakhr ibn Harb ibn Umayyah ibn 'Abd Shams, Al-Amawiyyah.

He sent 'Amr ibn Umayyah Ad-Damrī to convey the marriage proposal to her whilst she was in Abyssinia, and that was after the death of her husband 'Ubaydullāh ibn Jahsh. Khālid ibn Sa'īd ibn Al-'Ās took charge of marrying her off, or it is said that it was An-Najjāshī (Negus). What is correct though is the first (saying). However, An-Najjāshī provided a dower (*mahr*) for her on behalf of Allāh's Messenger (ﷺ), of four hundred dīnars; and he equipped her and sent her to him (رَضِيَ اللَّهُ عَنْهَا).[1] Then as for what Muslim reported in his *Sahīh*, from a hadīth of 'Ikrimah ibn 'Ammār Al-Yamānī: from Abū Zumayl Simāk ibn Al-Walīd: from Ibn 'Abbās: that when Abū Sufyān accepted Islām he said, speaking to Allāh's Messenger (ﷺ): "I have the finest and most beautiful of the Arabs: Umm Habībah bint Abī Sufyān: I will marry her to you..." — until the end of the hadīth.[2]

Then this has been held to be something strange from [Imām] Muslim (رَحِمَهُ اللَّهُ) — how could his attention not be drawn to it?! Since Abū Sufyān only accepted Islām on the night prior to the Conquest of Makkah; and this occurred more than a year after Allāh's Messenger (ﷺ) married Umm Habībah, and this is something about which there is no disagreement of the scholars.

So as for Ibn Hazm, then he declared that it was a fabrication, and he declared 'Ikrimah ibn 'Ammār to be weak, but this was not said by anyone before him or after him.

---

1 — SH Reported by Abū Dāwūd (no. 2107), An-Nasā'ī in *Al-Mujtabā* (6/119) and *Al-Kubrā* (5/220/no 5486), Ahmad (6/427) [and others] by way of 'Abdullāh ibn Al-Mubārak: from Ma'mar ibn Rāshid: from Ibn Shihāb: from 'Urwah: from Umm Habībah, with it.

Al-Hākim said: *"This hadīth is 'sahīh' to the standard of the two Shaikhs, and they did not report it"* — and adh-Dhahabī agreed with him. I say: It is just as they said.

2 — BJ SZ Reported by Muslim: *Book of the Virtues of the Companions* (4/1945/no. 2501)

As for Muhammad ibn Tāhir Al-Maqdisī, then he said: What Abū Sufyān meant was to renew the marriage contract so that it would not be the case that he was married to her without his permission, and so be a cause of shame for him; or that he wrongly thought that by his accepting Islām his daughter's marriage was dissolved.

He was followed upon this by Abū ʿAmr ibn As-Salāh, and by Abū Zakariyyā An-Nawawī in his explanation of Muslim.[1]

However, this is very far-fetched, since if that were the case he would not have said: *"I have the finest and the most beautiful of the Arabs"* — because Allāh's Messenger (صَلَّى ٱللَّهُ عَلَيْهِ وَسَلَّمَ) had already seen her for a year and more.

Also, the false assumption that her marriage would have been dissolved because of his Islām is very far-fetched. What is correct in that regard is that when Abū Sufyān saw that having Allāh's Messenger (صَلَّى ٱللَّهُ عَلَيْهِ وَسَلَّمَ) as his son-in-law was an honour for him, he wished to marry his other daughter — who was ʿIzzah — to him; and in that regard he sought the assistance of her sister, Umm Habībah, just as is reported in the two *Sahīhs*[2] from Umm Habībah that she said: "O Messenger of Allāh! Marry my sister, the daughter of Abū Sufyān."

So he said: "Would you like that?"

She said: "Yes" — until the end of the hadīth.[3]

And there occurs in *Sahīh Muslim* that she said: "O Messenger of Allāh! Marry my sister: ʿIzzah bint Abī Sufyān..." — until the end of the hadīth.[4]

So, based upon this, the first hadīth is authentic, however a mistake occurred from one of the narrators in his saying: *"And I have the finest and most beautiful of the Arabs: Umm Habībah,"* — and what he actually said was: *"ʿIzzah."*

---

1 — [SH] (16/62-63)

2 — [BJ] [SZ] Reported by Al-Bukhārī (no. 5101) & Muslim (no. 1449), as a hadīth of Umm Habībah.

3 — [DB] And it contains his (صَلَّى ٱللَّهُ عَلَيْهِ وَسَلَّمَ) statement: "That is not permissible for me."

4 — [SH] (no. 1449/16)

However the narrator mistook this; or otherwise that the Shaikh had said: *"Meaning his daughter"*, and the listener misunderstood that she was Umm Habībah, since he wasn't aware of another besides her.

There are many examples of this type of mistake, and I have detailed that in a treatise devoted to this hadīth, and all praise is for Allāh and favour is from Him.

Umm Habībah (رَضِيَ ٱللَّهُ عَنْهَا) died in the year 44H, according to what Abū 'Ubayd[1] stated; whereas Abū Bakr ibn Abī Khaythamah[2] said: "In the year 59, a year before her brother Mu'āwiyah."

Then in Dhul-Qa'dah of this year[3] he married Maymūnah bint Al-Hārith Al-Hilāliyyah, and there is disagreement about whether he was in a state of *ihrām* or not. So the compilers of the two *Sahīhs*[4] reported from Ibn 'Abbās that he was in a state of *ihrām*.[5]

So it is said: That was something specific to him (صَلَّى ٱللَّهُ عَلَيْهِ وَسَلَّمَ) because of what Muslim reported from 'Uthmān: that Allāh's Messenger (صَلَّى ٱللَّهُ عَلَيْهِ وَسَلَّمَ) said:

> "A person in a state of *ihrām* may not marry, nor marry someone else off, nor give a proposal of marriage."

So Abū Hanīfah relied upon the first (report), and took the hadīth of 'Uthmān to show dislike.

However, it is otherwise said: rather he was out of the state of *ihrām*, just as Muslim reported from Maymūnah that she said:

---

1 — BJ SZ He is Al-Qāsim ibn Sallām Al-Harawī, author of the book *Al-Amwāl* and *Al-Gharīb* and others. Refer for his biography to *Siyar A'lāmin-Nubalā'* (10/490).

2 — BJ SZ He is Ahmad ibn Zuhayr ibn Harb An-Nasā'ī. He wrote *Kitābut-Tārīkh*. For his biography refer to *Siyar A'lāmin-Nubalā'* (11/492).

3 — DB i.e. the seventh year.

4 — SH Reported by Al-Bukhārī (no. 5114) and Muslim (no. 1410).

5 — BJ SZ Reported by Muslim (no. 1411) from Maymūnah, without her saying *"and he consummated the marriage to her outside the state of ihrām."*

> "Allāh's Messenger (صَلَّى ٱللَّهُ عَلَيْهِ وَسَلَّمَ) married her outside the state of *ihrām*, and he consummated the marriage to her outside the state of *ihrām*."

Therefore, the great majority of the scholars gave precedence to this hadīth over the saying of Ibn ʿAbbās, since she was the person involved in the incident and therefore knew better.

The same was related by Abū Rāfiʿ, as At-Tirmidhī reported from him,[1] and he was the intermediary between them.

Then different responses have been given for the hadīth of Ibn ʿAbbās, but this is not the place for them.

She died at Sarif (at the same place where Allāh's Messenger صَلَّى ٱللَّهُ عَلَيْهِ وَسَلَّمَ had consummated the marriage to her) when she was returning from the ʿUmrah performed in accordance with the terms of the agreement, and her death occurred in the year 51H, or it is said: in 53H, or it is said: in 66H. The son of her sister — ʿAbdullāh ibn ʿAbbās (رَضِيَ ٱللَّهُ عَنْهُمَا) — led the [Funeral] Prayer over her.

So these nine, after Khadījah, are the ones referred to in what is mentioned in the two *Sahīhs*[2] that he (صَلَّى ٱللَّهُ عَلَيْهِ وَسَلَّمَ) died and left them behind.

And in a narration in the *Sahīh*[3] it is stated that he died and left eleven behind, but the first is more correct.[4]

---

1 — Imām Ahmad declared this hadīth to be weak — refer to ENDNOTE 121 ON PAGE 538 for more detail.

2 — BJ SZ Reported by Al-Bukhārī (no. 284) and Muslim (no. 1462) from Anas.

3 — The narraton reported in *Sahīh Al-Bukhārī* mentions eleven due to including Māriyah and Rayhānah as mentioned in ENDNOTE 122 ON PAGE 539.

4 — Refer to ENDNOTE 123 ON PAGE 539 for a mention of some of the virtues of Zaynab (رَضِيَ ٱللَّهُ عَنْهَا).

And Qatādah ibn Di'āmah said that he (صَلَّى ٱللَّٰهُ عَلَيْهِ وَسَلَّمَ) married fifteen wives, and consummated the marriage with thirteen, and gathered eleven together at one time, and died leaving nine behind.[1]

And Al-Hāfidh Abū 'Abdillāh Muhammad ibn 'Abdil-Wāhid Al-Maqdisī reported the like of this from Anas, in his book *Al-Mukhtārah*,[2] and this is what is well known.

And I have seen that some of the later scholars, from the Mālikīs and others, have enumerated in the book of marriage those wives he did not consummate the marriage with, and they come to more than twenty.

And he had two slave-girls, who were: Māriyah bint Sham'ūn Al-Qibtiyyah the mother of Ibrāhīm, the son of Allāh's Messenger (صَلَّى ٱللَّٰهُ عَلَيْهِ وَسَلَّمَ). Al-Muqawqas, the ruler of Iskandariyyah (Alexandria) and Egypt, sent her along with her sister, Shīrīn, and a eunuch called Ma'būr, and a mule called Ad-Duldul. So he (صَلَّى ٱللَّٰهُ عَلَيْهِ وَسَلَّمَ) gave Shīrīn as a gift to Hassān ibn Thābit, and she gave birth for him to 'Abdur-Rahmān.

Māriyah died in Muharram in the sixteenth year. So 'Umar ibn Al-Khattāb (رَضِيَ ٱللَّٰهُ عَنْهُ) himself gathered the people for her funeral, and he led the Funeral Prayer over her; and she was buried in Al-Baqī' (رَضِيَ ٱللَّٰهُ عَنْهَا).

As for the second, then she was Rayhānah bint 'Amr, or it is said: bint Zayd. He took her as his special share from Banū Quraydhah, and he took her as a slave-girl; or it is said: he married her; or it is said: rather he took her as a slave-girl, then he set her free, and she rejoined her family.

Some later people mentioned that he also took two other slave-girls,[2] and Allāh (the Most High) knows best.

---

1 — [SH] Reported by Al-Bayhaqī in *Dalā'ilun-Nubuwwah* (7/288-289) by way of 'Abdul-Wahhāb ibn 'Atā', who said: Sa'īd related to us: from Qatādah with it. I say: This is a mursal report, with a *'sahīh'* chain of narration.

2 — (7/106/2524) by way of Makkī ibn 'Abdān: from Muhammad ibn Al-Husayn ibn Tarkhān: from 'Umar ibn Sahl: from Yahyā ibn Abī Kathīr: from Qatādah: from Anas with it.

2 — [BJ][SZ] Ibnul-Qayyim said in *Az-Zād* (1/114): "Abū 'Ubaydah said: 'He had four: Māriyah, the mother of Ibrāhīm; and Rayhānah; and another beautiful slave-girl whom he acquired from some captives; and a slave-girl whom Zaynab gave him as a gift.'"

Chapter: The Slaves He Owned

264 A mention of the slaves owned by Allāh's Messenger (صَلَّىٱللَّهُعَلَيۡهِوَسَلَّمَ), arranged in alphabetical order (may Allāh be pleased with them all), and that is in accordance with what the great Hāfidh Abul-Qāsim ibn 'Asākir brought at the beginning of his *Tārīkh*[1]; and they are Ahmar, whose *kunyah* was Abū 'Usayb; and Aswad; and Aflah; and Anasah; and Ayman ibn Umm Ayman; and Bādhām; and Thawbān ibn Bujdud; and Hunayn; and Dhakwān (*or it is said: Tahmān, or it is said: Kaysān, or it is said: Marwān, or it is said: Mahrān*); and Rāfiʿ; and Rabāh; and Ruwayfiʿ; and Zayd ibn Bawlā'; and Zayd ibn Hārithah; and Zayd (*the grandfather of Hilāl ibn Yasār ibn Zayd*); and Sābiq; and Sālim; and Saʿīd; and Safīnah; and Salmān Al-Fārisī; and Sulaym, whose *kunyah* was Abū Kabshah (*he was mentioned amongst those who were present at Badr*); and Sālih (Shaqrān); and Dumayrah ibn Abī Dumayrah; and 'Ubaydullāh ibn Aslam; and 'Ubayd; and another 'Ubayd (*whose kunyah was Abū Safiyyah*); and Fudālah Al-Yamānī; and Qasīr; and Kirkirah (*or it is said: Karkarah*); and Ma'būr Al-Qibtī; and Midʿam; and Maymūn; and Nāfiʿ; and (Nubayh)[2]; and Hurmuz; and Hishām; and Wāqid; and Wardān; and Yasār (*who was a Nubian*); and Abū Uthaylah; and Abū Bakrah; and Abul-Hamrā'; and Abū Rāfiʿ (*and it is said that his name was Aslam*); and Abū 'Ubayd.

So these are the ones mentioned by Abū Zakariyyā An-Nawawī (رَحِمَهُٱللَّهُ) at the beginning of his book *Tahdhībul-Asmā' wal-Lughāt*,[3] except that I have arranged them in alphabetical order to make it easier.

As for the female slaves he owned, then (they were): Umaymah; and Barakah, Umm Ayman (*and she was the mother of Usāmah ibn Zayd*); and Khadrah; and Radwā; and Rayhānah; and Salmā' (*and she was Umm Rāfiʿ, the wife of Abū Rāfiʿ*); and Shīrīn; and her sister Māriyah,

---

1 — [SH] *Tārīkh Dimashq* (4/172-206).

2 — [SH] In the manuscripts, there occurs *"Nabīl"*, and what is written here is what is correct, as occurs in the biographies of the Companions and the reference works of sīrah.

3 — [BJ][SZ] (1/28).

the mother of Ibrāhīm (عَلَيْهِ السَّلَام); and Maymūnah bint Sa'd; and Umm Dumayrah; and Umm 'Ayyāsh.

Chapter: His (صَلَّى ٱللَّٰهُ عَلَيْهِ وَسَلَّمَ) Servants

A group of the Companions (رَضِيَ ٱللَّٰهُ عَنْهُمْ) devoted themselves to serving him, just as 'Abdullāh ibn Mas'ūd used to be the one who looked after his shoes; when he stood he would put them upon him, and when he sat down he would put them under his arms until he got up.

And Al-Mughīrah ibn Shu'bah was a sword-bearer who stood at his head.

And 'Uqbah ibn 'Āmir looked after his mule, leading it along upon journeys.

And Anas ibn Mālik; and Rabī'ah ibn Ka'b; and Bilāl; and Dhū Mikhbar, and it is said: Dhū Mikhmar — the son of the brother of An-Najjāshī, the King of Abyssinia, and it is said: the son of his sister; — and others.

Chapter: The Scribes of the Revelation

As for the scribes who wrote down the Revelation, then Abū Bakr wrote for him, and 'Umar, and 'Uthmān, and 'Alī, and Az-Zubayr, and Ubayy ibn Ka'b, and Zayd ibn Thābit, and Mu'āwiyah ibn Abī Sufyān, and Muhammad ibn Maslamah, and Al-Arqam ibn Abil-Arqam, and Abān ibn Sa'īd ibn Al-'Ās, and his brother Khālid, and Thābit ibn Qays, and Hanzalah ibn Ar-Rabī' Al-Usaydī (the scribe), and Khālid ibn Al-Walīd, and 'Abdullāh ibn Al-Arqam, and 'Abdullāh ibn Zayd ibn 'Abd Rabbihi, and Al-'Alā' ibn 'Utbah, and Al-Mughīrah ibn Shu'bah, and Shurahbīl ibn Hasanah.

Al-Hāfidh Abul-Qāsim mentioned this fully in his book,[1] and he reported what he was able to with fully connected chains from each one

---

1 — SH *Tārīkh Dimashq* (4/220-237) of Ibn 'Asākir.

of them, except for Shurahbīl ibn Hasanah; and he mentioned amongst them As-Sijill, just as Abū Dāwūd and An-Nasā'ī reported.[1]

And this hadīth was criticised by Imām Abū Ja'far ibn Jarīr in his *Tafsīr*, and he said: "No such person is known amongst the scribes of the Prophet (صَلَّى ٱللَّهُ عَلَيْهِ وَسَلَّمَ); indeed, there is no one amongst his Companions called Sijill."

I say: And it was criticised by more than one of the memorizers; and I have singled it out with a treatise, detailing its chains, its weaknesses, and those who have spoken about it from the imāms, and those of them who held it to be a fabricated hadīth; and Allāh (the Most High) knows best.

Chapter: The Mu'adhdhins

He (صَلَّى ٱللَّهُ عَلَيْهِ وَسَلَّمَ) had four mu'adhdhins: Bilāl ibn Rabāh; and 'Amr ibn Umm Maktūm, the blind-man (*Al-A'mā*) (and it is said: his name was 'Abdullāh). These two were in Al-Madīnah and they used to take turns to give the adhān. And Sa'd Al-Qaraz at Qubā'; and Abū Mahzūrah in Makkah (رَضِيَ ٱللَّهُ عَنْهُمْ).

Chapter: A Mention of the Emissaries he Sent to the Kings of the Distant Lands

He (صَلَّى ٱللَّهُ عَلَيْهِ وَسَلَّمَ) sent 'Amr ibn Umayyah Ad-Damrī to An-Najjāshī with his letter, and he accepted Islām (may Allāh be pleased with him and illuminate his grave);[2] and Dihyah ibn Khalīfah Al-Kalbī to Hiraql

---

1 — Shaikhul-Islām Ibn Taimiyyah (رَحِمَهُ ٱللَّهُ) stated that this hadīth is fabricated. See more reasons for this narration's weakness in Endnote 124 on page 540.

2 — [BJ] [SZ] Ibnul-Qayyim said in *Az-Zād* (1/120): "This is what a group said, from them Al-Wāqidī and others; however it is not as they said, since the Najjāshī whom he (صَلَّى ٱللَّهُ عَلَيْهِ وَسَلَّمَ) prayed over is not the one whom he wrote to. This second one is not known to have accepted Islām, contrary to the first one who died as a Muslim."

So Muslim reported in his *Sahīh* (3/1397/no. 1774), from Anas: "That the Prophet (صَلَّى ٱللَّهُ عَلَيْهِ وَسَلَّمَ) wrote to Kisrā (Khosrau), and to Qaysar (Caesar), and to An-Najjāshī, and to every tyrant-king, calling them to Allāh (the Most High); and he was not the Najjāshī whom the Prophet (صَلَّى ٱللَّهُ عَلَيْهِ وَسَلَّمَ) prayed over."

(Heraclius) the Byzantine emperor. So he came close to accepting Islām, but did not do so; and some said: he accepted Islām; and Sunayd ibn Dāwūd reported a *'mursal'* hadīth in his *Tafsīr* which indicates that he accepted Islām; and Abū 'Ubayd reported a hadīth which is also *'mursal'* in the book *Al-Amwāl*[1] which clearly states that he did not accept Islām.

And he sent 'Abdullāh ibn Hudhāfah As-Sahmī to Kisrā (Khosrau), the emperor of the Persians, so he displayed haughtiness and he tore up his (صَلَّى ٱللَّهُ عَلَيْهِ وَسَلَّمَ) letter.[2] So Allāh utterly tore him and his kingdom apart, due to the Messenger (صَلَّى ٱللَّهُ عَلَيْهِ وَسَلَّمَ) supplicating against him for that.[3]

And he sent Hātib ibn Abī Balta'ah to Al-Muqawqas, the ruler of Iskandariyyah (Alexandria) and Egypt; so he came close to accepting Islām, but it is not mentioned about him that he did accept Islām; and he sent gifts and valuable presents to him (صَلَّى ٱللَّهُ عَلَيْهِ وَسَلَّمَ).

And [he sent] 'Amr ibn Al-'Ās to the two kings of 'Umān (Oman), and they both accepted Islām; and they allowed 'Amr to collect the Zakāt, and to judge between the people — so may Allāh be pleased with them both.

And [he sent] Salīt ibn 'Amr Al-'Āmirī to Hawdhah ibn 'Alī Al-Hanafī in Al-Yamāmah.

And [he sent] Shujā' ibn Wahb Al-Asadī to Al-Hārith ibn Abī Shammar Al-Ghassānī, the king of Al-Balqā' in Shām.

And [he sent] Al-Muhājir ibn Abī Umayyah Al-Makhzūmī to Al-Hārith Al-Himyarī.

And [he sent] Al-'Alā' ibn Al-Hadramī to Al-Mundhir ibn Sāwā Al-'Abdī, the King of Bahrain, and he accepted Islām.

---

1 — Heraclius did not accept Islām according to an authentic hadīth — refer to ENDNOTE 125 ON PAGE 541.

2 — [SH] Reported by Al-Bukhārī (no.64), as a hadīth of Ibn 'Abbās (رَضِيَ ٱللَّهُ عَنْهُمَا).

3 — For more information regarding this, see ENDNOTE 126 ON PAGE 541.

And he sent both Abū Mūsā Al-Ashʿarī and Muʿādh ibn Jabal to the people of Yemen,[1] so most of their kings and their common-folk accepted Islām.

Chapter: His (صَلَّىٰٱللَّهُعَلَيْهِوَسَلَّمَ) She-Camels and Horses

The she-camels he (صَلَّىٰٱللَّهُعَلَيْهِوَسَلَّمَ) owned were: Al-ʿAdbāʾ, Al-Jadʿāʾ, and Al-Qaswāʾ[2] — and it is related from Muhammad ibn Ibrāhīm At-Taymī that he said: *"He had only a single she-camel which had these three characteristics"* — and this is very strange: An-Nawawī quoted it.[3]

As for horses, then he had *As-Sakb,*[4] which had a white blaze upon its forehead and white patches on its legs, but its right leg was of clear colour — and it was the first horse which he rode out to fight upon; and (he had) *Sabhah,*[5] and it was the one which he raced upon; and *Al-Murtajiz,*[6] and it was the one which he bought from the bedouin man, and Khuzaymah ibn Thābit bore witness regarding it.[7]

---

1 — SH Al-Bukhārī reported it (no. 2923) and Muslim (no. 1733), as a hadīth of Abū Mūsā, containing the wording that he sent him initially, and then sent Muʿādh after him (رَضِيَٱللَّهُعَنْهُمَا).

And Al-Bukhārī reported in his *Sahīh* (no. 1458), and Muslim (no. 19), as a hadīth of Ibn ʿAbbās: *"That when Allāh's Messenger (صَلَّىٰٱللَّهُعَلَيْهِوَسَلَّمَ) sent Muʿādh to Yemen..."* — until the end of the hadīth.

2 — Refer to the speech of Ibn Al-Qayyim (رَحِمَهُٱللَّهُ) regarding the camels of the Messenger (صَلَّىٰٱللَّهُعَلَيْهِوَسَلَّمَ) — ENDNOTE 127 ON PAGE 542.

3 — SH *Tahdhībul-Asmāʾ wal-Lughāt* (1/37).

4 — DB Ibnul-Athīr said in *An-Nihāyah*: *"Meaning profuse in galloping."* Ibnul-Qayyim said in *Zādul-Maʿād* (1/133): *"It was a dark reddish-brown, or it is said: It was blackish."*

5 — DB Ibnul-Athīr said in *An-Nihāyah*: "It is from their saying: *'A horse which glides'* (*sābih*) when it stretches forth its fore-legs in a fine manner when galloping."

6 — DB One who recites rhyming prose, Ibnul-Athīr said in *An-Nihāyah*: "It was so-called because of the fine sound it made when it neighed."

Ibnul-Qayyim said in *Zādul-Maʿād* (1/133): "And it was pale grey."

7 — For more detail regarding this chain of narration, see ENDNOTE 128 ON PAGE 542.

And Sahl ibn Sa'd said: "He had three horses: *Lizāz*,[1] and *Az-Zarib*,[2] and *Al-Lukhayf* — or it is said [that the name of the third was] with a *hā'* (ح) without the dot,[3] or it is said [that the name of the third was] *An-Nahīf* (the lean one)."

So these are six and there was a seventh, which was *Al-Ward*:[4] Tamīm Ad-Dārī presented it to him as a gift.

And he had a female mule called *Ad-Duldul;*[5] it was sent to him as a gift by Al-Muqawqas, and he rode it on the day of Hunayn. It lived on after him (صَلَّى ٱللَّهُ عَلَيْهِ وَسَلَّمَ) until barley had to be mashed for it with water, after its teeth had fallen out; and it was kept by 'Alī, and after him by 'Abdullāh ibn Ja'far.[6]

And a donkey called 'Ufayr[7] — with an *'ayn* (ع) without a dot,[8] or it is said with a dot (غ):[9] 'Iyād stated it; An-Nawawī said: "And they agree that he was mistaken in that."

I say: And stranger than all of this is Abul-Qāsim As-Suhaylī's narration in his *Rawd* of the well-known hadīth about the story of 'Ufayr, that it spoke to the Prophet (صَلَّى ٱللَّهُ عَلَيْهِ وَسَلَّمَ) and said that it was a descendant of

---

1 — DB That which unites and adheres — Ibnul-Athīr said in *An-Nihāyah fī Gharībil-Hadīth*: "As if it were joined to the desired goal because of its speed."

2 — DB Ibn Al-Athīr said: "Likening it to a small mountain because of its strength."

3 — DB [i.e. 'Al-Luhayf']. Ibnul-Athīr said: "Because of the length of its tail... It being as if it covered (*yalhafu*) the ground with its tail."

4 — DB Adh-Dhahabī said in *As-Sīratun-Nabawiyyah* (p. 359): "Al-Ward (tawny coloured) is between reddish-brown and reddish."

5 — DB Ibnul-Qayyim said in *Zādul-Ma'ād*: "It was pale grey."

6 — DB An-Nawawī said in *Tahdhībul-Asmā' wal-Lughāt* (1/60): "We have it narrated to us in *Tārīkh Dimashq*, through chains of narration, that it remained until 'Alī ibn Abī Tālib (رَضِيَ ٱللَّهُ عَنْهُ) fought against the Khawārij upon it during his caliphate." And he said: "It died at Yanbu'."

7 — DB An-Nawawī said in *Tahdhībul-Asmā' wal-Lughāt* (1/60): "'Ufayr died during the Farewell Pilgrimage."

8 — DB i.e. 'Ufayr.

9 — DB i.e. Ghufayr.

seventy donkeys — each one of which had been ridden by a Prophet, and that its name was Yazīd ibn Shihāb; and that the Prophet (صَلَّى ٱللَّٰهُ عَلَيْهِ وَسَلَّمَ) used to send it for any needs to his Companions.[1] And this is something false and futile: there is no basis for it through any authentic or weak chain of narration, except for what Abū Muhammad ibn Abī Hātim mentioned by way of a reprehensible and rejected chain.

So the people of knowledge of this affair do not doubt that it is a fabrication.

Abū Is-hāq Al-Isfarāyīnī also mentioned this (report), as did Imāmul-Haramayn. Even Al-Qādī ʿIyād mentioned it in passing, in his book *Ash-Shifā'*;[2] but it was more fitting that it should be left out, since it is a fabrication. I asked our Shaikh Abul-Hajjāj[3] about it and he said: "There is no basis for it, and it is a joke."

And at one time, he (صَلَّى ٱللَّٰهُ عَلَيْهِ وَسَلَّمَ) had twenty milking-camels[4] and one hundred sheep.

---

1 — [BJ][SZ] Ibn Hibbān mentions this report in *Al-Majrūhīn* (2/308), in the biography of Muhammad ibn Yazīd Abū Jaʿfar, and he said: "And this is a hadīth which has no foundation, and its chain of narration is nothing, and it is not permissible to use this Shaikh as proof."

Ibnul-Jawzī mentioned it in *Al-Mawdūʿāt* (2/26), and said: "This hadīth is a fabrication. So may Allāh curse the one who fabricated it, for he did not intend except to cause harm to Islām and to mock at it."

2 — [BJ][SZ] *Ash-Shifā' fī Huqūqil-Mustafā* (1/443).

3 — [DB] i.e. Al-Hāfidh Al-Mizzī.

4 — [BJ][SZ] He (i.e. Ibnul-Qayyim) said in *Az-Zād* (1/135): "He had forty-five milking camels."

Chapter: His Weaponry

With regard to armour and weapons, he had three spears, three bows, and six swords[1]; from them was *'Dhul-Fiqār'* (*'The Possessor of Backbone-like Ridges'*), which he took as part of the extra shares of booty on the day of Badr; and two coats of chain-mail,[2] a shield; a signet-ring, a sturdy wooden cup, a square black flag, and a white banner — or it is said that it was black.

---

1 — [BJ][SZ] Ibnul-Qayyim mentioned (1/130) nine swords of the Messenger, and he named them.

[DB] He said: "He had nine swords: [I] *Ma'thūr*, and it was the first sword which he possessed. He inherited it from his father; [II] *Al-'Adb* (*The Sharp One*); [III] *Dhul-Fiqār* (*The Possessor of Backbone-like Ridges*), with a *kasrah* on the *fā'* (فِقار), and also with a *fat-hah* on the *fā'* (فَقار)— and he would hardly be without it. Its hilt, pommel, carrying-ring, cord, decorative rings, and scabbard-tip were made of silver; [IV] *Al-Qala'ī* (*The Sword from Qala'*); [V] *Al-Battār* (*The Cutter*); [VI] *Al-Hatf* (*Death*); [VII] *Ar-Rasūb* (*The Penetrator*); [VIII] *Al-Mikhdham* (*The Fast Cutter*); and [IX] *Al-Qadīb* (*The Sharp Cutter*). The scabbard tip of his sword was made of silver, and in between, it had rings of silver. He acquired his sword *Dhul-Fiqār* as part of the extra share of booty on the day of Badr, and it is the one which he had the dream about."

2 — [BJ][SZ] Ibnul-Qayyim said (1/130): "And he had seven coats of chain-mail."

CHAPTER:

Regarding His Outward Appearance

The scholars have written works about this matter, and the one who compiled the finest work in that regard is the Imām Abū ʿĪsā Muhammad ibn ʿĪsā ibn Sawrah At-Tirmidhī (رَحِمَهُ ٱللَّهُ) by which I refer to the book *Ash-Shamā'il*,[1] and the scholars and Imāms followed him upon that.[2]

And this work has been dealt with thoroughly with its chains of narration, and explained at length by Al-Hāfidh Abul-Qāsim ibn ʿAsākir[3] (رَحِمَهُ ٱللَّهُ) and by our Shaikh, Al-Imām, Al-Hāfidh Abul-Hajjāj Al-Mizzī in *Tahdhībul-Kamāl*.[4]

And the Shaikh Abū Zakariyyā An-Nawawī compiled a short chapter about it in his *Tahdhīb*.[5]

He said:

....

---

1 — SH Our Shaikh, the great scholar, Al-Albānī (رَحِمَهُ ٱللَّهُ) abridged and researched it, and he referenced and verified its ahādīth and narrations. He also explained its difficult words, and he mentioned some points of benefit and rulings extracted from its ahādīth — may Allāh have mercy upon him, purify his soul, and fill his grave with light.

2 — For a list of books that have been written regarding the *"shamā'il"*, see ENDNOTE 129 ON PAGE 542.

3 — SH In *Tārīkh Dimashq* (3/139-217).

4 — SH (1/213-244)

5 — BJ SZ *Tahdhībul-Asmā' wal-Lughāt* (1/25-26).

"He (صَلَّى ٱللَّهُ عَلَيْهِ وَسَلَّمَ) was not extremely tall, nor was he short. He was not extremely white, nor was he brown. He was not curly-haired, nor was his hair straight. He died whilst not having twenty white hairs upon his head.

He was fine in build, and he had broad shoulders. His hair reached down to his shoulders, (and at some times it was down to his ear lobes), and at times it was half-way down his ears.

He had a thick beard; and his hands were sturdy, meaning that he had large fingers. He had a large head, and he had large joints.

His face was roundish; the pupils of his eyes were very black, and he had long eyelashes. The corners of his eyes were red.

He had fine hairs running from his chest to his navel, just like a downy twig.

When he walked, it was as if he was going down a slope, i.e. he walked forcefully; and a 'slope' (*sabab*) means an incline.

His face beamed like the shining of the full moon: it was as if his face was indeed like the moon.

He had a beautiful voice, his cheeks were not prominent, he had a broad mouth, and his chest and belly were equal.

He had hair upon his shoulders, forearms, and upper-chest. His wrists were long, and his palms were spacious.

He had some reddishness in the whites of his eyes, meaning that the corners were elongated.

He had lean heals, meaning that he had little flesh upon his heels.

Between his shoulder blades was the *'Seal of Prophethood'* (*Khātamun-Nubuwwah*) which was like a partridge egg, and like a pigeon's egg.

When he walked, it was as if the earth became rolled up for him; and they had to exert themselves to catch up with him, whereas he would not be exerting himself at all.

He used to allow his hair to fall upon his forehead, then afterwards he parted it; and he used to comb it, and he would comb his beard.

He used to apply antimony kohl every night, applying it thrice upon each eye before sleeping.[1]

The most beloved of clothes to him was the robe (*Al-Qamīs*), and the white ones, and the striped ones (*Al-Hibarah*) — and they are a type of striped cloaks containing redness. The sleeve of his robe was down to his wrist.

Once he wore a red outfit,[2] and a cloak (*ridā'*) and a waist-wrapper (*izār*); and on one occasion he wore two green garments.[3]

At one time, he wore a cloak with tight sleeves,[4] and one time he wore a tunic.

On an occasion, he wore a black turban (*'imāmah*), and he let its end hang down between his shoulder blades.[5]

On one occasion he wore a black woollen garment (*mirt*) — i.e. a cloak (*kisā'*).[6]

And he wore a signet-ring, leather socks, and shoes."

---

1 — See **Endnote 130 on page 543** for more detail regarding the usage of Kohl.

2 — See the speech of Imām Ibn Al-Qayyim (رَحِمَهُ ٱللَّهُ) regarding this clothing in **Endnote 131 on page 543**.

3 — [DB] Abū Dāwūd reported (no. 4206) from Abū Rimthah who said: "I came with my father towards the Prophet (صَلَّى ٱللَّهُ عَلَيْهِ وَسَلَّمَ), and he had his hair down to his ear-lobes — with a trace of henna; and he was wearing two green striped Yemeni garments." Shaikh Al-Albānī declared it *'sahīh'*.

4 — [DB] See *Sahīh Al-Bukhārī* (no. 363).

5 — [DB] Muslim reported (no. 1359/453) from 'Amr ibn Hurayth who said: "It is as if I am still looking at Allāh's Messenger (صَلَّى ٱللَّهُ عَلَيْهِ وَسَلَّمَ) upon the minbar wearing a black turban (*'imāmah*), letting its two ends hang down between his shoulder blades."

6 — [DB] Muslim reported (no.2081) from 'Ā'ishah who said: "The Prophet (صَلَّى ٱللَّهُ عَلَيْهِ وَسَلَّمَ) came out one morning wearing a black woollen cloak with camel-saddle designs upon it."

The end of that which he mentioned.

....

And Anas ibn Mālik (رَضِيَ اللَّهُ عَنْهُ) said: "I never touched any brocade or silk softer than the palm of Allāh's Messenger (صَلَّى اللَّهُ عَلَيْهِ وَسَلَّمَ); nor did I ever smell a fragrance finer than the fragrance of Allāh's Messenger (صَلَّى اللَّهُ عَلَيْهِ وَسَلَّمَ). I served Allāh's Messenger (صَلَّى اللَّهُ عَلَيْهِ وَسَلَّمَ) for ten years, and he never said to me: *'Uff!'*[1]

Nor did he say about anything which I had not done: *'Why did you not do such and such?!'*" Reported by Muslim.[2]

And ʿAbdullāh ibn Salām said: "When Allāh's Messenger (صَلَّى اللَّهُ عَلَيْهِ وَسَلَّمَ) came to Al-Madīnah the people hurried to him. So when I looked at him I knew that his face was not the face of a liar."[3] May Allāh extol him continually, until the Day of Recompensing, and grant him abundant peace and security.

Chapter: And as for his Pure Manners

Then Allāh (the Perfect) has said:

> نٓ ۚ وَالْقَلَمِ وَمَا يَسْطُرُونَ ۞ مَا أَنتَ بِنِعْمَةِ رَبِّكَ بِمَجْنُونٍ ۞ وَإِنَّ لَكَ لَأَجْرًا غَيْرَ مَمْنُونٍ ۞ وَإِنَّكَ لَعَلَىٰ خُلُقٍ عَظِيمٍ ۞
>
> MEANING: "*Nūn*. By the Pen and what they write. You are not mad [O Muhammad (صَلَّى اللَّهُ عَلَيْهِ وَسَلَّمَ)] by the Favour of Your Lord. And for

---

1 — An exclamation of disgust or impatience. In English: *'Fie!'*

2 — [BJ][SZ][SH] Reported by At-Tirmidhī [in his *Sunan*] (no. 2015), and by him in *Ash-Shamā'il* (no. 328); and by Muslim — separated in two places (nos. 2309 & 2330), and by Al-Bukhārī (no. 3561 & 6038).

3 — [BJ][SZ][SH] It is *sahīh*: Reported by At-Tirmidhī (no. 2485), Ibn Mājah (nos. 1334 & 3251), Ahmad (5/451), Ad-Dārimī (1/340, 341), and Al-Hākim (3/134 & 4/160) — and he declared it *'sahīh'*, and Adh-Dhahabī agreed; and Shaikh Al-Albānī agreed in *As-Sahīhah* (no. 569).

> you there shall be an endless reward. And you are certainly upon a tremendous standard of character." — **SŪRAH AL-QALAM (68): 1-4**

And there occurs in the *Sahīh*[1] from 'Ā'ishah (رَضِيَ ٱللَّهُ عَنْهَا) that she said: "The character of the Messenger (صَلَّى ٱللَّهُ عَلَيْهِ وَسَلَّمَ) was the Qur'ān."

The meaning of this is that he (صَلَّى ٱللَّهُ عَلَيْهِ وَسَلَّمَ) had made it a binding duty upon himself that he would not do except that which the Qur'ān commanded him with, and not leave except what the Qur'ān forbade him from. So compliance to the commands of his Lord became his character and his natural disposition — may Allāh extol him and grant him peace and security until the Day of Recompense.

And Allāh (the Most High) said:

> إِنَّ هَـٰذَا الْقُـرْآنَ يَهْـدِي لِلَّتِي هِيَ أَقْوَمُ
>
> MEANING: "Indeed this Qur'ān guides the one who follows it to the straightest path." — **SŪRAH AL-ISRĀ' (17): 9**

So his (صَلَّى ٱللَّهُ عَلَيْهِ وَسَلَّمَ) manners were the noblest, the most honourable, the most righteous, and the greatest of manners:

So he was the most courageous of the people,[2] and he was at his bravest when battles were fiercest.

He was the most generous of the people, and he would be at his most generous in Ramadān.[3]

He was the most knowledgeable one from the creation about Allāh, and the most eloquent of the creation in speech, and the sincerest one of the creation towards the creation, and the most forbearing of the people.

---

1 — (SH) *Sahīh Muslim* (no. 746).

2 — (BJ)(SZ) Reported by Al-Bukhārī (no. 2820) and Muslim (no. 2307), as a hadīth of Anas who said: "Allāh's Messenger (صَلَّى ٱللَّهُ عَلَيْهِ وَسَلَّمَ) was the finest of the people, and he was the most generous one of the people, and he was the most courageous one of the people."

3 — (BJ)(SZ) Reported by Al-Bukhārī (no. 6) and Muslim (no. 2308), from Ibn 'Abbās (رَضِيَ ٱللَّهُ عَنْهُمَا).

He (ﷺ) was the person having the greatest humility, along with dignified bearing — may Allāh extol and grant him peace and security until the Day of Recompense.

Qutaylah bint Makhramah said, in her hadīth reported by Abū Dāwūd: "So when I saw Allāh's Messenger (ﷺ) sitting in a humble state I trembled with fear."[1]

And there occurs in the Sīrah that when he (ﷺ) entered Makkah, on the day of the Conquest, he kept his head lowered from humility, to such an extent that the front part of his camel-saddle was touching the point of his beard (*'uthnūnah*)[2] — and that is from the hair of the beard.

He had greater sense of shame and shyness than a virgin-girl kept in seclusion,[3] yet along with this he was the sternest of the people concerning Allāh's commands. It is related from him that he said:

> "I am the one who frequently laughs and frequently slaughters."[4]

Likewise, Allāh (the Mighty and Majestic) praised his Companions. He (the Exalted and Most High) said:

> مُّحَمَّدٌ رَّسُولُ اللَّهِ ۚ وَالَّذِينَ مَعَهُ أَشِدَّاءُ عَلَى الْكُفَّارِ رُحَمَاءُ بَيْنَهُمْ
>
> MEANING: "Muhammad is the Messenger of Allāh; and those who are with him are stern against the Disbelievers, merciful amongst themselves." — **Sūrah Al-Fat-h (48): 29**

And the rest of his beautiful characteristic will follow if Allāh (the Most High) wishes, in detail, in the ahādīth, which we will bring after this, if Allāh (the Most High) wishes, and He is the One Whose aid is sought.

---

1 — For the authenticity of this narration, see **Endnote 132 on page 544**.

2 — See **Endnote 133 on page 544** for the authenticity of this narration.

3 — [BJ][SZ] Reported by Al-Bukhārī (no. 3562, 6102) and Muslim (no. 2320), as a hadīth of Abū Sa'īd Al-Khudrī (رضي الله عنه).

4 — [BJ][SZ] It is '*da'īf*': It was mentioned by Ibn Kathīr in his *Tafsīr* [Sūrah At-Tawbah (9): 123] (4/238), and reported by Ibn Fāris in *Asmā'ur-Rasūl wa Ma'ānīhā* (p. 31), from Ibn 'Abbās.

Chapter: A Mention of the Places Which he (ﷺ) Visited and These are the Prophetic Journeys.

He went to Ash-Shām[1] twice: The first time was along with his paternal uncle Abū Tālib, who went there to trade. At that time, he was twelve years old. So there occurred the incident of Bahīrā, and his announcing the good news of his being sent; and they saw such signs, which would astonish the minds. This is mentioned in detail in the hadīth which At-Tirmidhī reported from that which was narrated only by Qurād Abū Nūh, whose name was ʿAbdur-Rahmān ibn Ghazwān.

This is an authentic (*'sahīh'*) chain of narration; however, its text contains some strangeness, which has been spoken about at length elsewhere. It contains a mention of the cloud, which gave shade, and I have not seen this mentioned in any other hadīth, which is established, that I know of.[2]

The second time he went was on business for Khadījah bint Khuwaylid, and he was accompanied by her slave Maysarah. He reached the land of Busrā,[3] and he sold the goods there, and then returned. So Maysarah informed his lady-owner of the shining signs of Prophethood, which he had seen upon him (ﷺ), so she desired and married him. His age when he married her, as is mentioned by the historians, was twenty-five years.

And it has preceded that he was taken upon the Night-Journey from the Sacred Mosque to the Farthest Mosque (Al-Masjidul-Aqsā), so he met with the Prophets and led them in Prayer in it. Then he rode up to the heaven; and then to the subsequent heavens, one by one; and he

---

1 — DB Yāqūt Al-Hamawī in *Muʿjamul-Buldān* (3/213) defined the area of *'Shām'* as being from the Euphrates in the north, to the valley of ʿArīsh in the Sinai Peninsula in the south; and from the two mountains of Tayy in the east to the Mediterranean Sea in the west (i.e. present-day Syria, Lebanon, Jordan, and Palestine).

2 — DB Shaikh Al-Albānī declared the hadīth *'sahīh'* in *Sahīhus-Sīrah* (pp. 29-31); and in his checking of *Sunan At-Tirmidhī*, where he (no. 3620) said: "It is *'sahīh'*, however the mention of Bilāl in it is *'munkar'* (weak and contrary to what is correct) — as has been said."

3 — DB A town approximately sixty miles south of Damascus.

saw the Prophets there upon their levels, and he greeted them with the Salutation and they greeted him with the Salutation.

Then he ascended to the Farthest Lote-Tree (Sidratul-Muntahā), and he saw Jibrīl (عَلَيْهِ ٱلسَّلَامُ) there, in the form in which Allāh created him, having six hundred wings.

And the Exalted and All-Mighty Compellor, the Lord of Might and Honour, drew near — as He wished, as occurs in the hadīth.[1]

So he saw some of the greatest signs of his Lord, just as He (the Most High) said:

> لَقَدْ رَأَىٰ مِنْ آيَاتِ رَبِّهِ الْكُبْرَىٰ
>
> MEANING: "He certainly saw the greatest signs of His Lord." — **Sūrah An-Najm (53): 18**

And His Lord (the Perfect and Most High) spoke to him, upon the most famous of the two sayings of the people of hadīth.

And he saw his Lord (the Mighty and Majestic) with his eyesight, upon the saying of some of them, and it was the view preferred by Imām Abū Bakr ibn Khuzaymah — from the people of hadīth, and he was followed upon that by a group of the later people.

And Muslim reported from Ibn 'Abbās (رَضِيَ ٱللَّهُ عَنْهُمَا) that he saw Him with his heart, twice[2]; and 'Ā'ishah — the Mother of the Believers — denied his having seen (Him) with his eyes.[3]

And Muslim[4] reported from Abū Dharr who said: "O Messenger of Allāh! Did you see your Lord?"

---

1 — This wording is a mistake, and 'Ā'ishah, Ibn Mas'ūd, and Abū Hurairah (رَضِيَ ٱللَّهُ عَنْهُمْ) all held that it was actually the Angel Jibrīl who drew near. For a comprehensive discussion of this matter, see **Endnote 134 on page 544**.

2 — SH In his *Sahīh* (no. 176/285).

3 — SH Reported by Muslim in his *Sahīh* (no. 177).

4 — SH In his *Sahīh* (no. 178/291).

He said: ***"Light! How could I see Him?!"***

280 And this was the view inclined to by a large group of the imāms of the early and recent times, based upon this hadīth, and following the saying of ʿĀ'ishah (رَضِيَ ٱللَّهُ عَنْهَا). They said: This is famous from her, and no one is known to have disagreed with her from the Companions — except for what is related from Ibn ʿAbbās that he saw Him with his heart; and we hold that as our saying. As for what is related in that regard in affirmation of his, having seen Him with his eyes, then nothing from that is authentic: neither traced back to the Prophet (صَلَّى ٱللَّهُ عَلَيْهِ وَسَلَّمَ) nor even traced back to the Companions, and Allāh knows best.

And he saw Paradise and the Fire, and the tremendous signs; and Allāh (the Perfect) obligated the Prayer upon him that night, as fifty Prayers. Then He reduced them to five; and he went back and forth between Mūsā (عَلَيْهِ ٱلسَّلَامُ) and His Lord (the Mighty and Majestic) regarding that.

Then he was brought down to the earth; to Makkah; to the Sacred Mosque. So in the morning he informed the people of the signs which he had seen.

As for the hadīth which An-Nasā'ī reported at the start of the Book of Prayer: "ʿAmr ibn Hishām narrated to us: Makhlad — he is Ibn Yazīd narrated to us: from Saʿīd ibn ʿAbdil-ʿAzīz: Yazīd ibn Abī Mālik narrated to us: Mālik ibn Anas (رَضِيَ ٱللَّهُ عَنْهُ) narrated to us: that Allāh's Messenger (صَلَّى ٱللَّهُ عَلَيْهِ وَسَلَّمَ) said:

> "An animal larger than a donkey and smaller than a mule was brought to me. The distance between its steps was as far as it could see. So I rode it, and Jibrīl (عَلَيْهِ ٱلسَّلَامُ) was with me, and I travelled. So he said: *'Dismount and pray!'* So I did so. He said: *'Do you know where you have prayed? You have prayed at Taybah,*[1] *and the migration (Hijrah) will be to it.'*

---

1 — DB Yāqūt Al-Hamawī said in *Muʿjamul-Buldān*: "It is a name for the city (Madīnah) of Allāh's Messenger (صَلَّى ٱللَّهُ عَلَيْهِ وَسَلَّمَ). It is called *'Taybah'* and *'Tābah'* (The Fragrant) from *'At-Tīb'*, which means a fine fragrance, because of the fine fragrance of its soil, as is said."

> Then afterwards he said: *'Dismount and pray!'* So I prayed. He said: *'Do you know where you have prayed? You have prayed at Mount Sinai, where Allāh spoke to Mūsā.'*
>
> Then afterwards he said: *'Dismount and pray!'* So I prayed. He said: *'Do you know where you have prayed? You have prayed at Bethlehem, where 'Īsā was born.'*
>
> Then I entered Jerusalem, and the Prophets were gathered (for me). So Jibrīl put me forward so that I led them in Prayer. Then he ascended with me to the lowest heaven..."

— and he mentioned the rest of the hadīth. Then it is a hadīth which is strange (*gharīb*) and very *'munkar'* (incorrect and contrary to the authentic reports), but its chain of narration is close to acceptability. The authentic ahādīth contain that which indicates its incorrectness, and Allāh knows best.[1]

Likewise the hadīth which Bakr ibn Ziyād Al-Bāhilī, the abandoned narrator, is alone in reporting: from 'Abdullāh ibn Al-Mubārak: from Sa'īd ibn Abī 'Arūbah: from Qatādah: from Zurārah ibn Awfā: from Abū Hurairah (رَضِيَ ٱللَّهُ عَنْهُ): from the Prophet (صَلَّى ٱللَّهُ عَلَيْهِ وَسَلَّمَ) that he said:

> "On the night when I was taken on the Night-Journey Jibrīl said to me: *'This is the grave of your forefather Ibrāhīm. Dismount and pray at it.'*"[2]

This is not established either, because of the condition of the aforementioned Bakr ibn Ziyād.

---

1 — [DB] Shaikh Al-Albānī said in *Da'īf Sunanin-Nasā'ī* (no. 449): "It is *munkar*."

2 — Ibn Hibbān said: "Bakr ibn Ziyād Al-Bāhilī was a shaikh who was a *'dajjāl'* (great liar): he used to fabricate ahādīth upon reliable narrators." For the rest of his speech and the commentary of other scholars upon this unaccepted narration, see ENDNOTE 135 ON PAGE 546.

And likewise the hadīth which Ibn Jarīr reported at the beginning of his *Tārīkh*,[1] as a hadīth of Abū Nuʿaym ʿUmar ibn As-Subh, one of the great liars who admitted to fabrication: from Muqātil ibn Hayyān: from ʿIkrimah: from Ibn ʿAbbās that he (صَلَّىٱللَّهُعَلَيْهِوَسَلَّمَ), on the night of the Night Journey, went to Ya'jūj and Ma'jūj and called them to Allāh (the Mighty and Majestic), but they refused to respond to him. Then Jibrīl (عَلَيْهِٱلسَّلَامُ) took him to the two towns, meaning Jābalq — and it is a town in the east, and its people are the remnant of ʿĀd — from the descendants of those who believed from them; and then to Jābars, which is in the west, and its people are from the descendants of those who believed from Thamūd. So he called both of them to Allāh (the Mighty and Majestic) and they believed in him.

And there occurs in the hadīth that each of the towns has ten thousand gates, and between each two gates is a league.[2]

Each day ten thousand men take on the duty of guarding its gates, and then they do not guard again until the day when the Horn will be blown. So, by the One in Whose Hand is the soul of Muhammad, if it were not for the great number of those people (and the clamour of their voices) then all the people of the earth would hear the crashing sound of the sun when it rises and when it sets.

And beyond them are three nations: Mansik, (Tāwīl), and Tārīs.

And in it there occurs that he (صَلَّىٱللَّهُعَلَيْهِوَسَلَّمَ) called these three nations, but they disbelieved and rejected, so they are the Ya'jūj and Ma'jūj.

---

1 — SH (1/65-70). And Ibnul-Athīr mentioned it in *Al-Kāmil fit-Tārīkh* (1/15), and said: "Along with other things which there is no need to mention. So I have left them aside because they contradict the intellect, and if their chain of narration had been correct, we would have mentioned them and held them as our saying. However, the hadīth is not authentic; and it is not permissible to write the like of this tremendous matter in books, with such a weak chain of narration."

And As-Suyūtī said in *Al-Lāli'ul-Masnūʿah* (1/45): "It is *mawdūʿ* (fabricated)" — its chain of narration contains unknown people and weak narrators.

2 — DB A *'farsakh'* is approximately 3.4 miles.

And he mentioned a long hadīth; one who has the slightest knowledge will have no doubt about its being a fabrication.

So we have only drawn attention to it here so that its condition should be known and so that people are not fooled by it; and because it necessarily relates to the chapter heading which we have given to the chapter; and it pertains to the night of the Night Journey, and Allāh knows best.

Chapter: Summary of his Hijrah and Other Expeditions[1]

And he (ﷺ) migrated from Makkah to Al-Madīnah.

And we have already mentioned his military expeditions, and his ʿUmrahs, and his Hajj; and all of that pertains to this chapter. However what we have previously mentioned suffices us from having to repeat it.

Chapter: The Ways in Which he (ﷺ) Heard the Revelation

We have already mentioned that he (ﷺ) heard the Speech of Allāh (the Mighty and Majestic), and that He addressed him on the Night-Journey, since he (ﷺ) said:

> "I was called out to, that: *'I have completed My obligation, and I have made it lighter upon My servants. O Muhammad! The Saying will not be altered with Me. They are five, and they are fifty*'" — until the end of the hadīth.[2]

So the like of this cannot be said except by the Lord of the whole creation, just as is the case regarding His Saying (He the Most High) to Mūsā:

---

1 — Chapter title added by the publisher.

2 — [BJ][SZ] Reported by Al-Bukhārī (no. 3207), as a hadīth of Anas: from Mālik ibn Saʿsaʿah, with its like; and Al-Bukhārī reported it (no. 349), from Anas: from Abū Dharr; and Muslim (no. 162), as a hadīth of Anas.

[DB] In explanation of the phrase: *'They are five and they are fifty,'* Al-Hāfidh Ibn Hajr said in *Fat-hul-Bārī* (1/465): "It means: They are five in number, with regard to the action; and they are counted as fifty with respect to the reward."

إِنَّنِي أَنَا اللَّهُ لَا إِلَٰهَ إِلَّا أَنَا فَاعْبُدْنِي وَأَقِمِ الصَّلَاةَ لِذِكْرِي

MEANING: "I am Allāh, Who alone deserves to be worshipped, so worship Me alone, and establish the Prayer for My remembrance." — **Sūrah Tā-Hā (20): 14**

The scholars of the Salaf and their imāms said: "This is one of the clearest proofs that the Speech of Allāh is not created, since this (speech) could not emanate from a created being."

A group of them said: "Whoever claims that His Saying — the Most High: ***'I am Allāh, Who alone deserves to be worshipped, so worship Me alone'*** is created, then he is a Disbeliever (Kāfir). Since it would mean, according to his claim, that a part of the creation was therefore calling Mūsā to worship it; and this is explained fully elsewhere.[1]

And he (ﷺ) related many sayings from his Lord (the Mighty and Majestic), such as the saying: *"O My servants! Each one of you is hungry, except for the one whom I have fed..."* — until the end of the hadīth; and Muslim reported it.[2]

And there are many similar examples, and the scholars have devoted works to this topic, mentioning the *'Ahādīthul-Ilāhiyyah'*.[3]

---

1 — SH This is the creed and belief of the Ahlus-Sunnah and Jamā'ah, the followers of As-Salafus-Sālih (the Pious Predecessors), in every time and city. The matter has been explained in detail by Imām Al-Bukhārī in *Khalq Af'ālil 'Ibād*, and Imām Ibn Qutaybah in *Ikhtilāful-Lafz war Radd 'alal-Jahmiyyah*, and by others, such as Shaikhul-Islām Ibn Taymiyyah (رَحِمَهُ ٱللَّهُ).

2 — SH In his *Sahīh* (no. 2577), as a hadīth of Abū Dharr Al-Ghifārī (رَضِيَ ٱللَّهُ عَنْهُ).

3 — DB *'Ahādīth Ilāhiyyah'* are those ahādīth where the Prophet (ﷺ) directly reports Words, which have been said by Allāh (the Exalted and Most High). The term *'Hadīth Ilāhī'* is synonymous with the term *'Hadīth Qudsī'*. Shaikh Muhammad ibn Sālih Al-'Uthaymīn (رَحِمَهُ ٱللَّهُ) said in his book *Mustalahul-Hadīth* (p. 7): "The *'Hadīth Qudsī'* is that which the Prophet (ﷺ) narrated from his Lord (the Most High), and it is also called *'Al-Hādīthur-Rabbānī'* and *'Al-Hādīthul-Ilāhī'*."

So Zāhir ibn Tāhir compiled a work on that, and likewise Al-Hāfidh Ad-Diyā' (also)[1]; and 'Alī ibn Balbān[2] wrote a volume which I have seen, which comprises about one hundred hadīth.

And a group of the people of Hadīth and of Al-Usūl [the Principles of Fiqh] held that all of the Sunnah came as Revelation (*Wahy*), because of His Saying — He the Most High:

> وَمَا يَنطِقُ عَنِ الْهَوَىٰ ۝ إِنْ هُوَ إِلَّا وَحْيٌ يُوحَىٰ
>
> MEANING: "And Muhammad (ﷺ) does not speak from his own desires, rather it is Revelation conveyed to him." — **Sūrah An-Najm (53): 3-4**

So this matter is confirmed in the books of Usūl, and it was dealt with in a precise manner by Al-Hāfidh Abū Bakr Al-Bayhaqī in his book *Al-Madkhal ilas-Sunan.*

And he saw Jibrīl (عَلَيْهِ السَّلَام) there, in his true form; and he had seen him prior to that, descending from the heavens to the earth, in the form which he was created with; and that was at the beginning of Revelation, and it is what is meant by His Saying — He the Most High:

> عَلَّمَهُ شَدِيدُ الْقُوَىٰ ۝ ذُو مِرَّةٍ فَاسْتَوَىٰ ۝ وَهُوَ بِالْأُفُقِ الْأَعْلَىٰ ۝ ثُمَّ دَنَا فَتَدَلَّىٰ ۝ فَكَانَ قَابَ قَوْسَيْنِ أَوْ أَدْنَىٰ ۝

---

1 — (MM)(MK) Al-Hāfidh Ad-Diyā' is Abū 'Abdillāh Muhammad ibn 'Abdil-Wāhid Al-Maqdisī, who is well known as Diyā'-uddīn Al-Maqdisī. He was a scholar of hadīth and a historian, and from the people of Damascus — where he was born and died. He built the Dārul-Hadīth school there, and left his books there as a '*waqf*' (endowment). From his works are *Al-Muntaqā min Akhbāril- Asma'ī*, and *Al-Ahādīthul-Mukhtārah*. He died in the year 643H. See *Siyar A'lāmin-Nubalā'* (7/134) of Adh-Dhahabī.

2 — (SH) He is the scholar of hadīth, the great traveller, 'Alā'-uddīn 'Alī ibn Balbān. Abul-Qām Al-Maqdisī, An-Nāsirī, Al-Karkī. He was born in the year 612 H, and he heard from Al-Qatī'ī, Ibnul-Latī, and others. He gave great attention to ahādīth, and he brought out Al-'Awālī. He died at the beginning of Ramadān, in the year 684 AH.

> MEANING: "He was taught by one great in strength; one sound and beautiful in form. So he arose and was upon the highest part of the horizon. Then he approached and drew closer, and he was at a distance of two bows lengths or even closer." — **Sūrah An-Najm (53): 5-9**

So what is correct from the sayings of the scholars of Tafsīr, indeed what is stated with certainty, is that the one in this Āyah who drew closer is Jibrīl (عَلَيْهِ السَّلَامُ), just as both of them report in the two *Sahīhs.*[1]

So this hadīth ends the dispute and removes the problem. And we have already mentioned that he met with the Prophets, and he saw them in their levels; and he saw the custodian of Paradise and the custodian of the Fire. And the Angels drawn closer in every heaven accompanied him to the next one.

And there occurs in the *Sunan* that he said: "I did not pass by any company of Angels on the night when I was taken on the Night-Journey except that they said: *'O Muhammad! Command your nation with cupping (Al-Hijāmah).'*"[2]

'Abbād ibn Mansūr is alone in reporting this.

And there occurs in another authentic hadīth: "Except that, they said *'O Muhammad! Command your nation to plant many saplings in Paradise: (by saying:)* ***Subhānallāh!*** *(I declare Allāh free of all imperfections!), and* ***Alhamdulillāh*** *(All praise is for Allāh)...'*" — until the end of the hadīth,[3] and they are two singular (*gharīb*) narrations.

---

1 — BJ SZ Reported by Muslim (no. 177) as a hadīth of 'Ā'ishah, from the Prophet (صَلَّى ٱللَّهُ عَلَيْهِ وَسَلَّمَ); and by Al-Bukhārī (no. 3235) and Muslim (no. 177/290) as a hadīth of 'Ā'ishah, as her own saying.

2 — This narration is *'hasan lighairihi'*. For more detail regarding this narration, see Endnote 136 on page 546.

3 — This hadīth is acceptable. For the commentary of the scholars including Imām Al-Albānī, see Endnote 137 on page 547.

And Jibrīl (عَلَيْهِ ٱلسَّلَامُ) descended to him, bringing the Qur'ān from Allāh (the Mighty and Majestic), to his honourable heart.

And there occurs in the *Sīrah*[1] that the Angel of the mountains came to him on the day of Qarnuth-Tha'ālib[2] with a message from Allāh (the Most High) saying: "If he wishes, then the two mountains can be brought together to crush them."[3]

So he said: "Rather, I wish to be patient with them."[4]

And there occurs in *Sahīh Muslim*[5] that an Angel descended with the end of Sūratul-Baqarah.

And there occurs in *Maghāzī* of Al-Amawī:[6] from his father, who said: And Al-Kalbī claimed: from Abū Sālih: from Ibn 'Abbās: "Whilst the Prophet (صَلَّى ٱللَّهُ عَلَيْهِ وَسَلَّمَ) was gathering the booty, and Jibrīl was to his right, an Angel from the Angels came and said: *'O Muhammad! Allāh conveys the salutation of Salām to you.'* Allāh's Messenger (صَلَّى ٱللَّهُ عَلَيْهِ وَسَلَّمَ) said:

---

1 — (MM)(MK)(BJ)(SZ)(SH) In the 'Ārif Hikmah Library manuscript there occurs: *'in the Sunan'*, and in the Sulaymāniyyah Library (no. 59) manuscript there occurs: *'in the two Sahīhs'*.

2 — (BJ)(SZ)(SH) Qarnuth-Tha'ālib (Mountain of the Foxes): There occurs in *Mu'jamul-Buldān* that *'Qarn'* occurs in the language with a number of meanings, from them is that a *'Qarn'* is a small mountain. Al-Qādī 'Iyād said: "Qarnul-Manāzil, and it is Qarnuth-Tha'ālib, is the mīqāt for the people of Najd, facing Makkah." It is approximately 50 miles from Makkah.

3 — (SH) Al-Hāfidh said in *Al-Fat-h* (6/316): "They are the two mountains of Makkah: Abū Qubays, and the one which faces it [...] that they should be brought together upon the people in Makkah; and it is possible that he meant that they should be flattened (upon them)."

4 — (SH) Reported by Al-Bukhārī (no. 3231) and Muslim (no. 1795), as a hadīth of Ummul-Mu'minīn 'Ā'ishah (رَضِيَ ٱللَّهُ عَنْهَا).

(DB) With the wording: "Rather, I hope that Allāh will bring out from their loins those who will worship Allāh alone, and not associate anything with Him."

5 — (SH) (No. 806), as a hadīth of Ibn 'Abbās (رَضِيَ ٱللَّهُ عَنْهُمَا) with the wording: "Fātihatul-Kitāb and the concluding (Āyahs) of Sūratul-Baqarah."

6 — (BJ)(SZ) *Maghāzī Al-Amawī* is one of the lost books of Sīrah.

> 'He is the Flawless One (As-Salām), and peace and security come from Him, and peace returns to Him.'

So the Angel said: *'The affair is what Al-Hubāb ibn Al-Mundhir told you to do.'*

So Allāh's Messenger (صَلَّىٰ اللَّهُ عَلَيْهِ وَسَلَّمَ) said: *'O Jibrīl!*[1] *Do you recognize this one?'* He said: *'I do not know all of the inhabitants of the heavens, but he is truthful and he is not a devil.'*"

So this, even though its chain of narration is not sound,[2] has a supporting witness.

It is that when he (صَلَّىٰ اللَّهُ عَلَيْهِ وَسَلَّمَ) settled at the nearest well in Badr, Al-Hubāb ibn Al-Mundhir said to him: "O Messenger of Allāh! If you have settled at this place because of a command of Allāh then so be it, but if you have only settled at it as a war stratagem, then it is not the place to halt."

So he said: "Rather, as a war stratagem."

He said: *"Then proceed until we settle upon the nearest well to the enemy, and we can block up all the wells behind us"* — as has preceded in the story of Badr.[3] And it is related from him (صَلَّىٰ اللَّهُ عَلَيْهِ وَسَلَّمَ) that he narrated from Quss ibn Sāʿidah Al-Iyādī, narrating what he heard him say in the market of ʿUkāz, and its chain of narration is suspect.[4]

And there occurs in *Sahīh Muslim*[5] from Fātimah bint Qays that he (صَلَّىٰ اللَّهُ عَلَيْهِ وَسَلَّمَ) narrated upon the minbar from Tamīm Ad-Dārī, with the story of the Dajjāl.

---

1 — [BJ][SZ] There occurs in the ʿĀrif Hikmah Library manuscript: "So he (صَلَّىٰ اللَّهُ عَلَيْهِ وَسَلَّمَ) said to Jibrīl..."

2 — [SH] Because it contains Al-Kalbī and Abū Sālih, and he is not 'As-Sammān', and they are two liars.

3 — This hadīth is not authentic. Refer to **Endnote 138 on page 548** for more details.

4 — This narration is also inauthentic, and you can refer to **Endnote 139 on page 549** for the commentary of Imām Al-Bayhaqī and others.

5 — [BJ][SZ] No. 2942 and it is the hadīth of 'Al-Jassāsah' (The Story of the Dajjāl).

Chapter: Those Who Heard From him (صَلَّى ٱللَّهُ عَلَيْهِ وَسَلَّمَ)

His Companions heard from him in Makkah and Al-Madīnah, and in 289
other towns where he went on military expeditions or which he visited; and in ʿArafah, Minā, and in other places.

And the Jinn heard the Qurʾān from him when he was reciting with his Companions in ʿUkāz, and they came to him and asked him about some things.[1]

He remained with them [i.e. the Jinn] during a night witnessed by ʿAbdullāh ibn Masʿūd, except that he [i.e. Ibn Masʿūd] was not directly present with them. Rather, he awaited Allāh's Messenger (صَلَّى ٱللَّهُ عَلَيْهِ وَسَلَّمَ) in an encircled place, so that no evil would befall them.[2]

So a group of the Jinn of Nasībīn[3] accepted Islām — may Allāh be pleased with them all.

---

1 — [SH] Reported by Al-Bukhārī (no. 773), Muslim (no. 449), as a hadīth of Ibn ʿAbbās (رَضِيَ ٱللَّهُ عَنْهُمَا).

2 — The hadīth of the Jinn hearing from Allāh's Messenger (صَلَّى ٱللَّهُ عَلَيْهِ وَسَلَّمَ) in the market place of ʿUkāz is reported by Al-Bukhārī. Refer to **Endnote 140 on page 549** for a detailed discussion of the authenticity of the various chains which compose this report.

3 — [SH] A well-populated city in the land of Al-Jazīrah (Mesopotamia) upon the caravan-route between Al-Mawsil (Mosul) and Ash-Shām.

And we have it narrated to us, in *Al-Ghaylāniyyāt*,[1] a report of a man from them called ʿAbdullāh ibn Samhaj, and its chain of narration contains strangeness.

And Jibrīl came to him [Muhammad صَلَّى ٱللَّهُ عَلَيْهِ وَسَلَّمَ] in the form of a bedouin man, and he narrated to him about Islām, Īmān, Ihsān, and the signs of the (Last) Hour.[2]

Chapter: The Number of the Muslims When he (صَلَّى ٱللَّهُ عَلَيْهِ وَسَلَّمَ) Passed Away

Imām Abū ʿAbdillāh Ash-Shāfiʿī (رَحِمَهُ ٱللَّهُ) said: "Allāh's Messenger (صَلَّى ٱللَّهُ عَلَيْهِ وَسَلَّمَ) passed away and the Muslims were sixty thousand (in number): thirty thousand in Al-Madīnah, and thirty thousand in other places."

Al-Hāfidh Abū Zurʿah ʿUbaydullāh ibn ʿAbdil-Karīm Ar-Rāzī (رَحِمَهُ ٱللَّهُ) said: "Allāh's Messenger (صَلَّى ٱللَّهُ عَلَيْهِ وَسَلَّمَ) passed away when more than a hundred thousand people had seen him and heard from him."

---

1 — [BJ][SZ] Reported by Al-Bazzār in *Al-Ghaylāniyyāt* (p. 242, no. 663): Abū Bakr said: Al-Fadl ibn Al-Hasan ibn Al-Aʿyun, Abul-ʿAbbās Al-Ahwāzī narrated to me, saying: ʿAbdullāh ibn Al-Husayn Al-Missīsī narrated to me, saying: "I entered Tarsūs (Tarsus), and it was said: *'There is a woman here who saw the Jinn which came in a deputation to Allāh's Messenger (صَلَّى ٱللَّهُ عَلَيْهِ وَسَلَّمَ).'* So I went to her and I found a woman lying down on her back. So I said: *'What is your name?'* She said: *'Manūs.'*"

He said: "I said: *'O Manūs did you see any of the Jinn who came in a deputation to Allāh's Messenger (صَلَّى ٱللَّهُ عَلَيْهِ وَسَلَّمَ)?'* She said: *'Yes. ʿAbdullāh ibn Samhaj narrated to me, saying: "Allāh's Messenger (صَلَّى ٱللَّهُ عَلَيْهِ وَسَلَّمَ) named me ʿAbdullāh." He said: "O Messenger of Allāh! Where was our Lord (the Mighty and Majestic) before He created the heavens and the earth?"'*""

It chain of narration is very weak: it contains ʿAbdullāh ibn Husayn Al-Missīsī, about whom Ibn Hibbān said: *"He steals narrations and turns them around. What he is alone in reporting is not taken as proof"* — and it contains Manūs (the woman who saw the Jinn) and she is unknown; and the person from the Jinn is also unknown.

2 — [SH] Reported by Muslim (no. 8), as a longer hadīth of ʿUmar (رَضِيَ ٱللَّهُ عَنْهُ); and Al-Bukhārī reported it (no. 50) and Muslim (no. 9), as a hadīth of Abū Hurairah (رَضِيَ ٱللَّهُ عَنْهُ).

Al-Hāfidh Abū 'Abdillāh Muhammad 'Abdillāh Al-Hākim An-Naysābūrī said: "Four thousand Companions narrated from him (صَلَّى ٱللَّهُ عَلَيْهِ وَسَلَّمَ)."

I say: The imāms have devoted specific works to the names of the Companions, such as Al-Bukhārī, at the beginning of his *Tārīkhul-Kabīr*; and Ibn Abī Khaythamah, and Al-Hāfidh Abū 'Abdillāh Ibn Mandah, and Al-Hāfidh Abū Nu'aym Al-Asbahānī, and Ash-Shaikh (Al-Imām) Abū 'Umar ibn 'Abdil-Barr, and others.

And Abū Muhammad ibn Hazm recorded their names in a treatise[1] which he compiled from the book of the Imām Baqiyy ibn Makhlad Al-Andalusī (رَحِمَهُ ٱللَّهُ), and he mentioned what each one of them narrated.

So we will devote a section to that afterwards,[2] if Allāh (the Most High) wishes, and we will add to it whatever should be added; and if the Generous One, the Bestower, facilitates then I will mention the *'musnad'* narrations and the *'sunan'*:[3] those ahādīth narrated by each Companion, and I will speak about each one of them, and I will make clear its condition with regard to authenticity or weakness, if Allāh (the Most High) wishes; and in Him I trust, and upon Him I place my reliance, and there is no movement and no ability except with the aid of Allāh (the Mighty, the All-Wise).

---

1 — [BJ][SZ] It has been printed with the title *Asmā' As-Sahābah wa Mā Likulli Wāhid Minal-'Adad* (*The Names of the Companions, and How Many Narrations Each of them Reported*), and this has been appended to his book *Jawāmi'us-Sīrah*.

2 — [BJ][SZ] This chapter is not found in this book.

3 — [DB] In the *'musnad'* arrangement, all the narrations of a particular Companion are gathered together, irrespective of the subject matter. In the arrangement of the *'sunan'*, the narrations are arranged according to the subject, irrespective of the narrator.

CHAPTER:

The Matters Particular to Allāh's Messenger (ﷺ)

Containing a mention of the *'Khasā'is'* (those matters specific to) Allāh's Messenger (ﷺ), which no one else shared with him.

Our companions and others have frequently mentioned this chapter at the beginning of the book of marriage in their works, following the example of Imām Abū 'Abdillāh[1] — the progenitor of the *madh-hab*, since he mentioned something of that at that place.

As-Saymarī related[2] from Abū 'Alī ibn Khayrān[3] that he prevented speech about the affairs specific to Allāh's Messenger (ﷺ) with regard to the rulings of marriage, and likewise regarding leadership (*Al-Imāmah*).

His reason was that this is a matter, which is now finished, and therefore no action is connected to it; and that there are no subtle points of knowledge contained in it, which could instruct a person. So therefore, there is no way in which time should be spent upon surmising with regard to it.

---

1 — [SH] He means the Imām Muhammad ibn Idrīs Ash-Shāfi'ī (رَحِمَهُ ٱللَّهُ).

2 — [BJ][SZ][SH] He is Al-Qādī Abul-Qāsim 'Abdul-Wāhid ibn Al-Husayn As-Saymarī, the Shaikh of the Shāfi'īs. The jurists travelled to Al-Basrah to learn Fiqh from him; amongst his students was Al-Māwardī. He died in 405 H. (*Siyar A'lāmin-Nubalā'*: 17/14 of Adh-Dhahabī)

3 — [BJ][SZ][SH] He is the Imām, Shaikh of the Shāfi'īs, Abū 'Alī Al-Husayn ibn Sālih ibn Khayrān Al-Baghdādī. He was offered the post of Qādī (chief judge), and he refused it. He died in 320 H. Refer for his biography to *Siyar A'lāmin-Nubalā'* (15/58).

Shaikh Abū ʿAmr ibnus-Salāh said, after quoting that: "This is strange and fine, and Allāh knows best."

Imāmul-Haramayn said: "The verifiers have said: Mentioning disagreements regarding those matters specific to the Messenger (صَلَّى ٱللَّهُ عَلَيْهِ وَسَلَّمَ) is a mistake, containing no benefit, since no useful ruling which is needed is connected to it. Rather, disagreements are dealt with in those matters where a ruling has to be established. So here, there is no room for making analogy, and the ruling specific to him are matters requiring the following of clear texts. As for those matters where there are no clear texts, then disagreement in these matters is to rush into the unseen without any benefit being produced."

Shaikh Abū Zakariyyā An-Nawawī said[1]: "What is correct is to clearly state the permissibility of that — indeed, its being something recommended. Indeed if it were stated that it is something obligatory, then that would not be far from being correct, since there is no consensus to prevent it; and it may happen that an ignorant person sees something from those things particular [to the Messenger (صَلَّى ٱللَّهُ عَلَيْهِ وَسَلَّمَ)] established in the *Sahīh*, and act upon it — upon the basis of following the [Messenger's (صَلَّى ٱللَّهُ عَلَيْهِ وَسَلَّمَ)] example. So it is obligatory to explain these matters so that they are known, and so that no one else seeks to share in that; and what benefit can be greater than this?! As for what is found within the things particular to the Messenger (صَلَّى ٱللَّهُ عَلَيْهِ وَسَلَّمَ) from those things which contain no benefit today, then these are very few — and the different chapters of Fiqh each contain the like of that, for instruction, and to acquire awareness of evidences."

As for the great majority of the companions[2] then they have not taken the view mentioned by Ibn Khayrān and Imāmul-Haramayn, rather they mention this matter fully, to increase knowledge. This was particularly

1 — [SH] In *Tahdhībul-Asmā' wal-Lughāt* (1/43-43).

2 — [DB] i.e. the scholars of the Shāfiʿī *madh-hab*.

so with Imām Abul-ʿAbbās Ahmad ibn Abī Ahmad ibn Al-Qāss At-Tabarī, the author of the book *At-Talkhīs*.[1]

So Al-Hāfidh Abū Bakr Al-Bayhaqī utilized and arranged his speech about that in his *Sunanul-Kabīr*.[2] However, others have added many extra details to that based upon ahādīth which are suspect; and we will mention them, if Allāh (the Most High) wishes.

So they organized speech about that, dividing it into four aspects:

- **Firstly:** That which was obligatory upon him, and not upon others;
- **Secondly:** That which was prohibited for him, but not for others;
- **Thirdly:** That which was permissible for him, but not for others;
- **Fourthly:** Those virtues, which were specific to him, and were not possessed by others.

So in each one they mentioned the rulings relating to marriage, and to other matters; and I saw fit that I should arrange them in a different way, which is easier to learn than what they mentioned — if Allāh (the Most High) wishes.

So I say, and success is granted by Allāh: Those matters particular to the Messenger (صَلَّىٰ ٱللَّهُ عَلَيْهِ وَسَلَّمَ) (*Al-Khasāʾis*) are of two categories:

- **Firstly:** That which was specific to him, to the exclusion of the rest of his brothers from the Prophets — may Allāh extol him and them and bestow peace and security upon them.
- **Secondly:** Those rulings, which were specific to him, to the exclusion of his nation.

---

1 — [MM][MK] Ahmad ibn Abī Ahmad ibn Al-Qāss At-Tabarī, Ash-Shāfiʿī. He became the chief judge of Tarsūs, and he died there in the year 335 H.

[SH] The book of his, which is referred to, is *At-Talkhīs fil-Furūʿ*.

2 — [BJ][SZ] *As-Sunanul-Kubrā* of Al-Bayhaqī (7/36-76).

THE FIRST CATEGORY –

Those Matters Which Were Specific to him

to the Exclusion of the Other Prophets

As for the first category, then there occurs in the two *Sahīhs*:[1] from Jābir ibn ʿAbdillāh ibn ʿAmr Harām Al-Ansārī (رَضِيَٱللَّهُعَنْهُمَا) who said: Allāh's Messenger (صَلَّىٱللَّهُعَلَيْهِوَسَلَّمَ) said: "I have been given five things which no one from the Prophets before me was given: I have been aided by terror at the distance of a months journey; and the earth has been made for me a place of Prayer and a purification, so wherever the Prayer reaches a man from my nation, then let him pray; and the war-booties have been rendered lawful for me, and they were not lawful for anyone before me; and I have been granted Intercession (*Ash-Shafāʿah*); and a Prophet would be sent to his own people in particular, whereas I have been sent to the whole of mankind."

So concerning his (صَلَّىٱللَّهُعَلَيْهِوَسَلَّمَ) saying: *"I have been aided by terror at the distance of a month's journey"* — then it is said that when he intended to make an attack on a people they would be struck with terror of him a month before he reached them, and this did not occur for anyone else besides him.

---

1 — BJ SZ Reported by Al-Bukhārī (no. 335) and Muslim (no. 521), and the wording is that of Al-Bukhārī.

And as for what is reported in *Sahīh Muslim*,[1] regarding the story of the descent of ʿĪsā (عَلَيْهِ ٱلصَّلَاةُ وَٱلسَّلَامُ) to the earth, and that his breath will not reach any Disbeliever except that he will die, and that his breath will reach as far as his eye can see, then if this was a characteristic of his which he possessed even before he was raised up, then (still) it is not like this[2]; and otherwise it is something which will come about after he descends to the earth, when he will be one of the nation of Muhammad (صَلَّىٱللَّهُعَلَيْهِوَسَلَّمَ): meaning that he will judge by his revealed Law, and no Revelation contrary to it will be sent to him, and Allāh (the Most High) knows best.

As for his (صَلَّىٱللَّهُعَلَيْهِوَسَلَّمَ) saying: *"And the earth has been made for me a place of Prayer and a purification"* — then the meaning of that occurs in the hadīth which Imām Ahmad reported in his *Musnad*:

> "Those who came before us had not used to pray in their homes; rather, they used to pray in their churches."[3]

And his saying: *"A purification"* — means the *tayammum*,[4] since it was not present in any nation before us; rather it was only legislated for him (صَلَّىٱللَّهُعَلَيْهِوَسَلَّمَ) and for his nation, as an alleviation, a mercy, and a reduction.

And as for his (صَلَّىٱللَّهُعَلَيْهِوَسَلَّمَ) saying: *"And the war-booties have been rendered lawful for me,"* — then when those before him used to take any war-booty

---

1 — BJ SZ Reported by Muslim (no. 2937), as a hadīth of An-Nawwās ibn Samʿān (رَضِيَٱللَّهُعَنْهُ), and it contains the wording: "So it is certain that no Disbeliever will feel his breath except that he will die; and his breath will reach as far as his gaze."

2 — DB i.e. it is not the same as the characteristic given to the Prophet (صَلَّىٱللَّهُعَلَيْهِوَسَلَّمَ).

3 — BJ SZ It is *'hasan'*: Reported by Ahmad (11/639/7068), as a hadīth of ʿAmr ibn Shuʿayb: from his father: from his grandfather: from the Prophet (صَلَّىٱللَّهُعَلَيْهِوَسَلَّمَ), with its like. Al-Haythamī said (10/367): *"Its narrators are reliable"*, and Ibn Kathīr mentioned it in his tafsīr of Sūratul-Aʿrāf (verse 158), and said: "Its chain of narration is good and strong."

DB Declared *'hasan'* by Shaikh Al-Albānī in *Sahīhut-Targhīb wat-Tarhīb* (3/450/3634).

4 — DB *Tayammum*: 'Dry purification': striking the hands upon the earth and then wiping the face and hands.

they would take out a portion and place it to one side, then a fire would descend from the sky and consume it.[1]

And as for his (صَلَّى ٱللَّٰهُ عَلَيْهِ وَسَلَّمَ) saying: *"And I have been granted Intercession"* — then he (may Allāh extol him and grant him peace and security) meant by that the Praiseworthy Station (*Al-Maqāmul-Maḥmūd*), for which the earlier and later people will envy him; and it is the station in which everyone from the creation will eagerly turn to him so that he should intercede for them with their Lord, in order that He should pass judgement upon them, and relieve them from the standing in the Gathering-Place.[2]

And it is the Greater Intercession (*Ash-Shafā'atul-'Udhmā*) which the Messengers firmest in resolve (*Ulul-'Azm*) will shy-away from, because of the superiority in excellence and the honour and nobility which Allāh has given to him exclusively.

So he will go and knock at the gate of Paradise, and the gatekeeper will say: *"Who are you?"* So he will say: *"Muhammad."* So he will say: "I have been commanded concerning you that I should not open up to anyone before you."[3]

And this is a matter particular [to him (صَلَّى ٱللَّٰهُ عَلَيْهِ وَسَلَّمَ)] also; it is for no one else from the whole of mankind. So he will enter Paradise and intercede with Allāh (the Most High) for that, as occurs in the authentic ahādīth.[4]

And this is the first Intercession, which is particular to him, to the exclusion of the other Messengers besides him.

Then after that, he will have other intercessions to rescue whomever Allāh wishes, from those of his nation guilty of major sins, from the Fire.

---

1 — See **Endnote 141 on page 550** for the narration of the Prophet from the Prophets who went on a military expedition.

2 — [DB] See *Sahīhul-Bukhārī* (nos. 3340 & 7510).

3 — [SH] Reported by Muslim (no. 197) as a hadīth of Anas (رَضِيَ ٱللَّٰهُ عَنْهُ).

4 — [BJ][SZ] Reported by Al-Bukhārī (nos. 4476, 6565, & 7410) and Muslim (no. 193), from Anas. The ahādīth about Intercession are *'mutawātir'*. Ibn Khuzaymah mentioned them in *At-Tawhīd* (2/588,764: nos. 347, 491), as did Ibn Abī 'Āsim in *As-Sunnah* (nos. 803, 888: with the checking of Bāsim).

However, the (other) Messengers will share with him in this intercession: they will intercede for the sinful ones of their nations, and the Angels will do likewise. Indeed the Believers will do so as well, just as occurs in the two *Sahīhs* as a hadīth of Abū Hurairah and of Abū Sa'īd:

> "So Allāh (the Most High) will say: *'The Angels have interceded, and the Prophets have interceded, and the Believers have interceded, and none remains except for the Most Merciful One of those who are merciful...'*" — and he mentioned the hadīth.[1]

And these intercessions were mentioned fully by Al-Imām Abū Bakr Ibn Khuzaymah at the end of *Kitābut-Tawhīd*,[2] and likewise by Abū Bakr ibn Abī 'Āsim in his book *As-Sunnah*.[3]

It is likewise laid out in a fine manner in the hadīth of the Horn (As-Sūr) which At-Tabarānī reported in *Al-Mutawwalāt*,[4] and Abū Mūsā Al-Madīnī Al-Asbahānī, and others who compiled works on the long ahādīth.

Also, Al-Walīd ibn Muslim gathered a whole volume on it, and I devoted a treatise to its chain of narration. As for the narration of the compilers of the six books, such as the two *Sahīhs* and others besides them, then a hadīth frequently occurs with them in abridged form, or with rearrangement in the wording; and that is apparent to one who carefully examines it; and Allāh knows best.

---

1 — [BJ][SZ] Reported by Al-Bukhārī (no. 7439) and Muslim (no. 183), as a hadīth of Abū Sa'īd.

2 — [SH] (2/588-836)

3 — [SH] (2/369-414) with the checking of Shaikh Al-Albānī.

4 — [BJ][SZ][SH] Reported by At-Tabarānī in *Al-Mutawwalāt* (25/266/no. 36), Abush-Shaikh in *Al-'Azamah* (3/822/nos. 386, 387, 388), and At-Tabarī in his *Tafsīr*, Shaikh Al-Albānī said in his notes upon *Al-'Aqīdatut-Tahāwiyyah* (p. 265): "Its *isnād* is weak because it occurs by way of Ismā'īl ibn Rāfi': from Yazīd ibn Abī Ziyād, and both of them are weak — with their chain of narration from a man of the Ansār, and he is unknown as he is not named."

Then I saw in the *Sahīh* of Al-Bukhārī[1] a mention of the Greater Intercession. So he said in the *Book of Zakāt*:

> "Chapter: Whoever begs from the people in order to increase his wealth: Yahyā ibn Bukayr narrated to us: Al-Layth narrated to us: from 'Ubaydullāh ibn Abī Ja'far, who said: I heard Hamzah ibn 'Abdillāh ibn 'Umar say: I heard 'Abdullāh ibn 'Umar (رَضِيَ اللَّهُ عَنْهُمَا) say: Allāh's Messenger (صَلَّى اللَّهُ عَلَيْهِ وَسَلَّمَ) said: *'A man will continue begging from the people until he comes on the Day of Resurrection with no piece of flesh remaining upon his face.'*"

And he said:

> "The sun will draw close on the Day of Resurrection until a person's sweat reaches half-way up his ears. So whilst they are in that condition they will ask Ādam to seek relief for them, and then Mūsā, and then Muhammad."

'Abdullāh ibn Yūsuf added: Al-Layth narrated to me: from Ibn Abī Ja'far: "So he will intercede for judgement to be passed upon the creation. So he will take hold of the ring of the Gate. So on that day Allāh will raise him to a praiseworthy Station; all of the people gathered will praise him."

So this is the Greater Intercession, which he will be distinguished with, to the exclusion of all of the Messengers — those firmest in resolve. This will be after each one of them has been asked to take that station, and has said: "I am not the one for that, go to so and so."

So the people will go from one Messenger to the next, until they come to Muhammad (صَلَّى اللَّهُ عَلَيْهِ وَسَلَّمَ), and he will say: "I am the one for that."

So he will go and intercede for all the people of the standing place with Allāh (the Most High) in order that He should pass judgement upon them, and so that some may be given relief from the others.

---

1 — SH (Nos. 1474, 1475).

Then after that he will have four other intercessions.[1] From those is that [intercession] for some people who have been entered into the Fire to be rescued.[2]

Then he will also be the first one to intercede in Paradise, just as Imām Ahmad reported in his *Musnad*: from Al-Mukhtār ibn Fulful: from Anas who said: Allāh's Messenger (صَلَّى ٱللَّهُ عَلَيْهِ وَسَلَّمَ) said: "I will be the first interceder in Paradise."[3]

Furthermore, he will intercede for the levels of some of the people of Paradise to be raised, and this intercession is something about which the Ahlus-Sunnah and the Muʿtazilah agree; and its proof is what occurs in *Sahīhul-Bukhārī* as a narration of Abū Mūsā: that when his paternal uncle Abū ʿĀmir was killed at Awtās, Allāh's Messenger (صَلَّى ٱللَّهُ عَلَيْهِ وَسَلَّمَ) said:

> "O Allāh! Forgive ʿUbayd Abū ʿĀmir, and place him on the Day of Resurrection above many of Your creation."[4]

And he (عَلَيْهِ ٱلصَّلَاةُ وَٱلسَّلَامُ) said, when Abū Salamah ibn ʿAbdil-Asad died: "O Allāh! Raise his rank!"[5/6]

And we shall, if Allāh (the Most High) wishes, devote a treatise to Intercession, to clarify its categories and their number and its evidence.[7]

As for his (صَلَّى ٱللَّهُ عَلَيْهِ وَسَلَّمَ) saying: *"A Prophet would be sent to his own people, whereas I have been sent to the whole of mankind,"* — then its meaning

---

1 — Imām Ibn Abil-ʿIzz mentions that Intercession (Ash-Shafāʿah) is of eight categories — refer to **Endnote 142 on page 551**.

2 — Imām An-Nawawī mentions the Five Intercessions of the Prophet Muhammad (صَلَّى ٱللَّهُ عَلَيْهِ وَسَلَّمَ) — refer to **Endnote 143 on page 552**.

3 — [SH] Reported by Ahmad (3/140) with a chain of narration which is *'sahīh'* to the standard of Muslim; and Muslim in his *Sahīh* (no. 196/332) reported it.

4 — [BJ][SZ] *Sahīhul-Bukhārī* (nos. 4323 & 6383) & Muslim (no. 2498).

5 — [BJ][SZ][SH] Reported by Muslim (no. 920), as a hadīth of Umm Salamah (رَضِيَ ٱللَّهُ عَنْهَا).

6 — [BJ][SZ] What occurs between the decorative brackets is missing in the Sulaymāniyyah Library (no. 3339) manuscript.

7 — [SH] The author (رَحِمَهُ ٱللَّهُ) mentions this section at the end of the book, and it is present in the 'Sulaymāniyyah Library' manuscript (no. 3339) alone.

occurs in the Mighty Book, and it is His Saying (the Mighty and Majestic):

> وَمَا أَرْسَلْنَا مِن رَّسُولٍ إِلَّا بِلِسَانِ قَوْمِهِ لِيُبَيِّنَ لَهُمْ
>
> MEANING: "And We did not send a Messenger except with the language of his people, that he should make the affair clear to them." — **SŪRAH IBRĀHĪM (14): 4**

And His Saying -He the Most High:

> وَإِن مِّنْ أُمَّةٍ إِلَّا خَلَا فِيهَا نَذِيرٌ
>
> MEANING: "And there was never a nation except that it had a Warner." — **SŪRAH FĀTIR (35): 24**

So a Prophet in the times before us only had the duty of conveying the message and calling his own people to Allāh.

As for Muhammad (may Allāh extol him and them and bestow peace and security upon him), then Allāh (the Most High) said:

> قُلْ يَا أَيُّهَا النَّاسُ إِنِّي رَسُولُ اللَّهِ إِلَيْكُمْ
>
> MEANING: "O Mankind! I am Allāh's Messenger to you all." — **SŪRAH AL-AʿRĀF (7): 158**

And He (the Most High) said:

> لِأُنذِرَكُم بِهِ وَمَن بَلَغَ
>
> MEANING: "In order that I may warn you with the Qur'ān, and whomever it reaches." — **SŪRAH AL-ANʿĀM (6): 19**

And He (the Most High) said:

> وَمَن يَكْفُرْ بِهِ مِنَ الْأَحْزَابِ فَالنَّارُ مَوْعِدُهُ

> MEANING: "And whoever from the people of the religions of the Disbelievers, disbelieves in him (صَلَّى ٱللَّهُ عَلَيْهِ وَسَلَّمَ) then the Fire is his appointed destination." — **Sūrah Hūd (11): 17**

And He (the Most High) said:

> وَقُل لِّلَّذِينَ أُوتُوا الْكِتَابَ وَالْأُمِّيِّينَ أَأَسْلَمْتُمْ ۚ فَإِنْ أَسْلَمُوا فَقَدِ اهْتَدَوا ۖ وَّإِن تَوَلَّوْا
> فَإِنَّمَا عَلَيْكَ الْبَلَاغُ ۗ وَاللَّهُ بَصِيرٌ بِالْعِبَادِ
>
> MEANING: "And say to those who were given the Scripture, and to the illiterate Arab pagans without Scripture: *'Will you submit to Allāh, worshipping Him alone, as Muslims?'* So if they do submit to Allāh, worshipping Him alone, as Muslims, then they are rightly guided; but if they turn away, then your duty is just to convey the message; and Allāh is the All-Seer of His slaves." — **Sūrah Āli 'Imrān (3): 20**

Along with many Āyahs of the Qur'ān which prove the universality of his Messengership to the whole of the jinn and Mankind. So Allāh (the Most High) commanded him to warn the whole of His creation: the humans and the jinn, the Arabs and the non-Arabs. So he (may Allāh extol him and them and bestow peace and security upon him) did what he was commanded and conveyed the message from Allāh.

And from those things particular to him, over and above his brothers the Prophets (may Allāh extol him and them and bestow peace and security upon them) is that he is the most complete one of them, and their noble chief, and their orator, and their leader, and the last one of them.

So there was no Prophet except that the Covenant was taken from him that if Muhammad were to be sent whilst he was alive that he would certainly believe in him and aid him; and he was commanded to take that Covenant from his nation.

Allāh (the Most High) said:

> وَإِذْ أَخَذَ اللَّهُ مِيثَاقَ النَّبِيِّينَ لَمَا آتَيْتُكُم مِّن كِتَابٍ وَحِكْمَةٍ ثُمَّ جَاءَكُمْ رَسُولٌ
> مُّصَدِّقٌ لِّمَا مَعَكُمْ لَتُؤْمِنُنَّ بِهِ وَلَتَنصُرُنَّهُ ۚ

قَالَ أَأَقْرَرْتُمْ وَأَخَذْتُمْ عَلَىٰ ذَٰلِكُمْ إِصْرِي ۖ قَالُوا أَقْرَرْنَا ۚ قَالَ فَاشْهَدُوا
وَأَنَا مَعَكُم مِّنَ الشَّاهِدِينَ

MEANING: "And remember when Allāh took the Covenant from the Prophets: *'Whatever I have given you of the Scripture and Wisdom and then there comes to you a Messenger confirming what is with you; you must then believe in him and aid him.'* He said: *'Do you agree to it and take a solemn pledge to Me upon it?'* They said: *'We agree.'* He said: *'Then bear witness, and I am with you among the witnesses.'"* — **Sūrah Āli ʿImrān (3): 81**

He (the Most High) says: Whatever I have given you from Scripture and Wisdom, and then there comes to you a Messenger after all of that, then it is upon you to believe in him, and to aid him.

Then even though this covenant covered believing in each one of them, then it certainly included believing in Muhammad (ﷺ) from all of them; and this was something specific, which none of them besides him shared.

And from that was that he (ﷺ) was born with his umbilical-cord cut, already circumcised, as occurs in the hadīth which is reported through a number of chains, however they are weak (*gharīb*).[1]

However, it has been said that other Prophets shared with him in this, as Abul-Faraj Ibn Al-Jawzī said in his book *Tanqīhul-Fuhūm*.

And from that is that the miracle given to each Prophet ended with his passing away, whereas his (ﷺ) miracle will remain after him, for as long as Allāh wishes — and it is the Mighty Qurʾān, which is miraculous in its wording and its meaning. He challenged mankind and the jinn to produce the like of it, and they were unable to do so; and they will never be able to do that until the Day of Resurrection.

And from that is that he (ﷺ) was taken by night to the Farthest Lote-Tree (Sidratul-Muntahā), and then he returned to his home, in

1 — This narration is held to be weak by a number of scholars including Ibn Kathīr (the author of this book). See **Endnote 144 on page 552** for further details.

a single night, and this was something particular to him (ﷺ), except for what he mentioned in the hadīth in his saying that Jibrīl said to Al-Burāq, when he (ﷺ) wanted to ride it and it shied away from him:

> "Be calm! For Allāh, you have not been ridden by anyone better than him."[1]

And likewise his saying in the hadīth:

> "So I tethered the beast to the ring, which the Prophets used for tethering."[2]

So this indicates that they (the Prophets) used to be taken on such a journey, except that we know that none of them shared with him (ﷺ) in the extent to which he was brought near, and in closeness, and in the honour shown.[3]

And therefore his level in Paradise will be the highest level, and the closest one to the Throne, as occurs in the hadīth:

> "Then ask Allāh to grant me *'Al-Wasīlah'* (the position of highest status), for it is a level in Paradise which is not befitting except for a single servant from the servants of Allāh, and I hope that it will be me."[4]

So may Allāh extol him and grant him peace and security.

And from that is that if his nation unites upon a single saying relating to the rulings of the Legislation, then this saying of theirs is preserved

---

1 — This narration was declared *'sahīh'* by Imām Al-Albānī, and you can see more details in **Endnote 145 on page 553**.

2 — [BJ][SZ] Reported by Muslim (no. 162), as a hadīth of Anas (رضي الله عنه).

3 — [SH] This is what occurs in the 'Sulaymāniyyah Library' manuscript (no. 3339), whereas in the 'Sulaymāniyyah Library' manuscript (no. 59) and in the ''Ārif Hikmat Library' manuscript there occurs: *'In closeness to Him, to show honour'*, and both of them are correct.

4 — This narration is reported by Muslim and in it the Muslims are commanded to ask for Allāh to grant the Prophet Muhammad (ﷺ) this mighty position in Paradise. Read the narration in **Endnote 146 on page 553**.

from being erroneous. Rather, their agreement upon it means that it is correct and is the truth, as is confirmed in the books of Usūl; and this is a quality specific to them, on account of him, and is something which was not attained by any nation from the nations before it.[1]

And from that is that he (صَلَّى ٱللَّهُ عَلَيْهِ وَسَلَّمَ) will be the first one for whom the earth will split.[2]

And from that is that when the people are knocked unconscious on the Day of Resurrection he will be the first of them to regain consciousness, as the two report in the two *Sahīhs*,[3] as a hadīth of Abū Hurairah (رَضِيَ ٱللَّهُ عَنْهُ) concerning the incident of the Jew who said: "No, by the One Who chose Mūsā over the whole of the creation!"

So a man of the Muslims slapped him, and they took their case to Allah's Messenger (صَلَّى ٱللَّهُ عَلَيْهِ وَسَلَّمَ), and he said:

> "Do not declare my superiority over Mūsā, for the people will be knocked unconscious on the Day of Resurrection and I shall be the first one who regains consciousness. So I will find Mūsā grasping a support of the Throne, and I will not know whether he regained consciousness before me, or whether he was from those exempted by Allāh."

And in a narration: "Or whether he was sufficed by having been knocked unconscious at the mount."

---

1 — In a narration which Imām Al-Albānī (رَحِمَهُ ٱللَّهُ) declared to be authentic, the Prophet Muhammad (صَلَّى ٱللَّهُ عَلَيْهِ وَسَلَّمَ) states that his *'nation will not unite upon misguidance.'* See ENDNOTE 147 ON PAGE 553 for more.

2 — [SH] Reported by Al-Bukhārī (no. 2412) and Muslim (no. 2374), as a hadīth of Abū Sa'īd Al-Khudrī (رَضِيَ ٱللَّهُ عَنْهُ); and by Muslim (no. 2278), as a hadīth of Abū Hurairah (رَضِيَ ٱللَّهُ عَنْهُ).

[DB] The wording of the hadīth of Abū Hurairah (رَضِيَ ٱللَّهُ عَنْهُ) is: Allāh's Messenger (صَلَّى ٱللَّهُ عَلَيْهِ وَسَلَّمَ) said: "I shall be the noble chief of the descendants of Ādam on the Day of Resurrection, and the first one whose grave will be opened up for him, and the first one who will intercede, and the first one whose intercession will be accepted."

3 — [SH] Reported by Al-Bukhārī (no. 2411) and Muslim (no. 2373).

Some of those who have spoken about this hadīth have taken this awaking to mean the arising from the grave, and their evidence for that is what occurs in a narration of Al-Bukhārī's,[1] as a hadīth of Yahyā ibn ʿAmr Al-Madanī: from Abū Saʿīd (رَضِيَ ٱللَّهُ عَنْهُ) who said: Allāh's Messenger (صَلَّى ٱللَّهُ عَلَيْهِ وَسَلَّمَ) said:

> "Do not declare me better than the other Prophets, for the people will be knocked unconscious on the Day of Resurrection and I will be the first one for whom the earth will split open. So I will find Mūsā holding on to a support of the Throne, and I will not know whether he was one of those knocked unconscious or whether he was sufficed by his previous unconsciousness."

So this wording is problematic, and what is correctly preserved is the narration of Al-Bukhārī[2] from Yahyā ibn Qazʿah: from Ibrāhīm ibn Saʿd: from Az-Zuhrī: from Abū Salamah and ʿAbdur-Rahmān Al-Aʿraj: from Abū Hurairah. He mentioned the incident of the Jew, until he said: Allāh's Messenger (صَلَّى ٱللَّهُ عَلَيْهِ وَسَلَّمَ) said: *"Do not declare me to be better than Mūsā, for the people will be knocked unconscious on the Day of Resurrection, and I will be knocked unconscious, and I will be the first one who regains consciousness, and I will find Mūsā..."* — and he mentioned the hadīth.

So this is a clear text, which cannot be explained with an alternative meaning, that this will be an awakening from unconsciousness, not from death; and this is the reality of regaining consciousness (*Al-Ifāqah*). Then whoever carefully considers his saying: *"And I will not know whether he recovered consciousness before me, or whether he was sufficed by having been knocked unconscious at the mount"* — will state that with certainty, and Allāh (the Perfect and Most High) knows best.[3]

---

1 — SH It is the previous narration (no. 2412).

2 — SH (no. 2411).

3 — SH What occurs between the two [decorative] brackets is missing in the 'Sulaymāniyyah Library' manuscript (no. 3339).

And from that is that he will be the possessor of the greatest banner on the Day of Resurrection,[1] and he and his nation will be raised up upon an elevated part of the earth, apart from the rest of the nations; and Allāh will permit him and them to prostrate in the Gathering-Place, to the exclusion of all the other nations — as reported by Ibn Mājah[2] from Jubārah ibn Al-Mughallis Al-Himmānī: ʿAbdul-Aʿlā ibn Abil-Musāwir: from Abū Burdah: from his father Abū Mūsā who said: Allāh's Messenger (ﷺ) said:

> "When Allāh gathers the creation on the Day of Resurrection He will give permission to the nation of Muhammad to prostrate, and they will prostrate to Him for a long period. Then it will be said: *'Raise your heads, for We have made an equal number to you your ransom from the Fire.'*"

— and Jubārah is weak.

And it is authentic through other lines of transmission that they will be the first of the nations in having judgement passed upon them on the Day of Resurrection.[3]

---

1 — SH Reported by Ahmad 3/144), Ad-Dārimī in his *Musnad* (1/424/55: *Fat-hul-Mannān*), Ibn Khuzaymah in *At-Tawhīd* (2/710-711/454), Ibn Mandah in *Al-Īmān* (8/846-847/877) [and others] by way of Al-Layth ibn Saʿd: from Yazīd ibn Al-Hād: from ʿAmr ibn Abī ʿAmr mawlā Al-Muttalib: from Anas — with it. Our Shaikh Al-Imām Al-Albānī (رَحِمَهُ ٱللَّهُ) said in *As-Sahīhah* (4/100): *"And its chain of narration is good: its narrators are those of the two Shaikhs."* [...] And Ibn Mandah said: *"This is a 'sahīh' hadīth which is well-known from Ibnul-Hād."*

DB Its wording is: "And I will be given the Banner of Praise, and that is no boast..."

2 — Al-Albānī declares this chain of narration to be very weak, however there is another version of the narration in *Sahīh Muslim* which is authentic. Refer to **Endnote 148 on page 554**.

3 — See **Endnote 149 on page 554** for some of the narrations wherein Allāh's Messenger (ﷺ) mentions how his Ummah will be the first nation to enter Paradise.

And from that is that he will be the possessor of the Great Reservoir (Al-Hawd) to which people will come to drink; and At-Tirmidhī and others reported that every Prophet will have a Reservoir (Hawd).[1]

However, we know that his (صَلَّى ٱللَّٰهُ عَلَيْهِ وَسَلَّمَ) Reservoir will be the greatest of all the reservoirs, and have the greatest number of people coming to drink from it.

And from that is that the city in which he was raised as a Prophet is the most honourable part of the earth,[2] then the place to which he performed Hijrah (migrated), upon the saying of the majority; or it is said that the place to which he migrated is the most excellent of places, as is related from Mālik ibn Anas (رَحِمَهُ ٱللَّٰهُ) and the majority of his students.[3]

And Al-Qādī ʿIyād As-Sabtiyy quoted that[4] from Amīrul-Muʾminīn ʿUmar ibn Al-Khattāb (رَضِيَ ٱللَّٰهُ عَنْهُ) and Allāh knows best; and he quoted agreement upon the fact that his grave, which includes his body after his death, is the most excellent part of the earth. He was preceded in

---

1 — This narration is either *'hasan'* or *'sahīh'* according to Imām Al-Albānī — for more detail regarding the chains, see **Endnote 150 on page 555**. As for the Hawd (The Resevoir), then it is *'mutawātir'* and uncontested.

2 — [BJ][SZ] Indicating the hadīth of ʿAbdullāh ibn ʿAdiyy: from the Prophet (صَلَّى ٱللَّٰهُ عَلَيْهِ وَسَلَّمَ): "By Allāh! You are the most beloved part of Allāh's (the Most High) Earth to me, and if it were not that I were forced out of you, I would not have left." Reported by At-Tirmidhī (no. 4017), Ibn Mājah (no. 3108), Ahmad (4/305) [...] and it is a *'sahīh'* hadīth.

3 — [SH] And refer to *At-Tamhīd* (2/289) and *Al-Istidhkār* (26/17).

4 — [SH] In *Ash-Shifā'* (2/681-689).

quoting consensus upon this by Al-Qādī Abul-Walīd Al-Bājī,[1] Ibn Battāl,[2] and others.

The basis for that is what is related that when he (ﷺ) died they disagreed about where he should be buried. So it was said: [That it should be] in Al-Baqī', and it was said: in Makkah, and it was said: in Jerusalem. So Abū Bakr (رضي الله عنه) said: "Allāh did not take his soul except in the most beloved of places to Him."[3]

'Abdus-Samad ibn 'Asākir[4] mentioned it in his book *Tuhfatuz-Zā'ir*, and I have not seen it with a chain of narration.

And from that is that he was not to be inherited from after his death, just as Abū Bakr and Abū Hurairah (رضي الله عنهما) narrated from him (ﷺ) that he said:

---

1 — (MM)(MK)(SH) He is Abul-Walīd Sulaymān ibn Khalaf ibn Sa'd At-Tujībī, Al-Mālikī, Al-Bājī, Al-Qurtubī, Al-Andalusī; and 'Al-Bājī' is an ascription to Bājah (Beja) [c. 90miles SE of Lisbon, Portugal] the well-known city of Al-Andalus.

He was a major Mālikī jurist and muhaddith. He travelled to the Hijāz, and to Baghdād, Mosul, Aleppo, and Damascus. Then he returned to Andalusia. He wrote *Ahkāmul-Usūl*, and *Al-Muntaqā* in explanation of Imām Mālik's *Muwatta'*, and *Sharhul-Mudawwanah*. He was born in 403 H and died in 474 H. See *Siyar A'lāmin-Nubalā'* (18/535) of Adh-Dhahabī.

2 — (SH) He is the Shaikh, Al-'Allāmah, Abul-Hasan 'Alī ibn Khalaf ibn 'Abdil-Malik ibn Battāl, Al-Bakriyy, Al-Qurtubī, Al-Balansī — an ascription to the city of Balansiyah (Valencia). He died in 449 H. He wrote *Sharh Sahīhil-Bukhārī*, and a book on Zuhd and narrations that affect the heart.

3 — For a detailed report regarding the chains of this narration, refer to Endnote 151 on page 555.

4 — (MM)(MK)(SH) He is 'Abdus-Samad ibn 'Abdil-Wahhāb ibn Al-Hasan ibn Muhammad ibn 'Asākir, the grandson of the nephew of Al-Hāfidh, the historian Ibn 'Asākir. He was born in Damascus, and lived in Makkah for about forty years. He wrote *Fadā'il Ummil-Mu'minīn Khadījah*, and *Ahādīth 'Eidil-Fitr*, and *Fadā'il Ramadān*. He died in 686 H. See *Al-A'lām* (4/11).

> "We are not inherited from. Whatever we leave behind is charity (*sadaqah*)."[1]

The two of them reported it through two chains of transmission.

However, At-Tirmidhī reported, with a good chain of narration, in other than *Al-Jāmiʿ* from Abū Bakr (رَضِيَ ٱللَّهُ عَنْهُ) that he (صَلَّى ٱللَّهُ عَلَيْهِ وَسَلَّمَ) said: "We, the assembly of Prophets, are not inherited from."[2]

So therefore, they must have shared in this characteristic, to the exclusion of the rest of the servants.

Chapter: The State of the Prophets in their Sleep and in their Graves[3]

And from that which he and the other Prophets shared in is that his (صَلَّى ٱللَّهُ عَلَيْهِ وَسَلَّمَ) eyes would sleep but his heart would not sleep,[4] and the same was the case with the (rest of the) Prophets.[5]

---

1 — [BJ][SZ] Reported by Al-Bukhārī (nos. 3094, 6726) and Muslim (no. 1377), from Abū Bakr; and by Al-Bukhārī (no. 2776) and Muslim (no. 1762), from Abū Hurairah; and Al-Bukhārī (no. 6727) and Muslim (no. 1758) reported it from ʿĀʾishah; and it is a '*mutawātir*' hadīth.

2 — For the speech of Al-Hāfidh Ibn Hajr regarding this wording, see ENDNOTE 152 ON PAGE 557.

3 — Chapter title added by publisher.

4 — [BJ][SZ] Reported by Al-Bukhārī (no. 1147) and Muslim (no. 738), as a hadīth of ʿĀʾishah (رَضِيَ ٱللَّهُ عَنْهَا).

5 — [SH] Reported by Al-Bukhārī (no. 3570) as a saying of Anas, in the story of his (صَلَّى ٱللَّهُ عَلَيْهِ وَسَلَّمَ) ascension to the heavens. Al-Hāfidh said: "And the like of this has preceded as a statement of ʿUbayd ibn ʿUmayr, at the beginning of (the Book of) Purification, and its like could not have been said upon the basis of opinion."

And there occurs in the *Sahīh*[1]: *"Be close in the rows, for I can see you from behind my back"* — so many of them take it to mean what is apparent from it, and Allāh knows best.[2]

And Abū Nasr ibn As-Sabbāgh[3] said: *"He used to see behind him just as he could see in front of him"* — and the meaning of that is being able to observe and perceive.

And there occurs in a hadīth reported by Abū Ya'lā Al-Mawsilī in his *Musnad*: from Anas: from the Prophet (صَلَّىٱللَّهُعَلَيْهِوَسَلَّمَ): "The Prophets are alive in their graves, praying."[4]

---

1 — [BJ][SZ] Reported by Al-Bukhārī (nos. 718 & 719) and Muslim (no. 425), as a hadīth of Anas (رَضِيَٱللَّهُعَنْهُ); and reported by Al-Bukhārī (nos. 418 & 741) and Muslim (no. 424), as a hadīth of Abū Hurairah (رَضِيَٱللَّهُعَنْهُ), without his saying: "Be close together in the rows."

2 — [SH] Our Shaikh (Al-Albānī) (رَحِمَهُٱللَّهُ) said in *As-Sahīhah* (1/74): "The hadīth shows a clear miracle for the Prophet (صَلَّىٱللَّهُعَلَيْهِوَسَلَّمَ), in that he (صَلَّىٱللَّهُعَلَيْهِوَسَلَّمَ) could see what was behind him. However it should be known that this was specific to when he (صَلَّىٱللَّهُعَلَيْهِوَسَلَّمَ) was praying, since there is nothing in the Sunnah to say that he could see similarly outside the Prayer also, and Allāh knows best."

3 — [MM][MK][SH] He is the Imām, Al-'Allāmah, the Shaikh of the Shāfi'īs, Abū Nasr 'Abdus-Sayyid ibn Muhammad ibn 'Abdil-Wāhid ibn Ahmad ibn Ja'far, Al-Baghdādī. He was born in 400 H. He wrote *Ash-Shamā'il* in Fiqh, and *Al-Kāmil*, and other works. He was the first one taught in *Al-Madrasatun-Nizāmiyyah*, in the year 459 H. He died in 477 H.

4 — This narration was declared *'sahīh'* by Imām Al-Albānī — refer to **Endnote 153 on page 557** for more detail.

THE SECOND CATEGORY –

That Which was Particular to him, to the Exclusion of his Nation

though the other Prophets may share with him in some of it

This is what is of primary importance, so we shall mention it arranged in the order of the chapters of Fiqh:

The Book Of Īmān (True Faith):

So from that is that he was preserved from error (*maʿṣūm*) in his sayings and actions. It was not possible for him to err deliberately, nor by mistake, with regard to conveyance of the Message, nor in anything else — and then to be left upon that. So he did not speak from his own desire, rather it was just Revelation sent to him.

Therefore, many of the scholars have said that he did not possess the right to personally deduce rulings (*ijtihād*), since he had the revealed texts with him. Others said: Rather he did have the right to deduce rulings, but error was not possible for him. Others said: rather he would not be left upon it.

So upon any of the sayings it was certain that he was protected from error. It cannot be imagined that he could continue upon an error, contrary to the rest of his nation — for all of that is possible for every one of them individually. However, if they all unite upon a single saying, then in that case it is not possible for them to be upon error, as has preceded.

And from that is what Abul-ʿAbbās ibn Al-Qāss[1] mentioned: that he alone was given the responsibility of bearing the whole of the knowledge, which the rest of the people were jointly responsible for. Al-Bayhaqī used as evidence for this the hadīth of Ibn ʿUmar (رَضِيَ ٱللَّهُ عَنْهُمَا): from Allāh's Messenger (صَلَّى ٱللَّهُ عَلَيْهِ وَسَلَّمَ) who said: "Whilst I was sleeping, a container with milk in it was brought to me. So I drank from it until I could see its wetness coming out from my fingernails. Then I gave what remained to ʿUmar ibn Al-Khattāb (رَضِيَ ٱللَّهُ عَنْهُ)."

They said: "So what explanation do you give to that, O Messenger of Allāh?"

He said: "The knowledge." Reported by Muslim.[2]

And from that is that he could see that which the people around him could not see. So there occurs in the *Sahīh*[3] from ʿĀ'ishah (رَضِيَ ٱللَّهُ عَنْهَا) that Allāh's Messenger (صَلَّى ٱللَّهُ عَلَيْهِ وَسَلَّمَ) said to her: *"This is Jibrīl giving you the Salutation."* She said: "Upon him be the Salutation, O Messenger of Allāh! You see what we do not see."

And from her, in the hadīth of the eclipse which occurs in the two *Sahīhs*[4]: "By Allāh! If you knew what I knew you would laugh little and weep a great deal!"

And Al-Bayhaqī said: "Al-Hākim related to us: Muhammad ibn ʿAlī ibn Duhaym related to us: Ahmad ibn Hāzim Al-Ghifārī related to us: ʿUbayd ibn Mūsā narrated to us: Isrā'īl related to us from Ibrāhīm ibn Muhājir: from Mujāhid: from Muwarriq: from Abū Dharr (رَضِيَ ٱللَّهُ عَنْهُ) who said: Allāh's Messenger (صَلَّى ٱللَّهُ عَلَيْهِ وَسَلَّمَ) recited:

---

1 — [SH] He is the Imām, the jurist, Shaikh of the Shāfiʿīs, Abul-ʿAbbās Ahmad ibn Abī Ahmad At-Tabarī, Al-Baghdādī. Ibnul-Qāss. He wrote *Sharh Hadīth Abī ʿUmayr*, *Kitābul-Miftāh*, and other works. He died whilst guarding the frontier in Tarsus in 335 H.

2 — [BJ][SZ] Reported by Al-Bukhārī (nos. 82, 3681, & 7006) and Muslim (no. 2391).

3 — [SH] Reported by Al-Bukhārī (no. 3217), and Muslim (no. 2447), with the wording: *"She said: 'And he could see what I could not see'"* — and the wording of Al-Bukhārī is similar.

4 — [SH] Reported by Al-Bukhārī (no. 1044) and Muslim (no. 901).

هَلْ أَتَىٰ عَلَى الْإِنسَانِ حِينٌ مِّنَ الدَّهْرِ لَمْ يَكُن شَيْـًٔا مَّذْكُورًا

MEANING: "Has there not come upon a man a time period when he was nothing worthy of mention?" — **Sūrah Al-Insān (76): 1**

— until he completed it. Then he said:

"I see that which you do not see, and I hear that which you do not hear. The heavens creak, and they have a right to creak. There is not the space of a finger within them except that there is an Angel placing his forehead in prostration to Allāh. By Allāh! If you knew what I know you would laugh little and you would weep a great deal, and you would not take delight in women upon the beds; and you would go out upon the pathways beseeching Allāh."

"By Allāh! I would love to be a tree which will be cut down!" And Ibn Mājah reported it.[1]

Al-Bayhaqī said: *"It is said that his saying: 'a tree cut down' was the statement of Abū Dharr"* — and Allāh knows best.

And from that is that Allāh commanded him to choose the next life over this life.

---

1 — (BJ)(SZ) It is *'hasan'*: Reported by At-Tirmidhī (no. 2312) & Ibn Mājah (no. 4190), without a mention of the verse. At-Tirmidhī said: *"It is 'hasan gharīb'."* It is also related through other than this chain that Abū Dharr said: *"I would love to be a tree which will be cut down."* Also reported by Abū Nu'aym in *Al-Hilyah* (2/236), Al-Hākim (2/510), Al-Bayhaqī (7/52); and by Ahmad (5/173) — clearly stating that his saying: *"I would love to be..."* — was the saying of Abū Dharr.

And the hadīth has witnesses from the Companions and from the Prophet (ﷺ) which witness to its authenticity — without a mention of the Āyah, and without the last line which is *'mudraj'* [mistakenly included as a statement of the Prophet (ﷺ)], and it was declared *'sahīh'* by Shaikh Nāsir [ud-dīn Al-Albānī] in *As-Sahīhah* (no. 1722).

And it was forbidden for him to look to and desire the riches granted to the people of this world, and its proof is clear in the Mighty Book.[1]

And from that is that it was not right for him to learn poetry.

He (the Most High) said:

> وَمَا عَلَّمْنَاهُ الشِّعْرَ وَمَا يَنبَغِي لَهُ
>
> MEANING: "And We have not taught Muhammad (ﷺ) poetry, and it is not fitting for him." — **SŪRAH YĀ-SĪN (36): 69**

And from ʿAbdullāh ibn ʿAmr (رَضِيَ ٱللَّهُ عَنْهُمَا) who said: I heard Allāh's Messenger (ﷺ) say:

> "It would be all the same to me whether I drank a foul potion to repel poison, or I wore an amulet, or I myself composed poetry." Reported by Abū Dāwūd.[2]

So therefore, our companions said that it was forbidden for him to learn poetry.

And from that is that he could not write. They said: And that was forbidden for him.

Allāh (the Most High) said:

> الَّذِينَ يَتَّبِعُونَ الرَّسُولَ النَّبِيَّ الْأُمِّيَّ الَّذِي يَجِدُونَهُ مَكْتُوبًا عِندَهُمْ فِي التَّوْرَاةِ وَالْإِنجِيلِ
>
> MEANING: "Those who follow the Messenger: the Prophet who can neither read, nor write, whom they find written with them in the Tawrāt and the Injīl." — **SŪRAH AL-AʿRĀF (7): 157**

---

1 — Refer to ENDNOTE 154 ON PAGE 558 to read the verses wherein Allāh (the Most High) commands with refraining from looking longingly at the wealth and enjoyments given to the Disbelievers.

2 — Read ENDNOTE 155 ON PAGE 558 for more detail regarding the authenticity of this narration.

And He (the Most High) said:

> 316 وَمَا كُنتَ تَتْلُو مِن قَبْلِهِ مِن كِتَابٍ وَلَا تَخُطُّهُ بِيَمِينِكَ ۖ إِذًا لَّارْتَابَ الْمُبْطِلُونَ
>
> MEANING: "And you, O Muhammad (ﷺ) , were not able to read a book before this Qur'ān was sent down to you, nor could you write any book with your right hand; if you had been able to, then the followers of falsehood would have doubted." — **Sūrah Al-'Ankabūt (29): 48**

Some of them have claimed that he (ﷺ) did not die until he had learned to write. This is a saying which has no evidence to support it, so it is rejected — except for what Al-Bayhaqī[1] narrated as a hadīth of Abū 'Aqīl Yahyā ibn Al-Mutawakkil: from Mujālid: from 'Awn ibn 'Abdillāh: from his father who said: "Allāh's Messenger (ﷺ) did not die until he was able to write and read."

Mujālid said: So I mentioned that to Ash-Sha'bī, and he said: "He has spoken the truth, I have heard some of our companions mentioning that."

However, this Yahyā is weak (*'da'īf'*), and there is speech concerning Mujālid.

The same was claimed by one of the scholars of the West[2]: that he (ﷺ) wrote on the day of the Treaty of Al-Hudaybiyah. So he was severely criticized for his (claim), and they disassociated themselves from the one who said it from the pulpits, and they composed poetry against him.

He was misled in that regard on account of what occurs in one of Al-Bukhārī's narrations[3]: "So Allāh's Messenger (ﷺ) took (the document) and wrote: *'This is the agreement made by Muhammad ibn 'Abdillāh.'*"

---

1 — Refer to **Endnote 156 on page 559** for details regarding the authenticity of this report.

2 — [SH] He is Abul-Walīd Al-Bājī, as mentioned by Al-Hāfidh Ibn Hajr in *Fat-hul-Bārī* (7/503-504).

3 — [SH] It occurs with him in the *Sahīh* (no. 2699).

However, it is known that a restricted text is decisive over an unrestricted text, and there occurs in the other narration: "So he commanded 'Alī and he wrote: *'This is the agreement made by Muhammad ibn 'Abdillāh (صَلَّى ٱللَّٰهُ عَلَيْهِ وَسَلَّمَ).'*"[1]

And from that is that lying upon him is not like lying upon someone besides him. So it is *'mutawātir'* from him (may Allāh extol him and grant him peace and security) that whoever lies upon him deliberately must take his seat in the Fire.

This hadīth is reported by way of eighty and odd Companions. It occurs in the two *Sahīhs* as a hadīth of 'Alī,[2] and Anas,[3] and Abū Hurairah,[4] and Al-Mughīrah ibn Shu'bah;[5] and with Al-Bukhārī, as a narration of Az-Zubayr ibn Al-'Awwām,[6] and Salamah ibn Al-Akwa',[7] and 'Abdullāh ibn 'Amr[8] — and his wording is:

> "Convey from me even a single Āyah, and narrate from the Children of Isrā'īl, and there is no harm; and whoever lies upon me intentionally then let him take his seat in the Fire."

---

1 — SH It is the narration of Muslim in the *Sahīh* (1783/92).

2 — SH Reported by Al-Bukhārī (no. 106) and Muslim (no. 1).

3 — SH Reported by Al-Bukhārī (no. 108) and Muslim (no. 2).

4 — SH Reported by Al-Bukhārī (no. 110) and Muslim (no. 3).

5 — SH Reported by Al-Bukhārī (no. 1219) and Muslim (no. 4).

6 — SH In his *Sahīh* (no. 107).

7 — SH Reported by Al-Bukhārī (no. 109).

8 — SH Reported by Al-Bukhārī (no. 3461).

And there occurs in the *Musnad* of Ahmad from 'Uthmān,[1] and Ibn 'Umar,[2] and Abū Sa'īd,[3] and Wāthilah ibn Al-Asqa'[4] and Zayd ibn Arqam.[5]

And with At-Tirmidhī[6] from Ibn Mas'ūd.

And Ibn Mājah reported it from Jābir.[7]

And a group of the great preservers have written works about it, such as Ibrāhīm Al-Harbī, Yahyā ibn Sā'id, At-Tabarānī,[8] Al-Bazzār, Ibn Mandah, and others from the earlier (scholars). Likewise Ibnul-Jawzī and Yūsuf ibn Khalīl from the later (scholars). And the fact that it is *'mutawātir'* was clearly stated by Ibnus-Salāh, An-Nawawī, and others from the great preservers of hadīth; and it is the truth.

So therefore the scholars agreed by consensus (*ijmā'*) upon the Disbelief of one who lies deliberately upon him, whilst deeming that to be permissible; and they disagreed concerning the one who merely

---

1 — For detail regarding the authenticity of this chain, see **ENDNOTE 157 ON PAGE 559**.

2 — [SH] Reported by Ahmad (2/22, 103 & 144), [and others] by way of Bakr ibn Sālim: from his father: from his grandfather, 'Abdullāh — with it. I say: This is a chain of narration *'sahīh'* to the standard of the two Shaikhs.

3 — [SH] Reported by Ahmad (3/39, 44, & 46), and it is reported by Muslim in his *Sahīh* (no. 3304).

4 — [SH] Reported by Ahmad (3/490 & 491, & 4/106 & 107), and it occurs in Al-Bukhārī's *Sahīh* (no. 3509).

5 — [SH] Reported by Ahmad (4/367), [and others] from Abū Hayyān At-Taymī: from Yazīd ibn Hayyān: from Zayd — with it. I say: And this is a *'sahīh'* chain of narration, its narrators are reliable.

6 — For detail regarding the authenticity of this chain from Imām At-Tirmidhī, refer to **ENDNOTE 158 ON PAGE 560**.

7 — For detail regarding the authenticity of this chain from Imām Ibn Mājah, refer to **ENDNOTE 159 ON PAGE 560**.

8 — [BJ][SZ][SH] At-Tabarānī's book has been printed with the checking of 'Alī Al-Halabī and Hishām ibn Ismā'īl As-Saqā, and he has gathered chains of narration for the hadīth reaching sixty Companions.

does it deliberately.[1] So Shaikh Abū Muhammad[2] said: 'He becomes a Disbeliever also', but the majority disagreed with him.

Then if he repents, are his narrations to be accepted from him? There are two sayings: So Ahmad ibn Hanbal, Yahyā ibn Ma'īn, and Abū Bakr Al-Humaydī said: They are not to be accepted, because of his saying:

> "Lying upon me is not like lying upon anyone else. Whoever lies upon me then let him take his seat in the Fire."[3]

They said: And it is known that whoever lies upon someone other than him is sinful and is a sinner, and likewise one who lies upon him. However, if a person repents from lying upon someone else, then this is accepted, by consensus. So it is befitting that the narrations of one who lied upon him should not be accepted, in order to keep a distinction between lying upon him and lying upon anyone else.

As for the majority, then they said: His narrations are accepted, since the most that can be said is that he became a Disbeliever, and whoever repents from Disbelief, then his repentance and his narrations are accepted; and this is what is correct.

And from that is that whoever sees him in a dream has truly seen him, as occurs in the hadīth: "Because Satan cannot take my form."[4]

---

1 — [DB] i.e. but he does not deem it to be permissible.

2 — [BJ][SZ] He is the father of 'Imāmul-Haramayn', well known as 'Al-Juwaynī', and his name is 'Abdullāh ibn Yūsuf ibn 'Abdillāh. He died in the year 438 H. Refer to *Siyar A'lāmin-Nubalā'* (17/617).

3 — [BJ][SZ] Reported by Al-Bukhārī (no. 1291) and Muslim (no. 4), as a hadīth of Al-Mughīrah (رضي الله عنه).

4 — [SH] Reported by Al-Bukhārī (no. 6993), and Muslim (no. 2266), as a hadīth of Abū Hurairah (رضي الله عنه); and reported by Al-Bukhārī (no. 6995) and Muslim (no. 2267), from Abū Qatādah (رضي الله عنه); and reported by Al-Bukhārī (nos. 6994 & 6997), from Anas ibn Mālik and Abū Sa'īd Al-Khudrī (رضي الله عنهما).

[BJ][SZ] And it is *'mutawātir'*, as occurs in *Nadhmul-Mutanāthir* (no. 275) [of Al-Kattānī].

However, this is with the condition that he sees him in the form which was his form in the life of this world, as An-Nasā'ī reported from Ibn 'Abbās.[1]

However, they are agreed that whoever conveyed from him a saying by way of a dream, then this is not acted upon, since there is no precision in the narration of one who sees something in a dream; for dreams are a sphere where the soul and its precision is weakened, and Allāh (the Most High) knows best.

And from that is what Al-Hāfidh Abū Bakr Al-Bayhaqī mentioned in his *Sunanul-Kubrā*[2] from Abul-'Abbās ibn Al-Qāss regarding His Saying — He the Most High:

> لَئِنْ أَشْرَكْتَ لَيَحْبَطَنَّ عَمَلُكَ
>
> MEANING: "If you were to associate anything with Allāh then your deeds would be nullified." — **Sūrah Az-Zumar (39): 65**

Abul-'Abbās said: "And this is not the case with other than him until the person dies, because of His Saying — He the Most High:

> وَمَن يَرْتَدِدْ مِنكُمْ عَن دِينِهِ فَيَمُتْ وَهُوَ كَافِرٌ فَأُولَٰئِكَ حَبِطَتْ أَعْمَالُهُ
>
> MEANING: "And whomever of you turns back from his Religion and dies, as a Disbeliever, then his deeds are rendered null and void." — **Sūrah Al-Baqarah (2): 217**

Al-Bayhaqī said: "That is what Abul-'Abbās said, whereas others held that this was addressed to other than the Prophet (صَلَّى ٱللَّهُ عَلَيْهِ وَسَلَّمَ). Then the unrestricted text is taken in the light of the restricted text." This is the end of his words.

I say: There was no need to mention this issue in detail, since there is no benefit to be gained from it; and it would not be right for us to mention

---

1 — This hadīth was declared *'hasan'* by Imām Al-Albānī. Refer to **Endnote 160 on page 561**.

2 — SH (7/44)

it, if it were not for fear of giving the mistaken impression that by leaving it out we were also leaving out other things, which they have mentioned. Otherwise, it would have been better to leave out the like of this, and Allāh knows best.

And from that is that it was not right for him to make a treacherous hint with the eyes, meaning that it was not correct for him to indicate something with his eyes, which was contrary to what was apparent from his speech, such that it would be a case of making a concealed sign. The basis for this is the story of ʿAbdullāh ibn Saʿd ibn Abī Sarh, whose blood he (صَلَّى ٱللَّٰهُ عَلَيْهِ وَسَلَّمَ) declared lawful to shed amongst those whose blood he declared lawful to shed on the Day of the Conquest. So when his brother through breast-feeding, ʿUthmān ibn ʿAffān (رَضِيَ ٱللَّٰهُ عَنْهُ) came with him, he said: "O Messenger of Allāh! Take his pledge."

So he (صَلَّى ٱللَّٰهُ عَلَيْهِ وَسَلَّمَ) withheld, hoping that a man would get up and kill him. But then he took his pledge. Then he said to his Companions:

> "Was there not amongst you a wise man who could stand up to this one when he saw me withholding my hand, and kill him?!"

So they said: "O Messenger of Allāh! Would that you had made an indication to us!"

So he said:

> "It is not befitting for a Prophet to make a treacherous indication with the eyes."[1]

Chapter: The Book of Purification

So from that is that he had been commanded to make wudhū' for every Prayer, but when that became difficult for him he was then commanded to use the tooth-stick (*siwāk*). The evidence for this is what ʿAbdullāh ibn Hanzalah ibn Abī ʿĀmir narrated: that Allāh's Messenger (صَلَّى ٱللَّٰهُ عَلَيْهِ وَسَلَّمَ) was commanded to make wudhū' for every Prayer, whether he was upon a state of purification or not; but when this became difficult for him he

---

1 — This hadīth was declared *'sahīh'* by Imām Al-Albānī, and you can refer to Endnote 161 on page 561 for a detailed breakdown of this narration's authenticity.

was commanded to use the tooth-stick for every Prayer. Abū Dāwūd reported it.[1]

So what is apparent is that using the tooth-stick was made obligatory upon him, and that is the correct saying in the view of the companions.[2] It was stated by Abū Zakariyyā,[3] and Ash-Shaikh Abū ʿAmr ibn As-Salāh inclined towards its being strong, and it is supported by what Imām Ahmad reported from Ibn ʿAbbās: that Allāh's Messenger (ﷺ) said: "I was commanded with the tooth-stick to such an extent that I thought some Qur'ān or Revelation would come down to me concerning it."[4]

And from Umm Salamah who said: Allāh's Messenger (ﷺ) said: *"Jibrīl continued advising me with the tooth-stick until I feared for my teeth."*[5] Al-Bayhaqī reported it.

Al-Bukhārī said: "This is a *'hasan'* hadīth."

And ʿAbdullāh ibn Wahb said: Yahyā ibn ʿAbdillāh ibn Sālim narrated to us: from ʿAmr — the mawlā of Al-Muttalib: from Al-Muttalib ibn

---

1 — [BJ][SZ][SH] It is *'hasan'*: Reported by Abū Dāwūd (no. 48), Ahmad (5/225), Ibn Khuzaymah (1/11/no. 158, & 1/71-72/no. 138), ad-Dārimī (1/168-169), and Al-Hākim (1/155), by way of Muhammad ibn Is-hāq: Muhammad ibn Yahyā ibn Hibbān narrated to me: from ʿAbdullāh — or in some narrations: ʿUbaydullāh ibn ʿAbdillāh ibn ʿUmar: from Asmā' bint Zayd ibn Al-Khattāb: from ʿAbdullāh ibn Hanzalah, with it.

2 — [DB] i.e. the Shāfiʿī scholars.

3 — [DB] i.e. Imām An-Nawawī.

4 — [BJ][SZ] It is *'hasan'*: Reported by Ahmad (4/29/nos. 2125, 2573, & 2798), Abū Yaʿlā (4/218/no. 2330), Ibn Abī Shaybah (1/171), and Al-Bayhaqī (1/35); and it has a witness from a hadīth of Wāthilah ibn Al-Asqaʿ — reported by Ahmad (25/389/no. 16007) and At-Tabarānī in *Al-Kabīr* (22/76/nos. 189, 190).

5 — [BJ][SZ] It is *'hasan ligharihi'*: Reported by At-Tabarānī in *Al-Kabīr* (23/251/no. 510), and Al-Bayhaqī in *As-Sunan* (7/49). At-Tabarānī's chain of narration contains Muhammad ibn Humayd Ar-Rāzī, and he is weak; and the chain of narration of Al-Bayhaqī contains Khālid ibn ʿUbayd, and he is abandoned (*matrūk*) in hadīth. However it has a witness from a hadīth of Ibn ʿAbbās — reported by At-Tabarānī in *Al-Awsat*, as occurs in *Majmaʿul-Bahrayn* (The Prayer: 2/100/no. 779), and it has a witness from a hadīth of Sahl ibn Saʿd — reported by At-Tabarānī in *Al-Kabīr* (6/252/no. 6018).

ʿAbdillāh: from ʿĀʾishah (رَضِيَٱللَّهُعَنْهَا): that Allāh's Messenger (صَلَّىٱللَّهُعَلَيْهِوَسَلَّمَ) said: *"I continually used the tooth-stick until I feared that it would cause my teeth to fall out."* Al-Bayhaqī reported it.[1]

However, this is rendered problematic by what Imām Ahmad reported from Wāthilah ibn Al-Asqaʿ, who said: Allāh's Messenger (صَلَّىٱللَّهُعَلَيْهِوَسَلَّمَ) said: "I was commanded with the tooth-stick to such an extent that I feared that it would be written as an obligation upon me."[2]

So therefore, some of our companions said that it was not obligatory upon him, but rather something recommended.

And from that is that his wudhūʾ was not broken by sleep. Its proof is the hadīth of Ibn ʿAbbās in the two *Sahīhs*[3] that he (صَلَّىٱللَّهُعَلَيْهِوَسَلَّمَ) slept to the extent that his breathing was heavy, then the muʾadhdhin came to him, and he went out and prayed, and he did not perform wudhūʾ.

Its reason is what occurs in the hadīth of ʿĀʾishah (رَضِيَٱللَّهُعَنْهَا) that she asked him, saying: "O Messenger of Allāh! Will you sleep before you pray the Witr?"

So he said:

> "O ʿĀʾishah! My eyes sleep, but my heart does not sleep."

The two of them reported it.[4]

And they disagreed about whether his wudhūʾ would be broken by touching women. They had two sayings, and the more well known of the two is that it would be broken.

It is as if the evidence used by those who held that his wudhūʾ would not be broken is the hadīth of ʿĀʾishah occurring in *Sahīh Muslim*: that she missed Allāh's Messenger (صَلَّىٱللَّهُعَلَيْهِوَسَلَّمَ) when he was in the mosque, so her hand touched him whilst he was prostrating, and he was saying:

---

1 — For the details regarding this chain of narration, see **Endnote 162 on page 562**.

2 — SH However, it is *'daʿīf'*, as has preceded, so there is no problem.

3 — BJ SZ Reported by Al-Bukhārī (no. 138) and Muslim (no.763).

4 — SH Reported by Al-Bukhārī (no. 1147) and Muslim (no. 738).

> "O Allāh! I seek refuge in Your Pleasure from Your Wrath, and in Your protection from Your punishment, and with You from You. I cannot fully enumerate praise of You. You are just as You have praised Yourself."[1]

And there occurs, through more than one chain of transmission from her, that Allāh's Messenger (صَلَّى ٱللَّهُ عَلَيْهِ وَسَلَّمَ) used to kiss and then pray, and he would not perform wudhū'.[2]

And it is as if the one who said this held that this was something particular to him (صَلَّى ٱللَّهُ عَلَيْهِ وَسَلَّمَ), however the opponents will not be satisfied with accepting that from him. Rather they say: the basic rule in that regard is that it is not particular, unless there is an evidence.

AN ISSUE:

Did he used to experience wet dreams? There are two sayings, and An-Nawawī held its prevention.

A problem for this though is the hadīth of 'Ā'ishah occurring in the two *Sahīhs*: "Allāh's Messenger (صَلَّى ٱللَّهُ عَلَيْهِ وَسَلَّمَ) used to enter the morning in a state of *'janābah'* (post-coital state) because of other than a wet dream.[3] Then he would take a bath, and fast."[4]

However, what is most apparently correct is to make a distinction in this regard, and to say: if what is meant by 'wet-dreams' is fluid flowing from the body, then there is nothing to prevent this; but if what is meant is the disturbance caused by a devil, then he (صَلَّى ٱللَّهُ عَلَيْهِ وَسَلَّمَ) was protected from that.

---

1 — [BJ][SZ] Reported by Muslim (no. 486).

2 — This narration was declared *'sahīh'* by Imām Al-Albānī — refer to **Endnote 163 on page 563** for more detail.

3 — [BJ][SZ] This is what occurs in the 'Sulaymāniyyah Library' (no. 3339) manuscript, and this agrees with the narration of Muslim; and there occurs in the ''Ārif Hikmat Library' manuscript: *'because of other than sexual intercourse'* but what is correct is without the words *'other than'*, as occurs in *[Sahīh] Al-Bukhārī.*

4 — [SH] Reported by Al-Bukhārī (nos. 1930 & 1931) and Muslim (no. 1109).

Likewise, madness/jinn-possession was not possible for him, whereas falling unconscious was possible for him. Indeed, he fell unconscious, as occurs in the hadīth narrated by ʿĀʾishah (رَضِيَٱللَّهُعَنْهَا) which is in the *Sahīh*, and it mentions that he took a bath after falling unconscious. He did this a number of times, and the hadīth is well-known.[1]

And from that is what Abul-ʿAbbās ibn Al-Qāss mentioned: that it was not forbidden for him to remain in the mosque whilst he was in a post-coital state (*'junub'*). They use as evidence what At-Tirmidhī reported from a hadīth of Sālim ibn Abī Hafsah: from ʿAtiyyah: from Abū Saʿīd who said: Allāh's Messenger (صَلَّىٱللَّهُعَلَيْهِوَسَلَّمَ) said: "O ʿAlī! It is not permissible for anyone, besides me and you, to be in a post-coital state in this mosque."[2]

At-Tirmidhī said: "It is *'hasan-gharīb'*, we do not know it except through this chain, and Al-Bukhārī heard this hadīth from me."[3]

I say: ʿAtiyyah is weak in hadīth. Al-Bayhaqī said: *"He is not used as proof"* — and the narrator from him is weak.

Dirār ibn Surad[4] took it to refer to passing through [the mosque], as At-Tirmidhī related from his teacher ʿAlī ibn Mundhir At-Tarīqī from him.

This is problematic, since passing through is permissible for the people, so there is nothing particular in that regard. O Allāh! — unless it is claimed that it is not permissible for anyone else besides those two to pass through the Prophet's mosque, and therefore he said: *"It is not*

---

1 — BJ SZ Reported by Al-Bukhārī (no. 687 & no. 198) and Muslim (no. 418).

2 — BJ SZ It is *daʿīf*: Reported by At-Tirmidhī (no. 3727), Abū Yaʿlā (2/311/no. 1042), and Al-Bayhaqī in his *Sunan* (7/66).

SH Sālim ibn Abī Hafsah and ʿAtiyyah Al-ʿAwfī are both Shiites and are *'daʿīf'*. An-Nasāʾī said regarding Sālim: *"He is not reliable"*, and Al-Fallās said: *"Extreme in Shīʿism"*; and ʿAtiyyah was declared weak by Ahmad ibn Hanbal, ʿAlī ibn Al-Madīnī, An-Nasāʾī, and a group.

3 — SH There occurs in the printed version: "And Muhammad ibn Ismāʿīl heard this hadīth from me, and he deemed it *'gharīb' (singular/strange/weak).*"

4 — BJ SZ He is Abū Nuʿaym At-Tahhān Al-Kūfī, he was knowledgeable concerning the laws of inheritance.

DB He died in 229 H (*At-Taqrīb*).

permissible for anyone besides me and you to be in a post-coital state in this mosque" — and Allāh knows best.

And Mahdūj Adh-Dhuhlī said: from Jasrah bint Dajājah: from Umm Salamah who said: "The Prophet (ﷺ) entered the courtyard of this mosque and said:

> 'Indeed, this mosque is not lawful for one in a post-coital state (*'junub'*), nor for a menstruating woman, except for Allāh's Messenger (ﷺ), and 'Alī, and Fātimah, and Al-Hasan, and Al-Husayn. Indeed, I have explained the names to you so that you do not go astray.'"

Ibn Mājah reported it, and Al-Bayhaqī, and this is his wording.[1]

Then Al-Bayhaqī[2] reported it through another chain: from Ismā'īl ibn Umayyah: from Jasrah: from Umm Salamah, tracing it back to the Prophet (ﷺ) with its like; and nothing from that is authentic. Therefore Al-Qaffāl[3], from our companions, said that this was not from the characteristics specific to him (ﷺ); and Imāmul-Haramayn declared Abul-'Abbās ibn Al-Qāss to have been mistaken in that regard, and Allāh knows best.

---

1 — This hadīth is baseless and fabricated, as stated by Imām Al-Albānī and Imām Ibn Al-Qayyim. See **Endnote 164 on page 563** for a detailed explanation of why.

2 — [SH] (7/64) by way of Yahyā ibn Hamzah At-Tammār, who said: "I heard 'Atā' ibn Muslim mention: from Ismā'īl, with it."

Al-Bayhaqī said: "And this is related through another chain from Jasrah, and it contains weakness."

I say this is a weak chain, 'Atā' ibn Muslim Al-Khaffāf is weak [...] so in summary the hadīth is *'munkar'*, it is not authentic.

3 — [MM][MK] [BJ][SZ] He is Abū Bakr Muhammad ibn Ahmad ibn Al-Husayn Ash-Shāshī, Al-Imām, Al-'Allāmah. The Shaikh of the Shāfi'īs in Irāq in his time. He was born in 429 H and died in 507 H. He wrote a number of works, from them are: *Hilyatul-'Ulamā' bima'rifati madhāhibil-Fuqahā'*, and *Ash-Shāfī-Sharh Mukhtasaril-Muzanī*, and *Al-'Umdah* — on the details of the Shāfi'ī Fiqh.

Refer to *Siyar A'lāmin-Nubalā'* (19/393).

And from that is the purity of his (ﷺ) hair, as is established in *Sahīh Muslim* from Anas that when he (ﷺ) had his head shaved during his Hajj he commanded Abū Talhah to distribute his hair amongst the people.[1]

However, this will only be something specific to him if we judge the hair of others to be impure if it is cut from the person during his lifetime, and this is one of the two sayings.

Then as for the hadīth which Ibn 'Adiyy reported,[2] as a narration of Ibn Fudayk: from Buryah ibn 'Umar ibn Safīnah: from his father: from his grandfather who said: "The Prophet (ﷺ) was cupped, then he said to me: *'Take this blood and bury it away from animals and birds'* — or he said: *'people and animals.'*"

Ibn Abī Fudayk doubted. He said: "So I went off with it and I drank it."

He said: "Then he asked me, so I told him that I had drunk it, so he laughed."

Then it is a weak hadīth because of the condition of Buryah, whose name is Ibrāhīm, for he is very weak.

Al-Bayhaqī reported it through another chain,[3] saying: "Abul-Hasan ibn 'Abdān related to us: Ahmad ibn 'Ubayd related to us: Muhammad ibn Ghālib narrated to us: Mūsā ibn Ismā'īl (Abū Salamah) narrated to us:

---

1 — [SH] *Sahīh Muslim* (no. 1305/326).

2 — [SH] In *Al-Kāmil fid-Du'afā'* (2/496-497 & 5/1709), and by way of him by Al-Bayhaqī in *As-Sunanul-Kubrā* (7/67), and Abū Ya'lā in his *Musnad* [...] and Al-Bukhārī said in *At-Tārīkhul-Kabīr* (2/149): "Buryah ibn 'Umar ibn Safīnah — the mawlā of the Prophet (ﷺ): from his father. Ibn Abī Fudayk heard from him. Its chain is unknown."

And Al-Būsayrī said: "This is an unknown chain since some of its narrators are unknown."

I say: It is just as he said, since Ibrāhīm ibn 'Umar is unknown with regard to his condition, as occurs in *At-Taqrīb*.

3 — For more detail regarding the authenticity of this narration, see **Endnote 165 on page 564**.

Hunayd ibn Qāsim narrated to us: I heard ʿĀmir ibn ʿAbdillāh ibn Az-Zubayr narrate from his father, who said:

"The Prophet (ﷺ) was cupped, and he gave me his blood and said: *'Go and bury it so that no wild beast, or dog, or human should find it.'*"

He said: "So I went off to somewhere private and I drank it. Then I came to him, and he said: *'What have you done?'* I said: *'I have done what you commanded me to.'* He said: *'I do not think except that you have drunk it.'*"

"I said: *'Yes.'* He said: *'What will my nation experience from you?!'*"

This is a weak chain of narration because of the condition of Hunayd ibn Al-Qāsim Al-Asadī Al-Kūfī, because he is abandoned in hadīth, and he was declared a liar by Yahyā ibn Maʿīn.

However, Al-Bayhaqī said: "That is related through another chain, from Asmāʾ bint Abī Bakr and Salmān Al-Fārisī regarding Ibn Az-Zubayr drinking his (ﷺ) blood."[1]

I say: Therefore, some of our companions have said that the rest of his (ﷺ) bodily excretions are pure: even urine and excrement — [and they are] upon a strange saying.

They use as a witness for that what Al-Bayhaqī reported[2] from Abū Nasr ibn Qatādah: Abul-Hasan Muhammad ibn Ahmad ibn Hāmid Al-ʿAttār narrated to us: Ahmad ibn Al-Hasan ibn ʿAbdil-Jabbār narrated to us: Yahyā ibn Maʿīn narrated to us: Hajjāj narrated to us: from Ibn Juraij: Hukaymah bint Umaymah related to me: from Umaymah (her mother): that the Prophet (ﷺ) used to urinate in a wooden pot, and then

---

1 — The authenticity of this is questionable. See **Endnote 166 on page 564** for more detail.

2 — [BJ] [SZ] It is *daʿīf* with this full wording. It was reported by At-Tabarānī (24/189/ no. 477) and Al-Bayhaqī (7/67), and its chain contains Hukaymah, and she is unknown. It has a witness from a hadīth of Umm Ayman — reported by At-Tabarānī (25/89/ no. 230), Abū Nuʿaym in *Al-Hilyah* (2/67), and Al-Hākim in *Al-Mustadrak* (4/63-64). Al-Haythamī said in *Majmaʿuz-Zawāʾid* (8/271): "Abū Mālik is abandoned and Nubayh did not meet Umm Ayman."

[SH] In summary the hadīth is not authentic at all.

place it beneath his bed. (So he urinated in it and it was placed beneath his bed.)[1]

So he came, and he wanted it, and he found that the pot was empty. So he said to a woman (who was called Barakah) who used to serve him, belonging to Umm Ayman — she came with her from the land of Abyssinia: "Where is the urine which was in the pot?"

She said: "I drank it, O Messenger of Allāh!"

That is how he reported it, and it is an unknown chain of narration. So Abū Dāwūd and An-Nasā'ī reported it[2] as a hadīth of Hajjāj ibn Muhammad Al-A'war: from Ibn Juraij, and it does not contain the story concerning Barakah.

The Book of the Prayer

So from that is the Duhā (Forenoon Prayer) and the Witr (Prayer), because of what was reported by Imām Ahmad in his *Musnad* and by Al-Bayhaqī, from a hadīth of Abū Janāb Al-Kalbī (whose name was Yahyā ibn Abī Hayyah): from 'Ikrimah: from Ibn 'Abbās (رَضِيَٱللَّهُعَنْهُمَا): from the Prophet (صَلَّىٱللَّهُعَلَيْهِوَسَلَّمَ) that he said: "There are three matters which are obligatory upon me, and which are supererogatory for you: the Sacrifice (An-Nahr), the Witr (Prayer), and the two rak'ahs of the Duhā (Prayer)."[3]

The majority of the companions[4] rely upon this hadīth regarding these three, and therefore say that they were obligatory.

---

1 — BJ SZ What occurs between the brackets is missing in the "Ārif Hikmah Library' manuscript.

2 — BJ SZ Reported by Abū Dāwūd (no. 24), An-Nasā'ī (no. 32), Ibn Hibbān (no. 1426), and Al-Hākim (1/67), and its chain contains Hukaymah, and she is unknown; and it has a witness from a hadīth of 'Ā'ishah who said: *"He called for the bowl..."* — reported by Al-Bukhārī (no. 2741 & 4459) and Muslim (no. 1636) — without the drinking.

3 — This narration is very weak and rejected for a multitude of reasons, which are laid out in Endnote 167 on page 565.

4 — DB i.e. the Shāfi'ī scholars.

Shaikh Taqiyyuddīn Ibnus-Salāh (رَحِمَهُ ٱللَّهُ) said: "The companions hesitate concerning whether using the tooth-stick was obligatory upon him, but they clearly state that the Duhā (Prayer), the Adhā Sacrifice, and the Witr (Prayer) were obligatory upon him.

This is despite the fact that its basis is the hadīth whose weakness we have mentioned. So if they had reversed the matter and stated clearly the obligation of the tooth-stick upon him, and hesitated regarding the other three, then this would have been closer. The basis for hesitancy about that is that it is weak, because of the weakness of the narration of Abū Janāb Al-Kalbī; so there is disagreement between the imāms of hadīth concerning his weakness, and some of them declare him reliable — and Allāh knows best."

I say: The majority of the imāms of *'jarh and taʿdīl'* (the science of criticism of narrators and declaration of their reliability) hold that he was weak.

And Shaikh Abū Zakariyyā An-Nawawī quoted some hesitancy concerning the three aforementioned matters from the companions, and that some of them held that they were recommended matters for him (صَلَّى ٱللَّهُ عَلَيْهِ وَسَلَّمَ).

And this saying is more correct due to a number of reasons:

Firstly — The basis for that saying was this hadīth, and you have come to know that it is weak; and it has been related through another chain from a hadīth of Mandal ibn ʿAlī Al-ʿAnzī,[1] and he is worse in condition than Abū Janāb.

Secondly — Regarding the Witr, then it is established in the two *Sahīhs*[2] from Ibn ʿUmar: that he (صَلَّى ٱللَّهُ عَلَيْهِ وَسَلَّمَ) used to pray it upon the riding-beast.

So this is from our proofs against the Hanafīs that it is not obligatory, since if it were obligatory he would not have performed it upon the riding

1 — This narration is very weak — refer to Endnote 168 on page 566 for more detail.

2 — SH Reported by Al-Bukhārī (no. 999) and Muslim (no. 700).

beast. So this shows that it was with regard to him a recommended act, and Allāh knows best.

As for the Duhā (Forenoon Prayer) then there occurs in the *Sahīh*,[1] from 'Ā'ishah (رَضِيَ اللَّهُ عَنْهَا) that he had not used to pray the Duhā Prayer except when he returned from travelling.

So if it had been obligatory upon him then his being constant upon it would be a matter too well known to deny.

Then what occurs in this hadīth, and in the other hadīth: ***that he used to pray it as two rak'ahs, and then add whatever Allāh wished,***[2] then this is taken to mean that he would pray it in that manner when he returned from travelling, in order to harmonize between the two hadīths; and Allāh knows best.

AN ISSUE:

And so for the Night-Prayer (Qiyāmul-Layl), and it is the Tahajjud — and it is (other than)[3] the Witr Prayer (and An-Nasā'ī)[4] reported from Ibn 'Umar: that Allāh's Messenger (صَلَّى اللَّهُ عَلَيْهِ وَسَلَّمَ) said: *"The Witr is a single rak'ah at the end of the night"*[5] — and its chain of narration is good.

(So when that is confirmed, then you should know that)[6] the great majority of the companions[7] said the Tahajjud was obligatory (wājib) upon him, and they hold onto His Saying, the Most High:

وَمِنَ اللَّيْلِ فَتَهَجَّدْ بِهِ نَافِلَةً لَّكَ عَسَىٰ أَن يَبْعَثَكَ رَبُّكَ مَقَامًا مَّحْمُودًا

---

1 — [BJ][SZ] Reported by Muslim (no. 717).

2 — Refer to **Endnote 169 on page 567** for the narrations regarding the Duhā prayer.

3 — [BJ][SZ][SH] And addition from the "Ārif Hikmah Library' manuscript.

4 — [BJ][SZ][SH] And addition from the "Ārif Hikmah Library' manuscript.

5 — [BJ][SZ] Reported by Muslim (no. 752), An-Nasā'ī (no. 1688), and Ahmad (5/38/ no. 2836 & 5/480/no. 4878).

6 — [BJ][SZ][SH] What occurs between the brackets is missing in the 'Sulaymāniyyah Library' (no. 3339) manuscript.

7 — [DB] i.e. the Shāfi'ī scholars.

> MEANING: "And during the night awaken, and pray reciting the Qur'ān, as an extra Prayer for you. Your Lord will certainly raise you to a praiseworthy station." — **Sūrah Al-Isrā' (17): 79**

'Atiyyah ibn Sa'd Al-'Awfī said: from Ibn 'Abbās, regarding His Saying — He the Most High:

> نَافِلَةً لَّكَ
>
> MEANING: 'As an extra Prayer for you':

"'*Extra*' (*nāfilah*) — meaning that it was something particular to the Prophet (ﷺ). He was commanded with the Night Prayer, so it was written as a duty upon him."[1]

And 'Urwah said: from 'Ā'ishah (رَضِيَ ٱللَّهُ عَنْهَا): "When Allāh's Messenger (ﷺ) prayed he would stand for so long that his feet would crack open. So 'Ā'ishah said: *'O Messenger of Allāh! You do this when Allāh has forgiven for you all your earlier and later sins?!'*

He said:

> 'O 'Ā'ishah! Should I not be a thankful servant?!'"

Reported by Muslim[2] from Hārūn ibn Ma'rūf: from 'Abdullāh ibn Wahb: from Abū Sakhr: from Ibn Qusayt: from 'Urwah, with it.

And the two of them reported it[3] through another chain from Al-Mughīrah ibn Shu'bah.

---

1 — Refer to Endnote 170 on page 567 for detail regarding the authenticity of this narration.

2 — [BJ][SZ] Reported by Muslim (no. 2829); and reported by Al-Bukhārī (no. 4837), by way of Abul-Aswad: from 'Urwah: from 'Ā'ishah.

3 — [BJ][SZ] *Sahīh Al-Bukhārī* (no. 1130 & 4836), and Muslim (no. 2819).

And Al-Bayhaqī reported,[1] as a hadīth of Mūsā ibn ʿAbdir-Rahmān As-Sanʿānī: from Hishām ibn ʿUrwah: from his father: from ʿĀʾishah that she said: "Allāh's Messenger (ﷺ) said:

> 'Three are obligatory duties upon me, and they are sunnah for you: the Witr, the tooth-stick, and the Night-Prayer (Qiyāmul-Layl).'"

Then he said: "This narrator Mūsā ibn ʿAbdir-Rahmān is very weak, and no chain of narration is established concerning this, and Allāh knows best."

And Ash-Shaikh Abū Hāmid[2] (رَحِمَهُ ٱللَّهُ) quoted from Imām Abū ʿAbdillāh Ash-Shāfiʿī (رَحِمَهُ ٱللَّهُ) that having to perform the Night Prayer was abrogated for him (ﷺ), just as it was abrogated for the Ummah (nation), since it was obligatory in the beginning of Islām upon the whole nation.

I say: The hadīth which he indicated was reported by Muslim[3] as a hadīth of Hishām ibn Saʿd: that he entered upon ʿĀʾishah (the Mother of the Believers),[4] and said: "'O Mother of the Believers! Inform me about the Night-Prayer of Allāh's Messenger (ﷺ).'

She said: 'Do you not recite:

> يَا أَيُّهَا الْمُدَّثِّرُ
>
> MEANING: "O you wrapped in garments."?!'

I said: 'Yes indeed!'

---

1 — BJ SZ It is *daʿīf jiddan*. Reported by At-Tabarānī in *Al-Awsat* (6/155/no. 3525) and Al-Bayhaqī in his *Sunan* (7/39). Al-Haythamī said in *Al-Majmaʿ* (8/264): "It contains Mūsā ibn ʿAbdir-Rahmān As-Sanʿānī who was a liar."

2 — SH He is Muhammad ibn Muhammad ibn Ahmad At-Tūsī Al-Ghazzālī. He wrote widely circulated works, from the most famous of them is *Ihyāʾ ʿUlūmid-Dīn*; and the people of knowledge have spoken in criticism of him, and of his books, and they warned against him. He died in 505 H.

3 — BJ SZ (no. 746)

4 — SH An addition from the 'Sulaymāniyyah Library' manuscript (no. 59), and the 'Ārif Hikmah Library' manuscript.

She said: 'Then Allāh made the standing in the Night-Prayer obligatory at the beginning of this Sūrah, so Allāh's Messenger (صَلَّى ٱللَّهُ عَلَيْهِ وَسَلَّمَ) and his Companions prayed the Night-Prayer for one year, to the extent that their feet would split open; and Allāh kept back its concluding part for twelve months, in heaven. Then Allāh sent down the alleviation at the end of this Sūrah, so the Night-Prayer became superogatory after it had been an obligation.'"

And Ash-Shāfi'ī indicated that this be used as a proof to show abrogation, and also His Saying — He the Most High:

> وَمِنَ ٱلَّيْلِ فَتَهَجَّدْ بِهِۦ نَافِلَةً لَّكَ
>
> MEANING: "And during the night awaken and pray, reciting the Qur'ān, as an extra Prayer for you." — **Sūrah Al-Isrā' (17): 79**

He said: "So he informed him that the Night-Prayer was a supererogatory act, not an obligation; and Allāh (the Perfect and Most High) knows best."

AN ISSUE:

And he missed the performance of two rak'ahs, after the Zuhr Prayer, so he prayed them after the 'Asr Prayer — and he established that as his practice; and he used to perform it continuously, as is established in the *Sahīh*.[1]

So this was something particular to him (صَلَّى ٱللَّهُ عَلَيْهِ وَسَلَّمَ), in the most correct of the two sayings with our companions.

---

1 — [SH] Reported by Al-Bukhārī in his *Sahīh* (nos. 590, 591, 592, & 593), and Muslim in his *Sahīh* (nos. 835/299, 300 & 301), as a hadīth of Ummul-Mu'minīn 'Ā'ishah (رَضِيَ ٱللَّهُ عَنْهَا).

Or it is said: Rather it is for others to do so also, if this happens to a person: that he can then continue to pray them, and Allāh (the Most High) knows best.[1]

AN ISSUE:

And his praying supererogatory Prayer sitting was just like his praying it while standing; even without excuse, contrary to the case with others, since others besides him will receive only half the reward. They use as evidence for that what Muslim reported[2] from 'Abdullāh ibn 'Amr (رَضِيَ اللَّهُ عَنْهُمَا) who said: "It was narrated to me that Allāh's Messenger (صَلَّى اللَّهُ عَلَيْهِ وَسَلَّمَ) said: 'The Prayer of a man sitting is half of the Prayer.'

So then I came to him and found him praying whilst sitting, so I put my hands upon my head, and he said: 'What is wrong with you, O 'Abdullāh ibn 'Amr?'

So I said: 'It was narrated to me, O Messenger of Allāh, that you said: *"The Prayer of a man sitting is half of the Prayer."* But you are praying sitting!'

So he said: 'Yes indeed! But I am not like one of you.'"

---

1 — [SH] I say: This is what is correct, and is what is indicated in the authentic Sunnah and the narrations from the Companions. It also gathers the evidences, so that we are able to implement them, and not neglect any of them. And refer, if you wish to: *Fat-hul-Bārī* (2/63-66), *As-Sahīhah* (nos. 200, 314, & 2920), and my book *Al-Manāhiyyush-Shar'iyyah* (1/319-331).

2 — [BJ][SZ] (no. 735)

AN ISSUE:

336 And it was binding upon a person who was praying to respond if Allāh's Messenger (صَلَّى ٱللَّٰهُ عَلَيْهِ وَسَلَّمَ) called him, because of the hadīth of Abū Sa'īd ibn Al-Mu'allā occurring in *Sahīh Al-Bukhārī*.[1]

And this was not the case within anyone else besides him — O Allāh! — except for what Al-Awzā'ī related from his Shaikh, Makhūl: that he used to declare it obligatory to respond to one's mother whilst praying, because of the hadīth of Juraij the hermit: that his mother called him whilst he was standing in Prayer. So he said: "O Allāh! My mother and my Prayer!"

Then he continued praying. Then it happened for the second time, and he did the same. Then it happened for the third time, so she supplicated against him, and Allāh answered her supplication about him.

So his story occurred as is mentioned in the *Sahīh* of Al-Bukhārī[2] and elsewhere; and it is related in the context of affirmation and it was not criticized.

Whereas the great majority hold that this is not obligatory; indeed nothing from the speech of the people is correct in the Prayer, because of the authentic hadīth.[3]

---

1 — [BJ][SZ] Reported by Al-Bukhārī (no. 4474) from Abū Sa'īd ibn Al-Mu'allā who said: "I was praying in the mosque and Allāh's Messenger (صَلَّى ٱللَّٰهُ عَلَيْهِ وَسَلَّمَ) called me, and I did not respond. Then I said: 'O Messenger of Allāh! I was praying.' So he said: 'Did Allāh not say:

> اسْتَجِيبُوا لِلَّهِ وَلِلرَّسُولِ إِذَا دَعَاكُمْ
>
> MEANING: "Respond to Allāh, and to His Messenger when he calls you."'

2 — [BJ][SZ] Reported by Al-Bukhārī (nos. 2482 & 3436) and Muslim (no. 2550), as a hadīth of Abū Hurairah (رَضِيَ ٱللَّٰهُ عَنْهُ).

3 — [BJ][SZ] Reported by Muslim (no. 537) as a hadīth of Mu'āwiyah ibn Al-Hakam As-Sulamī (رَضِيَ ٱللَّٰهُ عَنْهُ), and it contains the wording: "Nothing from the speech of the people is correct in the Prayer, rather it is to be *'tasbīh'*, *'takbīr'*, and recitation of the Qur'ān."

O Allāh! Except for what Imām Ahmad permitted with regard to addressing the imām concerning parts of the Prayer that he has missed, because of the hadīth of Dhul-Yadayn.[1] So Allāh knows best.

AN ISSUE:

And he had not used to pray [the Funeral Prayer] over a person who had a debt upon him which would not be repaid, as reported by Al-Bukhārī in his *Sahīh*, through a chain of narration containing only three narrators, as a hadīth of Salamah ibn Al-Akwaʿ.[2]

However, our companions disagree about whether this was something forbidden for him to do, or disliked; upon two sayings. Then this was abrogated by his saying: "Whoever leaves behind a debt, or needy dependants, then that is upon me."[3]

So it is said: He used to pay it off for him as an obligation upon him, or it said: as an act of generosity.

And from that is that when he made supplication for the occupants of the graves, then Allāh filled them with light for their occupants, through the blessing resulting from his supplication (may Allāh extol and grant him peace and security) as is established in *Sahīh Muslim* from ʿĀʾishah (رَضِيَ اللَّهُ عَنْهَا).[4]

---

1 — [BJ][SZ] Reported by Al-Bukhārī (nos. 482, 714, & 1227) and Muslim (no. 573), as a hadīth of Abū Hurairah (رَضِيَ اللَّهُ عَنْهُ).

2 — [SH] Reported by Al-Bukhārī (no. 2289, 2295).

3 — [BJ][SZ] Reported by Al-Bukhārī (nos. 2298, 2398, & 2399), and Muslim (no. 1619), from Abū Hurairah (رَضِيَ اللَّهُ عَنْهُ); and reported by Muslim (no. 867) from Jābir (رَضِيَ اللَّهُ عَنْهُ).

4 — [BJ][SZ][SH] The hadīth of ʿĀʾishah occurs in *Sahīh Muslim* (no. 974), with the command for him to seek forgiveness for the occupant of the graveyard of Baqīʿ. As for the hadīth mentioned by the author, then it is a hadīth of Abū Hurairah (رَضِيَ اللَّهُ عَنْهُ) reported by Muslim (no. 956), with the story of his (صَلَّى اللَّهُ عَلَيْهِ وَسَلَّمَ) praying the Funeral Prayer over the woman who used to sweep the mosque, and at its end he (صَلَّى اللَّهُ عَلَيْهِ وَسَلَّمَ) said: "These graves are filled with darkness upon their occupants, but Allāh (the Mighty and Majestic) will illuminate them through my Prayer upon them."

And from that is that he passed by two graves, and said:

338 > "They are certainly being punished, and they are not being punished for something major."

Then he took a fresh date-palm branch and split it into two halves, and he placed a half on each grave. Then he said:

> "Perhaps Allāh will lighten their punishment for as long as these two do not wither."

The two of them reported it from Ibn ʿAbbās.[1]

AN ISSUE:

And from that is that he (صَلَّىٱللَّهُعَلَيْهِوَسَلَّمَ) experienced severe pain in his illness, so ʿAbdullāh ibn Masʿūd entered upon him and said: "O Messenger of Allāh! You are experiencing severe pain." So he said:

> "Indeed! I feel the pain that is felt by two men from amongst you."

I said: "Is it because there is double the reward for you?"

He said: "Yes." The two Shaikhs reported it.[2]

AN ISSUE:

He (صَلَّىٱللَّهُعَلَيْهِوَسَلَّمَ) did not die until Allāh (the Most High) had given him a choice between his being given extended life followed by Paradise; or, if he wished, to meet Allāh quickly. So he chose what is with Allāh over this world; and this is established in the two *Sahīhs* from ʿĀʾishah (رَضِيَٱللَّهُعَنْهَا).[3]

---

1 — Imām Al-Albānī explains in detail why this action of placing moist vegetation on the graves was limited to the Messenger (صَلَّىٱللَّهُعَلَيْهِوَسَلَّمَ), and why this narration does not prove that we should likewise place leaves on the graves. Refer to this essay in **Endnote 171 on page 568**.

2 — [BJ][SZ] Reported by Al-Bukhārī (no. 5647, 5648, & 5660) and Muslim (no. 2571).

3 — [BJ][SZ][SH] Al-Bukhārī (no. 4435) and Muslim (no. 244/86 and 87).

AN ISSUE:

And from that is that Allāh made it forbidden for the earth to devour the bodies of the Prophets. The proof for that is the hadīth of Shaddād ibn Aws, and it occurs in the *Sunan*.[1]

The Book of Zakāt

AN ISSUE:

It was forbidden for him to consume charity, whether it was obligatory or optional (charity), because of his (صَلَّى ٱللَّهُ عَلَيْهِ وَسَلَّمَ) saying: "Charity is not permissible for Muhammad, or for the family of Muhammad."[2]

And Muslim reported[3] from Abū Hurairah (رَضِيَ ٱللَّهُ عَنْهُ): *"That Allāh's Messenger (صَلَّى ٱللَّهُ عَلَيْهِ وَسَلَّمَ) would consume something given as a gift, but he would not consume charity"* — and this is general.

And Ash-Shāfi'ī has a saying regarding optional charity: that it is permissible for him. This was quoted by Shaikh Abū Hāmid[4] and Al-Qaffāl.[5]

---

1 — This narration has been declared as *'sahīh'* by a number of the scholars. See **Endnote 172 on page 573** for more detail.

2 — [SH] The ahādīth showing the prohibition of charity upon him (صَلَّى ٱللَّهُ عَلَيْهِ وَسَلَّمَ) are established in the two *Sahīhs* and elsewhere, from a group of the Companions; and this wording was reported by Muslim in his *Sahīh* (no. 1072), as a hadīth of 'Abdul-Muttalib ibn Rabī'ah ibn Al-Hārith (رَضِيَ ٱللَّهُ عَنْهُ).

3 — [BJ][SZ] (no. 1077)

4 — [SH] He is Al-Ustādh Abū Hāmid Ahmad ibn Abī Tāhir Muhammad ibn Ahmad Al-Isfarāyīnī, the Shaikh of the Shāfi'īs in Baghdad.

He excelled in the madh-hab and outstripped the earlier ones. He died in the year 406 H.

5 — [SH] He is the Shaikh of the Shāfi'īs, Abū Bakr 'Abdullāh ibn Ahmad ibn 'Abdillāh, Al-Marwazī, Al-Khurāsānī. He excelled in the profession of locksmithing. Then at the age of thirty, he noticed that he had outstanding intelligence, and he came to love Fiqh. So he studied it until he excelled in it, and came to be pointed out as an exemplary model regarding it. He died in the year 417 H.

Shaikh Abū ʿAmr ibn As-Salāh said: This saying was unknown to Imāmul-Haramayn and Al-Ghazzālī, and what is correct is the first (saying).

As for the mistaken idea of some of the bedouins, after his (صَلَّى ٱللَّٰهُ عَلَيْهِ وَسَلَّمَ) passing away, that the Zakāt was not to be handed over except to him (صَلَّى ٱللَّٰهُ عَلَيْهِ وَسَلَّمَ), and their withholding from handing it over to As-Siddīq until he fought them for it, though they eventually submitted to the truth and handed over the Zakāt, then the imāms have answered that in their books with a number of answers; and we have spoken about it in detail elsewhere.[1]

The Book of Fasting

Continuous fasting (*Al-Wisāl*) was permissible for him. Therefore, when he forbade his nation from continuous fasting they said: "But you fast continuously?!"

He said:

> "I am not like one of you, I spend the night in the presence of my Lord: He feeds me and gives me drink."

The two of them reported it.[2]

So following him upon that was prevented by its being made specific to him, because of the fact that Allāh (the Most High) fed him and gave him drink; and they disagree: was this physical food and drink, or spiritual? They have two sayings, and what is correct is that they were spiritual (food and drink), otherwise it would not have actually been continuous fasting.

---

1 — [BJ][SZ] Refer to *Tafsīr Ibn Kathīr*: Sūrah At-Tawbah (9): verse 103.

2 — [BJ][SZ] Reported by Al-Bukhārī (no. 1961) and Muslim (no. 1104), as a hadīth of Anas; and by Al-Bukhārī (no. 1964) and Muslim (no. 1105) from ʿĀʾishah; and by Al-Bukhārī (no. 1965) and Muslim (no. 1103) from Abū Hurairah.

AN ISSUE:

And he used to kiss whilst he was fasting.[1] So it is said: This was something specific to him. And is it disliked for other than him? Or forbidden? Or permissible? Or does it nullify the fast of one who does it, as Ibn Qutaybah said? Or is it recommended for him? Or is a distinction to be made between an old man and a youth? The scholars have different sayings, and presentation of them is for another place.[2]

AN ISSUE:

Some of our companions said: If he began a supererogatory act, it became binding upon him to complete it; and this is weak.[3] It is rebutted by the hadīth, which occurs in *Sahīh Muslim* from ʿĀʾishah (رَضِيَ اللَّهُ عَنْهَا) that Allāh's Messenger (صَلَّى اللَّهُ عَلَيْهِ وَسَلَّمَ) entered upon her, so she said: "O Messenger of Allāh! Here is some *'hays'*."[4]

So he said: *"Show it to me, for I began the day fasting"* — and he ate from it.[5]

The Book of Hajj

Some of our companions said: it was obligatory upon him, if he saw something which pleased him to say: 'لَبَّيـكَ إِنَّ العَيـشَ عَيـش الآخِـرَة' (*'Here I am at*

---

1 — [BJ][SZ] Reported by Al-Bukhārī (nos. 1927 & 1928) and Muslim (no. 1106), as a hadīth of ʿĀʾishah; and reported by Al-Bukhārī (no. 322 & 1929) and Muslim (no. 1108), from Umm Salamah, and it contains a proof that it is not something specific.

2 — [BJ][SZ] The correct saying in this matter is that it is not specific; rather, it is permissible for the person who can keep a hold of his desires and prevent himself from having intercourse.

3 — [BJ][SZ] There is written in the margin of the 'Sulaymāniyyah Library' (no. 3339) manuscript: "A marginal note in the handwriting of the author: *'It was likewise declared weak by An-Nawawī.'*"

4 — [DB] Ibnul-Athīr said in *An-Nihāyah fī Gharībil-Hadīth*: "It is a food made of dates, dried curd, and ghee; and sometimes flour or breadcrumbs are used in place of dried curd."

5 — [BJ][SZ] Reported by Muslim (no. 1154).

Your service! Indeed the true life is the life of the Hereafter'), and it is as if his basis for that is what Al-Bukhārī reported from Sahl ibn Sa'd who said: "We were with Allāh's Messenger (صَلَّى ٱللَّهُ عَلَيْهِ وَسَلَّمَ) on the day of the Trench. He was digging and we were carrying, so he looked upon us and said:

> 'There is no true life except the life of the Hereafter, so forgive the Ansār and the Muhājirs.'"[1]

And Ash-Shāfi'ī said[2]: Sa'īd[3] related to us: from Ibn Juraij: Humayd Al-A'raj related to us: from Mujāhid, that he said: Allāh's Messenger (صَلَّى ٱللَّهُ عَلَيْهِ وَسَلَّمَ) used to manifest the *talbiyah*:

> لَبَّيْكَ اللَّهُمَّ لَبَّيْكَ، لَبَّيْكَ لاَ شَرِيكَ لَكَ لَبَّيْكَ، إِنَّ الْحَمْدَ، وَالنِّعْمَةَ، لَكَ وَالْمُلْكَ، لاَ شَرِيكَ لَكَ
>
> "Here I am, answering Your call, O Allāh! Here I am answering Your call. Here I am answering Your call, You have no partner, here I am answering Your call. All praise is for You, all favours are from You, and Sovereignty is Yours. You have no partner."

Until one day, when the people were departing from him, it is as if he became pleased at his state, so he added to it: ' لَبَّيْكَ إِنَّ العَيْشَ عَيْشُ الآخِرَة ' — *'Here I am at Your service! Indeed the true life is the life of the Hereafter'*.

---

1 — (BJ)(SZ) Reported by Al-Bukhārī (nos. 3797 & 4098) and Muslim (no. 1804), as a hadīth of Sahl ibn Sa'd; and by Al-Bukhārī (no. 3795) and Muslim (no. 1805), from Anas.

2 — (SH)(BJ)(SZ) In his *Musnad* (no. 792 of its arrangement), and *Al-Umm* (2/156); and from him by Al-Bayhaqī in *As-Sunanul-Kubrā* (7/48), and in *Ma'rifatus-Sunan wal-Āthār* (4/4-5/2813). I say: And this is a weak chain of narration because it is *'mursal'*.

And the *talbiyah* of the Prophet (صَلَّى ٱللَّهُ عَلَيْهِ وَسَلَّمَ) is established in the two *Sahīhs* and the *Sunan*, and elsewhere, without the final addition. It is reported from Ibn 'Umar by Al-Bukhārī (no. 1549) and Muslim (no. 1184), and reported from 'Ā'ishah by Al-Bukhārī (no. 1550).

3 — (SH)(BJ)(SZ) In the 'Sulaymāniyyah Library' manuscript (no. 3339) there occurs "*Sufyān*", and it is a mistake; and what is affirmed here is what is correct, and conforms to what occurs in the *Musnad* of Ash-Shāfi'ī, and in *Al-Umm*; and he is Sa'īd ibn Sālim Al-Qaddāh.

Ibn Juraij said: "And I think that was on the day of ʿArafah."

I say: Its being an obligation is not apparent from these two hadīth. The most that could be said is that its like is recommended, and the same has been said regarding the rest of the people.

And the hadīth of Mujāhid is *'mursal'*, and the saying of Ibn Juraij is just his own saying, and Allāh knows best.

AN ISSUE:

Makkah was rendered lawful for him for a single day, so he entered it without being in a state of ihrām; and about twenty of its inhabitants were killed that day.

Then, was it conquered by force, or in accordance with a peace agreement? Ash-Shāfiʿī had two sayings in that regard, each one being supported by some people.

So, in summary, that was something particular to him, just as he (صَلَّى ٱللَّهُ عَلَيْهِ وَسَلَّمَ) mentioned in his address on the morning of that day, when he said:

> "If anyone claims to have a concession based upon the fighting of Allāh's Messenger (صَلَّى ٱللَّهُ عَلَيْهِ وَسَلَّمَ) in it, then say: *'Allāh gave permission to His Messenger but He did not give permission to you'*"[1] — and the hadīth is well known.

AN ISSUE:

Speech has already preceded about the hadīth which would mean that the sacrifice was obligatory upon him, and that it is *'daʿīf'* (weak). [2]

The Book of Foods

And with regard to foods:

---

1 — BJ SZ Reported by Al-Bukhārī (nos. 104, 1832, & 4295) and Muslim (no. 1354), as a hadīth of Abū Shuraih Al-Khuzāʿī, Al-Kaʿbī (رَضِيَ ٱللَّهُ عَنْهُ).

2 — DB It preceded on p. 208.

Some of our companions have said: It was forbidden for him to eat onions, garlic, and leeks. The basis for this is what the two of them reported from Jābir that a pot containing green vegetables was brought to Allāh's Messenger (صَلَّى ٱللَّٰهُ عَلَيْهِ وَسَلَّمَ), and he found that it gave off an odour. So he said to his Companions: "Eat! For I converse with those you do not converse with."[1]

However, a problem for the one who states this[2] is what At-Tirmidhī quoted from ʿAlī and Sharīk ibn Hanbal: that they held that only uncooked onions and garlic were forbidden.[3]

However, what is the correct and sound position is that it was not forbidden for him; rather, eating that was disliked for him. The proof for this is what Muslim reported[4] from Abū Ayyūb: that he placed some food for Allāh's Messenger (صَلَّى ٱللَّٰهُ عَلَيْهِ وَسَلَّمَ) which contained garlic, so he refused it and did not eat from it. So he said to him: "Is it forbidden?"

So he said: "No, however I dislike it."

So he said: "Then I dislike that which you dislike."

Ash-Shaikh Abū ʿAmr said: "And this negates the saying that it was forbidden" — and Allāh (the Most High) knows best.

AN ISSUE:

The same was the case with the spiny-tailed lizard (*dabb*). He (صَلَّى ٱللَّٰهُ عَلَيْهِ وَسَلَّمَ) said: *"I do not eat it, and I do not declare it to be forbidden."*[5] Meaning: for the people, and he only withheld from eating it because he had aversion to it.

---

1 — [BJ][SZ] Reported by Al-Bukhārī (no. 855) and Muslim (no. 564/73).

[DB] Al-Hāfidh Ibn Hajr said in *Fat-hul-Bārī* concerning his (صَلَّى ٱللَّٰهُ عَلَيْهِ وَسَلَّمَ) saying: "I converse with those whom you do not converse with," — "Meaning: the Angels..."

2 — [DB] i.e. that the prohibition was specific to the Prophet (صَلَّى ٱللَّٰهُ عَلَيْهِ وَسَلَّمَ).

3 — See **Endnote 173 on page 573** for more detail regarding the authenticity of this.

4 — [BJ][SZ] (no. 2053)

5 — [SH] Reported by Al-Bukhārī (no. 5536) and Muslim (no. 1943), as a hadīth of Ibn ʿUmar (رَضِيَ ٱللَّٰهُ عَنْهُمَا).

And Khālid said to him: "O Messenger of Allāh! Is it forbidden?" He said: "No, however it was not to be found in the land of my people, so I find myself having aversion to it."[1]

And it is likewise disliked for anyone to eat something which he dislikes, because of what Abū Dāwūd reported from him (ﷺ) that he said: "Destruction is caused by forcing oneself upon something disagreeable."[2]

And the physicians dislike that also because it leads to corruption of the person's constitution, and Allāh (the Most High) knows best.

AN ISSUE:

Al-Bukhārī reported from Abū Juhayfah that Allāh's Messenger (ﷺ) said: "I do not eat whilst reclining."[3]

Some of our companions said: "That was forbidden for him."

An-Nawawī said: "But what is correct is that it was disliked for him, not forbidden."

I say: So upon that basis, it will not remain something particular, since it is disliked for others to eat whilst reclining also. Whether reclining (*Al-Ittikā'*) is explained to mean lying down (as is immediately apparent to the minds of many — because of the harm which it may cause, just

1 — SH Reported by Al-Bukhārī (no. 5391) and Muslim (no. 1946), as a hadīth of Khālid ibn Al-Walīd (رَضِيَ اللَّهُ عَنْهُ).

2 — BJ SZ SH It is *'da'īf'*: Reported by Abū Dāwūd (no.3923), Ahmad (3/451) [and others] and by Al-Bayhaqī in *As-Sunanul-Kubrā* (9/347), and in *Shu'abul-Īmān* (2/125/1365), all of them by way of 'Abdur-Razzāq — and it occurs in his *Musannaf* (11/148/20163): Ma'mar related to us: from Yahyā ibn 'Abdillāh ibn Bahīr, who said: someone who heard Farwah ibn Musayk Al-Murādī (رَضِيَ اللَّهُ عَنْهُ) narrated to me (and he mentioned it) and in summary the hadīth is weak because of the fact that the man who is not named is therefore unknown, and because Yahyā ibn 'Abdillāh is unknown, and Allāh knows best.

3 — BJ SZ Reported by Al-Bukhārī (nos. 5398 & 5399).

as it is forbidden to drink whilst standing),[1] or whether it is explained to mean sitting cross-legged, as it was explained by Al-Khattābī[2] and others from the scholars of the language. And this [second one] is what is correct,[3] when it is carefully reflected upon and closely examined, because of the haughtiness and pride it involves, and Allāh (the Most High) knows best.[4]

AN ISSUE:

Abul-ʿAbbās ibn Al-Qāss said: "And he was forbidden to eat food to which he had not been invited. And Abud-Dardā' came unexpectedly to a meal he was eating, and he commanded him to eat; and that was something specific to him (صَلَّى ٱللَّهُ عَلَيْهِ وَسَلَّمَ)."

Al-Bayhaqī said: "I have not preserved [this hadīth of] the prohibition of food to which he was not invited through any chain [whose like is][5] established."

Then he brought the hadīth of Abū Dāwūd from the narration of Durust ibn Ziyād: from Abān ibn Tāriq: from Nāfiʿ: from Ibn ʿUmar, tracing it back to the Prophet (صَلَّى ٱللَّهُ عَلَيْهِ وَسَلَّمَ):

---

1 — [SH] As occurs in *Sahīh Muslim* (nos. 2024, 2025, & 2026), as a hadīth of Anas, and Abū Saʿīd Al-Khudrī, and Abū Hurairah (رَضِيَ ٱللَّهُ عَنْهُمْ); and for the Fiqh of this matter refer to the book of our Shaikh, Al-ʿAllāmah Al-Albānī (رَحِمَهُ ٱللَّهُ): *As-Silsilatus-Sahīhah* (nos. 175, 176, and 177).

2 — [BJ][SZ] As occurs in *Maʿālimus-Sunan*.

3 — [SH] Rather what is correct and clear is what is held by the majority [i.e. that it refers to reclining/leaning to one side whilst eating], and refer to *Mawsūʿatul-Manāhiyyish-Sharʿiyyah* (3/94-96).

4 — [SH] I say: Rather, the prohibition of eating whilst reclining is established from a saying of the Prophet (صَلَّى ٱللَّهُ عَلَيْهِ وَسَلَّمَ), in a hadīth narrated by Abud-Dardā', as occurs in *As-Sahīhah* (no. 3122), and refer to what our Shaikh, Al-Imām Al-Albānī (رَحِمَهُ ٱللَّهُ) wrote concerning the Fiqh of this matter in the same book.

5 — [SH] What occurs between brackets is an addition from the *Sunan* of Al-Bayhaqī, and the context demands it.

> "Whoever is invited and does not respond then he has disobeyed Allāh and His Messenger; and whoever enters without an invitation then he enters as a thief and departs as a raider."[1]

AN ISSUE:

They said: And it was obligatory upon anyone he requested some food from, and they had no other food besides it, to give it to him — in order to preserve the spirit of the Prophet (ﷺ), and to protect his noble soul with ones wealth and souls, because of His Saying (He the Most High):

> النَّبِيُّ أَوْلَىٰ بِالْمُؤْمِنِينَ مِنْ أَنفُسِهِ
>
> MEANING: "The Prophet has greater right over the Believers than their own selves." — **Sūrah Al-Ahzāb (33): 6**

I say: And this resembles the hadīth, which occurs in the two *Sahīhs*:

> "None of you truly believes until I am more beloved to him than his children, his parents, and the whole of mankind."[2]

AN ISSUE:

Al-Bukhārī reported from As-Saʿb ibn Jaththāmah, tracing it back to the Prophet (ﷺ): "There is to be no establishing private pasturing rights, except for Allāh and His Messenger."[3]

---

1 — BJ SZ It is *'daʿīf'*: Reported by Abū Dāwūd (no. 3741), and Abū Dāwūd said: *"Abān ibn Tāriq is unknown"*; and by Ibn ʿAdiyy in *Al-Kāmil* (1/381), and Al-Bayhaqī in his *Sunan* (7/68 & 765), and Al-Qudāʿī in *Musnadush-Shihāb* (1/314/ nos. 527 & 528), and Abān and Durust are both weak.

And it has a witness from a hadīth of ʿĀʾishah, reported by Ibn ʿAdiyy (7/2704) and Al-Bayhaqī (7/265), and its *isnād* contains an unknown narrator.

The first part of the hadīth is *'sahīh'*, being reported by Al-Bukhārī and Muslim.

2 — BJ SZ Reported by Al-Bukhārī (no. 15) and Muslim (no. 44), as a hadīth of Anas ibn Mālik (رَضِيَ ٱللَّهُ عَنْهُ).

3 — BJ SZ Reported by Al-Bukhārī (no. 2370).

Some of our companions said: It is something specific to him. And some of our companions said: Rather, it is permissible for others to do so for some benefit, just as Allāh's Messenger (صَلَّى ٱللَّٰهُ عَلَيْهِ وَسَلَّمَ) reserved An-Naqīʿ,[1] and ʿUmar (رَضِيَ ٱللَّٰهُ عَنْهُ) reserved Ash-Sharaf and Ar-Rabdhah,[2] except that whatever was reserved by Allāh's Messenger (صَلَّى ٱللَّٰهُ عَلَيْهِ وَسَلَّمَ) then it is not permitted to alter that at all.

And Regarding Gifts:

AN ISSUE:

He used to accept gifts, and he would give something in return for them.

That is established in the *Sahīh* from ʿĀʾishah (رَضِيَ ٱللَّٰهُ عَنْهَا),[3] and this is because of his hope that this would strengthen the attachment of the hearts of those who gave the gifts.

This is contrary to the case with others in authority besides him, since the hadīth is authentic in that regard stating that: "Gifts given to those employed in positions of authority are illegally acquired wealth."[4]

Since for them it will be like taking bribes, as they are open to that charge, and Allāh (the Most High) knows best.

---

1 — This narration was declared *'hasan'* by Imām Al-Albānī (refer to ENDNOTE 174 ON PAGE 574 for more detail). And An-Naqīʿ is a place twenty leagues (approx. seventy miles) from Al-Madīnah.

2 — [SH] Reported by Ibn Abī Shaybah in *Al-Musannaf* (7/304/3244): Yahyā ibn Saʿīd Al-Qattān narrated to us: from ʿUbaydullāh ibn ʿUmar: from Nāfiʿ: from Ibn ʿUmar: that ʿUmar reserved Ar-Rabdhah for the camels of Sadaqah.

I say: This is a chain of narration *'sahīh'* to the standard of the two Shaikhs. Al-Hāfidh Ibn Hajr said in *Al-Fat-h* (5/45): "And Ibn Abī Shaybah reported with a *'sahīh'* isnād from Nāfiʿ."

Ash-Sharaf is a place near to Al-Madīnah, and as for Ar-Rabdhah, then it is from the towns in the vicinity of Al-Madīnah.

3 — [BJ][SZ] Reported by Al-Bukhārī (no. 2585).

4 — Declared *'sahīh'* by Imām Al-Albānī — refer to ENDNOTE 175 ON PAGE 575 for more detail.

AN ISSUE:

Zakariyyā ibn ʿAdiyy said: Ibn Al-Mubārak narrated to us: from Al-Awzāʿī: from Ibn ʿAtāʾ; Zakariyyā said: I think that he was ʿUmar: from Ibn ʿAbbās, regarding His Saying (He the Most High):

> وَمَا آتَيْتُم مِّن رِّبًا لِّيَرْبُوَ فِي أَمْوَالِ النَّاسِ فَلَا يَرْبُو عِندَ اللَّهِ
>
> MEANING: "And whatever you give as a gift, hoping to gain more in return from people's property, then it will not increase with Allāh." — **Sūrah Ar-Rūm (30): 39**

He said: "It is the lawful increase (ribā): that he gives a gift, intending to receive more in return. So there is no reward for it, and no sin."

However, the Prophet (صَلَّى ٱللَّٰهُ عَلَيْهِ وَسَلَّمَ) was specifically forbidden from that:

> وَلَا تَمْنُن تَسْتَكْثِرُ
>
> MEANING: "And do not give something seeking an increase."[1] — **Sūrah Al-Muddaththir (74): 6**

Al-Bayhaqī reported it[2] from Al-Hākim and others: from Al-Asamm: from Muhammad ibn Is-hāq: from Zakariyyā; and it is a report which has a disconnected chain if ʿUmar ibn ʿAtāʾ is Ibn Warāz, and he was very weak; and if he is Ibn Abil-Khuwār, then Muslim used narrations from him, and he narrated from Ibn ʿAbbās. However, the matter is unclear.

And Regarding the Laws of Inheritance

AN ISSUE:

And it is that he (صَلَّى ٱللَّٰهُ عَلَيْهِ وَسَلَّمَ) was not inherited from, and that whatever he left behind was charity (*sadaqah*), as the two of them report in their

1 — See **Endnote 176 on page 575** for the statement of Ibn Kathīr regarding this affair.

2 — This narration is questionable, and you can refer to **Endnote 177 on page 576** for more detail.

Sahīhs: from Abū Bakr (رَضِيَ ٱللَّهُ عَنْهُ), that Fātimah (رَضِيَ ٱللَّهُ عَنْهَا) asked him for her share of inheritance from her father, so he said:

> "I heard Allāh's Messenger (صَلَّى ٱللَّهُ عَلَيْهِ وَسَلَّمَ) say: '*We are not inherited from. Whatever we leave behind is charity.*' Rather the family of Muhammad are to eat from this wealth. By Allāh I shall not alter anything from the charity which Allāh's Messenger (صَلَّى ٱللَّهُ عَلَيْهِ وَسَلَّمَ) used to give in his lifetime."[1]

And the two of them reported from Abū Hurairah (رَضِيَ ٱللَّهُ عَنْهُ) that Allāh's Messenger (صَلَّى ٱللَّهُ عَلَيْهِ وَسَلَّمَ) said:

> "My heirs will not receive any dīnars. Whatever I leave behind, excluding the adequate support of my wives and the wages for those I have appointed, is charity."[2]

And the notable people, whose saying is taken account of, agreed upon this by consensus, and no attention is given to the myths of the Shīʿah and the Rāfidah, for their ignorance is known far and wide.

The Book of Marriage

And it contains the majority of the rulings particular to the Prophet (صَلَّى ٱللَّهُ عَلَيْهِ وَسَلَّمَ) — may he be extolled in the best manner and may the best peace and security be upon him.

So we will mention them in order, in the categories, which the companions have mentioned, so that it becomes abridged and easy to take on.

The First Category: That Which was Obligatory Upon Him, and not Upon Others

AN ISSUE:

Allāh (the Most High) commanded him to give his wives the choice (of remaining married to him or separating), so He (the Most High) said:

---

1 — SH Reported by Al-Bukhārī in his *Sahīh* (no. 3093) and Muslim in his *Sahīh* (no. 1759).

2 — BJ SZ Reported by Al-Bukhārī (nos. 2776 & 2096) and Muslim (no. 1760).

> يَا أَيُّهَا النَّبِيُّ قُل لِّأَزْوَاجِكَ إِن كُنتُنَّ تُرِدْنَ الْحَيَاةَ الدُّنْيَا وَزِينَتَهَا فَتَعَالَيْنَ أُمَتِّعْكُنَّ
> وَأُسَرِّحْكُنَّ سَرَاحًا جَمِيلًا ۝ وَإِن كُنتُنَّ تُرِدْنَ اللَّهَ وَرَسُولَهُ وَالدَّارَ الْآخِرَةَ فَإِنَّ اللَّهَ
> أَعَدَّ لِلْمُحْسِنَاتِ مِنكُنَّ أَجْرًا عَظِيمًا
>
> MEANING: "O Prophet! Say to your wives: 'If you desire the life of this world and its glitter, then come. I will give you provision and set you free in a beautiful manner. But if you desire Allāh and His Messenger, and the Abode of the Hereafter, then Allāh has prepared for those of you who are doers of good a tremendous reward.'" — **Sūrah Al-Ahzāb (33): 28-29**

And the two of them report in the two *Sahīhs*[1] from ʿĀʾishah (رَضِيَ ٱللَّهُ عَنْهَا) a mention of this choice, and that Allāh commanded him with that.

And the companions differed: was this obligatory upon him or something recommended? There are two sayings. An-Nawāwī and others stated that what is correct is that it was obligatory.

And the companions differed: was it obligatory upon them to give an immediate response, or were they free to delay their response? There are two sayings. Ibnus-Sabbāgh said, to quote the meaning, that there is no disagreement that the choice, which he gave to ʿĀʾishah allowed for a delayed response, as occurs in his saying:

> "There will be no harm if you seek advice of your parents."[2]

They said:[3] So when they chose and preferred him [صَلَّى ٱللَّهُ عَلَيْهِ وَسَلَّمَ] then was it forbidden upon him to then divorce them? There are two sayings, and they declare that what is correct is that it was not forbidden.

Rather, it was just that Allāh (the Most High) forbade him to marry other women besides them, as a fitting recompense for their action. Then afterwards He allowed that for him, so that his action would be a favour upon them. ʿĀʾishah (رَضِيَ ٱللَّهُ عَنْهَا) said:

---

1 — [BJ][SZ] Reported by Al-Bukhārī (nos. 4785 & 4786) and Muslim (no. 1475).

2 — [BJ][SZ] It is (part of) the previous hadīth.

3 — [DB] i.e. the Shāfiʿī scholars referred to.

> "Allāh's Messenger (صَلَّى ٱللَّٰهُ عَلَيْهِ وَسَلَّمَ) did not die until (marrying other) women had been made permissible for him."[1]

(Ash-Shāfi'ī)[2] reported it.

The Second Category: That Which was Forbidden For Him, and not for Others, Pertaining To Marriage

AN ISSUE:

They said: It was forbidden for him to hold onto any wife who had chosen to separate from him, upon the correct saying. This is contrary to the case of anyone else who gives his wife such a choice, since if she chooses and prefers separation from him it does not become obligatory upon him to separate from her, and Allāh (the Most High) knows best.

And some of them said: Rather, he [صَلَّى ٱللَّٰهُ عَلَيْهِ وَسَلَّمَ] could release her, as an act of generosity.

AN ISSUE:

Was it permissible for him to marry a woman of the people of the Scripture? There are two sayings.

---

1 — [BJ][SZ] It is *'sahīh'*: Reported by Ahmad (6/41, 180), At-Tirmidhī (no. 3216), An-Nasā'ī (no. 3205), Al-Hākim (2/437), and At-Tabarī (10/320/nos. 28594-28598).

2 — [SH] An addition from the 'Ārif Hikmat Library' manuscript.

An-Nawawī[1] declared that what is correct is that it was forbidden, and this was the view preferred by Ibn Suraij,[2] Al-Istakhrī,[3] and Abū Hāmid Al-Marwarūdhī.[4]

Ash-Shaikh Abū Nasr ibn As-Sabbāgh derived evidence for this view, saying: "Because of his (صَلَّى ٱللَّهُ عَلَيْهِ وَسَلَّمَ) saying:

> 'My wives in this world will be my wives in the Hereafter.'"[5]

Then he quoted the other view, which is that it was permissible, and it is as if he inclined towards that; then he said: "The report is not a proof, since it is possible that if he married anyone from them that they could then have accepted Islām."

I say: This hadīth has no basis, which can be depended upon as being a saying of the Prophet (صَلَّى ٱللَّهُ عَلَيْهِ وَسَلَّمَ); rather it is from the speech of some of the Companions.[6]

---

1 — SH In the 'Sulaymāniyyah Library', (no. 3339) manuscript there occurs *"An-Nawāwī"*, and both of them are correct.

2 — BJ SZ SH He was the jurist of the people of 'Irāq, Abul-'Abbās Ahmad ibn 'Umar ibn Suraij, Al-Baghdādī, Al-Qādī, Ash-Shāfi'ī. He authored a number of works. He was born after the year 240 H, and he died in 306 H. Refer for his biography to *Siyar A'lāmin-Nubalā'* (14/201).

3 — BJ SZ He is the great scholar Abū Sa'īd, Al-Hasan ibn Ahmad ibn Yazīd Al-Istakhrī — an ascription to a district in Persia — Ash-Shāfi'ī; the Jurist of Al-'Irāq and the companion of Ibn Suraij. He wrote beneficial works, from them *Kitāb Adabil-Qadā'* He died in 328 H. Refer for his biography to *Siyar A'lāmin-Nubalā'* (15/250).

4 — BJ SZ SH He was the Shaikh of the Shāfi'iyyah, Abū Hāmid, Ahmad ibn Bishr ibn 'Āmir Al-Marwarūdhī. The muftī of Basrah and the author of a number of works. He studied Fiqh under Abū Is-hāq Al-Marwazī; and he authored *Al-Jāmi'* upon the Fiqh of the madh-hab, and an explanation of *Mukhtasar Al-Muzanī*, and concerning the principles of Fiqh. He died in 362 H. Refer for his biography to *Siyar A'lāmin-Nubalā'* (16/166).

5 — SH There is no basis for it with this wording.

6 — There are authentic narrations which prove that 'Ā'ishah (رَضِيَ ٱللَّهُ عَنْهَا) is from the wives of Muhammad (صَلَّى ٱللَّهُ عَلَيْهِ وَسَلَّمَ) both in this life and the Hereafter, and you can read some of them in Endnote 178 on page 576.

And Abū Is-hāq Al-Marwazī[1] said: "It was not forbidden."

354 And there are three sayings concerning the permissibility of his taking a woman from the people of the Scripture as a slave-girl, or of his marrying a Muslim slave-girl. The most correct view is that it was permissible for him to take a woman from the people of the Scripture as slave-girl, and that it was not permissible for him to marry a Muslim slave-girl: rather, that was forbidden.

As for the case of a slave-girl from the people of the Scripture, then the majority clearly state that marrying her was forbidden for him.

And Al-Hannātī[2] endorsed two sayings concerning it, and they are both very weak.

And they extract further details at this point, which are unsound, and abandoning them has more right than mentioning them; and this type of matter is from those matters mentioned as being particular which Ibn Khayrān[3] and the Imām[4] have criticised, and they are correct in that, and Allāh knows best.

---

1 — [BJ][SZ][SH] He was the Shaikh of the Shāfi'īs and the jurist of Baghdād, Abū Is-hāq Ibrāhīm ibn Ahmad Al-Marwazī; the companion of Abul-'Abbās Ibn Suraij and the greatest one of his students. He busied himself [in teaching and delivering verdicts] in Baghdād for a long period of time, and he wrote a number of works. He died in 340 H. Refer for his biography to *Siyar A'lāmin-Nubalā'* (15/429).

2 — [BJ][SZ][SH][DB] He was the great scholar, the muftī of the Shāfi'īs, Abū 'Abdillāh Al-Husayn ibn Muhammad ibn 'Abdillāh, At-Tabarī, Al-Hājī, Al-Bazzāzī. He came to Baghdād and narrated there. He became fully precise in the madh-hab, in the fundamental principles, and in the matters of disagreement. He died in Asbahān in the year 495 H, having exceeded the age of ninety. (*Tārīkh Baghdād*: 8/103; *Siyar A'lāmin-Nubalā'* (19/210); *Al-Kāmil fit-Tārīkh* (8/214).

3 — [BJ][SZ][SH] He is the Imām, Shaikh of the Shāfi'īs, Abū 'Alī Al-Husayn ibn Sālih ibn Khayrān, Al-Baghdādī. He was offered the post of chief judge and he refused it. He died in 320 H. Refer for his biography to *Siyar A'lāmin-Nubalā'* (15/58).

4 — [BJ][SZ] He is Imāmul-Haramayn Al-Juwaynī.

The Third Category: Those Marriages that were Permissible For him but not for Other than him

AN ISSUE:

He (may Allāh extol and bestow peace and security upon him) died whilst married to nine wives, and they agree that it was permissible for him to have nine. However, our companions disagree about whether it was permissible for him to have more.

What is correct is that this was allowed for him, and the proof for it is what occurs in Al-Bukhārī[1] from Bundār: from Muʿādh ibn Hishām: from his father: from Qatādah: from Anas who said: "Allāh's Messenger (صَلَّىٱللَّهُعَلَيۡهِوَسَلَّمَ) used to have relations with each of his wives in turn during a single hour of the night or the day, and they were eleven in number."

I said to Anas: "Was he able to do that?"

He said: "We used to say that he said he had been given the strength of thirty men" — and in a narration: "of forty."

Then Al-Bukhārī reported it[2] as a hadīth of Saʿīd: from Qatādah: from Anas: "And he had nine."

﴾ And Anas said: "He (صَلَّىٱللَّهُعَلَيۡهِوَسَلَّمَ) married fifteen women, and he consummated marriage with thirteen, and at one time he had gathered eleven, and he died leaving nine behind."[3] ﴿

And Qatādah said this also.

---

1 — (BJ)(SZ) *Sahīh Al-Bukhārī* (no. 268).

2 — (SH) (no. 284)

3 — (BJ)(SZ)(SH) What occurs between the [decorative] brackets is missing from the 'Sulaymāniyyah Library' (no. 3339) manuscript.

And Ibnus-Sabbāgh mentioned in his *Shāmil*, saying "And Abū 'Ubayd[1]

said: *'Allāh's Messenger (صَلَّى ٱللَّهُ عَلَيْهِ وَسَلَّمَ) married eighteen wives, and he had three slave girls.'*"

AN ISSUE:

They said: And it was correct for him to marry with the wording of being given a gift, because of His Saying (He the Most High):

> وَامْرَأَةً مُّؤْمِنَةً إِن وَهَبَتْ نَفْسَهَا لِلنَّبِيِّ إِنْ أَرَادَ النَّبِيُّ أَن يَسْتَنكِحَهَا خَالِصَةً لَّكَ مِن دُونِ الْمُؤْمِنِينَ
>
> MEANING: "If a believing woman offers herself to the Prophet (صَلَّى ٱللَّهُ عَلَيْهِ وَسَلَّمَ), and the Prophet (صَلَّى ٱللَّهُ عَلَيْهِ وَسَلَّمَ) wishes to marry her; as a special privilege for you alone, not for the rest of the Believers." — **Sūrah Al-Ahzāb (33): 50**

And if he were to establish the marriage upon the wording of her offering herself as a present (*hibah*), then no dower (*mahr*) would become due, neither by the marriage nor by its consummation, contrary to the case with others.

And was his divorcing restricted to three times? There are two views. The most correct of them is that yes, it was, because of the generality of the Āyah. It is otherwise said: No, because he was not restricted to marrying only four wives, and so his divorcing was not restricted to three times; but this is weak, since that does not necessarily follow.

AN ISSUE:

And it was permissible for him to marry without a guardian (for the woman), and without witnesses, upon the correct saying, because of the hadīth of Zaynab bint Jahsh that she used to boast to the wives of the

---

1 — [BJ][SZ][SH] There occurs in the 'Sulaymāniyyah Library' manuscript (no. 3339): "*Ubaydah*" and what is apparent is that what is correct is what we have affirmed and he is Al-Qāsim ibn Sallām.

Prophet (صَلَّى ٱللَّٰهُ عَلَيْهِ وَسَلَّمَ), and say: "*Your families married you off; whereas Allāh married me off, from above the seven heavens.*" Reported by Al-Bukhārī.[1]

AN ISSUE:

And was it permissible for him to marry whilst in a state of *ihrām*? There are two sayings:

The first of them is [that the answer is] no, because of the generality of the hadīth, which Muslim reported[2] from 'Uthmān: from Allāh's Messenger (صَلَّى ٱللَّٰهُ عَلَيْهِ وَسَلَّمَ) that he said:

> "The person in a state of *ihrām* may not marry, nor may anyone arrange marriage on his behalf, nor may he make a proposal of marriage."

And the person giving the address enters within it, if it pertains to him, upon the saying of the majority.

And those who hold it permissible base this upon the hadīth of Ibn 'Abbās: that he (صَلَّى ٱللَّٰهُ عَلَيْهِ وَسَلَّمَ) married Maymūnah whilst he was in the state of ihrām. The two of them reported it.[3]

However, this is contradicted by what Muslim reported from Maymūnah herself: that he married her when they were both outside the state of *ihrām*,[4] and the person actually involved in an incident knows better about it than others, and Allāh knows best.

AN ISSUE:

And if he desired to marry a woman, then it became obligatory upon her to respond to him, upon the correct saying with the companions; and it became forbidden for anyone else to propose to her.

---

1 — [SH] Reported by Al-Bukhārī in his *Sahīh* (nos. 7420 & 7421), as a hadīth of Anas (رَضِيَ ٱللَّٰهُ عَنْهُ).

2 — [SH] In his *Sahīh* (no. 1409).

3 — [SH] Reported by Al-Bukhārī (no. 5114) and Muslim (no. 1410).

4 — [BJ][SZ] Reported by Muslim (no. 1411).

AN ISSUE:

358 Was it obligatory upon him to have relations equally with his wives and slave-girls? There are two sayings.

What is apparent from the ahādīth is that it was obligatory; since when he (صَلَّى ٱللَّهُ عَلَيْهِ وَسَلَّمَ) became ill he took turns with them whilst he was in that state, until he requested their permission to remain for the period of his illness in the house of ʿĀʾishah (رَضِيَ ٱللَّهُ عَنْهَا) and they gave him permission.[1]

And Abū Saʿīd Al-Istakhrī said: "It was not obligatory, because of His Saying (He the Most High):

> تُرْجِي مَن تَشَاءُ مِنْهُنَّ وَتُؤْوِي إِلَيْكَ مَن تَشَاءُ
>
> MEANING: "You may postpone the turn of any wife you wish from them, or take to yourself whom you wish." — **SŪRAH AL-AHZĀB (33): 51**

So this was from the matters specific to him.

And all this follows on from whether or not marriage was for him (صَلَّى ٱللَّهُ عَلَيْهِ وَسَلَّمَ) the same as taking slave-girls is for the rest of us.[2] There are two sayings.

AN ISSUE:

And he set Safiyyah free, and he made her being set free her dower (*sadāq*), as is established in the two *Sahīhs* from Anas.[3]

So it is said: that means that he set her free, and he made it a condition upon her that she should marry him.

---

1 — [SH] Reported by Al-Bukhārī in his *Sahīh* (no. 4442) and Muslim in his *Sahīh* (no. 1637/22).

2 — [BJ][SZ] Taking slave-girls is something unlimited, so it is permissible for a Muslim to take as many slave-girls as he wishes; and a slave-girl does not have the right to a turn, which a wife has.

3 — [BJ][SZ] Reported by Al-Bukhārī (no. 5086) and Muslim (no. 1365/84 &85).

So it became obligatory upon her to fulfil the condition, contrary to the case with others besides him.

Or it is said: He made the act of freeing her itself her dower; and that was correct, contrary to the case with anyone else besides him. This was the view preferred by Al-Ghazālī.

I say: A problem for this is what At-Tirmidhī quoted from Ash-Shāfiʿī:[1] that this is permissible for other individuals, and it is a well-known saying.

And it is said: He set her free without any payment and married her without a dowry; neither there and then, nor later on. This is what is quoted from Abū Is-hāq, and it was clearly stated by Al-Hāfidh Abū Bakr Al-Bayhaqī,[2] and it was declared correct by Ibnus-Salāh and An-Nawāwī.

I say: And Ash-Shaikh Abū ʿAmr took his saying: *'And he made her being set free her dowry;'* to mean that he did not lay down a dower for her, he just set her free. So it was just like their saying: *'Hunger is the provision of the one who has no provision.'*

Or it is said: rather he gave her a slave-girl as a dowry, as Al-Bayhaqī reported[3] with a singular chain that is not authentic, and Allāh knows best.

The Fourth Category: Those Virtues Particular are to him (صَلَّىٰ اللَّهُ عَلَيْهِ وَسَلَّمَ), to the Exclusion of Others

So from that is that his wives are Mothers to the Believers (Ummahātul-Mu'minīn).

---

1 — [SH] In his *Sunan*, after the hadīth no. 1117, saying: "And action was upon this with some of the people of knowledge, from the Companions of the Prophet (صَلَّىٰ اللَّهُ عَلَيْهِ وَسَلَّمَ) and others; and it was the saying of Ash-Shāfiʿī, Ahmad, and Is-hāq. And some of the people of knowledge disliked making setting her free her dower, until he appoints a dower other than setting her free; but the first saying is more correct."

2 — [BJ][SZ] In *As-Sunanul-Kubrā* (7/128).

3 — This position is weak — refer to ENDNOTE 179 ON PAGE 578 for more detail.

Allāh (the Most High) said:

> النَّبِيُّ أَوْلَىٰ بِالْمُؤْمِنِينَ مِنْ أَنفُسِهِمْ ۖ وَأَزْوَاجُهُ أُمَّهَاتُهُمْ
>
> MEANING: "The Prophet has more right over the Believers than their own selves, and his wives are their mothers." — **Sūrah Al-Ahzāb (33): 6**

The meaning of this motherhood is that which necessitates respect, obedience, the forbiddance of acts of disobedience, and the obligation of honouring them. It does not mean that it is forbidden to marry their daughters, nor that it is permissible to be alone in seclusion with them; and their prohibited status does not pass on to others related to them.

And are they also mothers to the believing women? There are two sayings. They declare that what is correct is that this is not the case; and this was the saying of ʿĀ'ishah (رَضِيَ اللَّهُ عَنْهَا).[1]

So this follows on from the question of whether the external masculine plural includes the women also, and this is dealt with in the fundamental (of Fiqh).

And can their daughters be called *'Sisters of the Believers?'* Ash-Shāfiʿī is stated, as occurs in *Al-Mukhtasar*,[2] as having said that it is permissible; and some of the companions permit it, whereas others prohibit it; and Ibnus-Sabbāgh and others criticized Al-Muzanī for this, and said: It is a mistake.

---

1 — [SH] Ibn Saʿd reported in *At-Tabaqātul-Kubrā* (8/64), and Abū Nuʿaym in *Musnad Abī Yahyā Firās ibn Yahyā* (85/25), and Al-Bayhaqī in *As-Sunanul-Kubrā* (7/70), by way of ʿĀmir Ash-Shaʿbī: from Masrūq ibn Al-Ajdaʿ: from ʿĀ'ishah: that a woman said to her: *"O my mother!"* So she said: *"I am a mother to your men. I am not your mother."*

I say: This is a *'sahīh' isnād*: its narrators are reliable.

2 — [SH] It is *Mukhtasarul-Muzanī*, a book on the details of the Fiqh of the Shāfiʿī, written by the student of Imām Ash-Shāfiʿī: Ismāʿīl ibn Yahyā Al-Muzanī, who died in 264 H. It is one of the most famous books of Shāfiʿī Fiqh, and therefore the jurists of the Shāfiʿīs gave it a great deal of attention. [BJ][SZ] For the biography of Al-Muzanī refer to *Siyar Aʿlāmin-Nubalā'* (12/92).

AN ISSUE:

And can he (ﷺ) be called *'The Father of the Believers'*? Al-Baghawī related that some of the companions held this to be permissible.

I say: And it was the saying of Muʿāwiyah — and Ubayy recited, also Ibn ʿAbbās (رضي الله عنهم):[1]

> النَّبِيُّ أَوْلَىٰ بِالْمُؤْمِنِينَ مِنْ أَنفُسِهِمْ - **وَهُوَ أَبٌ لهُم** - وَأَزْوَاجُهُ أُمَّهَاتُهُمْ
>
> MEANING: "The Prophet has more right over the Believers than their own selves — *and he is a father to them* — and his wives are their mothers."

And Al-Wāhidī related from some of the companions that it is prohibited, because of His Saying (He the Most High):

> مَّا كَانَ مُحَمَّدٌ أَبَا أَحَدٍ مِّن رِّجَالِكُمْ
>
> MEANING: "Muhammad (ﷺ) is not the father of any of your men." — **Sūrah Al-Ahzāb (33): 40**

However, what it means is their father in lineage, otherwise Abū Dāwūd reported: *"I am to you just like a father..."* (the hadīth concerning cleaning oneself after relieving oneself).[2]

VARIOUS ISSUES

AN ISSUE:

And his wives are the most excellent of the women of the Ummah, due to their reward being multiplied, contrary to other than them; and then the most excellent of them were Khadījah and ʿĀ'ishah. Abū Saʿīd Al-

---

1 — This recitation was unusual, but it was established from Ubayy Ibn Kaʿb, and you can refer to **Endnote 180 on page 578** for more detail.

2 — [BJ][SZ] It is *'hasan'*: Reported by Abū Dāwūd (no. 8), An-Nasā'ī (no. 40), Ibn Mājah (no. 313), Ahmad (no. 3768), Al-Humaydī (no. 988), ad-Dārimī (1/138/no. 680), Ibn Hibbān (no. 1431), At-Tahāwī in *Sharh Maʿāniyyil-Āthār* (1/123), and others, all of them reporting it as a hadīth of Abū Hurairah (رضي الله عنه).

Mutawallī[1] said: "And our companions differ concerning which of the two of them was more excellent."

And the saying of Ibn Hazm that his (ﷺ) wives were more excellent than the rest of the Companions, even Abū Bakr As-Siddīq (رَضِيَ ٱللَّهُ عَنْهُ), is a saying which no one preceded him upon, and it is the weakest of the sayings.

AN ISSUE:

And it was forbidden to marry those wives whom he left behind when he died, by consensus; and that is because they will be his wives in Paradise. So if a wife does not remarry after the death of her husband, then she will be his wife in Paradise, just as it is related that Abud-Dardā''s wife[2] said to him when he was dying:

> "O Abud-Dardā'! You sought my hand in marriage from my family and they married me to you. So I ask you today to remain as my husband."

So he said: "Then do not get married after me."

So after his death Mu'āwiyah, who was the governor, sought her hand in marriage, and she refused him.[3]

---

1 — (SH)(BJ)(SZ) He was the Shaikh of the Shāfi'īs, Abū Sa'd 'Abdur-Rahmān ibn Ma'mūn ibn 'Alī ibn Muhammad Al-Abīwardī, Al-Mutawallī. He was one of the companions of Al-Qādī Husayn. He was a leader in Fiqh and Usūl, intelligent, a debater, fine in form, astute, and humble. He was born in Abīward in the year 427 H, and he died in 478 H.

Refer for his biography to *Siyar A'lāmin-Nubalā'* (18/585).

2 — (BJ)(SZ) She was the younger Ummud-Dardā', whose name was Hujaymah, or it is said: Juhaymah. She was a reliable jurist, from the Tābi'īn. She died in 81 H. Refer for her biography to *Siyar A'lāmin-Nubalā'* (4/277). As for Ummud-Dardā', the elder one, the female Companion, then her name was Khayrah. She died during the Khilāfah of 'Uthmān, before Abud-Dardā'. She has a biography in *Al-Isābah* (7/62).

3 — This was declared *'sahīh'* by Imām Al-Albānī, and there are other beneficial narrations and details which can be read in **Endnote 181 on page 580**.

And Al-Bayhaqī reported as a narration of ʿĪsā ibn ʿAbdir-Rahmān As-Sulamī: from Abū Is-hāq: from Silah: from Hudhayfah, that he said to his wife: "If you wish to be my wife in Paradise then do not remarry after me, for a woman in Paradise will be for her final husband in this world."[1]

So therefore it was forbidden for the wives of the Prophet (صَلَّى ٱللَّهُ عَلَيْهِ وَسَلَّمَ) (رَضِيَ ٱللَّهُ عَنْهُنَّ) to get married after him, because they will be his wives in Paradise.

And they disagree regarding those whom he divorced whilst he was alive, and they have three sayings. The third of them is that those whom he had relations with became forbidden for others; and Ash-Shāfiʿī stated that it was unrestrictedly forbidden, and this was supported by Ibn Abī Hurairah,[2] because of His Saying (He the Most High):

> وَأَزْوَٰجُهُۥٓ أُمَّهَٰتُهُمْ
>
> MEANING: "And his wives are their mothers." — **Sūrah Al-Ahzāb (33): 6**

So upon this basis there are two sayings regarding a slave-girl whom he left by death or otherwise, after having relations with her.

And it is said: his wives were not forbidden for others unless he died and left them behind. The proof for this is the Āyah of the choice,[3] since if she did not have the option of becoming the wife of someone else then there would be no benefit in his giving them a choice, and Allāh knows best.

---

1 — [BJ] [SZ] Reported by Al-Bayhaqī in his *Sunan* (7/69) and Shaikh Nāsir (Al-Albānī) said in *As-Silsilatus- Sahīhah* (no. 1281): *"Its narrators are reliable, except for the ʿanʿanah of Abū Is-hāq — who is As-Sabīʿī — and his ikhtilāt."* And the Shaikh mentioned another witness for it, reported by Ibn ʿAsākir.

2 — [SH] [BJ] [SZ] He was the Shaikh of the Shāfiʿīs, Abū ʿAlī, Al-Hasan ibn Al-Husayn ibn Abī Hurairah, Al-Baghdādī, Al-Qādī. He attained the leading position in the madhhab, and he wrote an explanation to *Mukhtasarul-Muzanī*, and he became famous throughout the lands. He died in 345 H. Refer for his biography to *Siyar Aʿlāmin-Nubalāʾ* (15/430).

3 — [DB] i.e. Verses 28-29 of Sūratul-Ahzāb, as has preceded.

AN ISSUE:

364 And whoever accuses ʿĀʾishah — the Mother of the Believers — of adultery is to be executed. As-Suhaylī and others mentioned it, because of the text of the Qurʾān stating her innocence; and with regard to the rest of the wives there are two sayings.

AN ISSUE:

And likewise, whoever insults him (صَلَّى ٱللَّهُ عَلَيْهِ وَسَلَّمَ) is to be executed, whether it be a man or a woman, because of the multiple ahādīth which collectively show that; and it would be too lengthy to mention them here.

So from that is the hadīth of Ibn ʿAbbās regarding the blind man who killed a slave-girl, from whom he had a child, when she spoke ill of the Prophet (صَلَّى ٱللَّهُ عَلَيْهِ وَسَلَّمَ). So he mentioned that to the Prophet (صَلَّى ٱللَّهُ عَلَيْهِ وَسَلَّمَ), and he said: "Bear witness that her blood has been lawfully spilled."[1]

And Shuʿbah said: from Tawbah Al-ʿAnbarī: from Abus-Siwār: from Abū Barazah: "That a man abused Abū Bakr, so I said: *'Will you not behead him?'*

So he said:

> 'This is not for anyone after the Prophet (صَلَّى ٱللَّهُ عَلَيْهِ وَسَلَّمَ).'"

An-Nasāʾī and Al-Bayhaqī reported it.[2]

---

1 — This narration was declared as *'sahīh'* by Imām Ibn Taimiyyah and Imām Al-Albānī. Refer to **Endnote 182 on page 580** for more detail.

2 — SH Reported by An-Nasāʾī in *Al-Mujtabā* (7/108-109), At-Tayālisī in his *Musnad* (1/7/4 Hajr Edn.), and from him by Al-Mizzī in *Tahdhībul-Kamāl* (15/443); and Ahmad (1/9), Abū Yaʿlā in his *Musnad* (1/84/81-82), [and others] through chains of narration from Shuʿbah, with it.

Al-Hākim said: *"This is a hadīth with a 'sahīh' isnād"* — and Adh-Dhahabī agreed with him.

I say: It is just as they said, and it was declared *'sahīh'* by our Shaikh Al-Imām Al-Albānī (رَحِمَهُ ٱللَّهُ) in *Sahīh Sunanin-Nasāʾī* (no. 3795).

And Ibn ʿAdiyy reported[1] a hadīth of Yahyā ibn Ismāʿīl Al-Wāsitī: Ibrāhīm ibn Saʿd narrated to us: from Az-Zuhrī: from Abū Salamah: from Abū Hurairah (رَضِيَٱللَّهُعَنْهُ) who said: "No one is to be executed for abusing anyone, except for abusing the Prophet (صَلَّىٱللَّهُعَلَيْهِوَسَلَّمَ)."

And Ash-Shaikh, Al-Imām, Abul-ʿAbbās Ibn Taimiyyah wrote his book *As-Sārimul-Maslūl ʿalā Sābbir-Rasūl* (*The Unsheathed Sword Against the One Who Abuses the Messenger*),[2] and it is one of the finest books written upon that topic, and Allāh knows best.

AN ISSUE:

It was from the characteristics particular to him that if he spoke ill of a man who was not, in reality, deserving of it, that the speech of Allāh's Messenger (صَلَّىٱللَّهُعَلَيْهِوَسَلَّمَ) against him was an expiation for him. Its proof is what the two of them report in their *Sahīhs* from Abū Hurairah (رَضِيَٱللَّهُعَنْهُ) who said: Allāh's Messenger (صَلَّىٱللَّهُعَلَيْهِوَسَلَّمَ) said:

> "O Allāh! I have taken a covenant with You, which You will never break: I am just a human; so whichever of the Believers I have harmed, or abused, or lashed, or cursed, then make it for him a supplication, a purification, and something by means of which You draw him closer on the Day of Resurrection."[3]

---

1 — [SH] In *Al-Kāmil* (7/2704), and from him by Al-Bayhaqī in *As-Sunanul-Kubrā* (7/60).

I say: This is a *'hasan' isnād* — if Allāh wills, and it is generally witnessed to by what preceded.

2 — [SH] And it is printed and widely available, and all praise is for Allāh.

3 — [BJ][SZ] Reported by Muslim (no. 2604), as a hadīth of Ibn ʿAbbās.

[SH] And refer to *As-Sahīhah* (1/164-167) to gain awareness of the virtues of Muʿāwiyah (رَضِيَٱللَّهُعَنْهُ), and a refutation of those who attack him; and refer to the treatise of our Shaikh, the great scholar, ʿAbdul-Muhsin Al-ʿAbbād (حفظه الله) entitled *Min-Aqwālil-Munsifīn fis-Sahābiyyil Khalīfah Muʿāwiyah* (رَضِيَٱللَّهُعَنْهُ) — *From the Sayings of the Trustworthy Scholars Regarding the Companion, the Khalīfah, Muʿāwiyah* (رَضِيَٱللَّهُعَنْهُ).

So these two together bring about a special virtue for Muʿāwiyah (رَضِيَ ٱللَّهُ عَنْهُ) and this is just one example of the leadership (in knowledge) of Muslim (رَحِمَهُ ٱللَّهُ).

And Regarding Jihād

AN ISSUE:

And when he (صَلَّى ٱللَّهُ عَلَيْهِ وَسَلَّمَ) put armour on, then it was not permissible for him to remove it until Allāh brought about His affair, because of the hadīth concerning the day of Uhud, when a group of the Believers advised him to go out to the enemy at Uhud. So he entered (his house) and put on his coat of chain mail.

Then when he came out to them they said: "O Messenger of Allāh! Do you think that you should go back?"

So he said:

> "It is not right for a Prophet, when he has put on his armour for fighting, to return until he has fought."[1]

So most of the companions said[2]: This was obligatory upon him, and it was forbidden for him to desist until he had fought; and they mention as a supplementary detail that whenever he began a supererogatory action then it became obligatory upon him to complete it, upon one of the two sayings — and it is weak, because of what we mentioned previously regarding fasting,[3] and Allāh knows best; and this supplementary detail was declared to be weak by Abū Zakariyyā[4] also.

---

1 — This hadīth is authentic — refer to Endnote 183 on page 581 for more detail regarding its reporting.

2 — [BJ][SZ] In the "Ārif Hikmat Library' Edn. there occurs *"our companions"*.

3 — See that which is mentioned regarding this on page 341.

4 — [DB] i.e. Imām An-Nawawī (رَحِمَهُ ٱللَّهُ).

AN ISSUE:

And they mention amongst those matters specific to him (صَلَّىٱللَّهُعَلَيْهِوَسَلَّمَ) is the obligation of consultation (*Al-Mushāwarah*) upon him, meaning his consulting his Companions regarding the affairs of war. 367

Allāh (the Most High) said:

> وَشَاوِرْهُمْ فِي الْأَمْرِ
>
> MEANING: "And consult with them concerning the affair." — **Sūrah Āli 'Imrān (3): 159**

Ash-Shāfi'ī said: "Sufyān ibn 'Uyainah narrated to us: from Az-Zuhrī, who said: Abū Hurairah (رَضِيَٱللَّهُعَنْهُ) said: 'I have not seen anyone who consulted his companions more than Allāh's Messenger (صَلَّىٱللَّهُعَلَيْهِوَسَلَّمَ) did.'"[1]

And Ash-Shāfi'ī (رَحِمَهُٱللَّهُ) said: Al-Hasan said: "Allāh's Messenger (صَلَّىٱللَّهُعَلَيْهِوَسَلَّمَ) had no need for consultation; however, he wished that the rulers after him should follow his example."[2]

I say: So upon this [position] it will not remain as something specific [only to Allāh's Messenger (صَلَّىٱللَّهُعَلَيْهِوَسَلَّمَ)].

AN ISSUE:

They said: And it was obligatory upon him to stand firm and face the enemy even if they were more than twice his number, and it is as if this is derived from the hadīth concerning Al-Hudaybiyah, and Allāh knows best, where he (عَلَيْهِٱلصَّلَاةُوَٱلسَّلَامُ) said:

---

1 — This narration is weak, and you can see more detail in **Endnote 184 on page 582**.

2 — [BJ][SZ] Reported by Ibn Abī Hātim (3/801/no. 4416), and Sa'īd Mansūr in *At-Tafsīr* (3/1098/no.534), and by Al-Bayhaqī in his *Sunan* (10/109): from Sufyān: from Ibn Shubrumah: from Al-Hasan; and its chain is *da'īf* (weak) because it is disconnected between Ibn Shubrumah and Al-Hasan Al-Basrī.

"So if they refuse, then by Allāh! I shall certainly fight them (meaning: the Quraysh) for this matter, even until I am killed" — and the hadīth is reported in the *Sahīh* of Al-Bukhārī. [1]

AN ISSUE:

And we have already mentioned his (صَلَّى ٱللَّٰهُ عَلَيْهِ وَسَلَّمَ) saying: "It is not befitting for a Prophet to make a treacherous indication with the eyes."[2]

They said: Yet along with this, it was permissible for him to deceive in war, because of his (صَلَّى ٱللَّٰهُ عَلَيْهِ وَسَلَّمَ) saying: "War is trickery."[3]

And just as he did on the *Day of the Allied Enemies* (*Al-Ahzāb*) when he ordered Nuʿaym ibn Masʿūd to cause trouble between Quraysh and Qurayzah; and he did what he did, until Allāh disunited them at his hands, and He put enmity between them. And Allāh caused them to disperse by means of that and by other means, and all praise is for Him and all favours are from Him.[4]

AN ISSUE:

And he (صَلَّى ٱللَّٰهُ عَلَيْهِ وَسَلَّمَ) had the right to choose (*As-Safiyy*) from the booty; and it was that he could choose and take whatever he wished: whether

1 — [SH] (nos. 2731 & 2732)

2 — [BJ][SZ] It is *'sahīh'*: Reported by Abū Dāwūd (nos. 2683 & 4359), An-Nasāʾī (no. 4078), [and others] as a hadīth of Saʿd ibn Abī Waqqās; and it has a supporting witness from a hadīth of Anas — reported by Ahmad (no. 12529) and Abū Dāwūd (no. 3194).

3 — [SH] Reported by Al-Bukhārī (no. 3030) & Muslim (no. 1739), as a hadīth of Jābir ibn ʿAbdillāh (رَضِيَ ٱللَّٰهُ عَنْهُمَا).

4 — The story has preceded (see page 156) as part of the history of the Battle of the Khandaq.

it be a slave, a slave-girl, or weaponry, or the like, prior to the division. And that is proven by ahādīth occurring in the *Sunan* and elsewhere.[1]

And likewise, he received a one-fifth share of the war spoils (*Al-Ghanīmah*), and four-fifths of the property forfeited by the enemy (*Al-Fai'*), as is our madh-hab. There is no disagreement about that.

And Regarding Rulings (Al-Ahkām):

AN ISSUE:

They said: He had the right to pass a legal judgement upon someone based upon his own knowledge, since he is free of any accusation of wrongdoing. Its witness is the hadīth of Hind bint 'Utbah when she complained that her husband Abū Sufyān was being miserly with his money, so he said:

> "Take from his wealth in a good manner what will suffice you and suffice your children."

And it occurs in the two *Sahīhs* from 'Ā'ishah (رَضِيَ ٱللَّهُ عَنْهَا).[2]

Whereas regarding other people besides him passing judgement based upon one's personal knowledge, there is well-known disagreement. It amounts to three sayings, the third of them being that such judgement

---

1 — BJ SZ Reported by Abū Dāwūd (no.2991), An-Nasā'ī (no. 4156), Sa'īd ibn Mansūr in his *Sunan* (nos. 2673 & 2674) from 'Āmir Ash-Sha'bī in *'mursal'* form: *"The Prophet (صَلَّى ٱللَّهُ عَلَيْهِ وَسَلَّمَ) had a share called 'As-Safiyy': if he wished a slave, and if he wished a slave-girl, and if he wished a horse, which he could choose before the division of the fifth."* And it also occurs as a *'mursal'* narration of Ibn Sīrīn with its like, reported by Abū Dāwūd (no. 2992); and as a *'mursal'* narration of Qatādah by Abū Dāwūd (no. 2993).

And it is indicated by the hadīth of 'Ā'ishah: *"Safiyyah was from the special share (As-Safiyy)"* — reported by Abū Dāwūd (no. 2994), Ibn Hibbān in his *Sahīh* (11/151/4822), and Al-Hākim (3/39).

SH And its chain of narration was declared *'sahīh'* by Al-Hākim, Adh-Dhahabī, and our Shaikh Al-Albānī (رَحِمَهُ ٱللَّهُ).

2 — BJ SZ Reported by Al-Bukhārī nos. 2211, 2460 and 3825) and Muslim (no. 1714).

may be passed in matters other than the punishments (*hudūd*) prescribed by Allāh. They said: So upon this he may pass judgement for himself or his children; and he may bear witness for himself and his children; and he may accept the testimony of one who bears witness in his favour, because of the hadīth of Khuzaymah ibn Thābit,[1] and it is a *'hasan'* hadīth which is mentioned fully elsewhere, and Allāh (the Most High) knows best.

AN ISSUE:

They said: And whoever, whilst in his presence, disrespects him or commits fornication, then he becomes a Disbeliever. Ash-Shaikh Abū Zakariyyā An-Nawawī said: "The matter of fornication is debatable, and Allāh knows best."[2]

AN ISSUE:

It is permissible to take his name, without any disagreement, but regarding his kunyah 'Abul-Qāsim', the scholars have three sayings:

The first: That this is unrestrictedly prohibited. This was the position of Ash-Shāfiʿī. It was quoted from him by Al-Bayhaqī, Al-Baghawī, and Abul-Qāsim ibn ʿAsākir Ad-Dimashqī. This is because of a hadīth occurring about it from Jābir who said: Allāh's Messenger (صَلَّى ٱللَّهُ عَلَيْهِ وَسَلَّمَ) said: *"Take my name, but do not take on my kunyah."* The two of them reported it.[3] And the two of them reported its like from Abū Hurairah.[4]

---

1 — For the story of when Khuzaymah Al-Ansārī bore witness that Allāh's Messenger (صَلَّى ٱللَّهُ عَلَيْهِ وَسَلَّمَ) was truthful, see **Endnote 185 on page 582**.

2 — [BJ][SZ][SH] Al-Hāfidh Ibn Hajr said in *At-Talkhīsul-Habīr* (3/143): "As for disrespecting, then that is by consensus (the case); but as for fornication, then if what is meant is its occurring where he could see it, then this is possible, since this is joined to disrespect; and if it means its occurring in his time, then this will not be correct because of the incident of Māʿiz and the woman of the Ghāmidī tribe."

3 — [BJ][SZ] Reported by Al-Bukhārī (nos. 3114 & 3538) and Muslim (no. 2133).

4 — [BJ][SZ] Reported by Al-Bukhārī (nos. 110, 3539 & 6188) and Muslim (no. 2134), from Abū Hurairah; and Al-Bukhārī reported it (no. 3537) and Muslim (no. 2131), from Anas.

The second: And it was the position of Mālik, and was what An-Nawawī (رَحِمَهُ ٱللَّهُ) preferred: that it is unrestrictedly permissible; since that was for a particular reason present during his lifetime, which passed away with his death.

The third: That it is permissible for someone whose name is not Muhammad, and it is not permissible for someone whose name is Muhammad — so that the person does not combine his name and his kunyah. This was the view preferred by Abul-Qāsim ʿAbdul-Karīm Ar-Rāfiʿī.[1]

AN ISSUE:

They mention amongst the matters particular to him: that the children of his daughters are ascribed to him. This is based upon what Al-Bukhārī reported from Abū Bakrah (رَضِيَ ٱللَّهُ عَنْهُ) who said: "I saw Al-Hasan ibn ʿAlī (رَضِيَ ٱللَّهُ عَنْهُمَا) with the Prophet (صَلَّى ٱللَّهُ عَلَيْهِ وَسَلَّمَ) upon the minbar, and he was looking towards him and then looking towards the people, and he said:

> 'This son of mine is a noble chief, and Allāh will bring about peace through him between two great groups of Muslims.'"[2]

AN ISSUE:

And from those matters specific to him is that every lineage and tie of kinship will have its benefit and good severed on the Day of Resurrection, except for lineage, ties of kinship, and relationship through marriages to him (صَلَّى ٱللَّهُ عَلَيْهِ وَسَلَّمَ).

Allāh (the Most High) said:

> فَإِذَا نُفِخَ فِي الصُّورِ فَلَا أَنسَابَ بَيْنَهُمْ يَوْمَئِذٍ وَلَا يَتَسَاءَلُونَ

---

1 — For the speech of Imām Al-Albānī (رَحِمَهُ ٱللَّهُ) regarding a person using the *kunyah* of "Abul-Qāsim", see **Endnote 186 on page 583**.

2 — [BJ] [SZ] *Sahīh Al-Bukhārī* (no. 2704), as a hadīth of Abū Bakrah (رَضِيَ ٱللَّهُ عَنْهُ).

> MEANING: "Then when the Horn is blown there will be no ties of kinship to benefit them on that day, nor will they ask about one another." — **SŪRAH AL-MU'MINŪN (23): 101**

And Imām Ahmad said: "Abū Sa'īd mawlā Banī Hāshim narrated to us: 'Abdullāh ibn Ja'far narrated to us: Umm Bakr bint Al-Miswar ibn Makhramah narrated to us: from 'Ubaydullāh ibn Abī Rāfi': from Al-Miswar: from Allāh's Messenger (صَلَّى ٱللَّهُ عَلَيْهِ وَسَلَّمَ) that he said:

> "Fātimah is a part of me: whatever angers her angers me, and whatever pleases her pleases me; and ties of kinship will be severed on the Day of Resurrection, except for my ties of kinship, lineage, and my ties to my in-laws."[1]

This hadīth occurs in the *Sahīhs* from Al-Miswar, with other than this wording, and without this addition.

Al-Hāfidh Abū Bakr Al-Bayhaqī said: "And a group narrated this hadīth with this addition from this 'Abdullāh ibn Ja'far — and he is Az-Zuhrī: from her father, and they did not mention Ibn Abī Rāfi', and Allāh knows best."[2]

And from 'Umar ibn Al-Khattāb (رَضِيَ ٱللَّهُ عَنْهُ) that when he sought to marry Umm Kulthūm bint 'Alī ibn Abī Tālib (رَضِيَ ٱللَّهُ عَنْهُ) and 'Alī said to him: "'*She is (too) young*', he said:

> 'I heard Allāh's Messenger (صَلَّى ٱللَّهُ عَلَيْهِ وَسَلَّمَ) say: "*Every tie of relationship and kinship will break on the Day of Resurrection, except for ties of relationship and kinship to me.*" So I loved that I should have a tie of relationship and kinship to Allāh's Messenger (صَلَّى ٱللَّهُ عَلَيْهِ وَسَلَّمَ).'

So 'Alī married (her) to me (رَضِيَ ٱللَّهُ عَنْهُمَا)."

---

1 — This narration is authentic — refer to **ENDNOTE 187 ON PAGE 584** for more detail regarding its chain.

2 — [SH] I say: At-Tabarānī reported it in *Al-Mu'jamul-Kabīr* (22/337/1014), and Ibn Abī 'Āsim in *Al-Āhād wal Mathānī* (5/362/2956), Abū Bakr Al-Khallāl in *As-Sunnah* (2/432-433/655), and Al-Bayhaqī (7/64) through chains of narration from 'Abdullāh ibn Ja'far, with it.

Al-Bayhaqī reported it as a hadīth of Sufyān ibn Wakī' — and he had some weakness, and from Rawh ibn 'Ubādah: from Ibn Juraij: from Ibn Abī Mulaykah: from Hasan ibn Hasan: from his father: that 'Umar [...], and he mentioned it.[1]

Our companions said: It is said that its meaning is that his nation will be ascribed to him on the Day of Resurrection, whereas the nations of the rest of the Prophets will not be ascribed to them.

And it is otherwise said: (It means that) there will be benefit to be derived from being ascribed to him on that Day, whereas there will be no benefit in all other ascriptions. This is preferable to the previous saying, indeed that other saying is weak. Allāh (the Most High) said:

> وَلِكُلِّ أُمَّةٍ رَّسُولٌ فَإِذَا جَاءَ رَسُولُهُمْ قُضِيَ بَيْنَهُم بِالْقِسْطِ وَهُمْ لَا يُظْلَمُونَ
>
> MEANING: "And for every nation there is a Messenger, so when their Messenger comes on the Day of Resurrection the matter will be judged between them with justice, and they will not be wronged." — SŪRAH YŪNUS (10): 47

1 — For more detail regarding the authenticity of this, see ENDNOTE 188 ON PAGE 585.

— along with many verses which prove that every nation will be called along with the Messenger who was sent to them, and Allāh (the Perfect and Most High) knows best (what is correct.)[1]

And Ash-Shaikh Abū ʿUmar ʿAbdil-Barr said in the book *Al-Istīʿāb*,[2] in the biography of ʿUthmān: "And it is established that the Messenger of Allāh (ﷺ) said: 'I asked my Lord that no one who becomes my in-law, or whose in-law I become, should enter the Fire.'"

This is *'gharīb'* (singular/strange).

AN ISSUE:

And from the matters particular to him (ﷺ), to the exclusion of the rest of his nation, is that he was the sternest of them in fighting, and the most courageous of them. He did not flee from any enemy, whether they were few or many.

Anas ibn Mālik said, when he mentioned that he (ﷺ) used to have relations with all his wives on a single night:

---

1 — [SH] An addition from the "ʿĀrif Hikmat Library' manuscript. Then there occurs in it: "And all praise is for Allāh, in the beginning and in the end; and may Allāh extol our noble chief Muhammad, and his true followers, and Companions, and grant peace and security.

This blessed manuscript was completed on the day of Wednesday, in the month of Jumādal-Ākhirah, in the year 1101; at the hand of the weakest one of the servants, and the one in the greatest need: Hasan ibn Al-Hāj Ramadān Al-Khattī, Al-Ayyūbī — may Allāh forgive him and his parents, and treat them and him in a fine manner."

And there occurs in the 'Sulaymāniyyah Library' (no. 59) manuscript: "The noble, blessed Sīrah is completed: through the subtle kindness of Allāh (the Most High); on the morning of the day of Wednesday, the thirteenth of Rabīʿul-Awwal, eight hundred and thirteen; may Allāh make its outcome good, through His Favour and His Clemency; and may He forgive its author, its owner, its scribe, and the one who reads it, and may He protect the Muslims. Amīn."

I say: And what follows on is missing from all of the manuscripts, and is a distinction of the 'Sulaymāniyyah Library' (no. 3339) manuscript.

2 — This narration is questionable. Refer to **Endnote 189 on page 585** for more detail.

> "And we used to estimate that he had the strength of thirty men from his nation."[1]

And from that is that he (صَلَّى ٱللَّهُ عَلَيْهِ وَسَلَّمَ) could see behind him just as he could see in front of him, as occurs in the hadīth, and it has preceded with that meaning.[2]

As for the hadīth which Al-Hāfidh Al-Bayhaqī reported in the book *Dalā'ilun-Nubuwwah* (Signs of Prophethood), when he said: "Abū Sa'd Al-Mālīnī related to us: Abū Ahmad ibn 'Alī Al-Hāfidh related to us: Ibn Salam[3] narrated to us: 'Abbās ibn Al-Walīd narrated to us: Zuhayr ibn 'Ubādah narrated to us: from 'Abdullāh ibn Muhammad ibn Al-Mughīrah: from Hishām ibn 'Urwah: from his father: from 'Ā'ishah that she said:

> 'Allāh's Messenger (صَلَّى ٱللَّهُ عَلَيْهِ وَسَلَّمَ) could see in the darkness just as he could see when it was light.'[4]

Then it is a weak hadīth; it was declared weak by the Hāfidhān: Ibn 'Adiyy and Al-Bayhaqī, and by others.

Al-Bayhaqī said: "And it is related through another chain which is not strong: Abū 'Abdillāh Al-Hāfidh related it to us: Abū 'Abdillāh Muhammad ibn Al-'Abbās narrated to me: Abū Is-hāq ibn Sa'īd narrated to us: Abū 'Abdillāh Muhammad ibn Al-Khalīl An-Naysābūrī narrated to us: Sālih ibn 'Abdillāh An-Naysābūrī narrated to us: 'Abdur-Rahmān ibn 'Ammār Ash-Shahīd narrated to us: Mughīrah ibn Muslim narrated to us: from 'Atā': from Ibn 'Abbās (رَضِيَ ٱللَّهُ عَنْهُ) who said: "Allāh's Messenger

---

1 — [SH] Reported by Al-Bukhārī (no. 268).

2 — Explanation of this has preceded. See page 311.

3 — [SH] In the manuscript, there occurs *"Aslam"*, and the correction is from the source books of hadīth-referencing, and the books of narrators.

4 — The *isnād* mentioned here is fabricated and unacceptable. Refer to **Endnote 190 on page 586** for details.

(صَلَّى ٱللَّهُ عَلَيْهِ وَسَلَّمَ) could see at night, in the darkness, just as he could see during the day, in the light."[1]

I say: As for what many of the storytellers and others narrate: that he (صَلَّى ٱللَّهُ عَلَيْهِ وَسَلَّمَ) used to see eight stars in the constellation of the Plough, whereas the people only see seven, then there is likewise no basis for that.[2]

AN ISSUE:

ʿUthmān ibn Abī Shaybah said: "From Jarīr: from Shaybah ibn Naʿāmah: from Fātimah bint Al-Husayn: from the major Fātimah, that she said: 'Allāh's Messenger (صَلَّى ٱللَّهُ عَلَيْهِ وَسَلَّمَ) said:

> "Every one of the descendants of Ādam will be ascribed to their paternal relations except for the sons of Fātimah: for they shall be ascribed to me, and I am their forefather."""[3]

Imām Ahmad ibn Hanbal and others criticized ʿUthmān ibn Abī Shaybah for it.

Al-Hāfidh Abū Bakr Al-Khatīb said: "However, others besides him report it from Jarīr."

---

1 — [BJ][SZ][SH] It is *'daʿīf jiddan'* (very weak): Al-Bayhaqī reported it in *Dalāʾilun-Nubuwwah* (6/75), and he said concerning it: *"And that is narrated through another chain which is not strong."* And our Shaikh, Al-Imām Al-Albānī (رَحِمَهُ ٱللَّهُ) said in *Ad-Daʿīfah* (no. 341): *"I say: And this is a gloomy isnād, since I do not find any biography at all for those beyond Al-Mughīrah."*

2 — [DB] The translation of this line is based upon the wording in the edition checked by Salīm Al-Hilālī (فَلَا أَصلَ لَهُ كَذَلِك). The wording in the edition checked by Samīr Az-Zuhayrī and Dr. Bāsim Al-Jawābirah (فَالأَصلُ كَذَلِك) could be translated as *"then that is basically how they are."*

3 — For detail regarding the authenticity of this narration, see **Endnote 191 on page 587**.

CHAPTER:

An Indication of the Types of Intercession (Ash-Shafāʿah) Which Our Prophet Muhammad (صَلَّى ٱللَّهُ عَلَيْهِ وَسَلَّمَ) Will Be Granted

[THE FIRST STATION:] So the highest of them, the greatest of them, and the most far-reaching of them will be *'Al-Maqāmul-Mahmūd'* (The Praiseworthy Station), which all of the creation will avidly petition him for, so that he should intercede for them with Allāh (the Exalted and Most High) for Him to come to pass judgement, and save the Believers from the standing in the Place of Gathering (*Al-Mahshar*), and rescue them from the company of the Disbelievers upon the open plain of the Resurrection. This will be after Ādam, Nūh, Ibrāhīm, Mūsā, and ʿĪsā (صلوات الله وسلامه عليهم) have been asked to do that, and each of them will say: "I am not the right person for that."

So then they will go to Muhammad (صلوات الله وسلامه عليه) and they will ask him to do that. So he will say: "I am the one for it! I am the one for it!"

So he will go and he will intercede with Allāh for that; and the details of that have preceded.[1]

THE SECOND STATION from the stations of Intercession (*Ash-Shafāʿah*) will be his interceding for some of his nation, about whom the command has been given that they are to be taken to the Fire: that they should not enter it.

That is clearly shown in the hadīth which is reported by Al-Hāfidh Abū Bakr ʿAbdullāh ibn Muhammad ibn Abid-Dunyā (رَحِمَهُ ٱللَّهُ) in his book

---

1 — It has preceded on page 297.

Ahwālul-Qiyāmah,[1] in the chapter on Intercession, towards its end, where he said:

"Saʿīd ibn Muhammad Al-Jarmī narrated to us: Abū ʿUbaydah[2] Al-Haddād narrated to us: Muhammad ibn Thābit Al-Bunānī narrated to us: from ʿUbaydullāh ibn ʿAbdillāh ibn Al-Hārith ibn Nawfal: from his father: from ʿAbdullāh ibn ʿAbbās who said: Allāh's Messenger (صَلَّىٰ اللَّهُ عَلَيْهِ وَسَلَّمَ) said:

> "Elevated seats of gold will be set up for the Prophets, and they will sit upon them, but my seat will remain — I will not sit upon it. I will be standing in front of Allāh (the Mighty and Majestic); standing upright with my nation, out of fear that I should be sent to Paradise whilst my nation remain behind after me.
>
> So I will say: 'O my Lord! My nation!'
>
> So Allāh (the Exalted and Most High) will say: 'O Muhammad! And what do you wish that I should do with your nation?'
>
> So I will say: 'O my Lord! Hasten their reckoning.'
>
> So they will be called, and their reckoning will be carried out. So some of them will enter Paradise by the Mercy of Allāh, and some of them will enter Paradise through my intercession. So I will continue interceding until I am given the judgements passed upon some men who have been sent to the Fire, to the extent that Mālik (the Custodian of the Hellfire) will say: 'O Muhammad! You have not left anyone for the torment of the Fire — the Fire that was due upon your nation because of your Lord's anger.'"

And he said also: "Ismāʿīl ibn ʿUnayd ibn ʿUmar[3] ibn Abī Karīmah narrated to us: Muhammad ibn Salamah narrated to me: from Abī

---

1 — For the details of this narration's authenticity, see Endnote 192 on page 587.

2 — [BJ][SZ] There occurs in the manuscript *"Abū ʿAbdillāh"*, and the correction is from the source-works of hadīth referencing.

3 — [SH] In the manuscript, and in *Al-Bidāyah wan-Nihāyah* (20/190) there occurs *"ʿUmayr"*, and the correction is from the books of narrators.

ʿAbdir-Rahīm: Zayd ibn Abī Unaysah narrated to me: from Al-Minhāl ibn ʿAmr: from ʿAbdullāh ibn Al-Hārith: from Abū Hurairah who said:

> "The people will be resurrected naked; and they will gather with their gaze fixed towards the sky, standing for forty years awaiting the Judgement. Then Allāh (the Most High) will descend from the Throne (*Al-ʿArsh*) to the Footstool (*Al-Kursī*). So the first one to be called will be Ibrāhīm Al-Khalīl (صَلَّى ٱللَّهُ عَلَيْهِ وَسَلَّمَ), and he will be clothed in two linen garments of Paradise. Then He will say: *'Call for Me, the Unlettered Prophet, Muhammad (صَلَّى ٱللَّهُ عَلَيْهِ وَسَلَّمَ).'"*

"He (صَلَّى ٱللَّهُ عَلَيْهِ وَسَلَّمَ) said:

> 'So I will stand and I will be dressed in an outfit from the garments of Paradise. He said: And the Great Reservoir (*Al-Hawd*) will be filled with water for me, and its width will be like that between Aylah (Eilat)[1] and the Kaʿbah. He said: So I will drink, and I will bathe, and the necks of the creation will be broken with thirst. Then I shall stand to the right of the footstool (*Al-Kursī*); no one else will stand at that station on that Day besides me. Then it will be said: *"Ask, and you will be given. Intercede and your intercession will be accepted."'"*

He said: "So a man said: 'Do you have any hope at all for your parents, O Messenger of Allāh?'

He (صَلَّى ٱللَّهُ عَلَيْهِ وَسَلَّمَ) said:

> 'I shall (try to) intercede for them, whether it is acceptable or not; but I do not have hope of anything for them.'"[2]

---

1 — [DB] A coastal town at the northern tip of the Gulf of ʿAqabah, 640 miles from Makkah. Yāqūt Al-Hamawī said in *Muʿjamul-Buldān*: "Aylah [Eilat] is a town on the coast of the sea of Qulzum (the Gulf of ʿAqabah), next to Shām. It is said that it is the end of the Hijāz and the beginning of Shām."

2 — [BJ][SZ] To this point, the hadīth is *mawqūf* (the statement of the Companion).

[SH] I say: And this hadīth has a *'hasan'* chain of narration since its narrators are all reliable, except for Al-Minhāl, about whom there is some slight speech, which will not take him below the level of the *'hasan'*.

Then Al-Minhāl said: "'Abdullāh ibn Al-Hārith also narrated to me that the Prophet of Allāh (صَلَّى ٱللَّهُ عَلَيْهِ وَسَلَّمَ) said: 'I will pass by some people of my nation, about whom the Command will have been given that they should be taken to the Fire. So they will say: *"O Muhammad! We implore you to intercede."'*

He said: 'So I will order the Angels to stop and wait with them.'

He said: 'And I will go and seek permission of the Lord (the Mighty and Majestic) and He will give me permission. So I shall prostrate and say: *"O my Lord, a people from my nation; You have commanded that they be taken to the Fire."'*

He said: 'So He will say:

> "Go, and take some of them away."

So I will go, and I will take whomever Allāh wishes me to take. Then those remaining will call out: *"O Muhammad! We implore you to intercede."*

So I shall return to the Lord (the Mighty and Majestic) and I will seek permission, and I will be granted permission. So I shall prostrate, and it will be said to me:

> "Raise you head! Ask, and you will be given. Intercede, and your intercession will be accepted."

So I will say: "A people from my nation; it has been commanded that they be taken to the Fire."'

He said: 'So He will say:

> "Go and take some of them away."'

He said: 'So I will go, and I will take out whomever Allāh wishes me to take out. Then those remaining will call out: "O Muhammad! We implore you to intercede."

So I shall return to my Lord (the Mighty and Majestic) and I will seek permission, and I will be granted permission, and I will prostrate. So He will say:

> "Raise your head! Ask, and you will be given. Intercede, and your intercession will be accepted."

So I will stand, and I will praise the Lord with words of praise, which no one has ever praised Him with. Then I will say: "A people from my nation; it has been commanded that they be taken to the Fire."

So He will say:

> "Go, and take some of them away."'

He said: 'So I shall say: "O my Lord, may I take from them whoever said '*None has the right to be worshipped except Allāh'* — and whoever has in his heart the weight of a mustard seed of Īmān (true Faith)?"'

He said: 'So He will say:

> "O Muhammad! That is not for you, that is for Me."'

He said: 'So I shall go, and I will take away whomever Allāh wishes me to take.'

He said: 'And a people will remain, and they will enter the Fire. So the inhabitants of the Fire will reproach them and say: *"You used to worship Allāh, and not associate anything with Him. Now He has entered you into the Fire."*'

He said: 'So they will feel grief because of that.'

He said: 'So Allāh (the Mighty and Majestic) will send an Angel with a handful of water, and it will be sprinkled into the Fire. So no one from the people of 'لَا إِلَٰهَ إِلَّا اللهُ' (*'None has the right to be worshipped except Allāh'*) will remain except that a drop of it will fall upon his face.'

He said: 'They will be recognized through it, and they will be envied by the inhabitants of the Fire. Then they will come out, and they will enter Paradise; and it will be said to them: *"Go and seek to settle with the people as guests."* So if all of them were to settle with a single man, then they would still have extensive space; and they will be called *"The Ones Set Free."*""[1]

So this hadīth, and the one which came before it, shows that he (ﷺ) will intercede for people about whom the command has been given that they should be taken to the Fire, so that they do not enter the Fire.

And this second hadīth shows that he will repeat the interceding; and that he will intercede for a group of them, then for others after others. All of this will be before their entering the Fire; therefore he said at the end of the hadīth: *"And a people will remain and they will enter the Fire"* — and this hadīth is *'mursal'*.[2]

[THE THIRD STATION:] And his saying in the first hadīth: *"So some of them will enter Paradise by the Mercy of Allāh, and some of them will enter Paradise through my intercession"* — is a proof for the Third Station: and it is the intercession for people whose good deeds and bad deeds are equal. So they do not deserve entry into Paradise, and they have not necessitated entry into the Fire. So he will intercede so that they enter Paradise.

AS FOR THE FOURTH STATION from the stations of Intercession, then it is the Intercession for the people guilty of major sins *(Ahlul-Kabā'ir)* who have entered the Fire, so that they come out from the Fire. The ahādīth about that are mutawātir from Allāh's Messenger (ﷺ) in the *Sahīh* books, and in the *Musnads*, and in other than them from the books of Islām; and the imāms of Islām, of the earlier and the later times, agreed upon acceptance of them.

No one disagreed concerning that except for the Khawārij and those who followed them upon their innovation, from the Mu'tazilah and others. So they are disproven by the *'mutawātir'* hadīth, which they hold it to be binding to adopt. However, their knowledge does not comprehend the fact that it is *'mutawātir'*, so therefore they deny that which their knowledge does not reach. So there is no excuse for them — rather,

---

1 — [SH] This hadīth with this wording is weak *(da'īf)*, because it is *'mursal'*; and it was declared weak for this reason by the author (رَحِمَهُ ٱللَّهُ).

2 — [BJ][SZ] Because it is a narration of 'Abdullāh ibn Al-Hārith, and he was a Tābi'ī.

whoever denies his honourable station will not attain it [i.e. they will not receive his Intercession].

Rather, by Allāh, he will certainly have the greatest station in that regard; and he will intercede for the people of major sins to come out, again and again, until it occurs four times, as occurs in the ahādīth.

And the Prophets will intercede for their nations; and the Believers for their families, and their companions — from the sinners; and the Angels will intercede also.

Then, after all of this, Allāh will take out from the Fire people who never did any good, but in their hearts was an atom's weight of Īmān (true Faith), and whoever upon a day, truly and sincerely said: 'لَا إِلَٰهَ إِلَّا اللّٰه' (*'None has the right to be worshipped except Allāh'*) .

The fifth station is his Intercession for the Believers, after they have crossed the *'Sirāt'* (the *'Bridge'* over the Fire), that permission be given for them to enter into Paradise. So he mentioned that they will go to Ādam, then Nūh, and to Ibrāhīm, and to Mūsā, then ʿĪsā. Then they will go to Muhammad (صَلَّى ٱللَّهُ عَلَيْهِ وَسَلَّمَ), and he will intercede for them, and his intercession will be accepted — may Allāh extol and grant him peace and security, until the Day of Recompense.

It is witnessed to by the hadīth of Anas in *Sahīh Muslim*[1]: that Allāh's Messenger (صَلَّى ٱللَّهُ عَلَيْهِ وَسَلَّمَ) said: "I will be the first to intercede in Paradise."

The sixth station from the stations of Intercession is his (عَلَيْهِ ٱلصَّلَاةُ وَٱلسَّلَامُ) intercession for the raising of the level of some of the Believers in Paradise, and this is something which the Muʿtazilah and others consent to.

Its proof is the hadīth of Umm Salamah, which occurs in *Sahīh Muslim*[2]: that when Abū Salamah died, Allāh's Messenger (صَلَّى ٱللَّهُ عَلَيْهِ وَسَلَّمَ) said:

> "O Allāh! Forgive Abū Salamah, and raise his level amongst the guided; and grant him good with regard to the offspring he leaves behind; and forgive us and him. O Lord of the whole of the creation! And extend his grave for him, and grant him light in it."

1 — BJ SZ (no. 196).

2 — BJ SZ (no. 920)

And likewise the other hadīth, from Abū Mūsā Al-Ash'arī (رَضِيَ ٱللَّهُ عَنْهُ) that when Allāh's Messenger (صَلَّى ٱللَّهُ عَلَيْهِ وَسَلَّمَ) was informed that Abū 'Āmir had been killed at Awtās, Allāh's Messenger (صَلَّى ٱللَّهُ عَلَيْهِ وَسَلَّمَ) performed wudhū', then he raised his hands, and said:

> "O Allāh! Forgive 'Ubayd, Abū 'Āmir, and place him on the Day of Resurrection above many from Your creation."

The two Shaikhs reported it in the two *Sahīhs*.[1]

---

1 — [SH] Reported by Al-Bukhārī (nos. 2884 & 4323) and Muslim (no. 2498).

This is the last part of what is found in this Prophetic Sīrah from that which was authored and written by the hand of the Shaikh, the Imām, the Hāfidh, the great scholar, Shaikhul-Islām, the blessing to mankind, the Shaikh: ʿImāduddīn, Ismāʿīl ibn Kathīr — may Allāh pardon him, by His Favour and Generosity, Indeed He is One Who forgives extensively, Merciful, Bountiful, and Generous.

It was transcribed by the poor servant: Sulaymān Al-Madīnī — servant of the apartments of the Prophet (صَلَّى ٱللَّهُ عَلَيْهِ وَسَلَّمَ) — may Allāh forgive him, and all of the Muslims. Āmīn.

And all praise is for Allāh, Lord of the whole of the creation. On the date of the tenth of Shawwāl, in the year seven-hundred and eighty-four, may Allāh seal it with good and with security from harm, indeed He is the Disposer of affairs.

— END —

Appendixes, Endnotes, and Translator's References

APPENDIX ONE

The Islamic Months

1ST MONTH:	Muharram
2ND MONTH:	Safar
3RD MONTH:	Rabīʿ Al-Awwal
4TH MONTH:	Rabīʿ Al-Ākhir
5TH MONTH:	Jumādā Al-Ūlā
6TH MONTH:	Jumādā Al-Ākhirah
7TH MONTH:	Rajab
8TH MONTH:	Shaʿbān
9TH MONTH:	Ramadān
10TH MONTH:	Shawwāl
11TH MONTH:	Dhul-Qaʿdah
12TH MONTH:	Dhul-Hijjah

APPENDIX TWO

Timeline of Key Events in the Life of the Messenger (صَلَّى ٱللَّٰهُ عَلَيْهِ وَسَلَّمَ)

2.1 – Events Before the Hijrah to Al-Madīnah

53 BH
The Year of the Elephant
The birth of Allāh's Messenger (صَلَّى ٱللَّٰهُ عَلَيْهِ وَسَلَّمَ)

49 BH
At the age of 4 years
The incident of the splitting open of his chest (صَلَّى ٱللَّٰهُ عَلَيْهِ وَسَلَّمَ).

47 BH
At the age of 6 years
His mother Āminah died at Al-Abwā'. He was then taken into the care of his grandfather; Abdul-Muttalib.

45 BH
At the age of 8 years
His grandfather died and he was taken into the care of his uncle; Abū Tālib.

41 BH
At the age of 12 years
He (صَلَّى ٱللَّٰهُ عَلَيْهِ وَسَلَّمَ) went on a trading trip with his uncle, Abū Tālib. Amazing signs were seen regarding him (صَلَّى ٱللَّٰهُ عَلَيْهِ وَسَلَّمَ), including the incident with Bahirah the Monk.

28 BH
At the age of 25 years
He married Khadijah (رَضِيَ ٱللَّٰهُ عَنْهَا).

18 BH
At the age of 35 years
The Ka'bah was rebuilt and the Black Stone was put in place by Allāh's Messenger (صَلَّى ٱللَّٰهُ عَلَيْهِ وَسَلَّمَ).

13 BH – 1 AB
1st Year of Prophethood
He received the first Revelation (the first verses of Sūrah Iqra'), at the age of 40.

BIRTH

BH = Before Hijrah

This refers to the years prior to the Hijrah of the Messenger (صَلَّى ٱللَّٰهُ عَلَيْهِ وَسَلَّمَ) to Al-Madinah; which took place in the 14th year of his Prophethood

AB = After Bi'thah

The Bi'thah is the "sending" of the Prophet Muhammad (صَلَّى ٱللَّٰهُ عَلَيْهِ وَسَلَّمَ), and it refers to the first time he received Revelation from the Angel Jibrīl (عَلَيْهِ ٱلسَّلَامُ).

3 AB

3rd Year of Prophethood

He received the 2nd Revelation (Sūrah Al-Muddaththir (74): 1-4). He was commanded to openly proclaim Islām. The Mushrikoon begin their persecution of the Muslims.

5 AB

5th Year of Prophethood

Rajab: The first Hijrah to Abyssinia (12 men and 4 women).

Shawwāl: The Muslims returned from Abyssinia.

6 AB

6th Year of Prophethood

Hamzah and 'Umar (رَضِيَ ٱللَّٰهُ عَنْهُ) accepted Islām.

7 AB

7th Year of Prophethood

The Quraysh boycotted Banū Hāshim and Banul-Muttalib. The boycott continued for 3 years.

9 AB

9th Year of Prophethood

- The Night Journey and the Ascent through the Heavens (*Al-Isrā' wal-Mi'rāj*).
- The Five Daily Prayers were prescribed.
- The miracle of the splitting of the moon.

10 AB

10th Year of Prophethood — also known as "The Year of Sorrow."

The end of the Boycott. 6 months later Abū Tālib died, and 3 days after that Khādijah (رَضِيَ ٱللَّٰهُ عَنْهَا) also died. Allāh's Messenger (صَلَّى ٱللَّٰهُ عَلَيْهِ وَسَلَّمَ) went to call the people of At-Tā'if. Allāh's Messenger (صَلَّى ٱللَّٰهُ عَلَيْهِ وَسَلَّمَ) married 'A'ishah (رَضِيَ ٱللَّٰهُ عَنْهَا), and also Sawdah (رَضِيَ ٱللَّٰهُ عَنْهَا).

12 AB

12th Year of Prophethood

The first Pledge of Al-'Aqabah, during the days of the Hajj.

13 AB

13th Year of Prophethood

The second Pledge of Al-'Aqabah, during the days of the Hajj.

HIJRAH

Timeline of Key Events in the Life of the Messenger (صَلَّى ٱللَّٰهُ عَلَيْهِ وَسَلَّمَ)

2.2 – Events After the Hijrah to Al-Madīnah

1ST YEAR OF THE HIJRAH

Safar
Before the arrival of the Prophet (صَلَّى ٱللَّٰهُ عَلَيْهِ وَسَلَّمَ) in Al-Madinah

Al-Barā' ibn Ma'rūr (one of the leaders of the people who gave the second pledge of Al-'Aqabah) died.

Rabī' Al-Awwal
The Month of the Hijrah.

- **12TH** — The arrival at Al-Madīnah. Allāh's Messenger (صَلَّى ٱللَّٰهُ عَلَيْهِ وَسَلَّمَ) settled in Qubā', in the house of Kulthūm ibn Al-Hidm, remaining there until the day of Jumu'ah when he (صَلَّى ٱللَّٰهُ عَلَيْهِ وَسَلَّمَ) proceeded to the place of Banū Sālim ibn 'Awf in the valley of Rānūnā. where he led them in the Jumu'ah prayer; then he (صَلَّى ٱللَّٰهُ عَلَيْهِ وَسَلَّمَ) proceeded to the place of Banun-Najjār and settled in the house of Abū Ayyūb.
- 'Abdullāh ibn Salām accepts Islām.
- The building of the mosque and the apartments for the Prophet (صَلَّى ٱللَّٰهُ عَلَيْهِ وَسَلَّمَ) and his wives.

Rabī' Al-Ākhir

- The death of Kulthūm ibn Hidm.
- The death of As'ad ibn Zurārah, who gave both of the pledges of Al-'Aqabah; (or it is otherwise said that he died in Shawwāl).
- Increase in the residence Prayer.
- The Companions suffer from the fever found in Al-Madīnah.
- The Zakāt established [upon the saying of the majority].

1 AH | *Muharram* | *Safar* | *Rabī' Al-Awwal* | *Rabī' Al-Ākhir* | *Jumādā Al-Ūlā* | *Jumādā Al-Ākhirah*

**— Indicates that Allāh's Messenger (صَلَّى ٱللَّٰهُ عَلَيْهِ وَسَلَّمَ) went along with the expedition, or took part in the battle himself.*

Ramadān

The expedition of Hamzah towards the coast to attack a caravan of Abū Jahl (or it is said that it occurred in Rabīʿ Al-Awwal in 2 H).

Shawwāl

- Allāh's Messenger (ﷺ) consummated his marriage with ʿĀʾishah (or it is said: in Shawwāl of the second year).
- The birth of ʿAbdullāh ibn Az-Zubayr.
- The expedition of ʿUbaydah ibn Al-Hārith against a party of Quraysh (or it is said: it occurred in Rabīʿ Al-Ākhir in 2 H).

Dhul-Qaʿdah

- The Raid of Saʿd ibn Abī Waqqās.
- Brotherhood established between the Muhājirīn and the Ansār.
- Legislation of the Adhān.

Rajab | *Shaʿbān* | *Ramadān* | *Shawwāl* | *Dhul-Qaʿdah* | *Dhul-Hijjah*

APPENDIX TWO – CONTINUED

Timeline of Key Events in the Life of the Messenger (صَلَّى ٱللَّٰهُ عَلَيْهِ وَسَلَّمَ)

2.2 – Events After the Hijrah to Al-Madīnah

2ND YEAR AFTER THE HIJRAH

Safar

- The Expedition of Abwa'/ Waddān.* Allāh's Messenger (صَلَّى ٱللَّٰهُ عَلَيْهِ وَسَلَّمَ) went out, leaving Sa'd ibn 'Ubādah in charge of Al-Madīnah].

Rabī' Al-Awwal

- The Expedition of Buwāt.*

Jumādā Al-Ūlā

- The Expedition of Ushayrah.*

Jumādā Al-Ākhirah

- The First Expedition of Badr.*

2 AH | *Muharram* | *Safar* | *Rabī' Al-Awwal* | *Rabī' Al-Ākhir* | *Jumādā Al-Ūlā* | *Jumādā Al-Ākhirah*

*— *Indicates that Allāh's Messenger (صَلَّى ٱللَّٰهُ عَلَيْهِ وَسَلَّمَ) went along with the expedition, or took part in the battle himself.*

Rajab

- The Raid of ʿAbdullāh ibn Jahsh.

Shaʿbān

- The changing of the Qiblah from Jerusalem to the Kaʿbah.
- The obligation of fasting in Ramadān.

Ramadān

- The Greater Battle of Badr.*
- The death of Ruqayyah, the daughter of Allāh's Messenger (صَلَّى ٱللَّهُ عَلَيْهِ وَسَلَّمَ).
- The Obligation of Zakāh Al-Fitr.

Shawwāl

- The Attack upon Banū Sulaym.*
- The Expedition of Banū Qaynuqāʿ.*

Dhul-Hijjah

- The Expedition of As-Sawīq.*

Rajab | *Shaʿbān* | *Ramadān* | *Shawwāl* | *Dhul-Qaʿdah* | *Dhul-Hijjah*

Timeline of Key Events in the Life of the Messenger (صَلَّى ٱللَّهُ عَلَيْهِ وَسَلَّمَ)

2.2 – Events After the Hijrah to Al-Madīnah

3RD YEAR AFTER THE HIJRAH

Muharram

- The Expedition of Dhī Amarr.*

Rabīʿ Al-Awwal

- ʿUthmān married Umm Kulthūm; daughter of the Prophet (صَلَّى ٱللَّهُ عَلَيْهِ وَسَلَّمَ).
- The killing of Kaʿb ibn Ashraf.

Rabīʿ Al-Ākhir

- The Expedition of Buhrān.*

Jumādā Al-Ākhirah

- ʿUthmān consumated his marriage with Umm Kulthūm; the daughter of Allāh's Messenger (صَلَّى ٱللَّهُ عَلَيْهِ وَسَلَّمَ)

3 AH | *Muharram* | *Safar* | *Rabīʿ Al-Awwal* | *Rabīʿ Al-Ākhir* | *Jumādā Al-Ūlā* | *Jumādā Al-Ākhirah*

**— Indicates that Allāh's Messenger (صَلَّى ٱللَّهُ عَلَيْهِ وَسَلَّمَ) went along with the expedition, or took part in the battle himself.*

Sha'bān

- Allah's Messenger (ﷺ) married Hafsah, the daughter of 'Umar.

Ramadān

- Fātimah gave birth to Al-Hasan ibn 'Alī ibn Abī Tālib, and in the same year she became pregnant with Al-Husayn.
- Allāh's Messenger (ﷺ) married Zaynab bint Khuzaymah Al-Hilāliyyah, who was known as *'Ummul-Masākīn' (The Mother of the Poor)* for her fine treatment of the poor and needy, and she died in his (ﷺ) lifetime, or it is said that she died a few months after the marriage.

Shawwāl

- The Battle of Uhud.*
- The Expedition of Hamrā' Al-Asad.*

Rajab | *Sha'bān* | *Ramadān* | *Shawwāl* | *Dhul-Qa'dah* | *Dhul-Hijjah*

APPENDIX TWO — CONTINUED

Timeline of Key Events in the Life of the Messenger (صَلَّى ٱللَّٰهُ عَلَيْهِ وَسَلَّمَ)

2.2 – Events After the Hijrah to Al-Madīnah

4TH YEAR AFTER THE HIJRAH

Safar

- The Expedition of Ar-Rajī'.
- The Incident of Bi'r Ma'ūnah.

Rabī' Al-Awwal

- The Expedition of Banu An-Nadīr.*
- The Qunūt of Allāh's Messenger (صَلَّى ٱللَّٰهُ عَلَيْهِ وَسَلَّمَ) for one month against those who had killed his Companions at Bi'r Ma'ūnah.

Jumādā Al-Ūlā

- 'Abdullāh ibn 'Uthmān ibn 'Affān — son of 'Uthmān and Ruqayyah (daughter of Muhammad صَلَّى ٱللَّٰهُ عَلَيْهِ وَسَلَّمَ) died at the age of 6. He (صَلَّى ٱللَّٰهُ عَلَيْهِ وَسَلَّمَ) prayed over him, and 'Uthmān put him in his grave.

Jumādā Al-Ākhirah

- Abū Salamah, 'Abdullāh ibn 'Abdil-Asad died (he had accepted Islām on the same day as 'Uthmān, Abū 'Ubaydah and Al-Akram ibn Abil-Akram). He died as a result of wounds suffered at Uhud.

4 AH | *Muharram* | *Safar* | *Rabī' Al-Awwal* | *Rabī' Al-Ākhir* | *Jumādā Al-Ūlā* | *Jumādā Al-Ākhirah*

**— Indicates that Allāh's Messenger (صَلَّى ٱللَّٰهُ عَلَيْهِ وَسَلَّمَ) went along with the expedition, or took part in the battle himself.*

Sha'bān

- The Expedition of Badr Al-Maw'id (Third Badr).*
- Al-Husayn ibn 'Alī ibn Abī Tālib was born.

Shawwāl

- Allāh's Messenger (صَلَّى ٱللَّٰهُ عَلَيْهِ وَسَلَّمَ) married Umm Salamah.

Dhul-Qa'dah

- The Prophet (صَلَّى ٱللَّٰهُ عَلَيْهِ وَسَلَّمَ) married Zaynab bint Jahsh; and the prescription of the Hijāb came about on the day after her wedding, (or it is said: this occurred in 3 H, or it is said: in 5 H).

Rajab | *Sha'bān* | *Ramadān* | *Shawwāl* | *Dhul-Qa'dah* | *Dhul-Hijjah*

Timeline of Key Events in the Life of the Messenger (صَلَّى ٱللَّٰهُ عَلَيْهِ وَسَلَّمَ)

2.2 – Events After the Hijrah to Al-Madīnah

5TH YEAR AFTER THE HIJRAH

Rabīʿ Al-Awwal

- The Expedition of Dūmatul-Jandal.*

5 AH: *Muharram* | *Safar* | *Rabīʿ Al-Awwal* | *Rabīʿ Al-Ākhir* | *Jumādā Al-Ūlā* | *Jumādā Al-Ākhirah*

**— Indicates that Allāh's Messenger (صَلَّى ٱللَّٰهُ عَلَيْهِ وَسَلَّمَ) went along with the expedition, or took part in the battle himself.*

Sha'bān

- The expedition of Banul-Mustaliq/ Al-Muraysī' (or it is said: it occurred in Sha'bān 6 H).*
- Allāh's Messenger (ﷺ) married Juwayriyah bint Al-Ḥārith.
- The incident of the slanderous lie against 'Ā'ishah. (She was fourteen years old).

Shawwāl

- The Battle of the Trench — Al-Khandaq / Al-Aḥzāb (The Confederates).*

Dhul-Qa'dah

- The Battle of Banū Qurayẓah.*

Dhul-Ḥijjah

- The death of Sa'd ibn Mu'ādh.

Rajab | *Sha'bān* | *Ramaḍān* | *Shawwāl* | *Dhul-Qa'dah* | *Dhul-Ḥijjah*

Timeline of Key Events in the Life of the Messenger (صَلَّى ٱللَّهُ عَلَيْهِ وَسَلَّمَ)

2.2 – Events After the Hijrah to Al-Madīnah

6TH YEAR AFTER THE HIJRAH

Jumādā Al-Ūlā

- The Expedition of Banū Lahyān.*

6 AH

Muharram | *Safar* | *Rabī' Al-Awwal* | *Rabī' Al-Ākhir* | *Jumādā Al-Ūlā* | *Jumādā Al-Ākhirah*

*— *Indicates that Allāh's Messenger (صَلَّى ٱللَّهُ عَلَيْهِ وَسَلَّمَ) went along with the expedition, or took part in the battle himself.*

Dhul-Qaʿdah

- The Expedition of Hudaybiyah.*
- The Pledge (*Bayʿah*) of Ridwān.
- The prohibition of Muslim women being married to Disbelieving men.

Timeline of Key Events in the Life of the Messenger (صَلَّىٱللَّهُعَلَيْهِوَسَلَّمَ)

2.2 – Events After the Hijrah to Al-Madīnah

7TH YEAR AFTER THE HIJRAH

Muharram

- The Raid of Dhī Qarad (or it is said: it occurred in Jumādal-Ūlā, 6 H).*
- The Expedition of Khaybar.*
- The marriage of Allāh's Messenger (صَلَّىٱللَّهُعَلَيْهِوَسَلَّمَ) to Safiyyah.
- The arrival of Ja'far and the Muslims of Abyssinia, and Abū Mūsā Al-Ash'arī, and Abū Hurairah.
- The incident of the poisoned sheep.
- The Expedition of Dhātur-Riqā'* (or it is said: it occurred in Jumādal-Ūlā 4 H; or it is said: in Muharram 5 H; or it is said at the end of 5 H; or it is said: there were two separate expeditions which bore this name: one before Al-Khandaq, and one afterwards).
- The Conquest of Wādī Al-Qurā.*
- The Conquest of Fadak.
- The marriage of Allāh's Messenger (صَلَّىٱللَّهُعَلَيْهِوَسَلَّمَ) to Umm Habībah Ramlah bint Abī Sufyān.
- Māriyah Al-Qibtiyyah was brought to Allāh's Messenger (صَلَّىٱللَّهُعَلَيْهِوَسَلَّمَ).

7 AH | *Muharram* | *Safar* | *Rabī' Al-Awwal* | *Rabī' Al-Ākhir* | *Jumādā Al-Ūlā* | *Jumādā Al-Ākhirah*

*— *Indicates that Allāh's Messenger (صَلَّىٱللَّهُعَلَيْهِوَسَلَّمَ) went along with the expedition, or took part in the battle himself.*

Dhul-Qaʿdah

- The ʿUmrah of the Agreement.
- The marriage of Allāh's Messenger (ﷺ) to Maymūnah.

Timeline of Key Events in the Life of the Messenger (صَلَّى ٱللَّٰهُ عَلَيْهِ وَسَلَّمَ)

2.2 – Events After the Hijrah to Al-Madīnah

8TH YEAR AFTER THE HIJRAH

Muharram

- At the start of the year: The death of Zaynab, the daughter of Allāh's Messenger (صَلَّى ٱللَّٰهُ عَلَيْهِ وَسَلَّمَ).

Safar

- 'Amr ibn Al-'Ās, Khālid ibn Al-Walīd, and 'Uthmān ibn Talhah accepted Islām.

Jumādā Al-Ūlā / Jumādā Al-Ākhirah

- The Battle of Mu'tah against the Byzantines.

8 AH | *Muharram* | *Safar* | *Rabī' Al-Awwal* | *Rabī' Al-Ākhir* | *Jumādā Al-Ūlā* | *Jumādā Al-Ākhirah*

**— Indicates that Allāh's Messenger (صَلَّى ٱللَّٰهُ عَلَيْهِ وَسَلَّمَ) went along with the expedition, or took part in the battle himself.*

Ramadān

- Abū Sufyān ibn Harb accepted Islām.
- The Conquest of Makkah.*
- The sending of Khālid ibn Al-Walīd to the tribe of Jadhīmah.
- The sending of Khālid ibn Al-Walīd to destroy the idol Al-'Uzzā.

Shawwāl

- The Battle of Hunayn.*
- The Siege of At-Tā'if.*

Dhul-Qa'dah

- Allāh's Messenger (صَلَّىٱللَّهُعَلَيْهِوَسَلَّمَ) performed the 'Umrah from Al-Ji'rānah, and then returned to Al-Madīnah at the end of the month.

Dhul-Hijjah

- The birth of Ibrāhīm; the son of Allāh's Messenger (صَلَّىٱللَّهُعَلَيْهِوَسَلَّمَ) from Māriyah Al-Qibtiyyah. He went on to die at the age of one year and ten months.

Rajab | *Sha'bān* | *Ramadān* | *Shawwāl* | *Dhul-Qa'dah* | *Dhul-Hijjah*

Timeline of Key Events in the Life of the Messenger (صَلَّى ٱللَّٰهُ عَلَيْهِ وَسَلَّمَ)

2.2 – Events After the Hijrah to Al-Madīnah

9TH YEAR AFTER THE HIJRAH

This year is known as 'The Year of the Deputations' — 'Āmul-Wafūd

9 AH	*Muharram*	*Safar*	*Rabī' Al-Awwal*	*Rabī' Al-Ākhir*	*Jumādā Al-Ūlā*	*Jumādā Al-Ākhirah*

**— Indicates that Allāh's Messenger (صَلَّى ٱللَّٰهُ عَلَيْهِ وَسَلَّمَ) went along with the expedition, or took part in the battle himself.*

Rajab

- The Expedition of Tabūk, also known as the Expedition of Al-ʿUsrah (Hardship).* They returned in Ramadān.
- The killing of ʿUrwah ibn Masʿūd Ath-Thaqafī, a chief of the people of At-Tāʾif, when he returned to call his people to Islām.

Shaʿbān

- The death of Umm Kulthūm, the daughter of Allāh's Messenger (صَلَّىٱللَّهُعَلَيْهِوَسَلَّمَ).

Ramadān

- Demolition of Masjid Ad-Dirār
- The arrival and departure of Thaqīf, and of many deputations.

Dhul-Qaʿdah

- The death of ʿAbdullāh ibn Ubayy ibn Salūl, the head of the Hypocrites.

Dhul-Hijjah

- The Hajj was led by Abū Bakr, who was accompanied by ʿAlī.

Rajab | *Shaʿbān* | *Ramadān* | *Shawwāl* | *Dhul-Qaʿdah* | *Dhul-Hijjah*

Timeline of Key Events in the Life of the Messenger (صَلَّى ٱللَّهُ عَلَيْهِ وَسَلَّمَ)

2.2 – Events After the Hijrah to Al-Madīnah

10TH YEAR AFTER THE HIJRAH

Rabīʿ Al-Awwal / Rabīʿ Al-Ākhir

- The sending of Khālid ibn Walīd to Banul-Hārith ibn Al-Kaʿb in Najrān to call them to Islām.
- The sending of Abū Mūsā and Muʿādh ibn Jabal to Yemen.
- The death of Ibrāhīm, the son of Allāh's Messenger (صَلَّى ٱللَّهُ عَلَيْهِ وَسَلَّمَ).

10 AH | *Muharram* | *Safar* | *Rabīʿ Al-Awwal* | *Rabīʿ Al-Ākhir* | *Jumādā Al-Ūlā* | *Jumādā Al-Ākhirah*

** — Indicates that Allāh's Messenger (صَلَّى ٱللَّهُ عَلَيْهِ وَسَلَّمَ) went along with the expedition, or took part in the battle himself.*

Ramadān

- The sending of ʿAlī ibn Abī Ṭālib and Khālid ibn Al-Walīd to Yemen.
- The sending of Jarīr ibn ʿAbdillāh Al-Bajalī to destroy Dhul-Khalasah in Yemen (an idol people had set up in rivalry to the Kaʿbah, known as *'The Kaʿbah of Yemen'*).

Dhul-Hijjah

- The Farewell Hajj (Hajjatul-Wadāʿ), and the return to Al-Madīnah.

Rajab | *Shaʿbān* | *Ramadān* | *Shawwāl* | *Dhul-Qaʿdah* | *Dhul-Hijjah*

Timeline of Key Events in the Life of the Messenger (صَلَّىٱللَّهُعَلَيْهِوَسَلَّمَ)

2.2 – Events After the Hijrah to Al-Madīnah

11TH YEAR AFTER THE HIJRAH

Rabīʿ Al-Awwal

- **12TH RABĪʿ AL-AWWAL** — The passing away of Allāh's Messenger (صَلَّىٱللَّهُعَلَيْهِوَسَلَّمَ).

11 AH | *Muharram* | *Safar* | *Rabīʿ Al-Awwal* | *Rabīʿ Al-Ākhir* | *Jumādā Al-Ūlā* | *Jumādā Al-Ākhirah*

*— *Indicates that Allāh's Messenger (صَلَّىٱللَّهُعَلَيْهِوَسَلَّمَ) went along with the expedition, or took part in the battle himself.*

APPENDIX THREE

The Lineage of the Prophet (صَلَّى ٱللَّهُ عَلَيْهِ وَسَلَّمَ)

This is the lineage of Allāh's Messenger (صَلَّى ٱللَّهُ عَلَيْهِ وَسَلَّمَ) up until ʿAdnān — and this lineage is generally agreed upon. Anything above ʿAdnān is differed over. Imām An-Nawawī said in *Tahdhīb Al-Asmāʾ wal-Lughāt*: "There is consensus of the Ummah upon this much."

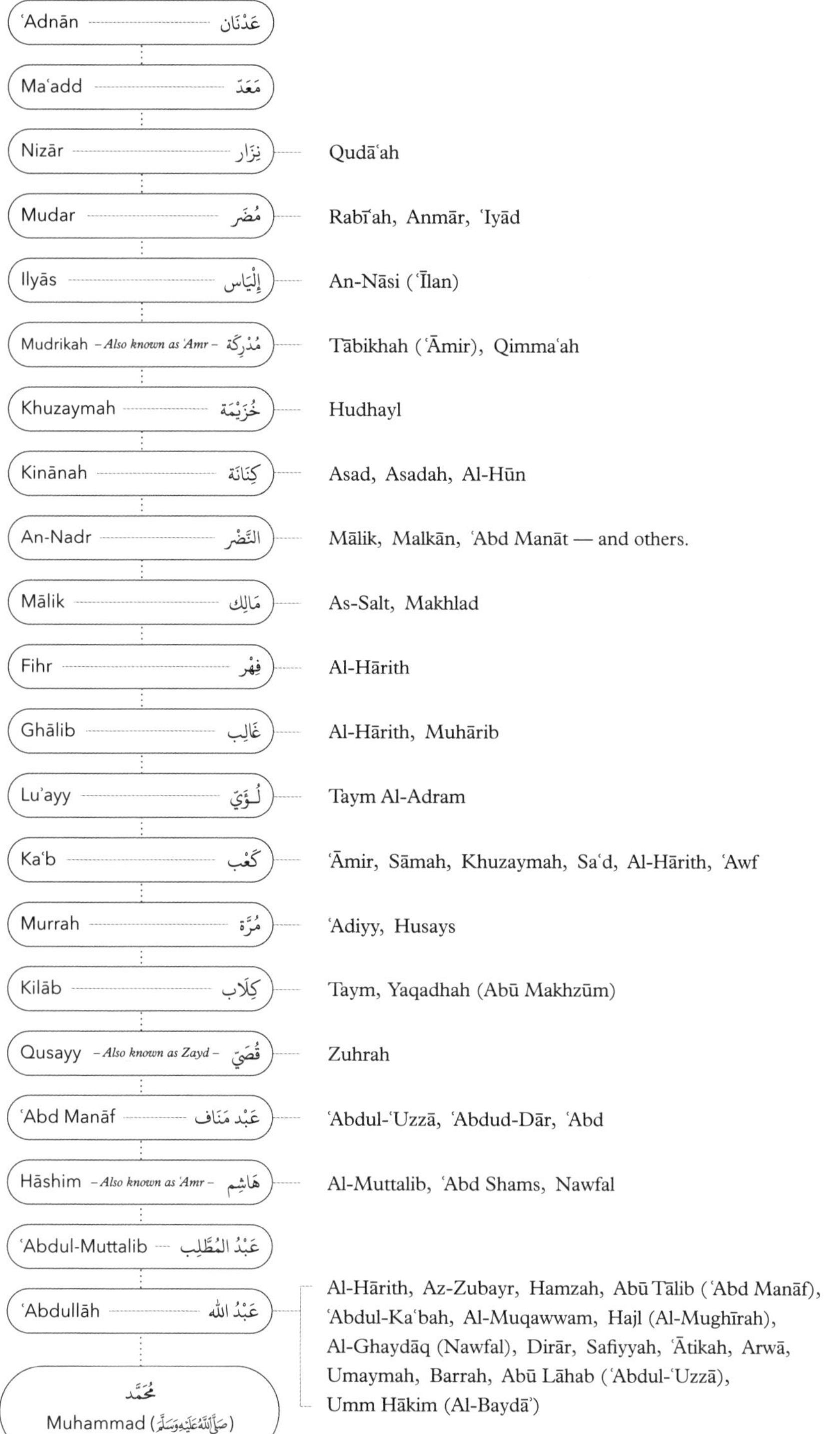
LINEAGE
SIBLINGS AT EACH LEVEL
ʿAdnān عَدْنَان
Maʿadd مَعَدّ
Nizār نِزَار
Qudāʿah
Mudar مُضَر
Rabīʿah, Anmār, ʿIyād
Ilyās إِلْيَاس
An-Nāsi (ʿĪlan)
Mudrikah – Also known as ʿAmr – مُدْرِكَة
Tābikhah (ʿĀmir), Qimmaʿah
Khuzaymah خُزَيْمَة
Hudhayl
Kinānah كِنَانَة
Asad, Asadah, Al-Hūn
An-Nadr النَّضْر
Mālik, Malkān, ʿAbd Manāt — and others.
Mālik مَالِك
As-Salt, Makhlad
Fihr فِهْر
Al-Hārith
Ghālib غَالِب
Al-Hārith, Muhārib
Luʾayy لُـؤَيّ
Taym Al-Adram
Kaʿb كَعْب
ʿĀmir, Sāmah, Khuzaymah, Saʿd, Al-Hārith, ʿAwf
Murrah مُرَّة
ʿAdiyy, Husays
Kilāb كِلَاب
Taym, Yaqadhah (Abū Makhzūm)
Qusayy – Also known as Zayd – قُصَيّ
Zuhrah
ʿAbd Manāf عَبْد مَنَاف
ʿAbdul-ʿUzzā, ʿAbdud-Dār, ʿAbd
Hāshim – Also known as ʿAmr – هَاشِم
Al-Muttalib, ʿAbd Shams, Nawfal
ʿAbdul-Muttalib عَبْدُ المُطَّلِب
ʿAbdullāh عَبْدُ الله
Al-Hārith, Az-Zubayr, Hamzah, Abū Tālib (ʿAbd Manāf), ʿAbdul-Kaʿbah, Al-Muqawwam, Hajl (Al-Mughīrah), Al-Ghaydāq (Nawfal), Dirār, Safiyyah, ʿĀtikah, Arwā, Umaymah, Barrah, Abū Lāhab (ʿAbdul-ʿUzzā), Umm Hākim (Al-Baydāʾ)
مُحَمَّد
Muhammad (ﷺ)

APPENDIX FOUR

The Ten Companions Promised Paradise

The First

NAME:	ʿAbdullāh ibn Abī Quhāfah (ʿUthmān) Ibn ʿĀmir
KUNYAH:	Abū Bakr
DEATH:	He died in Jumādal-Ākhirah 13H (aged 63), in the city of Al-Madīnah. He was the Caliph for 2 years and 3 months.

The Second

NAME:	ʿUmar ibn Al-Khattāb
KUNYAH:	Abū Hafs
DEATH:	He died in Dhul-Hijjah 23H (aged 63), in the city of Al-Madīnah. He was the Caliph for 10 years and 6 months.

The Third

NAME:	ʿUthmān ibn ʿAffān
KUNYAH:	Abū ʿAbdillāh
DEATH:	He died in Dhul-Hijjah 35H (aged 80+), in the city of Al-Madīnah. He was the Caliph for 11 years and 11 months.

The Fourth

NAME:	ʿAlī ibn Abī Tālib
KUNYAH:	Abul-Hasan; Abū Turāb
DEATH:	He died in Ramadān 40H (aged 63), in the city of Kūfah. He was the Caliph for 4 years and 9 months.

The Fifth

NAME:	Talhah ibn ʿUbaydillāh
KUNYAH:	Abū Muhammad
DEATH:	He died in Jumādal-Ākhirah 36H (aged 62), in or near to Basrah, at the battlefield wherein took place the Battle of the Camel.

The Sixth

NAME:	Az-Zubayr ibn Al-ʿAwwām
KUNYAH:	Abū ʿAbdillāh
DEATH:	He died in Jumādal-Ākhirah 36H (aged 66 or 67), in Wādī As-Sibāʾ, near Basrah. At the time of his death he was returning from the Battle of the Camel, which he did not take part in.

The Seventh

NAME:	ʿAbdur-Rahmān ibn ʿAwf
KUNYAH:	Abū Muhammad
DEATH:	He died in the year 32H (aged 72), in Al-Madīnah.

The Eighth

NAME:	Sa'd ibn Abī Waqqās
KUNYAH:	Abū Is-hāq
DEATH:	He died in the year 55H (aged 73), in the city of Al-Madīnah at his castle in Wādī Al-'Aqīq.

The Ninth

NAME:	Sa'īd ibn Zayd ibn 'Amr
KUNYAH:	Abul-A'war
DEATH:	He died in the year 51H (aged 70+), in the city of Al-Madīnah in Wādī Al-'Aqīq.

The Tenth

NAME:	'Āmir ibn 'Abdillāh ibn Al-Jarrāh
KUNYAH:	Abū 'Ubaydah
DEATH:	He died in the year 18H (aged 58), in Fihl, which is a village near Baysān in Palestine. He died during the plague of 'Amawās.

References:

Mukhtasar Sīratin-Nabī (صَلَّى ٱللَّٰهُ عَلَيْهِ وَسَلَّمَ) wa Sīrati As-hābihil-'Asharah of Al-Hāfidh 'Abdul-Ghanī Al-Maqdisī.

Taqrībut-Tahdhīb of Al-Hāfidh Ibn Hajr.

Tahdhībut-Tahdhīb of Al-Hāfidh Ibn Hajr.

Al-Kāshif of Adh-Dhahabī.

Al-Bidāyah wan-Nihāyah of Al-Hāfidh Ibn Kathīr.

Sharh Lum'atil I'tiqād of Shaikh Ibn 'Uthaymīn.

APPENDIX FIVE

The Wives of Allāh's Messenger (صَلَّىٱللَّهُعَلَيْهِوَسَلَّمَ)

May Allāh be pleased with them all

NAME:	Khadījah bint Khuwaylid
DETAIL:	Married in Makkah 15 years before Prophethood. Died in Makkah at the age of 64 years and 6 months and buried at Al-Hajūn, 3 years before the Hijrah (in Ramadān).
NAME:	ʿĀʾishah bint Abī Bakr As-Siddīq
DETAIL:	Married in Makkah, in Shawwāl in the tenth year of Prophethood, aged 6. Marriage consummated in Al-Madīnah, in Shawwāl of the first or second year after the Hijrah, at the age of 9. Died in 57H in Al-Madīnah.
NAME:	Sawdah bint Zamʿah
DETAIL:	Married in Makkah; it is said in Shawwāl in the tenth year of Prophethood. Died in Al-Madīnah at the end of the Khilāfah of ʿUmar (رَضِيَٱللَّهُعَنْهُ) — or it is said: in 55H.
NAME:	Hafsah bint ʿUmar ibn Al-Khattāb
DETAIL:	Married in Al-Madīnah, (in Shaʿbān) 3H. She died in Shaʿbān 45H, in the city of Al-Madīnah.

NAME:	Zaynab bint Khuzaymah Al-Hilāliyyah
DETAIL:	Married in Al-Madīnah (in Ramadān) 3AH. She died a few months later.
NAME:	Umm Salamah — Hind bint Abī Umayyah
DETAIL:	Married in Al-Madīnah in Shawwāl, 4AH. Died in Al-Madīnah, in the year 62AH.
NAME:	Zaynab bint Jahsh
DETAIL:	Married in Dhul-Qa'dah, 4AH (or it is said: in 3AH or 5AH). Died in Al-Madīnah, in the year 20AH.
NAME:	Juwayriyah bint Al-Hārith
DETAIL:	Married in 6AH. Died in 50AH in Al-Madīnah.
NAME:	Safiyyah bint Huyayy
DETAIL:	Married at the beginning of 7AH. Died in Ramadān, 50AH, in Al-Madīnah.
NAME:	Umm Habībah — Ramlah bint Abī Sufyān
DETAIL:	Married in 7AH whilst in Abyssinia. Died in Al-Madīnah, in the year 44AH.
NAME:	Maymūnah bint Al-Hārith
DETAIL:	Married in Dhul-Qa'dah 7AH at Sarif (near Makkah). Died at Sarif, in the same spot where her marriage was consummated, in 51AH.

References:

As-Sīratun-Nabawiyyah of Al-Hāfidh Ibn Kathīr.

Taqrībut-Tahdhīb of Al-Hāfidh Ibn Hajr.

Tahdhībut-Tahdhīb both by Al-Hāfidh Ibn Hajr.

Kitābu Azwājin-Nabī (صَلَّى ٱللَّهُ عَلَيْهِ وَسَلَّمَ) of Imām Muhammad ibn Yūsuf As-Sālihī.

APPENDIX SIX

The Children of Allāh's Messenger (صَلَّىٱللَّهُعَلَيْهِوَسَلَّمَ)

All except Ibrāhīm were born to Khadījah — رَضِيَٱللَّهُعَنْهَا.

NAME:	Al-Qāsim
DETAIL:	Born in Makkah before Islām. Died at the age of two after being able to walk. He was the first of the children to die.

NAME:	Zaynab
DETAIL:	Born in Makkah before Islām. She married Abul-'Ās ibn Ar-Rabī' ibn 'Abd-Shams (her cousin, son of her mother's sister Hālah) in the lifetime of her mother, after Prophethood. She accepted Islām and performed the Hijrah to Al-Madīnah, six years before her husband. He accepted Islām and joined her in Muharram 7H. She gave birth to a daughter Umāmah (who married 'Alī after the death of Fātimah) and a son 'Alī ibn Abil-'Ās (who it is said to have died as a child). She died in the beginning of 8H.

NAME: Ruqayyah

DETAIL: Born in Makkah before Islām. She married ʿUtbah ibn Abī Lahab, but after the revelation of *Sūrah Al-Lahab*, he separated from her on the orders of his father, doing so before having relations with her. She accepted Islām along with her mother and sisters, and married ʿUthmān ibn ʿAffān, and performed the two Hijrahs to Abysinnia with him. She gave birth to ʿUthmān's son ʿAbdullāh [who died at the age of six]. Then she performed the Hijrah to Al-Madīnah after ʿUthmān. She became ill before Badr, and died in Ramadān, 2H.

NAME: Umm Kulthūm

DETAIL: Born in Makkah before Islām. It is said that she married ʿUtaybah ibn Abī Lahab, who separated from her on the orders of his father, before having relations with her. She accepted Islām and performed the Hijrah to Al-Madīnah. After the death of Ruqayyah, she married ʿUthmān in Rabīʿ Al-Awwal, 3H. She did not give birth to any children and died in Shaʿbān, 9H.

NAME: Fātimah

DETAIL: Born in Makkah shortly before Prophethood. She married ʿAlī after Badr in 2H. She gave birth to Al-Hasan, Al-Husayn, Al-Muhassin, Umm Kulthūm and Zaynab. She died in 11H, six months after her father (صَلَّىٱللَّهُعَلَيْهِوَسَلَّمَ).

NAME: ʿAbdullāh — *At-Tayyib, At-Tāhir* (*The Good and Pure*)

DETAIL: Born in Makkah after Islām, and died as a baby. He was the second of the children to die.

NAME:	Ibrahīm
DETAIL:	His mother was Māriyah Al-Qibtiyyah. He was born in Al-Madīnah in Dhul-Hijjah 8H, and died at the age of 17 or 18 months, in 10H.

References:

As-Sīratun-Nabawiyyah of Al-Hāfidh Ibn Kathīr.

Siyar A'lāmin-Nubalā' of Adh-Dhahabī.

APPENDIX SEVEN

Maps & Diagrams

Note that these maps and diagrams are for illustrative purposes only. The topography and elevation indicators are not accurate, and are there only to provide a general idea of the terrain.

Map 1 — Old Makkah

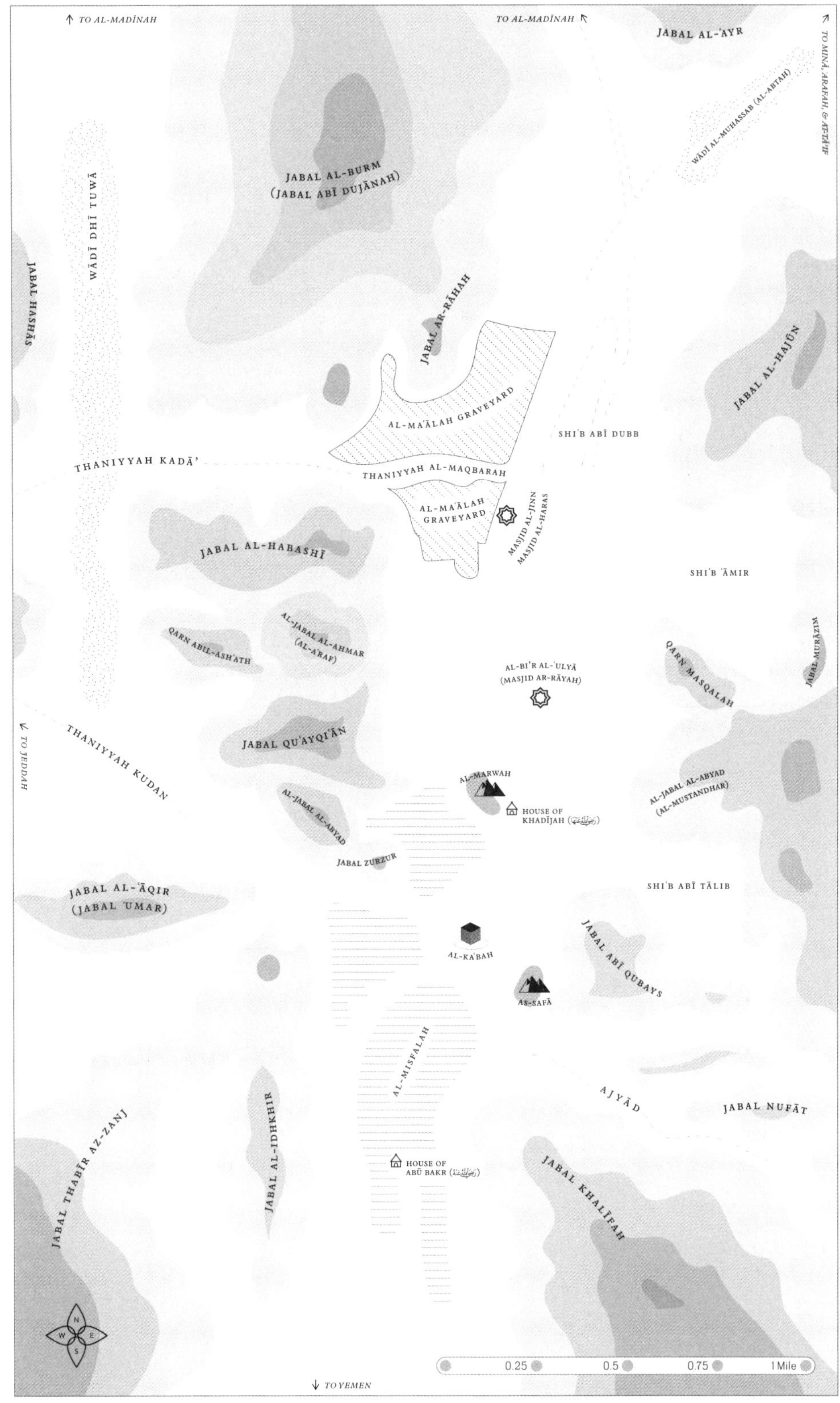

Map 2 — Old Madīnah

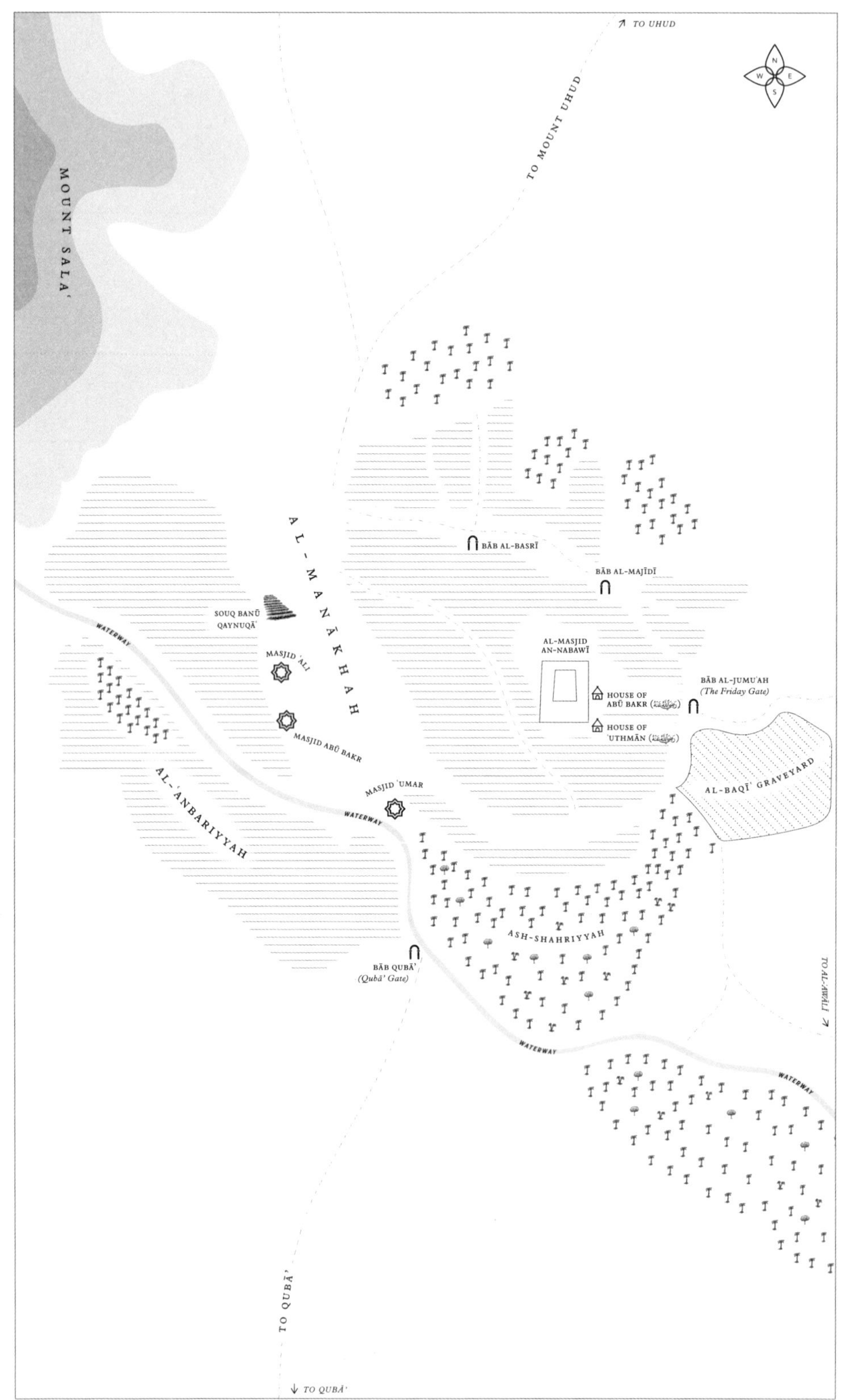

Diagram 1 — Diagram of the Al-Masjid An-Nabawī (before the King Fahad Expansion)

I *The room of Hafsah (رَضِيَ اللَّهُ عَنْهَا).*

II *The room of Sawdah (رَضِيَ اللَّهُ عَنْهَا).*

III *The room of 'Ā'ishah (رَضِيَ اللَّهُ عَنْهَا).*

IV *The room of Zaynab, & thereafter Umm Salamah (رَضِيَ اللَّهُ عَنْهَا).*

V *The room of 'Alī (رَضِيَ اللَّهُ عَنْهُ).*

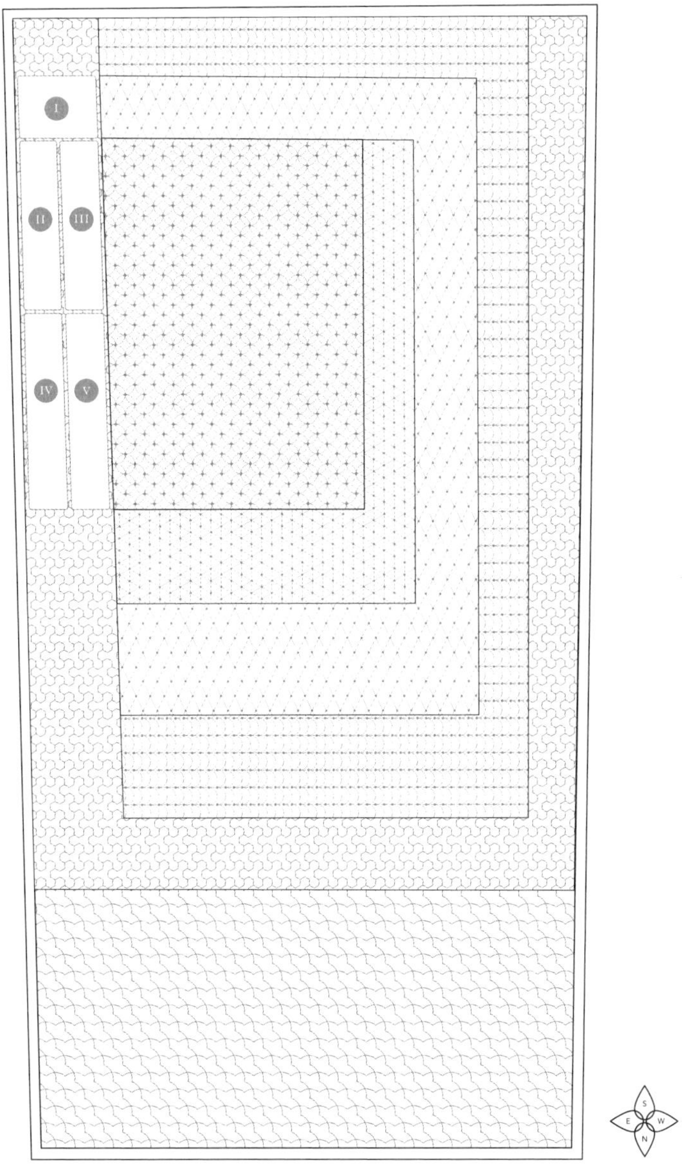

The mosque as originally built by Allah's Messenger (صَلَّى اللَّهُ عَلَيْهِ وَسَلَّمَ).

The expansion after Khaybar in the year 7 AH.

The extension of 'Umar (رَضِيَ اللَّهُ عَنْهُ) in 17 AH.

The extension of 'Uthmān (رَضِيَ اللَّهُ عَنْهُ) in 29 AH.

The extension of Al-Walīd Al-Amawī in 91 AH.

The extension of Al-Mahdī Al-'Abbāsī in 165 AH.

Endnotes

Endnote 1 – Source: Page 66

(DB) Muhammad and Ahmad are two names derived from *'Al-Hamd'* (praise). *'Muhammad'* meaning: the one who is, or who deserves to be praised repeatedly; and *'Ahmad'* meaning: the person most deserving of praise, and whose praise of his Lord is more excellent than the praise of all those who praise Him. See: *Jalā'ul-Afhām fī Fadlis-Salāti was-Salām 'alā Khairil-Anām* (صَلَّى ٱللَّهُ عَلَيْهِ وَسَلَّمَ) (pp. 183, 206 Dār 'Ālamil-Fawā'id' edition).

Endnote 2 – Source: Page 67

> *'Al-Māhī'* (the one through whom Disbelief was wiped away), and *'Al-Hāshir'* (the one after whom the people will be resurrected) and *'Al-'Āqib'* (the Prophet after whom there will be no other).

(SH) These three names *'Al-Māhī'*, *'Al-Hāshir'*, and *'Al-'Āqib'*, occur in the hadīth of Jubayr ibn Mut'im (رَضِيَ ٱللَّهُ عَنْهُ) reported by Al-Bukhārī (no. 3532) and Muslim (no. 2354).

> *'Al-Muqaffī'* (the one who follows on from the previous Prophets)

(SH) Its meaning is not far from the meaning of *'Al-'Āqib'*, so he is the one whom the rest of the Messengers comply to; and he is therefore the seal of them and the last one of them.

| *'Nabiyyur-Rahmah'* (the Prophet of Mercy),

(SH) The one whom Allāh sent as a mercy to the whole of creation, just as occurs in His Saying — He the Most High: "And We did not send you, O Muhammad (ﷺ), except as a mercy to the whole of the creation." — **Sūrah Al-Anbiyā' (21): 107**

| *'Nabiyyut-Tawbah'* (the Prophet of Repentance),

(SH) The one through whom Allāh opened the door to repentance for His servants. These three names occur in the hadīth of Abū Mūsā Al-Ash'arī (رضي الله عنه) reported by Muslim (no. 2355), and in the hadīth of Hudhayfah ibn Al-Yamān (رضي الله عنهما), whose referencing will follow.

| *Nabiyyul-Malhamah* (the Prophet of Great War),

(SH) The one sent to fight Jihād against the enemies of Allāh; and this name is established in the hadīth of Hudhayfah ibn Al-Yamān (رضي الله عنهما) reported by At-Tirmidhī in *Ash-Shamā'il* (no. 360), and by way of him by Al-Baghawī in *Sharhus-Sunnah* (13/212-213/no. 3631), and Ahmad (5/405) (by way of 'Āsim ibn Abin-Nujūd: from Abū Wā'il: from Hudhayfah, with it. This is a *'hasan'* chain, because of the well-known speech concerning 'Āsim).

Endnote 3 – Source: Page 69

(SH) He was famous as Ibn 'Abdil-Barr. His name was Yūsuf Ibn 'Abdillāh ibn Muhammad ibn 'Abdil-Barr. He was born in Qurtubah (Cordova). He advanced until he reached the level of being a *mujtahid*. His works brought benefit to the lands and to the servants; from them are:

- *At-Tamhīd*
- *Al-Istidhkār*
- *Al-Istī'āb*
- *Jāmi' Bayānil-'Ilm wa Fadlihī*

- *Ad-Durar fikhtisāril-Maghāzī was-Siyar*

- *Al-Inbā' bi Ma'rifati Qabā'ilir-Ruwāt.*

He died in 463H.

Endnote 4 – Source: Page 70

(DB) Imām Ibnul-Qayyim said in *Zādul-Ma'ād* (1/71-72): "Ismā'īl was the one due to be sacrificed (Adh-Dhabīh) upon the correct saying of the scholars from the Companions, the Tābi'īn, and those who came after them.

As for the saying it was Is-hāq, then this is futile from more then twenty aspects; and I heard Shaikhul-Islām Ibn Taymiyyah (may Allāh purify his soul) say:

> 'This saying was picked up from the People of the Book, despite its being false according to the text of their book, which states that Allāh commanded Ibrāhīm to sacrifice his first-born son, and in one version *"his only son"*. Then the People of the Book, along with the Muslims, have no doubt that Ismā'īl was his first-born son. So what has misled those who hold the saying is that there occurs in the Torah, which they have with them: *"Sacrifice your son Is-hāq."*'"

He said:

> 'And this addition is one of their textual distortions and lies, since it contradicts His saying: Sacrifice *'your first-born son'*, and *'your only son'*. However, the Jews envied the descendants of Ismā'īl because of this honour; and they desired it for themselves and sought to acquire it and misappropriate it for themselves to the exclusion of the Arabs. However, Allāh refuses except to bestow His Favour upon those deserving it.
>
> Then, further, how could it be correct to say that the one due to be sacrificed was Is-hāq when Allāh (the Most High) gave glad tidings to the mother of Is-hāq of his birth and the birth of his son Ya'qūb. So He (the Most High) said concerning the Angels, that they said to Ibrāhīm when they brought him the good news:

> لَا تَخَفْ إِنَّا أُرْسِلْنَا إِلَىٰ قَوْمِ لُوطٍ ۝ وَامْرَأَتُهُ قَائِمَةٌ فَضَحِكَتْ فَبَشَّرْنَاهَا بِإِسْحَاقَ وَمِن وَرَاءِ إِسْحَاقَ يَعْقُوبَ
>
> MEANING: "Do not fear! We have been sent against the people of Lūt. And his wife was standing and laughed. So we gave glad tidings to her of her son Is-hāq, and of his son Ya'qūb." — **SŪRAH HŪD (11): 70-71**
>
> So it is impossible that He should give her the glad tidings that she was to have a son, and then command that he be sacrificed, since there is no doubt that (the news of) Ya'qūb (عَلَيْهِ السَّلَامُ) entered into the glad tiding."

Endnote 5 – Source: Page 74

(SH) That is proven by many evidences. From them:

- The clear indication of the Qur'ān:

> أَلَمْ يَجِدْكَ يَتِيمًا فَآوَىٰ
>
> MEANING: "Did your Lord not find you an orphan, O Muhammad, and give you shelter?"

- That which Muslim reports (no. 1771/70): from Ibn Shihāb who said: "So when Āminah gave birth to Allāh's Messenger (صَلَّى ٱللَّهُ عَلَيْهِ وَسَلَّمَ) after his father died…"
- What Abū Nu'aym reports in *Dalā'ilun-Nubuwwah* (p.96) from Dāwūd ibn Abī Hind that he said: "The father of the Prophet (صَلَّى ٱللَّهُ عَلَيْهِ وَسَلَّمَ) died whilst his mother was pregnant with him." I say: "Its chain of narration is good."

Endnote 6 – Source: Page 75

Ad-Dārimī reported (1/8-9), and Al-Hākim (2/616-617), and Ahmad (4/184) from 'Utbah ibn Mas'ūd As-Sulamī, and he was from the Companions of Allāh's Messenger (صَلَّى ٱللَّهُ عَلَيْهِ وَسَلَّمَ), that he narrated that: a man said to Allāh's Messenger (ﷺ): "How did your affair begin, O Messenger of Allāh?"

So he said: "I was being taken care of by a woman from Banū Saʿd ibn Bakr. So I went off with a son of hers along with some of our goats, and we did not take any provision along with us. So I said: *'O my brother, go and bring us some provision from our mother.'*

So my brother went off and I remained with the goats. Then two white beings that were flying came, being as if they were two eagles. Then one of them said to the other: *'Is it him?'* The other one replied: *'Yes'*. So they hastened to me, took hold of me, and threw me upon the ground on my back.

Then they split open my chest and extracted two black clots from it, and one of them said to his companion: *'Bring me ice-water'*, and he washed my insides with it. Then he said: *'Bring me snow-water'*, and he washed my heart with it. Then he said: *'Bring me tranquility'*. And he planted it in my heart. Then one of them said to his companion: *'Sew it up'*, so he sewed it up and sealed it with the seal of Prophethood. Then one of them said to the other: *'Place him upon a scale, and place a thousand of his nation upon another scale.'*"

Allāh's Messenger (ﷺ) said : "So I saw a thousand people above me and feared that some of them were going to fall upon me. He said: *'If his whole nation were weighed against him he would outweigh them.'* Then they went off and left me."

Allāh's Messenger (ﷺ) said: "And I became very afraid, and I went back to my mother and informed her of what I had experienced. So I wished that I had been mistaken for someone else. She said: *'I entrust you to Allāh's protection.'* So she prepared a camel of hers for riding, placed me upon the saddle, and rode behind me until we reached my (true) mother. Then she said: *'I have fulfilled my trust and my responsibility,'* and she told her what had happened to me, and this did not alarm her. She said: *'When he came out from me I saw light which shone and revealed the palaces of Shām.'*"

Shaikh Al-Albānī said in *As-Sahīhah* (no.373): "This chain of narration is *'hasan'* (…) and this hadīth has many witnesses."

Endnote 7 – Source: Page 75

Muslim reported (976/105) from Abū Hurairah (رَضِيَٱللَّهُعَنْهُ) who said: "The Prophet (صَلَّىٱللَّهُعَلَيْهِوَسَلَّمَ) visited the grave of his mother, and he wept and those around him wept. So he said:

> 'I sought permission of my Lord to seek forgiveness for her, and He did not grant me permission; and I sought His permission to visit her grave, and He granted me permission. So visit the graves, for they will act as a reminder of death.'"

Ibn Kathīr said in *As-Sīratun-Nabawiyyah* (*Sahīhus-Sīratin-Nabawiyyah;* p. 23): "Imām Ahmad reported from Buraydah that he said: 'We went out with Allāh's Messenger (صَلَّىٱللَّهُعَلَيْهِوَسَلَّمَ) until we reached Waddān; he said: *"Remain where you are until I come back to you."*

So he went off, and then he later came back to us and he was troubled. So he said:

> "I went to the grave of the mother of Muhammad, and I asked my Lord for intercession (meaning: for her), but He prevented me from that; and I used to forbid you from visiting the graves, but now visit them."'"

Al-Bayhaqī also reported it. "The Prophet (صَلَّىٱللَّهُعَلَيْهِوَسَلَّمَ) came to the outline of a grave and sat down, and the people sat down around him. So he moved his head like one being spoken to, then he wept. So 'Umar went to him and said: 'What causes you to weep, O Messenger of Allāh?'

So he said:

> 'This is the grave of Āminah bint Wahb. I sought permission of my Lord to visit her grave, and He granted me permission; and I sought His permission to seek forgiveness for her and He refused me. So I felt pity for her and wept.'

He [Buraydah] said: 'So I have never seen more people weeping than at that time.'"

Shaikh Al-Albānī said (*Sahīhus-Sīrah* p. 23): "I say: It is an authentic hadīth when the two chains of narrations are brought together."

Endnote 8 – Source: Page 75

[SH] She was Barakah bint Tha'labah ibn Hisn. She was from Abyssinia, and was the nursemaid of Allāh's Messenger (صَلَّى ٱللَّهُ عَلَيْهِ وَسَلَّمَ). Then when he married Khadījah (رَضِيَ ٱللَّهُ عَنْهَا) he set her free and married her to Zayd ibn Hārith, whose son Usāmah (رَضِيَ ٱللَّهُ عَنْهُ) she gave birth to.

[BJ][SZ] And there occurs in *Sahīh Muslim* (no. 1771), as a hadīth of Anas ibn Mālik (رَضِيَ ٱللَّهُ عَنْهُ): "So Umm Ayman looked after him until Allāh's Messenger (صَلَّى ٱللَّهُ عَلَيْهِ وَسَلَّمَ) grew up."

Endnote 9 – Source: Page 78

[SH] Al-Bukhārī mentioned it as a statement of Az-Zuhrī, within his narration of the hadīth of the beginning of the Revelation, with the wording: *'According to what has reached us...'* So therefore, the incident of his trying to throw himself down from the mountaintops is unauthentic (*da'īf*), and is not established. Refer to: *Fat-hul-Bārī* (12/359-360), *Ash-Shifā'* of Al-Qādī 'Iyād (2/707-708), *Ad-Difā' 'anil-hadīthin-Nabawī* (p.41) and *Mukhtasar Sahīhil-Bukhārī* (1/17 — Al-Ma'ārif edition): the (last) two being by our Shaikh (Al-Albānī) (رَحِمَهُ ٱللَّهُ)."

[SH] Shaikh Al-Albānī (رَحِمَهُ ٱللَّهُ) concluded in *Ad-Difā'* (pp. 41-42):

"And you should know that this addition does not occur in any connected narration suitable as proof, as I have explained in *Silsilatul-Ahādīthid-Da'īfah* (no.4858) and I indicated that in a footnote to my *Mukhtasar Sahīhil-Bukhārī* (1/5)...

So when you are aware that this addition is not authentic, then we have the right to say that this addition is reprehensible with regard to its meaning, since it is not befitting that the Prophet (صَلَّى ٱللَّهُ عَلَيْهِ وَسَلَّمَ), who was safeguarded from error should try to kill himself by throwing himself down from a mountain, no matter what the motivation was, when he was the one who said: *'Whoever throws himself down from a mountain and kills himself will be in the Hell-Fire, throwing himself down in it, remaining in it forever'* — reported by the two Shaikhs and others, and I have referenced it in my book *Takhrījul-Halāli wal-Harām* (no. 447)."

Endnote 10 – Source: Page 83

DB Concerning An-Najjāshī's refusal to surrender the Muslims in his land to the Mushrikūn from Quraysh, and his refusal to accept gifts to bribe him to do that. Az-Zuhrī said: "I had this hadīth narrated by 'Urwah ibn Az-Zubayr (رَضِيَ اللَّهُ عَنْهُ), from Umm Salamah (رَضِيَ اللَّهُ عَنْهَا). So 'Urwah said:

> 'Do you know what he (i.e. An-Najjāshī) meant by his saying: *"Allāh did not take any bribe from me when He restored my kingdom to me, such that I should accept any bribe to keep my kingdom. And Allāh did not do what the people wanted with regard to me, such that I should obey the people against Him"*?'

So I said: *'No.'* So then 'Urwah explained it, saying: "Ā'ishah (رَضِيَ اللَّهُ عَنْهَا) narrated to me that:

....

"His father was previously king of his people, and he had a brother, and his brother had twelve sons. But the father of An-Najjāshī had no child besides An-Najjāshī.

So the people of Abyssinia started plotting together and they said: *'We ought to kill the father of An-Najjāshī, and give the kingship to his brother, for he has twelve sons. So then later, they can inherit the kingship and the Abyssinian people will remain for a long time without any infighting between them.'* So they attacked (the king) and killed him, and they made his brother king.

So then, An-Najjāshī entered upon his uncle, and he impressed him so much that he consulted nobody else besides him, and he was found to be a person of intellect and firm resolve. So when the rest of the Abyssinians saw the status which he now had with his uncle they said: *'This boy has got the better of his uncle now, so we do not feel safe that he will not make him king over us (after himself), and he knows that we have killed his father. So if that happens, he will not leave a single noble amongst us except he will kill him.'*

So they went to his uncle and said: *'You know that we killed his father, and put you in his place; and we do not feel safe that he will not become king over us (after you). So either you kill him, or you banish him from our land.'*

He said:

> 'Woe to you, you killed his father yesterday, and now I have to kill him today! Rather, I will send him away from your land.'

So they took him away, and put him in the market place; and they sold him as a slave to a trader from the traders who threw him into a ship, having bought him for 600 or 700 dirhams. Then he departed with him. Then when it was the evening of that same day, some clouds from the autumn clouds appeared. So his uncle went out to enjoy the rain, but he was struck by a lightening bolt, which killed him.

So the people quickly went to his children, but they found that they were stupid people. None of them had any good in him. So the affair of the Abyssinians was thrown into confusion. So some of them said to others: *'You know, by Allāh, that the only one who is suitable to be king over you is the one who you sold this morning. So if you have any concern for the affair of the Abyssinians, then go and get him before he leaves.'*

So they went searching for him. So they found him and brought him back; and they placed the crown upon his head, sat him upon his throne, and they made him the king. But the trader (came and) said: *'Give me back my money, for you have taken my slave!'*

They said: *'We will not give you anything.'*

So the trader said: *'Then by Allāh, I will go and speak to him.'*

So he went to him and spoke to him, and said: *'O king! I bought a slave and the people who sold him to me took the price, but then they seized the slave and took him away from me, and they won't give me my money back.'*

So this was the first case that was seen from the firmness, wisdom, and justice of An-Najjāshī that he said: *'You must either give him his money back, or hand over his slave to him so that he may take him wherever he wants.'*

So the people said: *'Rather we will give him his money.'* So they gave it to him.

So this is why (when the Najjāshī did not surrender the Muslims, and did not accept the bribe from the Quraysh to hand over the Muslims), he said:

> 'Allāh did not take any bribe from me, when He restored my kingdom to me, such that I should take any bribe to keep my kingdom; And Allāh did not do what the people wanted with regard to me, such that I should obey the people against Him.''''

....

Shaikh Al-Albānī mentioned that it is reported by Ibn Hishām in his abridgement of Ibn Is-hāq's *Sīrah* (1/363-364), and by Abū Nu'aym in *Ad-Dalā'il* (pp. 81-84), and that its chain of narration is *'hasan'*. [*Sahīhus-Sīrah*: p. 180]

This is the same Najjāshī who accepted Islām, and he died upon it (رَضِيَٱللَّهُعَنْهُ). He is the one who is mentioned in Al-Bukhārī and Muslim in a hadīth of Abū Hurairah (رَضِيَٱللَّهُعَنْهُ) that when he died, the Prophet (صَلَّىٱللَّهُعَلَيْهِوَسَلَّمَ) was told through Revelation, and he ordered the Companions to form rows and he prayed the Funeral Prayer for him, as no one in his land prayed the Funeral Prayer for him. [*Sahīhul-Bukhārī*: (nos. 3877-3881)]

Endnote 11 – Source: Page 86

(SH)/(DB) Al-Bukhārī (no. 3231) and Muslim (no. 1795) reported as a hadīth of 'Ā'ishah (رَضِيَٱللَّهُعَنْهَا) that she said to the Prophet (صَلَّىٱللَّهُعَلَيْهِوَسَلَّمَ): "Has there come upon you a day more severe than the day of Uhud?"

So he said: "I have encountered from your people that which I have encountered and the most severe thing that I encountered was on the day of the mountain pass (Al-'Aqabah) when I presented myself to Ibn 'Abd

Yālīl ibn ʿAbd Kulāl, but he did not respond as I wanted. So I departed, overwhelmed with sorrow, and I did not recover until I had arrived at Qarnuth-Thaʿālib. So I raised my head and saw a cloud shading me, and I looked and saw Jibrīl in it. So he called to me and said: *'Allāh has heard what your people said to you, and how they responded to you, and Allāh has sent to you the Angel of the mountains for you to command him as you wish concerning them.'*

So the Angel of the Mountains called to me and gave salutations to me, and then he said: *'O Muhammad! Order whatever you wish. If you wish, I shall crush the two mountains [i.e. Makkah] upon them.'"*

So the Prophet (صَلَّىٰ ٱللَّهُ عَلَيْهِ وَسَلَّمَ) said:

> "No, rather I hope that Allāh will bring out from their offspring those who worship Allāh alone, not associating anything along with Him."

Endnote 12 – Source: Page 87

BJ SZ Rather, it is as Al-Qādī ʿIyād said: "The truth, which most of the people are upon, and the great majority of the Salaf, and most of the later people from the jurists, the muhaddithīn, and the rhetorical theologians — is that he (صَلَّىٰ ٱللَّهُ عَلَيْهِ وَسَلَّمَ) was taken on the Night Journey bodily; and the narrators indicate this for the person who comes across them and researches them; and what is apparent from them is not to be diverted from, except because of a proof." [*Ash-Shifā*ʾ (1/248) — with its meaning.]

Also, Al-Hāfidh Ibn Hajr said in *Al-Fat-h*: "The Night-Journey and the ascent through the Heavens both occurred on a single night, whilst he was awake, with the body of the Prophet (صَلَّىٰ ٱللَّهُ عَلَيْهِ وَسَلَّمَ) and his soul, after he was sent as a Prophet. This was held by the majority of the muhaddithīn, the jurists, and the rhetorical theologians, and it is supported by what is clear from the multiple authentic narrations."

Endnote 13 – Source: Page 88

(SH) What is apparent is that there is no real disagreement between the Companions with regard to the affair of whether the Messenger (صَلَّى ٱللَّهُ عَلَيْهِ وَسَلَّمَ) saw his Lord; rather, it is merely a difference in wording. So there is an unrestricted narration from Ibn ʿAbbās (رَضِيَ ٱللَّهُ عَنْهُمَا) and another narration restricted to seeing with the heart, and there is no report from him that he said that he saw Him with the eyes of his head. So therefore, it is binding that we understand the unrestricted report in the sense of the restricted report. So in that case there is no disagreement, and Allāh knows best.

So with this it will be known that there is no disagreement between the Companions regarding the matter of the Messenger (صَلَّى ٱللَّهُ عَلَيْهِ وَسَلَّمَ) seeing his Lord on the Night of the Isrāʾ and Miʿrāj. This was held by Imām Ahmad ibn Hanbal, ʿUthmān ibn Saʿīd Ad-Dārimī, Shaikh-ul Islām Ibn Taimiyyah and others. And refer if you wish to *Minhājus-Sunnatin-Nabawiyyah* (2/636-637) and *Zādul-Maʿād*.

Endnote 14 – Source: Page 88

(DB) Ibn ʿAbbās (رَضِيَ ٱللَّهُ عَنْهُمَا) said, "Allāh's Messenger (صَلَّى ٱللَّهُ عَلَيْهِ وَسَلَّمَ) said:

> 'When it was the night when I was taken on the Night-Journey I entered the next morning feeling distressed at the seriousness of my affair, and I knew that the people would call me a liar. So I sat away from the people in a state of sadness.'"

He said: "So the enemy of Allāh — Abū Jahl — was passing by, so he came and sat with him. He said to him, in the manner of one making fun: *'Has anything happened?'*

So Allāh's Messenger (صَلَّى ٱللَّهُ عَلَيْهِ وَسَلَّمَ) said: *'Yes.'*

He said: *'What is it?'*

He said: *'I have been taken on a journey this night.'*

He said: *'Where to?'*

He said: *'To Jerusalem.'*

He said: *'And then you entered the morning amongst us?!'*

He said: *'Yes.'*

So he saw that he should not call him a liar for fear that he would then deny having said it when he called his people. He said: *'If I call your people will you narrate to them what you have narrated to me?'*

So Allāh's Messenger (صَلَّىٰٱللَّهُعَلَيۡهِوَسَلَّمَ) said: *'Yes.'*

So he said: *'Come! O assembly of Banū Ka'b ibn Lu'ayy!'*

So the gatherings left their places, and they came over and sat with the two of them. He said: *'Narrate to your people what you narrated to me.'*

So Allāh's Messenger (صَلَّىٰٱللَّهُعَلَيۡهِوَسَلَّمَ) said: *'I was taken on a journey this night.'*

They said: *'Where to?'*

He said: *'To Jerusalem.'*

They said: *'And then you entered the morning amongst us?!'*

He said: *'Yes.'*

He said: So some of them clapped their hands, and others put their hands upon their heads in amazement at the lie — as they claimed!

They said: *'And are you able to describe the mosque for us? And amongst the people, there were those who had travelled to that land and seen the mosque.'*

So Allāh's Messenger (صَلَّىٰٱللَّهُعَلَيۡهِوَسَلَّمَ) said: *'So I started describing it, until part of its description became difficult for me.'*

He said:

> 'So then, the mosque was brought to me whilst I was looking, and it was placed before the house of 'Iqāl, or 'Uqayl, so I described it whilst looking at it.'"

He said: "So the people said: *'As for the description, then he is correct.'*"

Shaikh Al-Albānī said in *As-Sahīhah* (no. 3021):

"Reported by An-Nasā'ī in *As-Sunanul-Kubrā* (6/377/11285), Ibn Abī Shaybah in *Al-Musannaf* (11/461/11746), Ahmad (1/309) — and from him by Ad-Diyā' Al-Maqdisī in *Al-Mukhtārah* (1/309), Al-Harbī in *Gharībul-Hadīth* (5/115/2), Al-Bazzār (1/45-46), At-Tabarānī in *Al-Mu'jamul-Kabīr* (12/167/12782) and in *Al-Awsat* (1/136/2/2623), and Al-Bayhaqī in *Dalā'ilun-Nubuwwah* (2/363), through chains by way of 'Awf: from Zurārah ibn Awfā: from Ibn 'Abbās who said: *"Allāh's Messenger* (صَلَّى ٱللَّهُ عَلَيْهِ وَسَلَّمَ) *said..."* — and he mentioned it.

So the chain of narration is *'sahīh'*, as As-Suyūtī said in *Ad-Durrul-Manthūr* (4/155)."

Endnote 15 – Source: Page 91

(BJ)(SZ) Al-Bukhārī (no. 18) and Muslim (no. 1709) reported as a hadīth of 'Ubādah ibn As-Sāmit (رَضِيَ ٱللَّهُ عَنْهُ) who said: "Allāh's Messenger (صَلَّى ٱللَّهُ عَلَيْهِ وَسَلَّمَ) said:

> 'Give me the pledge that you will not associate anything along with Allāh, and you will not steal, nor fornicate, nor kill your children, nor commit a slander which you invent from between your arms and legs, nor will you disobey in something good.
>
> So whoever amongst you fulfils his pledge, then his reward is with Allāh; and whoever falls into anything from that and is punished for it in this world, then it is an expiation for him.
>
> And whoever falls into anything from [those sins] and Allāh conceals it for him, then it is up to Allāh; if He wishes He will pardon him, and if He wishes He will punish him.'"

And the meaning of the 'Pledge of the Women,' is the taking from them a pledge and covenant which does not include fighting, as the pledge of the women used to be, as occurs in Sūratul-Mumtahanah (60): Verse 12.

Endnote 16 – Source: Page 92

(BJ)(SZ) It is not possible to take this hadīth to refer to 'Amr ibn Thābit, as Al-Hāfidh (Ibn Hajr) points out in *Al-Fat-h* (6/25), even though his story is reported by Ibn Is-hāq with a *'sahīh'* chain of narration, as a hadīth of Abū Hurairah (رَضِيَ ٱللَّهُ عَنْهُ). As for the hadīth mentioned here, then it is reported by Al-Bukhārī (no. 2808) and Muslim (no. 1900), and the wording of Muslim has: *'a man from Banun-Nabīt'*, and they are other than the Aws, which ʿAmr ibn Thābit was from.

Endnote 17 – Source: Page 92

Ahmad (3/322, 323 & 339), Al-Bazzār (no. 1756), Ibn Hibbān (nos. 6241 & 6973), Al-Bayhaqī (9/9) and in *Dalāʾilun-Nubuwwah* (2/442-444) report a hadīth of Jābir (رَضِيَ ٱللَّهُ عَنْهُ) who said:

"Allāh's Messenger (صَلَّى ٱللَّهُ عَلَيْهِ وَسَلَّمَ) remained in Makkah for ten years, and he would pursue the people in their gathering places in (the markets of) ʿUkāz and Majannah, and during the rites of pilgrimage in Minā, saying:

> 'Who will shelter me? Who will assist me so that I can convey the Message of My Lord, and Paradise will be for him?'

To the extent that a man would go out from Yemen or from Mudar, and his people would come to him saying: *'Beware of the young man of Quraysh, do not let him put you to trial.'*

So he (صَلَّى ٱللَّهُ عَلَيْهِ وَسَلَّمَ) would walk amongst their camps and they would point at him, until Allāh sent us to him from Yathrib. So we gave him shelter and believed him. So a man of us would depart and then believe in him, so he would recite the Qurʾān to him, and then he would return to his family and they would accept Islām because of his Islām. This continued until there remained no household from the households of the Ansār except that it contained a group of Muslims who openly displayed their Islām. Then they performed ʿUmrah together. So we said: *'For how long are we going to leave Allāh's Messenger (صَلَّى ٱللَّهُ عَلَيْهِ وَسَلَّمَ) as an outcast amongst the mountains of Makkah, and in a state of fear?'*

So seventy of us rode until we came to him during the pilgrimage. So we made an appointment to meet him in the mountain-pass of Al-ʿAqabah. So we went, one at a time, and two at a time, until we all gathered together with him. So we said: *'O Messenger of Allāh! Shall we give you our pledge of allegiance?'*

He said:

> 'Give me the pledge that you will hear and obey when energetic or sluggish, and that you will spend in charity in times of difficulty and ease, and upon commanding the good and forbidding the evil; and that you will speak out for Allāh's sake, not fearing the blame of any reproacher (for the sake of Allāh). And that you will aid me, and defend me if I come to you, from those things which you defend yourselves, your wives, and your children from; and you will have Paradise.'"

He said: "So we stood up to him and gave him the pledge, and Ibn Zurārah — and he was one of the youngest of them — took his hand and said:

> 'Steady on, O people of Yathrib! For we have not travelled upon camels except whilst we knew that he is indeed Allāh's Messenger; but his bringing us forth today will mean separating from all the Arabs, and your nobles being killed, and swords biting into you. So either you are a people who can have patience upon that — and your reward will be with Allāh, or you are a people who fear that they will show cowardice in which case you should make that clear, so that it may be an excuse for you with Allāh.'

They said: *'Desist, O Sa'd! For by Allāh we shall never leave this pledge, nor withhold from it ever.'"*

He said: "So we stood up to him and gave him the pledge, and he took it from us and made the conditions, and gave us the promise of Paradise for that."

Shaikh Al-Albānī said in *Silsilatul-Ahādīthis-Sahīhah* (no. 63): "I say: This is a chain of narration which is authentic to the standard of Muslim."

Endnote 18 – Source: Page 99

DB Al-Bukhārī (no. 3329) reported from Anas (رَضِيَ اللَّهُ عَنْهُ): "'Abdullāh ibn Salām heard of the arrival of the Prophet (صَلَّى اللَّهُ عَلَيْهِ وَسَلَّمَ) at Al-Madīnah, so he came to him and said: 'I am going to ask you about three things, which nobody but a Prophet will know.'

He said: 'What is the first of the signs of the Hour? And what will be the first food, which the people of Paradise will eat? And on account of what does a child resemble its father; and on account of what does a child resemble its maternal uncles?'

So Allāh's Messenger (صَلَّى ٱللَّهُ عَلَيْهِ وَسَلَّمَ) said: 'Jibrīl has just informed me of them.'"

He said: "'Abdullāh said: 'He is the enemy to the Jews from amongst the Angels.'

Allāh's Messenger (صَلَّى ٱللَّهُ عَلَيْهِ وَسَلَّمَ) said:

> 'As for the first of the signs of the Hour, then it will be a fire, which gathers the people from the east to the west. As for the first food which the people of Paradise will eat, then it will be the extra lobe of the liver of the fish. As for the resemblance of the child, then when the man has intercourse with the woman and his semen outstrips the fluid of the woman, then the child will resemble him; and if her fluid outstrips, then the resemblance will be towards her.'

He said: 'I testify that you are the Messenger of Allāh.' Then he said: 'O Messenger of Allāh! The Jews are a people who are great liars: if they know about my Islām before you ask them, then they will lie about me to you.'

So the Jews came, and 'Abdullāh ibn Salām entered the house. So Allāh's Messenger (صَلَّى ٱللَّهُ عَلَيْهِ وَسَلَّمَ) said: 'What sort of a man is 'Abdullāh ibn Salām amongst you?'

They said: 'He is the most knowledgeable one of us, and the son of the most knowledgeable one from amongst us; and he is the best one of us, and the son of the best one of us.'

So Allāh's Messenger (صَلَّى ٱللَّهُ عَلَيْهِ وَسَلَّمَ) said: 'What would you think if 'Abdullāh were to accept Islām?'

They said: 'May Allāh preserve him from that.'

So ʿAbdullāh came out to them and said: 'I testify that none has the right to be worshipped except Allāh, and I testify that Muhammad is the Messenger of Allāh.'

So they said: 'He is the most evil one of us, and the son of the most evil one of us' — and they spoke against him.'"

And Imām Ahmad reported (6/25) from ʿAwf ibn Mālik who said: "The Prophet (صَلَّى ٱللَّهُ عَلَيْهِ وَسَلَّمَ) went out one day, and I was with him, until we entered a synagogue of the Jews in Al-Madīnah on a festival day of theirs, and they disliked our entering upon them. So Allāh's Messenger (صَلَّى ٱللَّهُ عَلَيْهِ وَسَلَّمَ) said to them:

> 'O company of Jews! Show me twelve men who will bear witness that none has the right to be worshipped except Allāh, and that I am the Messenger of Allāh, and Allāh will remove from every Jew beneath the sky the Anger which He has upon them.'"

He said: "So they remained silent; no one responded to him. Then he repeated it to them, and no one responded. Then he did so for a third time, and no one responded. He said:

> 'You have refused; but, by Allāh, I am indeed the one after whom the people will be gathered, and I am the last Prophet, and I am the chosen Prophet — whether you believe or you reject the truth.'

Then he went off and I was with him, until, when we had almost left a man called out from behind us: 'Stay where you are, O Muhammad.' He said: So he came forward, and that man said: 'What sort of man do you know me to be amongst you, O company of Jews?'

They said: 'By Allāh! We do not know there to have been a man amongst us who knew the Scripture of Allāh better than you, nor anyone more knowledgeable than you, nor than your father before you, nor than your grandfather before your father.'

He said: 'Then I testify for him, by Allāh, that he is the Prophet of Allāh whom you find mentioned in the Tawrāt.'

They said: 'You have lied.' Then they rebutted his saying and spoke ill of him. Allāh's Messenger (صَلَّى ٱللَّهُ عَلَيْهِ وَسَلَّمَ) said:

> 'You people have lied. Your saying will never be accepted. You were just now praising him — as you did — with good. And when he believed you called him a liar, and said what you have said. So your saying will never be accepted.'

He said: So we went out and we were three: Allāh's Messenger (ﷺ), myself, and ʿAbdullāh ibn Salām; and Allāh (the Mighty and Majestic) sent down concerning him:

> قُلْ أَرَأَيْتُمْ إِن كَانَ مِنْ عِندِ اللَّهِ وَكَفَرْتُم بِهِ وَشَهِدَ شَاهِدٌ مِّن بَنِي إِسْرَائِيلَ عَلَىٰ مِثْلِهِ فَآمَنَ وَاسْتَكْبَرْتُمْ ۖ إِنَّ اللَّهَ لَا يَهْدِي الْقَوْمَ الظَّالِمِينَ
>
> MEANING: "Say: What do you think that Allāh will do with you if this Qur'ān is from Allāh, and you disbelieve in it, and a witness from the Children of Isrā'īl bears witness to its like, and he believes, whereas you are haughty. Indeed Allāh does not guide a people who are transgressors." — **Sūrah Al-Ahqāf (46): 10**

Shaikh Al-Albānī, in *Sahīhus-Sīratin-Nabawiyyah* (pp. 80-81), declared this hadīth to be authentic to the standard of Muslim.

Endnote 19 – Source: Page 102

(BJ)(SZ) It is also called 'The Expedition of Waddān'. Ibn Is-hāq said, as occurs in *Sīrah Ibn Hishām*: *"Until he reached Waddān, and it was the expedition of Al-Abwā'"*, and there is no disagreement about that, since Waddān and Al-Abwā' are two places that are close to each other; there being six or eight miles between them, and they are between Makkah and Al-Madīnah.

(MK)(MM) Waddān is a place between Makkah and Al-Madīnah. It is 29 miles from Rābigh, in the direction of Al-Madīnah.

(DB) Al-Abwā' is a village in the district of Al-Furʿ, situated 23 miles from Al-Juhfah, in the direction of Al-Madīnah. [*Fat-hul-Bārī*: (7/279)]

Endnote 20 – Source: Page 107

(DB) Al-Hāfidh Ibn Hajr said in *Fat-hul-Bārī* (1/155), commenting upon the hadīth containing this report: "The hadīth which he [i.e. Al-Bukhārī] alluded to is not brought in connected form by him in this book, however it is authentic; and I have found two chains of narrations for it. One of them is *'mursal'*, being mentioned by Ibn Is-hāq in *Al-Maghāzī* from Yazīd ibn Rūmān; and by Abul-Yamān in his manuscript from Shu'ayb: from Az-Zuhrī: both of them from 'Urwah ibn Az-Zubayr. The other is a fully connected report reported by At-Tabarānī [no.1670] as a hadīth of Jundab Al-Bajalī with a *'hasan'* chain. Then I found a witness for it as a hadīth of Ibn 'Abbās, reported by At-Tabarī in *At-Tafsīr*. So with these combined chains it is *'sahīh'*."

Shaikh Muqbil ibn Hādī Al-Wādi'ī said in his checking of *Tafsīr Ibn Kathīr* (2/466): "The hadīth has a number of chains in the Tafsīr of At-Tabarī, which prove that it is established."

Dr. Akram Diyā' Al-'Umarī said in *As-Sīratun-Nabawiyyatis-Sahīhah* (2/347): "Ibn Hishām's *Sīrah* (1/59-60) as a *'mursal'* narration of 'Urwah, and Al-Bayhaqī: *Sunan* (9/12, 58-59) with a *'sahīh'* chain to 'Urwah; and it has fully connected supporting witnesses with At-Tabarānī and others with a *'hasan'* chain. See: *Al-Isābah* (2/278); Ibn Kathīr (3/251); and Al-Haythamī: *Majma'uz-Zawā'id* (6/66-67); and with its chain of narration combined, the hadīth is raised to the level of *'sahīh lighairihi'*."

Endnote 21 – Source: Page 109

(BJ)(SZ) There is disagreement regarding his name, so Ibn Is-hāq and the scholars of Sīrah say 'Basbas', whereas there occurs in *Sahīh Muslim* (no. 1901): 'Busaysah', and in some manuscripts 'Basbasah' — and that occurs in *Sunan Abī Dāwūd* (no. 2618), except that Al-Hāfidh Ibn Hajr ascribed it to the Sunan with the wording 'Busaybasah', and Allāh knows best.

Endnote 22 – Source: Page 111

(SH) Reported by Ibn Abī Shaybah in his *Musannaf* (no. 18507) and Ibn Mardawaih — as occurs in *Al-Bidāyah wan-Nihāyah* (5/73), and *Tafsīrul-Qur'ānil-'Adhīm* (4/18-19) by way of Muhammad Ibn 'Amr 'Alqamah Al-Laythī: from his grandfather with it. I say: This chain of narration is weak, it contains two weaknesses: The first is *'irsāl'*, since 'Alqamah ibn Waqqās Al-Laythī was a tābi'ī who was alive in the time of the Prophet (صَلَّى ٱللَّهُ عَلَيْهِ وَسَلَّمَ) but is not a Companion; the second is that (the narrator) Muhammad did not meet his grandfather so it is a disconnected report. However, Ibn Mardawaih reports it, as occurs in *Tafsīrul-Qur'ānil-'Adhīm* (4/18-19) and *Fat-hul-Bārī* (7/288), by way of Muhammad ibn 'Amr ibn 'Alqamah: from his father: from his grandfather with it. So this narrator 'Amr ibn 'Alqamah is acceptable only if supported by others, as occurs in *At-Taqrīb*, so the hadīth is *'da'īf'* (weak)."

(BJ)(SZ) Reported by Ibn Is-hāq without a chain of narration, and he added at its end: *"By Allāh, it is as if I am looking, at this moment, at the places where those people will fall."* Refer to: *As-Sīrah* (2/227); and Ibn Kathīr said in *Al-Bidāyah* (3/261): "It has witnesses in many narrations."

(DB) From Anas who said: "At the time when Allāh's Messenger (صَلَّى ٱللَّهُ عَلَيْهِ وَسَلَّمَ) proceeded towards Badr, he came out and consulted the people. So Abū Bakr (رَضِيَ ٱللَّهُ عَنْهُ) gave him some advice. Then he consulted them, and 'Umar (رَضِيَ ٱللَّهُ عَنْهُ) gave him some advice. So he remained silent. Then a man from the Ansār said: *'He is only intending you people.'*

So they said: *'[Are you seeking our advice], O Messenger of Allāh?! By Allāh! We shall not say as was said by the Banū Isrā'īl to Mūsā* (عَلَيْهِ ٱلسَّلَامُ)*:*

> فَٱذْهَبْ أَنتَ وَرَبُّكَ فَقَٰتِلَآ إِنَّا هَٰهُنَا قَٰعِدُونَ
>
> MEANING: "Go, you and your Lord, and you two fight. We shall remain sitting here." — **Sūrah Al-Mā'idah (5): 24**

Rather, by Allāh! If you were to strike the livers of the camels until you reached Birkul-Ghimād we would be with you!'"

Shaikh Al-Albānī said in *As-Sahīhah* (no. 3340):

"Reported by An-Nasā'ī in *As-Sunanul-Kubrā* (5/170/8580 & 6/334/11141), Ahmad (6/105 & 188) — and the [bracketed] addition is his, and Abū Ya'lā (6/407/3766 & 430/3803), and from him by Ibn Hibbān in his *Sahīh* (11/23/4721: Al-Mu'assasah Edition), through two chains from Humayd: from Anas who said "..." — and he mentioned it.

I say: This is a chain of narration *'sahīh'* to the standard of the two Shaikhs.

And it has a witness from a *'mursal'* report of 'Alqamah ibn Waqqās with it, with fuller wording. Ibn Abī Shaybah reported it (14/355-356), and Ibn Mardawaih — as occurs in *Al-Fat-h* (7/288) — by way of Muhammad ibn 'Amr ibn 'Alqamah ibn Waqqās: from his father: from his grandfather — with its like; and it contains the wording that the person who said: *'We shall not say as was said...'* was Sa'd ibn Mu'ādh.

Al-Hāfidh remained silent concerning it, and its chain of narration is *'hasan'*."

Endnote 23 – Source: Page 111

(SH) Reported by Ibn Is-hāq in *As-Sīrah* (2/599-600: Ibn Hishām), and from him by Al-Bayhaqī in *Dalā'ilun-Nubuwwah* (3/31), and At-Tabarānī in *Al-Kabīr*, as occurs in *Majma'uz-Zawā'id* (6/73-74): "Yazīd ibn Rūmān narrated to us: from 'Urwah ibn Az-Zubayr with it."

I say: This is a mursal report, with a *'sahīh'* chain of narration, and with this context, it is not authentic. However, some parts of it have witnesses that cause them to become authentic. So from them are what Muslim reports in his *Sahīh* (no.1779): "He said: So Allāh's Messenger (صَلَّى ٱللَّهُ عَلَيْهِ وَسَلَّمَ) encouraged the people, and they proceeded until they camped at Badr. Then some water-carriers of Quraysh came to them. Amongst them there was a black boy belonging to Banul-Hajjāj so they seized him. So the Companions of Allāh's Messenger (صَلَّى ٱللَّهُ عَلَيْهِ وَسَلَّمَ) asked him about Abū Sufyān and his companions.

So he replied: *'I have no knowledge of Abū Sufyān, however here is Abū Jahl, 'Utbah, Shaybah, and Umayyah ibn Al-Khalaf.'* So when he said that they beat him. So he said: *'Yes, I will tell you. Here is Abū Sufyān.'*

But when they left him and then asked him, he said: *'I have no knowledge of Abū Sufyān. However, here is Abū Jahl, 'Utbah, Shaybah, and Umayyah ibn Al-Khalaf amongst the people.'*

So when he said that again they beat him, and Allāh's Messenger (صَلَّى ٱللَّهُ عَلَيْهِ وَسَلَّمَ) was standing in Prayer. So when he saw that, he completed his prayer and said: *'By the One in Whose Hand is my soul! You beat him when he told you the truth and you left him when he lied to you.'*"

This is what is authentic, and it does not specify who it was who went to the well of Badr to seek news, and it mentions that the one seized was a single slave, not two slaves — as was the wording of the text.

Then there is another witness as a hadīth of 'Alī containing the wording: "So he said to him: *'How many are the people?'*

He said: *'They are, by Allāh, many in number: a strong force.'*

So the Prophet (صَلَّى ٱللَّهُ عَلَيْهِ وَسَلَّمَ) tried to make him inform him of how many they were, but he refused. Then the Prophet (صَلَّى ٱللَّهُ عَلَيْهِ وَسَلَّمَ) asked him: *'How many camels do they slaughter?'*

He said: *'Ten every day.'*

So Allāh's Messenger (صَلَّى ٱللَّهُ عَلَيْهِ وَسَلَّمَ) said: *'The people are one thousand: each camel for a hundred.'*

Reported by Ahmad in his *Musnad* (1/117), Ibn Abī Shaybah in *Al-Musannaf* (no. 18526) — by way of Isrā'īl: from Abū Is-hāq As-Sabī'ī: from Hārithah ibn Mudarrib: from 'Alī (رَضِيَ ٱللَّهُ عَنْهُ) with it. I say this chain of narration is weak: Abū Is-hāq As-Sabī'ī is a *'mudallis'* whose memory deteriorated, and he mentions it by way of *'an'anah* in all the chains of narration which I have come across; and Isrā'īl heard from Abū Is-hāq after his memory deteriorated, in the most correct of the two sayings of the scholars.

However this final sentence: *"How many are the people..."* to the end, may be declared to be *'hasan lighairihi'* when taken along with the previous *'mursal'* narration of 'Urwah — Inshā-Allāh.

So in summary, the hadīth is established in the manner we have detailed, and Allāh knows best."

Endnote 24 – Source: Page 113

(BJ)(SZ) *'Munkar'* — Reported by Al-Hākim (3/426-427) and he was silent concerning it, whereas Adh-Dhahabī said: "A *'munkar'* hadīth" — and this story has no chain of narration which can validate it."

(SH) "It is reported by Ibn Is-hāq, as occurs in Sīrah Ibn Hishām (2/602), who said: 'It is narrated to me from some men of Banū Salamah: that they mentioned that Al-Hubāb...' So this chain of narration is weak (*da'īf*), having a series of weaknesses, and it was declared weak by our Shaikh [Al-Albānī] (رَحِمَهُ ٱللَّهُ) in his notes upon *Fiqhus-Sīrah* (pp. 81-83)."

Endnote 25 – Source: Page 113

(BJ)(SZ) "Ibn Kathīr said in his *Tafsīr* (2/280): 'The best report in that regard is what Imām Muhammad ibn Is-hāq ibn Yasār, the author of the *Maghāzī* (رَحِمَهُ ٱللَّهُ), reported, saying: Yazīd ibn Rūmān narrated to me: From 'Urwah ibn Az-Zubayr who said: "Allāh opened the heavens, and the valley was sandy and soft. So Allāh's Messenger (صَلَّى ٱللَّهُ عَلَيْهِ وَسَلَّمَ) and his Companions received rain in a manner which made the earth firm for them, and did not prevent them from moving about; but it struck the Quraysh in such a way that they couldn't proceed during it." Furthermore Allāh (the Mighty and Majestic) said:

> إِذْ يُغَشِّيكُمُ النُّعَاسَ أَمَنَةً مِّنْهُ وَيُنَزِّلُ عَلَيْكُم مِّنَ السَّمَاءِ مَاءً لِّيُطَهِّرَكُم بِهِ وَيُذْهِبَ
> عَنكُمْ رِجْزَ الشَّيْطَانِ وَلِيَرْبِطَ عَلَىٰ قُلُوبِكُمْ وَيُثَبِّتَ بِهِ الْأَقْدَامَ
>
> MEANING: "Remember when Allāh covered you with slumber which came as security from Him, and he caused rain to descend upon you from the sky, to cleanse you with it and to remove from you the whisperings of Satan, and to strengthen your hearts, and to make your feet firm thereby." — **Sūrah Al-Anfāl (8):11**

Endnote 26 – Source: Page 115

(SH) Reported by Abū Dāwūd (no.2665), Ahmad (1/117) — and others, by way of Isrā'īl: from Abū Is-hāq: from Hārithah ibn Mudarrib: from 'Alī ibn Abī Tālib (رَضِيَ اللَّهُ عَنْهُ).

The hadīth has a weakness in Ibn Is-hāq, since he was a *mudallis* whose memory deteriorated and he narrated it with *'an'anah;* and Isrā'īl narrated from him after his deterioration, in the more correct of the two sayings of the scholars. For this reason our Shaikh, the Imām Al-Albānī declared it weak in *Mishkātul-Masābīh.*

However, this basis of the hadīth is witnessed to by the hadīth coming after it, and also what Ibn Is-hāq reported in his *Sīrah*, as occurs in *Al-Isābah* (2/449), and from him by Al-Hākim in *Al-Mustadrak* (3/117), saying: "Yazīd ibn Rūmān narrated to me: from 'Urwah and others from our scholars: from 'Abdullāh ibn 'Abbās, with it."

I say: its chain of narration is *'hasan'*, Ibn Is-hāq is truthful/acceptable (*sadūq*), but is a *mudallis.* However, he clearly states that he had the hadīth narrated to him directly, so we are safe from the evil of his having performed *'tadlīs'*; and he is an Imām in affairs of Military Campaigns, as Al-Hāfidh said in *At-Taqrīb.* So, in summary, the basis of the story is authentic and Allāh knows best."

Endnote 27 – Source: Page 118

(SH) Reported by Ibn Is-hāq (2/619: Ibn Hishām), and Adh-Dhahabī related it from him in *Tārīkhul-Islām* (p.63: Al-Maghāzī) saying: "And some of the people of knowledge narrated to me: that Allāh's Messenger (صَلَّى اللَّهُ عَلَيْهِ وَسَلَّمَ)..."

I say: Its chain of narration is very weak, and it has a witness with its like as a hadīth of 'Ā'ishah (رَضِيَ اللَّهُ عَنْهَا) reported by Ahmad (6/170) with a weak chain of narration, which has two defects.

Firstly: Al-Haythamī said in *Majma' Az-Zawā'id* (6/90): "Ahmad reported it, and its narrators are reliable; however, Ibrāhīm did not hear from 'Ā'ishah."

Secondly: Mughīrah ibn Miqsam, who was reliable except when narrating from Ibrāhīm An-Nakhaʿī for his narrations from him are weak.

So in summary, the hadīth with this wording is *'daʿīf'* (weak)."

Endnote 28 – Source: Page 120

(DB) Ibn Hazm said in *Jawāmiʿus-Sīrah* (pp.117-118): "A mention of those martyred at Badr (may Allāh be pleased with them all):

- ʿUbaydah ibn Al-Hārith ibn Al-Muttalib ibn ʿAbd Manāf;
- ʿUmayr ibn Abī Waqqās, the brother of Saʿd ibn Abī Waqqās. He was killed that day at the age of sixteen;
- Dhush-Shimālayn ibn ʿAbd ʿAmr ibn Nadlah Al-Khuzāʿī, the confederate of Banū Zuhrah;
- ʿĀqil ibn Al-Bukayr Al-Laythī, the confederate of Banū ʿAdiyy ibn Kaʿb;
- Mihjaʿ, the mawlā of ʿUmar ibn Al-Khattāb;
- Safwān ibn Baydāʾ, who was from Banul-Hārith ibn Fihr.

So these six were from the Muhājirīn; and from the Ansār, and then from the Aws were:

- Saʿd ibn Khaythamah;
- Mubashshir ibn ʿAbdil-Mundhir ibn Zanbar.

So they were two men also; and from Banul-Hārith ibn Al-Khazraj:

- Yazīd ibn Al-Hārith, who was Ibn Fusham, from Banul-Hārith from the Khazraj.

And from the Banū Salimah:

- ʿUmayr ibn Al-Humām.

And from Banū Habīb ibn ʿAbd Hārithah:

- Rāfiʿ ibn Al-Muʿallā.

And from Banun-Najjār:

- Ḥārithah ibn Surāqah,
- ʿAwf, and
- Muʿawwidh, the two sons of Afrāʾ."

Endnote 29 – Source: Page 127

[BJ][SZ] This is authentic in a number of aḥādīth. From them is the ḥadīth of Az-Zubayr ibn Al-ʿAwwām reported by At-Tirmidhī (no. 1692); and as a ḥadīth of a man [i.e. from the Companions] reported by Abū Dāwūd (no. 2590); and Ibn Mājah reports it as a ḥadīth of As-Sāʾib ibn Yazīd (no. 2806); and concerning his saying: *'wearing two coats of chain-mail,'* — "[It] means that he was wearing one of them on top of the other."

[DB] Al-Qārī said in *Mirqātul-Mafātīḥ* (7/405): "It contains as an indication that it is permissible to strive in applying the means utilised in fighting, and that this does not negate reliance upon Allāh (*tawakkul*) and surrender to what has been decreed will occur."

Endnote 30 – Source: Page 129

[BJ][SZ] As is reported by Al-Bukhārī (no. 4043).

[DB] Adh-Dhahabī said in *Siyar Aʿlāmin-Nubalāʾ* (2/331): "ʿAbdullāh ibn Jubayr: he was present at Al-ʿAqabah with the seventy, and at Badr and Uḥud. Allāh's Messenger (صَلَّى ٱللَّهُ عَلَيْهِ وَسَلَّمَ) placed him in charge of the archers that day, and they were fifty men. He commanded them and they stood upon (the mount of) ʿAynayn. So he was martyred that day and mutilated; he was killed by ʿIkrimah ibn Abī Jahl."

Ibn Saʿd mentions in *At-Ṭabaqāt* (3/476): "So their leader ʿAbdullāh ibn Jubayr addressed them, and he had made himself recognizable that day by wearing white garments. So he praised and extolled Allāh, as He deserves, and then he commanded obedience to Allāh and obedience to His Messenger, and that they should not disobey any command of Allāh's Messenger. However, they disobeyed and went off, and none of the archers remained with ʿAbdullāh ibn Jubayr except for a small group who were less than ten in number, and amongst them was Al-Hārith ibn Anas ibn Rāfiʿ. So Khālid ibn Al-Walīd looked and saw the hill had been abandoned except for a few defenders, so he attacked with the cavalry, and ʿIkrimah ibn Abī Jahl followed him. So they came to the place of the archers and attacked those who remained. So the people defended with arrows until they were struck down, and ʿAbdullāh ibn Jubayr fired arrows until his arrows were finished. Then he fought with his spear until it broke. Then he broke the scabbard of his sword and fought them until he was killed."

Endnote 31 – Source: Page 133

(SH) Is-hāq ibn Rāhawaih reported it in his *Musnad*, as occurs in *Al-Matālibul-ʿĀliyah* (4/396/no. 4260), and from him by Ibn Hibbān in his *Sahīh* (15/436/6979: *Ihsān*) by way of Ibn Is-hāq: Yahyā ibn ʿAbbād ibn ʿAbdullāh ibn Az-Zubayr narrated to me: from his father: from his grandfather ʿAbdullāh ibn Az-Zubayr: from his father that he said:

> "Then Allāh's Messenger (صَلَّى ٱللَّٰهُ عَلَيْهِ وَسَلَّمَ) ordered ʿAlī ibn Abī Tālib (رَضِيَ ٱللَّٰهُ عَنْهُ), so he went to (the well/water trough of) Al-Mihrās and brought some water in his leather shield. So Allāh's Messenger (صَلَّى ٱللَّٰهُ عَلَيْهِ وَسَلَّمَ) wanted to drink from it, but he found that it had an odour so he refused to do so. So he washed the blood which was upon his face with it."

I say: Its chain of narration is *'hasan'*.

Endnote 32 – Source: Page 134

(SH) Al-Bukhārī reported in his *Sahīh* (3698 and 4066) from ʿUthmān ibn Mawhab who said: "A man came performing Hajj to the House and he saw some people sitting. So he said: *'Who are these people sitting?'*

They said: *'They are the Quraysh.'* He said: *'Who is the old man?'* They said: *'It is Ibn ʿUmar.'* So he went to him and said: *'I am going to ask you about something, so will you tell me?'* He said: *'I implore you by the respect due to this House; do you know that 'Uthmān ibn 'Affān fled on the Day of Uhud.'*

He said: *'Yes.'*

Ibn 'Umar said: *'Come and let me inform you and make clear to you what you asked about. As for his fleeing on the day of Uhud, then I bear witness that Allāh has pardoned him.'"*

Endnote 33 – Source: Page 134

DB Imām Ibnul-Qayyim (رَحِمَهُ ٱللَّهُ) in *Zādul-Ma'ād* (3/218) mentioned some of the points of wisdom to be taken from the Battle of Uhud, from them:

1 — Awareness of the bad consequences of sin, and of weak-heartedness and disagreement, and that what happened to them occurred as a result of that. [See: Sūrah Āli 'Imrān (3): 152].

2 — Allāh's Wisdom, and His pre-ordained way with regard to His Messengers and their followers, requires that sometimes they gain the upper hand and that sometimes others gain the upper hand over them. However, the final result will be in their favour. So if they were always victorious, then everybody would join them — the Believers, and those who are not Believers; and then those who are true and sincere would not be distinguished from the rest. Furthermore, what is intended by the sending of the Prophets and Messengers would not be attained.

3 — This is a sign for the Messengers: that sometimes they are victorious and sometimes their enemies are. Just as Heraclius said to Abū Sufyān: *"Have you fought against him?"* He said: *"Yes."* He asked: *"How was the war between you and him?"* He said: *"With alternate success: he would overcome us and we would overcome him."* So Heraclius said: *"That is how the Messengers are tried, and then the final victory is theirs."* [*Sahīhul-Bukhārī* no. 5].

4 — So that the truthful Believer is distinguished from the lying Hypocrite. Because when the Muslims had been victorious at Badr,

many people joined them and appeared to be Muslims, whereas inwardly they were not so. Therefore, Allāh in His Wisdom decreed for them a trial that would test them, and would distinguish the Believers from the Hypocrites. So in this battle the Hypocrites raised their heads and spoke openly with what they used to conceal. So then, the people were clearly divided into three groups: the Believers, the Disbelievers, and the Hypocrites.

Therefore, the Muslims became aware that besides their enemy from outside they also had enemies from within their ranks. So they therefore took precautions against them. [See: Sūrah Āli'Imrān (3):179]

5 — That Allāh should bring out those who truly love Him, fight for Him, and worship Him, at times of ease and times of hardship; and in situations which they love and situations they dislike, and in victory and in defeat.

So if they remain firm upon worship of Allāh in all such situations, then they are truly His worshippers; contrary to those who only worship Him in times of ease and comfort.

6 — If Allāh (the Perfect) always gave them victory over their enemies in every place; and if He established them and caused them to always overcome their enemies, then their souls would become overbearing, arrogant and proud.

7 — That when Allāh tests them with being overcome, routed, and defeated, they become humble and submissive to Him; then humbleness and submission to Him bring about His grant of victory. [Āli 'Imrān (3):123, and Sūrah Barā'ah (9):25]

So if Allāh (the Perfect) wishes to give honour, aid, and victory to His servant He first gives him a taste of defeat and humility, and then supports and grants him victory.

8 — That Allāh (the Perfect) has prepared high and honourable stations in Paradise for His believing servants; but these are such that they will not reach these stations by their actions. So Allāh provided for them tests and trials that will enable them to reach these high stations.

9 — If people's souls experience continual well-being, victory, and affluence, then they become unjust and start to love this world, and this is a disease that blocks the person's path towards his Lord and the Hereafter. So Allāh provides such tests and trials as will be a cure for this disease, and will allow the person's soul to proceed earnestly on its way towards its Lord.

10 — From the highest level of the beloved servants of Allāh is the level of martyrdom (*Ash-Shahādah*). So the martyrs are His especially close and chosen servants, and their level comes immediately after that of the '*Siddīqīn*' (the eminently true and truthful followers of the Messengers) [see Sūrah An-Nisā' (4):69].

So Allāh loves to take martyrs from His servants: those whose blood is spilled out of love for Him and seeking His Pleasure. They attain His Pleasure and His Love.

11 — That when Allāh (the Perfect) wishes to destroy and erase His enemies, He brings about those causes that will lead to their destruction. The most important of these, after their Disbelief itself, are: their injustice, their oppression, their extreme harm towards the Believers, and their fighting and overcoming the Believers.

So in this way Allāh purifies His chosen servants, and cleanses them from their sins and deficiencies; and at the same time He is adding to the causes of destruction for His enemies. [see: Sūrah Āli 'Imrān (3):139-140; and Sūrah An-Nisā' (4):104]

12 — So that the Hypocrites should be visible and known to the Believers, when previously they had been hidden.

13 — That Allāh should cleanse the Believers through what happened on that day from (I) their sins, (II) deficiencies in their souls, (III) from the Hypocrites, who pretended to be from them.

14 — That Allāh rewards the people in accordance with how they actually act, and not just in accordance with how He always knew they were going to act. [Sūrah Āli 'Imrān (3):142]

15 — That Uhud was a prelude, and a sign, prior to the death of the Prophet (صَلَّىٰ اللَّهُ عَلَيْهِ وَسَلَّمَ), so that they would remain firm when it occurred. So Allāh blamed those who turned and fled when they thought that he (صَلَّىٰ اللَّهُ عَلَيْهِ وَسَلَّمَ) had died in the battle. [see Sūrah Āli 'Imrān (3):144]

So it was made clear to them that what is obligatory upon them, if that should occur, was that they should remain firm upon his Religion, and upon Tawhīd, and that they should die upon that; because they are the worshippers not of Muhammad (صَلَّىٰ اللَّهُ عَلَيْهِ وَسَلَّمَ), but of his Lord — Who lives and never dies.

Endnote 34 – Source: Page 141

(SH) Reported by Al-Bukhārī (no. 3053) and Muslim (no. 1637), as a hadīth of Ibn 'Abbās, that he (صَلَّىٰ اللَّهُ عَلَيْهِ وَسَلَّمَ) said: *"Expel the Mushrikūn from the Arabian Peninsula,"* and Muslim reported (no.1767) as a hadīth of 'Umar ibn Al-Khattāb that the Prophet (صَلَّىٰ اللَّهُ عَلَيْهِ وَسَلَّمَ) said: "I shall certainly expel the Jews and the Christians from the Arabian Peninsula, so that I do not leave except a Muslim."

Al-Hāfidh said in *Al-Fat-h* (6/171): "And Al-Asma'ī said: 'The Arabian Peninsula (Jazīratul-'Arab) is between the farthest tip of 'Adan Abyan (Aden) and the fertile region of Al-'Irāq in length, and from Juddah (Jeddah) and whatever is adjacent to it to the limits of Shām in width. It is called *'Jazīratul-'Arab'* (lit. the Arabian Island) because it is surrounded by seas, i.e. the Indian Ocean, the Gulf of Aqabah, the Persian Sea, and the Red Sea. It is ascribed to the Arabs because they occupied it before Islām: their homelands and their dwelling places were there. However, the part which the Mushrikūn are to be prevented from residing in is the Hijāz in particular, and that is Makkāh, Al-Madīnah, Al-Yamāmah, and the adjacent area. It does not apply to the other areas covered by the term *'The Arabian Peninsula'*, since all agree that they are not to be prevented from Yemen, even though it is a part of the Arabian Peninsula. This is the position of the majority *(Al-Jumhūr)*.'"

Endnote 35 – Source: Page 144

[SH] Al-Hāfidh said in *Al-Fat-h* (7/417): "There is disagreement about when this expedition occurred, and there is disagreement about why it was called that name (...) Rather what is befitting is that it is stated that it occurred after the military expedition of Banū Qurayzah, since it has preceded that the Fear-Prayer was legislated at the battle of the Trench, and so was not to be found (at this point in time); and it is established that the Fear-Prayer occurred during the expedition of Dhātur-Riqāʿ. So this proves that it came after the Trench."

Endnote 36 – Source: Page 144

[DB] Al-Hāfidh Ibn Kathīr said in *As-Sīratun-Nabawiyyah* (3/158): "Ibn Is-hāq said: *'And he left Abū Dharr in charge of Al-Madīnah.'* Ibn Hishām commented: *'Or it is said: ʿUthmān ibn ʿAffān.'*"

[SH] Or it is said: ʿUthmān ibn ʿAffān, and that is what is more apparent, since it is established in *Sahīh Muslim* (no. 1825), from Abū Dharr (رَضِيَ ٱللَّهُ عَنْهُ) that he said: "I said: 'O Messenger of Allāh! Will you not appoint me to some position?'"

He said: "So he struck my shoulder with his hand, then he said:

> 'O Abū Dharr! You are weak, and it is a great responsibility; and on the Day of Resurrection it will be disgrace and regret, except for one who holds on to it rightfully, and who carries out what is due upon him with regard to it.'"

Endnote 37 – Source: Page 145

[BJ][SZ] There is disagreement about this point, and Al-Bukhārī (رَحِمَهُ ٱللَّهُ) was one of those who held the saying that it occurred after Khaybar. He said in *As-Sahīh* [*"The Book of Military Expeditions"* — Chapter 31]: *"And it occurred after Khaybar, since Abū Mūsā came after Khaybar"* — meaning; the arrival of Abū Mūsā (رَضِيَ ٱللَّهُ عَنْهُ) from Abyssinia after the conquest of Khaybar, as occurs in the hadīth, which he reported (no.4230).

This was also held by Al-Hāfidh ibn Hajr in *Al-Fat-h,* and it was supported by Ibnul-Qayyim in *Zādul-Ma'ād* (3/252-253), who declared the historians to be mistaken in placing it before Khaybar.

Endnote 38 – Source: Page 146

(SH) Reported by Ahmad (3/376), and Ibn Khuzaymah (...), Abū Ya'lā, Al-Bazzār, and Al-Bayhaqī in *Dalā'ilun-Nubuwwah* (3/382-383), all of them by way of Ibn Is-hāq (and it occurs in his *Sīrah* (3/888: Ibn Hishām): Wahb ibn Kaysān narrated to me: from Jābir with it.

This chain of narration is *'hasan':* Ibn Is-hāq is *'sadūq'* (truthful/acceptable) and a *'mudallis'*; however, he clearly states that he had it narrated to him directly, and he is a proof in expeditions and campaigns.

Endnote 39 – Source: Page 146

(SH) Reported by Ahmad (3/325 & 362), and Abū Ya'lā (3/329/ no. 1793) by way of 'Alī ibn Zayd ibn Jud'ān, who is weak because of his poor memory. It is also reported by Ibn 'Asākir in Tārīkh Dimashq (11/264-265). And its chain of narration has weaknesses. And it is reported by Al-Bukhārī (5/314) as a disconnected report. So in summary, it is not authentic that it occurred during the expedition of Tabūk.

Endnote 40 – Source: Page 146

(BJ)(SZ) This was the view preferred by Al-Hāfidh Ibn Hajr in *Fat-hul-Bārī* (5/320-321), who said: "This is the preferred saying in my view, since the military historians are more precise in that regard than others. Also, there occurs in the narration of At-Tahāwī (*Mushkilul-Āthār,* no. 4415) that this occurred whilst they were returning to Al-Madīnah upon the Makkah road; and the route to Tabūk does not meet up with the road to Makkah, as opposed to the road to Dhātur-Riqā'. Also, there occurs in many of its narrations that he (صَلَّى ٱللَّهُ عَلَيْهِ وَسَلَّمَ) asked him during this incident: *'Have you married?'* He said: *'Yes.'* He said: *'Did you marry a virgin, or a woman who had been previously married?'* — until the end of the hadīth.

And it contains his excusing himself for marrying a previously married woman with the fact that his father had been martyred at Uhud and had left behind his sisters, so he married a woman who could comb their hair and look after them. So this indicates that it happened soon after the death of his father. So it would appear to be more likely that the incident happened during Dhātur-Riqā', and not during Tabūk. So it is not surprising that Al-Bayhaqī clearly affirmed in *Dalā'ilun-Nubuwwah* (3/381) that which Ibn Is-hāq said."

(DB) For the details of the incident, refer to *Sahīh Al-Bukhārī* (no. 2097) and *Sahīh Muslim* (no 715).

Endnote 41 – Source: Page 147

(BJ)(SZ) A *'hasan'* hadīth. Ibn Is-hāq reported it, as occurs in *As-Sīratun-Nabawiyyah* (3/230), and Ahmad (3/343-344) by way of him, and Abū Dāwūd (no. 198): from Sadaqah ibn Yasār: from 'Aqīl ibn Jābir: from Jābir with it. No one narrates from 'Aqīl except for Sadaqah, and no one besides Ibn Hibbān declares him reliable.

It was declared authentic by Ibn Khuzaymah (no. 36), Ibn Hibbān (no.1096), Al-Hākim (1/156-157), and Ad-Diyā' in *Al-Mukhtārah.* Al-Bukhārī (*The Book of Wudhū:* Chapter 34) mentioned it in disconnected and abridged form, with a wording not indicating its being established.

It also has a supporting witness reported by Al-Bayhaqī in *Dalā'ilun-Nubuwwah* (3/378-379), and even though its chain of narration contains weakness then its basis occurs in the two *Sahīhs.*

(DB) Shaikh Al-Albānī said in *Sahīh Sunan Abī Dāwūd*: "It is *'hasan'*."

Endnote 42 – Source: Page 150

Shaikh Muhammad ibn Sālih Al-'Uthaymīn (رَحِمَهُ ٱللَّهُ) said in *Al-Qawlul-Mufīd 'alā Kitābit-Tawhīd* (1/30):

"The Decree of Allāh (the Mighty and Majestic) is of two categories:

1. The Legislative Decree (*Qadā' Shar'ī*),

2. The Universal/Creational Decree (*Qadā' Kawnī*).

So the Legislative Decree is such that it may result in what is decreed by it occurring, or not occurring; and it can only apply to that which is loved by Allāh. An example of that is this āyah:

> وَقَضَىٰ رَبُّكَ أَلَّا تَعْبُدُوا إِلَّا إِيَّاهُ
>
> MEANING: "And your Lord has decreed that you do not worship except Him alone." — **Sūrah Al-Isrā' (17): 23**

So *'decreed'* here means: He legislated, or: He enjoined, and their like.

As for the Universal/Creational Decree, then it must certainly occur; and it applies to that which Allāh loves and that which He does not love. An example of that is His Saying (He the Most High):

> وَقَضَيْنَا إِلَىٰ بَنِي إِسْرَائِيلَ فِي الْكِتَابِ لَتُفْسِدُنَّ فِي الْأَرْضِ مَرَّتَيْنِ وَلَتَعْلُنَّ عُلُوًّا كَبِيرًا
>
> MEANING: "And We decreed for the Banū Isrā'īl in the Scripture: you will cause corruption upon the earth twice, and you will behave with great insolence." — **Sūrah Al-Isrā' (17): 4**

So decree here is Creational and Universal (Decree), since Allāh did not legislate corruption upon the earth and does not love it."

Shaikh 'Abdul-'Azīz ibn Bāz (رَحِمَهُ ٱللَّهُ) said in his notes upon *At-Tanbīhātul-Latīfah 'Alā Mahtawat 'Alaihil-'Aqīdatul-Wāsitiyyah* (p. 41):

"From the fundamental principles of the Ahlus-Sunnah wal-Jamā'ah is to affirm the comprehensive Wish and Will (*Mashī'ah*) of the Lord; and that whatever He wishes occurs, and whatever He does not wish to occur does not occur; just as from their fundamental established principles is to affirm the attribute of 'Will' (*Al-Irādah*), and it is of two categories:

1. His Universal Decreeing Will (*Al-Irādatul-Kawniyyah Al-Qadariyyah*): and nothing can escape this Will, just as with His Wish and Will (*Mashī'ah*). So the Disbeliever and the Muslim equally fall under this Universal/Creational Will. So acts of obedience and sins,

provisions and life spans all occur by the Universal and Creational Wish and Will of the Lord.

2. The second category of Will is: The Legislative Will, which requires the affairs of the Religion. This comprises the Lord loving and being pleased with that which is willed. However, this Will does not necessitate the occurrence of what is willed by it: it may occur, or it may not occur. So Allāh (the Perfect) willed, in the Legislative sense, from His servants that they should worship Him alone and obey Him. So some of them worshipped him and obeyed Him, whereas others did not.

And whoever recognises the distinction between these two types of Will will be safe from many false doubts, on the basis of which people have erred and misunderstood."

Endnote 43 – Source: Page 156

(SH) Reported by Ibn Is-hāq in *As-Sīrah* (3/908-909: Ibn Hishām) who said: "And Yahyā ibn ʿAbbād ibn ʿAbdullāh ibn Az-Zubayr narrated to me: from his father ʿAbbād with it, as a longer narration. This chain of narration is weak (*'daʿīf'*) as it is *'mursal.'* However, his (صَلَّىٰ ٱللَّٰهُ عَلَيْهِ وَسَلَّمَ) saying: "*War is trickery,*" is authentic (*'sahīh'*) since it is reported by Al-Bukhārī in his *Sahīh* (no. 3029) and Muslim in his *Sahīh* (no. 1740) as a hadīth of Abū Hurairah (رَضِيَ ٱللَّٰهُ عَنْهُ). It is also reported by Al-Bukhārī (no. 3030) and Muslim (no. 1739) as a hadīth of Jābir ibn ʿAbdillāh (رَضِيَ ٱللَّٰهُ عَنْهُمَا).

Al-Hāfidh Ibn Hajr said in *Fat-hul-Bārī* (6/158): "In its origin *'khadʿ'* (trickery or deception) means making something apparent whilst hiding something contrary to it. So it shows an encouragement to take precautions in war, and the desirability of tricking the Disbelievers (therein); and that whoever is not alert to this will not be secure from having the matter turned against him."

An-Nawawī said: "They agree that it is permissible to trick the Disbelievers during war in whatever way that is possible, unless it involves breaking a treaty or a guarantee of security, in which cases it is not permissible."

Ibnul-Munayyir said: "The meaning of *'war is trickery'* is that the war which will be advantageous for its people, and which will fully attain the desired goals, is that of outwitting and not of openly facing the enemy. This is because of the risks involved in facing the enemy, as opposed to the victory obtained by means of outwitting which comes without risk."

Endnote 44 – Source: Page 157

(BJ)(SZ) Reported by Muslim in his *Sahīh* (1788) as a longer narration.

(DB) The narration is: "From Ibrāhīm At-Taymī: from his father who said: We were with Hudhayfah when a man said: *'If I had reached Allāh's Messenger (ﷺ) I would have fought along with him and striven hard.'*

So Hudhayfah said: 'Would you indeed have done that? I was with Allāh's Messenger (ﷺ) on the night of the allied enemies (Al-Ahzāb), and we were struck by a violent and freezing wind. So Allāh's Messenger (ﷺ) said: *"Which man can bring me news of the people, and then Allāh will place him with me on the Day of Resurrection?"*

So we remained silent and none of us responded to him. Then he said: *"Which man can bring me news of the people, and then Allāh will place him with me on the Day of Resurrection?"*

So we remained silent and none of us responded to him. Then he said: *"Which man can bring me the news of the people, and then Allāh will place him with me on the Day of Resurrection?"*

So we remained silent and none of us responded to him. So then, he said: *"Get up, O Hudhayfah! And bring me the news of the people."*

Since he had called me by my name I had no alternative but to get up. He said: *"Go and bring me news of the people, and do not do anything to provoke them against me."*

So when I left him I felt as if I were walking in a heated bath-house until I came to them. So I saw Abū Sufyān warming his back against the fire. So I placed an arrow in the middle of the bow and I wanted to shoot him, but then I remembered the saying of Allāh's Messenger (ﷺ): *"And do not do anything to provoke them against me"* — and if I had shot at him I would have struck him. So I came back walking as if I was in a heated bath-house. So when I came to him I informed him of the news of the people and when I had finished I felt the severe cold again.

So Allāh's Messenger (ﷺ) wrapped me in an extra cloak, which he had upon him, which he used to wear when he prayed. So I slept until it was dawn. So when it was dawn he said: *"Get up, O heavy sleeper!"*""

Endnote 45 – Source: Page 165

(DB) Ibn Is-hāq said in his *Sīrah* (3/264: Ibn Hishām): "On the Day of the Trench none of the Muslims were martyred except six men:

From Banū 'Abdil-Ash-hal: Sa'd ibn Mu'ādh; Anas ibn Aws ibn 'Atīk ibn 'Amr; and 'Abdullāh ibn Sahl.

And from Banū Jusham from the Khazraj, then from Banū Salamah: At-Tufayl ibn An-Nu'mān; and Tha'labah ibn Ghanamah.

And from Banun-Najjār, then from Banū Dīnār: Ka'b ibn Zayd who was struck and killed by a random arrow.

And on the Day of Banū Qurayzah, the Muslims who were martyred were:

From Banul-Hārith ibn Al-Khazraj: Khallād ibn Suwayd ibn Th'alabah ibn 'Amr who had a mill stone thrown upon him.

And Abū Sinān ibn Mihsan ibn Hurthān — the brother of Banū Asad ibn Khuzaymah — died whilst Allāh's Messenger (ﷺ) was besieging Banū Qurayzah. So he was buried in the graveyard of Banū Qurayzah where they bury today."

Endnote 46 – Source: Page 166

(SH) Reported by Ibn Is-hāq in *As-Sīrah* (3/951-953: Ibn Hishām) who said: Ibn Shihāb Az-Zuhrī narrated to me: from 'Abdullāh ibn Ka'b ibn Mālik with it; and Abdur-Razzāq reported it in his *Musannaf* (5/407/ no.9747): from Ma'mar; and Al-Bayhaqī in *Dalā'ilun-Nubuwwah* (3/221), by way of Ibrāhīm ibn Sa'd; both of them from Az-Zuhrī: from 'Abdur-

Rahmān ibn Kaʿb with it, in *'mursal'* form. So he said: *"Abdur-Rahmān'* in place of *"Abdullāh'* — and this is more authentic.

Al-Bayhaqī said after it: *"This is 'mursal' with a good chain of narration,"* and he said in *Al-Maʿrifah* (4/382): *"Even though this is 'mursal', then it is well-known to the people of knowledge of military expeditions."*

I say: Rather, its chain of narration is weak as it is *'mursal'*, and it contains things which contradict what is established. So it is established in *Sahīh Al-Bukhārī* (nos. 4038, 4039 & 4040) as a hadīth of Al-Barāʾ ibn ʿĀzib (رَضِيَ ٱللَّهُ عَنْهُ) that the one who killed him was ʿAbdullāh ibn ʿAtīk, and not ʿAbdullāh ibn Unays! And his report is completely different to the report of Ibn Is-hāq! So it is surprising how the author gave preference to mentioning something not authentic and not established over mentioning that which is authentic and established!

DB Imām Al-Bukhārī reported it (no. 4040) as a hadīth of Al-Barāʾ (رَضِيَ ٱللَّهُ عَنْهُ) with the wording:

"Allāh's Messenger (صَلَّى ٱللَّهُ عَلَيْهِ وَسَلَّمَ) sent ʿAbdullāh ibn ʿAtīk, ʿAbdullāh ibn ʿUtbah, and some men with them to attack Abū Rāfiʿ. So they went off until they came close to his fort. So ʿAbdullāh ibn ʿAtīk said: *'Wait whilst I go and have a look.'*

He said:

> 'So I used a trick to enter the fort. So they had lost a donkey of theirs and came out with a flaming torch to look for it. I feared that they would recognise me so I covered my head and my legs and made it look as if I was relieving myself. Then the gatekeeper called out: *"Whoever wants to enter then let him enter before I lock it."* So I entered and hid myself in a donkey stall near the gate of the fort.
>
> Then they ate their supper with Abū Rāfiʿ, and held conversation until an hour of the night had passed. Then they returned to their homes. So when the voices ceased and I could not hear any movement I came out. I had seen where the gatekeeper put the keys to the fort in a recess in the wall. So I took them and opened the gate of the fort, saying to myself: If the people notice me I can easily run away. Then I went to the houses and locked them upon their occupants from the

outside, and I ascended a staircase towards Abū Rāfiʿ. The house was in darkness, as its lights had been extinguished, so I did not know where he was.

So I called: *"O Abū Rāfiʿ!"*

He said: *"Who is this?"*

So I went towards the voice and struck him, and he called out, but my blow was in vain. Then I pretended to be someone coming to help him and I said: *"What is wrong with you, O Abū Rāfiʿ?"* — and I had changed my voice.

So he said: *"Shall I not astonish you? Woe to your mother! A man has just entered upon me and struck me with a sword."* So I went towards him again and struck him another time, but my blow was in vain.

So he shouted out and his wife got up. Then I came and changed my voice again as if I was someone coming to his aid, and I found him lying flat on his back. So I placed the sword into his belly and forced it down until I heard the sound of the (back) bone breaking. Then I came out in confusion until I reached the stairs. I wanted to descend but I fell and my leg became dislocated, so I tied it up tightly, and went limping to my companions.

So I said to them: *"Go and inform Allāh's Messenger (صَلَّى ٱللَّٰهُ عَلَيْهِ وَسَلَّمَ) of the good news, but I will not leave until I hear someone announcing his death."*

Then when the dawn broke an announcer climbed up and called out: *"I announce to you the death of Abū Rāfiʿ."* So I got up, walked, and could not feel any pain. So I reached my companions before they came to the Prophet (صَلَّى ٱللَّٰهُ عَلَيْهِ وَسَلَّمَ), so I told him the good news.'"

Endnote 47 – Source: Page 169

DB Ibn Is-hāq said: "So ʿĀsim ibn ʿUmar ibn Qatādah, ʿAbdullāh ibn Abī Bakr, and Muhammad ibn Yahyā ibn Habbān narrated to me: Each of them narrating to me a part of the story of Banul-Mustaliq, saying: *'News reached Allāh's Messenger (صَلَّى ٱللَّٰهُ عَلَيْهِ وَسَلَّمَ) that Banul-Mustaliq were gathering against him, being led by Al-Hārith ibn Abī Dirār, the father of*

Juwayriyah (who became) the wife of Allāh's Messenger (صَلَّىٰ ٱللَّٰهُ عَلَيْهِ وَسَلَّمَ). So when Allāh's Messenger (صَلَّىٰ ٱللَّٰهُ عَلَيْهِ وَسَلَّمَ) heard about them he went out against them.'" (*Sīrah Ibn Hishām*)

Al-Hāfidh Ibn Hajr said: *"This is how Ibn Is-hāq reported it, with 'mursal' chains."* (*Fat-hul-Bārī*: 7/430)

Endnote 48 – Source: Page 170

(SH) Reported by Ibn Is-hāq in *As-Sīrah* (3/970-971: Ibn Hishām), and from him by Abū Dāwūd (4/22/ no. 3931), and Ahmad (6/277) (...), that Muhammad ibn Ja'far ibn Az-Zubayr narrated to me: from 'Urwah: from 'Ā'ishah with it. I say: This chain of narration is *'hasan'*, and Ibn Is-hāq clearly stated that he heard it directly. Our Shaikh (Al-Albānī) (رَحِمَهُ ٱللَّٰهُ) said in *Sahīh Mawārididh-Dham'ān* (no. 1020): *"Hasan."*

Endnote 49 – Source: Page 170

(SH) Al-Bukhārī reported it in is *Sahīh* (no. 4900) and Muslim in his *Sahīh* (no.2772) as a hadīth of Zayd ibn Arqam (رَضِيَ ٱللَّٰهُ عَنْهُ). Al-Hāfidh (Ibn Hajr) said in *Al-Fat-h* (8/646): "It shows the permissibility of reporting forbidden speech to the one who has been spoken about; and that this is not considered blameworthy tale-carrying, unless the intention in doing so is to cause trouble. As for when the benefit outweighs the harm, then this is not (blameworthy)."

Endnote 50 – Source: Page 171

(BJ)(SZ) Refer to *Sahīh Al-Bukhārī* (no.4141) and *Sahīh Muslim* (no. 2770).

Narrated 'Ā'ishah (رَضِيَ ٱللَّٰهُ عَنْهَا): "Whenever Allāh's Messenger (صَلَّىٰ ٱللَّٰهُ عَلَيْهِ وَسَلَّمَ) intended to go on a journey, he used to draw lots amongst his wives, and Allāh's Messenger used to take with him the one to whom the lot fell. He drew lots amongst us for one of the military expeditions which he went on. The lot fell to me, so I proceeded with Allāh's Messenger after the (obligation of the) Hijāb had been sent down.

I was carried (on the back of a camel) in my howdah, and lifted down while still in it (when we came to a halt). So we went on until Allāh's Messenger (ﷺ) had finished from that expedition of his and returned. When we approached the city of Al-Madīnah, he announced at night that it was time for departure. So when they announced the news of departure, I got up and went away from the army camps, and after finishing from the call of nature, I came back to my riding animal. I touched my chest to find that my necklace, which was made of Zafār beads, was missing.

So I returned to look for my necklace, and my search for it detained me. (Meanwhile) the people who used to carry me on my camel came, took my howdah, and put it on the back of my camel on which I used to ride, as they considered that I was in it. In those days, women were light in weight for they did not get fat, and flesh did not cover their bodies in abundance, as they used to eat only a little food.

Those people, therefore, disregarded the lightness of the howdah while lifting and carrying it; and at that time, I was still a young girl. They made the camel rise and all of them left (along with it). I found my necklace after the army had gone. Then I came to their camping place and found no call maker from them, nor anyone who would respond to the call. So I intended to go to the place where I used to stay, thinking that they would miss me and come back to me (in search of me).

While I was sitting in my resting place, I was overwhelmed by sleep, and slept. Safwān ibn Al-Muʿattal As-Sulamī, then (known as) Adh-Dhakwānī, was behind the army. When he reached my place in the morning, he saw the figure of a sleeping person and he recognised me on seeing me, as he had seen me before the Hijāb (was prescribed). So I woke up when he said:

> إِنَّا للهِ وَ إِنَّا إِلَيهِ رَاجِعُون
>
> MEANING: 'Indeed, we belong to Allāh and to Him we shall return.'

— as soon as he recognised me.

I veiled my face with my jilbāb at once, and by Allāh, we did not speak a single word, and I did not hear him saying any word besides his saying: *'Indeed we belong to Allāh and to Him we shall return.'* He dismounted from his camel and made it kneel down, putting his leg on its front legs, and then I got up and rode on it.

Then he set out, leading the camel that was carrying me, until we overtook the army in the extreme heat of midday while they were at a halt (taking a rest). (Because of the event) some people brought destruction upon themselves, and the one who spread the slanderous lie was ʿAbdullāh ibn ʿUbayy ibn Salūl."

ʿUrwah said: "I was informed that it was propagated and talked about in his (i.e. ʿAbdullāh ibn ʿUbayy's) presence and he confirmed it, and listened to it, and asked about it, to let it prevail."

ʿUrwah also added: "None was mentioned as being a member of the group who spoke with the slander besides (ʿAbdullāh ibn ʿUbayy) — except Hassān ibn Thābit, Mistah ibn Uthāthah, and Hamnah bint Jahsh, along with others — about whom I have no knowledge, except that they were a group, as Allāh said. It is said that the one who carried most of the slander was ʿAbdullāh bin ʿUbayy ibn Salūl."

ʿUrwah added: "ʿĀ'ishah disliked to have Hassān abused in her presence and she used to say:

> 'It was he who said: *"My father and his father (i.e. Hassān's grandfather), and my honour — are all for the protection of Muhammad's honour from you."*'""

ʿĀ'ishah said: "After we returned to Al-Madīnah, I became ill for a month. The people were propagating the forged statements of the slanderers whilst I was unaware of anything of that, but I felt that in my present ailment I was not receiving the same kindness from Allāh's Messenger (ﷺ) as I used to receive when I became ill. (But now) Allāh's Messenger (ﷺ) would only enter upon me, greet me, and say: *'How is that (lady)?'* and leave.

That roused my doubts, but I did not discover the evil (i.e. the slander) until I went out, after my convalescence. I went out with Umm Mistah to Al-Manāsi', where we used to answer the call of nature, and we used not to go out (to answer the call of nature) except each night; and that was before we had toilets near to our houses. And this practice of ours concerning evacuating the bowels was the practice of the old 'Arabs living in the deserts, for we found it disagreeable for us to take toilets near to our houses. So I and Umm Mistah, who was the daughter of Abū Ruhm ibn Al-Muttalib ibn 'Abd-Manāf, whose mother was the daughter of Sakhr ibn 'Āmir, and the aunt of Abū Bakr As-Siddīq, and whose son was Mistah ibn Uthāthah ibn 'Abbād ibn Al-Muttalib, went out. Umm Mistah and I returned to my house after we had answered the call of nature. Umm Mistah stumbled when her foot caught in her covering sheet, and upon that she said, *'Let Mistah be ruined!'*

I said, *'What a hard word you have said. Do you abuse a man who took part in the battle of Badr?'*

On that she said, *'O woman! Haven't you heard what he (i.e. Mistah) said?'*

I said, *'What did he say?'*

Then she told me the slander of the people of the slanderous lie. So my ailment was aggravated, and when I reached my home, Allāh's Messenger (صَلَّى ٱللَّهُ عَلَيْهِ وَسَلَّمَ) came to me, and after greeting me, said, *'How is that (lady)?'*

I said, *'Will you allow me to go to my parents?'* I wanted to be sure about the news through them. Allāh's Messenger (صَلَّى ٱللَّهُ عَلَيْهِ وَسَلَّمَ) allowed me, so I said to my mother: *'O mother! What are the people talking about?'*

She said, *'O my daughter! Don't worry, for there is hardly any woman who is loved by her husband and whose husband has other wives besides her except that that they find faults with her.'*

I said: *'Subhān-Allāh (I declare Allāh free of all imperfections)! Are the people really talking in this way?'*

I kept on weeping that night until dawn — I could neither stop weeping, nor sleep. Then I continued weeping through the morning."

She (رَضِيَ ٱللَّهُ عَنْهَا) said: "Allāh's Messenger (صَلَّى ٱللَّهُ عَلَيْهِ وَسَلَّمَ) called 'Alī ibn Abī Tālib and Usāmah bin Zayd when Revelation was delayed in coming, to ask and consult them about divorcing me. Usāmah bin Zayd said what he knew of my innocence, and the respect he preserved in himself for me. Usāmah said: *'(O Allāh's Messenger!) She is your wife and we do not know anything except good about her.'*

As for ʿAlī ibn Abī Tālib, then he said: *'O Allāh's Messenger! Allāh does not put you in difficulty and there are plenty of women besides her, yet, ask the maid-servant who will tell you the truth.'*

On that, Allāh's Messenger (صَلَّى ٱللَّٰهُ عَلَيْهِ وَسَلَّمَ) called Barīrah (i.e. the maidservant) and said, *'O Barīrah! Did you ever see anything which aroused your suspicion?'*

Barīrah said to him, *'By Him Who has sent you with the Truth. I have never seen anything in her (i.e. ʿĀʾishah) which I could criticise, except that she is a young girl who sleeps leaving the dough of her family exposed so that the domestic goats come and eat it.'*

So, on that day, Allāh's Messenger (صَلَّى ٱللَّٰهُ عَلَيْهِ وَسَلَّمَ) got up on the minbar (pulpit) and complained about ʿAbdullāh bin ʿUbayy (ibn Salūl) before his Companions, saying, *'O you Muslims! Who will relieve me from that man who has hurt me with regard to my family? By Allāh, I know nothing except good about my family; and they have blamed a man about whom I know nothing except good, and he used never to enter my home except with me.'*

Saʿd ibn Muʿādh, the brother of Banū ʿAbd Al-Ash-hal, got up and said, *'O Allāh's Apostle! I will relieve you from him; if he is from the tribe of Al-Aws, then I will behead him, and if he is from our brothers from the Khazraj, then order us, and we will carry out your order.'*

On that, a man from Al-Khazraj got up. Umm Hassān, his cousin, was from his clan, and he was Saʿd ibn ʿUbādah, chief of Al-Khazraj. Before this incident, he was a pious man, but his love for his tribe goaded him into saying to Saʿd (ibn Muʿādh): *'By the eternity of Allāh, you have told a lie; you shall not and cannot kill him, and if he belonged to your people, you would not wish him to be killed.'*

On that, Usayd ibn Hudayr who was the cousin of Saʿd (ibn Muʿādh) got up and said to Saʿd ibn ʿUbādah, *'By Allāh! You are a liar! We will surely kill him, and you are behaving like a hypocrite, arguing on the behalf of Hypocrites.'*

On this, the two tribes of Al-Aws and Al-Khazraj were angered to such an extent that they wanted to fight each other, while Allāh's Messenger (صَلَّى ٱللَّهُ عَلَيْهِ وَسَلَّمَ) was standing on the minbar. Allāh's Messenger (صَلَّى ٱللَّهُ عَلَيْهِ وَسَلَّمَ) kept on calming them until they became silent, and he fell silent.

All that day I kept on weeping, with my tears never ceasing, and I could never sleep. In the morning, my parents were with me and I wept for two nights and a day with my tears never ceasing, and I could never sleep, until I thought that my liver would burst from weeping. So, while my parents were sitting with me and I was weeping, an Ansārī woman asked me to grant her admittance. I allowed her to come in, and when she came in, she sat down and started weeping with me. While we were in this state, Allāh's Messenger (صَلَّى ٱللَّهُ عَلَيْهِ وَسَلَّمَ) came, greeted us, and sat down.

He had never sat with me since that day of the slander. A month had elapsed and no Revelation had come to him about my case. Allāh's Messenger (صَلَّى ٱللَّهُ عَلَيْهِ وَسَلَّمَ) then recited Tashahhud and then said: *'To proceed, O 'Ā'ishah! Such and such has reached me concerning you; if you are innocent, then soon Allāh will reveal your innocence, and if you have committed a sin, then repent to Allāh and ask Him for forgiveness, for when a slave confesses his sins and asks Allāh for forgiveness, Allāh accepts his repentance.'*

When Allāh's Messenger (صَلَّى ٱللَّهُ عَلَيْهِ وَسَلَّمَ) finished his speech, my tears ceased flowing to the extent that I no longer felt a single tear flowing. I said to my father, *'Reply to Allāh's Messenger (صَلَّى ٱللَّهُ عَلَيْهِ وَسَلَّمَ) on my behalf concerning what he has said.'*

My father said: *'By Allāh, I do not know what to say to Allāh's Messenger (صَلَّى ٱللَّهُ عَلَيْهِ وَسَلَّمَ).'*

Then I said to my mother, *'Reply to Allāh's Messenger (صَلَّى ٱللَّهُ عَلَيْهِ وَسَلَّمَ) on my behalf concerning what he has said.'*

She said, *'By Allāh, I do not know what to say to Allāh's Messenger (صَلَّى ٱللَّهُ عَلَيْهِ وَسَلَّمَ).'*

In spite of the fact that I was a young girl and did not have a great amount of the Qur'ān, I said: *'By Allāh, no doubt I know that you heard this (slanderous) speech so that it has been planted in yourselves and you have taken it as a truth. Now if I tell you that I am innocent, you will not believe me; and if I confess to you about it, and Allāh knows that I am innocent, you will surely believe me.*

By Allāh, I find no similitude for me and you except that of the father of Yūsuf when he said, "(For me) patience is the most fitting against that which you assert; it is Allāh alone whose help can be sought."'

Then I turned to the other side and lay on my bed; and Allāh knew then that I was innocent and hoped that Allāh would reveal my innocence. But, by Allāh, I never thought that Allāh would reveal about my case revelation that would be recited (forever), as I considered myself too unworthy to be talked of by Allāh with something concerning me, but I hoped that Allāh's Messenger (ﷺ) might have a dream in which Allāh would prove my innocence.

But, by Allāh, before Allāh's Messenger (ﷺ) left his seat and before any of the household left, the Revelation came to Allāh's Messenger. So there overtook him the same hard condition which used to overtake him (when he used to receive Revelation). The sweat was dropping from his body like pearls, even though it was a wintry day, and that was because of the weighty statement which was being revealed to him. When that state of Allāh's Messenger (ﷺ) was over, he got up smiling, and the first word he said was, *'O 'Ā'ishah! Allāh has declared your innocence!'*

Then my mother said to me, *'Get up and go to him (i.e. Allāh's Messenger (ﷺ).'*

I replied, *'By Allāh, I will not go to him, and I praise none but Allāh.'*

So Allāh revealed the ten verses:

> إِنَّ الَّذِينَ جَاءُوا بِالْإِفْكِ عُصْبَةٌ مِّنكُمْ ۚ لَا تَحْسَبُوهُ شَرًّا لَّكُم ۖ بَلْ هُوَ خَيْرٌ لَّكُمْ ۚ
> لِكُلِّ امْرِئٍ مِّنْهُم مَّا اكْتَسَبَ مِنَ الْإِثْمِ ۚ وَالَّذِي تَوَلَّىٰ كِبْرَهُ مِنْهُمْ لَهُ عَذَابٌ عَظِيمٌ

۝ لَّوْلَا إِذْ سَمِعْتُمُوهُ ظَنَّ الْمُؤْمِنُونَ وَالْمُؤْمِنَاتُ بِأَنفُسِهِمْ خَيْرًا وَقَالُوا هَٰذَا إِفْكٌ
مُّبِينٌ ۝ لَّوْلَا جَاءُوا عَلَيْهِ بِأَرْبَعَةِ شُهَدَاءَ ۚ فَإِذْ لَمْ يَأْتُوا بِالشُّهَدَاءِ فَأُولَٰئِكَ عِندَ اللَّهِ
هُمُ الْكَاذِبُونَ ۝ وَلَوْلَا فَضْلُ اللَّهِ عَلَيْكُمْ وَرَحْمَتُهُ فِي الدُّنْيَا وَالْآخِرَةِ لَمَسَّكُمْ فِي
مَا أَفَضْتُمْ فِيهِ عَذَابٌ عَظِيمٌ ۝ إِذْ تَلَقَّوْنَهُ بِأَلْسِنَتِكُمْ وَتَقُولُونَ بِأَفْوَاهِكُم مَّا لَيْسَ
لَكُم بِهِ عِلْمٌ وَتَحْسَبُونَهُ هَيِّنًا وَهُوَ عِندَ اللَّهِ عَظِيمٌ ۝ وَلَوْلَا إِذْ سَمِعْتُمُوهُ قُلْتُم مَّا
يَكُونُ لَنَا أَن نَّتَكَلَّمَ بِهَٰذَا سُبْحَانَكَ هَٰذَا بُهْتَانٌ عَظِيمٌ ۝ يَعِظُكُمُ اللَّهُ أَن تَعُودُوا
لِمِثْلِهِ أَبَدًا إِن كُنتُم مُّؤْمِنِينَ ۝ وَيُبَيِّنُ اللَّهُ لَكُمُ الْآيَاتِ ۚ وَاللَّهُ عَلِيمٌ حَكِيمٌ ۝
إِنَّ الَّذِينَ يُحِبُّونَ أَن تَشِيعَ الْفَاحِشَةُ فِي الَّذِينَ آمَنُوا لَهُمْ عَذَابٌ أَلِيمٌ فِي الدُّنْيَا
وَالْآخِرَةِ ۚ وَاللَّهُ يَعْلَمُ وَأَنتُمْ لَا تَعْلَمُونَ ۝ وَلَوْلَا فَضْلُ اللَّهِ عَلَيْكُمْ وَرَحْمَتُهُ وَأَنَّ
اللَّهَ رَءُوفٌ رَّحِيمٌ ۝ يَا أَيُّهَا الَّذِينَ آمَنُوا لَا تَتَّبِعُوا خُطُوَاتِ الشَّيْطَانِ ۚ وَمَن يَتَّبِعْ
خُطُوَاتِ الشَّيْطَانِ فَإِنَّهُ يَأْمُرُ بِالْفَحْشَاءِ وَالْمُنكَرِ ۚ وَلَوْلَا فَضْلُ اللَّهِ عَلَيْكُمْ وَرَحْمَتُهُ مَا
زَكَىٰ مِنكُم مِّنْ أَحَدٍ أَبَدًا وَلَٰكِنَّ اللَّهَ يُزَكِّي مَن يَشَاءُ ۗ وَاللَّهُ سَمِيعٌ عَلِيمٌ ۝

MEANING: 'Verily! Those who brought forth the slander [against 'Āishah (رضي الله عنها), the wife of the Prophet (صلى الله عليه وسلم)] are a group among you. Consider it not a bad thing for you. Nay, it is good for you. Unto every man among them will be paid that which he had earned of the sin, and as for him among them who had the greater share therein, his will be a great torment.

Why then, did not the believers, men and women, when you heard it (the slander) think good of their own people and say: "*This (charge) is an obvious lie.*"

Why did they not produce four witnesses? Since they (the slanderers) have not produced witnesses, then with Allāh they are the liars.

Had it not been for the Grace of Allāh and His Mercy unto you in this world and in the Hereafter, a great torment would have touched you for that whereof you had spoken.

> When you were propagating it with your tongues, and uttering with your mouths that whereof you had no knowledge, you counted it a little thing, while with Allāh it was very great.
>
> And why did you not, when you heard it, say: *"It is not right for us to speak of this. Glory be to You (O Allāh) — this is a great lie."*
>
> Allāh forbids you from it and warns you not to repeat the like of it forever, if you are believers.
>
> Verily, those who like that (the crime of) illegal sexual intercourse should be propagated among those who believe, they will have a painful torment in this world and in the Hereafter. And Allāh knows and you know not.
>
> And had it not been for the Grace of Allāh and His Mercy on you, (Allāh would have hastened the punishment upon you). And Allāh is full of kindness, Most Merciful.
>
> O you who believe! Follow not the footsteps of Shaitān. And whosoever follows the footsteps of Shaitān, then, verily he commands with Al-Fahshā' (indecency), and Al-Munkar (evil and wicked deeds). And had it not been for the Grace of Allāh and His Mercy on you, not one of you would ever have been pure from sins. But Allāh purifies whom He wills, and Allāh is the All-Hearer, All-Knower.' — **Sūrah An-Nūr (24): 11-21**

So Allāh (the Most High) sent this down to declare my innocence. Abū Bakr As-Siddīq, who used to spend in charity upon Mistah ibn Uthāthah, because of his relationship to him and his poverty, said: *'By Allāh, I will never give anything to Mistah ibn Uthāthah after what he has said about 'Ā'ishah.'*

Then Allāh (the Most High) sent down:

> وَلَا يَأْتَلِ أُولُو الْفَضْلِ مِنكُمْ وَالسَّعَةِ أَن يُؤْتُوا أُولِي الْقُرْبَىٰ وَالْمَسَاكِينَ وَالْمُهَاجِرِينَ
> فِي سَبِيلِ اللَّهِ ۖ وَلْيَعْفُوا وَلْيَصْفَحُوا ۗ أَلَا تُحِبُّونَ أَن يَغْفِرَ اللَّهُ لَكُمْ ۗ وَاللَّهُ غَفُورٌ رَّحِيمٌ

> MEANING: 'And let not those among you who have virtue and wealth swear not to give (any sort of help) to their kinsmen who are in need, and those who have left their homes for Allāh's cause. Rather, let them pardon and overlook totally. Do you not love that Allāh should forgive you? And Allāh is Oft Forgiving, Most Merciful.' — **SŪRAH AN-NŪR (24): 22**

Abū Bakr As-Siddīq said, *'Yes, by Allāh, I would like that Allāh should forgive me,'* and he continued to give Mistah the money he used to give him before. He also added, *'By Allāh, I will never deprive him of it ever.'*"

'Ā'ishah further said: "Allāh's Messenger (صَلَّى ٱللَّهُ عَلَيْهِ وَسَلَّمَ) also asked Zaynab bint Jahsh (i.e. his wife) about my case. He said to Zaynab, *'What do you know and what did you see?'*

She replied, *'O Allāh's Messenger! I refrain from claiming falsely that I have heard or seen anything. By Allāh, I know nothing except good (about 'Ā'ishah).'*

Amongst the wives of the Prophet, Zaynab was my rival, but Allāh saved her from that evil because of her piety. Her sister Hamnah started struggling on her behalf, and she was destroyed along with those who were destroyed. The man who was blamed [alongside 'Ā'ishah] said, *'Subhān-Allāh! (I declare Allāh free of all imperfections!) By Him in Whose Hand is my soul, I have never removed the cover of any female.'* Later on he was martyred in Allāh's Cause."

Endnote 51 – Source: Page 177

(SH) The author (رَحِمَهُ ٱللَّهُ) said in *Tafsīrul-Qur'ānil-'Adhīm* (7/435): "And He declared that peace treaty to be a victory, because of the benefit it contained, and how it ended up. It is related from Ibn Mas'ūd (رَضِيَ ٱللَّهُ عَنْهُ), and from others, that he said: "You people consider the Victory to be the conquest of Makkah. However, we consider the Victory to be the Treaty of Al-Hudaybiyah."

I say: I have not found the narration of Ibn Mas'ūd (رَضِيَ ٱللَّهُ عَنْهُ), despite a lengthy search, and Allāh's aid is sought.

However, Al-Bukhārī reported in his *Sahīh* (no. 4150) from Al-Barā' ibn 'Āzib (رَضِيَ اللَّهُ عَنْهُمَا) that he said: "You people consider the Victory to be the Conquest of Makkah! And the Conquest of Makkah was a victory. However we consider the Victory to be *Bay'atur-Ridwān* on the day of Al-Hudaybiyah" — until the end of the hadīth.

And he reported likewise (nos. 4172 & 4834) from Anas ibn Mālik (رَضِيَ اللَّهُ عَنْهُ) that he said concerning:

> إِنَّا فَتَحْنَا لَكَ فَتْحًا مُّبِينًا
>
> MEANING: "We have certainly granted you a clear victory,"

— *"Al-Hudaybiyah."*

And At-Tabarī narrated in *Jāmi'ul-Bayān* (26/44): Muhammad ibn Al-Muthannā narrated to us: Yahyā ibn Hammād narrated to us Abū 'Awānah narrated to us: from Al-A'mash: from Abū Sufyān: from Jābir ibn 'Abdillāh (رَضِيَ اللَّهُ عَنْهُمَا) who said: "We had not used to consider the Victory of Makkah except as the Day of Al-Hudaybiyah."

I say: Its chain of narration is *'sahīh'* to the standard of Muslim. And he reported it through another chain from Al-A'mash with it, with the wording: "We had not used to consider the Victory except as being the Day of Al-Hudaybiyah." And its chain of narration is *'hasan'*.

Endnote 52 – Source: Page 180

(SH) A point of benefit: Our Shaikh, the great scholar, Al-Albānī (رَحِمَهُ اللَّهُ) said in *Tahrīm Ālātit-Tarb* (pp. 137-139):

....

It is obligatory upon you, O Muslim, to firmly believe that Allāh is Wise in everything which He has legislated for His servants with regard to commands, prohibitions, and allowances. Indeed, He has exceedingly wise purposes: they will be known by one who knows them and unknown to the one who is unaware of them. They can become apparent to some people, and yet remain hidden for others. Therefore, what is obligatory upon the true Muslim is that he hastens to obedience to Allāh, and does not hesitate until the wisdom in it becomes clear to him, for this negates Īmān, which is to submit totally and unreservedly to the All-Wise Legislator. Therefore, He (the Mighty and Majestic) said in the Noble Qur'ān:

> فَلَا وَرَبِّكَ لَا يُؤْمِنُونَ حَتَّىٰ يُحَكِّمُوكَ فِيمَا شَجَرَ بَيْنَهُمْ ثُمَّ لَا يَجِدُوا فِي أَنفُسِهِمْ حَرَجًا مِّمَّا قَضَيْتَ وَيُسَلِّمُوا تَسْلِيمًا
>
> MEANING: "So no, by your Lord, they will not be Believers until they make you, O Muhammad (ﷺ), the judge in all matters of dispute between them, then they do not find any resistance in themselves to your judgement, and they fully submit to it — outwardly and inwardly." — **Sūrah An-Nisā' (4):65**

So upon this basis our Salafus-Sālih (Pious Predecessors) lived; and therefore Allāh gave them strength and honour, and He opened up for them the lands and the hearts of the servants; and the latter part of this Ummah will not be rectified except by that which rectified its early part. And Abū Bakr As-Siddīq (رَضِيَ اللَّهُ عَنْهُ) had the distinction of precedence in that regard, and he was a righteous example for others. This is shown by his admirable stance in the incident of Al-Hudaybiyah. So Sahl ibn Hunayf (رَضِيَ اللَّهُ عَنْهُ) narrated, saying:

"O people! Doubt and suspect yourselves, for we were along with Allāh's Messenger (ﷺ) on the Day of Al-Hudaybiyah, and if we had seen any fighting we would have fought, and that was with regard to the peace treaty which came about between Allāh's Messenger (ﷺ) and the Mushrikīn. So 'Umar ibn Al-Khattāb came, and he went to Allāh's Messenger (ﷺ) and said: 'O Messenger of Allāh! Are we not upon the truth, whereas they are upon falsehood?!'

So he said: 'Yes indeed!'

He said: 'Is it not the case that those of us who are killed will be in the Paradise, whereas those of them who are killed will be in the Fire?!'

He said 'Yes indeed!'

He said: 'Are we to do that which demeans us for our Religion, and go back, when Allāh has not yet judged between us and them?!'

So he said:

> 'O Ibnul-Khattāb! I am Allāh's Messenger, and Allāh would never suffer me to be lost.'"

He said: "So 'Umar went off, and he could not control his rage, and he came to Abū Bakr, and said: 'O Abū Bakr! Are we not upon the truth whereas they are upon falsehood?!'

He said: 'Yes indeed!'

He said: 'Is it not the case that those of us who are killed will be in Paradise whereas those of them who are killed will be in the Fire?!'

He said; 'Yes indeed!'

So he said: 'Then why are we doing that which demeans us for our Religion, and we go back when Allāh has not yet judged between us and them?'

So he said: 'O Ibnul-Khattāb! He is Allāh's Messenger, and Allāh would never suffer him to be lost.'"

He said: "So the Qur'ān came down to Allāh's Messenger (صَلَّى ٱللَّهُ عَلَيْهِ وَسَلَّمَ) declaring it a victory. So he sent for 'Umar and read it to him. So he said: 'O Messenger of Allāh! Is it a victory?'

He said: '*Yes.*' So he became satisfied and returned."

It is reported by Al-Bukhārī (no. 3182: *'Fat-h'*), and Muslim (5/175-176) and the wording is his and Ahmad (3/486); and in a narration of the two of them, from him, there occurs: *"O people! Doubt and suspect your opinion..."* — and it is reported by Sa'īd ibn Mansūr (3/2/374), and Ibn Abī Shaybah (15/299).

Al-Hāfidh said: "It is as if he was saying: Accuse your opinion when it contradicts the Sunnah, just as happened with us when Allāh's Messenger (صَلَّى ٱللَّهُ عَلَيْهِ وَسَلَّمَ) ordered us to leave the state of ihrām. However, we wanted to continue in a state of ihrām, and we wanted to fight, in order to complete our rites and overcome our enemy. However, we were unaware of what was apparent to the Prophet (صَلَّى ٱللَّٰهُ عَلَيْهِ وَسَلَّمَ) from that which was going to occur as a consequence of it."

And the finest example which I have come across from the life-histories of his (صَلَّى ٱللَّٰهُ عَلَيْهِ وَسَلَّمَ) Companions, which shows how they gave precedence to obedience to him, even when that went against their desires and their personal benefit, is the saying of Zuhayr ibn Rāfiʿ who said:

> "Allāh's Messenger (صَلَّى ٱللَّٰهُ عَلَيْهِ وَسَلَّمَ) forbade us from something which used to benefit us; however, obedience to Allāh and His Messenger is more beneficial for us. He forbade us from renting out land in return for a share of the produce: for a third, or a quarter, or a specified amount of foodstuff."

It is reported by Muslim (no. 1548) and others, and it is referenced in *Al-Irwāʾ* (5/299).

So this obedience reminds me of that obedience, which amazed the Believers from the Jinn when they came to the Prophet (صَلَّى ٱللَّٰهُ عَلَيْهِ وَسَلَّمَ) to listen to his recitation in the Fajr Prayer, as is indicated at the beginning of Sūratul-Jinn:

> قُلْ أُوحِيَ إِلَيَّ أَنَّهُ اسْتَمَعَ نَفَرٌ مِّنَ الْجِنِّ فَقَالُوا إِنَّا سَمِعْنَا قُرْآنًا عَجَبًا ۝ يَهْدِي إِلَى الرُّشْدِ فَآمَنَّا بِهِ ۖ وَلَن نُّشْرِكَ بِرَبِّنَا أَحَدًا
>
> MEANING: "Say: It has been revealed to me that a group of the Jinn listened to this Qurʾān and said to their people: 'We have heard an amazing recitation. It guides to the true path, so we have believed in it, and we shall never associate anything along with our Lord.'" — **Sūrah Al-Jinn (72):1-2**

So they saw his (صَلَّى ٱللَّٰهُ عَلَيْهِ وَسَلَّمَ) Companions praying and following his Prayer: performing rukūʿ following his rukūʿ, and performing sujūd following his sujūd. Ibn ʿAbbās (رَضِيَ ٱللَّٰهُ عَنْهُمَا) said: "They were amazed at how carefully we obeyed him."

It is reported by Ahmad (1/270) and others with a '*sahīh*' chain of narration.

So what is intended is that this obedience must be actualised in every Muslim, outwardly and inwardly: whether it is something agreeing to his desire, or opposing it."

Endnote 53 – Source: Page 181

DB Imām Ibnul-Qayyim said in *Zādul-Ma'ād* (3/317): "He left Sibā' ibn 'Urfutah in charge of Al-Madīnah, and Abū Hurairah came to Al-Madīnah at that time and found Sibā' ibn 'Urfutah leading the Dawn prayer. So he heard him reciting *'Kāf Hā Yā 'Ayn Sād'* (i.e. Sūrah Maryam) in the first rak'ah, and in the second *'Waylun lil-Mutaffifīn'* (i.e. Sūratul-Mutaffifīn).

So he said to himself: *'Woe to so and so! He has two scales: When he takes he takes the fullest measure, and when he gives a measure he gives short measure.'*

So when he completed his Prayer he went to Sibā' and he gave him provisions so that he was able to go out to join Allāh's Messenger (صَلَّى ٱللَّهُ عَلَيْهِ وَسَلَّمَ). So he (صَلَّى ٱللَّهُ عَلَيْهِ وَسَلَّمَ) spoke to the Muslims and they gave him and his Companions a share of their spoils." [Reported by Imām Ahmad (2/345-346) and declared *'sahīh'* by Shaikh Ahmad Shākir in his checking of the *Musnad* (no. 8533)].

Al-Hāfidh Ibn Hajr said in *Fat-hul-Bārī* (7/465): "Ibn Hishām mentioned that he left Numaylah ibn 'Abdillāh Al-Laythī in charge of Al-Madīnah, whereas Ahmad and Al-Hākim have, in a hadīth of Abū Hurairah, that it was Sibā' ibn 'Urfutah, and that is more correct."

Endnote 54 – Source: Page 181

Al-Bukhārī reported (no.4198) from Anas bin Mālik (رَضِيَ ٱللَّهُ عَنْهُ) who said: "We attacked Khaybar in the early morning, and its people came out with their spades. So when they saw the Prophet (صَلَّى ٱللَّهُ عَلَيْهِ وَسَلَّمَ) they said: ***'Muhammad! By Allāh! Muhammad! Muhammad and the army!'***

So the Prophet (صَلَّى ٱللَّهُ عَلَيْهِ وَسَلَّمَ) said:

> 'Allāh is greater! Khaybar is destroyed! When we enter the land of an enemy then evil will be the morning for those who have been warned.'

So we obtained the meat of donkeys, but the caller of the Prophet (ﷺ) called out: 'Allāh and His Messenger forbid you from the meat of donkeys, for it is impure.'"

And Al-Bukhārī reported (no. 4210) from Abū Hāzim who said: "Sahl ibn Sa'd (رضي الله عنه) informed me that Allāh's Messenger (ﷺ) said on the day of Khaybar: *'I shall give this flag tomorrow to a man at whose hands Allāh will grant victory. He loves Allāh and His Messenger, and Allāh and His Messenger love him.'*

So in the morning the people went to Allāh's Messenger (ﷺ), all of them hoping to be given it. So he said: *'Where is 'Alī ibn Abī Tālib?'* So it was said: *'He is suffering from an eye complaint, O Messenger of Allāh.'* He said: *'Then send for him.'*

So he was brought, and Allāh's Messenger (ﷺ) spat into his eyes, and supplicated for him; and he was cured so that it was as if he had never suffered any ailment; and he gave him the flag. So 'Alī said: *'Shall I fight them until they become like us?'*

So he said:

> 'Proceed steadily until you enter their territory, then call them to Islām and inform them of Allāh's rights upon them. For by Allāh, that Allāh should guide a single man through you will be better for you than your having fine red camels.'"

Endnote 55 – Source: Page 182

(SH) Reported by Abū Dāwūd in his *Sunan* (no. 4511 & 4512), and from him by Al-Bayhaqī in *Dalā'ilun-Nubuwwah* (4/262), and Ad-Dārimī in his *Musnad* (1/471/71) by way of Khālid Al-Hadhdhā' and Ja'far ibn 'Awn: both of them from Muhammad ibn 'Amr: from Abū Salamah ibn 'Abdir-Rahmān with it, in *'mursal'* form. And this is a *'mursal'* report with a *'hasan'* chain of narration.

And Al-Hākim reports it in *Al-Mustadrak* (3/219) in connected form with a *'sahīh'* chain of narration, from Hammād ibn Salamah: from Muhammad ibn 'Amr: from Abū Salamah: from Abū Hurairah with it.

Al-Qādī ʿIyād said, as occurs in *Sharh Muslim* of An-Nawawī (14/179): "The way in which these narrations and saying are harmonised is that he did not kill her initially when he found out about the poison, and it was said to him: *'Kill her!'* So he said: *'No.'* But then, when Bishr ibn Al-Barāʾ died from that, he handed her over to his people, and they killed her in retribution. So their saying: *'He did not kill her'* — is correct, meaning at that time; and their saying: *'He killed her'* is (also) correct, meaning afterwards; and Allāh knows best."

And Al-Bayhaqī said in *Ad-Dalāʾil* (4/262): "It is possible that he did not kill her initially, and then, when Bishr ibn Al-Barāʾ died, he commanded that she be killed."

Al-Hāfidh said in *Al-Fat-h* (7/47): "This was the answer given by As-Suhaylī, and he added that he left her because he had not used to take revenge for himself, but then he killed her in retaliatory punishment for Bishr. I say: It is possible that he left her because she had accepted Islām, and postponed killing her until Bishr died; since with his death the obligation of retaliatory punishment was brought about by the occurrence of its condition."

Endnote 56 – Source: Page 183

(DB) Ibn Is-hāq said (*Sīrah Ibn Hishām*: 3/357-358): "These are the names of the Muslims who were martyred at Khaybar." He then proceeds to name them.

Those who died from the Quraysh, then from Banū Umayyah ibn ʿAbd Shams, and from their confederates:

- Rabīʿah ibn Aktham ibn Sakhbarah ibn ʿAmr ibn Bukayr ibn ʿĀmir ibn Ghanm ibn Dūdān ibn Asad;
- Thaqif ibn ʿAmr;
- Rifāʿah ibn Masrūh.

From those who died from Banū Asad ibn ʿAbdil-ʿUzzā was:

- ʿAbdullāh ibn Al-Hubayb (or it is said: Ibn Al-Habīb — as Ibn Hishām said) ibn Uhayb ibn Suhaym ibn Ghiyarah, who was from Banū Saʿd ibn Layth, the confederate of Banū Asad, and the son of their sister.

And from the Ansār, then from Banū Salimah died two men:

- Bishr ibn Al-Barāʾ ibn Maʿrūr (who died from the sheep through which Allāh's Messenger (ﷺ) was poisoned);
- Fudayl ibn An-Nuʿmān.

And from Banū Zurayq:

- Masʿūd ibn Saʿd ibn Qays ibn Khaladah ibn ʿĀmir ibn Zurayq.

And from the Aws, then from Banū ʿAbdil-Ash-hal:

- Mahmūd ibn Maslamah ibn Khālid ibn ʿAdiyy ibn Majdaʿah ibn Hārithah ibn Al-Hārith, a confederate of theirs from Banū Hārithah.

And from Banū ʿAmr ibn ʿAwf:

- Abū Dayyāh ibn Thābit ibn An-Nuʿmān ibn Umayyah ibn Umruʾul-Qays ibn Thaʿlabah ibn ʿAmr ibn ʿAwf;
- Al-Hārith ibn Hātib;
- ʿUrwah ibn Murrah ibn Surāqah;
- Aws ibnul-Qāʾid;
- Unayf ibn Habīb;
- Thābit ibn Athlah;
- Talhah [i.e. ibn Yahyā ibn Malīl ibn Damurah].

And from Banū Ghifār:

- ʿUmārah ibn ʿUqbah, who was struck by an arrow.

And from Aslam:

- ʿĀmir ibn Al-Akwaʿ;

- Al-Aswad — The Shepherd, and his name was Aslam. Ibn Hishām said: "Al-Aswad, The Shepherd, was from the people of Khaybar."

And from those who were martyred at Khaybar, as mentioned by Ibn Shihāb Az-Zuhrī, from Banū Zuhrah:

- Mas'ūd ibn Rabī'ah, a confederate of theirs from Al-Qārah.

And from the Ansār, from Banū 'Amr ibn 'Awf:

- Aws ibn Qatādah.

Ibn Hazm in *Jawāmi' As-Sīrah* (p. 171) adds to this list the name of Mubashshir ibn 'Abdil-Mundhir ibn Zanbar ibn Zayd ibn Umayyah ibn Zayd ibn Mālik ibn 'Awf ibn 'Amr ibn 'Awf.

Endnote 57 – Source: Page 184

(DB) Ibn Hazm said in *Jawāmi' As-Sīrah* (p.173): "When Allāh's Messenger (صَلَّى ٱللَّهُ عَلَيْهِ وَسَلَّمَ) returned from Khaybar he remained in residence for the two months of Rabī', and the two months of Jumādā, and Rajab, and Sha'bān, and Ramadān, and Shawwāl. So in this period he sent out military raiding parties..."

Ibnul Qayyim in *Zādul-Ma'ād* (3/359-370) mentions from these raiding parties:

- The raiding party of Abū Bakr As-Siddīq (رَضِيَ ٱللَّهُ عَنْهُ) to Najd, against Banū Fazārah.
- The raiding party of 'Umar ibn Al-Khattāb (رَضِيَ ٱللَّهُ عَنْهُ) along with thirty riders against Hawāzin.
- The raiding party of 'Abdullāh ibn Rawāhah (رَضِيَ ٱللَّهُ عَنْهُ) with thirty riders to repel the tribe of Ghatafān from attacking Khaybar.
- The raiding party of Bashīr ibn Sa'd Al-Ansārī (رَضِيَ ٱللَّهُ عَنْهُ) with thirty riders towards Banū Murrah at Fadak.
- The raiding party of Ghālib ibn 'Abdillāh Al-Kalbī (رَضِيَ ٱللَّهُ عَنْهُ) to attack Banul-Mulawwah at Al-Kadīd.

- The sending of Bashīr ibn Sa'd (رَضِيَ اللَّهُ عَنْهُ) with three hundred men towards Khaybar.
- The sending of the raiding party of Abū Hadrad Al-Aslamī to repel an enemy who reached Al-Ghābah.
- A raiding party containing Abū Qatādah and Muhallim ibn Jaththāmah (رَضِيَ اللَّهُ عَنْهُمَا) towards Idam.
- The raiding party of 'Abdullāh ibn Hudhāfah As-Sahmī (رَضِيَ اللَّهُ عَنْهُ).

Endnote 58 – Source: Page 185

(SH) Reported by Muslim in his *Sahīh* (no. 1411) as a hadīth of Yazīd ibn Al-Asamm who said: *"Maymūnah bint Al-Hārith narrated to me: that Allāh's Messenger (صَلَّى اللَّهُ عَلَيْهِ وَسَلَّمَ) married her having left the state of ihrām."* He said: *"And she was my maternal aunt and the maternal aunt of Ibn 'Abbās."*

Abū Dāwūd (no. 1843) added: "At Sarif" — and its chain of narration is '*sahīh*'.

As for what is established from Ibn 'Abbās contrary to this, then it is counted as a misunderstanding or a mistake. Refer to *Al-Fat-h* (4/52), *Tanqīhut-Tahqīq* (2/437-440), *Zādul-Ma'ād* (4/372-374), and *Irwā'ul-Ghalīl* (4/226-228).

(BJ)(SZ) So Sa'īd ibn Al-Musayyib, Ahmad ibn Hanbal and others said: *"Ibn 'Abbās misunderstood,"* and refer to *Bulūghul-Marām* (no. 993).

Endnote 59 – Source: Page 185

(DB) Al-Bukhārī reports in his *Sahīh* (nos. 4251 and 4256) from Al-Barā' (رَضِيَ اللَّهُ عَنْهُ) who said: "The Prophet (صَلَّى اللَّهُ عَلَيْهِ وَسَلَّمَ) performed 'Umrah in Dhul-Qa'dah, but the Quraysh refused to let him enter Makkah until he concluded a treaty with them which allowed him to stay there for three days. When the document was being written they wrote: *'This is the agreement concluded by Muhammad, Allāh's Messenger.'*

So they [i.e. the Disbelievers] said: *'We do not assent to this for you. If we knew you were the Messenger of Allāh we would not prevent you from anything. Rather, you are Muhammad the son of 'Abdullāh.'*

So he said : *'I am the Messenger of Allāh, and I am Muhammad the son of 'Abdullāh.'* Then he said to 'Alī ibn Abī Tālib (رَضِيَ ٱللَّهُ عَنْهُ): *'Erase "Allāh's Messenger."'*

So 'Alī said: *'No, by Allāh, I shall never erase you.'* So Allāh's Messenger (صَلَّى ٱللَّهُ عَلَيْهِ وَسَلَّمَ) took the document, and he could not write, so he had it written:

> 'This is the agreement concluded by Muhammad the son of 'Abdullāh. He may not bring weapons into Makkah except for swords in their sheaths, and he may not take out with him anyone from its people who want to follow him, and he may not prevent anyone from his Companions from settling in it if he so wishes.'

So when he entered and the time period expired, they came to 'Alī and said: *'Say to your companion: Get out and depart from us, for the time period has finished.'*

So the Prophet (صَلَّى ٱللَّهُ عَلَيْهِ وَسَلَّمَ) departed, and the daughter of Hamzah followed him and called out: *'O uncle! O uncle!'* So 'Alī took her by the hand and said to Fātimah (رَضِيَ ٱللَّهُ عَنْهَا): *'Take the daughter of your paternal uncle.'* So she made her ride with her..." — until the end of the hadīth.

Endnote 60 – Source: Page 185

(DB) Imām Ibnul-Qayyim said in *Zādul-Ma'ād* (3/381): "It is before Al-Balqā' (in present day Jordan), in the land of Shām, and its reason was that Allāh's Messenger (صَلَّى ٱللَّهُ عَلَيْهِ وَسَلَّمَ) had sent Al-Hārith ibn 'Umayr Al-Azdī, one of Banū Lihb, with his letter to Shām to the king of the Byzantines or of Busrā. So Shurahbīl ibn 'Amr Al-Ghassānī halted him, tied him up, and then led him along and beheaded him. So he was the only messenger sent by Allāh's Messenger (صَلَّى ٱللَّهُ عَلَيْهِ وَسَلَّمَ) to be killed, and he was greatly affected by that when he heard the news; so he sent out the armies, and placed Zayd ibn Hārithah in command of them."

Dr. Akram Diyā' Al-'Umarī said in *As-Sīratun-Nabawiyyatis-Sahīhah* (2/467): "Al-Wāqidī is alone in mentioning the reason for this battle (...) and Al-Wāqidī is weak and cannot be depended upon, particularly when he alone mentions a report."

Endnote 61 – Source: Page 187

[SH] Reported by Ibn Is-hāq in *As-Sīrah* (4/1047: Ibn Hishām), and from him by Abū Dāwūd (no. 2573), and Al-Bayhaqī in *Dalā'ilun-Nubuwwah* (4/363), saying: Yahyā ibn 'Abbād ibn 'Abdillāh ibn Az-Zubayr narrated to me: from his father 'Abbād who said: "My father (through breast-feeding) narrated to me — and he was someone from Banū Murrah ibn 'Awf, and he was present at that battle, the Battle of Mu'tah — saying..." [and the rest of the narration follows].

I say: And this is a *'hasan'* chain of narration, and it was declared *'hasan'* by Al-Hāfidh in *Al-Fat-h* (7/511) and by our Shaikh Al-Albānī (رَحِمَهُ ٱللَّهُ) in *Sahīh Sunan Abī Dāwūd* (no. 2243).

Endnote 62 – Source: Page 187

[SH] Reported by Ibn Hishām in *As-Sīrah* (4/1048) who said: "Someone I trust from the people of knowledge narrated it to me."

I say: This chain of narration is very weak.

Then there occurs in *Sahīh Al-Bukhārī* (no. 4261) from Ibn 'Umar (رَضِيَ ٱللَّهُ عَنْهُ) who said: "So we looked for Ja'far ibn Abī Tālib and we found him amongst those killed, and we found ninety and odd wounds upon his body, from thrusts (of spears) and from arrows."

And in one narration (no. 4660): "None of them were upon his back."

Endnote 63 – Source: Page 187

[DB] Ibn Is-hāq's narration (4/21-22: Ibn Hishām) states: "Then Thābit ibn Aqram, the brother of Banul-'Ajlān, took the flag and said: *'O Muslims! Agree upon a man from amongst you as your leader.'*

So they said: *'You!'*

So he said: *'I will not do so.'*

So the people agreed upon Khālid ibn Al-Walīd. So when he took the flag he repelled the enemy, and he pulled away from them. Then he drew back and they drew back from him, until he departed from the people."

Ibnul-Qayyim said in *Zādul-Maʿād* (3/383): "Ibn Saʿd mentions that the Muslims suffered defeat, however what occurs in *Sahīhul-Bukhārī* is that the defeat was suffered by the Byzantines. So what is correct is that which Ibn Is-hāq mentioned, that each group withdrew from the other."

Endnote 64 – Source: Page 188

DB Ibn Hishām said (4/30): "Here are the names of those who were martyred on the day of Muʾtah:

From the Quraysh, then from Banū Hāshim:

- Jaʿfar ibn Abī Tālib (رَضِيَٱللَّهُعَنْهُ);
- Zayd ibn Hārithah (رَضِيَٱللَّهُعَنْهُ).

And from Banū ʿAdiyy ibn Kaʿb:

- Masʿūd ibn Al-Aswad ibn Hārithah ibn Nadlah.

And from Banū Mālik ibn Hisl:

- Wahb ibn Saʿd ibn Abī Sarh.

And from the Ansār, then from Banul-Hārith ibn Al-Khazraj:

- ʿAbdullāh ibn Rawāhah;
- ʿAbbād ibn Qays.

And from Banū Ghanm ibn Mālik ibn An-Najjār:

- Al-Hārith ibn An-Nuʿmān ibn Asāf ibn Nadlah ibn ʿAbd ibn ʿAwf ibn Ghanam.

And from Banū Māzin ibn An-Najjār:

- Surāqah ibn ʿAmr ibn ʿAtiyyah ibn Khansā."

494 Ibn Hishām said: "And from those who were martyred on the Day of Mu'tah in what Ibn Shihāb mentioned are:

From Banū Māzin ibn An-Najjār:

- Abū Kulayb;
- Jābir;

[and these are] the two sons of ʿAmr ibn Zayd ibn ʿAwf ibn Mabdhūl, and they shared the same father and mother [both].

And from Banū Mālik ibn Afsā:

- ʿAmr;
- ʿĀmir;

[and these are] the two sons of Saʿd ibn Al-Hārith ibn ʿAbbād ibn Saʿd ibn ʿĀmir ibn Thaʿlabah ibn Mālik ibn Afsā."

Ibn Hishām said: "And it is said: *'Abū Kulāb and Jābir, the two sons of ʿAmr.'*"

Endnote 65 – Source: Page 190

(SH) Ibn Is-hāq mentioned it in *As-Sīrah* (4/1058-1059), and the author (رَحِمَهُ ٱللَّهُ) quoted it in *Al-Bidāyah wan-Nihāyah* (6/510-511) without a chain of narration. It is witnessed to, in general, by what Ibn Is-hāq reported — as occurs in *Al-Bidāyah wan-Nihāyah* (6/508-509) — and from him by At-Tabarī in *Tārīkhul-Umam wal-Mulūk* (2/3/111), and Al-Bayhaqī in *Dalā'ilun-Nubuwwah* (5/5-7): Az-Zuhrī narrated to me: from ʿUrwah ibn Az-Zubayr: from Al-Miswar ibn Makhramah and Marwān ibn Al-Hakam, who both said: "There occurred in the Treaty of Al-Hudaybiyah that whoever wanted to enter into a treaty and covenant with Muhammad could do so, and whoever wanted to enter into a treaty and a covenant with Quraysh could do so" — until the end of the hadīth.

And it contains the wording: "That Khuzāʿah entered into a treaty and a covenant with the Prophet (صَلَّىٱللَّهُ عَلَيْهِ وَسَلَّمَ), and Banū Bakr entered into a treaty and covenant with the Quraysh. So they remained upon that state of peace for about seventeen or eighteen months. Then Banū Bakr attacked Khuzā'ah by night, at a watering place of theirs called Al-Watīr, close to Makkah. So the Quraysh said: *'Muhammad will not know about us, and it is night and no one will see us.'* So they aided them against them with horses and weapons, because of their hatred for Allāh's Messenger (صَلَّى ٱللَّهُ عَلَيْهِ وَسَلَّمَ)."

I say: This chain of narration is *'hasan';* and Ibn Is-hāq clearly states that he heard it directly, and he is a proof with regard to military campaigns and expeditions.

Endnote 66 – Source: Page 190

(SH) Ibn Is-hāq reported it in is *As-Sīrah,* and At-Tabarī reported it from him in *Tārīkhul-Umam wal-Mulūk* (2/3/111-112) and Al-Bayhaqī in *Dalā'ilun-Nubuwwah* (5/5-7), with the chain of narration that has preceded a little while ago, from Al-Miswar ibn Makhramah and Marwān ibn Al-Hakam, within a long hadīth containing the wording: "When the incident occurred at Al-Watīr between Khuzā'ah and Banū Bakr, 'Amr ibn Sālim rode until he came to Allāh's Messenger (صَلَّى ٱللَّهُ عَلَيْهِ وَسَلَّمَ) to inform him of the news (...) So Allāh's Messenger (صَلَّى ٱللَّهُ عَلَيْهِ وَسَلَّمَ) said: *"You shall be aided, O 'Amr ibn Sālim"* — the hadīth.

As for the departure of Budayl ibn Warqā', then Ibn Is-hāq mentioned it in *As-Sīrah* (4/1064), and from him the author in *Al-Bidāyah wan Nihāyah* (6/513), without a chain of narration.

Endnote 67 – Source: Page 192

(SH) Reported by Ahmad (1/266 and 315) and by (...), and others, by way of Ibn Is-hāq, and it occurs in his *Sīrah* (4/1067): *"Ibn Shihāb Az-Zuhrī narrated to me: from 'Ubaydullāh ibn 'Abdillāh ibn 'Utbah: from Ibn 'Abbās with it,"* and this chain of narration is *'hasan',* and Ibn Is-hāq is a proof in *sīrah,* and he states that he heard it directly.

Endnote 68 – Source: Page 193

(SH) Reported by Ibn Is-hāq in *As-Sīrah* (4/1067-1068: Ibn Hishām), and from him by At-Tabarī in *Tārīkhul-Umam wal-Mulūk* (2/3/114-115), and At-Tabarānī in *Al-Muʿjamul-Kabīr* (8/9-10 no. 7264), and Al-Hākim in *Al-Mustadrak* (3/43), and from him by Al-Bayhaqī in *Dalāʾilun-Nubuwwah* (5/27-28): "Ibn Shihāb Az-Zuhrī narrated to me: from ʿUbaydullāh ibn ʿAbdillāh ibn ʿUtbah ibn Masʿūd: from ʿAbdullāh ibn ʿAbbās, as a longer narration."

I say: this is a *'hasan'* chain of narration, as preceded a short while ago.

(DB) Al-Hākim's narration contains the wording: "From Ibn ʿAbbās (رَضِيَ ٱللَّهُ عَنْهُمَا) who said:

> 'Allāh's Messenger (صَلَّى ٱللَّهُ عَلَيْهِ وَسَلَّمَ) proceeded with his Companions in the year of the Conquest until he stopped at Marraz-Zahrān.
>
> Abū Sufyān ibn Al-Hārith and ʿAbdullāh ibn Abī Umayyah ibn Al-Mughīrah had met Allāh's Messenger (صَلَّى ٱللَّهُ عَلَيْهِ وَسَلَّمَ) at Thaniyyatul-ʿIqāb, between Makkah and Al-Madīnah, so they sought to gain entry upon him, and Umm Salamah spoke to him, saying: "O Messenger of Allāh! It is the son of your paternal uncle, and the son of your paternal aunt and your brother in-law."
>
> So he said: "I have no need of them. As for the son of my paternal uncle, then he attacked my honour; and as for the son of my paternal aunt and my brother in law, then he is the one who said what he said about me in Makkah."
>
> So when they heard of this, and Abū Sufyān ibn Al-Hārith had a son of his with him, he said: *"By Allāh! Allāh's Messenger (صَلَّى ٱللَّهُ عَلَيْهِ وَسَلَّمَ) will grant us permission to enter or else I will take hold of the hand of this son of mine, and then we will wander upon the earth until we die of hunger or thirst."* So when that reached Allāh's Messenger (صَلَّى ٱللَّهُ عَلَيْهِ وَسَلَّمَ) he felt pity for them, and they were allowed to enter upon him. So Abū Sufyān composed a poem regarding his Islām and apologising for his previous behaviour."

The full narration is brought and declared *'hasan'* by Shaikh Al-Albānī in *As-Sahīhah.* (no. 3341)

Endnote 69 – Source: Page 195

(SH) It is reported by At-Tabarī in *Tārīkh Al-Umam wal-Mulūk* (2/115-117) with a weak chain of narration, and it has a witness from a mursal narration of ʿUrwah, in the *Sahīh* of Al-Bukhārī (no. 4280), so therefore it is *'sahīh'*; and it was declared *'sahīh'* because of its witness by our Shaikh, the great scholar, Al-Albānī (رَحِمَهُ ٱللَّهُ), in *Takhrīj Fiqhis-Sīrah* (p. 411).

(DB) Shaikh Al-Albānī (رَحِمَهُ ٱللَّهُ) said in *As-Sahīhah* (7/2/1023): "The story of the Conquest of Makkah, and the Islām of Abū Sufyān, in the most complete narration that is authentic: [3341]— *'Allāh's Messenger (صَلَّى ٱللَّهُ عَلَيْهِ وَسَلَّمَ) went forth, and he left Abū Ruhm Kulthūm ibn Husayn Al-Ghifārī in charge of Al-Madīnah'* — and it is the long narration of Ibn ʿAbbās (رَضِيَ ٱللَّهُ عَنْهُمَا), a mention of which has preceded."

Endnote 70 – Source: Page 196

(SH) Reported by Abū Yaʿlā in his *Musnad* (6/120/no.3393), and from him by Ibn ʿAdiyy in *Al-Kāmil* (4/1571), and Al-Hākim in *Al-Mustadrak* (3/47 and 4/317) and (...) from ʿAbdullāh ibn Bakr Al-Muqaddamī: from Jaʿfar ibn Sulaymān: from Thābit: from Anas with it.

Al-Hākim said: "It is *'sahīh'* to the standard of Muslim, and neither of the two reported it."

I say: He made a mistake, since Muslim did not report anything at all from Al-Muqaddamī, and he is weak. He was declared weak by Abū Yaʿlā, Ibn ʿAdiyy, Adh-Dhahabī, and others; and perhaps, and Allāh knows best, he confused him with his brother Muhammad ibn Abī Bakr Al-Muqaddamī who was reliable.

Al-Haythamī said in *Majmaʿuz-Zawāʾid* (6/169): "Abū Yaʿlā reported it, and it contains ʿAbdillāh ibn Abī Bakr Al-Muqaddamī, and he is weak."

It was also reported by Ibn Is-hāq in *As-Sīrah* — as occurs in *Al-Bidāyah wan-Nihāyah* (6/547) — and from him by Al-Bayhaqī in *Dalā'ilun-Nubuwwah* (5/68): *"Abdullāh ibn Abī Bakr narrated to me that Allāh's Messenger* (ﷺ)"—and he mentioned it. This is a weak chain of narration as it is *'mursal'*.

So overall, the hadīth with these two chains combined is *'hasan lighairihi'*, if Allāh wills.

Endnote 71 – Source: Page 197

(SH) It is reported by Abū Dāwūd (2/28/no.1290), Ibn Mājah (1/419/no. 1323), Ibn Khuzaymah in his *Sahīh* (2/234/no.1234), and Al-Bayhaqī in *As-Sunanul-Kubrā* (3/48), by way of 'Abdullāh ibn Wahb: from 'Iyād ibn 'Abdillāh: from Makhramah ibn Sulaymān: from Kurayb: from Umm Hāni', with it (...). Its chain of narration is weak, since 'Iyād was weak (...). And as for its text, then sometimes he mentioned the salutation, and sometimes he did not mention it (...). Add to this that more than eight narrators reported it from her, and none of them mentioned the salutation. So therefore, the mention of the salutation in the hadīth is *'munkar'* and not established.

Endnote 72 – Source: Page 198

(SH) Reported by Abū Dāwūd in *Al-Marāsīl* (83/23: *Ar-Risālah Edition* 129/23: *As-Sumay'ī Edition*), and Ibn Abī Shaybah in *Al-Musannaf* (1/224 and 14/497/no.18772), and Al-Bayhaqī in *Dalā'ilun-Nubuwwah* (5/78 and 79), and Ibn 'Asākir in *Tārīkh Dimashq* (10/358), by way of Abū Mu'āwiyah, and Abū Khālid Al-Ahmar, and Yūnus ibn Bukayr, and Ja'far ibn 'Awn; all of them from Hishām ibn 'Urwah: from his father, as a *'mursal'* narration. I say: This *'mursal'* narration has a *sahīh* chain (...).

And it has a witness from a *'mursal'* report of Ibn Abī Mulaykah with it, reported by Musaddad ibn Musarhad in his *Musnad* as occurs in *Al-Matālibul-'Āliyah* (...) with chains from Ayyūb As-Sakhtiyānī: from Ibn

Abī Mulaykah with it. I say: This is a *'mursal'* report with a *'sahīh'* chain (...).

And a fourth witness, reported by Al-Fākihī in *Akhbār Makkah*, as occurs in *Shifā'ul-Gharām bi Akhbāril-Baladil-Harām* (1/255): "Muhammad ibn Abī Al-Marwazī narrated to me: 'Ubaydullāh ibn Mūsā narrated to us: Mūsā ibn 'Ubaydah narrated to us: from 'Abdullāh ibn Dīnār: from Ibn 'Umar, with it." I say: this chain of narration is *'hasan'* as a witness, Mūsā ibn 'Ubaydah is weak (...).

So overall, the hadīth with all of that combined is at the very least *'hasan lighairihi'*, and Allāh knows best.

Endnote 73 – Source: Page 198

(SH) It is reported by 'Abdur-Razzāq in *Al-Musannaf* (5/85/no. 9076) from one of his companions: from Ibn Juraij: that Ibn Abī Mulaykah narrated it to me. I say: This chain of narration is weak because it is *'mursal'* and because of the fact that the shaikh of 'Abdur-Razzāq is unknown.

And it has a witness from a *'mursal'* narration of Az-Zuhrī, reported by 'Abdur-Razzāq in his *Musannaf* (5/83-84/no. 9073), and from him by At-Tabarānī, as occurs in *Al-Fat-h* (8/18): from Ma'mar: from Az-Zuhrī with it. I say: This is a *'mursal'* report with a *'sahīh'* chain.

And it is established in more than one hadīth that the keys were with 'Uthmān ibn Talhah, and that they (i.e. Banū 'Abdid-Dār) had the custodianship (...), so Al-Bukhārī reported (nos. 2988 and 4289) and Muslim (no. 1329/389) as a hadīth of Ibn 'Umar (رَضِيَ ٱللَّهُ عَنْهُمَا): "That Allāh's Messenger (صَلَّى ٱللَّهُ عَلَيْهِ وَسَلَّمَ) came on the Day of the Conquest from the upper part of Makkah upon his she-camel, with Usāmah ibn Zayd as his co-rider; and Bilāl was with him, and 'Uthmān ibn Talhah, one of the custodians, was with him. So he caused it to kneel down in the mosque, and he ordered him (meaning 'Uthmān) to bring the keys of the Ka'bah" — and in a wording: "And he sent a message to 'Uthmān ibn Talhah, so he brought the key, so he opened the door."

So in summary, with all of this combined, the hadīth is authentic without a doubt.

Endnote 74 – Source: Page 198

(SH) Reported by Abū Dāwūd (2/9-10/no.1229), and At-Tirmidhī with its like (2/430/no.545) and (...), and others with chains of narration from ʿAlī ibn Zayd ibn Judʿān: from Abū Nadrah: from ʿImrān, with it.

I say: Its isnād is *'daʿīf'*; it contains ʿAlī ibn Zayd ibn Judʿān who is weak, as occurs in *At-Taqrīb.*

Ibnul-Mundhir said: "The fact that the Prophet (صَلَّىٰ ٱللَّٰهُ عَلَيْهِ وَسَلَّمَ) shortened (the Prayers) in Makkah is established through other than this chain, since ʿAlī ibn Zayd is spoken about concerning his narrations; and this practice was done by ʿUmar ibn Al-Khattāb when he arrived in Makkah. He would pray two rakʿahs, and when he gave Salutation he said: *'O inhabitants of Makkah! We are travellers, so complete the Prayer.'"*

And the hadīth was declared weak by our Shaikh, Imām Al-Albānī (رَحِمَهُ ٱللَّٰهُ) in *Mishkātul-Masābīh* (2/87: Hidāyah).

And as for his (صَلَّىٰ ٱللَّٰهُ عَلَيْهِ وَسَلَّمَ) continuing to abstain from fasting for the rest of the month, then that is established in the *Sahīh* of Al-Bukhārī (no. 4275) as a hadīth of Ibn ʿAbbās (رَضِيَ ٱللَّٰهُ عَنْهُمَا).

And his continuing to pray the Prayers as two rakʿahs is established in *Al-Bukhārī* also (no. 4298) as a hadīth of Ibn ʿAbbās (رَضِيَ ٱللَّٰهُ عَنْهُمَا).

Endnote 75 – Source: Page 200

(SH) This portion is reported by Abū Dāwūd (3/20/no.2501), An-Nasāʾī in *As-Sunanul-Kubrā* (8/139-140/no.8819), and (...), through chains of narrations from Muʿāwiyah ibn Sallām: from Abū Kabshah As-Salūlī: from Sahl ibn Hanzalah with it.

I say: This is a *'sahīh'* chain of narration: its narrators are reliable; those of the *Sahīh.*

It was declared *'hasan'* by Al-Hāfidh Ibn Hajr in *Al-Fat-h* (8/27), and declared *'sahīh'* by our Shaikh (Al-Albānī) in *Sahīh Abī Dāwūd* (no. 2183) and *Takhrīj Fiqhis-Sīrah* (p. 421); and it is witnessed to by a hadīth of Anas ibn Mālik (رَضِيَ ٱللَّٰهُ عَنْهُ), reported by Ibn Abī Shaybah in *Al-Musannaf* (14/530-531/ no. 18845), and Ahmad (3/279), and Al-Bazzār in his *Musnad* (2/351/ no. 1835: *Kashf*) with a chain of narration *'sahīh'* to the standard of Muslim; and it is found in *Sahīhul-Bukhārī* (no. 4337) and *Sahīh Muslim* (no. 1059/135), through another chain from Anas.

Endnote 76 – Source: Page 201

(SH) Mentioned by Ibn Is-hāq in *As-Sīrah* (4/1100-1102) and from him by the author in *Al-Bidāyah wan-Nihāyah* (7/6-9) without a chain of narration.

It is also reported by Al-Hākim (3/48), and Al-Bayhaqī in *Dalā'ilun-Nubuwwah* (5/119-123), by way of Ahmad ibn 'Abdil-Jabbār: Yūnus ibn Bukayr narrated to us: from Ibn Is-hāq: 'Āsim ibn 'Umar ibn Qatādah narrated to us: from 'Abdur-Rahmān ibn Jābir ibn 'Abdillāh: from his father; and from 'Amr ibn Shu'ayb, and Az-Zuhrī, and 'Abdullāh ibn Abī Bakr ibn 'Amr ibn Hazm, and 'Abdullāh ibn Al-Mukaddam Ath-Thaqafī, concerning the story of Hunayn.

I say: Its chain of narration is weak; Ahmad ibn 'Abdil-Jabbār is *'da'īf'*, as occurs in *At-Taqrīb*.

Endnote 77 – Source: Page 201

(SH) Reported by Ahmad in his *Musnad* (4/222), Abū Dāwūd in his *Sunan* (no. 3566), An-Nasā'ī in *As-Sunanul-Kubrā* (nos. 5776 and 5777), Ibn Hibbān in his *Sahīh* (no. 4720: *Ihsān*), Ad-Dāraqutnī in his *Sunan* (3/39) by way of Hibbān ibn Hilāl: from Hammām ibn Yahyā: from Qatādah: from 'Atā': from Safwān ibn Ya'lā ibn Umayyah: from his father with it.

I say: This chain of narration is *'sahīh'* to the standard of the two Shaikhs, and it was declared *'sahīh'* by our Shaikh Al-Albānī (رَحِمَهُ ٱللَّٰهُ) in *As-Sahīhah* (no. 630).

Endnote 78 – Source: Page 202

(SH) Reported by Ibn Is-hāq in *As-Sīrah* (4/1104: Ibn Hishām), Ahmad in his *Musnad* (5/98), At-Tirmidhī in his *Sunan* (no. 2180), An-Nasā'ī in his *Tafsīr* (no. 205), and Ibn Hibbān in his *Sahīh* (no. 1835: *Mawārid*) and many others by way of Az-Zuhrī: from Sinān ibn Abī Sinān Ad-Du'alī: from Abū Wāqid Al-Laythī, with it. I say: This is a *'sahīh'* chain of narration, and it was declared *'sahīh'* by our Shaikh Al-Albānī (رَحِمَهُ ٱللَّهُ) in *Sahīh Mawārididh-Dham'ān* (no. 1540).

Endnote 79 – Source: Page 203

(SH) Reported by Al-Bazzār in his *Musnad* (2/346-347/ no.1827: *Kashf*): 'Alī ibn Shu'ayb and 'Abdullāh ibn Ayyūb Al-Makhzūmī narrated to us: 'Alī ibn 'Āsim narrated to us: Sulaymān At-Taymī narrated to us: from Anas, with it.

I say: Al-Haythamī said in *Majma'uz-Zawā'id* (6/178): "Reported by Al-Bazzār, and it contains 'Alī ibn 'Āsim who was weak."

And it has a witness from a *'mursal'* narration of Ar-Rabī' ibn Anas, reported by Al-Bayhaqī in *Dalā'ilun-Nubuwwah* (5/123-124) by way of Ahmad ibn 'Abdil-Jabbār: Yūnus ibn Bukayr narrated to us: from Abū Ja'far Ar-Rāzī: from Ar-Rabī', with it.

I say: This chain of narration is weak, and has two weaknesses besides its being *'mursal'*. Firstly: Abū Ja'far Ar-Rāzī, who had a very poor memory. Secondly: Ahmad ibn 'Abdil-Jabbār who was weak.

Endnote 80 – Source: Page 211

(SH) Reported by Ahmad in his *Musnad* (5/63), and in *Fadā'ilus-Sahābah* (nos. 846 and 847), At-Tirmidhī in his *Sunan* (no. 3701), Ibn Abī 'Āsim in *As-Sunnah* (no. 1279), and in *Al-Jihād* (no. 82) and (...), by way of Damurah ibn 'Abdillāh ibn Shawdhab: from 'Abdullāh ibn Al-Qāsim: from Kathīr (the mawlā of 'Abdur-Rahmān ibn Samurah) from 'Abdur-Rahmān ibn Samurah, with it.

I say: This is a *'hasan'* chain of narration. Kathīr ibn Abī Kathīr is *'sadūq'* (truthful), and *'hasan'* in narrating hadīth, if Allāh wills; since a group narrate from him, and he was declared reliable by Al-ʿIjlī and Ibn Hibbān, and he was from the elders amongst the Tābiʿīn.

Endnote 81 – Source: Page 211

(SH) Reported by Abū Dāwūd At-Tayālisī in his *Musnad* (no. 82), Ahmad in his *Musnad* (1/70), Ibn Abī ʿĀsim in *As-Sunnah* (no. 1303), An-Nasāʾī in his *Sunan* (6/46-47), and (...), with chains of narration from Husayn ibn ʿAbdir-Rahmān: from ʿAmr ibn Jāwān: from Al-Ahnaf ibn Qays, with it, with longer wording.

I say: This is a weak chain of narration; ʿAmr ibn Jāwān is *'maqbūl'* (acceptable only if supported), as occurs in *At-Taqrīb*.

However, overall it is witnessed to by what is reported by Al-Bukhārī in his *Sahīh* (no. 2778), as a hadīth of ʿUthmān ibn ʿAffān (رَضِيَ ٱللَّهُ عَنْهُ) himself.

It is also declared *'sahīh'* by our Shaikh, Al-Albānī (رَحِمَهُ ٱللَّهُ) in *Sahīh Sunanin-Nasāʾī*.

Al-Hāfidh said in *Al-Fat-h*: "Amongst the points of benefit of this hadīth is that it shows a clear virtue of ʿUthmān (رَضِيَ ٱللَّهُ عَنْهُ), and the permissibility of a man speaking of his own virtues, when there is a need for that, to repel some harm or attain some benefit, since this is only disliked when it is done for boasting, vying with others, or out of self-amazement."

(BJ)(SZ) His (رَضِيَ ٱللَّهُ عَنْهُ) equipping the Army of Hardship is something famous. So he (رَضِيَ ٱللَّهُ عَنْهُ) spent a tremendous amount upon it, such that no one has spent the like of it; and this is mentioned in a number of reports.

From them is what is reported by Ahmad (5/63) and At-Tirmidhī (no. 3701), as a hadīth of ʿAbdur-Rahmān ibn Samurah who said: "ʿUthmān ibn ʿAffān came to the Prophet (صَلَّى ٱللَّهُ عَلَيْهِ وَسَلَّمَ) with a thousand dīnars in his garment, when the Prophet (صَلَّى ٱللَّهُ عَلَيْهِ وَسَلَّمَ) was preparing the Army of Hardship. So he poured them out into the apartment of the Prophet (صَلَّى ٱللَّهُ عَلَيْهِ وَسَلَّمَ), and the Prophet (صَلَّى ٱللَّهُ عَلَيْهِ وَسَلَّمَ) began tossing them between his two hands and saying: *"Uthmān shall not be harmed by whatever he does after this day.*'" [Declared *'hasan'* by Shaikh Al-Albānī in *Sahīh Sunanit-Tirmidhī*]

[DB] Likewise in the aforementioned hadīth reported by Al-Bukhārī (no. 2778), as a hadīth of Abū 'Abdir-Rahmān who said: "When (the rebels) had surrounded 'Uthmān (رَضِيَ اللَّهُ عَنْهُ) he looked upon them from above, and said:

'I ask you, by Allāh, and I do not ask anyone except the Companions of the Prophet (صَلَّى اللَّهُ عَلَيْهِ وَسَلَّمَ): Do you not know that Allāh's Messenger (صَلَّى اللَّهُ عَلَيْهِ وَسَلَّمَ) said: *"Whoever digs the well of Rūmah, then he will be granted Paradise"*, and that I dug it?

'Do you not know that he said: *"Whoever equips the army of hardship will be granted Paradise"*, and I equipped it?!'"

He said: "So they attested to the truth of what he said."

Endnote 82 – Source: Page 212

[SH] Reported by Ibn Is-hāq, and by Ibnul-Mundhir and Abush-Shaikh in their *Tafsīrs*, as occurs in *Ad-Durrul-Manthūr* (4/264); from Az-Zuhrī, and Yazīd ibn Yasār, and 'Abdullāh ibn Abī Bakr, and 'Āsim ibn 'Umar ibn Qatādah with it, in *'mursal'* form.

And this is a *'mursal'* report with a *'sahīh'* chain of narration. It is also reported by At-Tabarī in *Jāmi'ul-Bayān* (10/239) and Al-Bayhaqī in *Dalā'ilun-Nubuwwah* (5/218), from Ibn Is-hāq, as his statement.

As for Al-'Irbād ibn Sāriyah, then it is something confirmed from him. It is reported by Ahmad in his *Musnad* (4/126-127), Abū Dāwūd in his *Sunan* (no. 4607) and (...) and others, with their chain of narration from Al-Walīd ibn Muslim: Thawr ibn Yazīd narrated to us: Khālid ibn Ma'dān narrated to me: 'Abdur-Rahmān ibn 'Amr and Hujr ibn Hujr narrated to me, saying: Al-'Irbād ibn Sāriyah came to us, and he was one of those about whom there came down:

وَلَا عَلَى الَّذِينَ إِذَا مَا أَتَوْكَ لِتَحْمِلَهُمْ قُلْتَ لَا أَجِدُ مَا أَحْمِلُكُمْ عَلَيْهِ

> MEANING: "Nor is there any blame on those who when they came to you to be provided with mounts you said: *'I can find no mounts for you.'*" — **SŪRAH AT-TAWBAH (9):92**

I say: This is a *'sahīh'* chain of narration. Al-Walīd ibn Muslim clearly states that the narration was heard directly at every stage of transmission; and it was declared *'sahīh'* by Ibn Hibbān, and by Al-Hāfidh Ibn Hajr in *Muwāfaqatul-Khabarul-Khabr* (1/137), and by our Shaikh Al-Albānī in *Silsilatus-Sahīhah* (no. 938).

Endnote 83 –Source: Page 212

(SH) Reported by Al-Bukhārī (no. 4418) and Muslim (no. 2769), as a hadīth of Ka'b ibn Mālik (رَضِيَ ٱللَّهُ عَنْهُ).

(DB) Al-Bukhārī reported (no. 4418) from 'Abdullāh ibn Ka'b ibn Mālik, who was the guide of Ka'b ibn Mālik when he became blind, who said: "I heard Ka'b ibn Mālik narrate about when he did not take part in the expedition of Khaybar. So Ka'b said:

....

I did not remain behind from Allāh's Messenger (صَلَّى ٱللَّهُ عَلَيْهِ وَسَلَّمَ) in any military expedition in which he took part, except for the Expedition of Tabūk; and except for the fact that I was not present on the Expedition of Badr, but no one was blamed for not going along with it, since Allāh's Messenger (صَلَّى ٱللَّهُ عَلَيْهِ وَسَلَّمَ) went out only intending to attack the caravan of Quraysh. However, Allāh caused them to meet their enemy without any prior engagement. And I witnessed the night of (the Pledge of) Al-'Aqabah with Allāh's Messenger (صَلَّى ٱللَّهُ عَلَيْهِ وَسَلَّمَ) when we gave a pledge upon Islām; and I would not like to exchange it for being present at Badr, even though Badr is more famous amongst the people than it.

So my story is that I had never been stronger or wealthier than I was when I remained behind from him in that expedition. By Allāh, I had never before possessed two riding camels, but I owned two during that expedition. Whenever Allāh's Messenger (صَلَّى ٱللَّهُ عَلَيْهِ وَسَلَّمَ) wanted to go on a military expedition he would disguise his intention and make it look as if he intended to attack somewhere else, until that expedition which

Allāh's Messenger (صَلَّى ٱللَّٰهُ عَلَيْهِ وَسَلَّمَ) entered upon in severe heat, and he faced a long journey across a waterless desert, and the enemy was large in number. So he announced the matter openly to the Muslims so that they could equip themselves for the expedition. So he informed them of the destination he intended, and the Muslims who were with Allāh's Messenger (صَلَّى ٱللَّٰهُ عَلَيْهِ وَسَلَّمَ) were so many in numbers that they could not be contained in a register.

So any man who wanted to absent himself thought that he could therefore remain hidden, as long as no Revelation came down from Allāh concerning him. Furthermore, Allāh's Messenger (صَلَّى ٱللَّٰهُ عَلَيْهِ وَسَلَّمَ) went on that expedition at the time when the fruits had ripened and there was shade (under the trees). So Allāh's Messenger (صَلَّى ٱللَّٰهُ عَلَيْهِ وَسَلَّمَ) made preparations, and likewise the Muslims along with him. I started to go out to equip myself along with them, but I would return not having done anything. So I would say to myself: "I will (still) be able to do that."

But I kept putting it off until the people were ready, and Allāh's Messenger (صَلَّى ٱللَّٰهُ عَلَيْهِ وَسَلَّمَ) and the Muslims along with him departed in the morning, and I had not made any preparations. So I said: "I can get ready a day or two after him, and then catch up with them."

So the next morning after they had departed I went out to get ready, but I came back having done nothing. Then I would go out and come back still having done nothing, and this continued with me until they had hastened away, and I had missed the expedition. I still intended to ride and catch up with them, and would that I had done it! But that was not decreed for me.

Then when I would go out amongst the people, after the departure of Allāh's Messenger (صَلَّى ٱللَّٰهُ عَلَيْهِ وَسَلَّمَ), and walk amongst them. And it would grieve me that I would not see anyone except a man who was accused of Hypocrisy, or those whom Allāh excused from the weak ones.

Allāh's Messenger (صَلَّى ٱللَّٰهُ عَلَيْهِ وَسَلَّمَ) did not remember me until he reached Tabūk, and said whilst he was sitting amongst the people at Tabūk: "What has happened to Kaʿb?"

So a man from Banū Salimah said: “O Messenger of Allāh! He has been detained by his garments and looking upon his own figure.”

So Muʿādh ibn Jabal said: “What a bad thing you have said! By Allāh, O Messenger of Allāh, we have not known anything but good about him.”

So Allāh’s Messenger (صَلَّى ٱللَّهُ عَلَيْهِ وَسَلَّمَ) was silent...

So when news reached me that he was returning I became worried, and I started thinking of false (excuses), and saying: “How can I escape his anger tomorrow?”

And I sought the assistance of everyone in my family who had sound opinion in that regard. However, when it was said: ***“Allāh’s Messenger (صَلَّى ٱللَّهُ عَلَيْهِ وَسَلَّمَ) is approaching”*** — all falsehood vanished from me, and I knew that I would never be able to evade him with falsehood. So I became determined to tell him the truth.

Then Allāh’s Messenger (صَلَّى ٱللَّهُ عَلَيْهِ وَسَلَّمَ) arrived in the morning, and when he arrived from a journey he would begin with the mosque and pray two rakʿahs in it; and then he would sit for the people. So when he did that those who had remained behind came to him and started making their excuses to him, and swearing oaths before him, and they were eighty and odd men. So Allāh’s Messenger (صَلَّى ٱللَّهُ عَلَيْهِ وَسَلَّمَ) accepted what was apparent from them, and accepted their pledge, and asked for forgiveness for them, and he entrusted their secrets to Allāh. So I went to him and when I greeted him with the Salutation, he smiled with the smile of one who is angry. Then he said: ***“Come!”*** So I walked until I sat down in front of him.

Then he said: “What prevented you from joining us? Had you not purchased a riding-beast?”

So I said: “Yes, O Messenger of Allāh! By Allāh, if I sat before anyone else besides you from the people of the world, I think that I would be able to evade his anger by making some excuse or other. By Allāh, I am able to speak eloquently; but by Allāh, I know that if I tell you a lie today to cause you to be satisfied with me, then Allāh will soon cause you to become angry with me. And if I speak truthfully to you, then you will be angry with me, but I hope that because of it Allāh may pardon me.

No, by Allāh, I had no excuse. By Allāh, I have never been stronger or wealthier than when I failed to join you."

So Allāh's Messenger (صَلَّى ٱللَّٰهُ عَلَيْهِ وَسَلَّمَ) said: "As for this one, then he has spoken the truth. So get up until Allāh ordains something concerning you."

So I got up and left, and some men from Banū Salimah got up, came after me, and said to me: "By Allāh! We do not know you to have committed a sin before this, and then on top of that you were unable to offer any excuse to Allāh's Messenger (صَلَّى ٱللَّٰهُ عَلَيْهِ وَسَلَّمَ) as the others who failed to join him have offered. Your sin could have been sufficed by Allāh's Messenger (صَلَّى ٱللَّٰهُ عَلَيْهِ وَسَلَّمَ) seeking forgiveness for you."

So, by Allāh, they kept rebuking me until I wanted to go back and say that I had lied. But then I said: "Has anyone else besides me experienced the same as myself?"

So they said; "Yes, two men who said the same as you said, and the same thing was said to both of them as was said to you."

So I said: "Who are they?"

So they said: "Murārah ibn Ar-Rabīʿ Al-ʿAmrī and Hilāl ibn Umayyah Al-Wāqifī."

So they mentioned to me two righteous men who had been present at Badr, and they were an example for me. So when they mentioned those two to me I persevered.

Allāh's Messenger (صَلَّى ٱللَّٰهُ عَلَيْهِ وَسَلَّمَ) forbade the Muslims from talking to us, we three out of all those who remained behind from him. So the people kept away from us, and their attitude towards us changed to such an extent that the land itself seemed strange to me, and it was unrecognisable to me. So we remained in that state for fifty nights.

So as for my two companions, then they became subdued and remained sitting in their houses, weeping. As for myself, then I was the youngest and strongest of them, so I used to go out and offer the Prayer along with the Muslims; and I would walk through the markets and no one would speak to me. I would also go to Allāh's Messenger (صَلَّى ٱللَّٰهُ عَلَيْهِ وَسَلَّمَ) and greet him with the salutation whilst he was in his sitting-place after the Prayer. So I would then say to myself: *"Did he move his lips in reply to my salutation or not?"*

Then I would pray near to him and would steal a glance towards him. When I was occupied in my Prayer, he would turn towards me, but if I turned my face towards him, he would turn away from me.

When the people's rebuffing me became prolonged for me, I walked until I climbed into the walled-garden of Abū Qatādah, and he was the son of my paternal uncle and the most beloved of the people to me, and I greeted him with the Salutation. So, by Allāh, he did not respond to my salutation. So I said: "O Abū Qatādah! I implore you by Allāh! Do you know that I love Allāh and His Messenger?"

So he was silent. So I repeated it to him, and implored him, but he was silent. So I repeated it again and implored him. So he said: "Allāh and His Messenger know best!"

So my eyes flowed with tears, and I went back and climbed back over the wall.

Then once, when I was walking in the market of Al-Madīnah, I found a Nabatean from the Nabatean farmers of Shām who had come to sell foodstuff in the market of Al-Madīnah, and he was saying: ***"Who can lead me to Kaʿb ibn Mālik?"*** So the people pointed me out to him, until he came to me and gave me a letter from the King of Ghassān. It said:

> To proceed. It has reached me that your companion is treating you severely. So Allāh does not force you to stay at a place where you are humiliated, or where you are deprived of your rights. So come and join us and we will console you.

So when I read it I said: *"This is also a trial."* So I took it to the oven and lit [the fire] with it.

Then when forty of the fifty nights had passed, a messenger came to me from Allāh's Messenger (صَلَّى ٱللَّهُ عَلَيْهِ وَسَلَّمَ) saying: "Allāh's Messenger (صَلَّى ٱللَّهُ عَلَيْهِ وَسَلَّمَ) commands that you keep away from your wife."

So I said: “Shall I divorce her or what should I do?”

He said: “No, just keep away from her and do not approach her.”

And he sent the same message to my two companions. So I said to my wife: “Go to your family, and remain with them until Allāh ordains something in this affair.”

So the wife of Hilāl ibn Umayyah went to Allāh’s Messenger (صَلَّى ٱللَّهُ عَلَيْهِ وَسَلَّمَ) and said: “O Messenger of Allāh! Hilāl ibn Umayyah is a helpless old man and has no one to serve him. Do you dislike that I should serve him?”

He said: “No, however do not let him approach you.”

She said: “By Allāh, he has no desire for anything. By Allāh, he has not ceased weeping from the start of his affair until this day.”

So then, one of my family said to me: “Why do you not seek permission of Allāh’s Messenger (صَلَّى ٱللَّهُ عَلَيْهِ وَسَلَّمَ) regarding your wife, just as he permitted the wife of Hilāl ibn Umayyah to serve him.”

So I said: “By Allāh, I will not seek the permission of Allāh’s Messenger (صَلَّى ٱللَّهُ عَلَيْهِ وَسَلَّمَ) with regard to her. I do not know what Allāh’s Messenger would say if I sought his permission regarding her, and I am a young man.”

So I remained ten nights after that, until fifty nights had been completed from the time when Allāh’s Messenger (صَلَّى ٱللَّهُ عَلَيْهِ وَسَلَّمَ) forbade that anyone should speak to us. So then when I had prayed the Fajr Prayer on the morning of the fiftieth night, and I was upon the roof of one of our houses — then whilst I was sitting in the condition which Allāh mentioned, my soul felt restricted upon me, and the earth felt tight around me, despite its extensiveness, I heard the voice of a caller who had climbed upon the mountain of Salʿ calling out at the top of his voice: ***“O Kaʿb ibn Mālik! Receive good news!”***

So I fell down in prostration, and I knew that relief had come. Allāh’s Messenger (صَلَّى ٱللَّهُ عَلَيْهِ وَسَلَّمَ) had announced that Allāh had accepted our repentance, when he had prayed the Fajr Prayer. So the people came to us to bring us the good news. Some bearers of glad tidings went towards my companions; and a man galloped upon a horse towards me, and another man from Aslam came running and ascended the mountain, and the voice was quicker than the horse. So when the one whose voice I had heard came to me to give me the good news, I took off my two garments and dressed him with them for conveying the good news to me. By Allāh, I did not own any others (of that type) on that day; and I borrowed two garments and wore them, and went off towards Allāh's Messenger (صَلَّى ٱللَّهُ عَلَيْهِ وَسَلَّمَ). The people met me in crowds and were congratulating me on the repentance (...).

So I entered the mosque and found Allāh's Messenger (صَلَّى ٱللَّهُ عَلَيْهِ وَسَلَّمَ) sitting with the people around him. Talhah ibn ʿUbaydillāh stood up, rushed over to me, and he shook hands with me, and congratulated me. By Allāh, no other man from the Muhājirīn besides him came up to me, and I shall not forget this action of Talhah. So when I gave the salutation to Allāh's Messenger (صَلَّى ٱللَّهُ عَلَيْهِ وَسَلَّمَ), Allāh's Messenger (صَلَّى ٱللَّهُ عَلَيْهِ وَسَلَّمَ) said, whilst his face was shining with joy: "Be happy at the best day that has come upon you since your mother gave birth to you."

So I said: "Is it from you, O Messenger of Allāh, or from Allāh?"

So he said: *"No, rather it is from Allāh."* And when Allāh's Messenger (صَلَّى ٱللَّهُ عَلَيْهِ وَسَلَّمَ) was happy, his face would shine as if it were a piece of the moon, and we would recognise that from him.

So when I sat before him I said: "O Messenger of Allāh! From my repentance is that I will give up all my wealth as charity for Allāh and His Messenger (صَلَّى ٱللَّهُ عَلَيْهِ وَسَلَّمَ)."

So Allāh's Messenger (صَلَّى ٱللَّهُ عَلَيْهِ وَسَلَّمَ) said: "Keep a part of your wealth, for that will be better for you."

I said: "I will keep my share from Khaybar," and I said: "O Messenger of Allāh! Allāh saved me through my telling the truth, so from my repentance is that I will only speak the truth for as long as I live."

So by Allāh, I do not know anyone from the Muslims whom Allāh has blessed with truthfulness in speech more then He has blessed me since I mentioned that to Allāh's Messenger (صَلَّى ٱللَّهُ عَلَيْهِ وَسَلَّمَ). I have never intended to tell a lie from the time I mentioned that to Allāh's Messenger

(صَلَّى ٱللَّهُ عَلَيْهِ وَسَلَّمَ) until this day, and I hope that Allāh will preserve me upon that for as long as I remain; and Allāh sent down to His Messenger:

> لَّقَد تَّابَ اللَّهُ عَلَى النَّبِيِّ وَالْمُهَاجِرِينَ وَالْأَنصَارِ
>
> MEANING: "Allāh has granted to the Prophet, and the Muhājirūn, and the Ansār, that they should turn to Him..."

up to His saying:

> وَكُونُوا مَعَ الصَّادِقِينَ
>
> MEANING: "And be with the truthful ones." — **SŪRAH AT-TAWBAH (9): 117-119**

So, by Allāh, Allāh never granted me any blessing, after having guided me to Islām, greater in my estimation than my speaking the truth to Allāh's Messenger (صَلَّى ٱللَّهُ عَلَيْهِ وَسَلَّمَ), so that I did not lie to him and thus perish as those who told lies perished. So when the Revelation was sent down, Allāh (the Most High) said, concerning those who lied, something more severe than He has said about anyone.

So He (the Exalted and Most High) said:

> سَيَحْلِفُونَ بِاللَّهِ لَكُمْ إِذَا انقَلَبْتُمْ
>
> MEANING: "They will swear oaths in Allāh's name to you when you return..."

up to His saying:

> فَإِنَّ اللَّهَ لَا يَرْضَىٰ عَنِ الْقَوْمِ الْفَاسِقِينَ
>
> MEANING: "...but Allāh is not pleased with the disobedient ones." — **SŪRAH AT-TAWBAH (9): 95-96**

....

Kaʿb said: "And we three differed totally from the case of those whose excuses were accepted by Allāh's Messenger (ﷺ) when they swore oaths to him. So he took their pledge and asked for forgiveness for them; whereas Allāh's Messenger (ﷺ) deferred our case until Allāh gave His judgement concerning it. So therefore He said:

> وَعَلَى الثَّلَاثَةِ الَّذِينَ خُلِّفُوا
>
> MEANING: "And the three whose case was deferred." — **SŪRAH AT-TAWBAH (9): 118**

So that which Allāh mentioned does not mean our remaining behind from the expedition; but rather, it means his deferring our case until later, and its being dealt with after those who came and swore oaths to him, and his excusing them and accepting that."

Endnote 84 – Source: Page 213

(SH) Reported by Ibn Khuzaymah in his *Sahīh* (no. 1010), Al-Bazzār in his *Musnad* (no. 1841: Kashf), Al-Hākim in *Al-Mustadrak* (1/159), and Al-Bayhaqī in *Dalāʾilun-Nubuwwah* (5/231) by way of Asbigh ibn Faraj, and Hurmulah ibn Yahyā, and Yūnus ibn ʿAbdil-Aʿlā, all of them: from Ibn Wahb: from ʿAmr ibn Al-Hārith: from Saʿīd ibn Abī Hilāl: from ʿUtbah ibn Abī ʿUtbah: from Nāfiʿ ibn Jubayr: from Ibn ʿAbbās, with it.

And it is reported by Ibn Hibbān in his *Sahīh* (no. 1383: *Ihsān*), by way of Hurmulah, from Ibn Wahb with [the narration], but (incorrectly) dropping ʿUtbah (from its chain).

(DB) Declared *'daʿīf'* by Shaikh Al-Albānī in *Daʿīf Mawārididh-Dhamʾān* (no. 1707/207) because of (1) the *'ikhtilāt'* of Saʿīd ibn Abī Hilāl, and (2) the weakness of ʿUtbah ibn Abī ʿUtbah.

Endnote 85 – Source: Page 214

(SH) Reported by Abū Yaʿlā in his Musnad, as occurs in *Al-Matālibul-ʿĀliyah* (4/427/4320: Al-Watn Edn. or 17/504/no. 4317: Al-ʿĀsimah Edn.), and Ibn Qāniʿ in *Muʿjamus-Sahābah* (2/351): from Jaʿfar ibn Humayd:

ʿUbaydullāh ibn Iyād ibn Laqīt narrated to us: from his father: from Qays ibn An-Nuʿmān (رَضِيَ اللَّهُ عَنْهُ), with it.

So this is a *'sahīh'* chain of narration; all of its narrators are reliable, and Al-Hāfidh declared it strong in *Al-Fat-h* (5/274).

Endnote 86 – Source: Page 214

(SH) It was built by the Hypocrites to cause separation between the Muslims, and as a base for their enemies, and to harm the Mosque founded upon dutifulness to Allāh: Qubā' Mosque. Concerning it Allāh (the Most High) sent down:

> وَالَّذِينَ اتَّخَذُوا مَسْجِدًا ضِرَارًا وَكُفْرًا وَتَفْرِيقًا بَيْنَ الْمُؤْمِنِينَ وَإِرْصَادًا لِّمَنْ حَارَبَ اللَّهَ وَرَسُولَهُ مِن قَبْلُ ۚ وَلَيَحْلِفُنَّ إِنْ أَرَدْنَا إِلَّا الْحُسْنَىٰ ۖ وَاللَّهُ يَشْهَدُ إِنَّهُمْ لَكَاذِبُونَ ۝ لَا تَقُمْ فِيهِ أَبَدًا ۚ لَّمَسْجِدٌ أُسِّسَ عَلَى التَّقْوَىٰ مِنْ أَوَّلِ يَوْمٍ أَحَقُّ أَن تَقُومَ فِيهِ ۚ فِيهِ رِجَالٌ يُحِبُّونَ أَن يَتَطَهَّرُوا ۚ وَاللَّهُ يُحِبُّ الْمُطَّهِّرِينَ ۝ أَفَمَنْ أَسَّسَ بُنْيَانَهُ عَلَىٰ تَقْوَىٰ مِنَ اللَّهِ وَرِضْوَانٍ خَيْرٌ أَم مَّنْ أَسَّسَ بُنْيَانَهُ عَلَىٰ شَفَا جُرُفٍ هَارٍ فَانْهَارَ بِهِ فِي نَارِ جَهَنَّمَ ۗ وَاللَّهُ لَا يَهْدِي الْقَوْمَ الظَّالِمِينَ ۝ لَا يَزَالُ بُنْيَانُهُمُ الَّذِي بَنَوْا رِيبَةً فِي قُلُوبِهِمْ إِلَّا أَن تَقَطَّعَ قُلُوبُهُمْ ۗ وَاللَّهُ عَلِيمٌ حَكِيمٌ
>
> MEANING: "And as for those who put up a mosque by way of harming and disbelief, and to disunite the believers, and as an outpost for those who warred against Allāh and His Messenger (Muhammad صَلَّى اللَّهُ عَلَيْهِ وَسَلَّمَ) aforetime, they will indeed swear that their intention is nothing but good. Allāh bears witness that they are certainly liars.
>
> Never stand you therein. Verily, the mosque whose foundation was laid from the first day on piety is more worthy that you stand therein (to pray). In it are men who love to clean and to purify themselves. And Allāh loves those who make themselves clean and pure.
>
> Is it then he, who laid the foundation of his building on piety to Allāh and His Good Pleasure, better, or he who laid the foundation of his

building on an undetermined brink of a precipice ready to crumble down, so that it crumbled to pieces with him into the Fire of Hell. And Allāh guides not the people who are the wrong-doers.

The building which they built will never cease to be a cause of hypocrisy and doubt in their hearts, unless their hearts are cut to pieces. (i.e. till they die). And Allāh is All-Knowing, All-Wise." — **Sūrah At-Tawbah (9): 107-110**

Endnote 87 – Source: Page 217

(SH) Reported by Ahmad in his *Musnad*; (4/21), Abū Dāwūd in his *Sunan* (no.531), An-Nasā'ī in *Al-Mujtabā* (2/23), and *Al-Kubrā* (no. 1648), and Ibn Mājah in his *Sunan* (no.987) and (...) — and others, all of them by way of Abul-'Alā': from Mutarrif ibn 'Abdillāh: from 'Uthmān with it. I say: Its chain of narration is *'sahīh'*, and it was declared *'sahīh'* by our Shaikh Al-Albānī (رَحِمَهُ ٱللَّهُ); and the hadīth was reported by Muslim in his *Sahīh* (no. 468), as a hadīth of 'Uthmān himself, without a mention of the mu'adhdhin.

Endnote 88 – Source: Page 219

(BJ)(SZ) This was the saying of Ibn Hazm. However, Ibnul-Qayyim preferred the saying that it was the day of Saturday, with five days remaining of the month. This was also supported by Ibn Kathīr himself in *Al-Bidāyah* (5/101-102).

(DB) Al-Hāfidh Ibn Hajr said in *Fat-hul-Bārī* (8/104): "In the hadīth of Ibn 'Abbās there occurs that their departure from Al-Madīnah was when five days of Dhul-Qa'dah remained. The author [i.e. Al-Bukhārī] reports it in (the Book of) Hajj; and he and Muslim reported its like as a hadīth of 'Ā'ishah. However, Ibn Hazm stated with certainty that their departure was on the day of Thursday, but this is questionable since the first day of Dhul-Hijjah was a Thursday. This is because it is established and mutawātir that his standing in 'Arafah was on the day of Jumu'ah (Friday). So therefore, it is certain that the beginning of the month was a Thursday, and hence they could not have departed on a Thursday.

Rather, what is apparent from the narrations is that it occurred on the day of Jumuʿah. However, it is established in the two *Sahīhs* from Anas: *'We prayed the Dhuhr Prayer along with the Prophet (ﷺ) in Al-Madīnah as four rakʿahs, and the ʿAsr Prayer in Dhul Hulayfah as two rakʿahs.'* So this shows that their departure was not on the day of Jumuʿah [DB *i.e. because they prayed the Dhuhr Prayer, and not the Jumuʿah Prayer*]

Therefore, all that remains is that they must have departed on Saturday. Then the saying of those who said *'with five days remaining'* is to be taken to mean if the month happened to be thirty days long, but it was actually twenty-nine days long.

Therefore, Thursday, the first day of Dhul-Hijjah, came after four nights had passed, not five. In this way, the reports are harmonized.

This was the manner in which Al-Hāfidh ʿImāduddīn Ibn Kathīr harmonized between the narrations; and this harmonization is further strengthened by the saying of Jābir: *'And he departed with five days remaining of Dhul-Qaʿdah, or four.'*

And his (ﷺ) entry into Makkah was on the morning of the fourth, as is established in the hadīth of ʿĀʾishah, and that was a Sunday. So this also supports his departure from Al-Madīnah having been on the day of Saturday, as has preceded. He therefore remained upon the road for eight nights, and that is the average journey time."

Endnote 89 – Source: Page 220

DB Shaikh Muhammad Nāsiruddīn Al-Albānī (رَحِمَهُ ٱللَّهُ) said in *Hajjatun-Nabiyy* (ﷺ) (p. 10-16):

....

We advise everyone who intends to perform the Hajj that he should study the rites of Hajj in the light of the Book and the Sunnah before beginning the actions of Hajj, so that it can be complete and acceptable to Allāh — the Exalted and Most High.

We say: *'in the light of the Book and the Sunnah'* since the rites of pilgrimage are something, unfortunately, which has been affected by disagreement, as has occurred with the rest of the acts of worship. So an example of this is (the question of) which is best for a person to intend to perform as his Hajj: Tamattu' ('Umrah followed by a separate Hajj), Qirān ('Umrah and Hajj together with a single ihrām), or Ifrād (Hajj on its own)? So they have three positions.

What we hold in that regard is the Tamattu' alone, as was the position of Imām Ahmad and others. Indeed, some of the verifying scholars held it to be an obligation if the person does not take a sacrificial animal along with him, and from them were Ibn Hazm and Ibnul-Qayyim, following the view of Ibn 'Abbās and others from the Salaf. So you will find the details of that in the book *Al-Muhallā* and *Zādul-Ma'ād* and elsewhere.

So I do not wish to enter into this matter with all its details now, rather I wish to mention a brief saying which may benefit, if Allāh (the Most High) wishes, one who is sincere and whose goal is to follow the truth, and not just to blindly follow forefathers or a madh-hab, then I say:

There is no doubt that the Hajj, when he (صَلَّى ٱللَّهُ عَلَيْهِ وَسَلَّمَ) first entered upon it, could lawfully be performed in any of the three aforementioned ways. Likewise, amongst the Companions, some were performing Tamattu', some were performing Qirān, and some were performing Ifrād; since he (صَلَّى ٱللَّهُ عَلَيْهِ وَسَلَّمَ) had given them a choice in that regard, as occurs in the hadīth of 'Ā'ishah (رَضِيَ ٱللَّهُ عَنْهَا):

> "We went out along with Allāh's Messenger (صَلَّى ٱللَّهُ عَلَيْهِ وَسَلَّمَ) and he said: '*Whoever amongst you wishes to declare that he is going to perform a Hajj and an 'Umrah, then let him do so; and whoever wishes to declare that he is going to perform a Hajj, then let him do so; and whoever wishes to declare that he is going to perform an 'Umrah, then let him do so...*'" — until the end of the hadīth, which is reported by Muslim.

So this choice occurred at the beginning of their ihrām, by the Tree [i.e. at Dhul-Hulayfah], as occurs in the narration of Ahmad (6/245). However, the Prophet (صَلَّى ٱللَّهُ عَلَيْهِ وَسَلَّمَ) did not persist upon this choice — rather he moved them on to that which was most excellent, which is the Tamattu', but he did not make it binding upon them or order them with it; and this was on different occasions on their way to Makkah. An example of that was what happened when they reached Sarif, which is a place close to At-Tan'īm and is about ten miles from Makkah. So 'Ā'ishah said, in a narration from her: "So we camped at Sarif."

She said: "So he came out to his Companions and said: '*Whoever has not brought a sacrificial animal with him, and he wishes to make it an 'Umrah, then let him do so; and whosoever has a sacrificial animal with him, then no.*'"

She said: "So some of his Companions did so, and others did not [from those who did not have a sacrificial animal]" — until the end of the hadīth, which is agreed upon; and the addition is Muslim's.

Likewise, when he (صَلَّى ٱللَّهُ عَلَيْهِ وَسَلَّمَ) reached Dhī Tuwā, which is a place near to Makkah and a gate from it, and had prayed the Dawn Prayer, he said to them: "*Whoever wishes to make it an 'Umrah then let him make it an 'Umrah*" — reported by the two Shaikhs as a hadīth of Ibn 'Abbās.

However, we see that when he (صَلَّى ٱللَّهُ عَلَيْهِ وَسَلَّمَ) entered Makkah and performed Tawāful-Qudūm along with his Companions he did not leave them upon that previous ruling (i.e. its being better). Rather, he led them on to a new ruling, which was its being an obligation. So he commanded those who had not brought a sacrificial animal to turn the Hajj into an 'Umrah, and to leave the state of ihrām. So 'Ā'ishah (رَضِيَ ٱللَّهُ عَنْهَا) said:

> "We went out along with Allāh's Messenger (صَلَّى ٱللَّهُ عَلَيْهِ وَسَلَّمَ) and we did not see except that it was a Hajj. So when we arrived at Makkah we performed Tawāf around the House. Then Allāh's Messenger (صَلَّى ٱللَّهُ عَلَيْهِ وَسَلَّمَ) commanded those who had not brought a sacrificial animal to leave the state of ihrām." She said: "So those who had not brought a sacrificial animal left the state of ihrām, and his wives had not brought sacrificial animals so they left the state of ihrām..." — until the end of the hadīth, which is agreed upon.

Also, its like is reported from Ibn 'Abbās with the wording: "So he ordered them to make it an 'Umrah. So they felt it to be a difficulty, which they were indisposed towards, and they said: '*Which leaving of ihrām?*' So he said: '*Leaving the state of ihrām altogether.*'"

It is agreed upon. Its like and something even clearer occurs in the hadīth of Jābir that follows.

I say: So whoever carefully considers these ahādīth will find that it becomes very clear to him, without any shadow of a doubt, that the choice which occurred in them came from him (صَلَّى ٱللَّٰهُ عَلَيْهِ وَسَلَّمَ) to ready and prepare the souls to accept the new ruling which may have been difficult, even if only upon some, for them to accept immediately (meaning the command to change the Hajj to an 'Umrah). This was the case in the days of Ignorance, as is established in the two *Sahīh*; they used to hold that it was not permissible to perform 'Umrah in the months of Hajj (Shawwāl, Dhul-Qa'dah, and Dhul-Hijjah).

So this view persisted, even though the Messenger of Allāh (صَلَّى ٱللَّٰهُ عَلَيْهِ وَسَلَّمَ) had nullified it by performing 'Umrah three times in three years: all of them in the month of Dhul-Qa'dah. So this on its own, even though it was sufficient to abolish that innovation of the days of Ignorance, was not sufficient here to prepare the souls to accept the new ruling (because he was performing Hajj Qirān — and Allāh knows best). So therefore, he (صَلَّى ٱللَّٰهُ عَلَيْهِ وَسَلَّمَ) prepared them for that by giving them a choice between Hajj and 'Umrah, whilst clarifying to them what was most excellent. Then he followed that with a definite command to change the Hajj to an 'Umrah, as preceded.

So when we are aware of this, then the command is one of obligation, for certain. This is proven by the following matters:

Firstly: The origin is that it brings about obligation, unless there is some contextual evidence proving otherwise, and there is no such contextual evidence proving otherwise here. Rather, the context here only confirms it, and it is the next matter:

Secondly: When he (صَلَّى ٱللَّٰهُ عَلَيْهِ وَسَلَّمَ) commanded them with that, they found themselves being indisposed and feeling difficulty in complying, as has preceded. So if it were not an obligation they would not have felt it to be a difficulty. Do you not see that he ordered them three times prior to that with a command of choice, and they did not feel any difficulty with that. So this proves that they understood an obligation from this command, which is what is intended.

Thirdly: In a narration of the hadīth of ʿĀʾishah (رَضِيَ اللَّهُ عَنْهَا) she said: "So ʿAlī entered and found him angry. So I said: *'Who has angered you, O Messenger of Allāh? May Allāh enter him into the Fire!'* He said:

> Are you not aware that I commanded the people with a command, and they are hesitant. If I had known before what I know now, I would not have brought the sacrificial animal along with me. Rather, I would have purchased one, then I could have left the state of ihrām just as they have left the state of ihrām." — Reported by Muslim, Al-Bayhaqī, and Ahmad (6/175).

So his (صَلَّى اللَّهُ عَلَيْهِ وَسَلَّمَ) anger is a clear proof that his command was one of obligation, especially since his (صَلَّى اللَّهُ عَلَيْهِ وَسَلَّمَ) anger was because of their hesitation, not because they were refusing outright to carry out his command — and how free they are from that. And therefore they all left the state of ihrām, except for those who had a sacrificial animal with them.

Fourthly: His (صَلَّى اللَّهُ عَلَيْهِ وَسَلَّمَ) saying when they asked him about changing it, as he had commanded them to: "Is it for this year of ours, or forever?"

So he (صَلَّى اللَّهُ عَلَيْهِ وَسَلَّمَ) joined his fingers together and said: "I have entered the ʿUmrah within Hajj until the Day of Resurrection. Rather, it is forever. Rather, it is forever."

So this is a clear statement that the ʿUmrah has become an essential part of the Hajj, and that this ruling was not specific to the Companions, as some people think, rather it continues forever.

Fifthly: If the command were not one of obligation then it would have been sufficient that some of the Companions carried it out. So how about when we see that Allāh's Messenger (صَلَّى اللَّهُ عَلَيْهِ وَسَلَّمَ) did not suffice with giving a general order for the people to change their Hajj to an ʿUmrah. Rather, he also commanded his daughter Fātimah (رَضِيَ اللَّهُ عَنْهَا) with it, and he commanded his wives with it, as occurs in the two *Sahīhs* from Ibn ʿUmar that Allāh's Messenger (صَلَّى اللَّهُ عَلَيْهِ وَسَلَّمَ) commanded his wives to leave the state of ihrām in the year of the Farewell Hajj. Hafsah said: "I said: *'What prevents you from leaving the state of ihrām?'* He said: *'I have matted my hair'* — until the end of the hadīth.

Also, when Abū Mūsā came to him from Yemen to perform Hajj, he (ﷺ) said: "With what have you declared?" He said: "I declared that I was going to do that which the Prophet (ﷺ) was doing." He said: "Did you bring a sacrificial animal along?" He said: "No." He said: "Then perform Tawāf around the House, and between Safā and Marwah, and then leave the state of ihrām…" — until the end of the hadīth.

So this great eagerness of the Prophet (ﷺ) to convey his command to change it to an ʿUmrah, does it not indicate an obligation?! O Allāh, obligation is established with less than that.

Endnote 90 – Source: Page 222

(SH) Yes; however, with regard to a person who takes the sacrificial animal along, as was the case with the Prophet (ﷺ) and others who took sacrificial animals along. As for a person who does not take a sacrificial animal along with him, then Tamattuʿ (performing ʿUmrah and then leaving the state of ihrām, and re-entering the state of ihrām at the time of Hajj) is obligatory upon him — as the author has mentioned. This is supported by the fact that when Abū Mūsā Al-Ashʿarī (رضي الله عنه) came from Yemen to perform Hajj and Allāh's Messenger (ﷺ) said: "What did you declare as your intent?" He said: "I declared that my intent was to do the same as Allāh's Messenger (ﷺ)," so he said: "Did you bring a sacrificial animal along?" He said: "No." He said: "Perform tawāf around the House, and between As-Safā and Al-Marwah, and then leave the state of ihrām." So this clearly shows Tamattuʿ.

So that which prevented ʿAlī (رضي الله عنه) from performing Tamattuʿ was that he had brought a sacrificial animal along. So when ʿAlī (رضي الله عنه) arrived from Yemen, he found that his wife Fātimah was performing Tamattuʿ and not Qirān, so he criticised her and said: "Who commanded you with this?" So she said: "My father commanded me with it," — meaning the Prophet (ﷺ).

So ʿAlī, being annoyed with her, went to the Prophet (ﷺ), and Allāh's Messenger (ﷺ) said: "She has spoken the truth. She has spoken the truth. I commanded her with it."

So this very clearly states Tamattuʿ; and refer necessarily to *Hajjatun-Nabī (ﷺ)*' (pp. 10-17, 66-67) of our Shaikh Al-Albānī (رَحِمَهُ ٱللَّهُ).

Endnote 91 – Source: Page 223

SH Reported by Abū Dāwūd (2/197/no. 1953), Al-Bukhārī in *Khalq Afʿālil-ʿIbād* (129/398: in abridged form), Ibn Saʿd in *At-Tabaqātul-Kubrā* (8/310) etc. By way of Abū ʿĀsim An-Nabīl: Rabīʿah ibn ʿAbdir-Rahmān Al-Ghanawī narrated to us: from his grandmother As-Sariyy bint Nabhān who said: "I heard Allāh's Messenger (ﷺ) say during the Farewell Pilgrimage: *'Do you know what day this is?'*"

She said: "And it was the day, which they call 'The Day of Heads.'"

"They said: *'Allāh and His Messenger know best.'*

He said: *'It is the middle one of the days of Tashrīq...'*" — until the end of the hadīth.

I say: This is a weak chain of narration, since Rabīʿah is unknown.

It has a witness as a hadīth of two men of Banū Bakr (رَضِيَ ٱللَّهُ عَنْهُمَا) who both said: "We saw Allāh's Messenger (ﷺ) giving a Khutbah in the middle one of the days of Tashrīq..." — until the end of the hadīth. It was reported by Abū Dāwūd (2/197/no. 1952) and Al-Bayhaqī (5/151) by way of Ibnul-Mubārak: from Ibrāhīm ibn Nāfiʿ: from Ibn Abī Najīh: from his father: from two men (from Banū Bakr) with it. I say: This is a *'sahīh'* chain of narration.

And it has a further witness from Abū Nadrah: "Someone who heard the Khutbah of Allāh's Messenger (ﷺ) on the middle day of Tashrīq narrated to me..." — until the end of the hadīth.

It was reported by Ahmad (5/411) and Al-Hārith ibn Abī Usāmah in his *Musnad* (1/193-194/51: *Bughyatul-Bāhith*) and (...) through two chains from Al-Jarīrī: from Abū Nadrah with it.

I say: This chain of narration is *'sahīh'*. Even though Al-Jarīrī's memory deteriorated, the narrator from him in Ahmad's chain (Ismāʿīl ibn ʿUlayyah) heard from him before the deterioration in his memory.

It also has a third witness, as a hadīth of Ibn ʿUmar (رَضِيَ ٱللَّهُ عَنْهُمَا) with its like, being reported by Al-Bayhaqī (5/152) with a chain of narration which is *'hasan'* as a witness, since it contains Mūsā ibn ʿUbaydah who is weak, as occurs in *At-Taqrīb*.

Imām Ibnul-Qayyim (رَحِمَهُ ٱللَّهُ) said in *Zādul-Maʿād* (2/288-289): "He (صَلَّى ٱللَّهُ عَلَيْهِ وَسَلَّمَ) gave two Khutbahs to the people in Mina: a Khutbah on the Day of Sacrifice, and a second Khutbah on the middle one of the days of Tashrīq. So it is said: it was the second day after the Day of Sacrifice, and it is the choicest one of them, meaning: the best of them. Those who hold that use as evidence the hadīth of Sarrāʾ bint Nabhān..."

He said: "And the 'Day of the Heads' is the second day after the Day of Sacrifice, by agreement."

I say: It was called that because on it they used to eat the heads of the sacrificed animals.

Endnote 92 – Source: Page 227

(SH) Reported by Ahmad in his *Musnad* (6/267), Is-hāq ibn Rāhawaih in his *Musnad* (no. 914), Abū Dāwūd in his *Sunan* (no. 3141), Ibn Mājah in his *Sunan* (no. 1464 in abridged form), Ibnul-Jārūd in *Al-Muntaqā* (no. 517), Ibn Hibbān in his *Sahīh* (nos. 2156 and 2157: 'Mawārid'), Al-Hākim (3/59-60), Al-Bayhaqī in *Al-Kubrā* (3/387) and in *Dalāʾilun-Nubuwwah* (7/242), and others, by way of Ibn Is-hāq — and it is found in his *Sīrah* (4/1302-1303: Ibn Hishām): Yahyā ibn ʿAbbād ibn ʿAbdillāh ibn Az-Zubayr narrated to me: from his father: from ʿĀʾishah with it, as part of a longer narration.

I say: This is a *'hasan'* chain of narration; Muhammad ibn Is-hāq is a proof in military expeditions and he states that he heard it directly; and it was declared *'sahīh'* by our Shaikh, the Imām, Al-Albānī (رَحِمَهُ ٱللَّهُ) in *Sahīh Mawārididh-Dhamʾān* (no. 1808).

Endnote 93 – Source: Page 227

(SH) Reported by Ahmad in his *Musnad* (1/260), by way of Ibn Is-hāq: Husayn ibn ʿAbdillāh narrated to me: from ʿIkrimah: from Ibn ʿAbbās, with it.

Shaikh Ahmad Shākir (رَحِمَهُ ٱللَّهُ) said in his notes upon the *Musnad* (4/104): "Its chain of narration is weak because of the weakness of Al-Husayn ibn ʿAbdillāh."

It also has another chain of narration from Ibn ʿAbbās with its like, reported by At-Tabarānī in *Al-Muʿjamul-Kabīr* (1/no. 629) with a chain of narration which is *'hasan'* as a witness and a support.

It also has a witness from a *'mursal'* narration of Ash-Shaʿbī with its like, reported by Ibn Saʿd in *At-Tabaqātul-Kubrā* (2/241) and Al-Bayhaqī in *Dalāʾilun-Nubuwwah* (7/243), and its chain of narration is *'sahīh.'*

It also has another from a *'mursal'* report of Ibn Shihāb Az-Zuhrī reported by Ibn Saʿd (2/241) with a *'sahīh'* chain of narration from him. So in summary the hadīth is *'hasan'*, at the very least.

Endnote 94 – Source: Page 228

(SH) The story of them praying over him individually is reported by At-Tirmidhī in *Ash-Shamāʾil* (no. 378), and from him by Al-Baghawī in *Al-Anwār fī Shamāʾil-in-Nabiyyil-Mukhtār* (no. 1209), and An-Nasāʾī in *As-Sunanul-Kubrā* (no.7081), ʿAbd ibn Humayd in his *Musnad* (no. 365: *'Muntakhab'*), At-Tabarānī in *Al-Muʿjamul-Kabīr* (7/6367), and Bahshal in *Tārīkh Wāsit* (pp. 51-52), by way of Salamah ibn Nubayt: from Nuʿaym ibn Abī Hind: from Nubayt ibn Sharīt: from Sālim ibn ʿUbayd (and he mentioned a long story).

I say: This is a *'sahīh'* chain of narration, and it was declared *'sahīh'* by our Shaikh Al-Albānī (رَحِمَهُ ٱللَّهُ) in *Mukhtasarush-Shamāʾil*; and it has a witness as a hadīth of Abū ʿAsīb (or it is said: Abū ʿAsīm) with it, reported by Ahmad (5/81), Ibn Saʿd in *At-Tabaqātul-Kubrā* (2/252 and 263) and Abū Nuʿaym Al-Asbahānī in *Maʿrifatus-Sahābah* (5/2969/6921), and others with a *'sahīh'* chain; and another witness as a hadīth of ʿAbdullāh ibn

ʿAbbās (رَضِيَ اللَّهُ عَنْهُ) with it, reported by Ibn Is-hāq in *As-Sīrah* (4/1303), and from him by Ibn Mājah (1/520-521/no.1628), with a chain of narration that is *'hasan'* as a witness since it contains Husayn ibn ʿAbdillāh who is weak.

Endnote 95 – Source: Page 228

(SH) In *Al-Bahr Az-Zakhkhār* (5/394-396/2028): Muhammad ibn Ismāʿīl Al-Ahmasī narrated to us: ʿAbdur-Rahmān ibn Muhammad Al-Muhāribī related to us: from Ibnul Asbahānī: that he informed him: from Murrah: from Ibn Masʿūd with it (...). And in summary, the chain of Al-Bazzār is extremely weak because of the weakness of Ibnul Asbahānī, meaning: ʿAbdul-Malik (...) and there is speech about Al-Muhāribī.

So in conclusion the hadīth is a fabrication (*mawdūʿ*), and is not authentic, and Allāh knows best.

Endnote 96 – Source: Page 234

(DB) An-Nawawī said in his explanation of the hadīth: "The scholars of military expeditions differ about the number of his military expeditions and the armies which he sent. So Ibn Saʿd and others mention their number in detail, in their order, and they number twenty-seven military expeditions and fifty-six army detachments sent.

They said: 'And he fought during nine of his military expeditions, and they are: Badr, Uhud, Al-Muraysīʿ, Al-Khandaq, Qurayzah, Khaybar, Al-Fat-h, Hunayn, and At-Tāʾif.'

So they counted Al-Fat-h [the Conquest of Makkah] amongst them, and this was upon the view of those who say that Makkah was conquered by force; and we have already mentioned the disagreement regarding that. So perhaps Buraydah meant, by his saying that he fought in eight of them, to exclude the Conquest (of Makkah), and that his view was that it was taken peacefully — as was said by Ash-Shāfiʿī and those who agreed with him."

Endnote 97 – Source: Page 234

Al-Hāfidh Ibn Hajr said in *Fat-hul-Bārī* (7/328), in explanation of hadīth no. 3949: "Ibn Saʿd widened the affair until he numbered the military expeditions upon which Allāh's Messenger went out himself as being twenty-seven, and he was following Al-Wāqidī in that. This accords with the number given by Ibn Is-hāq; however, he did not separate Wādī Al-Qurā from Khaybar. As-Suhaylī indicated this, and it is as if the six additional ones are like that."

Endnote 98 – Source: Page 238

(BJ)(SZ) Al-Bukhārī reported it (nos. 3636 and 4865) and Muslim (no. 2800), from ʿAbdullāh ibn Masʿūd (رَضِيَ اللَّهُ عَنْهُ).

Also, Al-Bukhārī (no. 3637) and Muslim (2802) reported it from Anas (رَضِيَ اللَّهُ عَنْهُ).

Also Al-Bukhārī (no. 3638) and (no. 2803) reported it from Ibn ʿAbbās (رَضِيَ اللَّهُ عَنْهُمَا).

Also Muslim reported it (no. 2801) from ʿUmar (رَضِيَ اللَّهُ عَنْهُ).

Also, At-Tirmidhī reported it (no. 3289), and Ahmad (4/81), and Ibn Hibbān (no. 6497) from Jubayr ibn Mutʿim, and as a hadīth of Hudhayfah (رَضِيَ اللَّهُ عَنْهُ) [*Sahīh Al-Isnād: Sahīh Sunanit-Tirmidhī*, no. 3289].

Also Ibn Abī Shaybah, Abū Nuʿaym in *Al-Hilyah*, and Ibn Jarīr reported it, as occurs in *Ad-Durrul-Manthūr* (6/134).

All of them mentioned the splitting of the moon, but they did not mention the Quraysh questioning those around them.

Their questioning those around them is reported by Ibn Jarīr At-Tabarī in his *Tafsīr* (11/545/no. 32699), and Al-Bayhaqī in *Ad-Dalāʾil* (2/266) from Ibn Masʿūd (رَضِيَ اللَّهُ عَنْهُ).

Endnote 99 – Source: Page 239

(SH) Reported by At-Tayālisī in his *Musnad* (no. 351), Ibn Abī Shaybah in his *Musnad* (nos. 379 and 462), Ibn Hibbān in his *Sahīh* (nos. 6504 and 7061: *'Ihsān'*), Abū Ya'lā in his *Musnad* (nos. 4985, 5096 and 5311) and others with chains of narration from 'Āsim ibn Abin-Nujūd: from Zirr ibn Hubaysh: from Ibn Mas'ūd, with it.

I say: This chain of narration is *'hasan'*; 'Āsim is *'sadūq'* (truthful) who has some mistakes, as occurs in *At-Taqrīb*.

And it was declared *'sahīh'* by Adh-Dhahabī in *As-Siyar* (1/465); and by the author in *Al-Bidāyah wan-Nihāyah* (3/195: *Al-Ma'ārif* edn.); and by Shaikh Ahmad Shākir in his checking of *Al-Musnad* (nos. 3598 and 3599); and by our Shaikh, the Imām Al-Albānī (رَحِمَهُ ٱللَّهُ) in *Sahīh Mawārididh-Dham'ān* (no. 1804).

Endnote 100 – Source: Page 239

(SH) Reported by Abū Nu'aym in *Ma'rifatus-Sahābah* (no 2265) who said: Al-Hasan ibn Anas narrated to us: Ahmad ibn Hamdān narrated to us: Yahyā ibn Nadlah narrated to us: Hizām ibn Hishām narrated to us: from his father Hishām ibn Hubaysh: from his father Hubaysh ibn Khālid, with it, within a long story.

I say: And this is a *'hasan'* chain of narration. Yahyā ibn Nadlah was *'sadūq'*, *'hasan'* in hadīth; and Hishām ibn Hubaysh was a Companion, as Ibn Hibbān said in *Ath-Thiqāt*, and Al-Hāfidh affirmed it in *Al-Isābah*, contrary to some people of the present day.

And it has other chains of narration from Hizām ibn Hishām, reported by At-Tabarānī in *Al-Mu'jamul-Kabīr* (no. 3605) and *Al-Ahādīthut-Tiwāl* (no. 30); and Al-Ājurrī in *Ash-Sharī'ah* (no. 1020); and Abū Nu'aym in *Dalā'ilun-Nubuwwah* (pp. 282-285); and Al-Hākim in *Al-Mustadrak* (no. 4333), and from him by Al-Bayhaqī in *Dalā'ilun-Nubuwwah* (1/276-281), and others, by way of Mihraz ibn Al-Mahdī, and Ayyūb ibn Al-Hakam, and Sālim ibn Muhammad, from Hizām with [the narration].

It also has witnesses from ahādīth of Abū Bakr As-Siddīq, and Qays ibn An-Nu'mān, and Jābir ibn 'Abdillāh (رَضِيَ ٱللَّهُ عَنْهُمْ).

Al-Hāfidh Ibn Kathīr said in *Al-Bidāyah wan-Nihāyah* (4/472): "And her story is well-known, being reported through chains of narration which strengthen each other."

Endnote 101 – Source: Page 239

(SH) Ibn Is-hāq mentioned it in *As-Sīrah* (2.23) without a chain of narration; and Ibn Sa'd narrated it in *At-Tabaqātul-Kubrā* (4/237), by way of Al-Wāqidī; and Ibn Jarīr in his *Tārīkh* (3/402) by way of Al-Kalbī, and these two are accused of lying.

So in summary, the hadīth is not authentic.

Endnote 102 – Source: Page 239

(BJ)(SZ) Reported by Al-Bukhārī (nos. 240, 520, 2934, and 3185), and Muslim (no. 1794), as a hadīth of Ibn Mas'ūd; and they were, as occurs in the two *Sahīhs*: Abū Jahl, 'Utbah ibn Rabī'ah Shaybah ibn Rabī'ah, Al-Walīd ibn 'Utbah, Umayyah ibn Khalaf, and 'Uqbah ibn Abī Mu'ayt. Then he said: "And he mentioned the seventh, and we have not remembered him."

Endnote 103 – Source: Page 239

(SH) Reported by Al-Hārith ibn Abī Usāmah in his *Musnad* (2/562/511: *Bughyatul-Bāhith*); and by way of him by Abū Nu'aym Al-Asbahānī in *Ma'rifatus-Sahābah* (5/2972/ no.6926), and Al-Hākim in *Al-Mustadrak* (2/539), and Al-Bayhaqī in *Dalā'ilun-Nubuwwah* (2/338): from Al-'Abbās ibn Al-Fadl Al-Azraq: Al-Aswad ibn Shaybān narrated to us: Abū Nawfal ibn Abī 'Aqrab narrated to us: from his father who said: Lahab ibn Abī Lahab used to abuse the Prophet (صَلَّى ٱللَّهُ عَلَيْهِ وَسَلَّمَ) and call against him. He said: *"So the Prophet (صَلَّى ٱللَّهُ عَلَيْهِ وَسَلَّمَ) said..."* and he mentioned it.

I say: this is a very weak (*da'īf jiddan*) chain of narration. It contains Al-'Abbās ibn Al-Fadl, about whom Al-Bukhārī said: *"His hadīth are gone"*, and Ibn Ma'īn said: *"A foul liar."*

Al-Hākim said: "This is a hadīth with a 'sahīh' chain of narration, and the two of them do not report it!"

And Adh-Dhahabī agreed!

And Al-Hāfidh said in *Fat-hul-Bārī* (4/39): "And it is a *'hasan'* hadīth! Reported by Al-Hākim."

And Al-Bayhaqī said: "This is what 'Abbās ibn Al-Fadl (and he is not so strong) said: *'Lahab ibn Abī Lahab'*, whereas the scholars of the military expeditions say: *"Utbah ibn Lahab'*, and some of them said: *"Utaybah'*."

I say: Abū 'Ubayd Al-Harawī said in *Gharībul-Hadīth* (2/169), and taking from him Al-Bayhaqī in *Al-Kubrā* (5/211): "Do you not see that they relate in the military expeditions that 'Utbah ibn Abī Lahab (...) and he mentioned it."

However, Ibnut-Turkumānī corrected him in *Al-Jawharun-Naqiyy* by saying: "Al-Bayhaqī was silent about it, in agreement with Abū 'Ubayd, and he mentioned from Ibnus-Salāh that he said: The saying *"Utbah'* is a mistake that has been made, and this incident occurred for 'Utaybah — the brother of 'Utbah. This is mentioned by the people of awareness of lineages and military expeditions. As for 'Utbah, then he remained until he accepted Islām on the Day of the Conquest, and he is mentioned in the books of the Companions (رَضِيَ ٱللَّهُ عَنْهُ)."

And the hadīth has witnesses; however, they are not authentic at all.

Refer to: *Al-Khilāfiyyāt* (1/241-242), and *Takhrījul-Ahādīth wal-Āthāril-Wāqi'ah fī Tafsīril-Kashshāf* of Az-Zayla'ī (3/377-378).

Endnote 104 – Source: Page 240

(SH) Reported by Ibn Is-hāq in *As-Sīrah* (2/609: Ibn Hishām), and from him by Al-Amawī in his *Maghāzī*, as occurs in *Al-Bidāyah wan-Nihāyah*

(3/284): Az-Zuhrī narrated to me: from ʿAbdullāh ibn Thaʿlabah ibn Suʿayr.

I say: This is a *'hasan'* chain of narration, and Ibn Is-hāq is a proof in military expeditions, and he has clearly stated that he had it narrated to him directly.

And it is reported by At-Tabarī in *Jāmiʿul-Bayān* (9/136), Ibn Abī Hātim in his *Tafsīr* (5/1672/no. 8906), At-Tabarānī in *Al-Muʿjamul-Kabīr* (nos. 3127 and 3128) and in *Al-Awsat* (no. 9097), etc.

I say: This is a weak chain of narration; this Mūsā [ibn Yaʿqūb Az-Zamʿī] was *'sadūq'* with a poor memory — as occurs in *At-Taqrīb.*

It also has a witness as a hadīth of Ibn ʿAbbās, reported by At-Tabarānī in *Al-Muʿjamul-Kabīr* (no. 11750).

And in summary, the hadīth is *'sahīh lighairihi'* (authentic because of its supporting narrations), and Allāh knows best.

Endnote 105 – Source: Page 240

(BJ)(SZ) It is *'hasan'*: Reported by Ahmad in *Al-Musnad* (5/335/no. 3310), Ibn Saʿd in *At-Tabaqāt* (4/15), At-Tabarī in his *Tārīkh* (2/463), Al-Bayhaqī in *Ad-Dalāʾil* (3/142-143), and Abū Nuʿaym in *Ad-Dalāʾil* (no. 409), all of them as a hadīth of Ibn ʿAbbās. These chains of narrations are not without points of criticism; and it has a witness as a hadīth of ʿĀʾishah — reported by Al-Hākim (3/324), and from him by Al-Bayhaqī in *As-Sunan* (6/322).

(SH) In summary the hadīth is *'hasan'* at the very least, when its chains of narration and witnesses are gathered, and Allāh knows best.

Endnote 106 – Source: Page 240

(SH) Reported by At-Tabarānī in *Al-Muʿjamul-Kabīr* (17/58/no.120), and Ibn Mandah in *Al-Maʿrifah* — as occurs in *Al-Isābah* (3/36-37), by way of Abdur-Razzāq: Jaʿfar ibn Sulaymān related to us: from Abū ʿImrān Al-Jūnī — I do not know it except from Anas Mālik with it.

I say: This is a *'hasan'* chain of narration.

And At-Tabarānī reported it in *Al-Muʿjamul-Kabīr* (17/54-56/118), and Abū Nuʿaym Al-Asbahānī in *Maʿrifatus-Sahābah* (4/2095/5269) and in *Dalāʾilun-Nubuwwah* (p. 413), by way of Ibn Is-hāq: Muhammad ibn Jaʿfar ibn Az-Zubayr narrated it to me — in *'muʿdal'* form (with at least two successive missing links).

However, Ibn Is-hāq reported it in *As-Sīrah* (2/640-64: Ibn Hishām): Muhammad ibn Jaʿfar ibn Az-Zubayr narrated to me: from ʿUrwah ibn Az-Zubayr, with it, in *'mursal'* form; and this *'mursal'* report has a *'sahīh'* chain of narration.

And it has a further witness from a *'mursal'* report of Ibn Shihāb Az-Zuhrī, reported by At-Tabarānī in *Al-Muʿjamul-Kabīr* (17/56-58/119), and Abū Nuʿaym Al-Asbahānī in *Maʿrifatus-Sahābah* (4/2093-2095/ 5267).

And it is a *'mursal'* report with a *'sahīh'* chain of narration.

It has a second witness from a *'mursal'* report of ʿIkrimah, reported by Ibn Saʿd in *At-Tabaqātul-Kubrā* (4/187): ʿAffān ibn Muslim narrated to us: from Hammād ibn Salamah: from Thābit: from ʿIkrimah with it; and this also is *'mursal'* with a *'sahīh'* chain of narration.

So, in summary, the hadīth is *'sahīh'* because of a combination of these factors, and Allāh knows best.

Endnote 107 – Source: Page 240

(SH) Reported by Abū Nuʿaym Al-Asbahānī in *Dalāʾilun-Nubuwwah* (p. 418): Ibrāhīm ibn Is-hāq Al-Harbī narrated to us: from Yūsuf ibn Bahlūl: from ʿAbdullāh ibn Idrīs: from Muhammad ibn Is-hāq: from ʿĀsim ibn ʿUmar ibn Qatādah: from Mahmūd ibn Labīd: from Qatādah ibn An-Nuʿmān with it.

I say: This is a *'sahīh'* chain of narration; its narrators are reliable, except that Ibn Is-hāq is a *'mudallis'* and performs *"anʿanah'*.

However, he is supported: Imām Mālik ibn Anas also narrated it from ʿĀsim. This is reported by Ibn Shāhīn and Ad-Dāraqutnī — as occurs in *Al-Isābah* (3/225), and Ibn ʿAsākir in *Tārīkh Dimashq* (52/189-190), by way of ʿAlī ibn Harb At-Tāʾī: from ʿAbdur-Rahmān ibn Yahyā Al-ʿUdhrī Al-Madanī with it.

However this ʿAbdur-Rahmān is not strong — as Ad-Dāraqutnī said; and Al-ʿUqaylī said: *"Unknown"*; and Ibn ʿAdiyy said: *"He narrates strange reports from reliable narrators"*; and Abū Ahmad Al-Hākim said: *"He is not relied upon."*

The hadīth has another chain of narration, reported by At-Tabarānī in *Al-Muʿjamul-Kabīr* (19/15/12 and 13). I say: And this is a weak chain of narration; ʿUmar ibn Qatādah is not known except by the narration of his son from him, as Adh-Dhahabī said; and there occurs in *At-Taqrīb*: *"(Maqbūl) Acceptable only if supported."*

And the hadīth has two witnesses.

The second is a *'mursal'* report from ʿĀsim ibn ʿUmar ibn Qatādah with it. Ibn Saʿd reported it in *At-Tabaqātul-Kubrā* (3/419) and by way of Ibn Is-hāq — and it occurs in his *Sīrah* (2/82: Ibn Hishām): from ʿĀsim with it; and its chain of narration is *'hasan'* as a witness.

So in summary the story, when the preceding chains of narration are gathered, is *'hasan'* at the very least — if Allāh wills.

Then it is also related that this incident happened with Qatādah on the Day of Badr! But what is correct is that it occurred at Uhud.

Endnote 108 – Source: Page 241

(BJ)(SZ) Reported by Ibn Is-hāq (3/180) who said: Saʿīd ibn Mīnāʾ narrated to us: that it was narrated to him that the daughter of Bashīr ibn Saʿd, the daughter of An-Nuʿmān ibn Bashīr, and he mentioned it; and by way of him Al-Bayhaqī reported it in *Ad-Dalāʾil* (3/427), and its chain of narration is disconnected.

Ibn Kathīr said in *As-Sīratun-Nabawiyyah* (3/190): "Ibn Is-hāq reported it, and it is disconnected."

Endnote 109 – Source: Page 241

(SH) Reported by At-Tirmidhī (5/685-686/no. 3839), Ahmad (2/352), Is-hāq ibn Rāhawaih in his *Musnad* — and from him Ibn Hibbān in his *Sahīh* (14/467/no. 6532: 'Ihsān'), and by way of Hammād ibn Zayd; and Abū Nu'aym Al-Asbahānī in *Dalā'ilun-Nubuwwah* (pp. 371-372), by way of Ayyūb As-Sakhtiyānī: both of them from Muhājir ibn Makhlad (the mawlā of Abī Bakrah): from Abul-'Āliyah: from Abū Hurairah with it. At-Tirmidhī said: "This is a *'hasan gharīb'* hadīth through this chain."

I say: It is just as he said, since its narrators are all reliable, the narrators of the two *Sahīh*, except for this Muhājir — about whom they differ. Wuhayb ibn Khālid said: *"He did not memorize."*

Abū Hātim said: "He was weakish. He was not such (in strength). He was not fully precise. His narrations may be noted."

And As-Sājī said: "He was a known, generally acceptable narrator (*sadūq*), those who said that he is unknown, then this is nothing."

Ibn Ma'īn said: *"Suitable"* and he was declared reliable by Ibn Hibbān. Ibn Shāhīn, and Al-'Ijlī; and Ibn Hibbān declared narrations of his *'sahīh'*, and At-Tirmidhī declared them *'hasan'*. So at the very least, he is *'sadūq'* (truthful) and his narrations are *'hasan'*.

It is also reported by Ahmad (2/324) by way of Ismā'īl ibn Muslim Al-'Abdī: from Abul-Mutawakkil An-Nājī: from Abū Hurairah — with it; and its chain of narration is *'sahīh'* to the standard of Muslim.

(DB) The wording of At-Tirmidhī is: from Abū Hurairah, who said: "I came to the Prophet (صَلَّىٰ ٱللَّهُ عَلَيْهِ وَسَلَّمَ) with some dates, and said: *'O Messenger of Allāh! Supplicate to Allāh to put blessing in them for me.'* So he held them and then he supplicated for me for blessing in them, and he said to me:

> 'Take them and put them in this leather bag of yours' — or *'in this leather bag'* — 'Whenever you want to take something from it, enter your hand into it and take it; and do not scatter it out.'

So I have taken many camel-loads from it in Allāh's cause. So we used to eat from it and feed others, and it would not leave my waist. This continued until the day when 'Uthmān was killed, when it broke."

Shaikh Al-Albānī (رَحِمَهُ ٱللَّهُ) said : "Its chain of narration is *'hasan'*."

Endnote 110 – Source: Page 242

[BJ][SZ][SH] Reported by Al-Bukhārī (no. 1020) and Muslim (2798), as a hadīth of ʿAbdullāh ibn Masʿūd (رَضِيَ ٱللَّهُ عَنْهُ).

[DB] A narration of Al-Bukhārī (no. 1007) has the wording: "When the Prophet (صَلَّى ٱللَّهُ عَلَيْهِ وَسَلَّمَ) saw the people refusing to accept Islām, he said:

> 'O Allāh! Give them seven years of famine, like the seven years of Yūsuf.'

So a famine struck them, which wiped out everything to the extent that they started eating animal hides, carcasses, and rotting dead animals. One of them would look to the sky and see what appeared to be smoke because of hunger. So Abū Sufyān went to him and said: *'O Muhammad! You command obedience to Allāh and maintaining ties of kinship, and your people are dying. So supplicate to Allāh for them.'*"

Endnote 111 – Source: Page 244

[BJ][SZ] It is *'sahīh'*: Reported by Ahmad in *Al-Musnad* (4/296/no. 2495), At-Tirmidhī (no. 3193), Al-Bukhārī in *Khalq Afʿālil-ʿIbād* (no. 115), and An-Nasāʾī in *Al-Kubrā*: *At-Tafsīr* (no. 11839), and others, as a hadīth of Ibn ʿAbbās.

[BJ][SZ][SH] And from Niyār ibn Mukram Al-Aslamī (رَضِيَ ٱللَّهُ عَنْهُ) — reported by At-Tirmidhī (5/344-345/ no. 3194), Al-Bukhārī in *At-Tārīkhul-Kabīr* (8/139-140), [and others] — and this chain of narration is *'hasan'*.

Endnote 112 – Source: Page 245

[BJ][SZ] Reported by Al-Bukhārī (no. 3120) and Muslim (no. 2918), as a hadīth of Abū Hurairah; and by Al-Bukhārī (no.3121) and Muslim (no. 2919), as a hadīth of Jābir ibn Samurah; and by Al-Bukhārī (no. 3595), as a hadīth of ʿAdiyy ibn Hātim.

Endnote 113 – Source: Page 245

(SH) The saying of the author (رَحِمَهُ ٱللَّهُ) *'and that is what happened'* is debatable from a number of angles:

Firstly: The Messenger (صَلَّى ٱللَّهُ عَلَيْهِ وَسَلَّمَ) informed that the rulership of his nation would reach whatever was shown to him from the earth, and he was shown the whole of it, but the rulership of the nation of Islām has not covered the whole earth. However, it will cover it, as Allāh wills.

Secondly: Allāh's Messenger (صَلَّى ٱللَّهُ عَلَيْهِ وَسَلَّمَ) informed that the rulership of his nation and his Religion would reach whatever is reached by the night and the day. So this emphasizes the first meaning: that the rulership of the nation of Islām will cover the whole of the globe — if Allāh wills, and news of it will be known after a time.

Thirdly: The ahādīth that show that the future is for Islām, which are *'mutawātir'* (reported by large numbers of narrators at every stage of transmission), emphasize the point that this will occur after the *'biting kingship'* and the *'tyrannical kingship'*.

Fourthly: There are ahādīth where Allāh's Messenger (صَلَّى ٱللَّهُ عَلَيْهِ وَسَلَّمَ) informed of the conquest of many lands, and these had not been realized by the time of the author. However some of them were realized after him, such as: the conquest of Constantinople; and some of them will come to be realized, if Allāh wills, such as the conquest of Rome; the Capital of Italy, and the city of the Vatican.

So what has preceded emphasizes the fact that what had occurred by the time of the author was just a part of what the Messenger (صَلَّى ٱللَّهُ عَلَيْهِ وَسَلَّمَ) informed of, and not all of it. However, it shall occur, by the permission of the Guardian Lord (the Mighty and Majestic) in spite of all the enemies of Allāh.

Endnote 114 – Source: Page 245

(BJ)(SZ) The ahādīth about fighting the Khawārij are *'mutawātir'*. To see them, refer to *As-Sunnah* of Ibn Abī 'Āsim (nos. 936-977).

536

(SH) As for the hadīth of Dhuth-Thudayyah, then it was reported by Al-Bukhārī (no. 3610), as a hadīth of Abū Sa'īd; and by Muslim (no. 1066/155), as a hadīth of 'Alī (رَضِيَ اللَّهُ عَنْهُمَا).

(BJ)(SZ) In the Sulaymāniyyah Library manuscript (no. 3339), the bracketed part occurs before the part about Al-Hasan ibn 'Alī.

Endnote 115 – Source: Page 246

(SH) Imām An-Nawāwī said in *Sharh Sahīh Muslim* (18/28): "A great fire appeared in our time in Al-Madīnah, in the year 654H. It was a tremendously huge fire, and came from the eastern side of Al-Madīnah, beyond the lava-plain. Knowledge of it is widespread amongst the people of Shām and the rest of the lands, and I have been informed about it by someone from the people of Al-Madīnah who witnessed it."

Endnote 116 – Source: Page 247

(BJ)(SZ) Reported by Al-Bukhārī (no. 2125) from 'Atā' ibn Yasār who said: "I met 'Abdullāh ibn 'Amr ibn Al-'Ās (رَضِيَ اللَّهُ عَنْهُمَا) and said: *'Tell me about the description of Allāh's Messenger in the Tawrāt.'*

He said: 'Indeed, by Allāh! He is described in the Tawrāt with some of the qualities mentioned about him in the Qur'ān:

> "O Prophet! We have sent you as a witness, a bearer of glad tidings, a warner, and a guardian for the illiterate ones. You are My Slave and My Messenger. I have called you the One Who depends (upon Allāh). He is not coarse, nor severe, nor one who shouts out in the market places. He does not repel an evil with an evil. Rather, he pardons and forgives."'"

Endnote 117 – Source: Page 253

(SH) Reported by 'Abdur-Razzāq in *Al-Musannaf* (3/410), and by way of 'Umārah ibn Al-Muhājir and 'Awn ibn Muhammad: both of them from Umm Ja'far bint Muhammad: from Asmā' bint 'Umays, with it.

Al-Jawriqānī said: "This is a hadīth which is well known, and *'hasan'*."

Al-Hāfidh said in *At-Talkhīsul-Habīr* (2/143): "Its chain of narration is *'hasan'*; Ahmad and Ibnul-Mundhir used it as evidence, and their stating it outright is a proof that they held it to be authentic."

Our Shaikh, Imām Al-Albānī — the Imām (رَحِمَهُ ٱللَّهُ) said in *Irwā'ul-Ghalīl* (3/162): "It is *hasan*. Its narrators are reliable and well known, except for this Umm Ja'far."

Endnote 118 – Source: Page 254

(SH) Ibn Sa'd reported it in *At-Tabaqātul-Kubrā* (8/53 & 169), and Abū Dāwūd in his *Sunan* (2/242-243/no. 2135), by way of Ahmad ibn Yūnus, Abū Bilāl Al-Ash'arī, 'Abdullāh ibn Wahb, and Al-Wāqidī; all four of them from Ibn Abiz-Zinād: from Hishām ibn 'Urwah: from his father: from 'Ā'ishah with it, as part of a story.

I say: And this is a *'hasan'* chain of narration, because Ibn Abiz-Zinād is *'sadūq'*, as occurs in *At-Taqrīb*. Al-Hākim said: *"This is a hadīth with a 'sahīh' chain of narration, and the two of them did not report it"* — and Adh-Dhahabī agreed with him.

And it was declared *'hasan'* by our Shaikh, the Imām Al-Albānī (رَحِمَهُ ٱللَّهُ) in *Al-Irwā'* (7/85), and the basis of the hadīth occurs with Al-Bukhārī (no. 5212) and Muslim (no. 1463), however it does not clearly state the reason for the coming down of the Āyah.

The author (رَحِمَهُ ٱللَّهُ) said in *Al-Bidāyah wan-Nihāyah* (8/73), whilst mentioning the events of the year 54H: "Ibnul-Jawzī mentioned her having died in this year, whereas Ibn Abī Khaythamah said: *'She died at the end of the khilāfah of 'Umar ibn Al-Khattāb'* — so Allāh knows best."

Endnote 119 – Source: Page 254

(DB) Imām An-Nawawī said in *Tahdhībul-Asmā' wal-Lughāt* (2/613): "She died at the end of the khilāfah of 'Umar (may Allāh be pleased with him and her), and this is the saying of most people; and Muhammad ibn Sa'd mentioned from Al-Wāqidī that she died in Shawwāl of the year

54H, in the khilāfah of Muʿāwiyah ibn Abī Sufyān, in Al-Madīnah. Al-Wāqidī said: *'That is sounder in our view, and Allāh knows best.'*"

Endnote 120 – Source: Page 255

(DB) An-Nawawī quoted in *Tahdhībul-Asmā' wal-Lughāt* (2/624-625) from Khalīfah ibn Khayyāt and others that Allāh's Messenger (صَلَّى ٱللَّهُ عَلَيْهِ وَسَلَّمَ) married her in Shawwāl of the fourth year.

Al-Hāfidh Ibn Hajr said in *Al-Isābah*: "He (i.e. Abū Salamah) died in Al-Madīnah after they had returned from Badr, this was stated by Ibn Mandah. However, Ibn Is-hāq said that it was after Uhud, and this is what is correct."

He also said in *Al-Isābah*: Abū Bakr ibn Zanjawaih said: Abū Salamah died in the fourth year after the Hijrah, after returning from Uhud. A wound that he suffered at Uhud burst open and he died from it, and Allāh's Messenger (صَلَّى ٱللَّهُ عَلَيْهِ وَسَلَّمَ) was present at his funeral. The same was said by Ibn Saʿd: that he was present at Badr and at Uhud, where he was wounded. Then the Prophet (صَلَّى ٱللَّهُ عَلَيْهِ وَسَلَّمَ) sent him in charge of an army detachment against Banū Asad in the fourth year. Then he returned and his wound burst open, and he died in Jumādal-Ākhirah. This was the saying of the majority, such as Ibn Abī Khaythamah, Yaʿqūb ibn Sufyān, Ibn Al-Buraqī, At-Tabarī, and others."

Endnote 121 – Source: Page 262

(BJ)(SZ) *Sunanut-Tirmidhī* (no. 841), Ahmad (6/392), Ibn Hibbān (9/438/no1430), Ad-Dārimī (2/38) [...] and others. At-Tirmidhī said: "A *'hasan'* hadīth; we do not know anyone to have reported it in fully connected form besides Hammād ibn Zayd: from Matar Al-Warrāq: from Rabīʿah."

I say: Its chain of narration contains Matar Al-Warrāq, who had a poor memory.

It was also reported by Mālik (Al-Hajj: 1/348), and from him by At-Tahāwī (2/272), and Ibn Saʿd (8/133): from Rabīʿah ibn Abī ʿAbdir-

Rahmān: from Sulaymān ibn Yasār (the mawlā of Maymūnah) in *'mursal'* form.

(SH) And in summary what is correct about the hadīth is that it is *'mursal'*. And the connected narration is not authentic — its chain is broken, since Sulaymān ibn Yasār did not reach Abū Rāfi' — as Ibn 'Abdil-Barr said. Then I saw that Imām Ahmad ibn Hanbal (رَحِمَهُ ٱللَّهُ) declared this hadīth of ours to be weak because of its being mursal.

Endnote 122 – Source: Page 262

(BJ)(SZ) Al-Bukhārī (no. 268) from Anas.

Al-Hāfidh said in *Al-Fat-h* (1/449), concerning his saying: *"And they were eleven"*:

> "This is reported only by Mu'ādh ibn Hishām: from his father; and Sa'īd ibn Abī 'Arūbah and others reported it from Qatādah, saying: *'Nine wives...'*"

Then he said:

"However, the narration of Hishām is taken to mean that he included Māriyah and Rayhānah — and she was a captive from Banū Qurayzah — along with them, and used the word *'wives'* to refer to the majority from them.

Ibnul-Qayyim said (1/114): "And there is no disagreement about the fact that he died and left nine behind, and used to share the nights between eight of them: 'Ā'ishah, Hafsah, Zaynab bint Jahsh, Umm Salamah, Safiyyah, Umm Habībah, Maymūnah, Sawdah, and Juwayriyah."

Endnote 123 – Source: Page 262

(DB) Ibn Hazm mentioned in *Jawāmi'us-Sīratin-Nabawiyyah* (1/31), after mentioning his marriage to Hafsah: "Then he married Zaynab bint Khuzaymah ibn Al-Hārith ibn 'Abdillāh ibn 'Amr ibn 'Abd Manāf ibn Hilāl ibn 'Āmir ibn Sa'sa'ah. Before him, she was married to 'Ubaydah ibn Al-Hārith ibn Al-Muttalib ibn 'Abd Manāf, who was killed on the

Day of Badr. Zaynab died during his (صَلَّى ٱللَّهُ عَلَيْهِ وَسَلَّمَ) lifetime, two months after he took her as his wife."

Az-Zuhrī said: "Rather, she was previously married to ʿAbdullāh ibn Jahsh Al-Asadī, who was martyred on the Day of Uhud."

Al-Hāfidh ibn Hajr said in *Al-Isābah* (4/309): "She was known as Ummul-Masākīn (the mother of the poor and needy) because she used to feed them and spend in charity upon them. He (صَلَّى ٱللَّهُ عَلَيْهِ وَسَلَّمَ) married her in the month of Ramadān in the third year. So she remained with him for eight months, and she died in Rabīʿul-Ākhir in the fourth year."

Endnote 124 – Source: Page 266

It is *'daʿīf'*: Reported by Abū Dāwūd (no. 2935), An-Nasāʾī in *Al-Kubrā* (nos. 1355 &1356), At-Tabarī in his *Tafsīr* (6/94/no. 24849), At-Tabarānī in *Al-Kabīr* (12/170/no. 1279), Ibn ʿAdiyy in *Al-Kāmil* (7/2662), and Al-Bayhaqī (10/126): all of them as a hadīth of Ibn ʿAbbās; and it has a witness from Ibn ʿUmar (whom there is speech concerning), reported by Al-Khatīb in his *Tārīkh* (8/175), and Abū Nuʿaym in *Maʿrifatus-Sahābah* (3/1453/3684).

Ibnul-Qayyim said: "I heard our Shaikh, Ibn Taimiyyah, say: 'This hadīth is a fabrication (*mawdūʿ*); Allāh's Messenger is not known to have ever had a scribe called As-Sijill, and the scribes of the Prophet are well-known, and they do not include anyone called As-Sijill; and His Saying (He the Most High):

> يَوْمَ نَطْوِي السَّمَاءَ كَطَيِّ السِّجِلِّ لِلْكُتُبِ
>
> MEANING: "The Day when We shall roll up the heavens just as a written scroll is rolled up," **[Sūrah Al-Anbiyāʾ (21): 104]**

— was sent down in Makkah, and the Messenger did not have any scribe in Makkah; and *'As-Sijill'* is a written parchment.'"

Endnote 125 – Source: Page 267

(SH) (No. 85), saying: Muʿādh narrated to us: from ʿAwn: from ʿUmayr ibn Is-hāq with it. I say: This is a *'mursal'* narration with a *'sahīh'* chain. And it has a witness from a hadīth of Anas ibn Mālik, reported by Ibn Hibbān in his *Sahīh* (10/357-358/4504 — *Ihsān*) [and others] by way of ʿAlī ibn Bahr: from Marwān ibn Muʿāwiyah: from Humayd: from Anas, with it.

And this is a *'sahīh'* chain, its narrators are reliable, and our Shaikh Al-Imām Al-Albānī (رَحِمَهُ ٱللَّهُ) declared it *'sahīh'* in *Sahīh Mawārididh-Dhamʾān* (no.1351).

(DB) This hadīth contains the clear statement of Allāh's Messenger (صَلَّىٰ ٱللَّهُ عَلَيْهِ وَسَلَّمَ) concerning Hiraql:

> "The enemy of Allāh has lied! He is not a Muslim, he remains upon his Christianity."

Endnote 126 – Source: Page 267

(SH) This part is also by Al-Bukhārī, along with the previous report. Al-Bukhārī said: "I think that Ibn Al-Musayyib said: *'So Allāh's Messenger (صَلَّىٰ ٱللَّهُ عَلَيْهِ وَسَلَّمَ) made supplication against them that they be torn to pieces.'*"

Al-Hāfidh said in *Al-Fat-h* (8/127): "It occurs through all the chains in *'mursal'* form, and it is possible that Ibn Al-Musayyib heard it from ʿAbdullāh ibn Hudhāfah — the companion of the incident, since Ibn Saʿd mentioned from his hadīth that he said: *'So he read to him the letter of Allāh's Messenger (صَلَّىٰ ٱللَّهُ عَلَيْهِ وَسَلَّمَ), and he took it and tore it up.'*"

And it has a witness from a hadīth of At-Tannūkhī, reported by Ahmad in his *Musnad* (3/441-442) [and others] by way of ʿAbdullāh ibn ʿUthmān ibn Khuthaym: from Saʿīd ibn Abī Rāshid: from At-Tannūkhī with it.

I say: This chain is *'hasan'* as a supporting chain, Saʿīd ibn Abī Rāshid is acceptable if supported, as occurs in *At-Taqrīb*.

So in summary the hadīth is *'hasan lighairihi'* when these two chains are gathered.

Endnote 127 – Source: Page 268

(DB) Ibnul Qayyim said in *Zādul-Ma'ād* (1/134): "And from camels he had were: Al-Qaswā' (*'The One with Clipped Ears'*), it is said that it is the one which he migrated upon; and 'Adbā' (*'The One with a Lopped Ear'*); and Al-Jad'ā' (*'The One with a Cut Nose'*) — and they did not have lopped ears or cut noses; rather they were just called that; or it is said: they had lopped ears, and were as a result named that. Also were Al-'Adbā' and Al-Jad'ā' one, or two?

There is disagreement concerning this. Al-'Adbā' was the one that could not be beaten in a race, and then a bedouin came upon a young riding-camel of his and surpassed it. So this grieved the Muslims, so Allāh's Messenger (صَلَّى ٱللَّهُ عَلَيْهِ وَسَلَّمَ) said:

> 'It is upon Allāh that He does not elevate anything from this world except that He (then) lowers it.'" [Al-Bukhārī (no. 2872)]

Endnote 128 – Source: Page 268

(SH) Reported by Abū Dāwūd (3/308/3608), An-Nasā'ī in *Al-Mujtabā* (7/301-302), and in *Al-Kubrā* (6/73-74/6198), Ibn Abī 'Āsim in *Al-Āhād wal-Mathānī* (4/116/2085), Ahmad (5/215-216) [and others] through chains of narration from Az-Zuhrī: from 'Umārah ibn Khuzaymah Al-Ansārī: that his paternal uncle — who was from the Companions of the Prophet (صَلَّى ٱللَّهُ عَلَيْهِ وَسَلَّمَ) — narrated it to him.

I say: And this chain of narration is *'sahīh'*.

Endnote 129 – Source: Page 272

(SH) A group of the scholars wrote on the *"shamā'il"* (characteristics of the Prophet صَلَّى ٱللَّهُ عَلَيْهِ وَسَلَّمَ), from them:

- *Akhlāqun-Nabī* of Shaikh Abū Bakr Muhammad ibn 'Abdillāh Al-Warrāq (d. 249H)
- *Akhlāqun-Nabī* of Abū Hātim Muhammad ibn Hibbān Al-Bustī (d. 354H)

- *Akhlāqun-Nabī* of Abush-Shaikh Al-Asbahānī (d. 369H)
- *Shamā'ilun-Nabī* of Abul-ʿAbbās Jaʿfar ibn Muhammad An-Nasafī (d. 432H)
- *Al-Anwār fī Shamā'ilin-Nabiyyil-Mukhtār* of Al-Baghawī (d. 516H)
- *Ash-Shamā'il* of Abul-Hasan ʿAlī ibn Muhammad Al-Fazārī, who was well known as Ibnul-Muqri' Al-Gharnātī (d. 552H).

Endnote 130 – Source: Page 274

DB See *Daʿīf Sunan Ibn Mājah* (no. 703/3564). In *As-Sahīhah* (no. 633) Shaikh Al-Albānī declares *'sahīh'* the hadīth of Anas (رَضِوَٱللَّهُعَنْهُ): "The Prophet (صَلَّىٱللَّهُعَلَيْهِوَسَلَّمَ) used to apply kohl to his right eye three times, and to his left eye twice." Reported by Ibn Saʿd [1/484], Abush-Shaikh in *Akhlāqun-Nabī (صَلَّىٱللَّهُعَلَيْهِوَسَلَّمَ)* [p. 183], and others.

He also declared *'sahīh'* the hadīth of Jābir (رَضِوَٱللَّهُعَنْهُ) that Allāh's Messenger (صَلَّىٱللَّهُعَلَيْهِوَسَلَّمَ) said: Use ithmid (antimony sulphide) when going to sleep, since it brightens the eyesight and causes the eyelashes to sprout." Reported by Ibn Abī Shaybah (8/599/5684), Ibn Mājah (no. 3496), Al-Mukhallas, Ibn ʿAdiyy in *Al-Kāmil* (143/2) and others. [*As-Sahīhah* no. 724].

Endnote 131 – Source: Page 274

DB See *Sahīh Al-Bukhārī* (no. 376). Ibnul-Qayyim said in *Zādul-Maʿād* (1/137): "And he wore a red outfit (hullah), and a *'hullah'* is a waist-wrapper (izār) and a cloak (ridā'). A *'hullah'* is a name only applied to the two garments together; and whoever thinks that it was purely red not mixed with another colour, is mistaken. Rather, the red outfit consisted of two woven Yemeni garments, which had red and black stripes, just like the rest of the striped Yemeni garments."

At-Tabārānī reported in *Al-Awsat* (no. 7609) from Ibn ʿAbbās who said: "Allāh's Messenger (صَلَّىٱللَّهُعَلَيْهِوَسَلَّمَ) used to wear a red outfit on the day of ʿEid." Shaikh Al-Albānī said in *As-Sahīhah* (no. 1279): "This is a good chain of narration."

Endnote 132 – Source: Page 277

[SH] Reported by Abū Dāwūd in his *Sunan* (no. 4847); At-Tirmidhī in his *Sunan* (no. 2814 in abridged form), and in *Ash-Shamā'il* (nos. 66 & 127); and Al-Bukhārī in *Al-Adabul-Mufrad* (no. 1178), by way of ʿAbdullāh ibn Hassān: from his two grandmothers — Safiyyah and Duhaybah: from Qaylah — with it. I say: And this is a *'hasan'* chain of narration.

[DB] Its wording has: "She saw Allāh's Messenger (صَلَّى ٱللَّهُ عَلَيْهِ وَسَلَّمَ) sitting in the manner of *'Al-Qurfusā'* (sitting upon the buttocks, with the legs upright and the hands wrapped around them)." [*ʿAwnul-Maʿbūd*]

Endnote 133 – Source: Page 277

[SH] Reported by Abū Yaʿlā in his *Musnad* (6/120/no. 3393) [...] from ʿAbdullāh ibn Abī Bakr Al-Muqaddamī: from Jaʿfar ibn Sulaymān: from Thābit: from Anas with it. Al-Haythamī said in *Majmaʿuz-Zawāid* (6/169): "Abū Yaʿlā reported it, and it contains ʿAbdullāh ibn Abī Bakr Al-Muqaddamī, and he is weak."

It was also reported by Ibn Is-hāq in *As-Sīrah*, as occurs in *Al-Bidāyah wan-Nihāyah* (6/547), and from him by Al-Bayhaqī in *Dalā'ilun-Nubuwwah* (5/68): "ʿAbdullāh ibn Abī Bakr narrated to me that Allāh's Messenger (صَلَّى ٱللَّهُ عَلَيْهِ وَسَلَّمَ)" — and he mentioned it. This is a weak chain of narration as it is *'mursal'*.

So overall, the hadīth with these two chains combined is *'hasan lighairihi'* — if Allāh wills.

Endnote 134 – Source: Page 279

[SH] This wording, i.e. *'The Lord — the Perfect — drew near'* is a mistake from Sharīk ibn ʿAbdullāh ibn Abī Namir. Our Shaikh, the Imām, Al-Albānī (رَحِمَهُ ٱللَّهُ) said in *Al-Isrā wal-Miʿrāj* (pp. 33-34):

....

"It is as if it was for this reason that Muslim does not quote the wording of his hadīth, as has preceded. Therefore, Ibn Kathīr said in his *Tafsīr*:

> 'And it is as Muslim said, because Sharīk ibn 'Abdillāh ibn Abī Namir reported contradictory things concerning this hadīth, and his memory became poor, and he did not precisely preserve it, as will be explained in the other ahādīth. Others declare this to have been a dream, as a preparation for what was to follow, and Allāh, knows best.'

And Al-Hāfidh Al-Bayhaqī said: "In the hadīth of Sharīk there is an addition which he is alone in reporting, upon the position of those who claim that he (صَلَّىٰ اللَّهُ عَلَيْهِ وَسَلَّمَ) saw his Lord (the Mighty and Majestic) meaning his saying: *'Then the Exalted and All-Mighty Compeller, the Lord of Might and Honour, approached and drew near:*

> فَكَانَ قَابَ قَوْسَيْنِ أَوْ أَدْنَىٰ
>
> MEANING: *"And he was at a distance of two lengths, or even nearer."*''" — **Sūrah An-Najm (53): 9**

He (Al-Bayhaqī) said: "And the saying of 'Ā'ishah, Ibn Mas'ūd, and Abū Hurayrah, who took these verses to mean his (صَلَّىٰ اللَّهُ عَلَيْهِ وَسَلَّمَ) seeing Jibrīl is more correct."

So what Al-Bayhaqī (رَحِمَهُ اللَّهُ) said about this matter is the truth, since Abū Dharr said: "O Messenger of Allāh! Have you seen your Lord?"

He said: *"Light! How could I see Him?!"* And in one narration: *"I saw light."* Reported by Muslim.

And His Saying:

> ثُمَّ دَنَا فَتَدَلَّىٰ
>
> MEANING: "Then he approached and drew near"

This refers to Jibrīl (عَلَيْهِ السَّلَامُ), as is established in the two *Sahīhs* from 'Ā'ishah, the Mother of the Believers, and from Ibn Mas'ūd. Likewise it occurs in *Sahīh Muslim* from Abū Hurairah, and no one from the

Companions is known to have disagreed with them in this explanation of the Āyah."

Endnote 135 – Source: Page 281

(SH) Reported by Ibn Hibbān in *Al-Majrūhīn* (1/225), and from him by Ibnul-Jawzī in *Al-Mawdū'āt* (1/113) by way of Bakr — this one, with it.

Ibn Hibbān said: "Bakr ibn Ziyād Al-Bāhilī was a shaikh who was a '*dajjāl*' (great liar): he used to fabricate ahādīth upon reliable narrators. It is not permissible to mention him in books, except in order to speak against him."

And he said about this hadīth of ours: "This is something which even the common folk from the people of hadīth will have no doubt about that it is a fabrication (*mawdū'*), then how about the precise verifiers of this affair?!" And Ibnul-Jawzī agreed with him.

Imām Adh-Dhahabī said in *Al-Mīzān* (1/435): *"Ibnul-Jawzī has spoken truly,"* and he said in *Talkhīsul-Mawdū'āt* (20/8): *"Bakr is a dajjāl."*

And Al-Qādī Badruddīn ibn Jamā'ah said in his book *At-Tanzīh fī Ibtāl Hujajit-Tashbīh*, as also occurs in *Tanzīhush-Sharī'ah* (1/137): "This is a very weak hadīth."

Endnote 136 – Source: Page 286

(BJ)(SZ) It is '*hasan lighairihi*': It was reported by At-Tirmidhī (no. 2053), Ahmad (5/340: no 3316), Ibn Shaybah (8/82, 84), and Al-Hākim (4/209) from Ibn 'Abbās, and its chain of narration contains 'Abbād ibn Mansūr who is '*da'īf*'.

However, it has a supporting witness from a hadīth of Anas, reported by Ibn Mājah (no. 3478); and its chain of narration is '*da'īf*'.

It also has a supporting witness from a hadīth of Ibn Mas'ūd, reported by At-Tirmidhī (no. 2052); and its chain of narration is '*da'īf*', containing 'Abdur-Rahmān ibn Is-hāq Al-Wāsitī who is weak.

It also has a supporting witness from a hadīth of Mālik ibn Sa'sa'ah, reported by At-Tabarānī in *Al-Kabīr* (19/no.600), and Al-Haythamī said: "At-Tabarānī reported it in *Al-Awsat* and in *Al-Kabīr*, and its narrators are those of the *Sahīh*."

And it has a supporting witness from a hadīth of Ibn 'Umar, reported by Al-Bazzār, as occurs in *Kashful-Astār* (3/388/no.3020).

Al-Haythamī said (5/91): "It contains 'Attāf ibn Khālid and he was *'thiqah'* (reliable), and there is some speech against him."

I say: And Ibn 'Abbās is mentioned in place of Ibn 'Umar: Shaikh Nāsir [ud-Dīn Al-Albānī] mentioned it in *As-Sahīhah* (no. 2262).

Endnote 137 – Source: Page 286

(SH) I have not seen it with this wording, and what is well known is that the one who said this to him was Ibrahīm Al-Khalīl (صَلَّى اللَّهُ عَلَيْهِ وَسَلَّمَ). So Ahmad (5/418) reported it, and Al-Hārith ibn Abī Usāmah in his *Musnad* (2/949/1047: *'Bughyah'*), and Al-Hāfidh said: *"This is a 'hasan' hadīth',"* and Al-Mundhirī said in *At-Targhīb wat-Tarhīb*: *"Its chain of narration is 'hasan'."*

Al-Haythamī said in *Majma'uz-Zawā'id* (10/97): "The narrators of Ahmad are the narrators of the *Sahīh*, except for 'Abdullāh ibn 'Abdir-Rahmān ibn 'Abdillāh ibn 'Umar ibn Al-Khattāb, and he was reliable. No one spoke against him, and he was declared reliable by Ibn Hibbān.

Our Shaikh, Al-Imām Al-Albānī (رَحِمَهُ اللَّهُ) said in *As-Sahīhah* (1/215-216): "So based upon the declaration of reliability by Ibn Hibbān he reported this hadīth in his *Sahīh*, and he said in *At-Targhīb*: *'Its chain of narration is 'hasan'.*"

I say: That is suspect in my view, because of what we have repeatedly confirmed — that Ibn Hibbān's declarations of reliability contain weakness."

– End –

I say: It is just as he (Al-Albānī) (رَحِمَهُ ٱللَّهُ) said, however the hadīth is alright as a narration, which has supports.

So from its supporting witnesses is what is reported by At-Tirmidhī (5/510/3462), At-Tabarānī [...] by way of ʿAbdul-Wāhid ibn Ziyād: from ʿAbdur-Rahmān ibn Is-hāq: from Al-Qāsim ibn ʿAbdir-Rahmān: from his father: from Ibn Masʿūd with it, tracing it back to the Prophet (صَلَّى ٱللَّهُ عَلَيْهِ وَسَلَّمَ).

At-Tabarānī said: "No one reports it from Al-Qāsim except for ʿAbdur-Rahmān ibn Is-hāq, nor from him except for ʿAbdul-Wāhid."

At-Tirmidhī said: "This is a hadīth which is *'hasan'*, but singular reported in this manner."

Al-Hāfidh said: "And he declared it *'hasan'* on account of its witnesses, and he declared it singular in a restricted sense, for ʿAbdur-Rahmān ibn Is-hāq was declared by them to be weak, and he is Abū Shaybah Al-Wāsitī."

This was the weakness mentioned for it by our Shaikh (رَحِمَهُ ٱللَّهُ) in *As-Sahīhah* (1/215).

So in summary the hadīth with these two chains combined is *'hasan'* at the very least, and it has other witnesses.

Endnote 138 – Source: 288

[SH] Reported by Ibn Is-hāq, as occurs in *Sīrah Ibn Hishām* (2/602). He said: *"It has been related to me from some men of Banū Salimah: that they mentioned that Al-Hubāb..."* — and this chain of narration is *'daʿīf'*, containing a string of weaknesses, and it was declared weak by our Shaikh [Al-Albānī] (رَحِمَهُ ٱللَّهُ) in his notes to *Fiqhus-Sīrah* (p. 240). And refer necessarily to *Difāʿ ʿanil-Hadīthin-Nabawī was-Sīrah* (pp. 81-83) by him.

And it has a witness from a hadīth of Al-Hubāb, reported by Al-Hākim (3/426-427), and it was declared weak by Adh-Dhahabī; and a hadīth of Ibn ʿAbbās, as occurs in *Al-Bidāyah wan-Nihāyah* (3/167). However they are not satisfactory because of their severe weakness.

So in summary the hadīth is not authentic, even when its witnesses are gathered, and Allāh knows best.

Endnote 139 – Source: Page 288

(SH) Reported by Al-Bazzār in his *Musnad* (3/286/2759: *'Kashf'*), and At-Tabarānī [...] by way of Muhammad ibn Al-Hajjāj Al-Lakhmī: from Mujālid: from Ash-Sha'bī: from Ibn 'Abbās, with it.

Ibn 'Adiyy said: "No one narrates this hadīth from Mujālid with this chain except for this Muhammad ibn Al-Hajjāj."

Al-Bayhaqī said: "This is reported by Muhammad ibn Al-Hajjāj Al-Lakhmī alone, and Muhammad ibn Al-Hajjāj is abandoned (*matrūk*)."

And the hadīth has many witnesses, but they are not authentic at all. [...] So in summary the hadīth is *'munkar'* and not authentic, and its witnesses only increase it in weakness.

Endnote 140 – Source: Page 289

(BJ)(SZ) The hadīth of the Jinn hearing from Allāh's Messenger (صَلَّىٰاللَّهُعَلَيْهِوَسَلَّمَ) in the market place of 'Ukāz is reported by Al-Bukhārī (nos. 773 & 4921) and Muslim (no. 449), as a hadīth of Ibn 'Abbās.

As for the narration of Ibn Mas'ūd, then it is narrated by Muslim (no. 450), and it contains the wording: "'Alqamah said: I asked Ibn Mas'ūd, saying: *'Did any of you witness the night of the Jinn along with Allāh's Messenger (صَلَّىٰاللَّهُعَلَيْهِوَسَلَّمَ)?'* So he said: *'No, however we were with Allāh's Messenger one night and we missed him. So we looked throughout the valleys and the mountain passes... so in the morning we found him in the direction of Hirā...'*" — until the end of the hadīth.

As for Ibn Mas'ūd awaiting the Messenger in a place with a circle drawn around it, then it has many chains of narration. Individually none of them is free from criticism, however together they reach the level of being *'hasan'*.

It is reported by Ahmad in *Al-Musnad* (7/367/no. 4353), Ad-Dāraqutnī (1/77), At-Tahāwī in *Sharh Mā'āniyyil-Āthār* (1/95) by way of 'Alī ibn Zayd: from Abū Rāfi': from Ibn Mas'ūd.

So its isnād contains 'Alī ibn Zayd ibn Jud'ān who is *'da'īf'*; and it is not established that Abū Rāfi' heard from Ibn Mas'ūd.

It is also reported by Ahmad (7/390/no. 4381), and At-Tabarānī (10/79/9966) by way of Abū Fazārah: from Abū Zayd the mawlā of 'Amr ibn Hurayth: from Ibn Mas'ūd. Its isnād contains Abū Zayd who is unknown.

And At-Tirmidhī reported it (no. 2861) by way of 'Uthmān: from Ibn Mas'ūd, and At-Tirmidhī said: "It is *'hasan sahīh'*."

And Ahmad reported it (6/332/no. 3788), by way of 'Amr Al-Bakkālī: from Ibn Mas'ūd — and its chain of narration is weak, since it is not established that 'Amr Al-Bakkālī heard from Ibn Mas'ūd.

And Al-Bayhaqī reported it in *Ad-Dalāil* (2/231), by way of Mūsā ibn 'Alī ibn Rabāh: from his father: from Ibn Mas'ūd.

And At-Tabarī reported it in the exegesis of Sūratul-Ahqāf (11/297/no. 31317), by way of Ma'mar: from Yahyā ibn Abī Kathīr: from 'Abdullāh ibn 'Amr ibn Ghaylān: from Ibn Mas'ūd; and 'Abdullāh ibn 'Amr is unknown. It has other chains of narration in *Tafsīr At-Tabarī.*

And the harmonization between the two narrations is that the first refers to a time when no one was with him, and on the second occasion Ibn Mas'ūd went out with him. So it occurred on more than one occasion, and Allāh knows best. Refer to *Fat-h Al-Bārī* (8/542/no. 4921).

Endnote 141 – Source: Page 297

[SH] Abū 'Awānah reported in his *Sahīh* (4/227/6605), and others, by way of Mu'ādh ibn Hishām Ad-Dastuwā'ī: from his father: from Qatādah: from Sa'īd ibn Al-Musayyib: from Abū Hurairah (رَضِيَ ٱللَّهُ عَنْهُ): that the Prophet (صَلَّى ٱللَّهُ عَلَيْهِ وَسَلَّمَ) said: "A Prophet from the Prophets went on a military expedition with his companions and said: *'No man from amongst you should follow me who has built a house but not taken up occupancy of it;*

nor one who has married a woman but has not consummated the marriage with her, and has a need to return.'"

"So he encountered the enemy at the time of the setting of the sun, and he said: *'O Allāh! It is under orders and I am under orders, so withhold it for me until You settle the affair between me and them!'* So Allāh withheld it for him, and they gained victory. So they gathered the spoils of war, but the fire did not consume it."

(He said): "And when they took the war spoils, fire would be sent upon it, and it would consume it." Declared *'sahīh'* by Shaikh Al-Albānī in *As-Sahīhah* (1/396).

DB For a longer and more detailed narration, refer to *Sahīhul-Bukhārī* (no. 3124).

Endnote 142 – Source: Page 300

DB Ibn Abil-ʿIzz in his *Sharhul-ʿAqīdatit-Tahāwiyyah* (pp. 229-235) mentions that Intercession (Ash-Shafāʿah) is of eight categories:

1. The Major Intercession, for judgement to be passed upon the people so that they are relieved from the standing;
2. His (صَلَّىٰٱللَّهُعَلَيْهِوَسَلَّمَ) intercession for those whose good and evil deeds are equal, so that they should be entered into Paradise:
3. His (صَلَّىٰٱللَّهُعَلَيْهِوَسَلَّمَ) intercession for the sinful Believers who deserve to enter the Fire, that they should not enter it;
4. His (صَلَّىٰٱللَّهُعَلَيْهِوَسَلَّمَ) intercession for the ranks of people of Paradise to be raised higher than was necessitated by the reward for their deeds;
5. His (صَلَّىٰٱللَّهُعَلَيْهِوَسَلَّمَ) intercession for some of the Believers to enter Paradise without any reckoning;
6. His (صَلَّىٰٱللَّهُعَلَيْهِوَسَلَّمَ) intercession for his uncle Abū Tālib, that his punishment in the fire be lessened in intensity;
7. His (صَلَّىٰٱللَّهُعَلَيْهِوَسَلَّمَ) intercession for the Believers to be entered into Paradise;

8. His (صَلَّى ٱللَّٰهُ عَلَيْهِ وَسَلَّمَ) intercession for those Believers guilty of major sins who have entered the Fire, that they be taken out from it.

Endnote 143 – Source: Page 300

DB This is the wording in the printed edition with the checking of Muhammad Al-'Eid Al-Khatrāwī and Muhiyyuddīn Mustū, and they add a footnote: "In the manuscript there occurs: *'Then after that he will have other intercessions, from them are four for rescuing...'* — but what is correct is what we have affirmed.

Also, there occurs in *Sharhul-Mawāhib* (5/342): 'And the wording used by An-Nawawī is:

> "The Prophet (صَلَّى ٱللَّٰهُ عَلَيْهِ وَسَلَّمَ) will have five intercessions: The Greater Intercession for the passing of judgement; and for a group of people to enter Paradise without any reckoning and for some people who deserved to enter the Fire, that they do not enter; and for some people who have entered the Fire, that they come out from it; and for the raising of the levels of some people in Paradise."'"

Endnote 144 – Source: Page 303

SH It is reported as a hadīth of Ibn 'Abbās, and Anas, and Ibn 'Umar, and Abū Hurairah, and Safiyyah, and Abū Bakr.

However, they are all unauthentic and not sufficient to establish this as a quality particular to the Prophet (صَلَّى ٱللَّٰهُ عَلَيْهِ وَسَلَّمَ).

The author (رَحِمَهُ ٱللَّٰهُ) said in *Al-Bidāyah wan-Nihāyah* (2/265): "Some have claimed that it is authentic, because of the chains of narration for it — to the extent that some of them have claimed that it is *'mutawātir'*! But all of this is suspect."

I say: Al-Hākim claimed in *Al-Mustadrak* (2/602) that it is *'mutawātir'*, but Adh-Dhahabī rebutted him with his saying: "I do not know that to be (even) authentic, so what about its being *mutawātir*?!"

And it was also declared to be *'da'īf'* by Imām Ibn Qayyim Al-Jawziyyah in *Zādul-Ma'ād* (1/81: Ar-Risālah Edn.).

So in summary, the hadīth is not established, and for a detailed discussion of that refer to my notes upon *Tuhfatul-Mawdūd* of Ibnul-Qayyim (pp. 334-341).

Endnote 145 – Source: Page 304

(SH) Reported by 'Abdur-Razzāq in his *Tafsīr* (1/2/372), and from him by 'Abd ibn Humayd in his *Musnad* (3/92-93/1183: *'Muntakhab'*), and Ahmad (3/164), At-Tirmidhī (5/301/3131) [...] Ma'mar narrated to us: from Qatādah: from Anas, with it.

I say: This chain is *'sahīh'* to the standard of the two Shaikhs.

At-Tirmidhī said: "This hadīth is *'hasan gharīb'*."

And our Shaikh, Imām Al-Albānī (رَحِمَهُ ٱللَّهُ) declared it *'sahīh'* in *Al-Isrā' wal-Mi'rāj* (p. 37).

Endnote 146 – Source: Page 304

(BJ)(SZ) Reported by Muslim (no. 384), as a hadīth of 'Abdullāh ibn 'Amr ibn Al-'Ās (رَضِيَ ٱللَّهُ عَنْهُ), and it begins: "When you hear the mu'adhdhin then say the like of what he says. Then supplicate for salāt upon me, since whoever supplicates for salāt upon me a single time then Allāh sends salāt upon him ten times over. Then ask Allāh to grant me *'Al-Wasīlah'*; for it is a level in Paradise that is not befitting except for a single servant from the servants of Allāh, and I hope that I am he. So whoever asks for *Al-Wasīlah* for me, then Intercession is binding for him."

Endnote 147 – Source: Page 305

(SH) The author (رَحِمَهُ ٱللَّهُ) is indicating what is authentic from the Prophet (صَلَّى ٱللَّهُ عَلَيْهِ وَسَلَّمَ) :

> "My nation will not unite upon misguidance."

And in a wording:

> "Allāh will never gather my nation (or he said: *'this nation'*) upon misguidance."

Reported by At-Tirmidhī (4/466/2166-in abridged form), and Al-Hākim (1/116), and from him by Al-Bayhaqī in *Al-Asmā' was-Sifāt* (2/136/702), [and others] — by way of 'Abdur-Razzāq: Ibrāhīm ibn Maymūn related to us: 'Abdullāh ibn Tāwūs narrated to me: from his father: from 'Abbās, with it.

I say: And this is a *'sahīh'* chain of narration..

Our Shaikh, Al-Imām Al-Albānī (may Allāh sanctify his soul — قَدَّسَ اللهُ رُوحَه) declared it *'sahīh'* in *Mishkātul-Masābīh* (1/135: *'Hidāyah'*).

Endnote 148 – Source: Page 307

SH [Reported] in his (Ibn Mājah's) *Sunan* (2/1434/4291). Our Shaikh, Al-Imām Al-Albānī (رَحِمَهُ ٱللَّهُ) said in *Ad-Da'īfah* (6/64/2549): "And this is a very weak chain of narration. Al-Hāfidh said concerning Ibn Abil-Musāwir: *'Abandoned, and declared by Ibn Ma'īn to be a liar';* and Jubārah ibn Al-Mughallis is weak. This was the weakness mentioned by Al-Būsayrī in *Az-Zawā'id* (mss. 265/1), and this is a clear case of falling short.

And the hadīth occurs in *Sahīh Muslim* (8/104/[2767]), and Ahmad (4/402 & 410) through chains of narration from Abū Burdah [from Abū Mūsā Al-Ash'arī] with it, from the Prophet (صَلَّى ٱللَّهُ عَلَيْهِ وَسَلَّمَ) with the wording: "On the Day of Resurrection Allāh (the Mighty and Majestic) will give a Jew or a Christian to every Muslim, and He will say: *'This is your ransom from the Fire.'*"

Endnote 149 – Source: Page 307

BJ SZ Reported by Muslim (no. 856), from Abū Hurairah and Hudhayfah that Allāh's Messenger (صَلَّى ٱللَّهُ عَلَيْهِ وَسَلَّمَ) said: *"Allāh misguided those who came before us away from the Jumu'ah..."*

Then he said:

> "And likewise, they will be followers to us on the Day of Resurrection. We are the last ones from the people of this world, and we will be the first ones on the Day of Resurrection; those upon whom judgement will be passed before the rest of the creation."

(SH) And Al-Bukhārī (no. 238) and Muslim (no. 855) reported, as a hadīth of Abū Hurairah (رَضِيَ ٱللَّهُ عَنْهُ), from the Prophet (صَلَّى ٱللَّهُ عَلَيْهِ وَسَلَّمَ):

> "We are the last ones, and we shall be the first ones on the Day of Resurrection; and we are the first ones who will enter Paradise."

Endnote 150 – Source: Page 308

(BJ)(SZ) It is *'hasan lighairihi'*: Reported by At-Tirmidhī (no. 2443), Al-Bukhārī in his *Tārīkh* (1/44), Ibn Abī 'Āsim in *As-Sunnah* (1/497/ no. 751), and At-Tabarānī in *Al-Kabīr* (7/256/no. 681), all of them by way of Samurah ibn Jundab. At-Tirmidhī said: *'[It is] gharīb (singular)'* — and it has another chain of narration from Samurah, reported by At-Tabarānī (7/312/no. 7053) with a weak chain of narration; and it has a witness from a hadīth of Abū Sa'īd Al-Khudrī, reported by Abū Nu'aym in *Akhbār Asbahān* (1/110) with a weak chain of narration; and it has a further witness from Ibn 'Abbās reported by Ibn Abid-Dunyā in *Al-Ahwāl*; and another witness from 'Awf ibn Mālik.

Our Shaikh Nāsir [ud-Dīn Al-Albānī] mentioned it in *As-Sahīhah* (no. 1589), and mentioned another mursal report, and then said: "And in summary, the hadīth, with its chains combined is *'hasan'* or *'sahīh'*, and Allāh knows best."

As for the Reservoir (Hawd) of the Prophet (صَلَّى ٱللَّهُ عَلَيْهِ وَسَلَّمَ), then it is *mutawātir*. Refer to *Sahīh Muslim* (nos. 1792-1802) and *As-Sunnah* of Ibn Abī 'Āsim (1/473-521).

Endnote 151 – Source: Page 309

(SH) Reported by At-Tirmidhī in his *Sunan* (4/98/1023: *Tuhfatul-Ahwadhī*), and in *Ash-Shamā'il* (400-481/391), [and others] by way of

ʿAbdur-Rahmān ibn Abī Bakr: from Abī Mulaykah: from ʿĀʾishah: from Abū Bakr, with it.

At-Tirmidhī said: "This is a *'gharīb'* hadīth, and ʿAbdur-Rahmān ibn Abī Bakr Al-Mulaykī is declared weak on account of his memory. And this hadīth is reported through other lines of transmission. Ibn ʿAbbās narrated it: from Abū Bakr As-Siddīq: from the Prophet (صَلَّى ٱللَّهُ عَلَيْهِ وَسَلَّمَ)."

And the narration of Ibn ʿAbbās which At-Tirmidhī indicated was reported by Ibn Mājah (no. 1628), and from him by Abū Yaʿlā in his *Musnad* (1/31-32/22 & 32/23) [and others] by way of Ibn Is-hāq (and it is in his *Sīrah:* 4/1303): Husayn ibn ʿAbdillāh narrated to me: from ʿIkrimah: from Ibn ʿAbbās; with it.

Al-Hāfidh Ibn Hajr said in *Fat-hul-Bārī* (1/529): "Its chain contains Husayn ibn ʿAbdillāh Al-Hāshimī, and he is weak."

And it has another witness, which is a *'mursal'* narration of ʿAbdul-ʿAzīz ibn Juraij. This is reported by ʿAbdur-Razzāq in *Al-Musannaf* (3/516-517/6534), and from him by Ahmad in *Al-Musnad* (1/7) [and others] from Juraij: my father narrated it to me. And its chain of narration is good.

In addition, it has another (witness) reported by Ibn Saʿd in *At-Tabaqātul-Kubrā* (2/292,) with a *'sahīh'* chain from ʿĀʾishah who said:

> "When the Prophet (صَلَّى ٱللَّهُ عَلَيْهِ وَسَلَّمَ) died, they said: *'Where should he be buried?'* Abū Bakr said: *'In the place where he died.'*"

This is a *'mawqūf'* report with a *'sahīh'* chain, and it carries the ruling of having come from the Prophet (صَلَّى ٱللَّهُ عَلَيْهِ وَسَلَّمَ), as will not be hidden.

And it has a third witness from a hadīth of Sālim ibn ʿUbayd Al-Ashjaʿī, who was a Companion, with it. It was reported by At-Tirmidhī in *Ash-Shamāʾil* (489-492/399), [and others].

Al-Hāfidh said in *Al-Fat-h* (1/529): "Its chain is *'sahīh'*, however it is *'mawqūf'*."

I say: However, it carries the ruling of having come from the Prophet (صَلَّى ٱللَّهُ عَلَيْهِ وَسَلَّمَ).

So, in summary, the hadīth is established when its chains and witnesses are combined.

(DB) The hadīth was declared *'sahīh'* by Shaikh Al-Albānī in *Sahīh Sunanit-Tirmidhī* (no. 1018).

Endnote 152 – Source: Page 310

(SH) Al-Hāfidh Ibn Hajr said in *Fat-hul-Bārī* (12/8): "As for what is famous in the books of the people of Al-Usūl and others, with the wording: *'We, the assembly of Prophets, are not inherited from'* (نَحْـنُ مَعَـاشِرَ الأَنبِيَـاء لَا نُـورَث), then it has been criticized as being unauthentic by a group of the imāms. And that is the case with regard to the particular wording *'nahnu'* (نَحْـنُ)."

However, the hadīth is established with the wording: *'We the assembly of Prophets...'* (إِنَّـا مَعَـاشِرَ الأَنبِيَـاء). It was reported by Imām Ahmad in his *Musnad* (2/463), and Al-Humaydī in his *Musnad* [and others] by way of Sufyān ibn 'Uyainah: from Abuz-Zinād: from Al-A'raj: from Abū Hurairah: from the Prophet (صَلَّىٰاللَّهُعَلَيْهِوَسَلَّمَ), with it.

I say: This is a chain of narration *'sahīh'* to the standard of the two Shaikhs.

Endnote 153 – Source: Page 311

(BJ)(SZ) It is *'sahīh'*: Reported by Abū Ya'lā (6/147/no. 3425), and Al-Bazzār — as occurs in *Kashful-Astār* (3/100/nos. 3339 & 2340), and Abū Nu'aym in *Akhbār Asbahān* (2/38), and Ibn 'Adiyy in *Al-Kāmil* (2/739). Al-Haythamī said (8/211): "Abū Ya'lā and Al-Bazzār reported it and the narrators of Abū Ya'lā are reliable."

And it is declared *'sahīh'* by Shaikh Nāsir [i.e. Al-Albānī] in *As-Silsilatus-Sahīhah* (no. 621).

And it is witnessed to by the hadīth of Anas, reported by Muslim (no. 2375): "I passed by Mūsā on the night when I was taken on the Night Journey, and he was standing praying in his grave, by the red sandhill."

Endnote 154 – Source: Page 315

He (the Most High) said:

> وَلَا تَمُدَّنَّ عَيْنَيْكَ إِلَىٰ مَا مَتَّعْنَا بِهِ أَزْوَاجًا مِّنْهُمْ زَهْرَةَ الْحَيَاةِ الدُّنْيَا لِنَفْتِنَهُمْ فِيهِ ۚ
> وَرِزْقُ رَبِّكَ خَيْرٌ وَأَبْقَىٰ
>
> MEANING: "And do not extend your eyes with longing towards the enjoyments which We have given to groups of the Disbelievers, from the splendour of the world, in order to test them with it. But the provision which your Lord has promised you in the Hereafter is better and longer lasting." — **Sūrah Tā-Hā (20): 131**

And He (the Most High) said:

> لَا تَمُدَّنَّ عَيْنَيْكَ إِلَىٰ مَا مَتَّعْنَا بِهِ أَزْوَاجًا مِّنْهُمْ
>
> MEANING: "And do not look with longing towards the enjoyments, which We have given to groups of the Disbelievers." — **Sūrah Al-Hijr (15): 88**

Endnote 155 – Source: Page 315

(BJ)(SZ) Reported by Abū Dāwūd (no. 3869), Ahmad (11/125/no. 6565 & 11/651/7081), Ibn Abī Shaybah (8/78), Al-Bayhaqī (9/355) [and others].

'At-Tiryāqī' (potions) were potions utilized to repel the effects of poison; and it is said: They were foul because snake-meat and forbidden things would be put into them.

'At-Tamīmah' ('amulet') was a string of beads which they would wear, thinking that they would repel calamities from them.

(DB) Shaikh Salīm Al-Hilālī declared its chain of narration to be *'da'īf'* because of the narrator 'Abdur-Rahmān ibn Rāfi' At-Tannūkhī, then he said: "However it has another chain of narration, reported by Ibn 'Abdil-Hakam in *Futūh Misr* (p. 255): from Abul-Aswad An-Nadr ibn

ʿAbdil-Jabbār: from Ibn Lahīʿah: from Sharāhīl ibn Yazīd: from Hanash ibn ʿAbdillāh As-Sanʿānī: from ʿAbdullāh ibn ʿAmr — with it, as part of a story.

I say: This is a *'hasan'* chain of narration, because of the well-known speech about Ibn Lahīʿah; and An-Nadr ibn ʿAbdil-Jabbār's narrations from Ibn Lahīʿah came before his memory deteriorated and his books were burned. Furthermore, his narrations from Ibn Lahīʿah were authentic, since he wrote from an authentic manuscript, just as Ahmad ibn Sālih Al-Misrī said, as his student Yaʿqūb ibn Sufyān quoted from him in *Al-Maʿrifah wat-Tārīkh* (2/184). So, in summary, the hadīth is *'sahīh'* when its chains are combined, and it was declared *'sahīh'* by Shaikh Ahmad Shākir in his explanation and checking of the *Musnad* (10/71/6565)."

Shaikh Al-Albānī said in *Daʿīf Sunan Abī Dāwūd*: "It is *'daʿīf.'*"

Endnote 156 – Source: Page 316

In *As-Sunanul-Kubrā* (7/42-43), and At-Tabarānī in *Al-Muʿjamul-Kabīr*, and from him by Adh-Dhahabī in *Tadhkiratul-Huffāz* (2/742). Al-Bayhaqī said: "So this is a hadīth which is *'munqati'* (disconnected), and its narrators contain a group of weak and unknown people, and Allāh (the Most High) knows best."

Adh-Dhahabī said in *Al-Muhadhdhab fikhtisāris-Sunan* (5/2603): "Its narrators include those who are weak, along with its being disconnected."

Al-Haythamī said in *Majmaʿuz-Zawāʾid* (8/271): "At-Tabarānī reported it and said: *'This is a 'munkar' hadīth'*, and Abū ʿAqīl is *'daʿīf'*, and this is contrary to the Book of Allāh, the Most High."

Endnote 157 – Source: Page 318

(SH) Reported by Ahmad (1/65 & 70) [and others] by way of Ibn Abiz-Zinād: from his father: from ʿĀmir ibn Saʿd: *"I heard ʿUthmān say..."* — and he mentioned it. This chain of narration is *'hasan'* because of the well-known speech concerning Ibn Abiz-Zinād, whose name is ʿAbdur-

Rahmān [...] and it was reported by Ahmad (1/70) [and others] by way of Abū Bakr Al-Hanafī: from ʿAbdul-Hamīd ibn Jaʿfar: from his father: from Mahmūd ibn Labīd: from ʿUthmān, with it.

And this chain of narration is *'sahīh'*.

Endnote 158 – Source: Page 318

(SH) In his *Sunan* (5/35/no. 2659) [and others] from ʿĀsim ibn Bahdalah: from Zirr ibn Hubaysh: from Ibn Masʿūd, with it.

I say: This is a *'hasan'* hadīth, because of the well-known disagreement concerning ʿĀsim.

And At-Tirmidhī reported it (4/524/ no. 2257), and Ibn Mājah (1/13/30), [and others] by way of Simāk ibn Harb: from ʿAbdur-Rahmān ibn ʿAbdullāh ibn Masʿūd: from his father, with it.

I say: This chain of narration is *'sahīh'*, its narrators are reliable and ʿAbdur-Rahmān ibn ʿAbdillāh heard from his father, in the view of the majority of the people of knowledge.

At-Tirmidhī said: "A *'hasan-sahīh'* hadīth."

Endnote 159 – Source: Page 318

(SH) Reported by Ibn Mājah (1/13/33) [and others] from Hushaym ibn Bashīr: Abuz-Zubayr narrated to us: from Jābir, with it.

I say: This is a chain of narration that is *'sahīh'* to the standard of Muslim, except for the fact that Abuz-Zubayr was a *'mudallis'*, and he reported it with *"anʿanah'*.

However At-Tabarānī reported it in his *Juz'* (95/93), and from him by Ibnul-Jawzī (1/72), by way of Abū Hishām Ar-Rifāʿī: Ismāʿīl ibn Shuʿayb narrated to us: Mansūr ibn Dīnār narrated to us: from Yazīd Al-Faqīr: from Jābir, with it.

So in summary, the hadīth, when these two chains are gathered, is *'hasan'* — Inshā'Allāh — and its text is *'sahīh'* without a doubt — indeed it is *'mutawātir'*.

Endnote 160 – Source: Page 320

(BJ)(SZ) I have not found it in the *Sunanus-Sughrā* of An-Nasā'ī, or in *Al-Kubrā*. However, it was reported by Ahmad (1/361), Ibn Abī Shaybah in his *Musannaf* (11/56), Ibn Sa'd(1/417), and At-Tirmidhī in *Ash-Shamā'il* (no. 392): from Yazīd Al-Fārisī who said (and Yazīd used to write the mus-hafs): "I saw Allāh's Messenger in a dream, in the time of Ibn 'Abbās, so I said to Ibn 'Abbās: I saw Allāh's Messenger in a dream. Ibn 'Abbās said: *'Then Allāh's Messenger used to say: "Satan..."'"* — [and he mentioned] the hadīth. Then he said: *'Then are you able to describe to us this man whom you saw?'*"

(SH) Shaikh Al-Albānī (رَحِمَهُ ٱللَّهُ) declared it *'hasan'* in *Mukhtasarush-Shamā'il* (no. 347).

Endnote 161 – Source: Page 321

(DB) Shaikh Al-Albānī said in *Sahīh Sunan Abī Dāwūd* (no. 4359): "[It is] *sahīh*."

(BJ)(SZ)(SH) Reported by Abū Dāwūd (nos. 2683 & 4359), An-Nasā'ī (no. 4078), Abū Ya'lā (no. 757), Ibn Abī Shaybah (no. 18, 759), and Al-Hākim (3/45), by way of Asbāt ibn Nasr: from As-Suddī: from Mus'ab ibn Sa'd: from his father (Sa'd ibn Abī Waqqās).

I say: This is a weak chain of narration; Asbāt ibn Nasr was a generally acceptable narrator (*sadūq*) who made many mistakes, and he reported strange things.

However, it has a witness from a hadīth of Sa'īd ibn Yarbū' Al-Makhzūmī (with it), reported by Abū Dāwūd (no. 2684), At-Tabarānī in *Al-Kabīr* (no. 5529), [and others] by way of 'Amr ibn 'Uthmān ibn 'Abdir-Rahmān ibn Sa'īd ibn Yarbū': from his grandfather: from his father, with it.

I say: This is a weak chain of narration: ʿAmr (or it is said: ʿUmar) is *ʻmaqbūl'* (acceptable only if supported), as occurs in *At-Taqrīb.*

It has another witness from a hadīth of Anas (رَضِيَ اللَّهُ عَنْهُ) with it, reported by Ibn Abī Shaybah in his *Musnad*, as occurs in *Al-Matālibul-ʿĀliyah* (17/453/4299: Al-ʿĀsimah Edn.) [...] and in *Al-Musannaf* (no. 18782) [...] with a chain of narration which is *ʻhasan'* as a witness, since it contains Al-Hakam ibn ʿAbdil-Malik, who was weak.

And it has a third (witness) from a *ʻmursal'* narration of Saʿīd ibn Al-Musayyib, reported by Ibn Saʿd in *At-Tabaqātul-Kubrā* (2/141) with a chain of narration which is *ʻhasan'* as a witness.

So in summary, the hadīth is established when all of that is combined, if Allāh wills.

Endnote 162 – Source: Page 323

(SH) In *As-Sunanul-Kubrā* (7/49-50), At-Tabarānī in *Al-Muʿjamul-Awsat* (6/323/no. 6526), and Ibnus-Sakan in his *Sahīh* — as occurs in *Al-Badrul-Munīr* (3/144) and in *At-Talkhīsul-Habīr* (1/67), and Abū Nuʿaym Al-Asbahānī in *Fadlul-Istiyāk wa Ādābuhu* — as occurs in *Al-Imām* (1/344), by way of Ibn Wahb — with it.

I say: Its chain of narration is *ʻdaʿīf'* because of its disconnection, as the author said.

It was reported likewise by Yahyā ibn ʿAbdillāh ibn Sālim — who is *ʻsadūq'* (truthful), however he was contradicted by Ismāʿīl ibn Jaʿfar — who was *ʻthiqatun thabt'* (reliable, firm), a narrator of the two *Sahīhs* — who reported it from ʿAmr (the mawlā of Al-Muttalib): from Al-Muttalib — with it, in *ʻmursal'* form. He did not make any mention of ʿĀʾishah.

This was reported by Ibn Khuzaymah in *Hadīth ʿAlī ibn Hujr* (424/363), and from him by Abū Nuʿaym in *Fadlul-Istiyāk wa Ādābuhu* — as occurs in *Al-Imām* (1/344): ʿAlī ibn Hujr narrated to us: from Ismāʿīl, with it.

This *ʻmursal'* report has a *ʻsahīh'* chain of narration, and it is more correct than the connected report.

Endnote 163 – Source: Page 324

(SH) Reported by Ibn Abī Shaybah in *Al-Musannaf* (1/61), Ahmad in *Al-Musnad* (6/210), Abū Dāwūd in his *Sunan* (no.179), At-Tirmidhī in his *Sunan* (no. 86), Ibn Mājah in his *Sunan* (no. 502), and others — by way of Wakī': from Al-A'mash: from Habīb: from 'Urwah: from 'Ā'ishah — with it.

I say: This is a *'sahīh'* chain of narration, and it was declared *'sahīh'* by Shaikh Ahmad Shākir (رَحِمَهُ ٱللَّهُ) in *Sharh Sunanit-Tirmidhī*, and he said: "And this is a *'sahīh'* hadīth with no weakness. Some mention as a defect for it something which does not affect its authenticity."

It was also declared *'sahīh'* by our Shaikh Al-'Allāmah Al-Albānī (رَحِمَهُ ٱللَّهُ).

Endnote 164 – Source: Page 326

(SH) Reported by Ibn Abī Shaybah in *Al-Musnad* — as occurs in *Al-Matālibul-'Āliyah* [...] and from him by Ibn Mājah in his *Sunan* (1/212/645), [and others] Al-Bayhaqī in *As-Sunanul-Kubrā* (7/65): from Abū Nu'aym Al-Fadl ibn Dukayn: 'Abdul-Malik ibn Abī Ghaniyyah: from Abul-Khattāb 'Umar Al-Hajarī: from Mahdūj Adh-Dhuhlī, with it.

And Ibn Mājah did not report this exception that is mentioned.

Ibn Hazm said in *Al-Muhallā* (2/186): "And this is baseless." [...] "As for Mahdūj, then he is worthless: he reports calamitous things from Jasrah; and Abul-Khattāb Al-Hajarī is unknown."

And our Shaikh, Al-Imām Al-Albānī (رَحِمَهُ ٱللَّهُ) said in *Ad-Da'īfah* (10/720-722/no. 4973): "It is *mawdū'* (fabricated)."

"This isnād is gloomy: Abul-Khattāb is unknown, and Mahdūj is like him [...] and they differ concerning Jasrah. Al-Bukhārī said: *'She had some very strange reports'*, and no one whose declaration of reliability can be trusted has declared her reliable."

"And Ibn Mājah reported it, except he did not mention the exception at all, and it is as if he deliberately omitted it because of its being *'munkar'*.

And therefore, Ibnul-Qayyim (رَحِمَهُ ٱللَّهُ) said [in *Tahdhīb Sunan Abī Dāwūd*

(1/158)]: 'So this exception is baseless, fabricated, an addition from some of the Shī'ah extremists, and Ibn Mājah did not report it in the hadīth.'"

Endnote 165 – Source: Page 327

(SH) In *As-Sunanul-Kubrā* (7/67), and from him by Ibn 'Asākir in *Tārīkh Dimashq* (30/126) [and others] by way of Mūsā ibn Ismā'īl, with it.

Ibn Daqīqil-'Eid said: "The isnād of Al-Bazzār does not contain anyone whose condition needs examining except for Hunayd."

I say: He is unknown (*majhūlul-'ayn*); no one narrates from him except for Mūsā ibn Ismā'īl, and no one declares him reliable except for Ibn Hibbān, who is over-lenient. Therefore Al-Hāfidh Ibn Hajr said in *At-Talkhīsul-Habīr* (1/30): *"He was passable, but he was not well-known for knowledge"*, — and Adh-Dhahabī said in *As-Siyar* (3/366): *"I have not known of any criticism of Hunayd."*

Therefore the saying of Al-Haythamī in *Majma'uz-Zawā'id* (8/273): *"Abū Ya'lā reported it, and Al-Bazzār — with abridgement; and the narrators of Al-Bazzār are those of the Sahīh, except for Hunayd ibn Al-Qāsim, and he is reliable!"* — is suspect; and close to it is the saying of Al-Būsayrī: "This is a *'hasan'* hadīth"!

Then if you are surprised, be surprised at the saying of the author (رَحِمَهُ ٱللَّهُ) about Hunayd: "Abandoned in hadīth, and he was declared a liar by Ibn Ma'īn."!

So this is not to be found at all, and perhaps he confused him with another narrator, so this should be examined.

Endnote 166 – Source: Page 328

(BJ)(SZ) Al-Hāfidh Al-Bayhaqī mentioned it in his *Sunan* (7/67), without a chain of narration.

As for the hadīth of Asmā' bint Abī Bakr, then it was reported by Ad-Dāraqutnī in his *Sunan* (1/228), and by At-Tabarānī, as occurs in *At-*

Talkhīsul-Habīr (1/31); and Al-Hāfidh said: "It contains 'Alī ibn Mujāhid, and he is *'da'īf'*."

I say: Rather, he is abandoned, and his Shaikh, Rabāh is such that it is not known who he is.

As for the hadīth of Salmān, then it was reported by Abū Nu'aym in *Al-Hilyah* (1/330), and by At-Tabarānī — as occurs in *At-Talkhīs* (1/31), and its chain contains Sa'd ibn Abī Ziyād. Abū Hātim said: *"His ahādīth can be noted, but he is not strong"* — and Kaysān is not known.

Endnote 167 – Source: Page 329

(SH) Reported by Ahmad ibn Manī' in his *Musnad,* [...] Imām Ahmad (1/231), and by way of him by Abū Nu'aym Al-Asbahānī in *Hilyatul-Awliyā'* (9/232) [...] and Al-Hākim (1/300) [...] by way of Abū Badr, Shujā' ibn Al-Walīd: from Abū Janāb Al-Kalbī, with it.

Al-Hākim remained silent about it, and Adh-Dhahabī commented by saying: "I say: Al-Hākim did not speak about it, and it is *'gharīb'*, *'munkar'*, and Yahyā was declared weak by An-Nasā'ī and Ad-Dāraqutnī."

Ibnul-Jawzī said: "As for Abū Janāb, then his name is Yahyā ibn Abī Hayyah. Yahyā Al-Qattān said: *'I do not hold it lawful to narrate from him'*, and Al-Fallās said: *'Abandoned in hadīth'*."

And it was also declared weak for that reason by our Shaikh, Al-Imām Al-Albānī (رَحِمَهُ ٱللَّهُ) in *Ad-Da'īfah* (6/494), and he added: "I say: And perhaps he actually took it from some of the liars, and performed *tadlīs*, since Al-Hāfidh Ibn 'Abdil-Hādī said in *Al-Furū'* (mss. 23/2): 'A fabricated (*mawdū'*) hadīth.'"

And the hadīth has another chain. So Ahmad reported it (1/232, & 234, & 317), and 'Abd Ibn Humayd in his *Musnad* (1/512/586: *'Muntakhab'*), and Abū Ya'lā [...] and Al-Bayhaqī (7/89 & 9/264), through chains of narration from Jābir Al-Ju'fī: from 'Ikrimah: from Ibn 'Abbās — with it.

I say: This chain of narration is very weak, Jābir Al-Ju'fī is abandoned (*matrūk*) in hadīth, accused of lying.

Al-Hāfidh said: "And this is also weak, because of the weakness of Jābir,who is Ibn Yazīd Al-Ju'fī."

And it has a third chain — reported by At-Tabarānī in *Al-Mu'jamul-Kabīr* (11/295/12044) by way of Hishām ibn 'Ammār: from Hammād ibn 'Abdir-Rahmān Al-Kalbī: from Al-Mubārak ibn Abī Hamzah Az-Zubaydī: from 'Ikrimah — with it.

Our Shaikh, Al-Imām Al-Albānī said: "Al-Mubārak is unknown, and Hammād Al-Kalbī is *'da'īf'*."

So, in summary, the hadīth is *'munkar'*; it is not authentic.

Endnote 168 – Source: Page 330

(BJ)(SZ) It is *'da'īf jiddan'*: Reported by Ibnul-Jawzī in *Al-'Ilalul-Mutanāhiyah* (1/453), and its chain contains Al-Waddāh ibn Yahyā; who is *'munkar'* in hadīth; and Mandal ibn 'Alī is weak.

(SH) And the hadīth has a witness which the author will mention, from a hadīth of 'Ā'ishah (رَضِيَ ٱللَّهُ عَنْهَا) traced back to the Prophet (صَلَّى ٱللَّهُ عَلَيْهِ وَسَلَّمَ):

> "Three things are obligatory duties upon me: the Witr, the tooth-stick, and 'Qiyāmul-Layl' (the Night Prayer)."

It was reported by At-Tabarānī in *Al-Mu'jamul-Awsat* (3/315/3266), and from him by Al-Hāfidh Ibn Hajr in *Muwāfaqatul-Khabarul-Khabar* (1/57), and Al-Bayhaqī in *As-Sunanul-Kubrā* (7/39), and in *Al-Khilāfiyyāt* (mss. 2/30/a): from Bakr ibn Sahl: 'Abdul-Ghanī ibn Sa'īd Ath-Thaqafī narrated to us: Mūsā ibn 'Abdir-Rahmān As-San'ānī narrated to us: from Hishām ibn 'Urwah: from his father: from her, with it.

At-Tabarānī said: "No one narrates it from Hishām except for Mūsā. 'Abdul-Ghanī is alone in narrating it."

Al-Bayhaqī said: "Mūsā ibn 'Abdir-Rahmān — this one is very weak. No isnād is established for this, and Allāh knows best."

Al-Hāfidh said: "Ibn Hibbān accused him of fabrication, and Ibn Hibbān said: *'His ahādīth are baseless, and the narrator from him is weak also.'*"

And Al-Haythamī said in *Majma'uz-Zawā'id* (8/264): "It contains Mūsā ibn 'Abdir-Rahmān As-San'ānī, and he was a liar."

I say: And Bakr ibn Sahl was *'da'īf'*, he was declared weak by An-Nasā'ī, Maslamah ibn Qāsim, and others.

Endnote 169 – Source: Page 331

(BJ)(SZ) Reported by Muslim (no. 719), from Mu'ādhah that she asked 'Ā'ishah (رَضِيَ اللَّهُ عَنْهَا): "How many (rak'ahs) had Allāh's Messenger (صَلَّى اللَّهُ عَلَيْهِ وَسَلَّمَ) used to pray for the Duhā?" She said: "Four rak'ahs, and he would add whatever Allāh wished."

And I do not find the two rak'ahs mentioned from 'Ā'ishah. Al-Bukhārī narrated (no. 1178), and Muslim (no. 721), from Abū Hurairah: *"My dear friend advised me with three things..."* — and from them was the two rak'ahs of Duhā; and the hadīth of Abū Dharr: *"Every morning a charitable act becomes due upon every joint of each one of you..."* — and it contains the wording that two rak'ahs which a person prays in the forenoon will suffice in that regard. Reported by Muslim (no. 720).

Endnote 170 – Source: Page 332

(SH) Reported by At-Tabarī in *Jāmi'ul-Bayān* (15/96), and by Ibn Abī Hātim and Ibn Mardawaih in their *Tafsīrs* — as occurs in *Ad-Durrul-Manthūr* (5/323), and by Al-Bayhaqī in *As-Sunanul-Kubrā* (7/39), by way of Muhammad ibn Sa'd ibn Muhammad ibn Al-Hasan ibn 'Atiyyah Al-'Awfī: my father narrated to me: my maternal uncle narrated to me: my father narrated to me: from his father: from Ibn 'Abbās, with it.

I say: And this is a very weak chain of narration: a chain of weak narrators of the 'Awf clan.

Endnote 171 – Source: Page 338

(SH) Reported by Al-Bukhārī in his *Sahīh* (nos. 216, 218, 1361), and Muslim in his *Sahīh* (no. 292).

A point of benefit: Our Shaikh, Al-Imām Al-Albānī (رَحِمَهُ ٱللَّهُ) said in his book *Ahkāmul-Janā'iz* (pp. 254-258):

....

And the fact that the placing of the date-palm leaf on the grave was something specific to him, and that the reduction in punishment was not on account of the moistness of its halves, is supported by a number of matters:

One:

The long hadīth of Jābir (رَضِيَ ٱللَّهُ عَنْهُ) in *Sahīh Muslim* (8/231-236), containing his (صَلَّى ٱللَّهُ عَلَيْهِ وَسَلَّمَ) saying: "I passed by two graves, and I wished that through my intercession it might be repelled from them for as long as the two twigs remain moist."

So this clearly shows the raising of the punishment was on account of his (صَلَّى ٱللَّهُ عَلَيْهِ وَسَلَّمَ) intercession and supplication, not on account of the moistness.

So it is all the same whether this story of Jābir is the same incident as the previous story of Ibn 'Abbās — as preferred by Al-'Aynī, or is a separate incident — as preferred by Al-Hāfidh in *Al-Fat-h*.

If the first is the case then the matter is clear, and if the latter possibility is the case, then correct examination necessitates that the underlying reason is one and the same in both incidents, because of their similarity. Also because moistness being a reason for the reduction in punishment for a deceased person is something not known in the Legislation or in the intellect. And if this were the case then those with the least punishment would be the Disbelievers: those who bury their dead in graveyards which are more like gardens because of the abundance of plants and trees which they grow [...] and which remain green through summer and winter!

In addition to what has preceded, then some of the scholars, such as As-Suyūtī, have mentioned that the reason why the moistness has an effect in reducing the punishment is that the moist plant glorifies and declares the perfection of Allāh (the Most High)!

They say: So when it passes away from the stick and it withers then its tasbīh (glorification and declaration of Allāh's perfection) ceases! However this reasoning is contrary to the generality of His Saying — He the Exalted and Most High:

> وَإِن مِّن شَيْءٍ إِلَّا يُسَبِّحُ بِحَمْدِهِ وَلَٰكِن لَّا تَفْقَهُونَ تَسْبِيحَهُمْ
>
> MEANING: "And there is nothing except that it glorifies, declares His Perfection, and praises Him; however you do not comprehend their glorification." — **Sūrah Al-Isrā' (17): 44**

Two:

In the hadīth of Ibn 'Abbās itself there is something which indicates that the underlying cause for the reduction of the punishment is not the moistness, or more exactly: that it is not the reason. This is his saying: *"Then he called for a palm branch, and he split it into two"* — meaning: lengthwise.

So, as is well known, splitting it will cause it to dry quickly. Therefore the time period for the reduction of punishment would be less than if it were not split. If this was the reason then, he (صَلَّى ٱللَّهُ عَلَيْهِ وَسَلَّمَ) would have left it without splitting it, and he would have placed a (whole) palm branch upon each grave (...) so the fact that he did not do so shows that its moistness was not the reason. Then it becomes certain that it was just a sign for the period of the reduction of punishment, which Allāh had permitted in response to the intercession of His Prophet (صَلَّى ٱللَّهُ عَلَيْهِ وَسَلَّمَ) , as is clearly stated in the hadīth of Jābir. So in this way the two hadīth are in agreement regarding determination of the reason, even if it is possible that they were separate events.

So reflect upon this, for it is an understanding which came to me, but I have not seen any of the scholars stating it or indicating it. So if it is correct then it is from Allāh (the Most High); and if it is a mistake then it is from me, and I seek His forgiveness for everything which is not pleasing to Him.

Three:

If moistness had been what was intended, then the Salafus-Sālih (Pious Predecessors) would have understood that; and they would have acted accordingly and planted date-palm stalks and myrtle plants and the like upon the graves when visiting them. Then if they had done that it would have become famous from them; and the reliable narrators would have transmitted it to us, since it is from those matters which would attract attention, and which would be reported. So since it is not reported, this indicates that it was not done, and that seeking nearness to Allāh by means of it is an innovation (bid῾ah). So what is intended is established.

So when this becomes clear, it is then easy to understand the falsity of that frail analogy which As-Suyūtī quoted from someone he did not name in *Sharhus-Sudūr*:

> "So if their punishment was reduced through the 'tasbīh' of the date-palm branch, then how about through the Believers recitation of the Qur'ān?! He said: And this hadīth is a fundamental evidence for planting trees by the graves!"

I say: Then it is said to him: *'First establish the throne, then embellish it!'* And: *'Can the shadow be straight when the stick is crooked?!'* So if this analogy were correct, then the Salaf would have hastened to it, since they were more eager upon doing good than we are.

So what has preceded shows that planting the date-stalk upon the grave was something specific to him, and that the underlying reason for the reduction of the punishment in the two graves was not the moistness of the branch; rather, it was his (صَلَّى ٱللَّهُ عَلَيْهِ وَسَلَّمَ) intercession, and his supplication for them. And this is something which cannot occur again, after his (صَلَّى ٱللَّهُ عَلَيْهِ وَسَلَّمَ) passing on to the highest company (of Angels), nor from someone else after him (صَلَّى ٱللَّهُ عَلَيْهِ وَسَلَّمَ), since becoming aware of punishment of the grave was something particular to him (عَلَيْهِ ٱلصَّلَاةُ وَٱلسَّلَامُ),

and it is from the Hidden and Unseen (Al-Ghayb) which no one but a Messenger is made aware of, as occurs in the text of the Qurʾān.

> عَالِمُ الْغَيْبِ فَلَا يُظْهِرُ عَلَىٰ غَيْبِهِ أَحَدًا ۝ إِلَّا مَنِ ارْتَضَىٰ مِن رَّسُولٍ
>
> MEANING: "He is the All-Knower of the Hidden and Unseen; and He does not disclose what he has kept hidden and unseen to anyone, except to a Messenger He has chosen." — **SŪRAH AL-JINN (72): 26-27**

And you should know that what we have clarified is not contradicted by what As-Suyūṭī brought in *Sharhus-Sudūr* (p.131): "And Ibn ʿAsākir reported by way of Hammād ibn Salamah: from Qatādah: that Abū Barzah Al-Aslamī (رَضِيَ اللَّهُ عَنْهُ) used to narrate that Allāh's Messenger (صَلَّى اللَّهُ عَلَيْهِ وَسَلَّمَ) passed by a grave whose inhabitant was being punished. So he took the branch of a date palm and planted it upon the grave and said: *'Perhaps it will be raised from him for as long as it remains moist,'* — and Abū Barzah left instructions: *'When I die, then place two palm branches with me in my grave.'*"

"He said: So he died in a waterless desert between Karmān and Qūmis, so they said: *'He left us instructions to place two palm-branches in his grave, and this is a place where we will be unable to find any.'*

However whilst they were in that state some riders came to them from Sijjistān, and they had with them some date-palm fronds; so they took two stalks and placed them along with him in his grave.

And Ibn Saʿd reported from Muwarriq, that Buraydah left instructions that two date-palm branches should be placed in his grave."

I say: The reason that there is no contradiction is that these two reports — even if we were to accept that they are both established — do not contain a prescription of placing date-palm branches when visiting the graves; which we assert to be an innovation, and we assert that the Salaf did not do it. Rather, the most that they contain is the placing of two date-palm branches along with the deceased in his grave. And this is another matter (even if it is just like that which preceded it with regard to its being something which is not legislated), since the hadīth narrated by Abū Barzah (like others besides him from the Companions) does not indicate that, especially when the hadīth mentions placing a single palm-branch and he instructed that two palm branches should be placed in his grave.

This, along with the fact that the chain of narration of the report is not authentic. So Ibn 'Asākir reported it in *Tārīkh Dimashq* at the end of the biography of Nadlah ibn 'Ubayd ibn Abī Barzah Al-Aslamī: from Ash-Shāh ibn 'Ammār, who said: Abū Sālih Sulaymān ibn Sālih Al-Laythī narrated to us, saying: An-Nadr ibn Al-Mundhir ibn Tha'labah Al-'Abdī related to us: from Hammād ibn Salamah, with it.

I say: This is a weak *(da'īf)* isnād, and it has two points of weakness:

Firstly: Ash-Shāh and An-Nadr are unknown, for I do not find any biography for them, and secondly: the *'an'anah* of Qatādah, since they do not mention his narrating anything from Abū Barzah. Then he is mentioned with *tadlīs*, so his *'an'anah* is to be feared in the like of this *isnād* of his.

As for the instructions left by Buraydah, then it is something established from him. Ibn Sa'd in *At-Tabaqāt* (vol. 7, leaf 1, p.4): "'Affān ibn Muslim related to us, saying: Hammād ibn Salamah narrated to us, saying: 'Āsim Al-Ahwal related to us: Muwarriq said: 'Buraydah Al-Aslamī left instructions that two date-palm fronds were to be placed in his grave. So he died in the nearest part of Khurāsān, and they could not find any except in the saddle-bags of a donkey.'"

This is a *'sahīh'* chain of narration, and it was brought in disconnected form by Al-Bukhārī (3/173), stating its ascription with certainty.

Al-Hāfidh said in his explanation: "It is as if Buraydah took the hadīth to be general, and did not hold it to be specific to those two men. Ibn Rushayd said: *'And from Al-Bukhārī's approach it appears that it was something specific to those two, since he quoted after it the saying of Ibn 'Umar: "A person will only be shaded by his own deeds."'*"

I say: And there is no doubt that the view taken by Al-Bukhārī is what is correct, due to what has previously been explained; and the view of Buraydah does not amount to proof since it was an opinion, and the hadīth does not prove it, even if it were general, since the Prophet (صَلَّى ٱللَّٰهُ عَلَيْهِ وَسَلَّمَ) did not place the date stalk within the grave but rather upon it — as has preceded; and *"the best way is the way of Muhammad"*.

Endnote 172 – Source: Page 339

(SH) Reported by Ahmad (4/8), ad-Dārimī (no. 1572), Abū Dāwūd (no. 1047), An-Nasā'ī (3/91), and Ibn Mājah (no.1085), by way of Husayn ibn 'Alī Al-Ju'fī: from 'Abdur-Rahmān ibn Yazīd ibn Jābir: from Abul Ash'ath As-San'ānī: from Aws ibn Abī Aws (and not Shaddād ibn Aws, as the author said, so that should be corrected), with it.

I say: This is a *'sahīh'* isnād; and it has been declared to have a weakness, but it is something which does not affect it in reality.

So it has been discussed in detail by the two great imāms: Ibn Qayyim Al-Jawziyyah in *Jalā'ul-Afhām* (pp. 149-156: Ibnul-Jawzī edn.), and Ibn 'Abdil-Hādī in *As-Sārimul-Munkī* (pp. 144-145) and he quoted Al-Bayhaqī as saying: *"It has supporting witnesses,"* and said: *"And it has more witnesses than those mentioned by Al-Bayhaqī (and he mentioned them)."*

And the hadīth was declared *'sahīh'* by a group of the scholars in earlier and later times; from them: Ibn Hibbān, Al-Hākim, Adh-Dhahabī, An-Nawawī, Shaikhul-Islām Ibn Taimiyyah, Ibnul-Qayyim, Ibn 'Abdil-Hādī, Al-Hāfidh Ibn Hajr, and our Shaikh Al-Albānī (رَحِمَهُ ٱللَّٰهُ).

Endnote 173 – Source: Page 344

(BJ)(SZ) It is *'sahīh'*: Reported by At-Tirmidhī (nos. 1808, 1809), and Abū Dāwūd (no. 3828), both of them by way of Abū Is-hāq: from Sharīk ibn Hanbal: from 'Alī that he said: "Eating garlic was prohibited, unless it is cooked."

At-Tirmidhī said: "The isnād of this hadīth is not that strong, and it has been reported from 'Alī as his own saying, and it has been related from Sharīk ibn Hanbal from the Prophet (صَلَّى ٱللَّٰهُ عَلَيْهِ وَسَلَّمَ) in *'mursal'* form."

I say: Its chain contains Abū Is-hāq As-Sabī'ī who was a *'mudallis'* and he reports it with *"an'anah'*, and his memory deteriorated towards the end of his life.

However it has a witness from a hadīth of Qurrah — reported by Abū Dāwūd (no. 2827), and An-Nasā'ī in *Al-Kubrā* (no. 6681); and a witness from a saying of 'Umar — reported by Muslim (no. 567).

Endnote 174 – Source: Page 348

(SH) Reported by Ahmad (2/91, 155, and 157), Abū 'Ubayd in *Al-Amwāl* (no. 740), Ibn Zanjawaih in *Al-Amwāl* (no. 1105), and Al-Bayhaqī in *As-Sunanul-Kubrā* (6/146): all of them by way of 'Abdullāh ibn 'Umar Al-'Umarī: from Nāfi': from Ibn 'Umar: that the Prophet (صَلَّى ٱللَّهُ عَلَيْهِ وَسَلَّمَ) reserved An-Naqī' for his horses.

I say: This is a weak chain of narration: it contains 'Abdullāh ibn 'Umar Al-'Umarī who is weak, as occurs in *At-Taqrīb*.

And the hadīth has another chain, reported by Ibn Hibbān in his *Sahīh* (no. 4683: *Al-Ihsān*) by way of 'Āsim ibn 'Umar: from 'Abdullāh ibn Dīnār: from Ibn 'Umar; and it contains the wording: "For the horses of the Muslims."

I say: This is a weak isnād: it contains 'Āsim ibn 'Umar and he is weak, as occurs in *At-Taqrīb*.

And it has a witness from a *'mursal'* hadīth of Az-Zuhrī, reported by Al-Bukhārī in his *Sahīh* (no. 2370), and Abū Dāwūd in his *Sunan* (no. 3083) with a *'sahīh'* chain.

And it is related from Az-Zuhrī in connected form from the Prophet (صَلَّى ٱللَّهُ عَلَيْهِ وَسَلَّمَ), and it is not authentic; rather, it is *'munkar'*.

So in summary, the hadīth is *'sahīh'* because of its supports, and it was declared *'sahīh'* by Al-'Allāmah Ahmad Shākir (رَحِمَهُ ٱللَّهُ) in his explanation and checking of the *Musnad* (8/41/5655), and declared *'hasan'* by our Shaikh Al-Albānī (رَحِمَهُ ٱللَّهُ).

BJ SZ And An-Naqī' is a place twenty leagues (approx. seventy miles) from Al-Madīnah.

Endnote 175 – Source: Page 348

BJ SZ It is *'sahīh lighairihi'*: Reported by Ahmad (5/424), Al-Bazzār, as occurs in *Kashful-Astār* (2/236/no. 599), Ibn 'Adiyy in *Al-Kāmil* (1/295), Al-Bayhaqī (10/138), as a hadīth of Abū Humayd As-Sā'idī. Al-Haythamī said (4/200): "Al-Bazzār reported it as a narration of Ismā'īl ibn 'Ayyāsh from the people of Hijāz, and these (narrations) are weak."

And it has a witness from a hadīth of Jābir, reported by Al-Bazzār, as occurs in *Kashful-Astār* (no. 1600), Ibn 'Adiyy in *Al-Kāmil* (1/281), Abū Nu'aym in *Al-Hilyah* (7/110), and At-Tabarānī in *Al-Awsat*, as occurs in *Majma'ul-Bahrayn* (4/93/nos. 2147, 2149).

And a witness from a hadīth of Abū Hurairah, reported by Ibn 'Adiyy in *Al-Kāmil* (1/177), At-Tabarānī in *Al-Awsat,* as occurs in *Majma'ul-Bahrayn* (4/94/2151); and Al-Haythamī said (4/151): "It contains Ahmad ibn Mu'āwiyah who was weak."

And a witness from a hadīth of Ibn 'Abbās, reported by At-Tabarānī in *Al-Awsat* — as occurs in *Majma'ul-Bahrayn* (4/93/no. 2150); and Al-Haythamī said (4/151): "It contains Yamān ibn Sa'īd who was weak."

And it was declared *'sahīh'* by Shaikh Nāsir [Ad-Dīn Al-Albānī] in *Al-Irwā'* (8/246/no. 2622).

Endnote 176 – Source: Page 349

BJ SZ Ibn Kathīr said in his exegesis of Sūrah Ar-Rūm: "Meaning whoever gives gifts intending that the people should give more than what he gave in return. So this will have no reward with Allāh. This was the explanation of Ibn 'Abbās, Mujāhid, Ad-Dahhāk, Qatādah, 'Ikrimah, Muhammad ibn Ka'b, and Ash-Sha'bī. And this practice is permissible, even though there is no reward in it; except that Allāh's Messenger (ﷺ) was specifically forbidden it: this was stated by Ad-Dahhāk."

Endnote 177 – Source: Page 349

(SH) In *As-Sunanul-Kubrā* (7/51), however it contains: *"From Al-Awzāʿī: from ʿAtāʾ."*

Zakariyyā said: "I think that it was from Ibn ʿAbbās."

And there is great difference between what the author (رَحِمَهُ ٱللَّهُ) mentioned here, and what occurs in the printed version of *As-Sunan*! And, furthermore, Al-Imām Adh-Dhahabī mentioned the chain of narration in *Al-Muhadhdhab fikhtisāris-Sunanil-Kabīr* (5/2614/no. 10663), just as it occurs in the printed version:

> "From Al-Awzāʿī: from ʿAtāʾ: from Ibn ʿAbbās."

So upon this basis, if ʿAtāʾ is "Ibn Abī Rabāh", then the chain is *'sahīh'* to the standard of the two Shaikhs; and if he is" Ibn Abī Muslim Al-Khurāsānī", then he is weak, because it would be disconnected. However, I am not, up to this moment, able to say which of the two possibilities is more correct. As for what the author (رَحِمَهُ ٱللَّهُ) stated, then it is most unlikely, and Allāh knows best.

Endnote 178 – Source: Page 353

(SH) I say: Al-Bukhārī reported in his *Sahīh* (7/106/no. 3772) from Abū Wāʾil Shaqīq ibn Salamah who said: 'When ʿAlī sent ʿAmmār and Al-Hasan to Al-Kūfah to urge the people to fight, ʿAmmār gave an address and said: "I certainly know that she is his wife in this world and the Hereafter. However, Allāh has tested you: will you follow him or her?"'

And he reported (no. 3771): from Al-Qāsim ibn Muhammad that ʿĀʾishah became ill, so Ibn ʿAbbās came and said: "O Mother of the Believers! You are advancing to meet true and sincere fore-runners: Allāh's Messenger (صَلَّى ٱللَّهُ عَلَيْهِ وَسَلَّمَ) and Abū Bakr."

And Ibn Hibbān reported in his *Sahīh* (16/7/no. 7095: *'Ihsān'*), and by Al-Hākim (4/10) by way of Saʿīd ibn Yahyā ibn Kathīr who narrated to me: from his father, who said: ʿĀʾishah narrated to us: that Allāh's Messenger (صَلَّى ٱللَّهُ عَلَيْهِ وَسَلَّمَ) mentioned Fātimah.

She said: "So I spoke, so he said:

> 'Are you not satisfied that you should be my wife in this world and in the Hereafter?'"

She said: "'Yes indeed, by Allāh!'

He said:

> 'Then you are indeed my wife in this world and in the Hereafter.'"

Al-Hākim said: *"Abul-'Anbas, this one, was reliable, and the hadīth is 'sahīh'"*, and Adh-Dhahabī agreed; and our Shaikh, Al-Imām Al-Albānī (رَحِمَهُ ٱللَّهُ) agreed with them in *As-Sahīhah* (7/27/3011).

And At-Tirmidhī reported (5/704/no.3880), and Ibn Hibbān in his *Sahīh* (16/6/no. 7094), through two chains: from Ibn Abī Mulaykah: from 'Ā'ishah that she said:

> "Jibrīl (عَلَيْهِ ٱلسَّلَامُ) came to Allāh's Messenger (صَلَّى ٱللَّهُ عَلَيْهِ وَسَلَّمَ) with me in a silk cloth, and said: 'This is your wife in this world and in the Hereafter.'"

At-Tirmidhī said: "This is a singular *'hasan'* hadīth."

I say: And its chain is *'sahīh'*.

And At-Tabarānī reported in *Al-Mu'jamul-Kabīr* (23/32/99), and Ibn Hibbān in his *Sahīh* (16/8/7096: *'Ihsān'*), and Al-Hākim (4/13), by way of Yūsuf ibn Ya'qūb ibn Al-Mājishūn: from his father: from 'Abdur-Rahmān ibn Ka'b ibn Mālik: from 'Ā'ishah that she said: "O Messenger of Allāh! Who are your wives in Paradise?"

He said: "You are from them" — until the end of the hadīth.

Al-Hākim said: *"This hadīth has a 'sahīh' chain, and the two of them did not report it"*, and Adh-Dhahabī agreed with him; and our Shaikh, Al-Imām Al-Albānī (رَحِمَهُ ٱللَّهُ) agreed with them in *As-Sahīhah* (7/27).

Endnote 179 – Source: Page 359

(BJ)(SZ) It is *'da'īf'*: Reported by At-Tabarānī in *Al-Kabīr* (24/227/no. 507), Abū Ya'lā (13/91/no. 7161), and Al-Bayhaqī in *As-Sunan* (7/28), as a hadīth of Razīnah — the slave-girl of Safiyyah, the wife of the Prophet (صَلَّىٰ ٱللَّٰهُ عَلَيْهِ وَسَلَّمَ).

Al-Haythamī said in *Majma'uz-Zawā'id* (9/251): "At-Tabarānī and Abū Ya'lā reported it by way of 'Alīlah bint Al-Kummayt: from her mother Amīnah: from Amatullāh bint Razīnah; and as for those three then I do not know them, and the rest of its narrators are reliable; and it is contrary to what is in the *Sahīh*, and Allāh knows best."

(SH) Al-Hāfidh said in *Al-Matālibul-'Āliyah* (16/611: 'Dārul-'Āsimah' Edn.): "A *'munkar'* hadīth by way of unknown women; whereas there occurs in the *Sahīh* from Anas (رَضِيَ ٱللَّٰهُ عَنْهُ) that he (صَلَّىٰ ٱللَّٰهُ عَلَيْهِ وَسَلَّمَ) made freeing her to be her dower."

And Al-Būsayrī said the like of this in *It-hāful-Khiyaratil-Maharah* (7/252: 'Dārul-Watan' Edn.)

I say: The hadīth of Anas, which they indicate, was reported by Al-Bukhārī in his *Sahīh* (no. 5086) and Muslim in his *Sahīh* (no. 1365), and others.

Endnote 180 – Source: Page 361

(SH) I say: This is an anomalous (*shādh*) recitation, and therefore it is not written in the mus-haf.

As for the recitation of Ubayy ibn Ka'b of it, then it is authentic and established from him. It was reported by 'Abdur-Razzāq in *Al-Musannaf* (10/181/18748), and from him by Is-hāq ibn Rāhawaih in *Al-Musnad*, as occurs in *Al-Matālibul-'Āliyah* [...] and Sufyān ibn 'Uyainah in his *Tafsīr* (p. 309), and Sa'īd ibn Mansūr in his *Sunan* — as occurs in *Ad-Durrul-Manthūr* (6/567), and from him Al-Bayhaqī in *As-Sunanul-Kubrā* (7/69), and Abū 'Ubayd in *Fadā'ilul-Qur'ān* (2/148/705): from 'Amr ibn Dīnār: from Bajālah ibn 'Abadah At-Tamīmī, who said: "'Umar ibn Al-Khattāb

(رَضِيَ ٱللَّهُ عَنْهُ) found a mus-haf in the room of a slave of his, and it contained (the wording):

> النَّبِيُّ أَوْلَى بِالْمُؤْمِنِينَ مِنْ أَنفُسِهِمْ - **وَهُوَ أَبٌ لَهُم** - وَأَزْوَاجُهُ أُمَّهَاتُهُمْ وَأُولُو الْأَرْحَامِ بَعْضُهُمْ أَوْلَى بِبَعْضٍ
>
> MEANING: "The Prophet has more right over the Believers than their own selves — *and he is a father to them* — and his wives are their mothers..."

So he said: 'Erase it, O slave-boy!'

So he said: 'No, by Allāh! I will not erase it when it is in the mus-haf of Ubayy ibn Ka'b (رَضِيَ ٱللَّهُ عَنْهُ)!'

So 'Umar (رَضِيَ ٱللَّهُ عَنْهُ) went off to Ubayy ibn Ka'b (رَضِيَ ٱللَّهُ عَنْهُ) and he [i.e. Ubayy] said: 'I have been occupied with the Qur'ān, and you have been occupied with transactions in the marketplaces, pulling your cloak upon your neck at the door of Ibnul-'Ajmā'.'"

Al-Hāfidh Ibn Hajr and Al-Būsayrī said: "This is a chain of narration '*sahīh*' to the standard of Al-Bukhārī."

And Al-Būsayrī said in *Al-Mukhtasarah* (8/407/6494): "Is-hāq narrated it with a chain of narration to the standard of Al-Bukhārī."

I say: It is as they said.

And the report from Ibn 'Abbās was reported by Al-Hākim (2/415) and from him by Al-Bayhaqī (7/69), with a weak chain of narration. It contains Mūsā ibn Mas'ūd An-Nahdī, and his memory was poor.

(BJ)(SZ) Ibn Kathīr said in his *Tafsīr* of Sūratul-Ahzāb; verse 6: "It is related from Ubayy ibn Ka'b, Ibn 'Abbās [...] and its like is related from Mu'āwiyah, Mujāhid, 'Ikrimah, and Al-Hasan; and it is one of the two sayings in the madh-hab of Ash-Shāfi'ī."

Endnote 181 – Source: Page 362

(SH) Reported by Ibn ʿAsākir in *Tārīkh Dimashq* (74/114-115), by way of Abul-ʿAbbās Al-Asamm: Muhammad ibn Is-hāq As-Sāghānī related to us: ʿAbdullāh ibn Sālih related to us: Muʿāwiyah ibn Sālih narrated to me: from Abuz-Zāhiriyyah: from Jubayr ibn Nufayr: from Ummud-Dardāʾ, with it.

I say: This is a *'hasan'* chain because of the slight speech concerning Muʿāwiyah ibn Sālih, and he is *'sadūq'* (truthful), from the narrators of Muslim; and as for what is to be feared from the weakness of ʿAbdullāh ibn Sālih, then the narrator from him here is one of the major scholars and memorizers, and Allāh knows best.

And it is authentic as a statement of the Prophet (صَلَّى ٱللَّهُ عَلَيْهِ وَسَلَّمَ). It is reported by Abū Yaʿlā Al-Mawsilī — the narration of Ibn Muqri — as occurs in *Al-Matālibul-ʿĀliyah* [...] and from him by Ibn ʿAsākir in *Tārīkh Dimashq* (74/116), [and others] through chains of narration from Ismāʿīl ibn ʿAbdillāh ibn Khālid Al-Qurashī Abī ʿAbdillāh As-Sukkarī: Abul-Malīh Al-Hasan ibn ʿUmar Ar-Raqqī narrated to us: from Maymūn ibn Mihrān who said: "Muʿāwiyah asked for Ummud-Dardāʾ's hand in marriage, but she refused to marry him, and she said:

> 'I heard Abud-Dardāʾ say: *"Allāh's Messenger (صَلَّى ٱللَّهُ عَلَيْهِ وَسَلَّمَ) said: 'The woman is for the last one of her husbands,'"* — and I do not want to exchange Abud-Dardāʾ for anyone.'"

Al-Būsayrī said: "The narrators of this isnād are reliable."

I say: It is just as he said, so the chain is *'sahīh'*, and it was declared *'sahīh'* also by our Shaikh, the Imām Al-Albānī (رَحِمَهُ ٱللَّهُ) and the hadīth has other chains and witnesses which our Shaikh (رَحِمَهُ ٱللَّهُ) mentioned is *As-Sahīhah* [3/275/1281].

Endnote 182 – Source: Page 364

(SH) Reported by Abū Dāwūd (4/129/4361), and from him by Ad-Dāraqutnī in his *Sunan* (3/39/3156 and 459/4425: 'Dārul-Maʿrifah' Edn.) and An-Nasāʾī in *Al-Mujtabā* (7/107-108), [and others] and Al-

Hākim (4/354): through chains of narration from Isrā'īl: from 'Uthmān Ash-Shahhām: from 'Ikrimah: from Ibn 'Abbās, with it.

Al-Hākim said: *"This is a hadīth with a 'sahīh' isnād, and the two of them did not report it"* — and Adh-Dhahabī agreed.

Al-Hāfidh Ibn Hajr said in *Bulūghul-Marām* (2/580/1253: 'Dārus-Sumay'ī' Edn.): "Its narrators are reliable."

And it was declared *'sahīh'* by Shaikhul-Islām Ibn Taimiyyah in *As-Sārimul-Maslūl*, and by our Shaikh Al-Imām Al-Albānī (رَحِمَهُ ٱللَّهُ) in *Sahīh Sunanin-Nasā'ī* (no. 3794).

Endnote 183 – Source: Page 366

(SH) Brought by Al-Bukhārī in disconnected form in his *Sahīh* (13/339) in the *Book of Adherence* [...] and reported in connected form by At-Tirmidhī (4/130), and Ibn Mājah (no. 2808) — both of them with abridged wording, and Ahmad in his *Musnad* (1/271), At-Tabarānī in *Al-Mu'jamul-Kabīr* (10/303/10733) — and from him by Ad-Diyā' Al-Maqdisī in *Al-Ahādīthul-Mukhtārah*, and from him by Al-Hāfidh Ibn Hajr in *Taghlīqut-Ta'līq* (5/330-331), and Al-Hākim in *Al-Mustadrak* (2/128-129), and from him by Al-Bayhaqī in *As-Sunanul-Kubrā* (7/41), and in *Dalā'ilun-Nubuwwah* (3/204-205): by way of 'Abdur-Rahmān ibn Abiz-Zinād: from his father: from 'Ubaydullāh ibn 'Abdillāh ibn 'Utbah: from Ibn 'Abbās, with it.

Al-Hākim said: *"This is a hadīth with a 'sahīh' chain, and the two of them did not report it"* — and Adh-Dhahabī and Al-Hāfidh Ibn Hajr agreed.

However, better than this is his saying in *Al-Fat-h*: *"This is a 'hasan' chain of narration"*, because of the well-known speech concerning Ibn Abiz-Zinād; and perhaps this is why At-Tirmidhī said: *"A singular 'hasan' hadīth."*

And it has a witness from a hadīth of Jābir ibn 'Abdillāh (رَضِيَ ٱللَّهُ عَنْهُ) with its like, reported by Ahmad in his *Musnad* (3/351), Ibn Sa'd in *At-Tabaqātul-Kubrā* (2/45), Ibn Abī Shaybah in *Al-Musannaf* (11/68-69/10538), Ad-Dārimī in his *Musnad* (8/342/2297: *Fat-hul-Mannān*), An-Nasā'ī in

As-Sunanul-Kubrā (7/114-115/7600), and Ibnul-Jārūd in *Al-Muntaqā* (3/313-314/1061): by way of Hammād ibn Salamah: from Abuz-Zubayr: Jābir narrated it to us.

I say: This is a chain *'sahīh'* to the standard of Muslim, and Abuz-Zubayr clearly stated that he heard the hadīth directly, in the narration of Imām Ahmad, as occurs in *Taghlīqut-Ta'līq* (5/332) and *Fat-hul-Bārī* (12/422); and the hadīth was declared *'sahīh'* by Al-Hāfidh Ibn Hajr (رَحِمَهُ ٱللَّٰهُ) in *Al-Fat-h* (13/341), and in *Taghlīqut-Ta'līq* (5/332).

Endnote 184 – Source: Page 367

(BJ)(SZ) It is *da'īf*: Ash-Shāfi'ī reported it [in *Al-Umm* (7/95), and in *Al-Musnad* (2/379/626 of its arranged version)], and from him it was reported by Al-Bayhaqī (7/45); and it was reported by 'Abdur-Razzāq in *Al-Musannaf* (5/331/no. 9720), and Ibn Abī Hātim in his tafsīr of verse 159 of Sūrah Āli 'Imrān (3/801/4413): by way of Ibn Wahb: from Sufyān: from Ma'mar: from Ibn Shihāb [Az-Zuhrī]: from Abū Hurairah.

Its isnād is disconnected: Az-Zuhrī did not meet Abū Hurairah.

Endnote 185 – Source: Page 370

(BJ)(SZ) Reported by Abū Dāwūd (no. 3607), An-Nasā'ī (no. 4661), and Ahmad (5/215, 216): from 'Umārah ibn Khuzaymah: that his paternal uncle narrated to him, and he was from the Companions of the Prophet (صَلَّىٰ ٱللَّٰهُ عَلَيْهِ وَسَلَّمَ): "That the Prophet (صَلَّىٰ ٱللَّٰهُ عَلَيْهِ وَسَلَّمَ) bought a horse from a bedouin man, and the Prophet (صَلَّىٰ ٱللَّٰهُ عَلَيْهِ وَسَلَّمَ) asked him to follow him so that he could pay him the price for his horse. So Allāh's Messenger (صَلَّىٰ ٱللَّٰهُ عَلَيْهِ وَسَلَّمَ) walked quickly and the bedouin was slower. So some men began making offers to buy the horse, and they were unaware that the Prophet (صَلَّىٰ ٱللَّٰهُ عَلَيْهِ وَسَلَّمَ) had bought it.

So the bedouin called to Allāh's Messenger (صَلَّىٰ ٱللَّٰهُ عَلَيْهِ وَسَلَّمَ) and said: 'Are you going to buy this horse, or otherwise I will sell it.'

So the Prophet (صَلَّىٰ ٱللَّٰهُ عَلَيْهِ وَسَلَّمَ) got up when he heard the call of the bedouin, and he said: 'Have I not already bought it from you?!'

So the bedouin said: 'No, by Allāh! I have not yet sold it to you.'

So the Prophet (صَلَّى ٱللَّٰهُ عَلَيْهِ وَسَلَّمَ) said: 'Rather, I have indeed bought it from you!'

So the bedouin began saying: 'Bring a witness!'

So Khuzaymah ibn Thābit said: 'I bear witness that you bought it from him.'

So the Prophet (صَلَّى ٱللَّٰهُ عَلَيْهِ وَسَلَّمَ) turned to Khuzaymah and said: 'Upon what basis do you bear witness?'

So he said: 'Upon the basis that I know you to be truthful, O Messenger of Allāh!'

So Allāh's Messenger (صَلَّى ٱللَّٰهُ عَلَيْهِ وَسَلَّمَ) made the witnessing of Khuzaymah equal to the witness of two men."

And there occurs in *Sahīh Al-Bukhārī* (no. 4784) from Zayd ibn Thābit who said: "When we were transcribing the written pages into the mus-hafs I did not find an Āyah from Sūratul-Ahzāb, which I used to frequently hear Allāh's Messenger (صَلَّى ٱللَّٰهُ عَلَيْهِ وَسَلَّمَ) reciting. I did not find it except with Khuzaymah Al-Ansārī, the one whose testimony Allāh's Messenger (صَلَّى ٱللَّٰهُ عَلَيْهِ وَسَلَّمَ) made equal to the testimony of two men."

Endnote 186 – Source: Page 371

(DB) Shaikh Al-Albānī (رَحِمَهُ ٱللَّٰهُ) said in *As-Sahīhah* (6/2/1081): "The scholars differed concerning the question of taking the kunyah of Abul-Qāsim, and they had three positions.

Al-Hāfidh quoted them in *Al-Fat-h*; and he brought evidence for them and discussed them, and he mentioned what there is for and against each of them; and I have no doubt after this that what is correct is the unrestricted prohibition: whether the person's name is Muhammad or not. This is because of the clear, authentic ahādīth which prohibit it, which are free of having anything decisive to oppose them — as has preceded. And it is what is established from Imām Ash-Shāfi'ī (رَحِمَهُ ٱللَّٰهُ).

So Al-Bayhaqī reported (9/309) with a *'sahīh'* chain from him that he said: "It is not permissible for anyone to take the kunyah 'Abul-Qāsim', whether his name is Muhammad or something else."

Al-Bayhaqī said: "And we have the meaning of that reported from Tāwūs Al-Yamānī (رَحِمَهُ ٱللَّهُ)."

Endnote 187 – Source: Page 372

[BJ][SZ] Reported by Ahmad in *Al-Musnad* (4/323), and from him by Al-Hākim (3/158), and from him by Al-Bayhaqī (7/64); and reported by At-Tabarānī in *Al-Kabīr* (20/25/no 30), and its isnād contains Umm Bakr bint Al-Miswar, whose condition is not known.

[SH] However, the first part of the hadīth is *'sahīh'* [...] from Al-Miswar ibn Makhramah that he heard Allāh's Messenger (صَلَّىٰ ٱللَّهُ عَلَيْهِ وَسَلَّمَ) say, whilst upon the minbar:

> "Banū Hishām ibn Al-Mughīrah sought permission to marry their daughter to ʿAlī ibn Abī Tālib. So I do not give permission, then I will not give permission, then I will not give permission, unless Ibn Abī Tālib wishes to divorce my daughter and to marry their daughter; for she is but a part of me. Whatever disturbs her disturbs me, and whatever annoys her annoys me."

Reported by Al-Bukhārī (no. 5230) and Muslim (no. 2449/93), by way of Ibn Abī Mulaykah: from Al-Miswar — with it.

And in a narration of Al-Bukhārī (no. 3729): "And Fātimah is a part of me, and I hate that she be troubled."

And in another narration (nos. 3714 & 3767): "Fātimah is a part of me, so whoever angers her angers me."

As for its second part, then it is *'sahīh'* also, because of its witnesses, which will follow with the author.

Endnote 188 – Source: Page 373

(BJ)(SZ) It is *'sahīh'*: Reported by Al-Bayhaqī in his *Sunan* (7/64, 114) with this chain, and it contains Sufyān ibn Wakī' who was *'sadūq'* (truthful/generally acceptable), however he suffered from having scribes who entered upon him narrations which were not from his ahādīth. However, the hadīth is *'sahīh'* because of its different chains of narration.

At-Tabarānī reported it (3/36/no. 2633), and Abū Nu'aym in *Al-Hilyah* (2/34) by way of Yūnus ibn Abī Ya'fūr: from his father: from 'Abdullāh ibn 'Umar who said: "I heard Allāh's Messenger (صَلَّى ٱللَّهُ عَلَيْهِ وَسَلَّمَ) say: 'Every tie of relationship and kinship on the Day of Resurrection...'"

And Al-Bazzār reported it, as occurs in *Kashful-Astār* (3/152/no. 3455) by way of 'Āsim ibn 'Ubaydillāh: from Ibn 'Umar: from 'Umar.

And Al-Bazzār reported it (no. 3456) by way of 'Abdullāh ibn Zayd ibn Aslam: from his father: from his grandfather: from 'Umar ibn Al-Khattāb.

And At-Tabarānī reported it (3/37/no. 2635) from Jābir: from 'Umar.

And 'Abdur-Razzāq reported it (no. 10354) from 'Ikrimah in *'mursal'* form; and At-Tabarānī connected it in *Al-Kabīr* (11/243/no. 11621), and Al-Khatīb (10/271).

And Shaikh Nāsir (Al-Albānī) (رَحِمَهُ ٱللَّهُ) mentioned it in *As-Silsilatus-Sahīhah* (no. 2036).

Endnote 189 – Source: Page 374

(SH) (3/71) And he did not mention its chain of narration, nor who reported it; and I do not find it with this wording.

However, it was reported by At-Tabarānī in *Al-Mu'jamul-Awsat* (6/50/no. 5762), Ibnul-A'rābī in *Al-Mu'jam* (2/431-432/842: Dār Ibnil-Jawzī Edn.) — and from him by Ibn 'Asākir in *Tārīkh Dimashq* (71/15), and Al-Hākim (3/137): by way of Qabīsah ibn 'Uqbah: from 'Ammār ibn Sayf: from Ismā'īl ibn Abī Khālid: from Ibn Abī Awfā who said: Allāh's Messenger (صَلَّى ٱللَّهُ عَلَيْهِ وَسَلَّمَ) said:

> "I asked my Lord (the Mighty and Majestic) that I should not marry anyone from my nation, and that no one should marry into my family, except that they will be with me in Paradise, and He granted it to me."

Al-Hākim said: *"This hadīth has a 'sahīh' isnād, and the two of them did not report it"* — and Adh-Dhahabī agreed with him!

Our Shaikh, Al-Imām Al-Albānī (رَحِمَهُ ٱللَّهُ) rebutted this in *Ad-Da'īfah* (7/40) saying: "I say: This is suspect, since Al-Hāfidh said concerning this narrator 'Ammār: *'Da'īf (weak) in hadīth, and he was a worshipper.'*"

And in summary, the hadīth is *'munkar'*, and is not authentic; and its witnesses will not strengthen it, since each of them is severely weak; and Allāh (the Most High) knows best.

Endnote 190 – Source: Page 375

(SH) Reported by Ibn Adiyy *Al-Kāmil* (4/1534) — and from him by Al-Bayhaqī in *Dalā'ilun-Nubuwwah* (6/74-75), and Ibnul-Jawzī in *Al-'Ilalul-Mutanāhiyah* (1/173-174/266), and Al-Khatīb in *Tārīkh Baghdād* (4/271-272), and Tammām in *Al-Fawā'id* (4/238/1430 — of its arrangement), Makkī Al-Mu'adhdhin in his *Hadīth* (236/1), and Ad-Diyā' Al-Maqdisī in *Al-Muntaqā min Hadīth Abī 'Alī Al-Awqī* (1/2), as occurs in *Ad-Da'īfah* (no. 341): by way of Zuhayr ibn 'Ubādah, with it.

And Al-Khatīb and Tammām added the narrator Al-Mu'allā ibn Hilāl between Zuhayr and 'Abdullāh ibn Muhammad ibn Al-Mughīrah.

I say this isnād is fabricated (*mawdū'*); it contains two weaknesses:

Firstly: Al-Mu'allā ibn Hilāl: the verifiers are agreed upon declaring him a liar.

Secondly: 'Abdullāh ibn Muhammad. Al-'Uqaylī said: "He narrates things which have no basis."

Ibn Yūnus said: "Munkar in hadīth."

Adh-Dhahabī brought some of his ahādīth, this being one of them, then he said: *"These are fabrications."* It was also declared weak by Ibn Dihyah in *Al-Āyātul-Bayyināt*, as occurs in *Faydul-Qadīr* (5/215); and our Shaikh, Al-Imām Al-Albānī (رَحِمَهُ ٱللَّهُ) said in *Ad-Da'īfah* (no. 341): "*Mawdū'* (fabricated)."

Endnote 191 – Source: Page 376

(BJ)(SZ) It is *'da'īf'*: Reported by At-Tabarānī in *Al-Kabīr* (3/36/2632), Abū Ya'lā in his *Musnad* (12/109/no. 6741), and Al-Khatīb in his *Tārīkh* (11/285). Al-Haythamī said in *Majma'uz-Zawā'id* (9/172): "Reported by At-Tabarānī and Abū Ya'lā; and it contains Shaybah ibn Na'āmah whom it is not permissible to use as evidence."

I say: And Fātimah bint Al-Husayn did not meet her grandmother Fātimah, the daughter of the Prophet (صَلَّى ٱللَّهُ عَلَيْهِ وَسَلَّمَ).

And Ibnul-Jawzī mentioned it in *Al-'Ilalul-Mutanāhiyah* (1/258), and he said: "*This hadīth is not authentic from the Prophet (صَلَّى ٱللَّهُ عَلَيْهِ وَسَلَّمَ).*" Ibn Hibbān said: *"It is not permissible to use Shaybah ibn Na'āmah as a proof."*

And it has a witness from a hadīth of Jābir, reported by At-Tabarānī — as occurs in *Majma'uz-Zawā'id* (9/172), and he said: "At-Tabarānī reported it; and it contains Yahyā ibn Al-'Alā', and he was abandoned (*matrūk*)."

Endnote 192 – Source: Page 378

(BJ)(SZ) It is *'da'īf'*: Reported by Ibn Abid-Dunyā in *Husn Adh-Dhann* (no. 60), and the verifier of *Kitābul-Ahwāl* mentioned it in the section on those narrations, which have been missed out (no. 5).

At-Tabarānī reported it in *Al-Kabīr* (10/385/10771), and in *Al-Awsat* — as occurs in *Majma'ul-Bahyrayn* (8/119/no. 4817), by way of Sa'īd ibn Muhammad Al-Jarmī, with it.

Al-Haythamī said (10/380): *"It contains Muhammad ibn Thābit Al-Bunānī, and he was weak."* And Adh-Dhahabī said in *Siyar A'lāmin-Nubalā* (13/82): *"This is 'gharīb, munkar', it is reported only by Muhammad ibn Thābit: one of the weak narrators."*

Translator's References

'Awnul-Ma'būd Sharh Sunan Abī Dāwūd — Muhammad Shamsul-Haqq Al-'Azīmābādī. **Dārul-Fikr, Beirut, 3rd edition, 1399 H.**

Āthārul-Madīnatil-Munawwarah — 'Abdul-Quddūs Al-Ansārī. **Al-Manhal, Jeddah, 5th edition, 1420 H.**

Ad-Durar fikhtisāril-Maghāzī was-Siyar — Ibn 'Abdil-Barr, Yūsuf ibn 'Abdillāh ibn 'Umar; verified by Mustafā Al-Bughā. **Mu'assasah 'Ulūmil-Qur'ān, Damascus, Beirut, 2nd edition, 1404 H.**

Akhbār Makkah — Muhammad ibn Ishāq Al-Fākihī; verified by 'Abdul-Malik ibn 'Abdillāh Duhaysh. **Jāmi'ah Ummil-Qurā, Makkah, 1419 H.**

Al-Bidāyah wan-Nihāyah — Ismā'īl ibn Kathīr. **Dārul-Kutubil-'Ilmiyyah, Beirut, 4th edition, 1408 H.**

Al-Isābah fī Tamyīzis-Sahābah — Ahmad ibn 'Alī Al-'Asqalānī. **Dārul-Kutubil-'Arabī, Beirut.**

Al-Istī'āb fī Bayānil-Asbāb — Salīm ibn 'Eid Al-Hilālī and Muhammad Mūsā Āl Nasr. **Dār Ibnil-Jawzī, Riyadh, 1425 H.**

Al-Jāmi'us-Sahīh — Muhammad ibn Ismā'īl Al-Bukhārī. **Dār Tawqin-Najāt, Beirut, 1422 H.**

Al-Kāshif — Adh-Dhahabī, Muhammad ibn Ahmad. **Dārul-Kutubil-'Ilmiyyah, Beirut, 1403 H.**

Al-Mawāhibul-Ladunniyyah — Ahmad ibn Muhammad Al-Qustalānī; verified by Ma'mūn Al-Jannān. **Dārul-Kutubil-'Ilmiyyah, Beirut, 1416 H.**

An-Nihāyah fī Gharībil-Hadīth — Ibn Al-Athīr, Al-Mubārak ibn Muhammad. Al-Maktabatul-'Ilmiyyah, Beirut.

Arabic-English Lexicon — E.W. Lane. The Islamic Texts Society, Cambridge, 1984.

Ar-Rawdul-Unuf — 'Abdur-Rahmān ibn 'Abdillāh As-Suhaylī; verified by Majdī Ash-Shūrī. Dārul-Kutubil-'Ilmiyyah, Beirut.

As-Sīratun-Nabawiyyah fī Daw'il-Masādiril-Asliyyah — Mahdī Rizqullāh Ahmad. Dār Imāmid-Da'wah, Riyadh, 2nd edition, 1424 H.

As-Sīratun-Nabawiyyah fī Fathil-Bārī — Muhammad Al-Amīn Al-Jaknī. Kuwait, 3rd edition, 1418 H.

As-Sīratun-Nabawiyyah wa Akhbārul-Khulafā' — Muhammad ibn Hibbān Al-Bustī; verified by 'Azīz Bek and others. Mu'assasatul-Kutubith-Thaqāfiyyah, Beirut, 2nd edition, 1411 H.

As-Sīratun-Nabawiyyah — Adh-Dhahabī, Muhammad ibn Ahmad; verified by Husāmuddīn Al-Qudsī. Dārul-Kutubil-'Ilmiyyah, Beirut, 1401 H.

As-Sīratun-Nabawiyyah — Ismā'īl ibn Kathīr; verified by Muhammad Al-Mu'tasim billāh Al-Baghdādī. Dārul-Kitābil-'Arabī, Beirut, 1417 H.

As-Sīratun-Nabawiyyah — 'Abdul-Malik ibn Hishām; verified by Mustafā As-Saqā, Ibrāhīm Al-Abyārī, and 'Abdul-Hafīz Shiblī. Dārul-Qalam, Beirut.

As-Sīratun-Nabawiyyatus-Sahīhah — Akram Diyā' Al-'Umarī. Maktabatul-'Ubaykān, Riyadh, 2nd edition, 1417 H.

At-Tanbīhātul-Latīfah 'alā Mahtawat 'alaihil-'Aqīdatul-Wāsitiyyah — 'Abdur-Rahmān ibn Nāsir As-Sa'dī; 'Abdul-'Azīz ibn Bāz. Dār Ibn Al-Qayyim, Ad-Dammām, 1409 H.

Buyūtus-Sahābah — Muhammad Ilyās 'Abdil-Ghanī. Markaz Taybah, Al-Madīnah, 2nd edition, 1418 H.

Dalā'ilun-Nubuwwah — Al-Bayhaqī, Ahmad ibn Al-Husayn; verified by 'Abdul-Mu'tī Al-Qal'ajī. Dārul-Kutubil-'Ilmiyyah, Beirut, 1408 H.

Fathul-Bārī Sharh Sahīhil-Bukhārī — Ahmad ibn 'Alī Al-'Asqalānī. Dārul-Ma'rifah, Beirut.

Fiqhus-Sīrah — Muhammad Al-Ghazālī; verified by Muhammad Nāsiruddīn Al-Albānī. Dārul-Kutubil-Hadīthiyyah, Cairo, 7th edition, 1976.

Hajjatun-Nabī (ﷺ) — Muhammad Nāsiruddīn Al-Albānī. **Al-Maktabul-Islāmī, Beirut, Damascus, 7th edition, 1405 H.**

Interpretation of the Meanings of the Noble Qur'ān — Taqī-ud-Dīn Al-Hilālī and Muhammad Muhsin Khan. **Darussalam, Riyadh, 1996.**

Irwā'ul-Ghalīl fī Takhrīj Ahādīth Manāris-Sabīl — Muhammad Nāsiruddīn Al-Albānī. **Al-Maktabul-Islāmī, Beirut, Damascus, 2nd edition, 1405 H.**

Jāmi'ul-Bayān 'an Ta'wīl Āyil-Qur'ān — Muhammad ibn Jarīr At-Tabarī; verified by 'Abdullāh ibn 'Abdil-Muhsin At-Turkī. **Hajr, Cairo, 1422 H.**

Jalā'ul-Afhām fī Fadlis-Salāti was-Salām 'alā Khayril-Anām — Muhammad ibn Abī Bakr, Ibn Qayyim Al-Jawziyyah; verified by Zā'id ibn Ahmad An-Nushayrī. **Dārul-'Ālamil-Fawā'id, Makkah, 1425 H.**

Jawāmi'us-Sīratin-Nabawiyyah — Ibn Hazm, 'Alī ibn Ahmad; verified by Nāyif Al-'Abbās. **Mu'assasah 'Ulūmil-Qur'ān, Damascus, Beirut, 1404 H.**

Kitāb Azwājin-Nabī (ﷺ) — Muhammad ibn Yūsuf As-Sālihī; verified by Muhammad Nazmuddīn Al-Futayyih. **Dār Ibn Kathīr, Damascus, Beirut, 4th edition, 1421 H.**

Lisānul-'Arab — Ibn Manzūr, Muhammad ibn Mukarram. **Dārul-Ma'ārif, Cairo.**

Ma'ālimut-Tanzīl — Al-Husayn ibn Mas'ūd Al-Baghawī; verified by Khālid Al-Ukk and Marwān Suwār. **Dārul-Ma'rifah, Beirut, 1406 H.**

Manāsikul-Hajj wal-'Umrah — Muhammad Nāsiruddīn Al-Albānī. **Maktabatul-Ma'ārif, Riyadh, 4th edition, 1410 H.**

Mirqātul-Mafātīh Sharh Mishkātil-Masābīh — 'Alī ibn Sultān Al-Qārī; verified by Jamāl 'Aytānī. **Dārul-Kutubil-'Ilmiyyah, Beirut, 1422 H.**

Mu'jamul-Buldān — Yāqūt ibn 'Abdillāh Al-Hamawī. **Dār Sādir, Beirut, 1404 H.**

Mukhtasar Sahīh Muslim — 'Abdul-'Azīm Al-Mundhirī; Muhammad Nāsiruddīn Al-Albānī. **Maktabatul-Ma'ārif, Riyadh, 3rd edition (reprinted), 1416 H.**

Mukhtasar Sīratin-Nabī (ﷺ) — 'Abdul-Ghanī Al-Maqdisī; verified by Khālid Ash-Shāyi'. **Dārul-Watan, Riyadh, 1413 H.**

Mukhtasarush-Shamā'ilil-Muhammadiyyah — Muhammad Nāsiruddīn Al-Albānī. **Al-Maktabatul-Islāmiyyah, Amman; Maktabatul-Ma'ārif, Riyadh, 2nd edition, 1406 H.**

Musnad Imām Aḥmad — Ahmad ibn Muhammad ibn Hanbal. **Baytul-Afkāril-Dawliyyah, Riyadh, 1419 H.**

Mustalahul-Hadīth — Muhammad ibn Sālih Al-ʿUthaymīn. **Maktabatul-Maʿārif, Riyadh, (reprinted) 1404 H.**

Sahīh Mawārididh-Dham'ān — Al-Haythamī; Muhammad Nāsiruddīn Al-Albānī. **Dārus-Sumayʿī, Riyadh, 1422 H.**

Sahīh Muslim bisharhin-Nawawī — Abū Zakariyyā An-Nawawī. **Dārul-Hadīth, Cairo, 1415 H.**

Sahīhus-Sīratin-Nabawiyyah — Muhammad Nāsiruddīn Al-Albānī. **Al-Maktabatul-Islāmiyyah, Amman, 1421 H.**

Sahīhut-Targhīb wat-Tarhīb — Al-Mundhirī; Muhammad Nāsiruddīn Al-Albānī. **Maktabatul-Maʿārif, Riyadh, 1421 H.**

Sharhul-ʿAqīdatit-Tahāwiyyah — Ibn Abil-ʿIzz Al-Hanafī; verified by Muhammad Nāsiruddīn Al-Albānī. **Al-Maktabul-Islāmī, Beirut, 9th edition, 1408 H.**

Silsilatul-Ahādīthis-Sahīhah — Muhammad Nāsiruddīn Al-Albānī. **Maktabatul-Maʿārif, Riyadh, (vols.1-7): 1415-1422 H.**

Siyar Aʿlāmin-Nubalā' — Adh-Dhahabī, Muhammad ibn Ahmad; verified by Shuʿayb Al-Arnawūt. **Mu'assasatur-Risālah, Beirut, 7th edition, 1408 H.**

Sunan Abī Dāwūd — Abū Dāwūd Sulaymān ibn Al-Ashʿath As-Sijjistānī; verified by Muhammad Nāsiruddīn Al-Albānī, prepared by Mashhūr Hasan Salmān. **Maktabatul-Maʿārif, Riyadh, 2nd edition.**

Sunan Ibn Mājah — Muhammad ibn Yazīd Al-Qazwīnī; verified by Muhammad Nāsiruddīn Al-Albānī, prepared by Mashhūr Hasan Salmān. **Maktabatul-Maʿārif, Riyadh.**

Sunanun-Nasā'ī — Ahmad ibn Shuʿayb ibn ʿAlī; verified by Muhammad Nāsiruddīn Al-Albānī, prepared by Mashhūr Hasan Salmān. **Maktabatul-Maʿārif, Riyadh.**

Sunanut-Tirmidhī — Muhammad ibn ʿĪsā At-Tirmidhī; verified by Muhammad Nāsiruddīn Al-Albānī, prepared by Mashhūr Hasan Salmān. **Maktabatul-Maʿārif, Riyadh.**

Tārīkhul-Umam wal-Mulūk — Muhammad ibn Jarīr At-Tabarī. **Dārul-Kutubil-ʿIlmiyyah, Beirut, 2nd edition, 1408 H.**

Tafsīrul-Qur'ānil-ʿAzīm — Ismāʿīl ibn Kathīr. **Dārul-Maʿrifah, Beirut, 1407 H.**

Tafsīrul-Qur'ānil-'Azīm — Ismā'īl ibn Kathīr; verified by Muqbil ibn Hadī Al-Wādi'ī. Dār Ar-Rāyah, Riyadh, 1414 H.

Tahdhībul-Asmā' wal-Lughāt — Abū Zakariyyā An-Nawawī. Dārul-Fikr, Beirut, 1416 H.

Taqrībut-Tahdhīb — Ahmad ibn 'Alī Al-'Asqalānī; verified by Abul-Ashbāl Saghīr Ahmad Shāghif. Dārul-'Āsimah, Riyadh, 1416 H.

Tarikatun-Nabī (صَلَّى ٱللَّٰهُ عَلَيْهِ وَسَلَّمَ) *was-Subulul-latī Wajjahahā Fīhā* — Hammād ibn Ishāq ibn Ismā'īl; verified by Akram Diyā' Al-'Umarī. Basāt, Beirut, 1404 H.

The Life of Muhammad, A Translation of Ibn Ishaq's Sirat Rasul Allah — A. Guillaume. Oxford University Press, 5th edition, 1978.

The Life of the Prophet Muhammad (As-Sīrah An-Nabawiyyah) — Ismā'īl ibn Kathīr; translated by Trevor Le Gassick. The Centre for Muslim Contribution to Civilization. Garnet Publishing, reprinted 2002.

The Qur'an, Arabic Text with Corresponding English Meanings — Saheeh International. Abul-Qāsim Publishing House, Jeddah, 1997.

The Translation of the Meanings of Sahih Al-Bukhari — Muhammad Muhsin Khan. Darussalam, Riyadh, 1997.

Zādul-Ma'ād fī Hadyi Khairil-'Ibād — Muhammad ibn Abī Bakr, Ibn Qayyim Al-Jawziyyah; Shu'ayb and 'Abdul-Qādir Al-Arnawūt. Mu'assastur-Risālah, Maktabatul-Manāril-Islāmiyyah, 13th edition, 1406 H.

ADDITIONAL

Notes and Points

FN

FN

ADDITIONAL
Notes and Points

FN

FN

ADDITIONAL

Notes and Points

FN

ADDITIONAL

Notes and Points

FN

FN

ADDITIONAL

Notes and Points

FN

ADDITIONAL

Notes and Points

FN

FN

ADDITIONAL
Notes and Points

EN

Donate to the Cause

ONLINE:

salafibookstore.com/donate

Make a one-time donation, or set up a monthly subscription. It takes less than a minute!

VIA BANK TRANSFER:

Account Name — Salafi Bookstore & Islamic Centre
Bank — Lloyds Bank Plc.
Branch — Erdington, Birmingham, UK.
Account Number — 002 312 60
Sort Code — 30-93-09
BIC/Swift Code — LOYDGB21282.

IBAN — GB14 LOYD 3093 0900 2312 60

Specify a reference such as: "books," "leaflets," "masjid", etc. Please also consider making this a recurring donation. Note: the IBAN and BIC codes are for foreign accounts.

Visit Our Websites

SALAFISOUNDS.COM — *For authentic Islamic audio.*

SALAF.COM — *Your starting point for Islām, Sunnah, & Salafiyyah online.*

AQIDAH.COM — *Learn the creed of Ahlus-Sunnah wal-Jamāʿah.*

SALAFIMASJID.COM — *The online home of the Salafi Masjid, on Wright St.*

AH-SP.COM — *The website of Abū Hakeem Bilāl Davis.*

ABUKHADEEJAH.COM — *The website of Abū Khadeejah ʿAbdul-Wāhid.*

SALAFIBOOKSTORE.COM — *Your one-stop-shop for Islamic literature and effects.*

SALAFIPUBS.COM — *Salafi Digital Media.*

We are a UK Registered Charity — No. 1083080